TI-83 and TI-83 Plus Quick Reference

Absolute value

MATH ▶ 1.

```
MATH NUM CPX PRB
1 abs(
2: round(
3: iPart(
4: fPart(
5: int(
6: min(
7↓max(
```

Complex numbers

MODE Select a+bi. Press ENTER
2nd QUIT.

```
Normal  Sci  Eng
Float  0123456789
Radian  Degree
Func  Par  Pol  Seq
Connected  Dot
Sequential  Simul
Real  a+bi  re^θi
Full  Horiz  G-T
```

Decimal to fraction

MATH 1 ENTER .

```
MATH NUM CPX PRB
1 ▶Frac
2: ▶Dec
3: 3
4: 3√(
5: x√
6: fMin(
7↓fMax(
```

Enter a function

The Y= key is used to enter an expression for a function.

```
Plot1 Plot2 Plot3
\Y1 ■0.IX^3-2X-1
\Y2 =
\Y3 =
\Y4 =
\Y5 =
\Y6 =
\Y7 =
```

Evaluate a function

Enter the expression into Y1. Press
2nd
QUIT. VARS
▶ 1 1.

```
Plot1 Plot2 Plot3
\Y1 ■X²/(X-1)
\Y2 =                Y1(-3)
\Y3 =                          -2.25
\Y4 =
\Y5 =
\Y6 =
\Y7 =
```

Home screen

2nd QUIT. Press
CLEAR to erase the
home screen

```
-2(3+5)-8/4
                  -18
```

Graph a function

Use the Y= key to enter the expression for the function, select a suitable viewing window, and then press GRAPH .

```
Plot1 Plot2 Plot3
\Y1 ■.IX^3-3X+1
\Y2 =
\Y3 =
\Y4 =
\Y5 =
\Y6 =
\Y7 =
```

```
ZOOM MEMORY
1: ZBox
2: Zoom In
3: Zoom Out
4: ZDecimal
5: ZSquare
6 ZStandard
7↓ ZTrig
```

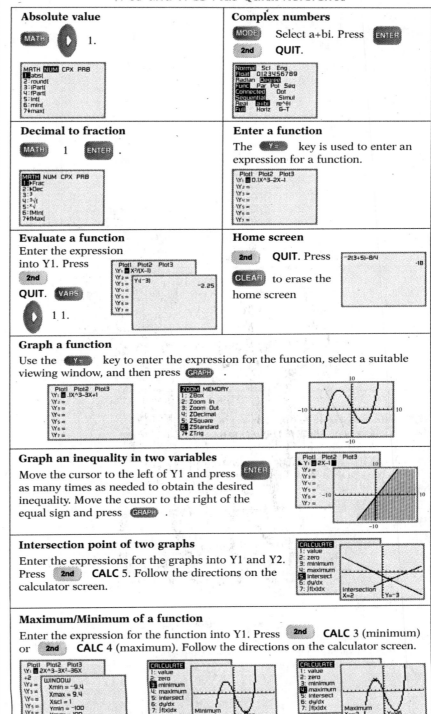

Graph an inequality in two variables

Move the cursor to the left of Y1 and press ENTER as many times as needed to obtain the desired inequality. Move the cursor to the right of the equal sign and press GRAPH .

```
Plot1 Plot2 Plot3
▶ Y1 ■2X-1
\Y2 =
\Y3 =
\Y4 =
\Y5 =
\Y6 =
\Y7 =
```

Intersection point of two graphs

Enter the expressions for the graphs into Y1 and Y2. Press 2nd CALC 5. Follow the directions on the calculator screen.

```
CALCULATE
1: value
2: zero
3: minimum
4: maximum
5 intersect
6: dy/dx
7: ∫f(x)dx
```

```
Intersection
X=2        Y=3
```

Maximum/Minimum of a function

Enter the expression for the function into Y1. Press 2nd CALC 3 (minimum) or 2nd CALC 4 (maximum). Follow the directions on the calculator screen.

```
Plot1 Plot2 Plot3
\Y1 ■2X^3-3X²-36X
+2
\Y2 =     WINDOW
\Y3 =     Xmin = -9.4
\Y4 =     Xmax = 9.4
\Y5 =     Xscl = 1
\Y6 =     Ymin = -100
          Ymax = 100
          Yscl = 10
          Xres = 1
```

```
CALCULATE
1: value
2: zero
3 minimum
4: maximum
5: intersect
6: dy/dx
7: ∫f(x)dx
```

```
Minimum
X=3        Y=-79
```

```
CALCULATE
1: value
2: zero
3: minimum
4 maximum
5: intersect
6: dy/dx
7: ∫f(x)dx
```

```
Maximum
X=-2       Y=46
```

TI-83 and TI-83 Plus Quick Reference

Radical Expressions

Square root: **2nd**

Cube root: **MATH** 4

Fourth root: 4 **MATH** 5

Fifth root: 5 **MATH** 5

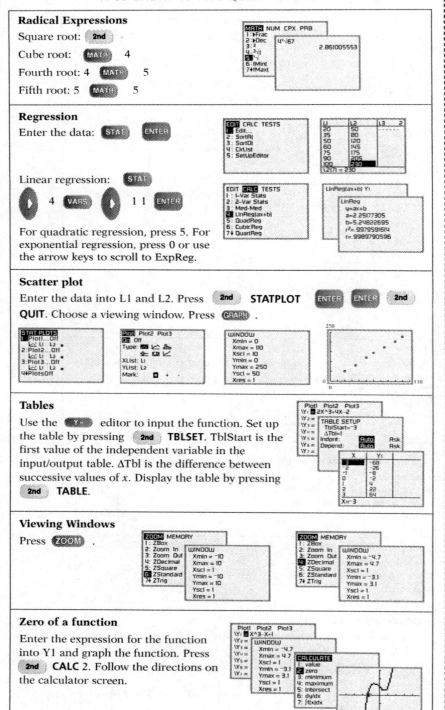

Regression

Enter the data: **STAT** **ENTER**

Linear regression: **STAT** ► 4 **VARS** ► 1 1 **ENTER**

For quadratic regression, press 5. For exponential regression, press 0 or use the arrow keys to scroll to ExpReg.

Scatter plot

Enter the data into L1 and L2. Press **2nd** **STATPLOT** **ENTER** **ENTER** **2nd** **QUIT**. Choose a viewing window. Press **GRAPH**.

Tables

Use the **Y=** editor to input the function. Set up the table by pressing **2nd** **TBLSET**. TblStart is the first value of the independent variable in the input/output table. ΔTbl is the difference between successive values of x. Display the table by pressing **2nd** **TABLE**.

Viewing Windows

Press **ZOOM**.

Zero of a function

Enter the expression for the function into Y1 and graph the function. Press **2nd** **CALC** 2. Follow the directions on the calculator screen.

Exploring Introductory and Intermediate
ALGEBRA

A Graphing Approach

Special Edition for Lansing Community College | MATH 107

RICHARD N. AUFMANN
Palomar College

JOANNE S. LOCKWOOD
Plymouth State College

LAURIE BOSWELL
Plymouth State College

Houghton Mifflin Company | Boston | New York

Publisher: Jack Shira
Senior Sponsoring Editor: Lynn Cox
Senior Development Editor: Dawn Nuttall
Assistant Editor: Lisa Pettinato
Project Editor: Merrill Peterson
Senior Production/Design Coordinator: Carol Merrigan
Manufacturing Manager: Florence Cadran
Senior Marketing Manager: Ben Rivera

PHOTOGRAPH CREDITS: p. 1 Paul Conklin/PhotoEdit; p. 14 David Young-Wolff/PhotoEdit; p. 71 Myrleen Ferguson Cate/PhotoEdit; p. 95 David Frazier/The Image Works; p. 112 Becky Luigart-Stayner/CORBIS; p. 135 Craig Lovell/CORBIS; p. 149 David Lees/CORBIS; p. 150 Cathy Charles/PhotoEdit; p. 161 Bill Lai/The Image Works; p. 181 Cathy MelleonResources/PhotoEdit; p. 182 Archivo Iconografico, S.A./CORBIS; p. 183 Morandi/Granata/The Image Works; p. 237 Tim David/CORBIS; p. 275 David Young-Wolff/PhotoEdit; p. 276 Michael Johnson; p. 278 Bettmann/CORBIS; p. 311 David Grossman/The Image Works; p. 371 Denis Scott/ CORBIS; p. 423 Tom Sanders/ CORBIS; p. 465 Donald C. Johnson/CORBIS; p. 531 Tom Wagner/CORBIS SABA; p. 535 James Marshall/CORBIS; p. 539 ER Productions/CORBIS; p. 551 Bill Bachman/PhotoEdit, Inc.; p. 574 Charles Krebs/CORBIS; p. 588 CORBIS; p. 607 Roy Marsch/CORBIS; p. 609 Richard Glover, Ecoscene/CORBIS; p. 616 AFP/CORBIS; p. 640 Joseph Sohm; ChromoSohm, Inc./CORBIS; p. 643 Dallas and John Heaton/CORBIS; p. 689 Bob Daemmrich/The Image Works

Custom Publishing Editor: Jan Scipio
Custom Publishing Production Manager: Christina Battista
Project Coordinator: Jennifer Feltri

Cover Design: Althea Chen
Cover Art: Kevin W. Fowler, Lansing Community College Media Services; Althea Chen

This book contains select works from existing Houghton Mifflin Company resources and was produced by Houghton Mifflin Custom Publishing for collegiate use. As such, those adopting and/or contributing to this work are responsible for editorial content, accuracy, continuity and completeness.

Printed in the United States of America.

ISBN 13: 978-0-618-81249-3
ISBN 10: 0-618-81249-0
N-06788

1 2 3 4 5 6 7 8 9 – CM – 08 07 06

Houghton Mifflin
Custom Publishing

222 Berkeley Street • Boston, MA 02116

Address all correspondence and order information to the above address.

CONTENTS

v

CHAPTER **4**

Linear Functions 237

CHAPTER **5**

Systems of Linear Equations and Inequalities 311

CHAPTER **6**   **Polynomials**   371

CHAPTER **7**   **Factoring**   423

Contents

CHAPTER **11**

Exponential and Logarithmic Functions 689

To: New Math Students

From: The Mathematical Skills Department Faculty and Staff

Welcome to the Mathematical Skills Department at Lansing Community College.

Thank you for selecting Lansing Community College and the Mathematical Skills Department.   Our mission is to help you acquire the math skills you need to succeed in your academic and career endeavors.

Whatever your learning style, we think you will find this text and associated learning materials to be very helpful. You can also choose from the variety of instructional methods offered by our Department. These methods are described on the following pages.

Our goal is to help you succeed in mathematics, regardless of your background in mathematics. If you encounter difficulty, or have questions, talk with your instructor(s). We have multiple resources and solutions to help you.

I wish you good luck in your endeavors.

Sincerely,

Todd Troutman
Chair, Mathematical Skills Department

Mathematical Skills Department
Contact Information

The department office is located in room 309(A), on the 3rd floor of Arts & Sciences.

24-hour Information Line	517-483-1900
Department Office	517-483-1073
Department Fax	517-483-1927
Lab Coordinator "Hotline"	mathlabcod@lcc.edu 517-267-5073

Write/phone to directly contact a Professor regarding main campus Lab issues

Mailing address: Lansing Community College
1300-Mathematical Skills
PO Box 40010
Lansing, MI   48901-7210

Web address: http://www.lcc.edu/mathskills

Lansing Community College
Contact Information

LCC Information Center: 517-483-1265

Mailing address: Lansing Community College
PO Box 40010
Lansing, MI   48901-7210

Web address: http://www.lcc.edu

LCC School Closing 517-483-9729
800-644-4522   X9729

MATHEMATICAL SKILLS DEPARTMENT
METHODS OF INSTRUCTION

The Mathematical Skills Department, located in the Arts and Sciences Building, room 309, offers instruction through a variety of delivery methods for Math 050, Math 107, and Math 112 courses. These instruction opportunities allow you to pick the method that best meets your learning style and personal situation. A brief description of each method is listed below.

Math Lab
The Math Lab provides a dynamic and adaptive instructional program to meet individual academic and personal schedule needs. The Math Lab emphasizes:

- Individual study with assignments and high-quality materials
- Flexible weekly schedules
- One-to-one faculty support from a variety of instructors
- Individualized test review appointments with faculty
- Options for re-taking tests
- Writing exercises
- Weekly Progress Checks

Math Lab courses are not 'self-paced'; however, Math Lab students have considerable flexibility each week while completing their course within the semester.

Students said that they appreciated the flexibility each week in scheduling their 4 contact hours in the lab (8 during the summer semester). They found the instructors extremely helpful in delivering 'just in time' instruction for anything from a specific problem to a mini-custom lecture on an entire concept. Un-timed testing and grade raising opportunities were praised!

Lab / Lecture
The Lab/Lecture approach combines the key features of the Math Lab with some features of a lecture class. The Lab/Lecture classes emphasize:

- A lecture presentation and testing schedules that provide structure
- Flexible access and support from a variety of instructors
- Options for re-taking tests
- Regular work with other students (collaborative learning)

Students reported that they liked the blend of having a set time to meet with their class and instructor and appreciated the added lab benefits of un-timed tests and convenient lab instruction.

Off-Campus Learning Centers

The Math Lab approach is used at Learning Centers located in Howell (LIVCEN), Mason (MHS), Owosso (OWOSSO), St. Johns (STJCCC), and East Lansing (LCCEAST). This approach utilizes a single assigned instructor to work with a group of students taking any of our three courses at one time, while following the Lab testing format.

"I chose to take Math as a lab so I would be able to go at my own pace. The lab allowed me to work through the chapters I knew at a fast pace. If I had a question, my instructor was there to help me along. I chose the off campus learning center because it worked with my schedule better and was not out of the way from my home." Ashley (student)

Lecture

The lecture option is for students who need more structure and specific timelines for accomplishing assignments and tests. This environment is also good for visual and auditory learners who benefit from lecture and demonstration activity.

"The advantages of a regular math lecture course are abundant. It allows for more personal contact and creates an environment conducive to putting theory into practice. Under the guidance of the instructor, a traditional math lecture empowers the student to ask questions in a group setting, which offers more of an interactive approach to learning and greater retention." Rick (student)

Online

Individuals who are independent learners and have good computer skills may utilize course offerings over the Internet. Students complete coursework on-line and then take tests at the on-campus Assessment Center. If students have travel restrictions, they may utilize an approved off-campus testing center and a test proctor. A fee may be assessed to test off-campus.

"Being able to go to class anytime during the day is one of the many reasons why I like online classes. I am able to go to class anywhere during a 24 hour period. I live in Grand Rapids, so online classes work best in order for me to attend LCC. It is also convenient that I am able to have my tests proctored to a location near my home." Miranda (student)

Lecture/Internet

This option combines the advantages of a lecture class with the flexibility of an online class. Students attend a once a week lecture along with completing on-line assignments, activities and/or discussions. This method is designed for the student who is self-motivated while offering the benefit of a lecture presentation.

"I really enjoyed this hybrid Lecture/Internet class. This type of class has a very convenient set-up. Students are allotted a large amount of time to do the homework and then the following class there is a teacher there to explain the old and new problems. The face-to-face interaction still exists, but with the convenience of an online class. There was also the opportunity to have questions answered whenever it was needed through the discussion board. However, the teacher absolutely needs to be attentive in order for this system to work." Bethany (student)

Geometric Relations

Perimeter of a **Triangle**: $P = a + b + c$

Perimeter of a **rectangle**: $P = 2l + 2w$

Circumference of a **circle**: $C = \pi d$ or $C = 2\pi r$

Area of a **Triangle**: $A = \dfrac{1}{2}bh$

Area of a **rectangle**: $A = lw$

Area of a **circle**: $A = \pi r^2$

Area of **a parallelogram**: $A = bh$

Volume of a **rectangular box**: $V = lwh$

Two angles are **complements** if the sum of the measures of the angles is **90°.**

Two angles are **supplements** if the sum of the measures of the angles is **180°.**

Diameter = twice the **radius:** $d = 2r$

The **sum** of the measures of the interior angles of a **triangle** is **180°.**

PREFACE

Exploring Introductory and Intermediate Algebra: A Graphing Approach is a new text designed to help students make connections between mathematics and its applications. Our goal is to develop a student's mathematical skills through appropriate use of applications and to use technology to establish links between abstract mathematical concepts and visual or concrete representations. In response to the more prevalent use of technology in the intermediate algebra curriculum, we have written this text as graphing calculator dependent. Although any calculator can be used, we have used the TI-83/TI-83 Plus in many of the examples.

Our hallmark *interactive approach*, which encourages students to practice a skill or concept as it is presented and get immediate feedback, is also highlighted in this text. Each section contains one or more sets of matched-pair Example/You Try It examples. The numbered example in each set is worked out; the second example, the *You Try It*, is for the student to work. By solving this problem, the student actively practices concepts as they are presented in the text. There are complete worked-out solutions to the You Try It problems in an appendix. Students can compare their solution to the solution in the appendix and thereby obtain immediate feedback on the concept.

Through the use of applications, we demonstrate to students that mathematics has a vast array of tools that can be used to solve meaningful problems. Modeling, analytic representation, and verbal representations of problems and their solutions are encouraged. We have also integrated numerous data analysis exercises throughout the text and encourage students to use technology to assist them in deriving meaningful conclusions about the data.

To promote and support problem solving, we offer students a systematic procedure to solve application problems. For each application example, we take students through a four-step process that asks the student to **State the goal**, **Devise a strategy**, **Solve the problem**, and **Check your work**. For the corresponding You Try It, we ask students to follow that procedure. To reinforce this process, the solution to the You Try It in the appendix demonstrates how the four-step approach could be used to solve the problem.

In some cases, we have incorporated into an exercise a writing component that asks the student to write a sentence explaining the meaning of an answer in the context of the problem. Additional writing exercises are integrated throughout every exercise set. These exercises ask students to make a conjecture based on some given facts, restate a concept in their own words, provide a written answer to a question, or research a topic and write a short report.

We have paid special attention to the standards suggested by AMATYC and have made a serious attempt to incorporate those standards in the text. Problem solving, critical analysis, the function concept, connecting mathematics to other disciplines through applications, multiple representations of concepts, and the appropriate use of technology are all integrated within this text. Our goal is to provide students with a variety of analytic tools that will make them more effective quantitative thinkers and problem solvers.

C H A P T E R

4 Linear Functions

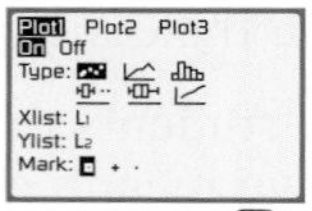

Press 2nd STAT PLOT ENTER to access the STAT PLOTS options.

In order to monitor species that are or are becoming endangered, scientists need to determine the present population of that species. Scientists have tracked the increase in the population of the grey wolf in regions of Idaho since its re-introduction in the mid-1990s. This has led to the modeling of the size of the population with a linear function, as shown in ***Exercise 9 on page 289.*** *From the equation, we can determine how fast the population is growing and make estimates about its future growth.*

Need help? For online student resources, visit this web site: Math.college.hmco.com

237

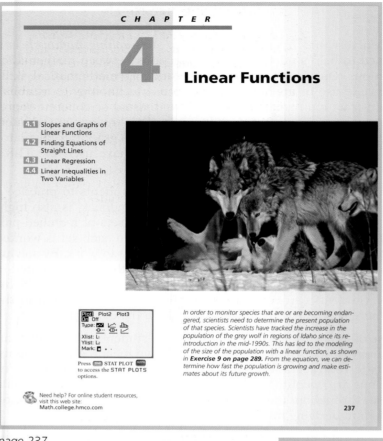

page 237

Chapter Opener

Each chapter begins with a **Chapter Opener** that illustrates a specific application of a concept from the chapter. There is a reference to a particular exercise in the chapter that asks the student to solve a problem related to the chapter opener topic.

The WWW icon at the bottom of the page lets students know of additional online resources at **math.college.hmco.com/students.**

Prep Test and Go Figure

Prep Tests occur at the beginning of each chapter and test students on previously covered concepts that they must understand in order to succeed in the upcoming chapter. Answers are provided in the Answer Appendix. Section references are also provided for students who need to review specific concepts.

The **Go Figure** problem that follows the *Prep Test* is a playful puzzle problem designed to engage students in problem solving.

96 CHAPTER 2 Introduction to Functions and Relations

PREP TEST

1. Simplify: $-\frac{6}{3} + 4$
2. Evaluate $-2x + 5$ for $x = -3$.
3. Evaluate $\frac{2r}{r-1}$ for $r = 5$.
4. Evaluate $2p^3 - 3p + 4$ for $p = -1$.
5. For what value of x is the expression $\frac{2x-5}{x}$ undefined?
6. Given $y = 6x - 5$, find the value of y when $x = -\frac{1}{3}$.

GO FIGURE

In a contest to guess how many jelly beans were in a jar, Hector guessed 223, Shannon guessed 215, Suki guessed 220, Deon guessed 221, Saul guessed 217, and Denise guessed 219. Two were off by 4, two were off by 2, one was off by 1, and one was correct. What was the correct number?

SECTION 2.1 **Rectangular Coordinates and Graphs**

- Introduction to Rectangular Coordinate Systems
- Input-Output Tables
- Graphs of Equations

Introduction to Rectangular Coordinate Systems

A cartographer (a person who makes maps) divides a city into little squares as shown on the map of Washington, DC below. Telling a visitor that the White

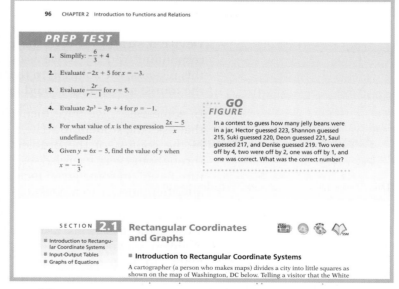

page 96

AUFMANN INTERACTIVE METHOD (AIM)

? QUESTION Why does it not make sense for the domain of $f(x) = -0.05x + 18$, discussed above, to exceed 360?

EXAMPLE 1

Suppose a 20-gallon gas tank contains 2 gallons when a motorist decides to fill up the tank. The gas pump fills the tank at a rate of 0.08 gallon per second. Find a linear function that models the amount of fuel in the tank x seconds after fueling begins.

Solution Because there are 2 gallons of gas in the tank when fueling begins (at $x = 0$), the y-intercept is $(0, 2)$.

The slope is the rate at which fuel is being added to the tank. Because the amount of fuel in the tank is increasing, the slope is positive and we have $m = 0.08$.

To find the linear function, replace m and b in $f(x) = mx + b$ by their values.

$$f(x) = mx + b$$
$$f(x) = 0.08x + 2 \quad \text{• Replace } m \text{ by 0.08; replace } b \text{ by 2.}$$

The linear function is $f(x) = 0.08x + 2$, where $f(x)$ is the number of gallons of fuel in the tank x seconds after fueling begins.

YOU TRY IT 1

The boiling point of water at sea level is 100°C. The boiling point decreases 3.5°C for each 1-kilometer increase in altitude. Find a linear function that gives the boiling point of water as a function of altitude.

Solution See page S14.

■ Find Equations of Lines Using the Point–Slope Formula

For each of the previous examples, the known point on the graph of the linear function was the y-intercept. This information enabled us to determine b for the linear function $f(x) = mx + b$. In some instances, a point other than the y-intercept is given. In this case, the *point–slope formula* is used to find the equation of the line.

Point–Slope Formula of a Straight Line

Let $P_1(x_1, y_1)$ be a point on a line, and let m be the slope of the line. Then the equation of the line can be found using the point–slope formula

$$y - y_1 = m(x - x_1)$$

? ANSWER If $x > 360$, then $f(x) < 0$. This would mean that the tank contained negative gallons of gas. For instance, $f(400) = -2$.

page 261

■ An Interactive Approach

Exploring Introductory and Intermediate Algebra: A Graphing Approach uses an interactive approach that provides the student with an opportunity to try a skill as it is presented. Each section contains one or more sets of matched-pair examples. The first example in each set is worked out; the second example, called *You Try It*, is for the student to work. By solving this problem, the student actively practices concepts as they are presented in the text.

There are <u>complete worked-out</u> solutions to these problems in an appendix. By comparing their solution to the solution in the appendix, students obtain immediate feedback on, and reinforcement of, the concept.

YOU TRY IT 1 Let x represent the number of kilometers above sea level and y represent the boiling point of water.

Since the boiling point of water at sea level is 100°C, $x = 0$ when $y = 100$. The y-intercept is $(0, 100)$.

The slope is the decrease in the boiling point per kilometer increase in altitude.

Since the boiling point decreases 3.5°C per 1-kilometer increase in altitude, the slope is negative; $m = -3.5$.

To find the linear function, replace m and b in $f(x) = mx + b$ by their values.

$$f(x) = mx + b$$
$$f(x) = -3.5x + 100$$

The linear function is $f(x) = -3.5x + 100$, where $f(x)$ is the boiling point of water x kilometers above sea level.

page S14

■ Question/Answer

At various places during a discussion, we ask the student to respond to a **Question** about the material being read. This question encourages the reader to pause and think about the current discussion and to answer the question. To make sure the student does not miss important information, the **Answer** to the question is provided as a footnote at the bottom of the page.

■ *AIM for Success* Student Preface

This "how to use this book" student preface explains what is required of a student to be successful in mathematics and how this text has been designed to foster student success through the Aufmann Interactive Method (AIM). *AIM for Success* can be used as a lesson on the first day of class or as a project for students to complete to strengthen their study skills. There are suggestions for teaching this lesson in the *Instructor's Resource Manual* and on the *Class Prep* CD.

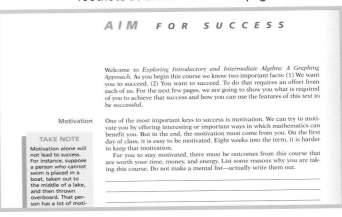

AIM   FOR   SUCCESS

Welcome to *Exploring Introductory and Intermediate Algebra: A Graphing Approach*. As you begin this course we know two important facts: (1) We want you to succeed. (2) You want to succeed. To do that requires an effort from each of us. For the next few pages, we are going to show you what is required of you to achieve that success and how you can use the features of this text to be successful.

Motivation

One of the most important keys to success is motivation. We can try to motivate you by offering interesting or important ways in which mathematics can benefit you. But in the end, the motivation must come from you. On the first day of class, it is easy to be motivated. Eight weeks into the term, it is harder to keep that motivation.

For you to stay motivated, there must be outcomes from this course that are worth your time, money, and energy. List some reasons why you are taking this course. Do not make a mental list—actually write them out.

TAKE NOTE

Motivation alone will not lead to success. For instance, suppose a person who cannot swim is placed in a boat, taken out to the middle of a lake, and then thrown overboard. That person has a lot of moti-

page xxv

PROBLEM SOLVING

YOU TRY IT 3

Find the equation of the line that passes through $P(4, 3)$ and whose slope is undefined.

Solution   See page S14.

EXAMPLE 4

Judging on the basis of data from the Kelley Blue Book, the value of a certain car decreases approximately $250 per month. If the value of the car 2 years after it was purchased was $14,000, find a linear function that models the value of the car after x months of ownership. Use this function to find the value of the car after 3 years of ownership.

State the goal.   Find a linear model that gives the value of the car after x months of ownership. Then use the model to find the value of the car after 3 years.

Devise a strategy.   Because the function will predict the value of the car, let y represent the value of the car after x months.

Then $y = 14,000$ when $x = 24$ (2 years is 24 months).

The value of the car is decreasing $250 per month. Therefore, the slope is -250.

Use the point–slope formula to find the linear model.

To find the value of the car after 3 years (36 months), evaluate the function when $x = 36$.

Solve the problem.

$$y - y_1 = m(x - x_1)$$
$$y - 14,000 = -250(x - 24)$$
$$y - 14,000 = -250x + 6000$$
$$y = -250x + 20,000$$

A linear function that models the value of the car is $V(x) = -250x + 20,000$.

$$f(x) = -250x + 20,000$$
$$f(36) = -250(36) + 20,000 \quad \bullet \text{ Evaluate the function at } x = 36.$$
$$= -9000 + 20,000$$
$$= 11,000$$

The value of the car is $11,000 after 36 months of ownership.

Check your work.   An answer of $11,000 seems reasonable. This value is less than $14,000, the value of the car after 2 years.

The graph of the function is shown at the right. Pressing TRACE 24 shows that the or-

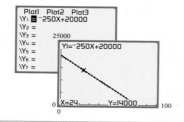

Problem-Solving Strategies

The text features a carefully developed approach to problem solving. Students are encouraged to develop their own strategies—drawing diagrams, for example, or writing out the solution steps in words—as part of their solution to a problem. In each case, model solutions consistently encourage students to

State the goal.
Devise a strategy.
Solve the problem.
Check your work.

Having students describe a strategy is a natural way to incorporate writing into the math curriculum.

EXAMPLE 5

In 2002, the computer service America Online offered its customers the option of paying $23.90 per month for unlimited use. Another option was a rate of $4.95 per month with 3 free hours plus $2.50 per hour thereafter (*Source:* AOL web site, March 2002). How many hours per month can you use this second option if it is to cost you less than the first option? Round to the nearest whole number.

State the goal. The goal is to determine how many hours you can use the second option ($4.95 per month plus $2.50 per hour after the first 3 hours) if it is to cost you less than the first option ($23.90 per month).

Devise a strategy. Let x represent the number of hours per month you use the service. Then $x - 3$ represents the number of hours you would be paying $2.50 per hour for service under the second option.

$$\text{Cost of first plan: } 23.90$$
$$\text{Cost of second plan: } 4.95 + 2.50(x - 3)$$

Write and solve an inequality that expresses that the second plan is less expensive (less than) the first plan.

Solve the problem.
$$4.95 + 2.50(x - 3) < 23.90$$
$$4.95 + 2.50x - 7.50 < 23.90$$
$$2.50x - 2.55 < 23.90$$
$$2.50x < 26.45$$
$$x < 10.58$$

The greatest whole number less than 10.58 is 10.

In order for the second option to cost you less than the first option, you can use the service for up to 10 hours per month.

Check your work. One way to check ... racy of our work. We can also make a p...

page 207

■ Real Data

Real-data examples and exercises, identified by 🔵, ask students to analyze and solve problems taken from actual situations. Students are often required to work with tables, graphs, and charts drawn from a variety of disciplines.

■ Applications

One way to motivate an interest in mathematics is through applications. Wherever appropriate, the last portion of a section presents applications that require the student to use problem-solving strategies, along with the skills covered in that section, to solve practical problems. This carefully integrated applied approach generates student awareness of the value of algebra as a real-life tool.

Applications are taken from many disciplines, including agriculture, business, carpentry, chemistry, construction, Earth science, education, manufacturing, nutrition, real estate, and sociology.

Fit a Line to Data

8. 🔵 *Demography* The table and scatter diagram show the projected number of U.S. high school graduates, in millions (*Source:* National Center for Education Statistics).

Year, x	'01	'03	'05	'07	'09
Number of graduates, y (in millions)	2.90	2.98	2.99	3.13	3.25

a. Find the equation of a line that approximately fits the data by selecting two data points and finding the equation of the line through those two points.
b. What does the slope of your line mean in the context of the problem?
c. What does the y-intercept mean in the context of the problem?

9. 🔵 *Zoology* The table and scatter diagram show the increase in the grey wolf population in regions of Idaho after that species's re-introduction in the mid-1990s (*Source:* U.S. Fish and Wildlife Service).

Year, x	'95	'96	'97	'98	'99	'00
Number of wolves, y	14	42	71	114	141	185

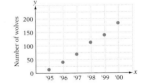

a. Find the equation of a line that approximately fits the data by selecting two data points and finding the equation of the line through those two points.
b. What does the slope of your line mean in the context of the problem?

page 289

INTEGRATION OF TECHNOLOGY

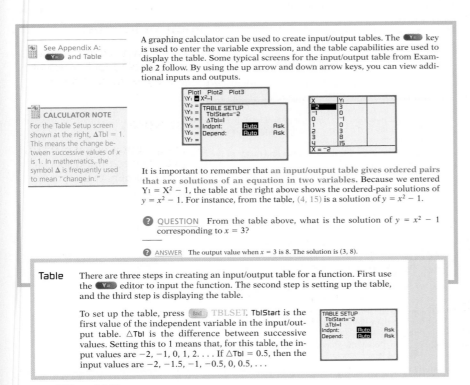

page 205

pages 100 and 841

■ Integration of Technology

We have used a TI-83/TI-83 Plus graphing calculator throughout the text to help students make connections between abstract mathematical concepts and a concrete representation provided by technology. This is one way in which students are encouraged to think about and use multiple representations of a concept.

For appropriate examples within the text, we have provided both an algebraic solution and a graphical representation of the solution. This enables the student to visualize the algebraic solution. For other graphing calculator examples, an algebraic verification of a graphing calculator solution is presented. This promotes the link between the algebraic and graphical components of a solution.

■ Calculator Note

These margin notes provide suggestions for using a calculator in certain situations.

■ Graphing Calculator Appendix A

A TI-83/TI-83 Plus graphing calculator appendix contains some of the common calculator keystrokes that are used in the text. Students are referred to this appendix by appropriately placed *See Appendix A* notes indicating which calculator feature is in use.

In addition, a convenient **calculator bookmark** containing a synopsis of major calculator functions is included in the front of the text. The calculator bookmark can be removed from the text and used to mark the student's current lesson.

STUDENT PEDAGOGY

This text was designed as a resource for students. Special emphasis was given to readability and effective pedagogical use of color to highlight important words and concepts.

■ Icons

The 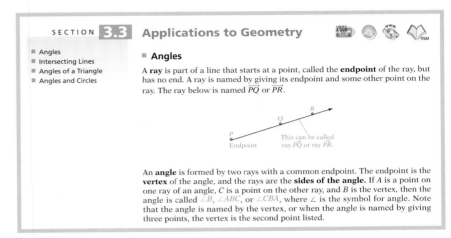, at each objective head remind students of the many and varied additional resources available for each objective.

■ Key Terms and Concepts

Key terms, in bold, emphasize important terms.

SECTION 3.3 **Applications to Geometry**

- Angles
- Intersecting Lines
- Angles of a Triangle
- Angles and Circles

■ Angles

A **ray** is part of a line that starts at a point, called the **endpoint** of the ray, but has no end. A ray is named by giving its endpoint and some other point on the ray. The ray below is named $\overrightarrow{PQ}$ or $\overrightarrow{PR}$.

An **angle** is formed by two rays with a common endpoint. The endpoint is the **vertex** of the angle, and the rays are the **sides of the angle.** If A is a point on one ray of an angle, C is a point on the other ray, and B is the vertex, then the angle is called $\angle B$, $\angle ABC$, or $\angle CBA$, where $\angle$ is the symbol for angle. Note that the angle is named by the vertex, or when the angle is named by giving three points, the vertex is the second point listed.

page 187

SECTION 2.2 Relations and Functions **119**

For the relation between an exam score and a letter grade, the domain is all possible exam scores, and the range is all possible letter grades.

Domain = {0, 1, 2, 3, 4, . . . , 97, 98, 99, 100}   and   Range = {A, B, C, D, F}

Here is one more example of a relation. Consider the situation of a paleontologist trying to determine how fast a dinosaur could run. By studying the relation between the stride lengths of living creatures and the speed at which those creatures run, the scientist can infer the speed of a dinosaur. The table below shows the results of measuring the stride length and speed of various horses.

▼ *Point of Interest*
Studies of foot imprints of dinosaurs suggest they traveled between 2 mph and 7 mph. However, some dinosaurs could run about 25 mph. To put this in perspective, the fastest human can run about 23.5 mph. The fastest land animal (the cheetah) can run about 65 mph.

Stride length (in meters)	2.5	3.2	2.8	3.4	3.2	3.5	4.5	5.2
Speed (in meters per second)	2.6	2.7	2.5	2.8	2.6	2.8	3.2	3.0

This relation is the set of ordered pairs {(2.5, 2.6), (3.2, 2.7), (2.8, 2.5), (3.4, 2.8), (3.2, 2.6), (3.5, 2.8), (4.5, 3.2), (5.2, 3.0)}.

❓ QUESTION What is the meaning of the ordered pair (3.5, 2.8) for the relation above?

Although relations are important in mathematics, the concept of *function* is especially useful in applications.

TAKE NOTE
The idea of *function* is one of the most important concepts in math. It is a concept you will encounter throughout this text.

Definition of a Function
A **function** is a relation in which no two ordered pairs have the same first coordinate and different second coordinates.

The relation between stride length and speed given earlier is *not* a function because the ordered pairs (3.2, 2.7) and (3.2, 2.6) have the same first coordinate and different second coordinates.

Key Concepts are presented in green boxes in order to highlight these important concepts and to provide for easy reference.

■ Point of Interest

These margin notes contain interesting sidelights about mathematics, its history, or its application.

■ Take Note

These margin notes either alert students to a point requiring special attention or amplify the concept under discussion.

page 119

■ Annotated Examples

Examples indicated by ➡ use annotations in blue to explain what is happening in key steps of the complete, worked-out solutions.

As shown in the example that follows, the Addition Property of Inequalities applies to variable terms as well as to constants.

➡ Solve $3x - 4 \leq 2x - 1$. Write the solution set in interval notation.

$$3x - 4 \leq 2x - 1$$
$$3x - 2x - 4 \leq 2x - 2x - 1 \quad \text{• Subtract } 2x \text{ from each side of the inequality.}$$
$$x - 4 \leq -1 \quad \text{• Simplify.}$$
$$x - 4 + 4 \leq -1 + 4 \quad \text{• Add 4 to each side of the inequality.}$$
$$x \leq 3 \quad \text{• Simplify.}$$

The solution set is $(-\infty, 3]$. ⬅

page 203

xix

Exercises

The exercise sets of *Exploring Introductory and Intermediate Algebra: A Graphing Approach* emphasize skill building, skill maintenance, and applications. Concept-based writing or developmental exercises have been integrated with the exercise sets.

Icons identify appropriate writing , group , and data analysis exercises.

Before each exercise set are **Topics for Discussion**, which ask students to discuss or write about a concept presented in the section. Used as oral exercises, these can lead to interesting classroom discussions.

page 288

4.3 EXERCISES

Topics for Discussion

1. What does it mean to "fit a line to data"?

2. What is a regression line?

3. What might be the purpose of determining the regression equation for a set of data?

4. Determine whether the statement is always true, sometimes true, or never true.
   a. For linear regression to be performed on two-variable data, the points corresponding to the data values must lie on a straight line.
   b. If the correlation coefficient is equal to 1, the data exactly fit the regression line. If the correlation coefficient is equal to -1, the data do not fit the regression line.
   c. A scatter diagram is a graph of ordered pairs.

58. *Sound* The distance sound travels through air when the temperature is 75°F can be approximated by $d(t) = 1125t$, where d is the distance, in feet, that sound travels in t seconds. What is the slope of this function? What is the meaning of the slope in the context of this problem?

59. *Biology* The distance that a homing pigeon can fly can be approximated by $d(t) = 50t$, where $d(t)$ is the distance, in miles, flown by the pigeon in t hours. What is the slope of this function? What is the meaning of the slope in the context of this problem?

60. *Construction* The American National Standards Institute (ANSI) states that the slope for a wheelchair ramp must not exceed $\frac{1}{12}$.
    a. Does a ramp that is 6 inches high and 5 feet long meet the requirements of ANSI?
    b. Does a ramp that is 12 inches high and 170 inches long meet the requirements of ANSI?

page 254

Applying Concepts

In Exercises 25 to 36, you were asked to find the number in the domain of function for which the output was the given number. Frequently in mathematics, we express directions such as these by using a combination of words and symbols. For instance, in Exercise 25, we could have written "Find the value of a in the domain of $f(x) = 3x - 4$ for which $f(a) = 5$." Recall that $f(a)$ is output of a function for a given input a. Thus $f(a) = 5$ says the output is 5 an input of a. We will use this terminology in Exercises 70 to 75.

70. Find the value of a in the domain of $f(x) = 2x + 5$ for which $f(a) = -3$

71. Find the value of a in the domain of $g(x) = -2x - 1$ for which $g(a) =$

72. Find the value of a in the domain of $h(x) = \frac{3}{2}x - 2$ for which $h(a) = 4$

73. Find the value of a in the domain of $F(x) = -\frac{5}{4}x - 1$ for which $F(a) =$

74. For $f(x) = x^3 - 4x - 1$, how many different values, a, in the domain satisfy the condition that $f(a) = 1$? (You do not have to find the valu just determine number of possible values for a.)

75. For $f(x) = 0.01(x^4 - 49x^2 + 36x + 252)$, how many different values, a, the domain of f satisfy the condition that $f(a) = 1$? (You do not have find the values; just determine number of possible values for a.)

In Exercises 76 to 79, find two numbers in the domain of the functions for which the values of the functions are equal. *Hint:* Apply the method of finding the point of intersection of two graphs twice, once to each point of intersection.

76. $f(x) = x^2 + 4x - 1, g(x) = 3x + 5$

77. $f(x) = x^2 - x - 1, g(x) = -3x + 2$

78. $f(x) = 2x - 7, g(x) = x^2 - 4x - 2$

79. $f(x) = x + 4, g(x) = x^2 + 3x - 4$

EXPLORATION

1. *Calculator Viewing Windows* A graphing calculator screen consists of **pixels,**[2] which are small rectangles of light that can be turned on or off. When a calculator draws the graph of an equation, it is turning on the pixels that represent the ordered-pair solutions of the equation. The jagged appearance of the graph is a consequence of the solutions being approximations; the pixel nearest the ordered pair is turned on.

[2] Digital cameras are rated in pixels; some cameras have over 3 million pixels. A typical graphing calculator has just over 5800 pixels. Because of this, the graphs on these screens are not so sharp as an image in a digital camera.

3.1

−4.7 · · · · · · · · 4.7

−3.1

Pixel off

Pixel on

Included in each exercise set are **Applying Concepts,** which present extensions of topics, require analysis, or offer challenge problems.

Explorations are extensions of a concept presented in the section. These Explorations can be used in cooperative learning situations or as extra-credit assignments.

■ Chapter Summary

At the end of each chapter there is a Chapter Summary that includes **Key Terms** and **Essential Concepts** that were covered in the chapter. These chapter summaries provide a single point of reference as the student prepares for a test. Each concept is accompanied by the page number from the lesson where the concept is introduced.

CHAPTER **4** SUMMARY

Key Terms

coefficient of determination [p. 281]
constant function [p. 243]
correlation coefficient [p. 281]
half-plane [p. 294]
linear function [p. 235]
linear inequality in two variables [p. 294]
linear regression [p. 280]
line of best fit [p. 278]

negative reciprocals [p. 265]
parallel lines [p. 262]
perpendicular lines [p. 264]
regression line [p. 280]
scatter diagram [p. 277]
slope [p. 236]
solution set of a linear inequality in two variables [p. 294]

Essential Concepts

Slope of a Line
Let $P_1(x_1, y_1)$ and $P_2(x_2, y_2)$ be two points on a line. Then the slope m of the line through the two points is the ratio of the change in the y-coordinates to the change in the x-coordinates. [p. 237]

$$m = \frac{\text{change in } y}{\text{change in } x} = \frac{y_2 - y_1}{x_2 - x_1}, x_1 \neq x_2$$

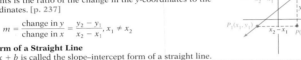

Slope–Intercept Form of a Straight Line
The equation $y = mx + b$ is called the slope–intercept form of a straight line. The slope of the line is m, the coefficient of x. The y-intercept is $(0, b)$.

page 305

■ Chapter Review Exercises

Review exercises are found at the end of each chapter. These exercises are selected to help the student integrate all of the topics presented in the chapter.

306 CHAPTER 4 Linear Functions

CHAPTER **4** REVIEW EXERCISES

1. Find the slope of the line that contains the points $(-1, 3)$ and $(-2, 4)$.

2. Find the slope of the line that passes through the points $(-6, 5)$ and $(-6, 4)$.

3. Graph the line that has slope $\frac{1}{2}$ and passes through the point $(-2, 4)$.

4. Graph $y = -\frac{2}{3}x + 4$ by using the slope and y-intercept.

5. Graph $x + 2y = -4$.

6. Graph $y = 3$.

■ Chapter Test

The Chapter Test exercises are designed to simulate a possible test of the material in the chapter.

CHAPTER **4** TEST

1. Find the slope of the line that contains the points $(-2, 6)$ and $(-1, 4)$.

2. Find the slope of the line that passes through the points $(-4, 3)$ and $(-8, 3)$.

■ Cumulative Review Exercises

Cumulative Review Exercises, which appear at the end of each chapter (beginning with Chapter 2), help students maintain skills learned in previous chapters.

The answers to all Chapter Review Exercises, all Chapter Test exercises, and all Cumulative Review Exercises are given in the Answer Section. Along with the answer, there is a reference to the section that pertains to each exercise.

◀ CUMULATIVE REVIEW EXERCISES

1. In how many different ways can a panel of four on–off switches be set if no two adjacent switches can be off?

2. Given the operation $a @ b = a + ab$, evaluate $(x @ y) @ z$ for $x = 2, y = 3, z = 4$.

3. Let $E = [0, 5, 10, 15]$ and $F = [-10, -5, 0, 5, 10]$. Find $E \cup F$ and $E \cap F$.

pages 306, 307, 309

INSTRUCTOR RESOURCES

Exploring Introductory and Intermediate Algebra: A Graphing Approach has a complete set of teaching aids for the instructor.

Instructor's Annotated Edition   This edition contains a replica of the student text and additional items just for the instructor. These include *Instructor Notes, Suggested Activity* notes, *PowerPoint transparency icons,* and *Suggested Assignments*. Answers to all exercises are also provided.

Instructor's Resource Manual with Testing   The *Instructor's Resource Manual* includes a lesson plan for the *AIM for Success* student preface as well as the complete *Student Activity Manual,* with answers. The testing consists of a *Printed Test Bank* providing a printout of one example of each of the algorithmic items in *HM Testing* and four ready-to-use printed *Chapter Tests* per chapter.

Instructor's Solutions Manual   The *Instructor's Solutions Manual* contains worked-out solutions for all exercises in the text.

HM ClassPrep with HM Testing CD-ROM   *HM ClassPrep* contains a multitude of text-specific resources for instructors to use to enhance the classroom experience. These resources can be easily accessed by chapter or resource type and can also link you to the text's web site. *HM Testing* is our computerized test generator and contains a database of algorithmic test items as well as providing **on-line testing** and **gradebook** functions.

Instructor Text-specific website   The resources available on the *Class Prep CD* are also available on the instructor web site at math.college.hmco.com/instructors. Appropriate items are password protected. Instructors also have access to the student part of the text's web site.

STUDENT RESOURCES

Student Activity Manual   This manual contains worksheets for the optional *Suggested Activities* referenced in the Instructor's Annotated Edition.

Student Solutions Manual   The *Student Solutions Manual* contains complete solutions to all odd-numbered exercises in the text.

Math Study Skills Workbook by Paul D. Nolting   This workbook is designed to reinforce skills and minimize frustration for students in any math class, lab, or study skills course. It offers a wealth of study tips and sound advice on note taking, time mangement, and reducing math anxiety. In addition, numerous opportunities for self-assessment enable students to track their own progress.

HM eduSpace® online learning environment   *eduSpace®* is a text-specific online learning environment that combines an algorithmic tutorial program with homework capabilities. Specific content is available 24 hours a day to enhance your understanding of your textbook.

HM mathSpace™ Tutorial CD-ROM   This tutorial CD ROM allows you to practice skills and review concepts as many times as necessary by providing algorithmically generating exercises and step-by-step solutions for practice.

SMARTHINKING™ live, online tutoring   Houghton Mifflin has partnered with SMARTHINKING to provide an easy-to-use and effective online tutorial service. **Whiteboard Simulations** and **Practice Area** promote real-time visual interaction.

Three levels of service are offered:

- **Text-specific Tutoring** provides real-time, one-on-one instruction with a specially qualified "e-structor."
- **Questions Any Time** allows students to submit questions to the tutor outside the scheduled hours and receive a reply within 24 hours.
- **Independent Study Resources** connect students with around-the-clock access to additional educational services, including interactive web sites, diagnostic tests and Frequently Asked Questions posed to SMARTHINKING e-structors.

Houghton Mifflin Instructional Videos and DVDs   This text offers text-specific videos and DVDs, hosted by Dana Mosely, covering all sections of the text and providing a valuable resource for further instruction and review. Next to every objective head, [VIDEO & DVD] serves as a reminder that the objective is covered in a video/DVD lesson.

Student Text-specific web site   Online student resources can be found at this text's web site at **math.college.hmco.com/students.**

ACKNOWLEDGMENTS

· ·

The authors would like to thank all the people who reviewed this manuscript and provided many valuable suggestions.

Dianne Adams, *Hazard Community College, KY*
Richard B. Basich, *Lakeland Community College, OH*
Laurette Blakey Foster, *Prairie View A&M University, TX*
Anne Haney
Sandeep H. Holay, *Southeast Community College-Lincoln, NE*
Glenn Hunt, *Riverside Community College, CA*
Jerry Kissick, *Portland Community College, OR*
Charyl Link, *Kansas Community College, KS*
Michelle Merriweather, *Southern Connecticut State University, CT*
Kim Nunn, *Northeast State Technical Community College, TN*
Scott Reed, *College of Lake County, IL*
Russ Reich, *Sierra Nevada College, NV*
Deana Richmond
Karl Zilm, *Lewis & Clark Community College, IL*

Special thanks to Christi Verity for her diligent preparation of the solutions manuals and for her contribution to the accuracy of the textbook.

AIM FOR SUCCESS

Welcome to *Exploring Introductory and Intermediate Algebra: A Graphing Approach*. As you begin this course we know two important facts: (1) We want you to succeed. (2) You want to succeed. To do that requires an effort from each of us. For the next few pages, we are going to show you what is required of you to achieve that success and how you can use the features of this text to be successful.

Motivation

One of the most important keys to success is motivation. We can try to motivate you by offering interesting or important ways in which mathematics can benefit you. But in the end, the motivation must come from you. On the first day of class, it is easy to be motivated. Eight weeks into the term, it is harder to keep that motivation.

For you to stay motivated, there must be outcomes from this course that are worth your time, money, and energy. List some reasons why you are taking this course. Do not make a mental list—actually write them out.

_____

_____

_____

> **TAKE NOTE**
>
> Motivation alone will not lead to success. For instance, suppose a person who cannot swim is placed in a boat, taken out to the middle of a lake, and then thrown overboard. That person has a lot of motivation to swim, but there is a high likelihood the person will drown without some help. Motivation gives us the desire to learn but is not the same as learning.

Although we hope that one of the reasons you listed was an interest in mathematics, we know that many of you are taking this course because it is required for graduation, because it is a prerequisite for a course you must take, or because it is required for your major. Although you may not agree that this course is necessary, it is! If you are motivated to graduate or complete the requirements for your major, then use that motivation to succeed in this course. Do not become distracted from your goal to complete your education!

Commitment

To be successful, you must make a commitment to succeed. This means devoting time to math so that you achieve a better understanding of the subject.

List some activities (sports, hobbies, talents such as dance, art, or music) that you enjoy and at which you would like to become better.

ACTIVITY	*TIME SPENT*	*TIME WISHED SPENT*

Thinking about these activities, put next to each activity the number of hours that you spend every week practicing that activity. Then indicate how many hours per week you would like to spend on each activity.

Whether you listed surfing or sailing, aerobics or restoring cars, or any other activity you enjoy, note how many hours a week you spend doing it. To succeed in math, you must be willing to commit the same amount of time. Success requires some sacrifice.

The "I Can't Do Math" Syndrome

There may be things you cannot do, such as lift a 2-ton boulder. You can, however, do math. It is much easier than lifting the 2-ton boulder. When you first learned the activities you listed above, you probably could not do them well. With practice, you got better. With practice, you will be better at math. Stay focused, motivated, and committed to success.

It is difficult for us to emphasize how important it is to overcome the "I Can't Do Math" Syndrome. If you listen to interviews of very successful athletes after a particularly bad performance, you will note that they focus on the positive aspect of what they did, not the negative. Sports psychologists encourage athletes to always be positive—to have a "Can Do" attitude. Develop this attitude toward math.

Strategies for Success

Textbook Reconnaissance   Right now, do a 15-minute "textbook reconnaissance" of this book. Here's how:

First, read the table of contents. Do it in three minutes or less. Next, look through the entire book, page by page. Move quickly. Scan titles, look at pictures, notice diagrams.

A textbook reconnaissance shows you where a course is going. It gives you the big picture. That's useful because brains work best when going from the general to the specific. Getting the big picture before you start makes details easier to recall and understand later on.

Your textbook reconnaissance will work even better if, as you scan, you look for ideas or topics that are interesting to you. List three facts, topics, or problems that you found interesting during your textbook reconnaissance.

_____

_____

_____

The idea behind this technique is simple: It's easier to work at learning material if you know it's going to be useful to you.

Not all the topics in this book will be "interesting" to you. But that is true of any subject. Surfers find that on some days the waves are better than others; musicians find some music more appealing than other music; computer gamers find some computer games more interesting than others; car enthusiasts find some cars more exciting than others. Some car enthusiasts would rather have a completely restored 1957 Chevrolet than a new Ferrari.

Know the Course Requirements   To do your best in this course, you must know exactly what your instructor requires. Course requirements may be stated in a *syllabus*, which is a printed outline of the main topics of the course, or they may be presented orally. When they are listed in a syllabus or on other printed pages, keep them in a safe place. When they are presented orally, make sure to take complete notes. In either case, it is important that you understand the requirements completely and follow them exactly. Be sure you can answer the following questions.

1. What is your instructor's name?
2. Where is your instructor's office?
3. At what times does your instructor hold office hours?
4. Besides the textbook, what other materials does your instructor require?
5. What is your instructor's attendance policy?
6. If you must be absent from a class meeting, what should you do before returning to class? What should you do when you return to class?
7. What is the instructor's policy regarding collection or grading of homework assignments?
8. What options are available if you are having difficulty with an assignment? Is there a math tutoring center?
9. Is there a math lab at your school? Where is it? What hours is it open?
10. What is the instructor's policy if you miss a quiz?
11. What is the instructor's policy if you miss an exam?
12. Where can you get help when studying for an exam?

Remember: Your instructor wants to see you succeed. If you need help, ask! Do not fall behind. If you are running a race and fall behind by 100 yards, you may be able to catch up, but it will require more effort than if you had not fallen behind.

TAKE NOTE

Besides time management, there must be realistic ideas of how much time is available. There are very few people who can *successfully* work full-time and go to school full-time. If you work 40 hours a week, take 15 units, spend the recommended study time given at the right, and sleep 8 hours a day, you will use over 80% of the hours in a week. That leaves less than 20% of the hours in a week for family, friends, eating, recreation, and other activities.

Time Management   We know that there are demands on your time. Family, work, friends, and entertainment all compete for your time. We do not want to see you receive poor job evaluations because you are studying math. However, it is also true that we do not want to see you receive poor math test scores because you devoted too much time to work. When several competing and important tasks require your time and energy, the only way to manage the stress of being successful at both is to manage your time efficiently.

Instructors often advise students to spend twice as much time outside of class studying as they spend in the classroom. Time management is important if you are to accomplish this goal and succeed in school. The following activity is intended to help you structure your time more efficiently.

List the name of each course you are taking this term, the number of class hours each course meets, and the number of hours you should spend studying each subject outside of class. Then fill in a weekly schedule like the one below. Begin by writing in the hours spent in your classes, the hours spent at work (if you have a job), and any other commitments that are not flexible with respect to the time that you do them. Then begin to write down commitments that are more flexible, including hours spent studying. Remember to reserve time for activities such as meals and exercise. You should also schedule free time.

We know that many of you must work. If that is the case, realize that working 10 hours a week at a part-time job is equivalent to taking a three-unit

	Monday	Tuesday	Wednesday	Thursday	Friday	Saturday	Sunday
7–8 a.m.							
8–9 a.m.							
9–10 a.m.							
10–11 a.m.							
11–12 p.m.							
12–1 p.m.							
1–2 p.m.							
2–3 p.m.							
3–4 p.m.							
4–5 p.m.							
5–6 p.m.							
6–7 p.m.							
7–8 p.m.							
8–9 p.m.							
9–10 p.m.							
10–11 p.m.							
11–12 a.m.							

class. If you must work, consider letting your education progress at a slower rate to allow you to be successful at both work and school. There is no rule that says you must finish school in a certain time frame.

Schedule Study Time   As we encouraged you to do by filling out the time management form above, schedule a certain time to study. You should think of this time the way you would the time for work or class—that is, reasons for missing study time should be as compelling as reasons for missing work or class. "I just didn't feel like it" is not a good reason to miss your scheduled study time.

Although this may seem obvious, list a few reasons why you might want to study.

_____

_____

_____

Of course we have no way of knowing what reasons you listed, but from our experience, one reason given quite frequently is "To pass the course." There is nothing wrong with that reason. If that is the most important reason for you to study, then use it to stay focused.

One method of keeping to a study schedule is to form a **study group.** Look for people who are committed to learning, who pay attention in class, and who are punctual. Ask them to join your group. Choose people with similar educational goals but different methods of learning. You can gain insight from seeing the material from a new perspective. Limit groups to four or five people; larger groups are unwieldy.

There are many ways to conduct a study group. Begin with the following suggestions and see what works best for your group.

1. Test each other by asking questions. Each group member might bring two or three sample test questions to each meeting.
2. Practice teaching each other. Many of us who are teachers learned a lot about our subject when we had to explain it to someone else.
3. Compare class notes. You might ask other students about material in your notes that is difficult for you to understand.
4. Brainstorm test questions.
5. Set an agenda for each meeting. Set approximate time limits for each agenda item and determine a quitting time.

And finally, probably the most important aspect of studying is that it should be done in relatively small chunks. If you can study only three hours a week for this course (probably not enough for most people), do it in blocks of one hour on three separate days, preferably after class. Three hours of studying on a Sunday is not as productive as three hours of paced study.

Text Features That Promote Success

Preparing for a Chapter Before you begin a new chapter, you should take some time to review previously learned skills. There are two ways to do this. The first is to complete the ***Cumulative Review,*** which occurs after every chapter (except Chapter 1). For instance, turn to page 309. The questions in this review are taken from the previous chapters. The answers for all these exercises can be found on page A15. Turn to that page now and locate the answers for the Chapter 4 Cumulative Review. After the answer to the first exercise, which is 8 you will see the section reference [1.1]. This means that this question was taken from Chapter 1, Section 1. If you missed this question, you should return to that section and restudy the material.

A second way of preparing for a new chapter is to complete the ***Prep Test.*** This test focuses on the particular skills that will be required for the new chapter. Turn to page 238 to see a Prep Test. The answers for the Prep Test are the first set of answers in the answer section for a chapter. Turn to page A12 to see the answers for the Chapter 4 Prep Test. Note that a section reference is given for each question. If you answer a question incorrectly, restudy the section from which the question was taken.

Before the class meeting in which your professor begins a new section, you should browse through the material, being sure to note each word in bold type. These words indicate important concepts that you must know in order to learn the material. Do not worry about trying to understand all the material. Your professor is there to assist you with that endeavor. The purpose of browsing through the material is so that your brain will be prepared to accept and organize the new information when it is presented to you.

Turn to page 2. Write down the title of Section 1.1. Under the title of the section, write down the words in the section that are in bold print. It is not necessary for you to understand the meaning of these worlds. You are in this class to learn their meaning.

_____ _____ _____ _____

_____ _____ _____ _____

_____ _____ _____ _____

_____ _____ _____ _____

_____ _____ _____ _____

See Appendix A:
Graphing Linear
Inequalities

page 299

Using Technology There are many places in the text where a graphing calculator is used to assist you in making connections between abstract mathematical concepts and a graphical representation provided by the calculator. To benefit from this feature, you must be able to use your calculator effectively. Whenever appropriate, there are *See Appendix A* margin notes. These refer you to a **graphing calculator appendix** at the end of the text that demonstrates many of the major keystrokes you will need in this course. An abbreviated **calculator bookmark** at the beginning of the text can be removed and used to mark your current lesson. The calculator bookmark is a quick keystroke reference for many of the calculator's functions.

Math Is Not a Spectator Sport To learn mathematics you must be an active participant. Listening and watching your professor do mathematics is not enough. Mathematics requires that you interact with the lesson you are studying. If you filled in the blanks above, you were being interactive. There are other ways this textbook has been designed to help you be an active learner.

Annotated Examples A green arrow indicates an example that has explanatory remarks next to solution steps. These examples are used for two purposes. The first is to provide additional examples of important concepts. Second, these examples illustrate important techniques or principles that are often used in the solution of other types of problems.

⟶ Find the equation of the line that contains the point $(4, -1)$ and has slope $-\frac{3}{4}$.

$$y - y_1 = m(x - x_1)$$
• The slope and a point other than the y-intercept are given. Use the point–slope formula.

$$y - (-1) = -\frac{3}{4}(x - 4)$$
• $(x_1, y_1) = (4, -1)$ and $m = -\frac{3}{4}$.

$$y + 1 = -\frac{3}{4}x + 3$$
• Simplify the left side. Use the Distributive Property on the right side.

$$y = -\frac{3}{4}x + 2$$
• Subtract 1 from each side of the equation. The equation is now in the form $y = mx + b$. ⟵

page 262

After you review the example, get a clean sheet of paper. Write down the example, and then try to complete the solution without referring to your notes or the book. When you can do that, move on to the next part of the section. Leaf through the book now, and write down the page numbers of two other occurrences of an "arrowed" example.

Example/You Try It Pairs One of the key instructional features of this text is Example/You Try It pairs. Note that each example is completely worked out and the You Try It following the example is not. Study the worked-out example carefully by working through each step. Then work the You Try It. If you get stuck, refer to the page number following the You Try It, which directs you to the page on which the You Try It is solved—a complete worked-out solution is provided. Try to use the given solution to get a hint for the step you are stuck on. Then try to complete the solution yourself.

You Try It 2

$$y - y_1 = m(x - x_1)$$
$$y - 2 = -\frac{1}{2}[x - (-2)]$$
$$y - 2 = -\frac{1}{2}x - 1$$
$$y = -\frac{1}{2}x + 1$$

page S15

EXAMPLE 2

Find the equation of the line that passes through $P(1, -3)$ and that has slope -2.

Solution $y - y_1 = m(x - x_1)$ • Use the point–slope formula.
$$y - (-3) = -2(x - 1)$$ • $m = -2, (x_1, y_1) = (1, -3)$
$$y + 3 = -2x + 2$$
$$y = -2x - 1$$

In this example, we wrote the equation of the line as $y = -2x - 1$. We could have written the equation in functional notation as $f(x) = -2x - 1$.

YOU TRY IT 2

Find the equation of the line that passes through $P(-2, 2)$ and has slope $-\frac{1}{2}$.

Solution   See page S15.

page 262

When you have completed your solution, check your work against the solution we provided. (Turn to page S15 to see the solution of You Try It 2.) Be aware that frequently there is more than one way to solve a problem. Your answer, however, should be the same as the given answer. If you have any question about whether your method will "always work," check with your instructor or with someone in the math center.

Browse through the textbook and write down the page numbers where two other Example/You Try It pairs occur.

Remember: Be an active participant in your learning process. When you are sitting in class watching and listening to an explanation, you may think that you understand. However, until you actually try to do it, you will have no confirmation of the new knowledge or skill. Most of us have had the experience of sitting in class thinking we knew how to do something, only to get home and realize that we didn't.

Word Problems Word problems are difficult because we must read the problem, determine the quantity we must find, think of a method to find it, actually solve the problem, and then check the answer. In short, you must *state the goal, devise a strategy, solve the problem,* and *check your work.*

TAKE NOTE

There is a strong connection between reading and being a successful student in math or in any other subject. If you have difficulty reading, consider taking a reading course. Reading is much like other skills. There are certain things you can learn that will make you a better reader.

Note in the example below that solving a word problem includes stating the goal, devising a strategy, solving an equation, and checking the answer. If you have difficulty with a word problem, write down the known information. Be very specific. Write out a phrase or sentence that states what you are trying to find. Ask yourself whether there are known formulas that relate the known and unknown quantities. Do not ignore the word problems. They are an important part of mathematics.

EXAMPLE 4

A doctor has prescribed 2 cc (cubic centimeters) of medication for a patient. The tolerance is 0.03 cc. Find the lower and upper limits of the amount of medication to be given.

State the goal.   The goal is to find the lower and upper limits of the amount of medication to be given.

Devise a strategy.   Let p represent the prescribed amount of medication, T the tolerance, and m the given amount of medication. Solve the absolute value inequality $|m - p| \le T$ for m.

Solve the problem.
$$|m - p| \le T$$
$$|m - 2| \le 0.03$$
$$-0.03 \le m - 2 \le 0.03$$
$$1.97 \le m \le 2.03$$

The lower and upper limits of the amount of medication to be given to the patient are 1.97 cc and 2.03 cc.

Check your work.   Be sure to check your work by doing a thorough check of your calculations. As an estimate, the answers appear reasonable in that the amounts of medication are close to 2 cc.

YOU TRY IT 4

A machinist must make a bushing that has a tolerance of 0.003 inch. The diameter of the bushing is 2.55 inch. Find the lower and upper limits of the diameter of the bushing.

Solution   See page S14.

page 223

TAKE NOTE

If a rule has more than one part, be sure to make a notation to that effect.

Rule Boxes Pay special attention to rules placed in boxes. These rules give you the reasons why certain types of problems are solved the way they are. When you see a rule, try to rewrite the rule in your own words.

Find and write down two page numbers on which there are examples of rule boxes.

Absolute Value Inequalities of the Form $|ax + b| < c$

To solve an absolute value inequality of the form $|ax + b| < c$, $c > 0$, solve the equivalent compound inequality $-c < ax + b < c$.

---

page 220

Chapter Exercises When you have finished studying a section, do the exercises in the exercise set that correspond to that section. Math is a subject that needs to be learned in small sections and practiced continually in order to be mastered. Doing all of the exercises in each exercise set will help you master the problem-solving techniques necessary for success. As you work through the exercises for a section, check your answers to the odd-numbered exercises with those at the back of the book.

Preparing for a Test There are important features of this text that can be used to prepare for a test.

- Chapter Summary
- Chapter Review Exercises
- Chapter Test

After completing a chapter, read the Chapter Summary. This summary is divided into two sections: *Key Terms* and *Essential Concepts*. (See page 305 for the Chapter 4 Summary.) This summary highlights the important topics covered in the chapter. The page number following each topic refers you to the page in the text on which you can find more information about the concept.

Following the Chapter Summary are Chapter Review Exercises (see page 306) and a Chapter Test (see page 307). Doing the review exercises is an important way of testing your understanding of the chapter. The answer to each review exercise is given at the back of the book, along with its section reference. After checking your answers, restudy any section from which a question you missed was taken. It may be helpful to retry some of the exercises for that section to reinforce your problem-solving techniques.

The Chapter Test should be used to prepare for an exam. We suggest that you try the Chapter Test a few days before your actual exam. Take the test in a quiet place, and try to complete the test in the same amount of time you will be allowed for your exam. When taking the Chapter Test, practice the strategies of successful test takers: (1) Scan the entire test to get a feel for the questions; (2) Read the directions carefully; (3) Work the problems that are easiest for you first; And, perhaps most important, (4) try to stay calm.

When you have completed the Chapter Test, check your answers. If you missed a question, review the material in that section and rework some of the exercises from that section. This will strengthen your ability to perform the skills in that section.

Your career goal goes here. →

Is it difficult to be successful? YES! Successful music groups, artists, professional athletes, chefs, and _____ have to work very hard to achieve their goals. They focus on their goals and ignore distractions. The things we ask you to do to achieve success take time and commitment. We are confident that if you follow our suggestions, you will succeed.

1

Fundamental Concepts

```
ERR:SYNTAX
1: Quit
2: Goto
```

Be sure to use the correct symbol for a minus sign ⊟ versus a negative sign (−) or your calculator will display this error message.

*What cargo might this freighter be carrying? Agricultural goods, cars, computers, tobacco products? These are only a few of the products exported from the United States each year. The more goods a country exports, the better the likelihood for a favorable balance of trade. In order to avoid a trade deficit, a country needs to export more than it imports. The **Exploration on page 49** shows how to calculate a country's balance of trade and determine whether it is favorable or unfavorable. These calculations involve operations with integers.*

Need help? For online student resources, visit this web site: Math.college.hmco.com

PREP TEST

For Exercises 1 to 4, add, subtract, multiply, or divide.

1. $875 + 49$

2. $1602 - 358$

3. $39(407)$

4. $456 \div 19$

5. What is 127.1649 rounded to the nearest hundredth?

6. Which of the following numbers are greater than -8?

    a. -6 **b.** -10 **c.** 0 **d.** 8

7. Match each fraction with its decimal equivalent.

    a. $\dfrac{1}{2}$ **A.** 0.75

    b. $\dfrac{7}{10}$ **B.** 0.89

    c. $\dfrac{3}{4}$ **C.** 0.5

    d. $\dfrac{89}{100}$ **D.** 0.7

8. What is the least whole number that both 8 and 12 divide evenly into?

9. What is the greatest whole number that divides into both 16 and 20 evenly?

10. Without using 1, write 21 as a product of two whole numbers.

GO FIGURE

If $\boxed{5} = 4$ and $\textcircled{5} = 6$ and $y = x - 1$, which of the following has the greatest value?

    $\boxed{x}$ $\textcircled{x}$ $\boxed{y}$ $\textcircled{y}$

SECTION **1.1** ## Problem Solving

- Problem Solving
- Inductive Reasoning
- Deductive Reasoning

▪ Problem Solving

A group of students is standing, equally spaced, around a circle. The 43rd student is directly opposite the 89th student. How many students are there in the group?

Solving a problem like the one above requires problem-solving strategies. One way to organize these strategies was expressed by George Polya (1887–1985) as a four-step process.

1. **Understand the problem and state the goal.**
2. **Devise a strategy to solve the problem.**
3. **Solve the problem by executing the strategy, and state the answer.**
4. **Review the solution and check your work.**

▼ *Point of Interest*

George Polya was born in Hungary and moved to the United States in 1940. He lived in Providence, Rhode Island, where he taught at Brown University until 1942, when he moved to California. There he taught at Stanford University until his retirement. While at Stanford, he published 10 books and a number of articles for mathematics journals. Of the books Polya published, How To Solve It *(1945) is one of his best known. In this book, Polya outlines a strategy for solving problems. This strategy, although frequently applied to mathematics, can be used to solve problems from virtually any discipline.*

Each of these steps is described below.

Understand the Problem and State the Goal.

This part of problem solving is often overlooked. You must have a clear understanding of the problem.

- Read the problem carefully and try to determine the goal.
- Make sure you understand all the terms or words used in the problem.
- Make a list of known facts.
- Make a list of information that, if known, would help you solve the problem. Remember that it may be necessary to look up information you do not know in another book, in an encyclopedia, at the library, or perhaps on the Internet.

Devise a Strategy to Solve the Problem.

Successful problem solvers use a variety of techniques when they attempt to solve a problem.

- Draw a diagram.
- Work backward.
- Guess and check.
- Solve an easier problem.
- Look for a pattern.
- Make a table or chart.
- Write an equation.
- Produce a graph.

Solve the Problem.

- If necessary, define what each variable represents.
- Work carefully.
- Keep accurate and neat records of your attempts.
- When you have completed the solution, state the answer carefully.

Review the Solution and Check Your Work.

Once you have found a solution, check the solution against the known facts and check for possible errors. Be sure the solution is consistent with the facts of the problem. Another important part of this review process is to ask whether your solution can be used to solve other types of problems.

We will apply this process to the problem stated earlier: A group of students is standing, equally spaced, around a circle. The 43rd student is directly opposite the 89th student. How many students are there in the group?

State the goal.   We need to determine the number of students standing around the circle, given that the 43rd student is standing directly opposite the 89th student.

Devise a strategy. One strategy for this problem is to draw a diagram of the situation. This approach might lead to a method by which to solve the problem.

Solve the problem. First draw a diagram of the students standing around a circle.

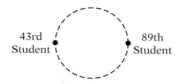

Note that if the 43rd and 89th students are standing opposite each other, then these two students divide the group into two equal parts. The difference between 89 and 43 is one-half of the total number of students.

$$89 - 43 = 46$$

There are 46 students in half of the group.

Multiply 46 by 2 to find the total number of students in the group.

$$46(2) = 92$$

There are 92 students in the group.

Check your work. The answer "92 students" makes sense in the context of this problem. For example, we know that there have to be more than 89 students because we are told the 89th student is in the group.

EXAMPLE 1

Find the sum of the first 10,000 natural numbers.

State the goal. Do you understand the meaning of all terms in the problem? For instance, do you know the meaning of the term *natural number*? Do you know the meaning of the word *sum*?[1] If you do, you will know this problem is asking you to find $1 + 2 + 3 + \ldots + 9998 + 9999 + 10{,}000$.

Devise a strategy. One strategy for this problem would be to use a calculator and just start adding the numbers. However, this plan may lead to mistakes because of all the numbers to enter and then add. Even if we

---

[1] A *natural number* is one of the numbers 1, 2, 3, 4, 5, 6, . . . , where the . . . means that the list of natural numbers continues on and on and that there is no largest natural number. A *sum* is the result of adding numbers.

could enter numbers accurately and quickly—say, one number every two seconds—it would take over 5 hours to get the answer. Therefore, we will try a different strategy: try to solve an easier problem first. The idea is to see whether solving an easier problem will lead to a strategy for solving the original problem.

Solve the problem.   Our easier problem will be to find the sum of the first 10 natural numbers. Note that when the natural numbers are paired as shown below, each pair has the same sum.

$$
\begin{array}{c}
11 \\
11 \\
11 \\
11 \\
11 \\
1 + 2 + 3 + 4 + 5 + 6 + 7 + 8 + 9 + 10
\end{array}
$$

There are 5 pairs ($10 \div 2 = 5$) whose sum is 11.

Because there are 5 pairs whose sum is 11, the sum of the first 10 natural numbers is the product 11 times 5.

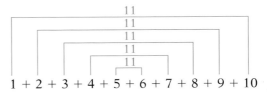

$$1 + 2 + 3 + 4 + 5 + 6 + 7 + 8 + 9 + 10 = 11 \cdot 5 = 55$$

Using the easier problem as a model suggests that a strategy we can use to find the sum of the first 10,000 natural numbers is to pair the numbers, find the sum of one pair, and then multiply that sum by the number of pairs.

Extending the pattern for the easier problem to the original problem, we have

$$
\begin{array}{c}
10,001 \\
10,001 \\
10,001 \\
1 + 2 + 3 + \ldots + 9998 + 9999 + 10,000
\end{array}
$$

There are 5000 pairs ($10,000 \div 2 = 5000$) whose sum is 10,001. Thus,

$$1 + 2 + 3 + \ldots + 9998 + 9999 + 10,000 = 10,001 \cdot 5000 = 50,005,000$$

The sum of the first 10,000 natural numbers is 50,005,000.

Check your work.   By repeating the calculations, you can verify that the solution is correct and is consistent with the problem we were given to solve.

YOU TRY IT 1

The product of the ages of three teenagers is 4590. How old is the oldest if none of the teens are the same age?

Solution   See page S1.

■ Inductive Reasoning

Looking for patterns is one of the techniques used in *inductive reasoning*. Let's look at an example.

Suppose you take 6 credit hours each semester. The total number of credit hours you have taken at the end of each semester can be described in a list of numbers.

$$6, 12, 18, 24, 30, 36, \ldots$$

The list of numbers that indicates the total credit hours is an ordered list of numbers called a **sequence.** Each number in a sequence is called a **term** of the sequence. The list is ordered because the position of a number in the list indicates the semester at the end of which that number of credit hours has been completed. For example, the 5th term of the sequence is 30, and a total of 30 credit hours have been completed after the 5th semester.

? QUESTION   What is the 3rd term of the sequence?*

Now consider another student who is taking courses each semester. The total number of credit hours taken by this student at the end of each semester is given by the sequence

$$9, 18, 27, 36, 45, 54, \ldots$$

? QUESTION   Assuming that the pattern continues in the same manner, what will be the total number of credit hours completed after the 8th semester?†

The process you used to discover the next number in the above sequence is inductive reasoning. **Inductive reasoning** involves making generalizations from specific examples; in other words, we reach a conclusion by making observations about particular facts or cases.

EXAMPLE 2

Use inductive reasoning to find the three missing terms in the sequence.

<u>A</u> <u>2</u> <u>3</u> <u>4</u> <u>B</u> <u>6</u> <u>7</u> <u>8</u> <u>C</u> <u>10</u> <u>11</u> <u>12</u> <u>D</u> <u>14</u> <u>15</u> <u>16</u> . . . __ __ __ <u>64</u>

Solution   The pattern of the sequence is that the numbers 1, 5, 9, 13, . . . are replaced by consecutive letters of the alphabet, beginning with the letter A.

Think of each four terms as a group. The groups end with 4, 8, 12, 16, . . . , which are the multiples of 4.

$64 \div 4 = 16$. Because 64 is the 16th multiple of 4, we are looking for the 16th group. The 16th letter of the alphabet is P.

The missing terms in __ __ __ <u>64</u> are P, 62, 63.

? ANSWERS   * The 3rd term of the sequence is 18. † The 6th term is 54. The 7th term is 63. The 8th term is 72. The total number of credit hours taken after the 8th semester will be 72.

YOU TRY IT 2

A portion of the beads on the string shown below is not visible. How many beads are not visible along the dashed portion of the string?

Solution   See page S1.

EXAMPLE 3

Using a calculator, determine the decimal representation of several proper fractions that have a denominator of 11. For instance, you may use $\frac{2}{11}$, $\frac{5}{11}$, and $\frac{9}{11}$. Then use inductive reasoning to explain the pattern, and use your reasoning to find the decimal representation of $\frac{8}{11}$ without a calculator.

Solution $\frac{2}{11} = 0.181818\ldots$; $\frac{5}{11} = 0.454545\ldots$; $\frac{9}{11} = 0.818181\ldots$

Note that $2(9) = 18$, $5(9) = 45$, and $9(9) = 81$. The repeating digits of the decimal representation of the fraction equal 9 times the numerator of the fraction.

The decimal representation of a proper fraction with a denominator of 11 is a repeating decimal in which the repeating digits are the product of the numerator and 9.

Using this reasoning, we know that $\frac{8}{11} = 0.727272\ldots$

YOU TRY IT 3

Using a calculator, determine the decimal representation of several proper fractions that have a denominator of 33. For instance, you may use $\frac{2}{33}$, $\frac{10}{33}$, and $\frac{25}{33}$. Then use inductive reasoning to explain the pattern, and use your reasoning to find the decimal representation of $\frac{19}{33}$ without a calculator.

Solution   See page S1.

TAKE NOTE

In a proper fraction, the numerator is greater than 0 but less than the denominator.

 CALCULATOR NOTE

To find the decimal representation of $\frac{2}{11}$, press

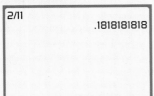

The conclusion formed by using inductive reasoning is often called a **conjecture** because the conclusion may or may not be correct. For example, predict the next letter in the following list.

O, T, T, F, F, S, S, E, . . .

You might predict that the next letter is E because you see two T's, followed by two F's, followed by two S's. However, note that there is only one O at the beginning of the list.

The next letter in the pattern is N, because the letters are chosen by using the first letter in the English words used to name the counting numbers.

One, **T**wo, **Th**ree, **F**our, **F**ive, **S**ix, **S**even, **E**ight, **N**ine, . . .

■ Deductive Reasoning

Another type of reasoning that is used to reach conclusions is called deductive reasoning. **Deductive reasoning** is the process of reaching a conclusion by applying a general principle or rule to a specific example.

For example, suppose that during the last week of your math class, your instructor tells you that if you receive an 88 or better on the final exam, you will earn an A in the course. When grades for the final exam are posted, you learn that you received an 89 on the final exam. By using deductive reasoning, you can conclude that you will earn an A in the course.

Deductive reasoning is also used to reach a conclusion from a sequence of known facts. For example, consider the following:

If Gary completes his thesis, he will pass the course. If Gary passes the course, he will graduate.

From these statements, we can conclude that "If Gary completes his thesis, he will graduate." This is shown in the diagram below.

Gary completes his thesis. $\xrightarrow{\text{means}}$ Gary passes the course. $\xrightarrow{\text{means}}$ Gary will graduate.

Gary completes his thesis. $\xrightarrow{\qquad\qquad\text{means}\qquad\qquad}$ Gary will graduate.

Example 4 is another example of reaching a conclusion from a sequence of known facts.

EXAMPLE 4

If ◇◇◇◇◇ = ‡‡‡ and ‡‡‡ = ▽▽▽▽, how many ◇'s equal ▽▽▽▽▽▽▽▽?

Solution   We are given that ◇◇◇◇◇ = ‡‡‡ and that ‡‡‡ = ▽▽▽▽.

These are the same.

◇◇◇◇◇ = ‡‡‡   and   ‡‡‡ = ▽▽▽▽

Therefore, these are equal.

◇◇◇◇◇ = ▽▽▽▽

Because 4 ▽'s = 5 ◇'s, 8 ▽'s = 10 ◇'s. That is,
▽▽▽▽▽▽▽▽ = ◇◇◇◇◇◇◇◇◇◇.

YOU TRY IT 4

Given that ¥¥¥ = △△△△ and that △△△△ = ΩΩ, how many Ω's equal ¥¥¥¥¥¥¥¥¥?

Solution   See page S1.

EXAMPLE 5

Determine whether the following argument is an example of inductive reasoning or deductive reasoning:

During the past 10 years, this tree has produced fruit every other year. Last year this tree did not produce fruit, so this year the tree will produce fruit.

Solution   The conclusion is based on observation of a pattern. Therefore, it is an example of inductive reasoning.

YOU TRY IT 5

Determine whether the following argument is an example of inductive reasoning or deductive reasoning:

All kitchen remodeling jobs cost more than the contractor's estimate. The contractor estimated the cost of remodeling my kitchen at $35,000. Therefore, it will cost more than $35,000 to have my kitchen remodeled.

Solution   See page S1.

Deductive reasoning, along with a chart, is used to solve problems like the one in Example 6.

EXAMPLE 6

Each of four neighbors, Chris, Dana, Leslie, and Pat, has a different occupation (accountant, banker, chef, or dentist). From the following statements, determine the occupation of each neighbor.

1. Dana usually gets home from work after the banker but before the dentist.
2. Leslie, who is usually the last to get home from work, is not the accountant.
3. The dentist and Leslie usually leave for work at about the same time.
4. The banker lives next door to Pat.

Solution   From statement 1, Dana is not the banker or the dentist. In the chart on the next page, write X1 (which stands for "ruled out by statement 1") for these conditions.

From statement 2, Leslie is not the accountant. We know from statement 1 that the banker is not the last to get home, and we know from statement 2 that Leslie usually is the last to get home; therefore, Leslie is not the banker. In the chart, write X2 for these conditions.

From statement 3, Leslie is not the dentist. Write X3 for this condition. There are now X's for three of the four occupations in Leslie's row; therefore, Leslie must be the chef. Place a √ in that box. Since Leslie is the chef, none of the other three people can be the chef. Write X3 for these conditions. There are now X's for three of the four occupations in Dana's row; therefore, Dana must be the accountant. Place a √ in that box. Since Dana is the accountant, neither Chris nor Pat is an accountant. Write X3 for these conditions.

From statement 4, Pat is not the banker. Write X4 for this condition. Since there are three X's in the banker's column, Chris must be the banker. Place a √ in that box. Now Chris cannot be the dentist. Write X4 in that box. Since there are 3 X's in the dentist's column, Pat must be the dentist. Place a √ in that box.

	Accountant	Banker	Chef	Dentist
Chris	X3	√	X3	X4
Dana	√	X1	X3	X1
Leslie	X2	X2	√	X3
Pat	X3	X4	X3	√

Chris is a banker, Dana is an accountant, Leslie is a chef, and Pat is a dentist.

YOU TRY IT 6

Mike, Clarissa, Roger, and Betty were recently elected as the new officers of the Wycliff Neighborhood Association. From the following statements, determine which position each holds.

1. Mike and the treasurer are next-door neighbors.
2. Clarissa and the secretary have lived in the neighborhood for 5 years, Roger has lived there for 8 years, and the president has lived there for 10 years.
3. Betty has lived in the neighborhood for fewer years than Mike.
4. The vice president has lived in the neighborhood for 5 years.

Solution   See page S1.

1.1 EXERCISES

Topics for Discussion

1. List the four steps involved in Polya's problem-solving process.

2. Discuss some of the strategies used by good problem solvers.

3. When solving a problem, why is it important to write neatly?

4. What is inductive reasoning? Provide an example in which inductive reasoning is used.

5. What is deductive reasoning? Provide an example in which deductive reasoning is used.

■ **Problem Solving**

6. Find the units digit of 7^{97}.

7. A square floor is tiled with congruent square tiles. The tiles on the two diagonals of the floor are blue. The rest of the tiles are green. If 101 blue tiles are used, find the total number of tiles on the floor.

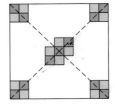

8. What is the least natural number greater than 1 that divides evenly into the sum $3^{11} + 5^{13}$?

9. How many of the first one hundred natural numbers are divisible by all of the numbers 2, 3, 4, and 5?

10. An ewok was visiting an island on which there lived knights, who only make true statements, and knaves, who only make false statements. The ewok needed to find a knight to be a trusty guide. While walking along the shore, the ewok came upon three natives, named Arthur, Bernard, and Charles. The ewok first asked Arthur, "Are Bernard and Charles both knights?" Arthur replied, "Yes." The ewok then asked, "Is Bernard a knight?" To his surprise, Arthur answered, "No." Who is a knight and who is a knave? [Modified from a puzzle by Raymond Smallyan.]

11. What are the next two letters of the sequence A, B, E, F, I, J, ⸬⸰ ?

12. What is the 96th digit in the decimal equivalent of $\frac{1}{7}$?

13. One hundred college seniors were interviewed about their reading habits. The responses revealed that 63 read the *New York Times*, 41 read the *Wall Street Journal*, and 10 read both newspapers. How many students read neither newspaper?

14. What three-digit natural number is equal to 11 times the sum of its digits?

15. How many natural numbers greater than ten and less than one hundred are increased by nine when their digits are reversed?

16. A perfect number is one for which the sum of the proper divisors is equal to the number. (The proper divisors are the ones that are less than the number and divide evenly into the number.) For instance, 496 is a perfect number. The proper divisors of 496 are 1, 2, 4, 8, 16, 31, 62, 124, and 248. The sum of the divisors is

$$1 + 2 + 4 + 8 + 16 + 31 + 62 + 124 + 248 = 496.$$

Find a perfect number between 20 and 30.

17. A car has an odometer reading of 15951 miles, which is a palindrome. (A palindrome is a whole number that remains unchanged when its digits are written in reverse order.) After 2 hours of continuous driving at a constant speed, the odometer reading is the next palindrome. How fast, in miles per hour, was the car being driven during these 2 hours?

18. If all of the digits must be different, how many three-digit odd numbers greater than 700 can be written using only the digits 1, 2, 3, 5, 6, 7?

19. A square is divided into a 100-by-100 grid of smaller squares. If 100 squares are shaded in the top row, 99 in the second row, 98 in the third row, and so on, what is the ratio of the squares shaded to the squares not shaded? Write the answer as a fraction in simplest form.

20.  Suppose you have a balance scale and 8 coins. One of the coins is counterfeit and weighs slightly more than the other 7 coins. Explain how you can find the counterfeit coin in two weighings.

21. How many children are there in a family wherein each girl has as many brothers as sisters, but each boy has twice as many sisters as brothers?

22. The natural numbers greater than 1 are arranged in five columns as shown below. In which column, 1, 2, 3, 4, or 5, will the number 1000 fall?

	2	3	4	5
9	8	7	6	
	10	11	12	13
17	16	15	14	
	18	19	20	21

23. Which terms must be removed from $\frac{1}{2} + \frac{1}{4} + \frac{1}{6} + \frac{1}{8} + \frac{1}{10} + \frac{1}{12}$ if the sum of the remaining terms is to equal 1?

24. The number of a certain type of bacteria doubles every minute. If one of these bacteria is placed in a jar at 1:00 P.M. and starts doubling, the jar will be full in one hour. At what time was the jar half full?

25. A new product, Super-Yeast, causes bread to double in volume each minute. If it takes one loaf of bread 30 minutes to fill an oven, how many minutes would it take two loaves to fill half the oven?

26. September 9, 1981 (9/9/81) was a square-root year date because both the month and the day are square roots of the last two digits of the year. How many square-root dates will there be during the 21st century?

■ Inductive and Deductive Reasoning

For Exercises 27 to 34, use inductive reasoning to predict the next term of the sequence.

27. 5, 11, 17, 23, 29, 35, . . .   **28.** 3, 5, 9, 15, 23, 33, . . .   **29.** 1, 8, 27, 64, 125, . . .

30. $\frac{3}{5}, \frac{5}{7}, \frac{7}{9}, \frac{9}{11}, \frac{11}{13}, \cdots$ **31.** 2, 3, 7, 16, 32, 57, . . .   **32.** $2, 7, -3, 2, -8, -3, -13, -8, \ldots$

33. a, b, f, g, k, l, p, q, . . .   **34.** Z, X, V, T, R, P, . . .

35. Use a calculator to evaluate each of the following.

$$12{,}345{,}679 \cdot 9$$
$$12{,}345{,}679 \cdot 18$$
$$12{,}345{,}679 \cdot 27$$
$$12{,}345{,}679 \cdot 36$$
$$12{,}345{,}679 \cdot 45$$

Then use inductive reasoning to explain the pattern, and use your reasoning to evaluate

$$12{,}345{,}679 \cdot 54 \text{ and } 12{,}345{,}679 \cdot 63$$

without a calculator.

36. Use a calculator to evaluate 15^2, 25^2, 35^2, 45^2, 55^2, 65^2, and 75^2. Then use inductive reasoning to explain the pattern, and use your reasoning to evaluate 85^2 and 95^2 without a calculator.

37. Draw the next figure in the sequence:

38. Draw the next figure in the sequence: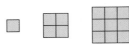

39. Given that ▽▽ = ⊕⊕⊕ and that ⊕⊕⊕ = ΛΛΛΛ, how many Λ's equal ▽▽▽▽▽▽?

40. Given that ⇑ = ◇◇ and ΩΩΩ = ◇◇, how many Ω's equal ⇑⇑⇑?

41. If ♠♠ = ♦♦♦♦♦, and ♦♦♦ = ♣♣, and ♣♣♣♣ = ♥, then how many ♥'s equal ♠♠♠♠♠♠?

42. If ⇊⇊ = ΩΩΩΩΩ, and Ω = ◇◇◇, and ◇◇ = ⊕⊕⊕⊕⊕⊕, then how many ⊕'s equal ⇊⇊?

43. Take the number 7654 and reverse the digits to form the number 4567. Now subtract the smaller number from the larger one ($7654 - 4567 = 3087$). Try this for other four-digit numbers whose digits are consecutive integers written in descending order (largest to smallest). Make a conjecture from your observations.

44. There are four weights labeled A, B, C, and D. A weighs more than B, and B weighs more than D. B and D together weigh more than B and C together. Which weight is the lightest?

45. The year 1998 was unusual in at least one respect: Friday the 13th occurred in two consecutive months. What were the months? (You should be able to do this problem without looking at a calendar for 1998.)

For Exercises 46 to 50, determine whether the argument is an example of inductive or deductive reasoning.

46. All Mark Twain novels are worth reading. *The Adventures of Tom Sawyer* is a Mark Twain novel. Therefore, *The Adventures of Tom Sawyer* is worth reading.

47. Every English setter likes to hunt. Duke is an English setter, so Duke likes to hunt.

48. $2 \cdot 3 + 1 = 7$
$2 \cdot 3 \cdot 5 + 1 = 31$
$2 \cdot 3 \cdot 5 \cdot 7 + 1 = 211$
$2 \cdot 3 \cdot 5 \cdot 7 \cdot 11 + 1 = 2311$

Therefore, the product of the first n prime numbers increased by 1 is always a prime number.

49. I have enjoyed each of Tom Clancy's novels. Therefore, I know that I will like his next novel.

50. The Atlanta Braves have won eight games in a row. Therefore, the Atlanta Braves will win their next game.

51. Each of four siblings (Anita, Tony, Maria, and Jose) is given $5000 to invest in the stock market. Each chooses a different stock. One chooses a utility stock, another an automotive stock, another a technology stock, and the other an oil stock. From the following statements, determine which sibling bought which stock.

    a. Anita and the owner of the utility stock purchased their shares through an online brokerage, whereas Tony and the owner of the automotive stock did not.

    b. The gain in value of Maria's stock is twice the gain in value of the automotive stock.

    c. The technology stock is traded on NASDAQ, whereas the stock that Tony bought is traded on the New York Stock Exchange.

52. The Changs, Steinbergs, Ontkeans, and Gonzaleses were winners in the All-State Cooking Contest. There was a winner in each of four categories: soup, entrée, salad, and dessert. From the following statements, determine in which category each family was the winner.

    a. The soups were judged before the Ontkeans' winning entry.

    b. This year's contest was the first for the Steinbergs and for the winner in the dessert category. The Changs and the winner in the soup category entered last year's contest.

    c. The winning entrée took 2 hours to cook, whereas the Steinberg's entrée required no cooking at all.

53. The cities of Atlanta, Chicago, Philadelphia, and Seattle held conventions this summer for collectors of coins, stamps, comic books, and baseball cards. From the following statements, determine which collectors met in which city.

    a. The comic book collectors convention was in August, as was the convention held in Chicago.

    b. The baseball card collectors did not meet in Philadelphia, and the coin collectors did not meet in Seattle or Chicago.

    c. The convention in Atlanta was held during the week of July 4, whereas the coin collectors convention was held the week after that.

    d. The convention in Chicago had more collectors attending it than did the stamp collectors convention.

54. Each of the Little League teams in a small rural community is sponsored by a different local business. The names of the teams are the Dodgers, the Pirates, the Tigers, and the Giants. The businesses that sponsor the teams are the bank, the supermarket, the service station, and the drug store. From the following statements, determine which business sponsors each team.

    a. The Tigers and the team sponsored by the service station have winning records this season.

    b. The Pirates and the team sponsored by the bank are coached by parents of the players, whereas the Giants and the team sponsored by the drug store are coached by the director of the Community Center.

    c. Jake is the pitcher for the team sponsored by the supermarket and coached by his father.

    d. The game between the Tigers and the team sponsored by the drug store was rained out yesterday.

Applying Concepts

55. It is a fact that the fourth power of any number ends with a 1, a 5, or a 6. On the basis of this, can you conclude that 134,512,357,186 is the fourth power of some number?

56. Predict the next term of the sequence 1, 5, 12, 22, 35, . . .

57. $1K31K4$ represents a six-digit number that is a multiple of 12 but not a multiple of 9. Find the value of K. *Note:* All K's represent the same digit.

58. Let x be the least of three natural numbers whose product is 720. Find the greatest possible value of x.

59. Find the least value of d that satisfies $a^2 + b^2 + c^2 = d^2$, where a, b, c, and d are natural numbers, not necessarily different.

60. During the spring campus clean-up day, four students (Daisy, Heather, Lily, and Rose) each did different chores (painting, pruning, raking, or washing). Each worked a different number of hours (5, 6, 7, or 8 hours). From the following statements, determine each student's chore and the length of time each worked. You might find it helpful to use the chart provided below the statements.

    a. Lily and the student who did the pruning worked the longest hours.

    b. Daisy and the student who did the washing started working at the same time, but Daisy worked 3 hours longer.

    c. Rose, Lily, and the student who did the washing all worked at the campus clean-up day last year.

    d. The student who did the raking worked 2 hours less than the student who did the pruning and 1 hour more than Heather.

	Painting	Pruning	Raking	Washing	5 hours	6 hours	7 hours	8 hours
Daisy								
Heather								
Lily								
Rose								
5 hours								
6 hours								
7 hours								
8 hours								

EXPLORATION

1. *The Game of Sprouts*   The mathematician John H. Conway has created
    several games that are easy to play but complex enough to be challeng-
    ing. For instance, in 1967, Conway, along with Michael Paterson, created
    the two-person, paper-and-pencil game of Sprouts. After more than 30
    years, the game has not been completely analyzed.

    Here are the rules for Sprouts.

    - Begin by drawing a few dots on a piece of paper. (Keep the number
      small to ensure that you can complete the game.)
    - The players alternate turns. A turn consists of drawing an arc between
      two dots or drawing a curve that starts at a dot and ends at the same
      dot. The active player then draws a new dot at the midpoint of the
      new arc.
    - No dot can have more than three arcs coming from it.
    - No arc can cross itself or any previously drawn arc.
    - The winner is the player to draw the last possible arc.

    Here is an example of a game of Sprouts that begins with two dots.

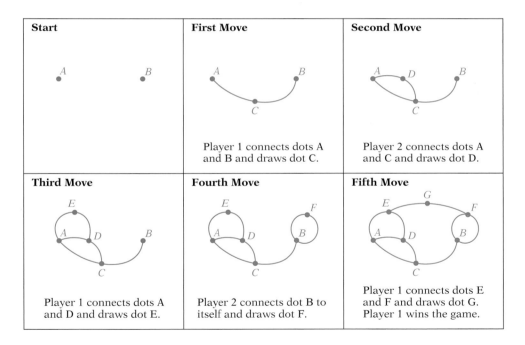

Start	First Move	Second Move
	Player 1 connects dots A and B and draws dot C.	Player 2 connects dots A and C and draws dot D.

Third Move	Fourth Move	Fifth Move
Player 1 connects dots A and D and draws dot E.	Player 2 connects dot B to itself and draws dot F.	Player 1 connects dots E and F and draws dot G. Player 1 wins the game.

    A dot with no arc emanating from it is said to have three lives. A dot with
    one arc emanating from it has two lives. A dot with two arcs emanating
    from it has one life. A dot is dead and cannot be used if it has three arcs
    emanating from it.

    Note in the game above that dot G has only two arcs emanating from it,
    so it has one life. But every other dot has three arcs emanating from it
    and is therefore dead. Thus there is no dot to connect to G, and the game

is over. (Dot G cannot be connected to itself, because it would then have more than three arcs coming from it.)

a. Play a few games of one-spot Sprouts. How many moves are needed to determine a winner?

b. In a two-dot game, how many initial moves are possible?

c. Try to play out all possible two-dot games. How many moves are needed to determine a winner?

d. In a two-dot game, which player is guaranteed a win? Did you use inductive or deductive reasoning to answer this question?

e. In a three-dot game, how many initial moves are possible?

f. Play several three-dot games. How many moves are needed to determine a winner?

g. In a three-dot game, which player is guaranteed a win? Did you use inductive or deductive reasoning to answer this question?

SECTION **1.2** # Sets

- Sets of Numbers
- Union and Intersection of Sets
- Interval Notation

■ Sets of Numbers

The tendency to group similar items seems to be a typical human trait. For instance, a botanist groups plants with similar characteristics in groups called species. Nutritionists classify foods according to food groups; for example, pasta, crackers, and rice are among the foods in the bread group.

Mathematicians place objects with similar properties in groups called sets. A **set** is a collection of objects. The objects in a set are called the **elements** of the set.

The **roster method** of writing sets is to enclose a list of the elements in braces. The set of sections within an orchestra is written {brass, percussion, string, woodwind}.

The numbers that we use to count objects, such as the number of students enrolled in a university or the number of stars in a constellation, are the natural numbers.

Natural numbers = {1, 2, 3, 4, 5, 6, 7, 8, 9, 10, . . .}

The set of natural numbers is an example of an **infinite set;** the pattern of numbers continues without end. It is impossible to list all the elements of an

▼ *Point of Interest*

Georg Cantor (1845–1918) was a German mathematician who developed many new concepts that dealt with the theory of sets. At the age of 15 he had decided that he wanted to become a mathematician, but his father coerced him into the field of engineering because it was a more lucrative profession. After
(continued)

▼ *Point of Interest (cont.)*
a few years, Cantor's father realized that his son was not suited to engineering, and he permitted Georg to seek a career in mathematics.

Much of Cantor's work was controversial. One of the simplest of the controversial concepts concerned points on a line segment. For instance, consider the line segment AB and the line segment CD shown below.

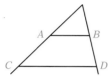

Which line segment do you think contains the most points? Cantor was able to show that they both contain the same number of points. In fact, he was able to show that any line segment—no matter how short—contains the same number of points as a line, or as a plane, or as all of three-dimensional space.

infinite set. The set of even natural numbers less than 9 is written {2, 4, 6, 8}. This is an example of a **finite set;** all the elements of the set can be listed.

Each natural number greater than 1 is either a prime number or a composite number. **A prime number** is a natural number greater than 1 that is evenly divisible only by itself and 1. The first six prime numbers are 2, 3, 5, 7, 11, 13. A natural number greater than 1 that is not a prime number is a **composite number.** The numbers 4, 6, 8, 9, and 10 are the first five composite numbers.

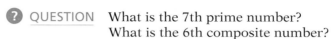

? QUESTION   What is the 7th prime number?
What is the 6th composite number?

The natural numbers do not have a symbol to denote the concept of none—for instance, the number of college students at Providence College that are under the age of 10. The whole numbers include zero and the natural numbers.

Whole numbers = {0, 1, 2, 3, 4, 5, 6, 7, 8, 9, 10, . . .}

The whole numbers do not provide all the numbers that are useful in applications. For example, a meteorologist also needs numbers less than zero.

Integers = {. . ., −5, −4, −3, −2, −1, 0, 1, 2, 3, 4, 5, . . .}

The integers . . ., −5, −4, −3, −2, −1 are **negative integers.** The integers 1, 2, 3, 4, 5, . . . are **positive integers.** Note that the natural numbers and the positive integers are the same set of numbers. The integer zero is neither a positive nor a negative integer.

EXAMPLE 1

Use the roster method to write the set of whole numbers less than 7.

Solution   {0, 1, 2, 3, 4, 5, 6}

YOU TRY IT 1

Use the roster method to write the set of positive odd integers less than 10.

Solution   See page S2.

Still other numbers are necessary to solve the variety of application problems that exist. For instance, a plumber may need to purchase drain pipe that has a diameter of $\frac{5}{8}$ inch. The set of numbers that include fractions are called rational numbers.

Rational numbers = $\left\{ \dfrac{p}{q}, \text{ where } p \text{ and } q \text{ are integers and } q \neq 0 \right\}$

Examples of rational numbers include $\frac{2}{3}$, $-\frac{9}{2}$, and $\frac{5}{1}$. Note that $\frac{5}{1} = 5$; all integers are rational numbers. The number $\frac{4}{\pi}$ is not a rational number because π is not an integer.

? ANSWER   The 7th prime number is 17. The 6th composite number is 12.

A fraction can be written in decimal notation by dividing the numerator by the denominator. For example, $\frac{7}{20} = 7 \div 20 = 0.35$ and $\frac{5}{9} = 5 \div 9 = 0.\overline{5}$. The number 0.35 is an example of a **terminating decimal.** $0.\overline{5}$ is an example of a **repeating decimal;** the bar over 5 indicates that this digit repeats. Every rational number can be written as either a terminating or a repeating decimal.

Some numbers cannot be written as terminating or repeating decimals; examples include 0.02002000200002 . . ., $\sqrt{7} = 2.645751\ldots$, and $\pi = 3.1415926\ldots$. These numbers have decimal representations that neither terminate nor repeat. They are called **irrational numbers.**

The rational numbers and the irrational numbers taken together are the **real numbers.**

The relationship among sets of numbers is shown in the figure below.

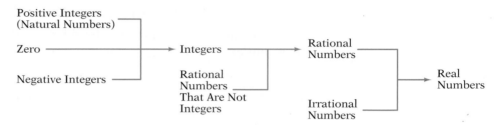

The **real number line** is used as a graphical representation of the real numbers. Although usually only integers are shown on the real number line, it represents the real numbers. The **graph of a real number** is made by placing a heavy dot on a number line directly above the number. The graphs of some real numbers are shown below.

It is common to designate a set by a capital letter. For instance, if A is the set of the first four letters of the alphabet, then $A = \{a, b, c, d\}$.

To refer to the elements of a set, the symbol $\in$ is used. This symbol is read "is an element of." The symbol $\notin$ means "is not an element of."

Given $B = \{1, 3, 5\}$, then $1 \in B$, $3 \in B$, and $6 \notin B$.

The **empty set,** or **null set,** is the set that contains no elements. The symbol $\varnothing$ or $\{\}$ is used to represent the empty set. The set of people who have run a 2-minute mile is the empty set.

A second method of representing a set is **set-builder notation.** Set-builder notation can be used to describe almost any set, but it is especially useful for writing infinite sets. In set-builder notation, the set of integers greater than -4 is written

$$\{x \mid x > -4, x \in \text{integers}\}$$

This is read "the set of all x such that x is greater than -4 and x is an element of the integers." Recall that the symbol $>$ means "is greater than."

The set of real numbers less than 5 is written

$$\{x \,|\, x < 5, x \in \text{real numbers}\}$$

which is read "the set of all x such that x is less than 5 and x is an element of the real numbers." Recall that the symbol $<$ means "is less than."

> ### EXAMPLE 2
>
> Use set-builder notation to write the set of integers greater than -6.
>
> **Solution** $\{x \,|\, x > -6, x \in \text{integers}\}$

> **YOU TRY IT 2**
>
> Use set-builder notation to write the set of real numbers greater than 19.
>
> **Solution**   See page S2.

The inequality symbols $>$ and $<$ are sometimes combined with the equality symbol.

$a \geq b$ is read "a is greater than or equal to b" and means $a > b$ or $a = b$.

$a \leq b$ is read "a is less than or equal to b" and means $a < b$ or $a = b$.

Sets described using set-builder notation and the inequality symbols $>$, $<$, $\geq$, and $\leq$ can be graphed on the real number line.

The graph of $\{x \,|\, x > -2, x \in \text{real numbers}\}$ is shown at the right. The set is the real numbers greater than -2. The parenthesis on the graph indicates that -2 is not included in the set.

The graph of $\{x \,|\, x \geq -2, x \in \text{real numbers}\}$ is shown at the right. The set is the real numbers greater than or equal to -2. The bracket at -2 indicates that -2 is included in the set.

For the remainder of this section, all variables will represent real numbers unless otherwise stated. Using this convention, the set above would be written $\{x \,|\, x \geq -2\}$.

> ### EXAMPLE 3
>
> Graph $\{x \,|\, x \leq 3\}$.
>
> **Solution**   The set is the real numbers less than or equal to 3. Draw a right bracket at 3, and darken the number line to the left of 3.
>
>

TAKE NOTE

A parenthesis is used to indicate that the number is not included in the set. A bracket is used to indicate that the number is included in the set.

YOU TRY IT 3

Graph $\{x | x > -3\}$.

Solution   See page S2.

■ Union and Intersection of Sets

Just as operations such as addition and multiplication are performed on real numbers, operations are performed on sets. Two operations performed on sets are union and intersection.

The **union of two sets,** which is written $A \cup B$, is the set of all elements that belong to either A or B. In set-builder notation, this is written

$$A \cup B = \{x | x \in A \text{ or } x \in B\}$$

Given $A = \{2, 3, 4\}$ and $B = \{0, 1, 2, 3\}$, $A \cup B = \{0, 1, 2, 3, 4\}$. Note that an element that belongs to both sets is listed only once in their union.

> **TAKE NOTE**
>
> When we list the elements of a set, the order is not important. Thus the set $\{2, 3, 4, 0, 1\}$ is the same as the set $\{0, 1, 2, 3, 4\}$. However, numerical elements are generally listed in increasing order so that it is easier to read and compare sets.

EXAMPLE 4

Find $C \cup D$ given $C = \{1, 5, 9, 13, 17\}$ and $D = \{3, 5, 7, 9, 11\}$.

Solution $C \cup D = \{1, 3, 5, 7, 9, 11, 13, 17\}$

YOU TRY IT 4

Find $E \cup F$ given $E = \{-2, -1, 0, 1, 2\}$ and $F = \{-5, -1, 0, 1, 5\}$.

Solution   See page S2.

The set $\{x | x \le -1\} \cup \{x | x > 3\}$ is the set of real numbers that are either less than or equal to -1 or greater than 3.

The set is written $\{x | x \le -1 \text{ or } x > 3\}$.

The set $\{x | x > 2\} \cup \{x | x > 4\}$ is the set of real numbers that are either greater than 2 or greater than 4.

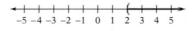

The set is written $\{x | x > 2\}$.

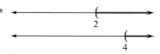

The union is the numbers greater than 2.

▼ Point of Interest

Some mathematics that concerns sets has led to paradoxes. For example, in 1902 Bertrand Russell developed the following paradox: "Is the set A of all sets that are not elements of themselves an element of itself?" Both the assumption that A is an element of A and the assumption that A is not an element of A lead to a contradiction.

Russell's paradox has been popularized in the following form: "The town barber shaves all males who do not shave themselves, and he shaves only those males. The town barber is a male who shaves. Who shaves the barber?" The assumption that the barber shaves himself leads to a contradiction, and the assumption that the barber does not shave himself also leads to a contradiction.

EXAMPLE 5

Graph $\{x\,|\,x \le 0\} \cup \{x\,|\,x \ge 4\}$.

Solution   The set is the numbers less than or equal to 0 or greater than or equal to 4.

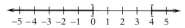

YOU TRY IT 5

Graph $\{x\,|\,x \ge 1\} \cup \{x\,|\,x \le -3\}$.

Solution   See page S2.

The **intersection of two sets,** which is written $A \cap B$, is the set of all elements that are common to both A and B. In set-builder notation, this is written

$$A \cap B = \{x\,|\,x \in A \text{ and } x \in B\}$$

Given $A = \{2, 3, 4\}$ and $B = \{0, 1, 2, 3\}$, $A \cap B = \{2, 3\}$.

EXAMPLE 6

a. Find $C \cap D$ given $C = \{3, 6, 9, 12\}$ and $D = \{0, 6, 12, 18\}$.
b. Find $E \cap F$ given $E = \{x\,|\,x \in \text{natural numbers}\}$ and $F = \{x\,|\,x \in \text{negative integers}\}$.

Solution   **a.** $C \cap D = \{6, 12\}$
                b. There are no natural numbers that are also negative integers.
                $E \cap F = \varnothing$

YOU TRY IT 6

a. Find $A \cap B$ given $A = \{-2, -1, 0, 1, 2\}$ and $B = \{-10, -5, 0, 5, 10\}$.
b. Find $C \cap D$ given $C = \{x\,|\,x \in \text{odd integers}\}$ and $D = \{x\,|\,x \in \text{even integers}\}$.

Solution   See page S2.

The set $\{x\,|\,x > -2\} \cap \{x\,|\,x < 5\}$ is the set of real numbers that are greater than -2 and less than 5.

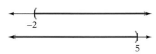

The intersection is the numbers between -2 and 5.

The set can be written $\{x\,|\,x > -2 \text{ and } x < 5\}$. However, it is more commonly written $\{x\,|\,-2 < x < 5\}$, which is read "the set of all x such that x is greater than -2 and less than 5."

The set $\{x \mid x < 4\} \cap \{x \mid x < 5\}$ is the real numbers that are less than 4 and less than 5.

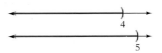

The set is written $\{x \mid x < 4\}$.

The intersection is the numbers less than 4.

EXAMPLE 7

Graph $\{x \mid x < 0\} \cap \{x \mid x > -3\}$.

Solution   The set is $\{x \mid -3 < x < 0\}$.

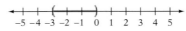

YOU TRY IT 7

Graph $\{x \mid x \leq 2\} \cap \{x \mid x \geq -1\}$.

Solution   See page S2.

■ Interval Notation

Some sets can also be expressed using **interval notation.** For example, the interval notation $(-3, 2]$ indicates the interval of all real numbers greater than -3 and less than or equal to 2. As on the graph of a set, the left parenthesis indicates that -3 is not included in the set. The right bracket indicates that 2 is included in the set.

An interval is said to be **closed** if it includes both endpoints; it is **open** if it does not include either endpoint. An interval is **half-open** if one endpoint is included and the other is not. In each of the following examples, -3 and 2 are the endpoints of the interval. In each case, the set notation, the interval notation, and the graph of the set are shown.

$\{x \mid -3 < x < 2\}$	$(-3, 2)$ Open interval	
$\{x \mid -3 \leq x \leq 2\}$	$[-3, 2]$ Closed interval	
$\{x \mid -3 \leq x < 2\}$	$[-3, 2)$ Half-open interval	
$\{x \mid -3 < x \leq 2\}$	$(-3, 2]$ Half-open interval	

To indicate an interval that extends forever in one or both directions using interval notation, we use the **infinity symbol** ∞ or the **negative infinity symbol** $-\infty$. The infinity symbol is not a number; it is simply used as a notation to indicate that the interval is unlimited. In interval notation, a parenthesis is always used to the right of an infinity symbol or to the left of a negative infinity symbol, as shown in the following examples.

Set-Builder Notation	Interval Notation	Graph
$\{x \mid x > 1\}$	$(1, \infty)$	
$\{x \mid x \geq 1\}$	$[1, \infty)$	
$\{x \mid x < 1\}$	$(-\infty, 1)$	
$\{x \mid x \leq 1\}$	$(-\infty, 1]$	
$\{x \mid -\infty < x < \infty\}$	$(-\infty, \infty)$	

EXAMPLE 8

a. Write $\{x \mid 0 < x \leq 5\}$ using interval notation.
b. Write $(-\infty, 9]$ using set-builder notation.

Solution   **a.** The set is the real numbers greater than 0 and less than or equal to 5.
$(0, 5]$

b. The set is the real numbers less than or equal to 9.
$\{x \mid x \leq 9\}$

YOU TRY IT 8

a. Write $\{x \mid -8 \leq x < -1\}$ using interval notation.
b. Write $(-12, \infty)$ using set-builder notation.

Solution   See page S2.

EXAMPLE 9

Graph $(-\infty, 3) \cap [-1, \infty)$.

Solution $(-\infty, 3) \cap [-1, \infty)$ is the set of real numbers greater than or equal to -1 and less than 3.

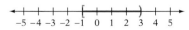

YOU TRY IT 9

Graph $(-\infty, -2) \cup (-1, \infty)$.

Solution   See page S2.

1.2 EXERCISES

Topics for Discussion

1. Explain the similarities and differences between rational and irrational numbers.

2. Explain the difference between the union of two sets and the intersection of two sets.

3. Explain the difference between $\{x \,|\, x < 5\}$ and $\{x \,|\, x \leq 5\}$.

4. Explain the similarities and differences between open intervals and closed intervals.

5. **a.** Is the intersection of two infinite sets always an infinite set? Explain your reasoning.
   b. Is the union of two infinite sets always an infinite set? Explain your reasoning.

■ Sets of Numbers

Determine which of the numbers are **a.** natural numbers, **b.** whole numbers, **c.** integers, **d.** positive integers, **e.** negative integers, **f.** prime numbers. List all that apply.

6. $-14, 9, 0, 53, 7.8, -626$

7. $31, -45, -2, 9.7, 8600, \dfrac{1}{2}$

Determine which of the numbers are **a.** integers, **b.** rational numbers, **c.** irrational numbers, **d.** real numbers. List all that apply.

8. $-\dfrac{15}{2}, 0, -3, \pi, 2.\overline{33}, 4.232232223\ldots, \dfrac{\sqrt{5}}{4}, \sqrt{7}$

9. $-17, 0.3412, \dfrac{3}{\pi}, -1.010010001\ldots, \dfrac{27}{91}, 6.1\overline{2}$

Use the roster method to list the elements of each set.

10. The integers between -3 and 5

11. The integers between -4 and 0

12. The even natural numbers less than or equal to 10

13. The odd natural numbers less than 15

14. The letters in the word Mississippi

15. The letters in the word banana

16. The odd numbers evenly divisible by 2

17. The natural numbers less than 0

Use set-builder notation to write the set.

18. The integers greater than 7

19. The integers less than -5

20. The real numbers less than or equal to 0

21. The real numbers greater than or equal to -4

22. The real numbers between -1 and 4

23. The real numbers between -2 and 5

For Exercises 24 to 29, answer True or False.

24. $7 \in \{2, 3, 5, 7, 9\}$

25. $4 \notin \{-8, -4, 0, 4, 8\}$

26. $\varnothing \in \{0, 1, 2, 4\}$

27. $\{a\} \in \{a, b, c, d, e\}$

28. $5 \in \{x \mid x \in \text{prime numbers}\}$

29. $0 \in \varnothing$

Graph.

30. $\{x \mid x < 2\}$

31. $\{x \mid x < -1\}$

32. $\{x \mid x \geq 1\}$

33. $\{x \mid x \leq -2\}$

■ Union and Intersection of Sets

For Exercises 34 to 37, find $A \cup B$.

34. $A = \{1, 4, 9\}, B = \{2, 4, 6\}$

35. $A = \{2, 3, 5, 8\}, B = \{9, 10\}$

36. $A = \{x \mid x \in \text{whole numbers}\}$
$B = \{x \mid x \in \text{positive integers}\}$

37. $A = \{x \mid x \in \text{rational numbers}\}$
$B = \{x \mid x \in \text{real numbers}\}$

For Exercises 38 to 41, find $A \cap B$.

38. $A = \{6, 12, 18\}, B = \{3, 6, 9\}$

39. $A = \{2, 4, 6, 8, 10\}, B = \{4, 6\}$

40. $A = \{x \mid x \in \text{rational numbers}\}$
$B = \{x \mid x \in \text{real numbers}\}$

41. $A = \{x \mid x \in \text{rational numbers}\}$
$B = \{x \mid x \in \text{irrational numbers}\}$

42. Let $B = \{2, 4, 6, 8, 10\}$ and $C = \{2, 3, 5, 7\}$. Find $B \cup C$ and $B \cap C$.

43. Let $M = \{1, 4, 6, 8, 9, 10\}$ and $C = \{2, 3, 5, 7\}$. Find $M \cup C$ and $M \cap C$.

Graph.

44. $\{x \mid x > 1\} \cup \{x \mid x < -1\}$

45. $\{x \mid x \leq 2\} \cup \{x \mid x > 4\}$

46. $\{x \mid x \leq 2\} \cap \{x \mid x \geq 0\}$

47. $\{x \mid x > -1\} \cap \{x \mid x \leq 4\}$

48. $\{x \mid 0 \leq x \leq 3\}$

49. $\{x \mid -1 < x < 5\}$

50. $\{x \mid 1 < x < 3\}$

51. $\{x \mid -1 \leq x \leq 1\}$

52. $\{x \mid x > 1\} \cap \{x \mid x \geq -2\}$

53. $\{x \mid x < -2\} \cup \{x \mid x < -4\}$

■ **Interval Notation**

For Exercises 54 to 59, write the interval in set-builder notation.

54. $(0, 8)$ **55.** $[-5, 7]$ **56.** $[-3, 6)$

57. $(-9, 5]$ **58.** $(-\infty, 4]$ **59.** $[-2, \infty)$

For Exercises 60 to 68, write the set of real numbers in interval notation.

60. $\{x \mid -2 < x < 4\}$ **61.** $\{x \mid 0 \le x \le 3\}$ **62.** $\{x \mid -4 \le x < -1\}$

63. $\{x \mid -2 \le x < 7\}$ **64.** $\{x \mid -10 < x \le -6\}$ **65.** $\{x \mid x \le -5\}$

66. $\{x \mid x < -2\}$ **67.** $\{x \mid x > 23\}$ **68.** $\{x \mid x \ge -8\}$

Graph.

69. $[0, 3]$ **70.** $(-1, 4]$ **71.** $(1, \infty)$

72. $(-\infty, 2] \cup [4, \infty)$ **73.** $(-3, 4] \cup [-1, 5)$ **74.** $[-1, 2] \cap [0, 4]$

75. $[-5, 4) \cap (-2, \infty)$ **76.** $(2, \infty) \cup (-2, 4]$ **77.** $(-\infty, 2] \cup (4, \infty)$

Applying Concepts

78. Let $C = \{5, 12, 15, 17\}$. If $A = \{5, 12\}$ and $A \cap B = \{5\}$ and $A \cup B = C$, find the sum of the numbers that are elements of set B.

79.   Some search engines on the World Wide Web make use of the operators "AND" and "OR." For instance, using the search engine Excite, a recent search for

"chocolate" produced 105,512 sites that mention the word *chocolate*
"dessert" produced 40,209 sites that mention the word *dessert*
"chocolate AND dessert" produced 9162 sites that mention the word
  chocolate and the word *dessert*

a. Explain this search in the context of the intersection of two sets.
b. Explain how a search engine might respond to a search for "chocolate OR dessert." How is this related to the union of two sets?

80.   Why are 2 and 5 the only prime numbers whose difference is 3?

81. What is a well-defined set? Provide examples of sets that are not well defined.

1. *Examining a Set of Positive Integers*   Let S be the set of positive integers that have the following property:

when divided by 6 leaves a remainder of 5
when divided by 5 leaves a remainder of 4
when divided by 4 leaves a remainder of 3
when divided by 3 leaves a remainder of 2
when divided by 2 leaves a remainder of 1

a.   Find three elements of set S.

b.   Find the minimum value of S.

c.   Suppose the property is extended further to also include

when divided by 7 leaves a remainder of 6
when divided by n leaves a remainder of $n - 1$

Express in terms of n the least positive integer that satisfies this set of properties.

Operations on Integers

■ Opposites and Absolute Value

Two numbers that are the same distance from zero on the number line but are on opposite sides of zero are **opposite numbers,** or **opposites.** The opposite of a number is also called its **additive inverse.**

The opposite of 5 is −5.

The opposite of −5 is 5.

The negative sign can be used to indicate "the opposite of."

$$-(2) = -2.$$ The opposite of 2 is negative 2.

$$-(-2) = 2.$$ The opposite of −2 is 2.

▼ Point of Interest

The topic of this section is integers. Recall that the integers are the numbers . . ., −3, −2, −1, 0, 1, 2, 3, . . .

The word integer *comes directly from the Latin word* integer, *which means "whole, complete, perfect, entire." In fact,* integer *and* entire *have the same word origin.*

? QUESTION   **a.** What is the opposite of −43?
b. What is the additive inverse of 51?
c. What is the opposite of 0?

The **absolute value** of a number is its distance from zero on the number line. The symbol for absolute value is two vertical bars, | |.

The distance from 0 to 4 is 4. Therefore, the absolute value of 4 is 4.

$$|4| = 4$$

The distance from 0 to −4 is 4. Therefore, the absolute value of −4 is 4.

$$|-4| = 4$$

Note that because the absolute value of a number is its distance from zero on the number line, **the absolute value of a number is nonnegative.**

Absolute Value

The absolute value of a positive number is the number itself.

The absolute value of zero is zero.

The absolute value of a negative number is the opposite of the negative number.

? ANSWERS   **a.** The opposite of −43 is 43.   **b.** The additive inverse of 51 is −51.
c. The opposite of 0 is 0.

To **evaluate an expression** means to determine what number the expression is equal to. Example 1 below illustrates evaluating absolute value expressions.

EXAMPLE 1

Evaluate. **a.** $|-14|$ **b.** $|38|$ **c.** $-|-26|$

Solution **a.** $|-14| = 14$
b. $|38| = 38$
c. $-|-26| = -26$ • The negative sign *in front of* the absolute value sign means the opposite of $|-26|$.

YOU TRY IT 1

Evaluate. **a.** $|47|$ **b.** $|-50|$ **c.** $-|-89|$

Solution See page S2.

An expression containing absolute value can be evaluated by using the 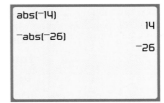 key. A check of the evaluation of the expressions in Example 1a and 1c above is shown below.

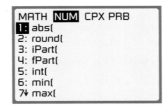

See Appendix A:
Basic Operations

Note that on a graphing calculator there is a difference between the minus key ![minus key] and the negative key ![negative key]. The negative key was used above to enter negative numbers.

■ Addition of Integers

A number can be represented by an arrow. A positive number is represented by an arrow pointing to the right, and a negative number is represented by an arrow pointing to the left. The magnitude (absolute value) of the number is represented by the length of the arrow. Arrows representing -6 and 4 are shown below.

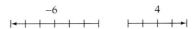

▼ *Point of Interest*

Arrows are also used to represent numbers in engineering. Engineers call these arrows vectors and use them in many different situations.

? QUESTION What number is represented by the arrow shown at the right?

Addition is the process of finding the total of two numbers. The numbers being added are called **addends.** The total is called the **sum.** We can find rules

---

? ANSWER Because the arrow points to the left and is of length 5, the number is -5.

for adding integers by using a number line and the arrow representation of numbers.

To add two integers, find the point on the number line that corresponds to the first addend. At that point, draw an arrow representing the second addend. The sum is the number directly below the tip of the arrow.

$3 + 5 = 8$

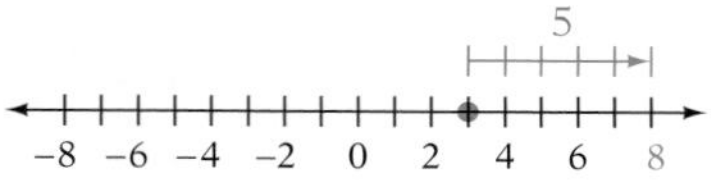

$-3 + (-5) = -8$

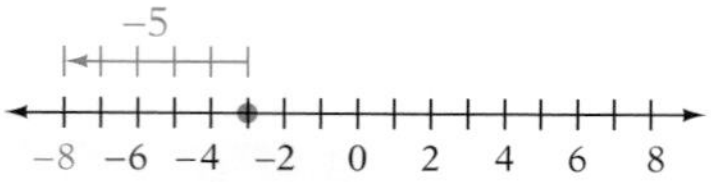

$3 + (-5) = -2$

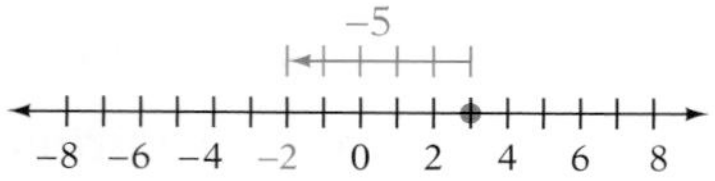

$-3 + 5 = 2$

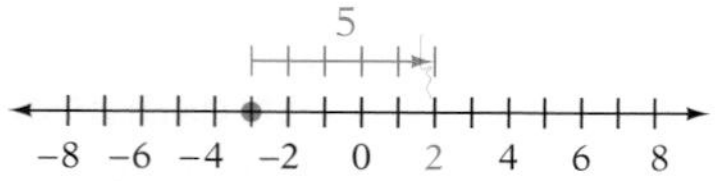

The arrow models for adding integers suggest the following rule.

Addition of Integers

Integers with the same sign

To add two numbers with the same sign, add the absolute values of the numbers. Then attach the sign of the addends.

Integers with different signs

To add two numbers with different signs, find the absolute value of each number. Then subtract the lesser of these absolute values from the greater. Attach the sign of the number with the greater absolute value.

? QUESTION Which number has the greater absolute value, 37 or -62?

EXAMPLE 2

a. Add: $23 + (-51)$
b. Find the sum of -14 and -48.

Solution

a. $|23| = 23, |-51| = 51$
- The signs are different. Find the absolute value of each number.

$51 - 23 = 28$
- Subtract the lesser of the absolute values from the greater.

$23 + (-51) = -28$
- Because $|-51| > |23|$, the answer has the same sign as -51.

? ANSWER $|37| = 37$ and $|-62| = 62$. $62 > 37$. Therefore, -62 has a greater absolute value than 37.

b. The word *sum* indicates addition.

$$-14 + (-48)$$

$$|-14| = 14, \ |-48| = 48$$ • The signs are the same. Find the absolute value of each number.

$$14 + 48 = 62$$ • Add the absolute values of the numbers.

$$-14 + (-48) = -62$$ • Both numbers are negative. The answer is negative.

Check: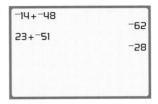

YOU TRY IT 2

a. Add: $(-18) + 9$

b. What is the sum of -52 and 36?

Solution See page S2.

■ Subtraction of Integers

The $-$ sign is used in two different ways: to mean *subtract*, as in $9 - 4$ (9 **minus** 4), and to mean *the opposite of*, as in -4 (the **opposite** of 4 or **negative** 4).

Look at the next four examples and be sure you understand the difference between *minus* (meaning subtract) and *negative* (meaning the opposite of).

$9 - 4$	positive 9 minus positive 4
$-9 - 4$	negative 9 minus positive 4
$9 - (-4)$	positive 9 minus negative 4
$-9 - (-4)$	negative 9 minus negative 4

? QUESTION   Write the expression in words.   **a.** $-6 - 4$ **b.** $8 - (-7)$

▼ Point of Interest

In mathematics manuscripts dating from the 1500s, an m was used to indicate minus. Some historians believe that, over time, the m went from m to ᴎ to ∼ to —.

Subtraction is the process of finding the difference between two numbers. Look at the following three problems. Opposites are used to rewrite subtraction problems as related addition problems. Note below that the subtraction of whole numbers is the same as the addition of the opposite number.

Subtraction		**Addition of the Opposite**	
$8 - 4$	$=$	$8 + (-4)$	$= 4$
$7 - 5$	$=$	$7 + (-5)$	$= 2$
$9 - 2$	$=$	$9 + (-2)$	$= 7$

? ANSWERS   **a.** Negative 6 minus positive 4.   **b.** Positive 8 minus negative 7.

Subtraction of integers can be written as the addition of the opposite number. To subtract two integers, rewrite the subtraction expression as the first number plus the opposite of the second number. Some examples follow.

first number	−	second number	=	first number	+	opposite of the second number	
15	−	20	=	15	+	(−20)	= −5
15	−	(−20)	=	15	+	20	= 35
−15	−	20	=	−15	+	(−20)	= −35
−15	−	(−20)	=	−15	+	20	= 5

Subtraction of Integers
To subtract two numbers, add the opposite of the second number to the first number.

EXAMPLE 3

a. Subtract: $-43 - 25$
b. What is the difference between 9 and -17?
c. Evaluate: $2 - (-24) - 18 - (-3)$

Solution

a. $-43 - 25 = -43 + (-25)$ • Add the opposite of 25 to -43.
$= -68$

b. The word *difference* indicates subtraction.
$9 - (-17) = 9 + 17$ • Add the opposite of -17 to 9.
$= 26$

c. $2 - (-24) - 18 - (-3)$
$= 2 + 24 + (-18) + 3$ • Rewrite each subtract as addition of
$= 26 + (-18) + 3$ the opposite. Then add the numbers.
$= 8 + 3$
$= 11$

Check:

```
9--17
                    26
2--24-18--3
                    11
-43-25
                   -68
```

CALCULATOR NOTE
Recall that on a graphing calculator, the ⬛ key is the "minus" key; it is used for subtraction. The (−) key is the "negative" key; it is used to enter a negative sign. You will notice in the display that the negative sign is slightly higher and shorter than the minus sign.

See Appendix A:
Basic Operations

YOU TRY IT 3

a. Subtract: $46 - 72$
b. Find the difference between -8 and -26.
c. Evaluate: $-15 - 12 - 9 - (-36)$

Solution See page S2.

■ Multiplication and Division of Integers

One method of developing rules for multiplication of integers is to look for a pattern. Consider multiplying a decreasing sequence of integers by 5.

Decreasing sequence of integers

→

4	3	2	1	0	−1	−2	−3	−4
5(4)	5(3)	5(2)	5(1)	5(0)	5(−1)	5(−2)	5(−3)	5(−4)
20	15	10	5	0	?	?	?	?

Using inductive reasoning, it appears that each term of the sequence of products (20, 15, 10, 5, 0) is 5 less than the previous term. To continue this pattern, the question marks should be replaced by $-5, -10, -15$, and -20.

Decreasing sequence of integers

→

4	3	2	1	0	−1	−2	−3	−4
5(4)	5(3)	5(2)	5(1)	5(0)	5(−1)	5(−2)	5(−3)	5(−4)
20	15	10	5	0	−5	−10	−15	−20

This suggests that the product of a positive number and a negative number is a negative number.

Now consider multiplying a decreasing sequence of integers by −5.

Decreasing sequence of integers

→

4	3	2	1	0	−1	−2	−3	−4
−5(4)	−5(3)	−5(2)	−5(1)	−5(0)	−5(−1)	−5(−2)	−5(−3)	−5(−4)
−20	−15	−10	−5	0	?	?	?	?

Using inductive reasoning, it appears that each term of the sequence of products $(-20, -15, -10, -5, 0)$ is 5 more than the previous term. To continue this pattern, the question marks should be replaced by 5, 10, 15, and 20.

Decreasing sequence of integers

→

4	3	2	1	0	−1	−2	−3	−4
−5(4)	−5(3)	−5(2)	−5(1)	−5(0)	−5(−1)	−5(−2)	−5(−3)	−5(−4)
−20	−15	−10	−5	0	5	10	15	20

This suggests that the product of two negative numbers is a positive number.

Multiplication of Integers

Integers with the same sign

To multiply two numbers with the same sign, multiply the absolute values of the numbers. The product is positive.

Integers with different signs

To multiply two numbers with different signs, multiply the absolute values of the numbers. The product is negative.

EXAMPLE 4

a. Multiply: $6(-13)$
b. Find the product of -4 and -27.

Solution

a. $6(-13) = -(6 \cdot 13) = -78$ • Multiply the absolute values. The signs are different, so the product is negative.

b. The word *product* indicates multiplication.

$-4(-27) = 4 \cdot 27 = 108$ • Multiply the absolute values. The signs are the same, so the product is positive.

Check:

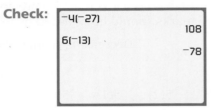

YOU TRY IT 4

a. Multiply: $(-18)(-21)$
b. What is -5 times 33?

Solution   See page S2.

For every division problem there is a related multiplication problem. For instance,

Division		Related Multiplication
$\dfrac{12}{4} = 3$	because	$3 \cdot 4 = 12$

Extending this to negative integers, we have

$$\frac{-12}{4} = -3 \quad \text{because} \quad -3 \cdot 4 = -12$$

$$\frac{-12}{-4} = 3 \quad \text{because} \quad 3 \cdot (-4) = -12$$

$$\frac{12}{-4} = -3 \quad \text{because} \quad -3 \cdot (-4) = 12$$

This suggests the following rules for dividing integers.

Division of Integers

Integers with the same sign

To divide two numbers with the same sign, divide the absolute values of the numbers. The quotient is positive.

Integers with different signs

To divide two numbers with different signs, divide the absolute values of the numbers. The quotient is negative.

The relationship between division and multiplication can be used to illustrate principles of division involving zero and one.

$0 \div 3 = 0$ because $0 \cdot 3 = 0$.   **Zero divided by any number except zero is zero.**

$3 \div 3 = 1$ because $1 \cdot 3 = 3$.   **A number other than zero divided by itself is 1.**

$3 \div 1 = 3$ because $3 \cdot 1 = 3$.   **A number divided by 1 is the number.**

$3 \div 0 = ?$ $? \cdot 0 = 3$.   What number can be multiplied by 0 to get 3? There is no number whose product with 0 is 3 because the product of a number and zero is 0. **Division by zero is undefined.**

EXAMPLE 5

a. Simplify: $\dfrac{-72}{-9}$

b. What is the quotient of 36 and -12?

c. What is -18 divided by 1?

Solution

a. $\dfrac{-72}{-9} = 8$ • The fraction bar can be read "divided by." $\frac{-72}{-9}$ means -72 divided by -9. Divide the absolute values of the numbers. The signs are the same, so the quotient is positive.

b. The word *quotient* indicates division.

$36 \div (-12) = -3$ • Divide the absolute values. The signs are different, so the quotient is negative.

c. $-18 \div 1 = -18$ • A number divided by 1 is the number.

Check:

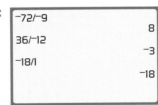

```
-72/-9
              8
36/-12
             -3
-18/1
            -18
```

YOU TRY IT 5

a. Simplify: $\dfrac{96}{-8}$

b. Find the quotient of -121 and -11.

c. What is -24 divided by 0?

Solution   See page S2.

■ Exponential Expressions

Genealogy is the study of the history of a family. A genealogist uses a family tree as a pictorial history of your ancestors. A sample of a family tree follows.

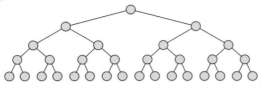

You

Parents

Grandparents

Great-grandparents

Great-great-grandparents

In each generation, you have twice as many ancestors as in the previous generation.

$$2 \text{ Parents}$$
$$2 \cdot 2 = 4 \text{ Grandparents}$$
$$2 \cdot 2 \cdot 2 = 8 \text{ Great-grandparents}$$
$$2 \cdot 2 \cdot 2 \cdot 2 = 16 \text{ Great-great-grandparents}$$

Instead of writing the number of ancestors as a product, in what is called **expanded form,** we could have written each product in **exponential form.**

Expanded form		Exponential form	Read as
2	$=$	2^1	"2 to the first power" or just "two."
$2 \cdot 2$	$=$	2^2	"2 squared" or "2 to the second power."
$2 \cdot 2 \cdot 2$	$=$	2^3	"2 cubed" or "2 to the third power."
$2 \cdot 2 \cdot 2 \cdot 2$	$=$	2^4	"2 to the fourth power."

▼ *Point of Interest*

René Descartes (1596–1650) was the first mathematician to use exponential notation as it is used today.

In an exponential expression, the **exponent** indicates the number of times the **base** is used in a product.

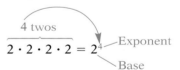

$$\overbrace{2 \cdot 2 \cdot 2 \cdot 2}^{4 \text{ twos}} = 2^4 \text{—Exponent}$$
Base

Look at the following examples of exponential expressions involving negative signs.

$(-3)^2 = (-3)(-3) = 9$ The (-3) is squared. Multiply -3 by -3.

$-(3^2) = -(3 \cdot 3) = -9$ Read $-(3^2)$ as "the opposite of three squared." 3^2 is 9. The opposite of 9 is -9.

$-3^2 = -(3^2) = -9$ The expression -3^2 is the same as $-(3^2)$.

❓ QUESTION   How is each of the following expressions simplified?

   a. -4^2 **b.** $(-4)^2$ **c.** $-(4^2)$

The caret key ⬛^ on a graphing calculator is used to enter an exponent. The expressions -4^2, $(-4)^2$, and $-(4^2)$ are evaluated on the graphing calculator screen at the left.

❓ ANSWERS   **a.** $-4^2 = -(4 \cdot 4) = -16$ **b.** $(-4)^2 = (-4)(-4) = 16$ **c.** $-(4^2) = -(4 \cdot 4) = -16$

There is a second method of squaring a number on a graphing calculator: press . For example, to evaluate -4^2, press

$$\boxed{(-)} \quad 4 \quad \boxed{x^2} \quad \boxed{\text{ENTER}}$$

The $\boxed{x^2}$ key displays the exponent 2 to the right of the 4.

EXAMPLE 6

Evaluate.   **a.** 5^3 **b.** $2^3 \cdot 3^2$ **c.** -6^4

Solution

a. $5^3 = (5 \cdot 5 \cdot 5)$
- Write the exponential expression in expanded form.

$ = 25 \cdot 5$
- Multiply.

$ = 125$

b. $2^3 \cdot 3^2 = (2 \cdot 2 \cdot 2) \cdot (3 \cdot 3)$
- Write each exponential expression in expanded form.

$ = 8 \cdot 9$
- Multiply.

$ = 72$

c. $-6^4 = -(6 \cdot 6 \cdot 6 \cdot 6) = -1296$

Check:

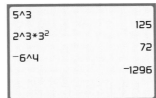

```
5^3
                    125
2^3*3²
                     72
-6^4
                  -1296
```

YOU TRY IT 6

Evaluate.   **a.** 4^3 **b.** $3^3 \cdot 5^2$ **c.** $(-8)^4$

Solution   See page S2.

■ The Order of Operations Agreement

You buy a poster for $7 and two CDs, each priced at $18. The total cost of the items purchased is

$$7 + 2(18)$$

Note that the expression we use to find the total cost of the two purchases includes two arithmetic operations, addition and multiplication. Which operation should be performed first?

The correct answer is that we multiply first to find the cost of the two CDs. We then add the cost of the two CDs (36) to the cost of the poster (7) to determine that the total cost of the three items is $43.

Whenever an expression contains more than one operation, the operations must be performed in a specified order, as listed below in the Order of Operations Agreement.

> **The Order of Operations Agreement**
>
> **Step 1**   Perform operations inside grouping symbols. Grouping symbols include parentheses (), brackets [], braces {}, the absolute value symbol ‖, and fraction bars.
>
> **Step 2**   Simplify exponential expressions.
>
> **Step 3**   Do multiplication and division as they occur from left to right.
>
> **Step 4**   Do addition and subtraction as they occur from left to right.

? QUESTION   What operations are in the expression $67 - 3 \cdot 9$? Which operation must be performed first?

In algebra, the $\times$ sign is seldom used for multiplication. Instead, we use a raised (centered) dot or parentheses with no operation sign. Here are some examples:

$$-5 \cdot 6 = -30 \qquad -5(6) = -30 \qquad (-5)(6) = -30 \qquad (-5)6 = -30$$

EXAMPLE 7

Evaluate.   **a.** $\frac{4 - 8}{2} + 3(4^2)$ **b.** $-2(7 - 3)^2 + 4 - 2(5 - 2)$

Solution

a. $\dfrac{4 - 8}{2} + 3(4^2) = \dfrac{-4}{2} + 3(4^2)$ • Simplify the expression in the numerator of the fraction.

$\qquad\qquad\qquad = \dfrac{-4}{2} + 3(16)$ • Simplify the exponential expression.

$\qquad\qquad\qquad = -2 + 3(16)$ • Do the multiplication and division from left to right. Recall that the fraction bar can be read "divided by."

$\qquad\qquad\qquad = -2 + 48$

$\qquad\qquad\qquad = 46$ • Add.

b. $-2(7 - 3)^2 + 4 - 2(5 - 2)$

$\qquad = -2(4)^2 + 4 - 2(3)$ • Perform operations inside the parentheses.

$\qquad = -2(16) + 4 - 2(3)$ • Simplify the exponential expression.

$\qquad = -32 + 4 - 2(3)$ • Do the multiplication and division from left to right.

$\qquad = -32 + 4 - 6$

$\qquad = -28 - 6$ • Do the addition and subtraction from left to right.

$\qquad = -28 + (-6) = -34$

? ANSWER   The expression contains the operations of subtraction and multiplication. The multiplication must be performed first.

Check: *Note:* The numerator $(4 - 8)$ in part a must be in parentheses so that the calculator understands that the entire expression, not just the number 8, is in the numerator. This is related to Step 1 of the Order of Operations Agreement; the fraction bar is a grouping symbol.

```
(4−8)/2+3(4²)
                          46
−2(7−3)²+4−2(5−2)
                         −34
```

YOU TRY IT 7

Evaluate.   **a.** $48 \div 2^3 - 2 \cdot 3$ **b.** $(-4)(6 - 8)^2 - |-12 \div 4|$

Solution   See page S2.

EXAMPLE 8

The daily low temperatures, in degrees Celsius, for a 1-week period were recorded as $-8°$, $-12°$, $-6°$, $-13°$, $5°$, $-10°$, $2°$. What was the average daily low temperature for the week?

State the goal.   We must determine the average of the seven recorded temperature readings.

Devise a strategy.   To find the average, add the seven temperatures and divide by the number of temperatures (7).

Solve the problem.

$$\text{Average temperature} = \frac{-8 + (-12) + (-6) + (-13) + 5 + (-10) + 2}{7}$$

$$= \frac{-42}{7}$$

$$= -6$$

The average daily low temperature for the week was $-6°C$.

Check your work.   You should check to see that the answer is reasonable. You can also repeat the calculations to verify that the solution is correct or use a calculator to check the answer.

YOU TRY IT 8

To discourage guessing on a true/false test, a psychology professor awards 2 points for a correct answer, takes off 4 points for an incorrect answer, and takes off 2 points if an answer is left blank. What is the score for a student who answered 48 questions correctly, answered 14 questions incorrectly, and left 8 questions unanswered?

Solution   See page S3.

1.3 EXERCISES

Topics for Discussion

For Exercises 1 to 6, determine whether the statement is always true, some-times true, or never true. If the statement is sometimes true or never true, explain your answer.

1. A number and its opposite are different numbers.

2. The absolute value of a number is positive.

3. The natural numbers plus the opposites of the natural numbers equals the integers.

4. If two integers are added, the sum is greater than either of the two integers.

5. If two integers are subtracted, the difference is less than either of the two integers.

6. If two integers are multiplied, the product is greater than either of the two integers.

7. Explain why division by zero is not allowed.

8. Explain why the absolute value of -24 is greater than the absolute value of 7.

9. **a.** Explain how to add two integers with the same sign.
    b. Explain how to add two integers with different signs.

10. Explain how to rewrite the subtraction $-9 - (-5)$ as addition of the opposite.

11. **a.** Explain how to multiply two integers with the same sign.
    b. Explain how to multiply two integers with different signs.

12. Why must there be an Order of Operations Agreement?

■ Opposites and Absolute Value

Find the opposite of the number.

13. 25

14. 42

15. −34

16. −45

17. 0

18. −7

19. 12

20. −3

Evaluate.

21. $-(-16)$

22. $-(-30)$

23. $-(49)$

24. $-(32)$

25. $|16|$

26. $|25|$

27. $|-32|$

28. $|-21|$

29. $-|86|$

30. $-|40|$

31. $-|-54|$

32. $-|-27|$

■ Addition and Subtraction of Integers

Use the number line to illustrate the sum.

33. $-4 + 6$

34. $-3 + 7$

35. $2 + (-8)$

36. $5 + (-10)$

37. $-1 + (-5)$

38. $-4 + (-2)$

Simplify.

39. $-6 + 15$

40. $12 + (-16)$

41. $(-23) + (-17)$

42. $30 + (-21)$

43. $-17 + (-3) + 29$

44. $-3 + (-8) + 110$

45. $13 + (-38) + 62$

46. $-32 + (-42) + (-18)$

47. $13 + (-22) + 4 + (-5)$

48. $22 + 10 + (-18) + 2$

49. $-6 - 8$

50. $2 - (-2)$

51. $12 - (-7)$

52. $-12 - 16$

53. $-12 - (-3) - (-15)$

54. $-6 - 19 - (-31)$

55. $4 - 12 - (-8)$

56. $-30 - (-65) - 29 - 6$

57. $13 - 7 - (-15) - 9$

58. $42 - (-82) - 65 - 7$

59. $-16 - 47 - 63 - 12$

60. $-47 - (-67) - 13 - 15$

61. Find the sum of -8 and 11.

62. What is the total of -12 and -5?

63. Find -9 added to -11.

64. What is the sum of 17 and -21?

65. Add -16, -8, and 14.

66. Find the total of 32, -61, 17, and -44.

67. Find the difference between 7 and 14.

68. Subtract -3 from -6.

69. What is -4 minus -12?

70. What is the difference between -15 and 24?

71. Subtract -24 from 24.

72. What is 32 minus -27?

Sports   The following table shows the top nine golfers in the 2001 Masters Golf Tournament. The golfers' scores in relation to par are given for the four rounds of play. Use this table for Exercises 73 and 74.

Name	Round 1	Round 2	Round 3	Round 4	Final Score
Calcavecchia, M.	0	-6	-4	0	
Duval, D.	-1	-6	-2	-5	
Els, E.	-1	-4	-4	0	
Furyk, J.	-3	-1	-2	-3	
Izawa, T.	-1	-6	2	-5	
Langer, B.	1	-3	-4	-3	
Michelson, P.	-5	-3	-3	-2	
Triplett, K.	-4	-2	-2	-1	
Woods, T.	-2	-6	-4	-4	

73. **a.** Complete the table by filling in the final score for each of the nine players. (Add the player's four scores.)

   b. Rank the players from lowest score to highest. For players with identical scores, list them alphabetically.

74. For the golf course on which the tournament was played, par is 72. If a player's score in relation to par for one round was -4, then he completed the course in $72 + (-4) = 68$ strokes. For each player listed above, find the number of strokes taken throughout the four rounds of golf.

75. *Economics*   The Bureau of Economic Analysis provides data on per capita personal income in the United States. **Per capita income** is total personal income divided by total population. For the year 2000, the per capita personal income in the United States was $29,676. Listed below is the dollar difference for some states from the national average. The dollar difference is a positive number if the per capita income for that state is above the national average. The dollar difference is negative if the per capita income for that state is below the national average. Calculate a state's per capita income by adding the dollar difference to the national average. Iowa's per capita personal income is calculated in the table. Find the per capita income for each of the other plains states listed.

Per Capita Personal Income for the United States in 2000: $29,676

State	Dollar Difference from National Average	Per Capita Personal Income
Iowa	−$2953	$29,676 + (−$2953) = $26,723
Kansas	−$1860	
Minnesota	$2425	
Missouri	−$2231	
Nebraska	−$1847	
North Dakota	−$3561	
South Dakota	−$4608	

▪ Multiplication and Division of Integers

Use the number line to illustrate the product.

76. $5(-1)$

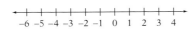

77. $3(-2)$

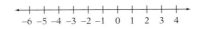

Simplify.

78. $-6(14)$

79. $-8 \cdot 12$

80. $(-12)(-11)$

81. $24(-14)$

82. $12(0)$

83. $0(-41)$

84. $-5(-4)(-8)$

85. $6(-7)(4)$

86. $6(-5)(-3)$

87. $-4(-3)(-7)$

88. $8(-2)(-1)(10)$

89. $-4(-4)(-3)(-5)$

90. $54 \div (-6)$

91. $-56 \div 7$

92. $-72 \div (-12)$

93. $(-48) \div (-8)$

94. $\dfrac{27}{-27}$

95. $-\dfrac{0}{17}$

96. $\dfrac{-30}{-15}$

97. $\dfrac{-63}{9}$

98. Find the product of -8 and 17.

99. What is 12 times -7?

100. What is 9 multiplied by -18?

101. What is the product of 10 and -11?

102. Multiply -3, -5, and 6.

103. Find the product of 21, -4, and -3.

104. Find the quotient of -12 and 4.

105. Divide 64 by -8.

106. What is -84 divided by -6?

107. What is the quotient of 98 and -14?

108. Divide -51 by -17.

109. Find the quotient of -168 and -7.

Mathematics A **geometric sequence** is a list of numbers in which each number after the first is found by multiplying the preceding number in the list by the same number. For example, in the sequence 1, 3, 9, 27, 81, . . ., each number after the first is found by multiplying the preceding number in the list by 3. To find the multiplier in a geometric sequence, divide the second number in the sequence by the first number; for the example above, 3 ÷ 1 = 3. Geometric sequences are given in Exercises 110 to 113. Find the next three numbers in each geometric sequence.

110. −4, 12, −36, . . .

111. 1, −4, 16, . . .

112. −3, −15, −75, . . .

113. −1, −6, −36, . . .

Business The following table shows the net incomes for the first quarter of 2001 and the first quarter of 2000 for five Internet companies (*Source:* **www.wsj.com**). Profits are shown as positive numbers; losses are shown as negative numbers. One quarter of a year is 3 months. Use this table for Exercises 114 to 117.

Company	First-Quarter 2001 Net Income	First-Quarter 2000 Net Income
Adam.com	44,000	−4,187,000
Buy.com	−45,172,000	−32,846,000
Hotjobs.com	−13,600,000	−12,300,000
iVillage, Inc.	−12,175,000	−25,168,000
Tickets.com	−27,992,000	−21,610,000

114. If earnings were to continue throughout the year at the same level, what would the 2001 annual net income be for Buy.com?

115. If earnings were to continue throughout the year at the same level, what would the 2001 annual net income be for Tickets.com?

116. Find the difference between Adam.com's first-quarter net income for 2001 and its first-quarter net income for 2000.

117. For the first quarter of 2000, what was the average monthly net income for Hotjobs.com?

▪ **Exponential Expressions**

Evaluate.

118. 3^4 **119.** 2^5 **120.** 1^{20} **121.** 0^{17}

122. 6^2 **123.** 7^4 **124.** 14^2 **125.** 9^3

126. -7^2 **127.** -4^3 **128.** $(-2)^3$ **129.** $(-3)^4$

130. $(-5)^3$ **131.** $2^2 \cdot 3^3$ **132.** $5^2 \cdot 3^2$ **133.** $(-3) \cdot 2^2$

134. $(-5) \cdot 3^4$ **135.** $(-4) \cdot (-2)^3$ **136.** $(-6) \cdot (-2)^2$ **137.** $2^3 \cdot 3^3 \cdot (-4)$

138. $(-3)^3 \cdot 5^2 \cdot 10$ **139.** $(-7) \cdot 4^2 \cdot 3^2$ **140.** $(-2) \cdot 2^3 \cdot (-3)^2$ **141.** $8^2 \cdot (-3)^3 \cdot 5$

■ The Order of Operations Agreement

Evaluate.

142. $15 - 3 \cdot 4$ **143.** $37 - 6 \cdot 5$ **144.** $4 - 8 \div 2$

145. $2^2 \cdot 3 - 3$ **146.** $5^2 - 4(5)$ **147.** $3^4 + \frac{15}{5}$

148. $\frac{16(2 + 3)}{10}$ **149.** $12 + 4 \cdot 2^3$ **150.** $3^3 + 5(8 - 6)$

151. $2^2(3^2) - 2 \cdot 3$ **152.** $12 - (12 - 4) \div 4$ **153.** $(8 - 2)^2 - 3 \cdot 4 + 6$

154. $5(3 + 4)^2 - 6(7 - 5)^3$ **155.** $2(8 - 5)^3 + 6(1 + 3)^3 - 9^2$ **156.** $2(3 - 4) - (-3)^2$

157. $8 - 2(3)^2$ **158.** $16 - 2 \cdot 4^2$ **159.** $27 - 18 \div (-3^2)$

160. $16 + 15 \div (-5) - 2$ **161.** $14 - 2^2 - (4 - 7)$ **162.** $-2^2 + 4[16 \div (3 - 5)]$

163. $24 \div \frac{3^2}{5 - 8} - (-5)$ **164.** $18 \div 2 - 4^2 - (-3)^2$ **165.** $18 \div (2^3 - 9) + (-3)$

166. $16 - 3(3 - 8)^2 \div (-5)$ **167.** $4(-8) \div [2(7 - 3)^2]$ **168.** $16 - 4 \cdot \frac{3^3 - 7}{2^3 + 2} - (-2)^2$

169. *Temperature*   The daily low temperatures, in degrees Celsius, in Fargo, North Dakota, for a 7-day period were $-4°$, $2°$, $7°$, $-5°$, $-4°$, $-2°$, and $-1°$. What was the average daily low temperature for this 7-day period?

170. *Temperature*   The daily low temperatures, in degrees Celsius, in Billings, Montana, for a 5-day period were $-8°$, $-6°$, $-5°$, $2°$, and $-3°$. What was the average daily low temperature for this 5-day period?

171. *Aptitude Tests*   The score on an aptitude test is the sum of 8 times the number of correct answers and -2 times the number of incorrect answers. Questions that are not answered are not counted in the score. What score does a person receive who answered 28 questions correctly, answered 5 questions incorrectly, and left 7 questions unanswered?

172. *Education*   To discourage guessing, a professor scores a multiple-choice exam by awarding 6 points for a correct answer, -2 points for an incorrect answer, and -1 point for a question that is not answered. What score does a student receive who answered 37 questions correctly, answered 5 questions incorrectly, and left 8 questions unanswered?

173. *Physics*   If a rock is dropped from a cliff, the distance the rock has fallen, in feet, after 5 seconds is given by the expression $16 \cdot 5^2$. Find the distance the rock falls in 5 seconds. Is this more or less than the length of a football field?

Final Scores from the PGA Seniors' Championship	
D. Tewell	-15
H. Irwin	-8
T. Kite	-8
D. Quigley	-8
L. Nelson	-8
H. Green	-7
V. Fernandez	-7
J. Mahaffey	-5
J. Ahern	-5
J. Bland	-3
K. Zarley	-3

174. *Sports*   The scores, in relation to par, of the top 11 golfers in a recent PGA Seniors' Championship golf tournament are shown at the right. What was the average score of these 11 golfers?

Temperature   The following table shows the record low temperatures, in degrees Fahrenheit, in four cities in the United States for each of the first 6 months of the year (*Source:* **www.weather.com**). Use this table for Exercises 175 to 177.

Record Low Temperatures (in degrees Fahrenheit)

	January	February	March	April	May	June
Boston, MA	-12	-18	1	13	34	41
Chicago, IL	-24	-12	0	13	32	41
Jackson, WY	-46	-42	-25	-10	7	20
Minneapolis, MN	-34	-33	-32	2	18	33

175. Find Jackson's average record low temperature for the first 6 months of the year.

176. For the city of Boston, what is the difference between the average record low temperature for the first 4 months of the year and the average record low temperature for the first 2 months of the year?

177. What is the difference between Chicago's average record low temperature for the first 3 months of the year and Minneapolis's average record low temperature for the first 3 months of the year?

Applying Concepts

178. a. On the number line, what number is 5 units to the right of -3?
   b. On the number line, what number is 6 units to the left of 4?

179. a. Name two numbers that are 5 units from 1 on the number line.
    b. Name two numbers that are 6 units from 2 on the number line.

180. *A* is a point on the number line halfway between -11 and 5. *B* is a point halfway between *A* and the graph of 1 on the number line. *B* is the graph of what number?

181. Write each expression in words.
    a. -7 **b.** $-(-10)$ **c.** $-|9|$ **d.** $-|-24|$

182. Consider the numbers 5, -6, -3, 16, and -10. Find the greatest difference that can be obtained by subtracting one number in the list from a different number in the list. What is the least difference?

183. Fill in the blank squares at the right with integers so that the sum of the integers along any row, column, or diagonal is zero. The resulting square is called a magic square.

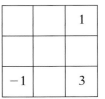

184. The sum of two negative integers is -9. Find the integers.

185. a. Find the largest possible product of two negative integers whose sum is -18.
    b. Find the smallest possible sum of two negative integers whose product is 16.

EXPLORATION

1. *Balance of Payments*   An **export** is a good or service produced in one's own country and sold for consumption in another country. An **import** is a good or service that is consumed in one's own country but was bought from another country. A nation's **balance of payments** or **balance of trade** is the difference between the value of its exports and the value of its imports during a particular period of time.

A **favorable balance of trade** exists when the value of the exports is greater than the value of the imports. In this case, the balance of trade is a positive number. An **unfavorable balance of trade** exists when the value of the imports is greater than the value of the exports. In this case, the balance of trade is a negative number. An unfavorable balance of trade is referred to as a **trade deficit.** A trade deficit is considered unfavorable because more money is going out of the country to pay for goods imported than is coming into the country to pay for goods exported.

The U.S. government provides data on international trade. On the Internet, go to **www.fedstats.gov** and click on "Search." When the next screen loads, type in "balance of payments" in the space provided, and then click "Search." Find tables that provide data on the value of U.S. imports and exports.

All figures in the tables provided on this web site are in millions of dollars. The first two columns are annual figures. Subsequent columns are for quarters (3-month periods).

We located the following data for the first quarter of the year 2000.

Exports: Total, all countries   183,659
Imports: Total, all countries   289,699

We then calculated the balance of trade as follows:

Balance of trade = value of exports − value of imports
= 183,659 − 289,699
= 183,659 + (−289,699)
= −106,040

The balance of trade for the first quarter of 2000 was −106,040 million dollars. This figure is provided in the table under "Balance: Total, all countries."

a. Show the calculation of the balance of trade for each of the four quarters of last year. Use the calculation shown above as a model.
b. Show the calculation of the annual balance of trade for last year.
c. Show that the sum of the four quarterly figures is equal to the annual figure.

SECTION **Operations on Rational Numbers**

- Addition and Subtraction of Rational Numbers
- Multiplication and Division of Rational Numbers
- The Order of Operations Agreement

■ Addition and Subtraction of Rational Numbers

Fractions with the same denominator are added by adding the numerators and placing the sum over the common denominator.

> **Addition of Fractions**
> To add two fractions with the same denominator, add the numerators and place the sum over the common denominator.

For example, $\frac{2}{6} + \frac{1}{6} = \frac{2+1}{6} = \frac{3}{6} = \frac{1}{2}$.

Note that after adding the fractions, we write the sum in simplest form.

To add fractions with different denominators, first rewrite the fractions as equivalent fractions with a common denominator. Then add the fractions.

The least common denominator is the **least common multiple** (LCM) of the denominators. This is the least number that is a multiple of each of the denominators.

? QUESTION   What is the LCM of 6 and 8?

The sign rules for adding and subtracting fractions are the same as those for adding and subtracting integers.

CALCULATOR NOTE
A graphing calculator can be used to find the LCM of two numbers.

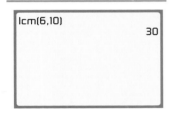

See Appendix A: Math

EXAMPLE 1

Add: $-\dfrac{5}{6} + \dfrac{3}{10}$

Solution   The LCM of 6 and 10 is 30. Rewrite the fractions as equivalent fractions with the denominator 30. Then add the fractions.

$$-\frac{5}{6} + \frac{3}{10} = -\frac{5}{6} \cdot \frac{5}{5} + \frac{3}{10} \cdot \frac{3}{3} = -\frac{25}{30} + \frac{9}{30} = \frac{-25 + 9}{30} = -\frac{16}{30} = -\frac{8}{15}$$

Note: You can find the LCM by multiplying the denominators and then dividing by the greatest common factor of the two denominators. In the case of 6 and 10, $6 \cdot 10 = 60$. Now divide by 2, the common factor of 6 and 10. $60 \div 2 = 30$.

Check:

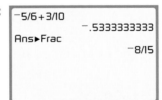

• Note that the sum is first displayed as a decimal. Use the FRAC command in the MATH menu to convert the decimal to a fraction. (A **menu** gives a list of additional functions the calculator performs.)

YOU TRY IT 1

Add: $-\dfrac{3}{8} + \left(-\dfrac{1}{3}\right)$

Solution   See page S3.

Subtraction of Fractions
To subtract two fractions with the same denominator, subtract the numerators and place the difference over the common denominator.

? ANSWER   The LCM of 6 and 8 is 24, because 24 is the least number that both 6 and 8 divide evenly into.

EXAMPLE 2

Subtract: $-\dfrac{4}{9} - \dfrac{7}{12}$

Solution   The LCM of 9 and 12 is 36. Rewrite the fractions as equivalent fractions with the denominator 36. Then subtract the fractions.

$$-\frac{4}{9} - \frac{7}{12} = -\frac{16}{36} - \frac{21}{36} = \frac{-16 - 21}{36} = \frac{-37}{36} = -\frac{37}{36}$$

Check:

```
-4/9-7/12
               -1.027777778
Ans►Frac
                      -37/36
```

YOU TRY IT 2

Subtract: $-\dfrac{3}{4} - \dfrac{3}{16}$

Solution   See page S3.

EXAMPLE 3

Simplify: $-\dfrac{3}{4} + \dfrac{1}{6} - \dfrac{5}{8}$

Solution   The LCM of 4, 6, and 8 is 24.

$$-\frac{3}{4} + \frac{1}{6} - \frac{5}{8} = -\frac{18}{24} + \frac{4}{24} - \frac{15}{24} = \frac{-18 + 4 - 15}{24} = -\frac{29}{24}$$

Check:

```
-3/4+1/6-5/8
               -1.208333333
Ans►Frac
                       -29/24
```

YOU TRY IT 3

Simplify: $-\dfrac{7}{8} - \dfrac{5}{6} + \dfrac{3}{4}$

Solution   See page S3.

The sign rules for adding and subtracting decimals are the same as those for adding and subtracting integers.

EXAMPLE 4

Subtract: $42.987 - 98.61$

Solution $42.987 - 98.61$

$$= 42.987 + (-98.61)$$

• Rewrite subtraction as addition of the opposite.

$$= -55.623$$

• The signs are different. Find the difference between the absolute values of the numbers. Attach the sign of the number with the greater absolute value.

YOU TRY IT 4

Subtract: $-16.127 - 67.91$

Solution   See page S3.

■ Multiplication and Division of Rational Numbers

Fractions are multiplied and divided as described below.

> **Multiplication and Division of Fractions**
>
> To multiply two fractions, multiply the numerators and place the product over the product of the denominators.
>
> To divide fractions, rewrite the division as multiplication by the reciprocal of the second fraction. Then multiply the fractions.

The **reciprocal** of a fraction is the fraction with the numerator and denominator interchanged. The reciprocal of $\frac{4}{5}$ is $\frac{5}{4}$.

? QUESTION   What is the reciprocal of $-\dfrac{7}{10}$?

EXAMPLE 5

a. Multiply: $\dfrac{3}{8} \cdot \dfrac{4}{15}$

b. Divide: $\dfrac{3}{10} \div \left(-\dfrac{18}{25} \right)$

? ANSWER   The reciprocal of $-\frac{7}{10}$ is $-\frac{10}{7}$.

Solution **a.** $\dfrac{3}{8} \cdot \dfrac{4}{15} = \dfrac{3 \cdot 4}{8 \cdot 15}$

- Multiply the numerators. Multiply the denominators.

$$= \dfrac{\overset{1}{\cancel{3}} \cdot \overset{1}{\cancel{4}}}{\underset{2}{\cancel{8}} \cdot \underset{5}{\cancel{15}}}$$

- Divide by the common factors.

$$= \dfrac{1}{10}$$

- Write the answer in simplest form.

Check:

```
3/8*4/15
                        .1
Ans▸Frac
                      1/10
```

b. $\dfrac{3}{10} \div \left(-\dfrac{18}{25}\right) = -\left(\dfrac{3}{10} \div \dfrac{18}{25}\right)$

- Because the signs are different, the quotient is negative.

$$= -\left(\dfrac{3}{10} \cdot \dfrac{25}{18}\right)$$

- Rewrite division as multiplication by the reciprocal.

$$= -\dfrac{\overset{1}{\cancel{3}} \cdot \overset{5}{\cancel{25}}}{\underset{2}{\cancel{10}} \cdot \underset{6}{\cancel{18}}}$$

- Multiply the fractions. Divide by the common factors.

$$= -\dfrac{5}{12}$$

- Write the answer in simplest form.

Check:

```
(3/10)/(-18/25)
             -.4166666667
Ans▸Frac
                    -5/12
```

YOU TRY IT 5

a. Multiply: $-\dfrac{3}{8} \cdot \left(-\dfrac{5}{12}\right)$

b. Divide: $-\dfrac{5}{8} \div \left(-\dfrac{5}{40}\right)$

Solution See page S3.

As stated above, the sign rules are the same for decimals as for integers. These rules are used in Example 6 below to multiply and divide numbers written in decimal notation.

EXAMPLE 6

a. Multiply: $(-0.23)(0.04)$

b. Divide $0.0527 \div (-0.27)$. Round to the nearest hundredth.

Solution

a. $(-0.23)(0.04) = -0.0092$ • The signs of the factors are different, so the product is negative.

b. $0.0527 \div (-0.27) \approx -0.20$ • The signs of the numbers are different, so the quotient is negative.

TAKE NOTE

The symbol $\approx$ is used to indicate that the quotient is an approximate value that has been rounded off.

YOU TRY IT 6

a. Multiply $-4.027(0.49)$. Round to the nearest hundredth.

b. Divide: $(-2.835) \div (-1.35)$

Solution   See page S3.

The table that follows shows the net incomes, in millions of dollars, for the first quarter of 2001 and the first quarter of 2000 for two U.S. companies (*Source:* **www.wsj.com**). Profits are shown as positive numbers; losses are shown as negative numbers. One quarter of a year is three months. Use this table for Example 7 and You Try It 7.

Company	First-Quarter 2001 Net Income	First-Quarter 2000 Net Income
Cisco Systems, Inc.	−2,693	641
Friendly Ice Cream	−3.203	−18.510

EXAMPLE 7

If earnings were to continue throughout the year at the same level as in the first quarter, what would be the 2001 annual net income for Cisco Systems?

State the goal.   You need to find the annual net income for Cisco Systems for 2001, assuming the income were to continue throughout the year at the same level as in the first quarter.

Devise a strategy.   To find the annual net income, multiply the net income in the first quarter of 2001 ($-2{,}693$) by the number of quarters in 1 year (4).

Solve the problem. $-2{,}693(4) = -10{,}772$

Cisco System's annual net income for 2001 would be $-\$10{,}772$ million.

Check your work.   You should check to see that the answer is reasonable. For example, using estimation, $-2693 \approx -2700$, and -2700 times 4 is $-10{,}800$, which is close to our answer of $-10{,}772$.

YOU TRY IT 7

For the first quarter of 2001, what was the average monthly net income for Friendly Ice Cream?

Solution   See page S3.

■ The Order of Operations Agreement

Recall the Order of Operations Agreement from Section 1.3. This agreement is used for all numerical expressions.

The Order of Operations Agreement

Step 1 Perform operations inside grouping symbols. Grouping symbols include parentheses (), brackets [], braces {}, the absolute value symbol | |, and fraction bars.

Step 2 Simplify exponential expressions.

Step 3 Do multiplication and division as they occur from left to right.

Step 4 Do addition and subtraction as they occur from left to right.

EXAMPLE 8

Evaluate: $(1.3 - 1.75)^2 \div 0.025 - 16.1$

Solution $(1.3 - 1.75)^2 \div 0.025 - 16.1$

$= (-0.45)^2 \div 0.025 - 16.1$ • Simplify the expression in the parentheses.

$= 0.2025 \div 0.025 - 16.1$ • Simplify the exponential expression.

$= 8.1 - 16.1$ • Do the division.

$= 8.1 + (-16.1)$ • Do the subtraction.

$= -8$

YOU TRY IT 8

Evaluate: $(4.7 - 6.9)^2 + 4.5 \div (-0.05)$

Solution   See page S3.

1.4 EXERCISES

Topics for Discussion

For Exercises 1 to 7, determine whether the statement is always true, sometimes true, or never true. If the statement is sometimes true or never true, explain your answer.

1. The sum of two fractions is the sum of the numerators over the sum of the denominators.

2. The sum of a number and its additive inverse is zero.

3. The rule for multiplying two fractions is to multiply the numerators and place the product over the least common multiple of the denominators.

4. To multiply two fractions, you must first rewrite the fractions as equivalent fractions with a common denominator.

5. To divide two fractions, multiply the first fraction by the reciprocal of the second fraction.

6. To evaluate the expression $-6 + 7(10)^2$ means to determine what number it is equal to.

7. The Order of Operations Agreement is used for natural numbers, integers, rational numbers, and real numbers.

8. Given both a fraction and a decimal, how can you determine which is the greater number?

9. **a.** Are there any integers that are not rational numbers?
    b. Are there any rational numbers that are not integers?

10. **a.** Is there a least positive rational number?
    b. Is there a greatest negative rational number?

11. Give some examples of how rational numbers are used in everyday experiences.

■ **Addition and Subtraction of Rational Numbers**

Add or subtract.

12. $\dfrac{5}{8} - \dfrac{5}{6}$

13. $\dfrac{1}{9} - \dfrac{5}{27}$

14. $-\dfrac{5}{12} - \dfrac{3}{8}$

15. $-\dfrac{5}{6} - \dfrac{5}{9}$

16. $-\dfrac{6}{13} + \dfrac{17}{26}$

17. $-\dfrac{7}{12} + \dfrac{5}{8}$

18. $\dfrac{5}{8} - \left(-\dfrac{3}{4}\right)$

19. $-\dfrac{5}{8} - \left(-\dfrac{11}{12}\right)$

20. $\dfrac{1}{3} + \dfrac{5}{6} - \dfrac{2}{9}$

21. $-\dfrac{5}{16} + \dfrac{3}{4} - \dfrac{7}{8}$

22. $\dfrac{1}{2} - \dfrac{3}{8} - \left(-\dfrac{1}{4}\right)$

23. $\dfrac{3}{4} - \left(-\dfrac{7}{12}\right) - \dfrac{7}{8}$

24. $\dfrac{1}{3} - \dfrac{1}{4} - \dfrac{1}{5}$

25. $\dfrac{5}{16} + \dfrac{1}{8} - \dfrac{1}{2}$

26. $-32.1 - 6.7$

27. $-16.92 - 6.925$

28. $5.13 - 8.179$

29. $2.54 - 3.6$

30. $-13.092 + 6.9$

31. $-3.87 + 8.546$

32. $2.09 - 6.72 - 5.4$

33. $-18.39 + 4.9 - 23.7$

34. $19 - (-3.72) - 82.75$

35. $-3.09 - 4.6 - (-27.3)$

36. Find the sum of $-\dfrac{1}{2}$ and $\dfrac{3}{8}$.

37. Find the total of $\dfrac{2}{3}$, $-\dfrac{1}{2}$, and $\dfrac{5}{6}$.

38. Find the difference between $\dfrac{5}{6}$ and $\dfrac{11}{12}$.

39. What is 6.9027 minus 17.692?

40. Which is greater, $\dfrac{5}{8} - \left(-\dfrac{5}{6}\right)$ or $-\dfrac{5}{6} - \dfrac{5}{9}$?

41. Which is greater, $-\dfrac{1}{8} - \dfrac{3}{4}$ or $\dfrac{11}{12} - \left(-\dfrac{1}{4}\right)$?

42. *The Stock Market* At the close of the stock markets on April 2, 2002, the indexes were posted as shown below, along with the decreases for that day, shown as negative numbers. At what levels were the indexes at the close of the day on April 1, 2002?

Index	Points at Market Close	Decrease for the Day
Dow Jones Industrial Average	10,313.70	−49.00
Standard & Poor 500	1,136.77	−9.77
NASDAQ	1,804.41	−58.21

Multiplication and Division of Rational Numbers

Multiply or divide.

43. $-\dfrac{2}{9}\left(-\dfrac{3}{14}\right)$

44. $\left(-\dfrac{3}{8}\right)\left(-\dfrac{4}{15}\right)$

45. $\left(-\dfrac{3}{4}\right)\left(-\dfrac{8}{27}\right)$

46. $\dfrac{5}{12}\left(-\dfrac{8}{15}\right)$

47. $\dfrac{5}{8}\left(-\dfrac{7}{12}\right)\dfrac{16}{25}$

48. $\dfrac{1}{2}\left(-\dfrac{3}{4}\right)\left(-\dfrac{5}{8}\right)$

49. $\dfrac{5}{6} \div \left(-\dfrac{3}{4}\right)$

50. $-\dfrac{5}{12} \div \dfrac{15}{32}$

51. $-\dfrac{7}{10} \div \dfrac{2}{5}$

52. $\dfrac{1}{8} \div \left(-\dfrac{5}{12}\right)$

53. $-\dfrac{4}{9} \div \left(-\dfrac{2}{3}\right)$

54. $-\dfrac{6}{11} \div \dfrac{4}{9}$

55. $1.06(-3.8)$

56. $-2.7(-3.5)$

57. $-2.4(6.1)(0.9)$

58. $2.3(-0.6)(0.8)$

59. $-3.4(-22.1)(-0.5)$

60. $4.5(-0.22)(-0.8)$

For Exercises 61–64, divide. Round to the nearest hundredth.

61. $-1.27 \div (-1.7)$

62. $9.07 \div (-3.5)$

63. $-6.904 \div 1.35$

64. $-7.894 \div (-2.06)$

65. What is $-\dfrac{1}{2}$ times $\dfrac{8}{9}$?

66. Find the product of $\dfrac{5}{12}$, $-\dfrac{8}{15}$, and $-\dfrac{1}{3}$.

67. Find the quotient of $-\dfrac{3}{8}$ and $\dfrac{1}{4}$.

68. Divide -24.3 by 0.09.

69. Which is greater, $\left(-\dfrac{8}{9}\right)\left(-\dfrac{3}{4}\right)$ or $-\dfrac{5}{16} \div \dfrac{3}{8}$?

70. Which is greater, $-\dfrac{5}{6} \div (-5)$ or $-\dfrac{3}{4}\left(\dfrac{2}{9}\right)$?

Business   The following table shows the net incomes for the first quarter of 2001 and the first quarter of 2000 for three companies in the entertainment industry (*Source:* **www.wsj.com**). Figures are in millions of dollars. Profits are shown as positive numbers, losses as negative numbers. One quarter of a year is 3 months. Use this table for Exercises 71 to 76.

Company	First-Quarter 2001 Net Income	First-Quarter 2000 Net Income
Fox Entertainment	−9.0	19.0
Midway Games, Inc.	−25.852	−11.481
Six Flags, Inc.	−130.752	−113.892

71. If earnings were to continue throughout the year at the same level, what would the 2001 annual net income be for Midway Games?

72. If earnings were to continue throughout the year at the same level, what would the 2000 annual net income be for Six Flags?

73. For the first quarter of 2001, what was the average monthly net income for Six Flags?

74. For the first quarter of 2000, what was the average monthly net income for Midway Games?

75. Find the difference between Fox Entertainment's first-quarter net income for 2000 and Midway Games's first-quarter net income for 2000.

76. Find the difference between Fox Entertainment's first-quarter net income for 2001 and Six Flags's first-quarter net income for 2001.

Commerce   The table at the right shows the U. S. balance of trade, in billions of dollars, for the years 1970 to 2000 (*Source:* U.S. Dept. of Commerce). See page 49 for a discussion of balance of trade. Use the table for Exercises 77 to 84.

77. For which year was the trade balance lowest? For which was it highest?

78. In which years did the trade balance increase from the previous year?

Year	Trade Balance
1970	2.3
1971	−1.3
1972	−5.4
1973	1.9
1974	−4.3
1975	12.4
1976	−6.1
1977	−27.2
1978	−29.8
1979	−24.6
1980	−19.4
1981	−16.2
1982	−24.2
1983	−57.8
1984	−109.2
1985	−122.1
1986	−140.6
1987	−153.3
1988	−115.9
1989	−92.2
1990	−81.1
1991	−30.7
1992	−35.7
1993	−68.9
1994	−97.0
1995	−95.9
1996	−102.1
1997	−104.7
1998	−166.9
1999	−265.0
2000	−369.7

79. Calculate the difference between the trade balance in 1990 and that in 2000.

80. What was the difference between the trade balance in 1970 and that in 2000?

81. During which two consecutive years was the difference in the trade balance greatest?

82. How many times greater was the trade balance in 1990 than in 1980? Round to the nearest whole number.

83. Calculate the average trade balance per quarter for the year 2000.

84. By examining the data, would you expect the trade balance to have increased or decreased from 1995 to the year 2000? Support your answer.

■ The Order of Operations Agreement

Evaluate.

85. $(0.2)^2 \cdot (-0.5) + 1.72$

86. $0.3(1.7 - 4.8) + (-1.2)^2$

87. $(-1.6)^2 - 2.52 \div (1.8)$

88. $(1.05 - 1.65)^2 \div 0.4 - 2$

89. $-\dfrac{7}{12} + \dfrac{5}{6}\left(\dfrac{1}{6} - \dfrac{2}{3}\right)$

90. $-\dfrac{3}{4}\left(\dfrac{11}{12} - \dfrac{7}{8}\right) + \dfrac{5}{16}$

91. $\dfrac{11}{16} - \left(-\dfrac{3}{4}\right)^2 + \dfrac{7}{8}$

92. $\left(-\dfrac{2}{3}\right)^2 - \dfrac{7}{18} + \dfrac{5}{6}$

93. $\left(-\dfrac{1}{3}\right)^2 \cdot \left(-\dfrac{9}{4}\right) + \dfrac{3}{4}$

94. $\left(-\dfrac{2}{3}\right)^2 + \left(-\dfrac{1}{6}\right) \div \dfrac{3}{8}$

95. $\left(\dfrac{1}{3} - \dfrac{5}{6}\right) + \dfrac{7}{8} \div \left(-\dfrac{1}{2}\right)^3$

96. $\left(-\dfrac{1}{4}\right)^2 \div \left(\dfrac{1}{2} - \dfrac{3}{4}\right) + \dfrac{3}{8}$

 Temperature The following table shows the average low temperatures and the record low temperatures, in degrees Fahrenheit, in Anchorage, Alaska, and Fairbanks, Alaska, for each month of the year (*Source:* **www.weather.com**). Use this table for Exercises 97 to 102.

	Anchorage, Alaska		Fairbanks, Alaska	
	Average Low Temperature	*Record Low Temperature*	*Average Low Temperature*	*Record Low Temperature*
January	8	−34	−18	−61
February	11	−28	−14	−58
March	18	−24	−1	−49
April	28	−4	20	−24
May	38	17	38	−1
June	47	33	49	30
July	51	36	52	35
August	49	31	47	27
September	41	19	36	3
October	28	−5	18	−27
November	15	−21	−5	−46
December	10	−30	−14	−62

97. For Anchorage, what is the difference between the average low temperature for March and the record low temperature for March?

98. For Fairbanks, what is the difference between the average low temperature for January and the record low temperature for January?

99. Calculate the difference between the average low temperature for December in Anchorage and the average low temperature for December in Fairbanks.

100. What is the average of the average low monthly temperatures for Fairbanks? Round to the nearest tenth.

101. Find the average of the record low monthly temperatures for Fairbanks. Round to the nearest tenth.

102. Find the average of the record low monthly temperatures for Anchorage. Round to the nearest tenth.

Federal Budget   The table at the right shows the surplus or deficit, in billions of dollars, for the federal budget every fifth year from 1945 to 1995 and every year from 1995 to 2000 (*Source:* U.S. Office of Management and Budget). The negative sign (−) indicates a deficit. Use this table for Exercises 103 to 110.

Year	Federal Budget Surplus or Deficit
1945	−47.533
1950	−3.119
1955	−2.993
1960	0.301
1965	−1.411
1970	−2.842
1975	−53.242
1980	−73.835
1985	−212.334
1990	−221.194
1995	−163.899
1996	−107.450
1997	−21.940
1998	69.246
1999	79.263
2000	117.305

103. Find the difference between the deficits in the years 1980 and 1985.

104. Calculate the difference between the surplus in 1960 and the deficit in 1955.

105. How many times greater was the deficit in 1985 than in 1975? Round to the nearest whole number.

106. What was the average deficit, in billions of dollars, per month for the year 1985?

107. What was the average deficit, in millions of dollars, per quarter for the year 1970?

108. What was the average annual change in the deficit from 1980 to 1985? Round to the nearest billion.

109. Find the average surplus or deficit for the years 1996 through 2000.

110. Find the average surplus or deficit for the years 1995 through 2000. Round to the nearest billion.

Applying Concepts

111. Find the average of $\dfrac{5}{6}$ and $\dfrac{3}{4}$.

112. If the same positive number is added to both the numerator and denominator of $\frac{4}{7}$, is the new fraction less than, equal to, or greater than $\frac{4}{7}$?

113.   A student simplified the expression $6 + 2(4 - 9)$ as shown below.

$$6 + 2(4 - 9) = 6 + 2(-5)$$
$$= 8(-5)$$
$$= -40$$

Is this a correct simplification? Explain your answer.

114. A magic square is one in which the sum of the numbers in every row, column, and diagonal is the same number. Complete the magic square at the right.

$\frac{2}{3}$		
	$\frac{1}{6}$	$\frac{5}{6}$
		$-\frac{1}{3}$

115. Given any two distinct rational numbers, is it always possible to find a rational number between the two numbers? If so, explain how to find one.

116. Suppose the numerator of a fraction is a fixed number—for instance, 5. How does the value of the fraction change as the denominator increases?

117. Explain why you need a common denominator when adding two fractions and why you don't need a common denominator when multiplying two fractions?

EXPLORATION

1. *The Kelvin Scale*   The Celsius temperature scale was devised by Anders Celsius, a Swedish astronomer. On the Celsius scale, the temperature at which water freezes is represented as 0°C, and the temperature at which water boils is represented as 100°C. The interval between 0°C and 100°C is divided into 100 equal parts. Temperatures below 0°C are represented as negative numbers.

Theoretically, there is a temperature that is the lowest possible temperature. Scientists refer to the lowest possible temperature as **absolute zero.** An English physicist, Lord William Kelvin, devised a temperature scale, called the **Kelvin scale,** on which the zero point is absolute zero and each degree (which in the Kelvin scale is called a kelvin) is the same size as the Celsius degree. The letter K denotes a temperature on the Kelvin scale.

It is estimated that the temperature of absolute zero is −273.15°C, or 273.15 degrees below 0°C, the temperature at which water freezes. Thus, on the Kelvin scale, the temperature at which water boils is 373.15 K. Generally, these values are rounded to −273°C and 373 K, respectively. To convert temperatures from the Celsius scale to the Kelvin scale, add 273 to the Celsius temperature.

$$-50°C = (-50 + 273) \text{ K} = 223 \text{ K}$$

To convert temperatures from the Kelvin scale to the Celsius scale, subtract 273 from the Kelvin temperature.

$$250 \text{ K} = (250 - 273)°C = -23°C$$

Convert each of the following to Kelvin temperature.

a. 67°C   **b.** −15°C   **c.** −38°C   **d.** −200°C

Convert each of the following to Celsius temperature.

e. 320 K   **f.** 245 K   **g.** 189 K   **h.** 76 K

SECTION **1.5**

■ Evaluate Variable Expressions

Evaluating Variable Expressions

■ Evaluate Variable Expressions

Suppose that gasoline costs $1.50 per gallon. Then the amount you spend for gas for your car depends on how many gallons you purchase. Here are some examples:

A purchase of 5 gallons costs 1.50(5) = $7.50.
A purchase of 7 gallons costs 1.50(7) = $10.50.
A purchase of 11.3 gallons costs 1.50(11.3) = $16.95.

If you decide to fill the tank, you may not know how many gallons of gas will be required. In that case, you might use a letter, such as *g*, to represent the number of gallons that will be purchased.

A purchase of *g* gallons costs 1.50*g*.

A **variable** is a letter that represents a quantity that can change, or vary. The expression 1.50*g* (which means 1.50 times *g*) is a **variable expression.** The number 1.50 is the **coefficient** of the variable.

The expression 1.50*g* represents the cost to purchase *g* gallons of gas. As *g* (the number of gallons purchased) changes, the cost of the purchase changes.

EXAMPLE 1

Use the variable expression 1.50g to find the cost to purchase 12.5 gallons of gas.

Solution   1.50g

$$1.50(12.5) \quad \bullet \text{ Replace the variable } g \text{ by } 12.5.$$
$$= 18.75 \quad \bullet \text{ Multiply } 1.50 \text{ times } 12.5.$$

The cost for 12.5 gallons of gas is $18.75.

YOU TRY IT 1

Use the variable expression 1.50g to find the cost to purchase 9.7 gallons of gas.

Solution   See page S3.

Replacing a variable in a variable expression, as we did in Example 1, by a number and then simplifying the resulting numerical expression is called **evaluating the variable expression.** The number substituted for the variable (12.5) is called the **value of the variable.** The result (18.75) is called the **value of the variable expression.**

We could also use a variable expression to represent the total cost of a gasoline purchase. If we let T represent the total cost, in dollars, for a gasoline purchase, then

$$T = 1.50g$$

This *equation* shows the relationship between g, the number of gallons of gas purchased, and T, the total cost of the purchase.

g	1.50g	T
1	1.50(1)	1.50
2	1.50(2)	3.00
3	1.50(3)	4.50
4	1.50(4)	6.00
5	1.50(5)	7.50
6	1.50(6)	9.00

We can also use the equation $T = 1.50g$ to prepare an **input/output** table, which shows how T changes as g changes. The input is g, the number of gallons of gas purchased. The output is T, the total cost of the purchase. For the input/output table at the left, we have chosen 1, 2, 3, 4, 5, and 6 as the values of g, but other values of g could have been used.

? QUESTION   In the table at the left, what is the meaning of the number 7.50?

See Appendix A:
Y =

A graphing calculator can be used to create input/output tables for equations such as $T = 1.50g$. This is accomplished by using the **Y =** editor screen. The output variable is designated as one of the calculator's Y variables. For this example, we will designate T as Y_1. The input variable is usually designated by X. Thus the equation would appear as $Y_1 = 1.50X$.

```
Plot1  Plot2  Plot3
\Y1 ■1.50X
\Y2 =
\Y3 =
\Y4 =
\Y5 =
\Y6 =
\Y7 =
```

? ANSWER   7.50 is the output when the input is 5. The 7.50 means that it costs $7.50 for 5 gallons of gas.

See Appendix A:
Table

To create the table, we use the TABLE feature of the calculator. Some typical screens for the gasoline purchase follow.

In the Table Setup screen, TblStart is the beginning value of X, and △Tbl is the difference between successive values of X. The difference between any two successive X values is called the **change in X** or the **increment in X.** The symbol Δ is frequently used to represent the phrase *the change in.*

You can scroll down the screen by repeatedly pressing the down arrow key ⬇ to view greater values of X. Use the up arrow key to scroll up the screen to view lesser values of X.

X	Y₁	
5	7.5	
6	9	
7	10.5	
8	12	
9	13.5	
10	15	
11	16.5	
X = 11		

EXAMPLE 2

When a rock is dropped off a cliff, the distance the rock falls is given by the equation $d = 16t^2$, where d is the distance in feet that the rock has fallen and t is the time in seconds that the rock has been falling.

a. Create an input/output table for this equation. Use increments of 0.5 second, beginning with $t = 0$.

b. What is the meaning of the number 64 in the table?

Solution

a. The input variable is t, the number of seconds the rock has been falling. The output variable is d, the distance the rock falls.

ALGEBRAIC SOLUTION

t	d
0	0
0.5	4
1	16
1.5	36
2	64
2.5	100
3	144
3.5	196
4	256

GRAPHICAL CHECK

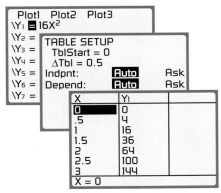

b. The number 64 is the output when the input is 2.

The number 64 means that the rock falls 64 feet in 2 seconds.

YOU TRY IT 2

Suppose that the average speed of an American Airlines flight from Los Angeles to Boston is 525 mph. Then the distance, in miles, that the plane is from Boston is given by the equation $d = 2650 - 525t$, where t is the number of hours since the plane left Los Angeles.

a. Create an input/output table for this equation. Use increments of 0.5 hour, beginning with $t = 0$.
b. What is the meaning of the number 1862.5 in the table?

Solution See page S3.

EXAMPLE 3

The fuel economy of a car is given by the equation $M = -0.02v^2 + 1.6v + 3$, where M is the fuel economy in miles per gallon (mpg) and v is the speed of the car in miles per hour (mph). Use a graphing calculator to create an input/output table for this equation with TblStart = 25 and ΔTbl = 5. Use the table to answer the following questions.

a. What is the fuel economy when the speed of the car is 50 mph?
b. What is the speed of the car when the fuel economy is 35 mpg?

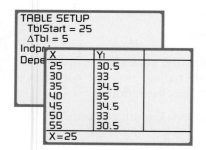

Solution The input variable is X, the speed of the car. The output variable is Y₁, the fuel economy of the car. The input/output table should look like the one at the left.

a. Because the question asks for the fuel economy (Y₁) when the speed is 50 mph (X), look in the table for an input value of 50. The corresponding output value is 33.

When the speed of the car is 50 mph, the fuel economy is 33 mpg.
b. Because the question asks for the speed (X) when the fuel economy is 35 mpg (Y₁), look in the table for an output value of 35. The corresponding input value is 40.

When the fuel economy is 35 mpg, the speed of the car is 40 mph.

YOU TRY IT 3

The amount of garbage generated by each person living in the United States is given by the equation $A = 0.05x - 95$, where A is the amount of garbage generated, in pounds per person per day, and x is the year. Use a graphing calculator to create an input/output table for this equation with TblStart = 1970 and ΔTbl = 5. Use the table to answer the following questions.

a. What was the amount of garbage generated per person per day in 1990?
b. In what year will the amount of garbage generated per person per day be 5.75 pounds?

Solution See page S4.

A **formula** is a special type of equation that states a rule about measurements. For instance, the formula for the area of a rectangle is $A = LW$. This formula shows the relationship between the area, A, of a rectangle and its length, L, and width, W. In this formula, two variables L and W, are written together. **When two or more variables are written together in an expression, the operation is multiplication.** Thus $A = LW$ means $A = L \cdot W$.

In a similar manner,

$$xyz \quad \text{means} \quad x \cdot y \cdot z$$

$$7rs \quad \text{means} \quad 7 \cdot r \cdot s$$

$$\frac{2ab}{3} \quad \text{means} \quad \frac{2}{3} \cdot a \cdot b$$

When evaluating expressions with more than one variable, replace each of the variables by its given value. Then use the Order of Operations Agreement to simplify the numerical expression. You can check your work using a graphing calculator, as shown in the check to Example 4.

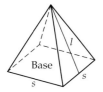

TAKE NOTE

When two variables are written together in an expression, the operation is multiplication. Thus $2sl$ in Example 4 means 2 times s times l.

 See Appendix A: Evaluating Variable Expressions

EXAMPLE 4

The formula for the surface area of a regular pyramid is $S = s^2 + 2sl$, where S is the surface area, s is the length of a side of the square base, and l is the slant height. Find the surface area of the regular pyramid shown at the right.

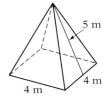

Solution $S = s^2 + 2sl$

$S = 4^2 + 2(4)(5)$ • Replace the variables s and l by their given values, $s = 4$ and $l = 5$.

$S = 16 + 2(4)(5)$ • Use the Order of Operations Agreement to simplify the numerical expression.

$S = 16 + 8(5)$

$S = 16 + 40$

$S = 56$

The surface area is 56 m².

Check: As an alternative method of checking the evaluation of a variable expression, store the value of each variable in the calculator. A typical screen for the evaluation of the expression $s^2 + 2sl$ in Example 4 follows.

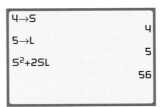

Note: Generally a variable that is a capital letter cannot be changed to lower case, and a lower-case variable cannot be capitalized. However, some graphing calculators cannot represent variables as lower-case letters.

YOU TRY IT 4

A rectangle has a length of 8.5 meters and a width of 3.5 meters. Find the perimeter of the rectangle. Use the formula $P = 2L + 2W$, where P is the perimeter, L is the length, and W is the width of a rectangle.

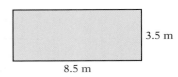

3.5 m

8.5 m

Solution   See page S4.

A more general variable expression is evaluated in Example 5 below.

EXAMPLE 5

Evaluate $5ab^3 + 2a^2b^2 - 4$ when $a = 3$ and $b = -2$.

Solution $5ab^3 + 2a^2b^2 - 4$

$5(3)(-2)^3 + 2(3)^2(-2)^2 - 4$ • Replace a by 3 and b by -2.

$= 5(3)(-8) + 2(9)(4) - 4$ • Use the Order of Operations Agreement to simplify the numerical expression.

$= -120 + 72 - 4$

$= -48 - 4$

$= -52$

Check: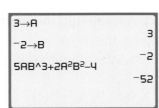

YOU TRY IT 5

Evaluate $3xy^2 - 3x^2y$ when $x = -2$ and $y = 5$.

Solution   See page S4.

1.5 EXERCISES

Topics for Discussion

1.   What is a variable?

2.   What is a variable expression?

3. What does it mean to evaluate a variable expression?

4. Can the value of a variable ever equal 0? If not, why not? If so, give an example of an actual situation where it makes sense for the value of a variable to be 0.

5. What is an input/output table?

For Exercises 6 and 7, determine whether the statement is always true, sometimes true, or never true. If the statement is sometimes true or never true, explain your answer.

6. The Order of Operations Agreement is used in evaluating a variable expression.

7. The result of evaluating a variable expression is a single number.

▪ Evaluate Variable Expressions

Evaluate the variable expression when $a = 2$, $b = 3$, and $c = -4$.

8. $a - 2c$ **9.** $-3a + 4b$ **10.** $3b - 3c$

11. $-3c + 4$ **12.** $16 \div (2c)$ **13.** $6b \div (-a)$

14. $2a - (c + a)^2$ **15.** $(b - a)^2 + 4c$ **16.** $(b - 2a)^2 + bc$

Evaluate the variable expression when $a = -2$, $b = 4$, $c = -1$, and $d = 3$.

17. $\dfrac{b + c}{d}$ **18.** $\dfrac{d - b}{c}$ **19.** $\dfrac{2d + b}{-a}$

20. $\dfrac{b - d}{c - a}$ **21.** $2(b + c) - 2a$ **22.** $3(b - a) - bc$

23. $\dfrac{-4bc}{2a - b}$ **24.** $\dfrac{abc}{b - d}$ **25.** $(b - a)^2 - (d - c)^2$

26. $(b + c)^2 + (a + d)^2$ **27.** $4ac + (2a)^2$ **28.** $3cd - (4c)^2$

Evaluate the variable expression when $a = 2.7$, $b = -1.6$, and $c = -0.8$.

29. $c^2 - ab$ **30.** $(a + b)^2 - c$ **31.** $\dfrac{b^3}{c} - 4a$

Evaluate the variable expression when $a = -2$ and $b = -3$.

32. $|2a + 3b|$ **33.** $|-4ab|$ **34.** $|5a - b|$

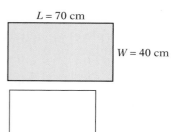

L = 70 cm

W = 40 cm

35. *Geometry* The formula for the perimeter of a rectangle is $P = 2L + 2W$, where P is the perimeter, L is the length, and W is the width. Find the perimeter of the rectangle shown at the right.

36. *Geometry* The formula for the perimeter of a square is $P = 4s$, where P is the perimeter and s is the length of one of the equal sides. Find the perimeter of the square shown at the right.

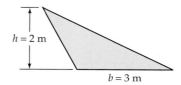

37. *Geometry* The formula for the area of a rectangle is $A = LW$, where A is the area, L is the length, and W is the width. Find the area of the rectangle in Exercise 35.

38. *Geometry* The formula for the area of a square is $A = s^2$, where A is the area and s is the length of one of the equal sides. Find the area of the square in Exercise 36.

39. *Geometry* The formula for the area of a triangle is $A = \frac{1}{2}bh$, where A is the area, b is the base, and h is the height. Find the area of the triangle shown at the right.

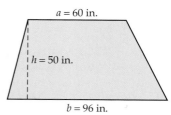

h = 2 m

b = 3 m

40. *Geometry* The formula for the area of a trapezoid is $A = \frac{1}{2}h(a + b)$, where A is the area, h is the height, and a and b are the lengths of the bases. Find the area of the trapezoid shown at the right.

a = 60 in.

h = 50 in.

b = 96 in.

41. *Depreciation* To determine the depreciated value of an X-ray machine, an accountant uses the formula $V = C - 5500t$, where V is the depreciated value of the machine in t years and C is the original cost. Find the depreciated value after 4 years of an X-ray machine that cost $70,000.

42. *Sports* The world record time for a 1-mile race can be approximated by the formula $t = 17.08 - 0.0067y$, where y is the year of the race and t is the time, in minutes, of the race. Find the time predicted by this formula for the year 1954. Round to the nearest tenth.

43. *Automotive Technology* Black ice is an ice covering on roads that is especially difficult to see and therefore extremely dangerous for motorists. The distance D, in feet, that a car traveling 30 mph will slide after its brakes are applied is related to the outside air temperature by the formula $D = 4C + 180$, where C is the Celsius temperature. Find the distance a car will slide on black ice when the outside temperature is $-11°C$.

44. *Geometry* Find the surface area of a rectangular solid that has a length of 5 meters, a width of 8 meters, and a height of 4 meters. Use the formula $S = 2LW + 2LH + 2WH$, where S is the surface area, L is the length, W is the width, and H is the height of the rectangular solid.

SECTION 1.5   Evaluating Variable Expressions   **71**

For Exercises 45 to 52, use a graphing calculator to create an input/output table for the equation using the given instructions. Use the input/output table to answer the questions.

45. $y = 3x + 2$, TblStart $= 0$, ΔTbl $= 1$

    a. What is the value of y when $x = 3$?
    b. What is the value of x when $y = 5$?

46. $y = 2x - 3$, TblStart $= 2$, ΔTbl $= 1$

    a. What is the value of y when $x = 6$?
    b. What is the value of x when $y = 5$?

47. $y = x^2$, TblStart $= 1$, ΔTbl $= 0.5$

    a. What is the value of y when $x = 2$?
    b. What is the value of x when $y = 12.25$?

48. $y = x^2 - 1$, TblStart $= 2$, ΔTbl $= 0.5$

    a. What is the value of y when $x = 4.5$?
    b. What is the value of x when $y = 5.25$?

49. $y = 2x^2 + 1$, TblStart $= 1.5$, ΔTbl $= 0.25$

    a. What is the value of y when $x = 1.75$?
    b. What is the value of x when $y = 16.125$?

50. $y = 12 - x^2$, TblStart $= 1$, ΔTbl $= 0.25$

    a. What is the value of y when $x = 1.5$?
    b. What is the value of x when $y = 8.9375$?

51. $y = x^2 + 3x + 1$, TblStart $= 0$, ΔTbl $= 1$

    a. What is the value of y when $x = 3$?
    b. What is the value of x when $y = 29$?

52. $y = x^2 + 5x - 2$, TblStart $= 1$, ΔTbl $= 1$

    a. What is the value of y when $x = 4$?
    b. What is the value of x when $y = 48$?

53. *Architecture*   An architect charges a fee of $500 plus $2.65 per square foot to design a house. The equation that represents the architect's fee is $F = 2.65s + 500$, where F is the fee, in dollars, and s is the number of square feet in the house. Use a graphing calculator to create an input/output table for this equation for increments of 100 square feet, beginning with $s = 1200$. What is the meaning of the number 4740 in the table?

54. *Business*   A rental car company charges a drop-off fee of $50 to return a car to a location different from that at which it was rented. It also charges a fee of $.18 per mile the car is driven. The equation that represents the total cost to rent a car from this company is $C = 0.18m + 50$, where C is the total cost, in dollars, and m is the number of miles the car is driven. Use a graphing calculator to create an input/output table for this equation for increments of 10 miles beginning with $m = 100$. What is the meaning of the number 77 in the table?

55. *Temperature*   In June, the temperature at various elevations of the Grand Canyon can be approximated by the equation $T = -0.005x + 113.25$, where T is the temperature in Fahrenheit and x is the elevation, or distance above sea level. Use a graphing calculator to create an input/output table for this equation. Use ΔTbl = 500 and TblStart = 2450.

 a.   According to this equation, what is the temperature at an elevation of 4450 feet (about halfway down the south rim of the canyon)?

 b.   At Inner Gorge, or the bottom of the canyon, the temperature is 101°F. What is the elevation of Inner Gorge?

56. *Temperature*   The equation $F = \frac{9}{5}C + 32$ can be used to convert Celsius temperatures (C) to Fahrenheit temperatures (F). Use a graphing calculator to create an input/output table for this equation. Use ΔTbl = 5 and TblStart = 0.

 a.   Find the Fahrenheit temperature when the Celsius temperature is 20°C.

 b.   Find the Celsius temperature when the Fahrenheit temperature is 50°F.

57. *Geology*   Old Faithful is a geyser in Yellowstone National Park that was so named because of its regular eruptions for the past 100 years. An equation that can predict the approximate time until the next eruption is $T = 12.4L + 32$, where T is the time (in minutes) to the next eruption and L is the length of time (in minutes) of the last eruption. Use a graphing calculator to create an input/output table for this equation for increments of 0.5 minute, beginning with $L = 1$.

 a.   According to this equation, how long will it be until the next eruption if the last eruption lasted 3.5 minutes?

 b.   If the time between two eruptions is 63 minutes, what was the length of time of the last eruption?

58. *Aeronautics*   The altitude, or height above sea level, of a hot-air balloon is given by the equation $H = 100t + 1250$, where H is the altitude of the balloon in feet t seconds after it has been released. Create an input/output table for this equation for increments of 1 second, beginning with $t = 0$.

 a.   What is the altitude of the balloon 3 seconds after it is released?

 b.   How many seconds after it is released is the balloon at an altitude of 1750 feet?

59. *Sports*   The equation $h = -16t^2 + 64t + 5$ gives the height of a baseball thrown straight up, where h is the height of the baseball in feet and t is the time in seconds since the baseball was released. Create an input/output table for this equation for increments of 0.5 second, beginning with $t = 0$.

    a. What is the height of the baseball 2 seconds after it is released?

    b. The baseball is 65 feet above the ground at two different times, once on the way up and once on the way down. What are the two times?

60. *Sports*   The distance d (in feet) of a platform diver above the water t seconds after the dive begins is given by the equation $d = 50 - 16t^2$. Create an input/output table for this equation for increments of 0.25 second, beginning with $t = 0$.

    a. How many feet above the water is the diver 0.25 second after the dive begins?

    b. After how many seconds is the diver 25 feet above the water?

61. *Geometry*   The formula for the perimeter of a square is $P = 4s$, where P is the perimeter and s is the length of one of the equal sides.

    a. Create an input/output table for this equation for increments of 2 inches, beginning with $s = 2$.

    b. What does the output value of 48 represent?

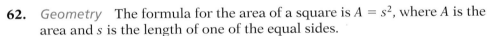

62. *Geometry*   The formula for the area of a square is $A = s^2$, where A is the area and s is the length of one of the equal sides.

    a. Create an input/output table for this equation for increments of 2 feet, beginning with $s = 2$.

    b. What does the output value 64 represent?

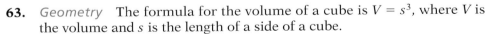

63. *Geometry*   The formula for the volume of a cube is $V = s^3$, where V is the volume and s is the length of a side of a cube.

    a. Create an input/output table for this equation for increments of 1 meter, beginning with $s = 1$.

    b. Write a sentence that describes the meaning of the numbers 3 and 27.

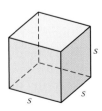

64. *Geometry*   The formula for the surface area of a cube is $S = 6s^2$, where S is the surface area and s is the length of a side of a cube.

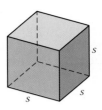

   a.   Create an input/output table for this equation for increments of 1 centimeter beginning with $s = 1$.
   b.   Write a sentence that describes the meaning of the numbers 4 and 96.

Applying Concepts

Evaluate the variable expression when $a = \frac{2}{3}$ and $b = -\frac{3}{2}$.

65. $\frac{1}{3}a^5b^6$ **66.** $\dfrac{(2ab)^3}{2a^3b^3}$ **67.** $|5ab - 8a^2b^2|$

Evaluate the variable expression when $x = 2$, $y = 3$, and $z = -2$.

68. $3^x - x^3$ **69.** $2^y - y^2$ **70.** z^y

71. z^x **72.** $x^x - y^y$ **73.** $y^{(x^2)}$

EXPLORATION

1. *Patterns in Mathematics*   For each of the following, determine the first natural number x, greater than 2, for which the second expression is greater than the first. On the basis of your answers, make a conjecture that appears to be true about the expressions x^n and n^x, where $n = 3, 4, 5, 6, 7, \ldots$ and x is a natural number greater than 2.
   a. $x^3, 3^x$ **b.** $x^4, 4^x$
   c. $x^5, 5^x$ **d.** $x^6, 6^x$

2. *Making Conjectures*   Consider the following expressions: $(a + b)^2, a^2 + b^2, (a + b)^3, a^3 + b^3,$ and $(a + b)^4, a^4 + b^4$.
   a.   By trying different values of a and b, determine whether $(a + b)^2 = a^2 + b^2$ is always true.
   b.   By trying different values of a and b, determine whether $(a + b)^3 = a^3 + b^3$ is always true.
   c.   By trying different values of a and b, determine whether $(a + b)^4 = a^4 + b^4$ is always true.
   d.   Using inductive reasoning, make a conjecture about whether $(a + b)^n = a^n + b^n$ is always true when n is a natural number.

Simplifying Variable Expressions

■ Properties of Real Numbers

In the last two sections, we *evaluated* variable expressions. That is, we replaced the variables by numbers and then simplified the resulting numerical expressions. Now we will look at *simplifying* variable expressions. This is accomplished by using the Properties of Real Numbers, presented below.

Note that numbers can be added in either order and the result is the same.

$$9 + (-12) = -3 \quad \text{and} \quad -12 + 9 = -3$$

This is the **Commutative Property of Addition,** which states that if a and b are any two numbers, then $a + b = b + a$.

When three numbers are added together, the numbers can be grouped in any order and the sum will be the same.

$$-6 + (3 + 7) = -6 + 10 = 4 \quad \text{and} \quad (-6 + 3) + 7 = -3 + 7 = 4$$

This is the **Associative Property of Addition,** which states that if a, b and c are any three numbers, then $a + (b + c) = (a + b) + c$.

Two other properties of addition are also important. The first says that the sum of a number and its opposite is zero.

$$-8 + 8 = 0 \quad \text{and} \quad 8 + (-8) = 0$$

This is the **Inverse Property of Addition,** which states that $a + (-a) = 0$ and $-a + a = 0$. Recall that a and $-a$ are opposites, or additive inverses, of each other.

The second of these two other properties expresses the fact that the sum of a number and zero is the number.

$$-3 + 0 = -3 \quad \text{and} \quad 0 + (-3) = -3$$

This is the **Addition Property of Zero,** which states that if a is any number, then $a + 0 = a$ and $0 + a = a$.

Note that numbers can be multiplied in either order and the result is the same.

$$9(-8) = -72 \quad \text{and} \quad (-8)9 = -72$$

This is the **Commutative Property of Multiplication,** which states that if a and b are any two numbers, then $ab = ba$.

When three numbers are multiplied together, the numbers can be grouped in any order and the product will be the same.

$$3(5 \cdot 2) = 3(10) = 30 \quad \text{and} \quad (3 \cdot 5)2 = 15 \cdot 2 = 30$$

This is the **Associative Property of Multiplication,** which states that if a, b, and c are any three numbers, then $a(bc) = (ab)c$.

Two other properties of multiplication are also important. The first says that the product of a number and its reciprocal is 1.

$$\frac{1}{8} \cdot 8 = 1 \quad \text{and} \quad 8\left(\frac{1}{8}\right) = 1$$

This is the **Inverse Property of Multiplication,** which states that for $a \neq 0$, $a \cdot \frac{1}{a} = 1$ and $\frac{1}{a} \cdot a = 1$. The terms a and $\frac{1}{a}$ are **reciprocals.** They are also called **multiplicative inverses** of each other.

The second of these other two properties expresses the fact that the product of a number and 1 is the number.

$$9 \cdot 1 = 9 \quad \text{and} \quad 1 \cdot 9 = 9$$

This is the **Multiplication Property of One,** which states that if a is any number, then $a \cdot 1 = a$ and $1 \cdot a = a$.

Recall that the coefficient of a variable is the number that multiplies the variable. Note from the Multiplication Property of One that when the coefficient is 1, the 1 is not written. Thus we write x instead of $1x$ or $1 \cdot x$. A coefficient of -1 is treated in much the same way. For instance, we normally write $-1x$ and $-1 \cdot x$ as $-x$.

By the Order of Operations Agreement, the expression $6(4 + 7)$ is simplified by first adding the numbers inside the parentheses and then multiplying. However, we can multiply each number inside the parentheses by the number outside the parentheses and then add the products, and the result is the same.

$$6(4 + 7) = 6(11)$$
$$= 66$$
$$6(4 + 7) = 6(4) + 6(7)$$
$$= 24 + 42$$
$$= 66$$

This is an example of the **Distributive Property,** which states that if a, b, and c are any numbers, then $a(b + c) = ab + ac$.

> **TAKE NOTE**
>
> Here is a summary of the discussion at the right. If a coefficient is 1 or −1, the 1 is usually not written. For instance, we write 1*x* as *x* and write −1*xy* as −*xy*.

EXAMPLE 1

a. Complete the statement by using the Commutative Property of Addition:

$$4 + x = ?$$

b. Complete the statement by using the Distributive Property:

$$4(6 + 9) = ?(6) + ?(9)$$

Solution　**a.** $4 + x = x + 4$　　• The Commutative Property of Addition states that the order of addends can be interchanged.

b. $4(6 + 9)$
$= 4(6) + 4(9)$　　• The Distributive Property states that each number inside the parentheses is multiplied by the number outside the parentheses.

> **YOU TRY IT 1**
>
> **a.** Complete the statement by using the Associative Property of Multiplication:
>
> $$4(3x) = ?$$
>
> **b.** Complete the statement by using the Inverse Property of Addition.
>
> $$12 + ? = 0$$
>
> **Solution**   See page S4.

> **TAKE NOTE**
>
> Recall that we can rewrite subtraction as addition of the opposite. This step is rarely written when simplifying variable expressions but is always done mentally.
> $3x^2 + 3x - 6 - 7x + 9$
> equals
> $3x^2 + 3x + (-6) + (-7x) + 9.$

■ Simplify Variable Expressions

A variable expression is shown at the right. The expression can be rewritten by writing subtraction as addition of the opposite.

$$3x^2 - 4xy + 5z - 2$$
$$3x^2 + (-4xy) + 5z + (-2)$$

Note that the expression has 4 addends. The **terms** of a variable expression are the addends of the expression. The expression has 4 terms.

$$\overbrace{3x^2 - 4xy + 5z}^{\text{4 terms}}\quad \overbrace{-2}$$
Variable terms   Constant term

The terms $3x^2$, $-4xy$, and $5z$ are **variable terms.** The term -2 is a **constant term,** or simply a **constant.**

Like terms of a variable expression are the terms that have the same variable parts. The terms $3x$ and $-7x$ are like terms. Constant terms are also like terms. Thus -6 and 9 are like terms. The terms $3x^2$ and $3x$ are not like terms, because $x^2 = x \cdot x$ and thus the variable parts are not the same.

Like terms

$$3x^2 + 3x - 6 - 7x + 9$$

Like terms

Terms such as $4xy$ and $-7yx$ are like terms because, by the Commutative Property of Multiplication, $xy = yx$. The same is true for the like terms $-4abc$ and $12bca$.

> **TAKE NOTE**
>
> Combining like terms is an operation we do quite naturally, probably everyday. For instance,
> 4 apples + 7 apples
>   = 11 apples
> $5 + $2 = $7
> 6 pounds + 3 pounds
>   = 9 pounds
> Equally natural is the idea of *not* combining items that are not similar.
> 4 apples + 7 oranges
> 2 dogs + 5 cats

? **QUESTION**   Which of the following pairs of terms are like terms?

    a. $3a$ and $3b$ **b.** $7z^2$ and $7z^3$ **c.** $6ab$ and $3a$ **d.** $-4c^2$ and $6c^2$

By using the Commutative Property of Multiplication, we can rewrite the Distributive Property as $ba + ca = (b + c)a$. This is sometimes called the *factoring form* of the Distributive Property. This form of the Distributive Property is used to **combine like terms** of a variable expression by adding their coefficients. For instance,

$$7x + 9x = (7 + 9)x$$ • Use the Distributive Property:
$$= 16x$$ $ba + ca = (b + c)a$

Combining like terms of a variable expression is referred to as **simplifying the variable expression.**

———

? ANSWERS **a.** Not like terms; the variable parts are not the same. **b.** Not like terms; $z^2 = z \cdot z$ and $z^3 = z \cdot z \cdot z$. **c.** Not like terms; the variable parts are not the same. **d.** These are like terms; the variable parts are the same.

? QUESTION   What is the result when the expression $9y + 5y$ is simplified?

Because subtraction is defined as addition of the opposite, the Distributive Property also applies to subtraction. Thus, we can write $a(b - c) = ab - ac$ and $ac - bc = (a - b)c$. Here are the steps to simplify $8z - 12z$.

$$8z - 12z = (8 - 12)z \qquad \bullet \text{ Use the Distributive Property: } ac - bc = (a - b)c$$
$$= -4z \qquad\qquad \bullet \textit{Note: } 8 - 12 = 8 + (-12) = -4$$

Some variable expressions cannot be simplified. For instance, the variable expression $4a + 7b$ cannot be rewritten in a simpler form. The terms $4a$ and $7b$ do not have the same variable part. Therefore, the Distributive Property cannot be used. We say that $4a + 7b$ is in *simplest form*. As another example, $5x^2 + 8x$ is in simplest form because $5x^2$ and $8x$ are not like terms.

EXAMPLE 2

Simplify.   **a.** $2(-y)$ **b.** $-\dfrac{1}{3}(-3y)$

Solution   **a.** $2(-y) = 2(-1y)$ $\bullet$ Recall: $-y = -1 \cdot y$

$\qquad\qquad\quad = [2(-1)]y$ $\bullet$ Use the Associative Property of Multiplication to regroup factors.

$\qquad\qquad\quad = -2y$ $\bullet$ Multiply.

b. $-\dfrac{1}{3}(-3y) = \left[-\dfrac{1}{3}(-3)\right]y$ $\bullet$ Use the Associative Property of Multiplication to regroup factors.

$\qquad\qquad\quad\quad = 1y$ $\bullet$ Use the Inverse Property of Multiplication.

$\qquad\qquad\quad\quad = y$ $\bullet$ Use the Multiplication Property of One.

YOU TRY IT 2

Simplify.   **a.** $-5(-3a)$ **b.** $\left(-\dfrac{1}{2}c\right)2$

Solution   See page S4.

EXAMPLE 3

Simplify.   **a.** $5y + 3x - 5y$ **b.** $4x^2 + 5x - 6x^2 - 7x$

Solution   **a.** $5y + 3x - 5y$

$\qquad\qquad = 3x + 5y - 5y$ $\bullet$ Use the Commutative Property of Addition to rearrange the terms.

$\qquad\qquad = 3x + (5y - 5y)$ $\bullet$ Use the Associative Property of Addition to group like terms.

$\qquad\qquad = 3x + 0$ $\bullet$ Use the Inverse Property of Addition.

$\qquad\qquad = 3x$ $\bullet$ Use the Addition Property of Zero.

? ANSWER $9y + 5y = (9 + 5)y = 14y$

TAKE NOTE

After simplifying an expression, it is customary to rewrite addition of the opposite as subtraction. That is why, in the solution to Example 3b, we write $-2x^2 + (-2x)$ as $-2x^2 - 2x$.

b. $4x^2 + 5x - 6x^2 - 7x$

$= 4x^2 - 6x^2 + 5x - 7x$	• Use the Commutative Property of Addition to rearrange the terms.
$= (4x^2 - 6x^2) + (5x - 7x)$	• Use the Associative Property of Addition to group like terms.
$= -2x^2 + (-2x)$	• Use the Distributive Property to combine like terms.
$= -2x^2 - 2x$	• Rewrite addition of the opposite as subtraction.

YOU TRY IT 3

Simplify.   **a.** $3a - 2b + 5a$ **b.** $2z^2 - 5z - 3z^2 + 6z$

Solution   See page S4.

? QUESTION   Suppose you correctly simplify an expression and write the answer as $x + 7$, and another person writes the answer as $7 + x$. Are both answers correct?

The Distributive Property also is used to remove parentheses from a variable expression. Here is an example.

$4(2x + 5z) = 4(2x) + 4(5z)$	• Use the Distributive Property: $a(b + c) = ab + ac$
$= (4 \cdot 2)x + (4 \cdot 5)z$	• Use the Associative Property of Multiplication to regroup factors.
$= 8x + 20z$	• Multiply $4 \cdot 2$ and $4 \cdot 5$.

When a negative number precedes the parentheses, be especially careful that all of the operations are performed correctly. Here are two examples.

$-5(3x - 7) = -5(3x) - (-5)(7)$	• Use the Distributive Property.
$= -15x - (-35)$	• Multiply.
$= -15x + 35$	• Rewrite subtraction of a negative number as addition of the opposite.

$-3(-7a + 4) = -3(-7a) + (-3)(4)$	• Use the Distributive Property.
$= 21a + (-12)$	• Multiply.
$= 21a - 12$	• Rewrite addition of a negative number as subtraction.

The Distributive Property can be extended to expressions containing more than two terms. For instance,

$$4(2x + 3y + 5z) = 4(2x) + 4(3y) + 4(5z)$$
$$= 8x + 12y + 20z$$

? ANSWER   Yes. By the Commutative Property of Addition, $x + 7 = 7 + x$.

EXAMPLE 4

Simplify. **a.** $-3(2x + 4)$ **b.** $-(3z - 4)$
c. $(4a - 2c)5$ **d.** $6(3x - 4y + z)$

Solution **a.** $-3(2x + 4) = -3(2x) + (-3)(4)$ • Use the Distributive
$= -6x - 12$ Property.

b. $-(3z - 4) = -1(3z - 4)$ • Just as $-x = -1x$,
$-(3z - 4) = -1(3z - 4)$.

$= -1(3z) - (-1)(4)$ • Use the Distributive
$= -3z + 4$ Property.

c. $(4a - 2c)5 = (4a)(5) - (2c)(5)$ • Use the Distributive
$= 20a - 10c$ Property:
$(b + c)a = ba + ca$

d. $6(3x - 4y + z)$
$= 6(3x) - 6(4y) + 6(z)$ • Use the Distributive
$= 18x - 24y + 6z$ Property.

YOU TRY IT 4

Simplify. **a.** $-3(5y - 2)$ **b.** $-(6c + 5)$
c. $(3p - 7)(-3)$ **d.** $-2(4x + 2y - 6z)$

Solution See page S4.

TAKE NOTE

When we simplified
$5 + 12x - 6$ (shown at
the right), we wrote
$12x - 1$. That is, the
variable term was
written first. Through-
out the text, we use
this convention of
writing variable terms
first and then the con-
stant term. If there is
more than one vari-
able term, we arrange
the variable terms al-
phabetically. There is
no mathematical rea-
son to do this. It is just
a convention that de-
veloped over time.

To simplify the expression $5 + 3(4x - 2)$, use the Distributive Property to re-move the parentheses. Remember that $3(4x - 2)$ means $3 \cdot (4x - 2)$. Thus, by the Order of Operations Agreement, perform the multiplication $3(4x - 2)$ be-fore doing the addition.

$5 + 3(4x - 2) = 5 + 3(4x) - 3(2)$ • Use the Distributive Property
$= 5 + 12x - 6$
$= 12x - 1$ • Add the like terms 5 and -6.

In Example 5a and 5b below, the Distributive Property is used twice to sim-plify each expression.

EXAMPLE 5

Simplify. **a.** $3(2x - 4) - 5(3x + 2)$ **b.** $3a - 2[7a - 2(2a + 1)]$

Solution **a.** $3(2x - 4) - 5(3x + 2)$ • Use the Distributive Property
$= 6x - 12 - 15x - 10$ to remove parentheses.
$= -9x - 22$ • Combine like terms.

b. $3a - 2[7a - 2(2a + 1)]$ • Use the Distributive Property
$= 3a - 2[7a - 4a - 2]$ to remove parentheses.

• Combine like terms inside the
brackets.
$= 3a - 2[3a - 2]$
• Use the Distributive Property
to remove the brackets.
$= 3a - 6a + 4$

$= -3a + 4$ • Combine like terms.

YOU TRY IT 5

Simplify.   **a.** $7(-3x - 4y) - 3(3x + y)$ **b.** $2y - 3[5 - 3(3 + 2y)]$

Solution   See page S4.

■ Translate Phrases into Variable Expressions

Creating a variable expression is an important goal in the applications of mathematics. Many application problems are given in verbal or written form and must be translated into a mathematical expression. A partial list of the verbal phrases used to indicate the different mathematical operations follows.

> **TAKE NOTE**
>
> Note the translation of 12 *less than b* at the right as $b - 12$. It would be incorrect to write $12 - b$.

Addition	added to	7 added to z	$z + 7$
	more than	8 more than w	$w + 8$
	the sum of	the sum of z and 9	$z + 9$
	the total of	the total of r and s	$r + s$
	increased by	x increased by 7	$x + 7$
Subtraction	minus	t minus 3	$t - 3$
	less than	12 less than b	$b - 12$
	the difference between	the difference between x and 1	$x - 1$
	decreased by	17 decreased by a	$17 - a$
Multiplication	times	negative 2 times c	$-2c$
	the product of	the product of x and y	xy
	of	three fourths of m	$\frac{3}{4}m$
	twice	twice d	$2d$
	multiplied by	6 multiplied by y	$6y$
Division	divided by	v divided by 15	$\frac{v}{15}$
	the quotient of	the quotient of y and 3	$\frac{y}{3}$
Power	the square of *or* the second power of	the square of x	x^2
	the cube of *or* the third power of	the cube of r	r^3
	the fifth power of	the fifth power of a	a^5

Translating a phrase that contains the word *sum, difference, product,* or *quotient* can sometimes cause a problem. In the examples at the right, note that the operation symbol replaces the word *and.*

the *sum* of x and y $x + y$

the *difference* between x and y $x - y$

the *product* of x and y $x \cdot y$

the *quotient* of x and y $\dfrac{x}{y}$

⟹ Translate "the difference between three times a number and seven" into a variable expression.

Assign a variable, say x, to the unknown quantity.

Underline words that indicate mathematical operations.

Use the operations and the assigned variable (x) to write the variable expression.

the <u>difference between</u> three <u>times</u> a number and seven

$3x$ $-$ 7

The variable expression is $3x - 7$.

EXAMPLE 6

Translate into a variable expression.

a. eight less than five times a number
b. the product of four times a number and the sum of the number and five

Solution   **a.** Let the unknown number be x.

eight <u>less than</u> five <u>times</u> a number

$5x - 8$

- Underline the words that indicate mathematical operations.
- Use the operations and the assigned variable to write the variable expression.

b. Let the unknown number be x.

the <u>product</u> of four <u>times</u> a number and the <u>sum</u> of the number and five

four times a number: $4x$
the sum of the number and 5: $x + 5$

$4x(x + 5)$

- Underline the words that indicate mathematical operations.
- Use the operations and the assigned variable to write variable expressions for internal phrases.
- Write the variable expression.

YOU TRY IT 6

Translate into a variable expression.

a. seven more than the product of a number and twelve
b. the total of eighteen and the quotient of a number and nine

Solution   See page S4.

After translating a verbal expression into a variable expression, simplify the variable expression by using the Properties of Real Numbers.

EXAMPLE 7

Translate and simplify: "the total of four times an unknown number and twice the difference between the number and eight."

Solution   Let the unknown number be x.

the <u>total</u> of four <u>times</u> an unknown number and <u>twice</u> the <u>difference between</u> the number and eight

four times an unknown number: $4x$
twice the difference between the number and eight: $2(x - 8)$

$4x + 2(x - 8)$

$= 4x + 2x - 16$
$= 6x - 16$

• Underline the words that indicate mathematical operations.

• Use the operations and the assigned variable to write variable expressions for internal phrases.
• Write the variable expression.
• Simplify the variable expression.

YOU TRY IT 7

Translate and simplify: "a number minus the difference between the number and seventeen."

Solution   See page S4.

Many of the applications of mathematics require that you identify an unknown quantity, assign a variable to that quantity, and then express another unknown quantity in terms of that variable.

➡ A wire for a guitar is 12 feet long and is cut into two pieces. Use one variable to express the lengths of the two pieces.

Suppose that 4 feet are cut from the wire. Then the remaining piece would be

$$12 - 4 = 8 \text{ feet}$$

If 5 feet are cut from the wire, then the remaining piece would be

$$12 - 5 = 7 \text{ feet}$$

▼ **Point of Interest**

The way in which expressions are symbolized has changed over time. Here are some expressions as they may have appeared in the early 16th century.
   R p. 9 *for* x + 9*. The symbol* ***R*** *was used for a variable to the first power. The symbol* ***p.*** *was used for plus.*
   R m. 3 *for* x − 3*. The symbol* ***R*** *represented a variable. The symbol* ***m.*** *was used for minus.*
   The square of a variable was designated by Q*, and the cube was designated by* C*. The expression* x³ + x² *was written* ***C p. Q.***

Extend this idea by letting x feet represent the length of the piece cut from the wire. Then the remaining piece would be

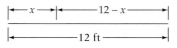

$$(12 - x) \text{ feet}$$

The lengths of the two pieces are x feet and $(12 - x)$ feet.

Note in this example that the sum of the two lengths of wire is 12, the length of the original wire.

$$x + (12 - x) = x + 12 - x = 12$$

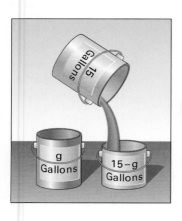

EXAMPLE 8

Fifteen gallons of paint were poured into two containers of different sizes. Express the amount of paint poured into the smaller container in terms of the amount poured into the larger container.

Solution   the number of gallons poured into the larger container: g

the number of gallons of paint poured into the smaller container: $15 - g$

YOU TRY IT 8

The sum of two numbers is 10. Express both numbers in terms of the same variable.

Solution   See page S4.

If you are having difficulty writing a variable expression for a problem, first try using numbers for the quantity that is changing. For instance, suppose the cost to rent a pair of skis is $10 plus $15 per day. Then the cost to rent the skis for 3 days is $10 + 15(3)$ or $55. The cost to rent the skis for 8 days is $10 + 15(8)$ or $130. Now replace the quantity that is changing with a variable. The variable expression is $10 + 15d$, where d is the number of days the skis are rented.

EXAMPLE 9

The cost to rent a car is $39.95 plus $.15 per mile driven. Express the cost of renting the car in terms of the number of miles driven.

Solution   Let m represent the number of miles driven.

$39.95 + 0.15$ for each mile driven:

$39.95 + 0.15m$

YOU TRY IT 9

A chef is paid $640 per week plus $32 for each hour of overtime worked. Express the chef's weekly pay in terms of the number of hours of overtime worked.

Solution   See page S4.

1.6 EXERCISES

Topics for Discussion

For Exercises 1 to 12, determine whether the statement is always true, sometimes true, or never true. If the statement is sometimes true or never true, explain your answer.

1. The Multiplication Property of One states that multiplying a number by 1 does not change the number.

2. The sum of a number and its additive inverse is zero.

3. The product of a number and its multiplicative inverse is 1.

4. The terms x and x^2 are like terms because both have a coefficient of 1.

5. Like terms are terms with the same variables.

6. To add like terms, add the coefficients; the variable part remains unchanged.

7. The expression $3x^2$ is a variable expression.

8. In the expression $8y^2 - 4y$, the terms are $8y^3$ and $4y$.

9. For the expression x^3, the value of x is 1.

10. For the expression $6a + 7b$, 7 is a constant term.

11. If the sum of two numbers is 15 and one of the two numbers is x, then the other number can be expressed as $x - 15$.

12. The expressions $7y - 8$ and $(7y) - 8$ are equivalent.

13. Explain the difference between the Commutative and Associative Properties of Addition.

14. Explain the difference between the Commutative and Associative Properties of Multiplication.

▪ Properties of Real Numbers

Use the given property to complete the statement.

15. The Commutative Property of Multiplication
$2 \cdot 5 = 5 \cdot ?$

16. The Addition Property of Zero
$? + x = x$

17. The Commutative Property of Addition
$9 + 17 = ? + 9$

18. The Distributive Property
$2(4 + 3) = 8 + ?$

19. The Associative Property of Multiplication

$4(5x) = (? \cdot 5)x$

20. The Multiplication Property of One

$? \cdot 1 = -4$

21. The Associative Property of Addition

$(4 + 5) + 6 = ? + (5 + 6)$

22. The Inverse Property of Addition

$8 + ? = 0$

23. The Multiplication Property of Zero

$y \cdot ? = 0$

24. The Inverse Property of Multiplication

$\left(-\frac{1}{5}\right)(-5) = ?$

Identify the Property of Real Numbers that justifies the statement.

25. $1 \cdot a = a$

26. $3(4x) = (3 \cdot 4)x$

27. $0 + c = c$

28. $z + (-z) = 0$

29. $\left(-\frac{2}{3}\right)\left(-\frac{3}{2}\right) = 1$

30. $3(4 + 7) = 12 + 21$

31. $2 + (4 + w) = (2 + 4) + w$

32. $(-3 + 9)8 = -24 + 72$

33. $(3x)(4) = 4(3x)$

34. $(x + y) + z = z + (x + y)$

■ Simplify Variable Expressions

Name the terms of the variable expression. Then underline the constant term.

35. $2x^2 + 5x - 8$

36. $-3a^2 - 4a + 7$

37. $6 - n^4$

Name the variable terms of the expression. Then underline the variable part of each term.

38. $9b^2 - 4ab + a^2$

39. $7x^2y + 6xy^2 + 10$

40. $5 - 8n - 3n^2$

Name the coefficients of the variable terms.

41. $x^2 - 9x + 2$

42. $12a^2 - 8ab - b^2$

43. $n^3 - 4n^2 - n + 9$

Simplify each of the following. If the expression is already in simplest form, write "simplest form" as the answer.

44. $6x + 8x$

45. $12y + 9y$

46. $8b - 5b$

47. $4y - 10y$

48. $2a + 7$

49. $x + y$

50. $-12a + 17a$

51. $-12xy + 17xy$

52. $3x + 5x + 3x$

53. $-5x^2 - 12x^2 + 3x^2$

54. $7x - 3y + 10x$

55. $3x - 8y - 10x + 4x$

56. $5a + 6a - 2a$

57. $-5x + 7x - 4x$

58. $2a - 5a + 3a$

59. $12y^2 + 10y^2$

60. $3x^2 - 15x^2$

61. $9z^2 - 9z^2$

62. $\dfrac{3}{4}x - \dfrac{1}{4}x$

63. $\dfrac{2}{5}y - \dfrac{3}{4}y$

64. $3x - 7 + 4x$

65. $4(3x)$

66. $-2(-3y)$

67. $(3a)(-2)$

68. $-5(3x^2)$

69. $\dfrac{1}{8}(8x)$

70. $\dfrac{12x}{5}\left(\dfrac{5}{12}\right)$

71. $\dfrac{1}{7}(14x)$

72. $-\dfrac{5}{8}(24a^2)$

73. $(33y)\left(\dfrac{1}{11}\right)$

74. $-(z + 2)$

75. $-2(a + 7)$

76. $(5 - 3b)7$

77. $3(5x^2 + 2x)$

78. $(-3x - 6)5$

79. $-3(2y^2 - 7)$

80. $4(x^2 - 3x + 5)$

81. $4(-3a^2 - 5a + 7)$

82. $5(2x^2 - 4xy - y^2)$

83. $6a - (5a + 7)$

84. $8 - (12 + 4y)$

85. $6(2y - 7) - 3(3 - 2y)$

86. $2[x + 2(x + 7)]$

87. $-2[3x - (5x - 2)]$

88. $4a - 2[2b - (b - 2a)] + 3b$

■ Translate Phrases into Variable Expressions

Translate each phrase into a variable expression.

89. four divided by the difference between p and six

90. the product of seven and the total of r and eight

91. three-eighths of the sum of t and fifteen

92. the total of nine times the cube of m and the square of m

93. thirteen less a number

94. forty more than a number

95. three-sevenths of a number

96. the quotient of twice a number and five

97. eight subtracted from the product of five and a number

98. the sum of four-ninths of a number and twenty

99. fourteen added to the product of seven and a number

100. the product of a number and ten more than the number

101. six less than the total of a number and the cube of the number

102. the quotient of twelve and the sum of a number and two

103. eleven plus one-half of a number

104. a number multiplied by the difference between the number and nine

105. eighty decreased by the product of thirteen and a number

106. the difference between sixty and the quotient of a number and fifty

107. four less than seven times the square of a number

108. the sum of the square of a number and three times the number

Translate into a variable expression. Then simplify the expression.

109. a number increased by the total of the number and ten

110. a number added to the product of five and the number

111. a number decreased by the difference between nine and the number

112. eight more than the sum of a number and eleven

113. the difference between one-fifth of a number and three-eighths of a number

114. the sum of one-eighth of a number and one-twelfth of the number

115. four more than the total of a number and nine

116. a number minus the sum of the number and fourteen

117. twice the sum of three times a number and forty

118. seven times the product of five and a number

119. sixteen multiplied by one-fourth of a number

120. the total of seventeen times a number and twice the number

121. the difference between nine times a number and twice the number

122. a number plus the product of the number and twelve

123. nineteen more than the difference between a number and five

124. seven minus the sum of the number and two

125. *Aviation*   The cruising speed of a jet plane is twice the cruising speed of a propeller-driven plane. Express the cruising speed of the jet plane in terms of the cruising speed of the propeller-driven plane.

126. *Sports*   In football, the number of points awarded for a touchdown is three times the number of points awarded for a safety. Express the number of points awarded for a touchdown in terms of the number of points awarded for a safety.

127. *Food Mixtures*   A mixture contains four times as many peanuts as cashews. Express the amount of peanuts in the mixture in terms of the amount of cashews.

128. *Coin Problem*   In a coin bank, there are ten more dimes than quarters. Express the number of dimes in the coin bank in terms of the number of quarters.

129. *Stamp Problem*   A 5¢ stamp in a stamp collection is 25 years older than an 8¢ stamp in the collection. Express the age of the 5¢ stamp in terms of the age of the 8¢ stamp.

130. *Geometry*   The length of a rectangle is five meters more than twice the width. Express the length of the rectangle in terms of the width.

131. *Geometry*   In a triangle, the measure of the smallest angle is three degrees less than one-half the measure of the largest angle. Express the measure of the smallest angle in terms of the measure of the largest angle.

132. *Mathematics*   The sum of two numbers is twenty-three. Use one variable to represent the two numbers.

133. *Coin Problem*   A coin purse contains thirty-five coins in nickels and dimes. Use one variable to express the number of nickels and the number of dimes in the coin purse.

134. *Natural Resources*   Twenty gallons of oil was poured into two containers of different sizes. Use one variable to express the amount of oil poured into each container.

135. *Wages*   An employee is paid $640 per week plus $24 for each hour of overtime worked. Express the employee's weekly pay in terms of the number of hours of overtime worked.

136. *Repair Bills*   An auto repair bill is $92 for parts and $45 for each hour of labor. Express the amount of the repair bill in terms of the number of hours of labor.

Applying Concepts

Simplify.

137. $C - 0.7C$ **138.** $\dfrac{1}{3}(3x + y) - \dfrac{2}{3}(6x - y)$ **139.** $-\dfrac{1}{4}[2x + 2(y - 6y)]$

For each of the following, write a phrase that would translate into the given expression.

140. $2x + 3$

141. $5y - 4$

142. $2(x + 3)$

143. $5(y - 4)$

144. *Travel*   Two cars start at the same point and travel in opposite directions and at different rates. Two hours later the cars are two hundred miles apart. Express the distance traveled by the slower car in terms of the distance traveled by the faster car.

145. *Coin Problem*   A coin bank contains nickels and dimes. Using n for the number of nickels in the bank and d for the number of dimes in the bank, write an expression for the value, in pennies, of the coins in the bank.

146. *Chemistry*   Each molecule of octyl acetate, which gives air fresheners an orange scent, contains 10 carbon atoms, 20 hydrogen atoms, and 2 oxygen atoms. If x represents the number of atoms of oxygen in one gram of octyl acetate, express the number of carbon atoms in one gram of octyl acetate in terms of x.

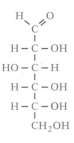

147. *Chemistry*   Each molecule of glucose (sugar) contains 6 carbon atoms, 12 hydrogen atoms, and 6 oxygen atoms. If x represents the number of atoms of oxygen in a pound of sugar, express the number of hydrogen atoms in the pound of sugar in terms of x.

148. *Metalwork*   A wire whose length is given as x inches is bent into a square. Express the length of a side of the square in terms of x.

EXPLORATION

1.   *Investigation into Even and Odd Integers*   Complete each statement with the word *even* or *odd*.

   a.   If k is an odd integer, then $k + 1$ is an _____ integer.
   b.   If k is an odd integer, then $k - 2$ is an _____ integer.
   c.   If n is an integer, then $2n$ is an _____ integer.
   d.   If m and n are even integers, then $m - n$ is an _____ integer.
   e.   If m and n are even integers, then mn is an _____ integer.
   f.   If m and n are odd integers, then $m + n$ is an _____ integer.
   g.   If m and n are odd integers, then $m - n$ is an _____ integer.
   h.   If m and n are odd integers, then mn is an _____ integer.
   i.   If m is an even integer and n is an odd integer, then $m - n$ is an _____ integer.
   j.   If m is an even integer and n is an odd integer, then $m + n$ is an _____ integer.

2.   *Investigation into Properties*   Determine whether the statement is true or false. If the statement is false, give an example that illustrates that it is false.

   a.   Division is a commutative operation.

   b.   Division is an associative operation.

   c.   Subtraction is an associative operation.

   d.   Subtraction is a commutative operation.

   e.   Addition is a commutative operation.

CHAPTER **1** *SUMMARY*

Key Terms

absolute value [p. 30]
addends [p. 31]
addition [p. 31]
additive inverse [p. 30]
base [p. 38]
change in X [p. 65]
closed interval [p. 24]
coefficient [p. 63]
combine like terms [p. 77]
composite number [p. 19]
constant terms [p. 77]
deductive reasoning [p. 8]
difference [p. 34]
elements of a set [p. 18]
empty set [p. 20]
evaluate an expression [p. 31]
evaluate a variable expression
  [p. 64]
expanded form [p. 38]
exponent [p. 38]
exponential form [p. 38]
finite set [p. 19]
formula [p. 67]
graph of a real number [p. 20]
half-open interval [p. 24]
increment in X [p. 65]
inductive reasoning [p. 6]
infinite set [p. 18]
infinity symbol [p. 24]
input/output table [p. 64]
integers [p. 19]
intersection of two sets [p. 23]
interval notation [p. 24]
irrational numbers [p. 20]
least common multiple [p. 51]
like terms [p. 77]
multiplicative inverse [p. 76]

natural numbers [p. 18]
negative infinity symbol [p. 24]
negative integers [p. 19]
null set [p. 20]
open interval [p. 24]
opposites [p. 30]
positive integers [p. 19]
power [p. 38]
prime number [p. 19]
product [p. 36]
quotient [p. 37]
rational numbers [p. 19]
real number line [p. 20]
real numbers [p. 20]
reciprocal [pp. 53 and 76]
repeating decimal [p. 20]
roster method [p. 18]
sequence [p. 6]
set [p. 18]
set-builder notation [p. 20]
simplify a variable expression
  [p. 77]
subtraction [p. 33]
sum [p. 31]
terminating decimal [p. 20]
term of a sequence [p. 6]
terms of a variable expression
  [p. 77]
union of two sets [p. 22]
value of the variable [p. 64]
value of the variable expression
  [p. 64]
variable [p. 63]
variable expression [p. 63]
variable terms [p. 77]
whole numbers [p. 19]

Essential Concepts

The four-step process in problem solving:
  1. Understand the problem and state the goal.
  2. Devise a strategy to solve the problem.
  3. Solve the problem.
  4. Review the solution and check your work. [p. 3]

To add two numbers with the same sign, add the absolute values of the numbers. Then attach the sign of the addends. [p. 32]

To add two numbers with different signs, find the absolute value of each number. Then subtract the lesser of these absolute values from the greater one. Attach the sign of the number with the greater absolute value. [p. 32]

To subtract two numbers, add the opposite of the second number to the first number. [p. 34]

To multiply two numbers with the same sign, multiply the absolute values of the numbers. The product is positive. [p. 35]

To multiply two numbers with different signs, multiply the absolute values of the numbers. The product is negative. [p. 35]

To divide two numbers with the same sign, divide the absolute values of the numbers. The quotient is positive. [p. 36]

To divide two numbers with different signs, divide the absolute values of the numbers. The quotient is negative. [p. 36]

The Order of Operations Agreement

Step 1   Perform operations inside grouping symbols.
Step 2   Evaluate exponential expressions.
Step 3   Do multiplication and division as they occur from left to right.
Step 4   Do addition and subtraction as they occur from left to right. [p. 40]

Properties of Real Numbers
If a, b, and c are real numbers, then the following properties hold true. [pp. 75 and 76]

Commutative Property of Addition	$a + b = b + a$
Associative Property of Addition	$(a + b) + c = a + (b + c)$
Inverse Property of Addition	$a + (-a) = (-a) + a = 0$
Addition Property of Zero	$a + 0 = 0 + a = a$
Commutative Property of Multiplication	$ab = ba$
Associative Property of Multiplication	$(ab)c = a(bc)$
Inverse Property of Multiplication	$a \cdot \dfrac{1}{a} = \dfrac{1}{a} \cdot a = 1, a \neq 0$
Multiplication Property of One	$a \cdot 1 = 1 \cdot a = a$
Distributive Property	$a(b + c) = ab + ac$

CHAPTER **1** *REVIEW EXERCISES*

1. I have one brother and two sisters. My mother's parents have 10 grandchildren, while my father's parents have 11 grandchildren. If no divorces or remarriages occurred, how many first cousins do I have?

2. Use inductive reasoning to predict the next term in the sequence 1, 2, 4, 7, 11, 16, . . .

3. Given that ♠♠♠♠ = ♦♦, and ♦♦♦♦ = ♣♣, and ♣♣♣ = ♥♥♥♥♥♥, how many ♠'s equal ♥♥?

4. Use the roster method to write the set of integers between -9 and -2.

5. Use set-builder notation to write the set of real numbers less than or equal to -10.

6. Find $C \cap D$ given $C = \{0, 1, 2, 3\}$ and $D = \{2, 3, 4, 5\}$.

7. Write $[-2, 3]$ in set-builder notation.

8. Write $\{x \mid x < -44\}$ in interval notation.

9. Graph: $(-2, 4]$

10. Graph: $\{x \mid x \le 3\} \cup \{x \mid x < -2\}$

11. Graph: $\{x \mid x < 3\} \cap \{x \mid x > -2\}$

12. Multiply: $\left(-\dfrac{1}{3}\right) \cdot \dfrac{3}{7}$

13. Divide and round to the nearest tenth: $-6.8 \div 47.92$

14. Find the sum of -247.8 and -193.4.

15. Subtract: $\dfrac{7}{8} - \left(-\dfrac{5}{6}\right)$

16. Divide: $\dfrac{5}{9} \div \left(-\dfrac{2}{3}\right)$

17. Simplify: $3 - (8 - 10) \div 2$

18. Simplify: $4 + 2|3 - 6|$

19. Find the temperature after an increase of $5°C$ from $-8°C$.

20. The boiling point of mercury is $356.58°C$. The melting point of mercury is $-38.87°C$. Find the difference between the boiling point and the melting point of mercury.

21. The formula for the perimeter of a rectangle is $P = 2L + 2W$, where P is the perimeter, L is the length, and W is the width. Find the perimeter of the rectangle with a length of 12.5 centimeters and a width of 6.25 centimeters.

22. The pressure P, in pounds per square inch, at a certain depth in the ocean can be approximated by the equation $P = 15 + 0.5D$, where D is the depth in feet.

   a. Create an input/output table for this equation for increments of 2 feet, beginning with $D = 2$.

   b. Write a sentence that describes the meaning of the numbers 6 and 18.

23. Evaluate $a - b(c + d)$ for $a = 6$, $b = 2$, $c = 1$, and $d = -7$.

24. Evaluate $ab^2 - c$ when $a = 4$, $b = -\dfrac{1}{2}$, and $c = \dfrac{5}{7}$.

25. Identify the property that justifies the statement: $-4(3) = 3(-4)$

26. Simplify: $(-6d)(-4)$

27. Simplify: $7a^2 + 10a - 4a^2$

28. Simplify: $4(6a - 3) - (5a + 1)$

29. Translate and simplify: "eight times the quotient of twice a number and 16."

30. The distance from Neptune to the Sun is thirty times the distance from Earth to the sun. Express the distance from Neptune to the sun in terms of the distance from Earth to the sun.

CHAPTER **1** TEST

1. Find the greatest prime number between 210 and 220.

2. Use the roster method to write the set of integers between -7 and 1.

3. Use set-builder notation to write the set of real numbers greater than or equal to -2.

4. Find $A \cap B$ given $A = \{-2, -1, 0, 1, 2, 3\}$ and $B = \{-1, 0, 1\}$.

5. Write $[-4, 6]$ in set-builder notation.

6. Write $\{x \mid x \geq -20\}$ in interval notation.

7. Graph: $(-\infty, -1]$

8. Graph: $\{x \mid x \leq -3\} \cup \{x \mid x > 0\}$

9. Simplify: $12 - 4(3 - 5)^2 \div (-1)$

10. Multiply: $-\frac{3}{8}\left(-\frac{4}{15}\right)$

11. Find the sum of $\frac{3}{4}$ and $-\frac{2}{3}$.

12. Find the difference between -3.597 and -4.826.

13. Evaluate $x \div y$ for $x = \frac{1}{8}$ and $y = -\frac{5}{12}$.

14. Evaluate $m + n(p - q)^2$ for $m = -3$, $n = 4$, $p = 2$, and $q = -1$.

15. A business analyst has determined that the cost per unit for a stereo amplifier is $127 and that the fixed costs per month are $20,000. Find the total cost during a month in which 147 amplifiers were produced. Use the formula $T = UN + F$, where T is the total cost, U is the cost per unit, N is the number of units produced, and F is the fixed cost.

16. The distance d, in feet, of a platform diver above the water t seconds after the dive begins is given by the equation $d = 50 - 16t^2$. Create an input/output table for this equation for increments of 0.25, beginning with $t = 0$.
    a. How many feet above the water is the diver 0.25 second after the dive begins?
    b. After how many seconds is the diver 25 feet above the water?

17. Simplify: $-3y^2 + 9y - 5y^2$

18. Simplify: $3(4w - 1) - 7(w + 2)$

19. Translate and simplify: "two more than a number added to the difference between the number and three."

20. One car was driven 15 mph faster than a second car. Express the speed of the first car in terms of the speed of the second car.

2

Introduction to Functions and Relations

```
TABLE SETUP
  TblStart = 40
  ∆Tbl = 5
Indpnt:    Auto    Ask
Depend:    Auto    Ask
```

Press **2nd** TBLSET to access the **TABLE SETUP** options.

Officers investigating the scene of a traffic accident have a number of factors to analyze. For example, the skid marks, along with the type of street surface and the weather at the time of the accident, can give clues as to what happened. A quadratic function with variables representing the speed of the car and the length of the skid marks appears in **Exercise 30 on page 113**. Note that the length of the skid marks can potentially reveal whether or not the driver of the car was speeding.

Need help? For online student resources, visit this web site:
Math.college.hmco.com

PREP TEST

1. Simplify: $-\dfrac{6}{3} + 4$

2. Evaluate $-2x + 5$ for $x = -3$.

3. Evaluate $\dfrac{2r}{r-1}$ for $r = 5$.

4. Evaluate $2p^3 - 3p + 4$ for $p = -1$.

5. For what value of x is the expression $\dfrac{2x-5}{x}$ undefined?

6. Given $y = 6x - 5$, find the value of y when $x = -\dfrac{1}{3}$.

GO FIGURE

In a contest to guess how many jelly beans were in a jar, Hector guessed 223, Shannon guessed 215, Suki guessed 220, Deon guessed 221, Saul guessed 217, and Denise guessed 219. Two were off by 4, two were off by 2, one was off by 1, and one was correct. What was the correct number?

SECTION **2.1**

- Introduction to Rectangular Coordinate Systems
- Input-Output Tables
- Graphs of Equations

Rectangular Coordinates and Graphs

■ Introduction to Rectangular Coordinate Systems

A cartographer (a person who makes maps) divides a city into little squares as shown on the map of Washington, DC below. Telling a visitor that the White House is located in square A3 enables the visitor to locate the White House within a small area of the map.

(1) Department of State
(2) FBI Building
(3) Lincoln Memorial
(4) National Air and Space Museum
(5) National Gallery of Art
(6) Vietnam Veterans Memorial
(7) Washington Monument
(8) White House

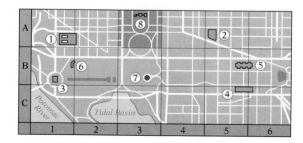

▼ *Point of Interest*

The concept of a coordinate system developed over time, culminating in 1637 with the publication of Discourse on the Method for Rightly Directing One's Reason and Searching for Truth in the Sciences *by René Descartes (1596–1650) and* Introduction to Plane and Solid Loci *by Pierre de Fermat (1601–1665). Of the two mathematicians, Descartes is usually given more credit. In fact, he became so famous in Le Haye, the town in which he was born, that the town was renamed Le Haye-Descartes.*

In mathematics we have a similar problem, that of locating a point in a plane. One way to solve the problem is to use a *rectangular coordinate system*.

A **rectangular coordinate system** is formed by two number lines, one horizontal and one vertical, that intersect at the zero point of each line. The point of intersection is called the **origin.** The two number lines are called the **coordinate axes** or simply the **axes.** Frequently, the horizontal axis is labeled the x-axis, and the vertical axis is labeled the y-axis. In this case, the axes form what is called the xy-**plane**.

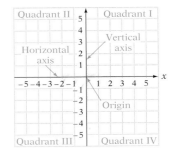

The two axes divide the plane into four regions called **quadrants** that are numbered counterclockwise, using Roman numerals I to IV, starting at the upper right.

Each point in the plane can be identified by a pair of numbers called an **ordered pair.** The first number of the ordered pair measures a horizontal change from the y-axis and is called the **abscissa,** or x**-coordinate**. The second number of the pair measures a vertical change from the x-axis and is called the **ordinate,** or y**-coordinate.** The ordered pair (x, y) associated with a point is also called the **coordinates** of the point.

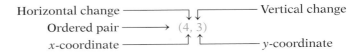

To **graph,** or **plot,** a point means to place a dot at the coordinates of the point. For example, to graph the ordered pair $(4, 3)$, start at the origin. Move 4 units to the right and then 3 units up. Draw a dot. To graph $(-3, -4)$, start at the origin. Move 3 units left and then 4 units down. Draw a dot.

The **graph of an ordered pair** is the dot drawn at the coordinates of the point in the plane. The graphs of the ordered pairs $(4, 3)$ and $(-3, -4)$ are shown at the right.

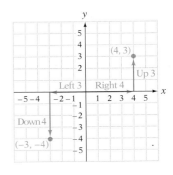

The graphs of the points whose coordinates are $(2, 3)$ and $(3, 2)$ are shown at the right. Note that they are different points. **The order in which the numbers in an ordered pair appear is important.**

If the axes are labeled other than as x and y, then we refer to the ordered pair by the given labels. For instance, if the horizontal axis is labeled t and the vertical axis is labeled d, then the ordered pairs

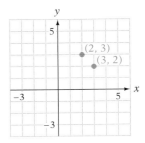

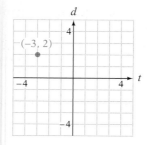

are written as (t, d). In any case, we sometimes just refer to the first number in an ordered pair as the **first coordinate** of the ordered pair and to the second number as the **second coordinate** of the ordered pair.

EXAMPLE 1

Give the coordinates of the four points in the figure at the right.

Solution A: $(-4, 2)$, B: $(4, 3)$, C: $(0, -1)$, D: $(2, 0)$, E: $(-1, -3)$.

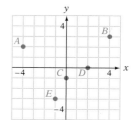

YOU TRY IT 1

Plot the points $A(-2, 4)$, $B(4, 0)$, $C(0, 3)$, and $D(-3, -4)$.

Solution See page S5.

■ Input/Output Tables

One purpose of a coordinate system is to draw a picture of the solutions of an **equation in two variables.** Examples of equations in two variables are shown at the right.

$$y = 3x - 2$$
$$x^2 + y^2 = 25$$
$$s = t^2 - 4t + 1$$

A **solution of an equation in two variables** is an ordered pair that makes the equation a true statement. For instance, as shown below, $(2, 4)$ is a solution of $y = 3x - 2$ but $(3, -1)$ is not a solution of the equation.

> **TAKE NOTE**
>
> An ordered-pair solution of the equation $y = 3x - 2$ is of the form (x, y). The first number in an ordered pair is the x value; the second number is the y value.

$y = 3x - 2$	
4	$3(2) - 2$
4	$6 - 2$
$4 = 4$	

• $x = 2, y = 4$

• Checks.

$y = 3x - 2$	
-1	$3(3) - 2$
-1	$9 - 2$
$-1 \neq 7$	

• $x = 3, y = -1$

• Does not check.

There are many solutions of the equation $y = 3x - 2$. By choosing any value of x, we can calculate the corresponding value of y. The resulting ordered pair is a solution of the equation. For instance, we can choose $x = \frac{2}{3}$. Then, as shown at the right, $y = 0$. Thus $\left(\frac{2}{3}, 0\right)$ is also a solution of $y = 3x - 2$.

$$y = 3x - 2$$
$$y = 3\left(\frac{2}{3}\right) - 2$$
$$= 2 - 2$$
$$= 0$$

? QUESTION   What is the solution of $y = 2x + 5$ corresponding to $x = 4$?

An **input/output table** shows some of the ordered-pair solutions of an equation in two variables. The values of x are the *inputs*; the values of y are the *outputs*.

Here is an input/output table for the equation $y = 3x - 2$. The graph of the ordered pairs is shown on the coordinate grid next to the table.

x	$3x - 2 = y$	(x, y)
-2	$3(-2) - 2 = -8$	$(-2, -8)$
-1	$3(-1) - 2 = -5$	$(-1, -5)$
0	$3(0) - 2 = -2$	$(0, -2)$
1	$3(1) - 2 = 1$	$(1, 1)$
2	$3(2) - 2 = 4$	$(2, 4)$
3	$3(3) - 2 = 7$	$(3, 7)$

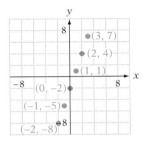

You may choose any values of x you wish. Generally, we do not choose fractional values for x because they are more difficult to graph.

The numbers do not have to be in sequence. For the input/output table above, we showed all the calculations for the ordered pairs. Normally an input/output table would show only the results, as illustrated below. The table can be displayed vertically or horizontally.

x	y
-2	-8
-1	-5
0	-2
1	1
2	4
3	7

x	-2	-1	0	1	2	3
y	-8	-5	-2	1	4	7

Note that in finding ordered-pair solutions of an equation, we determine a value of y after choosing a value of x. The value of y (the output) *depends* on the value of x (the input). Therefore, we say that y is the **dependent variable** and x is the **independent variable.**

? ANSWER   Replace x in $y = 2x + 5$ by 4 and then simplify: $y = 2(4) + 5 = 8 + 5 = 13$. The solution is $(4, 13)$.

EXAMPLE 2

Create an input/output table for $y = x^2 - 1$ for $x = -2, -1, 0, 1, 2$, and 3. Graph the resulting ordered pairs.

Solution   Evaluate the expression $x^2 - 1$ for $x = -2, -1, 0, 1, 2$, and 3.

x	$x^2 - 1 = y$	(x, y)
-2	$(-2)^2 - 1 = 3$	$(-2, 3)$
-1	$(-1)^2 - 1 = 0$	$(-1, 0)$
0	$(0)^2 - 1 = -1$	$(0, -1)$
1	$(1)^2 - 1 = 0$	$(1, 0)$
2	$(2)^2 - 1 = 3$	$(2, 3)$
3	$(3)^2 - 1 = 8$	$(3, 8)$

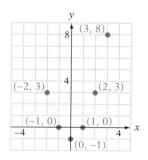

YOU TRY IT 2

Create an input/output table for $y = x^2 + 2x$ for $x = -4, -3, -2, -1, 0, 1$, and 2. Graph the resulting ordered pairs.

Solution   See page S5.

See Appendix A:
Y= and Table

A graphing calculator can be used to create input/output tables. The **Y=** key is used to enter the variable expression, and the table capabilities are used to display the table. Some typical screens for the input/output table from Example 2 follow. By using the up arrow and down arrow keys, you can view additional inputs and outputs.

CALCULATOR NOTE
For the Table Setup screen shown at the right, ΔTbl = 1. This means the change between successive values of x is 1. In mathematics, the symbol Δ is frequently used to mean "change in."

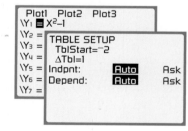

It is important to remember that **an input/output table gives ordered pairs that are solutions of an equation in two variables.** Because we entered $Y_1 = X^2 - 1$, the table at the right above shows the ordered-pair solutions of $y = x^2 - 1$. For instance, from the table, $(4, 15)$ is a solution of $y = x^2 - 1$.

❓ QUESTION   From the table above, what is the solution of $y = x^2 - 1$ corresponding to $x = 3$?

❓ ANSWER   The output value when $x = 3$ is 8. The solution is $(3, 8)$.

EXAMPLE 3

Without using a calculator, create an input/output table for $y = \frac{2}{3}x + 1$ for $x = -6, -3, 0, 3,$ and 6. Then check your table by using a graphing calculator. Graph the resulting ordered pairs.

Solution

ALGEBRAIC SOLUTION

GRAPHICAL CHECK

The input/output table is created by evaluating $\frac{2}{3}x + 1$ for the given values of x.

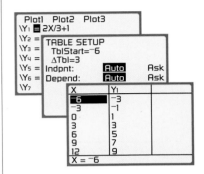

x	$\frac{2}{3}x + 1 = y$	(x, y)
-6	$\frac{2}{3}(-6) + 1 = -3$	$(-6, -3)$
-3	$\frac{2}{3}(-3) + 1 = -1$	$(-3, -1)$
0	$\frac{2}{3}(0) + 1 = 1$	$(0, 1)$
3	$\frac{2}{3}(3) + 1 = 3$	$(3, 3)$
6	$\frac{2}{3}(6) + 1 = 5$	$(6, 5)$

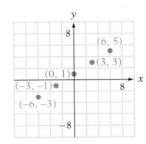

The calculator screens verify that our calculations are correct. Note that ΔTbl $= 3$ because the difference between successive input values is 3.

In this example, we chose input values that are multiples of 3 so that after we multiplied by $\frac{2}{3}$, the result would be an integer. This made graphing the points easier. However, we could have chosen any numbers for x.

YOU TRY IT 3

Without using a calculator, create an input/output table for $y = -\frac{x}{2} - 2$ for $x = -6, -4, -2, 0, 2,$ and 4. Check your results using a graphing calculator. Graph the resulting ordered pairs.

Solution See page S5.

Input/output tables are also used in application problems.

EXAMPLE 4

The height h, in feet, t seconds after a certain rocket used in fireworks celebrations is launched is given by $h = -16t^2 + 350t$.

a. Complete the input/output table below.

Input, time t (in seconds)	0	2	4	6	8	10
Output, height h (in feet)						

b. Write a sentence that explains the meaning of the ordered pair (6, 1524).

Solution

a. Evaluate the expression $-16t^2 + 350t$ for the given values of t.

Input, time t (in seconds)	0	2	4	6	8	10
Output, height h (in feet)	0	636	1144	1524	1776	1900

b. The ordered pair (6, 1524) means that 6 seconds after the rocket is launched it is 1524 feet above the ground.

CALCULATOR NOTE

This table can be created using a graphing calculator. Use the Y= editor to input Y₁ as $-16X^2 + 350X$.
TblStart = 0, ΔTbl = 2
Note, in this case, that although the independent variable is time, t, the variable X is used with a graphing calculator.

YOU TRY IT 4

The temperature T, in degrees Fahrenheit, h hours after 4:00 P.M. one summer day was given by $T = \frac{960}{h + 12}$.

a. Complete the input/output table below. Round to the nearest tenth.

Input, time h (in hours)	0	0.5	1	1.5	2	2.5	3
Output, temperature T (in degrees Fahrenheit)							

b. Write a sentence that explains the meaning of the ordered pair (2, 68.6).

Solution   See page S5.

▪ Graphs of Equations

The input/output table below was produced for the equation $y = 2x - 1$ using an increment of ΔTbl = 0.5. Scrolling through the table and graphing the ordered pairs produces the graph of the ordered pairs in the input/output table.

X	Y₁	
-2	-5	
-1.5	-4	
-1	-3	
-.5	-2	
0	-1	
.5	0	
1	1	
X = -2		

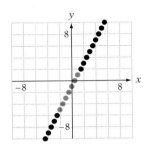

The points shown in red are from this table. The coordinates of the remaining points were found by scrolling through the table and then graphing the points displayed.

One observation we can make from the graph is that the points appear to lie on a straight line. If we change the increment to ΔTbl = 0.25, there will be even more points to graph.

X	Y₁	
-1	-3	
-.75	-2.5	
-.5	-2	
-.25	-1.5	
0	-1	
.25	-.5	
.5	0	
X = -1		

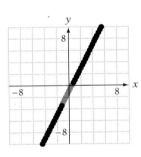

The points shown in red are from the table above. Plotting additional points seems to confirm our earlier observation that the graph is a straight line.

Note that as we use smaller and smaller increments, the graph of the ordered pairs of the input/output table begins to look more and more like a straight line. If we graph *all* of the ordered-pair solutions of $y = 2x - 1$, the resulting graph is a straight line. This line is called the **graph of the equation** and is shown at the right. Because the graph is a straight line, $y = 2x - 1$ is called a **linear equation in two variables.**

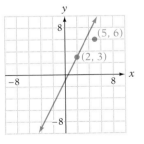

As shown below, $(2, 3)$ is a solution of $y = 2x - 1$, and note that the point $(2, 3)$ is on the graph of the equation. The ordered pair $(5, 6)$ is not a solution of the equation and is not a point on the graph.

$y = 2x - 1$	
3	$2(2) - 1$
3	$4 - 1$
$3 = 3$	

• $x = 2, y = 3$

• Checks.

$y = 2x - 1$	
6	$2(5) - 1$
6	$10 - 1$
$6 \neq 9$	

• $x = 5, y = 6$

• Does not check.

It is important to remember that **any ordered pair on a graph is a solution of the equation of the graph, and any ordered-pair solution of the equation is a point on the graph.**

A graphing calculator can be used to draw the graph of an equation by entering an expression in the Y= editor window. The portion of the rectangular coordinate grid that is shown on the calculator's screen is called the **viewing window** or just the **window.** All graphing calculators have some built-in viewing windows. One of these windows is called the **standard viewing window.** For the standard viewing window, the coordinate grid is shown for x-coordinates that are between -10 and 10 and y-coordinates that are between -10 and 10. The graph of $y = 2x - 1$ is shown below in the standard viewing window.

See Appendix A:
Graph

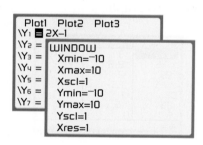

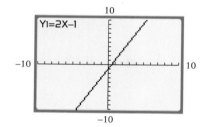

EXAMPLE 5

Let $y = -\dfrac{3}{4}x + 2$.

a. Complete the input/output table below.

x	-8	-4	0	4	8
y					

b. Graph the equation.
c. Use a graphing calculator to verify the input/output table and the graph.

Solution

a. Evaluate $-\dfrac{3}{4}x + 2$ for the given values of x.

x	-8	-4	0	4	8
y	8	5	2	-1	-4

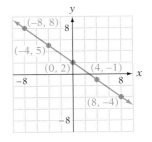

b. To graph the equation, graph the ordered pairs of the input/output table and draw a straight line through the points. The graph is shown at the right.

c. Some typical graphing calculator screens are shown below. Note that ΔTbl = 4 because the values of x (the input) in the table differ by 4. We are using the standard viewing window.

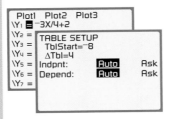
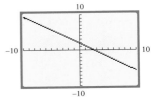

YOU TRY IT 5

Let $y = \dfrac{2}{3}x - 3$.

a. Complete the input/output table below.

x	-6	-3	0	3	6	9
y						

b. Graph the equation.
c. Use a calculator to verify the input/output table and the graph.

Solution   See page S5.

See Appendix A:
Window and Trace

The graph of an equation is a drawing of all the ordered pair solutions of the equation. Besides using the TABLE feature, the TRACE feature of a graphing calculator can be used to find some of those solutions. To use this feature, enter the equation to be graphed using the Y= editor and graph the equation.

The graph of $y = -\frac{x}{2} + 1$ is shown at the right in the decimal viewing window. When the **TRACE** key is pressed, a small cursor is placed on the graph. **The coordinates of the point under the cursor are shown at the bottom of the screen. These coordinates are a solution of the graphed equation.**

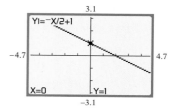

A solution is (0, 1).

Using the left and right arrow keys moves the cursor along the graph. As the arrow key is pressed, the coordinates of the point on which the cursor rests are shown at the bottom of the screen. Two examples follow.

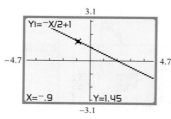

A solution is (−0.9, 1.45).

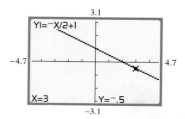

A solution is (3, −0.5).

The first shows that $(-0.9, 1.45)$ is a solution of the equation. The second shows $(3, -0.5)$ is a solution of the equation.

EXAMPLE 6

Let $y = 2x + 4$.

a. Graph the equation in the integer viewing window.
b. Trace along the graph to find the value of y when x is -6.
c. Trace along the graph to find the value of x when y is 16.

Solution

a. Enter $2x + 4$ for Y_1, select the integer viewing window, and press **ENTER**. Typical screens are shown below.

 See Appendix A:
Window and Trace

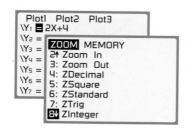

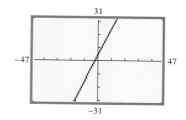

b. To find the value of y when x is -6, press (TRACE) and use the left and right arrow keys until the value of x at the bottom of the screen is -6. The corresponding value of y is -8.

A solution of the equation is $(-6, -8)$.

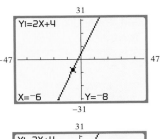

c. To find the value of x when y is 16, press (TRACE) and use the left and right arrow keys until the value of y at the bottom of the screen is 16. The corresponding value of x is 6.

A solution of the equation is $(6, 16)$.

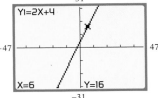

YOU TRY IT 6

Let $y = -\dfrac{2}{3}x + 4$.

a. Graph the equation in the integer viewing window.
b. Trace along the graph to find the value of y when x is 9.
c. Trace along the graph to find the value of x when y is 8.

Solution   See page S5.

The TRACE feature can also be used to jump to any point on the graph in the viewing window by inputting the x-coordinate of that point. After you press the (TRACE) key, you can just enter the x value. The **X =** automatically appears on the screen. This procedure will work for any viewing window that contains the value of x that you input. If you input a value of x that is not in the viewing window, you will get an error message.

EXAMPLE 7

Let $y = -\dfrac{3}{2}x - 3$.

a. Use a graphing calculator to find the ordered-pair solution of the equation when $x = -\dfrac{13}{4}$.
b. Check the results algebraically.

See Appendix A:
Trace

Solution

a. Graph $y = -\frac{3}{2}x - 3$ in any viewing window that contains an x value of $-\frac{13}{4}$. We will use the standard viewing window. Use the TRACE feature to find the ordered pair whose x-coordinate is $-\frac{13}{4}$. The screens below show the result of graphing the equation and using the TRACE feature to enter the value $-\frac{13}{4}$.

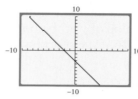 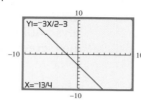 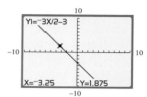

The ordered-pair solution is $(-3.25, 1.875)$.

Note that the calculator automatically converted the fraction $-\frac{13}{4}$ to a decimal. To write the ordered pair in fraction form, convert the decimals to fractions.

The ordered-pair solution in fraction form is $\left(-\frac{13}{4}, \frac{15}{8}\right)$.

b. To check the results algebraically, evaluate $-\frac{3}{2}x - 3$ when $x = -\frac{13}{4}$.

$$y = -\frac{3}{2}x - 3$$

$$y = -\frac{3}{2}\left(-\frac{13}{4}\right) - 3 \qquad \bullet \text{ Replace } x \text{ by } -\frac{13}{4}.$$

$$= \frac{39}{8} - 3 \qquad \bullet \text{ Multiply the fractions.}$$

$$= \frac{39}{8} - \frac{24}{8} \qquad \bullet \text{ Subtract the fractions. The common denominator is 8.}$$

$$= \frac{15}{8}$$

The result checks. The ordered-pair solution is $\left(-\frac{13}{4}, \frac{15}{8}\right)$.

See Appendix A:
Operations

YOU TRY IT 7

Let $y = \frac{1}{2}x + 2$.

a. Use a graphing calculator to find the ordered-pair solution of the equation when $x = -5$.

b. Check the results algebraically.

Solution   See page S5.

There is a similar problem of trying to find x for a given value of y. When tracing along the curve, the cursor may not stop at the particular value of y that you need. The solution to this problem is more complicated both with and without a calculator. We will discuss this in more detail later in the text.

2.1 EXERCISES

Topics for Discussion

1. Describe a rectangular coordinate system. Include in your description the concepts of axes, ordered pairs, and quadrants.

2. What is the graph of an ordered pair?

3. What is a solution of an equation in two variables?

4. What is an input/output table?

5. For the equation $s = 3t - 4$, what is the input variable? What is the output variable?

6. What is the graph of an equation?

■ Introduction to Rectangular Coordinate Systems

7. Graph the ordered pairs $A(2, -3)$, $B(0, 3)$, $C(-2, 0)$, and $D(-3, -4)$.

8. Graph the ordered pairs $A(-3, 4)$, $B(3, 0)$, $C(0, -3)$, and $D(3, -2)$.

9. Name the x-coordinates for points A and B. Name the y-coordinates for points C and D.

10. Name the x-coordinates for points A and B. Name the y-coordinates for points C and D.

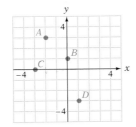

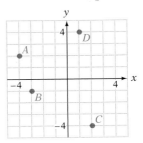

■ Input/Output Tables

11. Is $(3, -4)$ a solution of $y = 2x - 10$?

12. Is $(-2, 3)$ a solution of $y = -2x - 2$?

13. Is $(-2, 5)$ a solution of $y = \dfrac{3}{2}x + 7$?

14. Is $(4, -2)$ a solution of $y = -\dfrac{3}{4}x + 1$?

15. Without using a calculator, create an input/output table for $y = -2x + 1$ for $x = -3, -2, -1, 0, 1, 2,$ and 3. Check your results using a graphing calculator. Graph the resulting ordered pairs.

16. Without using a calculator, create an input/output table for $y = 2x - 3$ for $x = -3, -2, -1, 0, 1, 2,$ and 3. Check your results using a graphing calculator. Graph the resulting ordered pairs.

17. Without using a calculator, create an input/output table for $y = \frac{3}{4}x + 1$ for $x = -8, -4, 0, 4,$ and 8. Check your results using a graphing calculator. Graph the resulting ordered pairs.

18. Without using a calculator, create an input/output table for $y = -\frac{2}{3}x - 3$ for $x = -9, -6, -3, 0, 3,$ and 6. Check your results using a graphing calculator. Graph the resulting ordered pairs.

19. Without using a calculator, create an input/output table for $y = x^2 + 1$ for $x = -3, -2, -1, 0, 1, 2,$ and 3. Check your results using a graphing calculator. Graph the resulting ordered pairs.

20. Without using a calculator, create an input/output table for $y = -x^2 + 2$ for $x = -3, -2, -1, 0, 1, 2,$ and 3. Check your results using a graphing calculator. Graph the resulting ordered pairs.

21. Without using a calculator, create an input/output table for $y = x^2 + 4x - 3$ for $x = -5, -4, -3, -2, -1, 0,$ and 1. Check your results using a graphing calculator. Graph the resulting ordered pairs.

22. Without using a calculator, create an input/output table for $y = -x^2 + 2x + 3$ for $x = -2, -1, 0, 1, 2, 3,$ and 4. Check your results using a graphing calculator. Graph the resulting ordered pairs.

23. *Sports*   If a jogger is running at a rate of 11 feet per second, then the distance d traveled by the jogger in t seconds is given by $d = 11t$.

   a. Complete the input/output table below.

Input, time t (in seconds)	0	5	10	15	20	25	30
Output, distance d (in feet)							

   b. ✒ Write a sentence that explains the meaning of the ordered pair (20, 220).

24. *Geometry*   Sand, dumped from a conveyor belt, is forming a cone-shaped mound. The relationship between the height h, in feet, of the cone and the diameter of the base b, in feet, is given by $h = \frac{4}{3}b$.

   a. Complete the input/output table below.

Input, diameter of base b (in feet)	0	6	12	18	24	30
Output, height h (in feet)						

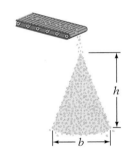

   b. ✒ Write a sentence that explains the meaning of the ordered pair (18, 24).

25. *Physics*   Assuming no air resistance, the distance d, in feet, that an object will fall in t seconds is given by $d = 16t^2$.

   a. Complete the input/output table below.

Input, time t (in seconds)	0	0.5	1	1.5	2	2.5	3
Output, distance d (in feet)							

   b. ✒ Write a sentence that explains the meaning of the ordered pair (1.5, 36).

26. *Food Mixtures*   Suppose a flavored drink contains 10% fruit juice. Then the quantity Q, in ounces, of fruit juice in a serving size of s ounces is given by $Q = 0.10s$.

 a. Complete the input/output table below.

Input, serving size s (in ounces)	0	2	4	6	8	10	12	14
Output, quantity of fruit juice Q (in ounces)								

 b. Write a sentence that explains the meaning of the ordered pair (12, 1.2).

27. *Metallurgy*   Gold jewelry that is made with 18-carat gold contains 75% gold. The quantity Q, in grams, of gold in a piece of jewelry weighing w grams is given by $Q = 0.75w$.

 a. Complete the input/output table below.

Input, weight of jewelry w (in grams)	0	5	10	15	20	25	30
Output, quantity of gold Q (in grams)							

 b. Write a sentence that explains the meaning of the ordered pair (15, 11.25).

28. *Fuel Consumption*   If a car averages 25 miles per gallon, then the number of miles m that a car can travel on g gallons of gasoline is given by $m = 25g$.

 a. Complete the input/output table below.

Input, quantity of gas g (in gallons)	0	3	6	9	12	15	18	21
Output, distance traveled m (in miles)								

 b. Write a sentence that explains the meaning of the ordered pair (9, 225).

29. *Sports*   The height h of a baseball thrown upward at an initial velocity of 70 feet per second is given by $h = -16t^2 + 70t + 5$, where t is the time in seconds since the baseball was released.

 a. Complete the input/output table below.

Input, time t (in seconds)	0	0.5	1	1.5	2	2.5	3
Output, height h (in feet)							

 b. Write a sentence that explains the meaning of the ordered pair (2.5, 80).

30. *Automotive Technology*   When the driver of a car is presented with a dangerous situation that requires braking, the distance the car will travel before stopping depends on the driver's reaction time and the speed of the car at the time the brakes are applied. The distance d, in feet, is given by $d = 0.05s^2 + 1.1s$, where s is the speed of the car in miles per hour.

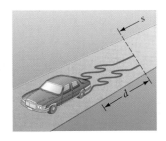

a.   Complete the input/output table below.

Input, speed s (in miles per hour)	40	45	50	55	60	65	70
Output, distance d (in feet)							

b.   Write a sentence that explains the meaning of the ordered pair (60, 246).

Graphs of Equations

For Exercises 31 to 38, complete the input/output table and graph the equation without using a calculator. Then use a calculator to verify the table and graph.

31. $y = 2x - 4$

x	−2	−1	0	1	2
y					

32. $y = -2x + 2$

x	−2	−1	0	1	2
y					

33. $y = \dfrac{x}{2} + 1$

x	−4	−2	0	2	4
y					

34. $y = \dfrac{2x}{3} - 2$

x	−3	0	3	6	9
y					

35. $y = \dfrac{-5x}{4}$

x	−8	−4	0	4	8
y					

36. $y = -\dfrac{3}{2}x + 4$

x	−2	0	2	4	6
y					

37. $y = \dfrac{3}{4}x - 4$

x	-8	-4	0	4	8
y					

38. $y = -\dfrac{2}{3}x + 4$

x	-6	-3	0	3	6
y					

In Exercises 39 to 44, create your own input/output table for the equation and then graph the equation.

39. $y = 2x + 2$

40. $y = -x - 1$

41. $y = \dfrac{3}{2}x - 3$

42. $y = -\dfrac{5}{2}x + 5$

43. $y = -\dfrac{3}{4}x + 1$

44. $y = \dfrac{2}{3}x - 4$

In Exercises 45 to 54, graph the equation in the integer viewing window. Then trace along the graph to find the requested values.

45. Let $y = 3x - 2$.
  a. Find y when $x = 4$.
  b. Find x when $y = 13$.

46. Let $y = 3 - 2x$.
  a. Find y when $x = -2$.
  b. Find x when $y = 7$.

47. Let $y = -\dfrac{x}{2} + 5$.
  a. Find y when $x = 10$.
  b. Find x when $y = -6$.

48. Let $y = \dfrac{2}{3}x + 6$.
  a. Find y when $x = -12$.
  b. Find x when $y = -10$.

49. Let $y = 5 - \dfrac{7x}{4}$.
  a. Find y when $x = -8$.
  b. Find x when $y = -9$.

50. Let $y = \dfrac{3x}{2} - 5$.
  a. Find y when $x = -8$.
  b. Find x when $y = 10$.

51. Let $y = -\dfrac{3}{4}x + 7$.

    a. Find y when $x = 24$.
    b. Find x when $y = -14$.

52. Let $y = \dfrac{5}{7}x - 6$.

    a. Find y when $x = -14$.
    b. Find x when $y = 14$.

53. Let $y = \dfrac{5}{3}x + 10$.

    a. Find y when $x = 0$.
    b. Find x when $y = 0$.

54. Let $y = -\dfrac{2}{5}x - 8$.

    a. Find y when $x = 0$.
    b. Find x when $y = 0$.

In Exercises 55 to 64, graph the equation in any viewing window that contains the given value of x. Use the TRACE feature of the calculator to find the ordered-pair solution of the equation for the given value of x. Check the results algebraically.

55. $y = 2x + 5$; $x = 7.5$

56. $y = -3x + 2$; $x = -6.4$

57. $y = 2 - 3x$; $x = -6.3$

58. $y = 3 - 5x$; $x = 8.4$

59. $y = \dfrac{3}{4}x + 3$; $x = -\dfrac{16}{3}$

60. $y = -\dfrac{3}{5}x - 5$; $x = -\dfrac{10}{3}$

61. $y = \dfrac{5}{3}x + 5$; $x = -\dfrac{57}{10}$

62. $y = -\dfrac{5}{4}x + 3$; $x = -\dfrac{16}{5}$

63. $y = -2.3x + 4.8$; $x = 12.1$

64. $y = 1.95x - 4.5$; $x = -12.3$

Applying Concepts

65. What is the y-coordinate of a point at which a graph crosses the x-axis?

66. What is the x-coordinate of a point at which a graph crosses the y-axis?

67. Name any two points on a horizontal line that is 2 units above the x-axis.

68. Name any two points on a vertical line that is 3 units to the left of the y-axis.

69. If $(-3, 4)$ and $(5, -1)$ are coordinates of two opposite vertices of a rectangle, what are the coordinates of the other two vertices?

70. If $(0, -3)$ and $(-5, 4)$ are coordinates of two opposite vertices of a rectangle, what are the coordinates of the other two vertices?

For Exercises 71 to 76, determine the distance from the given point to **a.** the
x-axis and **b.** the *y*-axis.

71. $(3, 5)$ **72.** $(-1, 6)$ **73.** $(7, -4)$

74. $(-4, -8)$ **75.** $(-2, 0)$ **76.** $(0, 6)$

For Exercises 77 to 82, draw a graph in the *xy*-plane that satisfies the stated
conditions.

77. The *x*-coordinate is always -3;
the *y*-coordinate is any real
number.

78. The *x*-coordinate is any real
number; the *y*-coordinate
always is 5.

79. The *x*-coordinate is any real
number; the *y*-coordinate is
always -2.

80. The *x*-coordinate is always 4;
the *y*-coordinate is any real
number.

81. The *x*-coordinate always
equals the *y*-coordinate.

82. The *y*-coordinate is always
the opposite of the
x-coordinate.

83. There is a coordinate system on Earth that consists of *longitude* and *latitude*.
Write a report on how location is determined on the surface of Earth.

EXPLORATION

Properties of Graphs of Straight Lines

1. Using a graphing calculator, enter $Y_1 = 2x + 3$, $Y_2 = -x + 3$, $Y_3 = \frac{3}{4}x + 3$,
$Y_4 = -\frac{5}{3}x + 3$, and $Y_5 = x + 3$. Graph all of these in the standard viewing window.

    a. What are the similarities among the graphs?

    b. What are the differences among the graphs?

    c. Without graphing $y = -2.7x + 3$, determine through which point on
the *y*-axis the graph will pass.

    d. From the answers you have given and without graphing each equation, determine through which point on the y-axis each graph will pass.

        i. $y = 2x + 4$ **ii.** $y = -2x + 1$

        iii. $y = \dfrac{1}{2}x - 3$ **iv.** $y = -3.1x - 5$

2. Using a graphing calculator, enter $Y_1 = 2(x - 2) + 1$, $Y_2 = -\dfrac{1}{2}(x - 2) + 1$, $Y_3 = -3(x - 2) + 1$, $Y_4 = -(x - 2) + 1$, and $Y_5 = \dfrac{2}{3}(x - 2) + 1$. Graph all of these in the decimal viewing window.

    a. What are the similarities among the graphs?

    b. What are the differences among the graphs?

    c. Without graphing $y = 3.4(x - 2) + 1$, determine through which point in the rectangular coordinate system the graph will pass.

    d. From the answers you have given and without graphing each equation, determine through which point in the plane each graph will pass.

        i. $y = 3(x - 1) + 2$ **ii.** $y = -2(x - 3) + 4$

        iii. $y = \dfrac{5}{2}(x - 5) + 1$ **iv.** $y = -1.2(x - 4) + 3$

3. Using a graphing calculator, enter $Y_1 = 2x + 3$, $Y_2 = 2x - 1$, $Y_3 = 2x + 2.5$, $Y_4 = 2x - 3.5$ and $Y_5 = 2x + 6$. Graph all of these in the standard viewing window.

    a. What are the similarities among the graphs?

    b. What are the differences among the graphs?

    c. How are the equations the same?

    d. How are they different?

4. Using a graphing calculator, enter $Y_1 = -2x + 2$, $Y_2 = -2x - 2$, $Y_3 = -2x + 6$, $Y_4 = -2x - 4$, and $Y_5 = -2x + 3$. Graph all of these in the standard viewing window.

    a. What are the similarities among the graphs?

    b. What are the differences among the graphs?

    c. How are the equations the same?

    d. How are they different?

Relations and Functions

Introduction to Relations and Functions

Exploring relationships between known quantities frequently results in sets of ordered pairs. For instance, the amount of air resistance R, in pounds, experienced by a certain car is given by $R = 0.024s^2$, where s is the speed of the car in miles per hour. The table below shows how the resistance on the car depends on the speed of the car for various values of s.

Speed, s (in miles per hour)	10	15	25	35	55	70
Resistance, R (in pounds)	2.4	5.4	15	29.4	72.6	117.6

▼ *Point of Interest*

Automotive engineers use equations such as $R = 0.024s^2$ to study the flow of air over a car. By understanding the relationship between speed and resistance, engineers can design more fuel-efficient cars.

The numbers in the table can also be written as ordered pairs where the first coordinate of the ordered pair is the speed of the car and the second coordinate is the air resistance. The ordered pairs are (10, 2.4), (15, 5.4), (25, 15), (35, 29.4), (55, 72.6) and (70, 117.6). The ordered pairs from the table above are only some of the possible ordered pairs. Other possibilities include (31, 23.064), (52, 64.896), (65, 101.4) and many more.

A table is another way of describing the relationship between two quantities. The table at the right shows a grading scale for an exam. Some possible ordered pairs for the relationship between exam scores and letter grades are (91, A), (87, B), (78, C), (98, A), (68, D), and (85, B).

Test Score	Grade
90–100	A
80–89	B
70–79	C
60–69	D
0–59	F

A third way of describing a relationship between two quantities is a graph. The bar graph below, based on data from the U.S. Census Bureau, shows the increase of the median price of a house in the United States. The ordered pairs can be approximated by reading the graph as

(1996, 140,000), (1997, 146,000), (1998, 153,000), (1999, 161,000), (2000, 169,000), and (2001, 175,000).

For each of these situations, ordered pairs were used to show the relationship between two quantities. In mathematics, a set of ordered pairs is called a *relation*.

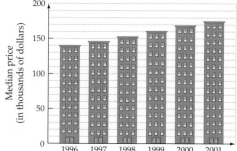

Definition of a Relation

A **relation** is any set of ordered pairs. The **domain** of the relation is the set of first coordinates of the ordered pairs. The **range** of the relation is the set of second coordinates of the ordered pairs.

For the relation between an exam score and a letter grade, the domain is all possible exam scores, and the range is all possible letter grades.

Domain = {0, 1, 2, 3, 4, . . ., 97, 98, 99, 100}   and   Range = {A, B, C, D, F}

Here is one more example of a relation. Consider the situation of a paleontologist trying to determine how fast a dinosaur could run. By studying the relation between the stride lengths of living creatures and the speed at which those creatures run, the scientist can infer the speed of a dinosaur. The table below shows the results of measuring the stride length and speed of various horses.

Stride length (in meters)	2.5	3.2	2.8	3.4	3.2	3.5	4.5	5.2
Speed (in meters per second)	2.6	2.7	2.5	2.8	2.6	2.8	3.2	3.0

This relation is the set of ordered pairs {(2.5, 2.6), (3.2, 2.7), (2.8, 2.5), (3.4, 2.8), (3.2, 2.6), (3.5, 2.8), (4.5, 3.2), (5.2, 3.0)}.

❓ QUESTION What is the meaning of the ordered pair (3.5, 2.8) for the relation above?

Although relations are important in mathematics, the concept of *function* is especially useful in applications.

> **Definition of a Function**
> A **function** is a relation in which no two ordered pairs have the same first coordinate and different second coordinates.

The relation between stride length and speed given earlier is *not* a function because the ordered pairs (3.2, 2.7) and (3.2, 2.6) have the same first coordinate and different second coordinates.

Now consider the relation between exam scores and letter grades. If there were two ordered pairs with the same first coordinate and different second coordinates, it would mean that two students with the same exam score (first coordinate) would receive different letter grades (second coordinate). For example, one student with an exam score of 72 could receive a D, and another student with an exam score of 72 could receive an A. But this does not happen with a grading scale. Thus there are no two ordered pairs with the same first coordinate and different second coordinates. The relationship between exam scores and letter grades is a function.

TAKE NOTE

The idea of *function* is one of the most important concepts in math. It is a concept you will encounter throughout this text.

TAKE NOTE

Note, however, that two students can receive different exam scores (first coordinates) and the same letter grade (second coordinates). For example, the ordered pairs (84, B) and (86, B) belong to the function.

❓ ANSWER A horse with a stride length of 3.5 meters ran at a speed of 2.8 meters per second.

EXAMPLE 1

Give the domain and range of the following relation. Is the relation a function?

$$\{(2, 4), (3, 6), (4, 7), (5, 4), (3, 2), (6, 8)\}$$

Solution   Domain = {2, 3, 4, 5, 6}   Range = {2, 4, 6, 7, 8}

The relation is not a function because there are two ordered pairs, (3, 6) and (3, 2), with the same first coordinate and different second coordinates.

YOU TRY IT 1

Give the domain and range of the following relation. Is the relation a function?

$$\{(1, 1), (2, 1), (3, 1), (4, 1), (5, 1), (6, 1), (7, 1)\}$$

Solution   See page S6.

TAKE NOTE

Recall that when listing elements of a set, duplicate elements are listed only once.

CALCULATOR NOTE

A graphing calculator can be used to find ordered pairs of $s = 16t^2$ for arbitrary values of t by using the *ASK* feature.

See Appendix A: Table

Some typical screens are shown below.

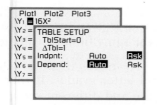

Although a function can be described in terms of ordered pairs, in a table, or by a graph, a major focus of this text will be functions defined by equations in two variables. For instance, when gravity is the only force acting on a falling body, a function that describes the distance s, in feet, that an object will fall in t seconds can be given by the equation $s = 16t^2$.

Given a value of t (time), the value of s (the distance the object falls) can be found. For instance, given $t = 3$, then

$$s = 16t^2$$
$$s = 16(3)^2 \qquad \bullet \text{ Replace } t \text{ by 3.}$$
$$= 16(9) = 144$$

In 3 seconds, an object falls 144 feet.

Because the distance the object falls depends on how long it has been falling, s is the dependent variable and t is the independent variable. We can find some of the ordered pairs of this function by evaluating $16t^2$ for various values of t. Here are the calculations for $t = 2, \frac{1}{2}$, and 4.5.

$$s = 16t^2 \qquad\qquad s = 16t^2 \qquad\qquad s = 16t^2$$

$$s = 16(2)^2 \qquad\qquad s = 16\left(\frac{1}{2}\right)^2 \qquad\qquad s = 16(4.5)^2$$

$$= 64 \qquad\qquad\qquad = 4 \qquad\qquad\qquad = 324$$

$$(2, 64) \qquad\qquad \left(\frac{1}{2}, 4\right) \qquad\qquad (4.5, 324)$$

The ordered pairs can be written as (t, s), where $s = 16t^2$. By substituting $16t^2$ for s, we can also write the ordered pairs as $(t, 16t^2)$.

For the equation $s = 16t^2$, we say that "distance is a function of time."

Not all equations in two variables define a function. For instance, $y^2 = x^2 + 9$ is not an equation that defines a function. As shown below, the ordered pairs $(4, 5)$ and $(4, -5)$ belong to the equation.

$y^2 = x^2 + 9$	
5^2	$4^2 + 9$
25	$16 + 9$
$25 = 25$	

- Let $(x, y) = (4, 5)$.
  Replace x by 4 and y by 5.
- $(4, 5)$ checks.

$y^2 = x^2 + 9$	
$(-5)^2$	$4^2 + 9$
25	$16 + 9$
$25 = 25$	

- Let $(x, y) = (4, -5)$.
  Replace x by 4 and y by -5.
- $(4, -5)$ checks.

Thus there are two ordered pairs with the *same* first coordinate, 4, but *different* second coordinates, 5 and -5; the equation does not define a function.

The phrase "*y* is a function of *x*," or a similar phrase with different variables, **is used to describe those equations in two variables that define functions.**

■ Functional Notation

Functional notation is frequently used for those equations that define functions. Just as x is commonly used as a variable, the letter f is commonly used to name a function.

To describe the relationship between a number and its square using functional notation, we can write $f(x) = x^2$. The symbol $f(x)$ is read "the *value* of f at x" or "*f* of x." The symbol $f(x)$ is the **value of the function** and represents the value of the dependent variable for a given value of the independent variable. We will often write $y = f(x)$ to emphasize the relationship between the independent variable, x, and the dependent variable, y. **Remember: y and $f(x)$ are different symbols for the same number.**

Also, **the *name* of the function is f; the *value* of the function at x is $f(x)$.** For instance, the equation $R = 0.024s^2$ discussed at the beginning of this section could be written as $R(s) = 0.024s^2$. The name of the function is R.

The letters used to represent a function are somewhat arbitrary. All of the following equations represent the same function.

$$f(x) = x^2 \qquad g(t) = t^2 \qquad P(v) = v^2$$

All three equations represent the square function.

The process of finding $f(x)$ for a given value of x is called **evaluating the function.** For instance, to evaluate $f(x) = x^2$ when x is 4, replace x by 4 and simplify.

$$f(x) = x^2$$
$$f(4) = 4^2 \qquad \text{• Replace } x \text{ by 4.}$$
$$= 16 \qquad \text{• Simplify.}$$

The *value* of the function is 16 when $x = 4$.

An ordered pair of the function is $(4, 16)$.

TAKE NOTE

The notation $f(x)$ does not mean f *times x*. The letter f stands for the name of the function, and $f(x)$ is the value of the function at *x*.

In many cases, you can think of a function as a machine that performs an operation on a number. For instance, you can think of the square function as taking an input (a number from the domain) and creating an output (a number in the range) that is the square of the input.

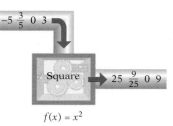

$f(x) = x^2$

? QUESTION What is the value of the function $f(x) = x^2$ when $x = -5$?

➡ Evaluate $p(s) = s^2 - 4s - 1$ when $s = -2$.

$$p(s) = s^2 - 4s - 1$$
$$p(-2) = (-2)^2 - 4(-2) - 1 \quad \bullet \text{ Replace } s \text{ by } -2.$$
$$= 11 \quad \bullet \text{ Simplify.}$$

The value of the function is 11 when $s = -2$.

See Appendix A:
Evaluating Functions

A graphing calculator can be used to check the evaluation of the function above. Some typical screens are shown at the right.

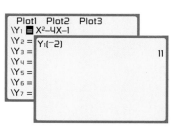

EXAMPLE 2

Let $g(t) = \dfrac{t^2}{t + 1}$.

a. Find $g(-2)$.
b. Find the value of g when $t = 3$.

Solution

ALGEBRAIC SOLUTION

$$g(t) = \frac{t^2}{t + 1}$$

a. $g(-2) = \dfrac{(-2)^2}{(-2) + 1}$ • Replace t by -2.

$$= \frac{4}{-1} = -4 \quad \bullet \text{ Simplify.}$$

$g(-2) = -4$

GRAPHICAL CHECK

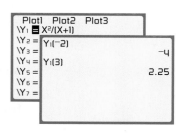

? ANSWER $f(-5) = (-5)^2 = 25$. The value of the function is 25 when $x = -5$.

b. To find the value of g when $t = 3$ means to evaluate the function when t is 3.

$$g(t) = \frac{t^2}{t + 1}$$

$$g(3) = \frac{(3)^2}{3 + 1} \qquad \bullet \text{ Replace } t \text{ by } 3.$$

$$= \frac{9}{4} \qquad \bullet \text{ Simplify.}$$

The value of g when $t = 3$ is $\frac{9}{4}$.

Note the use of parentheses when inputting the function. If the parentheses were missing, the calculator, using the Order of Operations Agreement, would have interpreted the expression as $\frac{x^2}{x} + 1$, which is not correct. Also note that the decimal value was given for $Y_1(3)$. You can use the calculator to convert this to a fraction.

YOU TRY IT 2

Let $f(z) = 2z^3 - 4z$.

a. Find $f(-1)$.
b. Find the value of f when $z = -3$.

Solution See page S6.

■ Graphs of Functions

The **graph of a function** is the graph of the ordered pairs that belong to the function. The graph of the speed–resistance function $R(s) = 0.024s^2$ given earlier is shown at the right. **The horizontal axis represents the domain of the function, or the independent variable** (the speed of the car); **the vertical axis represents the range of the function, or the dependent variable** (air resistance).

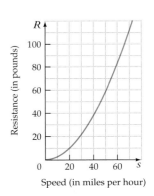

The graph of a function can be drawn by finding ordered pairs of the function, plotting the ordered pairs, and then connecting the points with a curve.

➡ Graph $f(x) = x^2 - 4x - 2$ by completing the table below, plotting the ordered pairs, and then connecting the points with a curve.

TAKE NOTE

We are creating the graph of an equation in two variables as we did earlier. The only difference is the use of functional notation.

x	$f(x) \quad = x^2 - 4x - 2$	(x, y)
-1	$f(-1) = (-1)^2 - 4(-1) - 2 = 3$	$(-1, 3)$
0		
1		
2		
3		
4		
5		

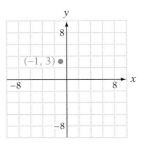

Complete the table by evaluating the function for the remaining values of x. Remember that $f(x)$ and y are two different symbols for the same number, the value of the dependent variable.

x	$f(x) = x^2 - 4x - 2$	(x, y)
-1	$f(-1) = (-1)^2 - 4(-1) - 2 = 3$	$(-1, 3)$
0	$f(0) \;\; = (0)^2 - 4(0) - 2 = -2$	$(0, -2)$
1	$f(1) \;\; = (1)^2 - 4(1) - 2 = -5$	$(1, -5)$
2	$f(2) \;\; = (2)^2 - 4(2) - 2 = -6$	$(2, -6)$
3	$f(3) \;\; = (3)^2 - 4(3) - 2 = -5$	$(3, -5)$
4	$f(4) \;\; = (4)^2 - 4(4) - 2 = -2$	$(4, -2)$
5	$f(5) \;\; = (5)^2 - 4(5) - 2 = 3$	$(5, 3)$

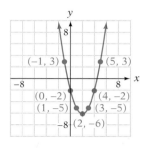

Plot the ordered pairs and draw a smooth curve through the points. ⬅

EXAMPLE 3

Let $f(x) = -\dfrac{3}{4}x + 2$.

a. Complete the following input/output table.

x	-8	-4	0	4	8
$f(x)$					

b. Graph the ordered pairs and then draw a line through the points.

Solution

a. Evaluate the function for the given values of x. The calculations for evaluating $f(-8)$ are shown at the right.

x	-8	-4	0	4	8
$f(x)$	8	5	2	-1	-4

$$f(x) = -\frac{3}{4}x + 2$$

$$f(-8) = -\frac{3}{4}(-8) + 2$$

$$= 6 + 2 = 8$$

b. Graph the ordered pairs $(-8, 8)$, $(-4, 5)$, $(0, 2)$, $(4, -1)$, and $(8, -4)$. Then draw a line through the points. The graph is shown at the right.

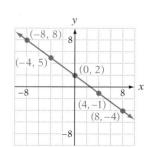

YOU TRY IT 3

Let $h(x) = 2x - 3$.

a. Complete the following input/output table.

x	-2	-1	0	1	2
$h(x)$					

b. Graph the ordered pairs and then draw a line through the points.

Solution   See page S6.

The equation $f(x) = 4$ is an example of a *constant function*. No matter what value of x is chosen, the value of the function is 4. For instance,

$$f(-3) = 4 \qquad f(0) = 4 \qquad f(2) = 4$$

The graph of $f(x) = 4$ is shown at the right. It is a horizontal line passing through $(0, 4)$.

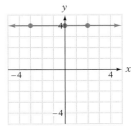

The **constant function** is written as $f(x) = c$, where c is a real number. No matter what value of x is chosen, the value of the constant function is c. **The graph of the constant function $f(x) = c$ is a horizontal line passing through $(0, c)$.**

EXAMPLE 4

Graph $h(x) = -1$.

Solution

The graph is a horizontal line through $(0, -1)$, as shown at the right.

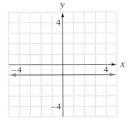

YOU TRY IT 4

Graph $g(x) = 2$.

Solution   See page S6.

The graphs of many functions can be created by using a graphing calculator. The calculator uses the same procedure we would use by hand. That is, the calculator chooses values of x, evaluates the function for that value, plots the corresponding point, and then connects the points with a curve. The advantage of using a calculator is that we can produce the graph quickly and then investigate its properties.

The following typical graphing calculator screens could be used to graph the function in Example 3 in the standard viewing window.

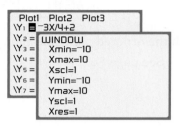
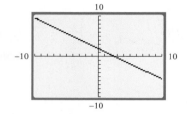

See Appendix A:
Trace

In Example 2, we showed one method of evaluating a function by using a graphing calculator. It is also possible to evaluate a function using **TRACE** on a calculator.

➡ Graph $f(x) = x^3 - 2x + 5$ in the standard viewing. Use the **TRACE** feature to find $f(-3)$, the value of the function when $x = -3$. Verify the result algebraically.

Graph the function in the standard viewing window. Now use the **TRACE** feature to find the value of the function when $x = -3$.

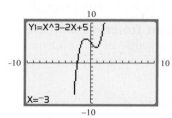
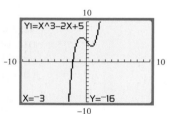

From the graph on the right, when $x = -3$, $y = -16$. Therefore, $f(-3) = -16$.

Algebraic check:

$$f(x) = x^3 - 2x + 5$$
$$f(-3) = (-3)^3 - 2(-3) + 5$$
$$= -27 + 6 + 5$$
$$= -16$$

■ Domain and Range

Recall that the domain of a function is the set of first coordinates of the ordered pairs of the function, and the range is the set of second coordinates. Another way of saying this is that **the domain is the set of all possible inputs, and the range is the set of corresponding outputs.** When the domain is a finite set of numbers, we can find the range by evaluating the function at each element of the domain.

EXAMPLE 5

Given $f(x) = x^2 - 4x$ with domain $\{-1, 0, 1, 2, 3, 4\}$, find the range of f.

Solution   Evaluate the function for each element of the domain.

$$f(x) = x^2 - 4x$$
$$f(-1) = (-1)^2 - 4(-1) = 1 + 4 = 5$$
$$f(0) = 0^2 - 4(0) = 0 + 0 = 0$$
$$f(1) = 1^2 - 4(1) = 1 - 4 = -3$$
$$f(2) = 2^2 - 4(2) = 4 - 8 = -4$$
$$f(3) = 3^2 - 4(3) = 9 - 12 = -3$$
$$f(4) = 4^2 - 4(4) = 16 - 16 = 0$$

The range is $\{-4, -3, 0, 5\}$.

YOU TRY IT 5

Given $f(x) = -x^2 + 2x + 2$ with domain $\{-2, -1, 0, 1, 2, 3\}$, find the range of f.

Solution   See page S6.

In Example 5, the domain was given as a finite set. In many instances, we will assume that the domain of a function is all the real numbers for which the value of the function is a real number. For instance, the number 3 is not in the domain of $h(x) = \frac{2x}{x-3}$ because when $x = 3$, $h(3) = \frac{6}{3-3} = \frac{6}{0}$, which is not a real number.

EXAMPLE 6

For $f(x) = \frac{x}{x-2}$, which of the following numbers, if any, are *not* in the domain of f?

a. -4 **b.** 2   **c.** 0   **d.** 4

Solution   When $x = -4$, $f(-4) = \dfrac{-4}{-4-2} = \dfrac{-4}{-6} = \dfrac{2}{3}$, a real number.

When $x = 2$, $f(2) = \dfrac{2}{2-2} = \dfrac{2}{0}$, which is not a real number.

When $x = 0$, $f(0) = \dfrac{0}{0-2} = \dfrac{0}{-2} = 0$, a real number.

When $x = 4$, $f(4) = \dfrac{4}{4-2} = \dfrac{4}{2} = 2$, a real number.

The number 2 is not in the domain of f.

YOU TRY IT 6

For $P(t) = \frac{t}{t^2 + 1}$, which of the following numbers, if any, are *not* in the domain of f?

a. 4 **b.** −4 **c.** 0 **d.** 3

Solution   See page S6.

When $x = 2$ for the function $f(x) = \frac{x}{x-2}$ in Example 6, the value of the function is undefined. In this case, given an input of 2, there is no output because division by zero is undefined. Therefore, 2 is *not* in the domain of the function. The domain of this function is all real numbers except 2.

The graph of $f(x) = \frac{x}{x-2}$ is shown at the right.

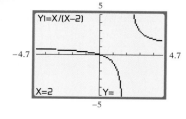

Note that when we try to evaluate this function at 2 using the TRACE feature, there is no output shown for y. This indicates that 2 is not in the domain of the function. If you trace along the curve, there is an output value for other input values.

A portion of an input/output table for $f(x) = \frac{x}{x-2}$ is shown at the right. Note that when $x = 2$, the output shows **ERROR**. This again demonstrates that 2 is not in the domain of f.

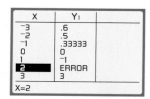

EXAMPLE 7

Graph $f(x) = \frac{x}{x^2 - 4}$ using the decimal viewing window. Trace along the curve to find two numbers that are not in the domain of f. Algebraically verify that the value of the function is undefined at these two numbers.

Solution   Graph the function and trace along the graph to find where no value of y is shown.

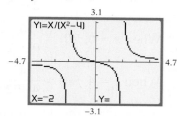

−2 is not in the domain of f.

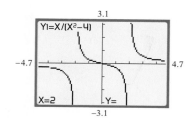

2 is not in the domain of f.

TAKE NOTE

Because of the way a graphing calculator graphs a function, use the viewing windows we suggest. Other windows can be used, but we have chosen these windows so that it is possible to trace to the necessary numbers.

An input/output table for

$f(x) = \dfrac{x}{x^2 - 4}$ is shown

below.

Note the word **ERROR** in the Y₁ column for the input values of −2 and 2. This is another indication that these two numbers are not in the domain of f.

X	Y₁
−3	−.6
−2	ERROR
−1	.33333
0	0
1	−.3333
2	ERROR
3	.6

X = −3

We can algebraically verify that these numbers are not in the domain of f by attempting to evaluate the function for the two numbers.

$$f(x) = \frac{x}{x^2 - 4} \qquad\qquad f(x) = \frac{x}{x^2 - 4}$$

$$f(-2) = \frac{-2}{(-2)^2 - 4} \qquad\qquad f(2) = \frac{2}{2^2 - 4}$$

$$= \frac{-2}{0} \;\; \text{Undefined} \qquad\qquad = \frac{2}{0} \;\; \text{Undefined}$$

Because the value of the function is undefined when x equals -2 and when x equals 2, these numbers are not in the domain of f.

YOU TRY IT 7

Graph $f(x) = \dfrac{3}{x^2 - x - 6}$ using the decimal viewing window. Trace along the curve to find two numbers that are not in the domain of f. Algebraically verify that the value of the function is undefined at these two numbers.

Solution See page S6.

■ Applications

Any letter or combination of letters can be used to name a function. In the next example, the letters SA are used to represent a Surface Area function. In this case, SA is the name of the function and does not mean S times A.

EXAMPLE 8

The surface area of a cube (the sum of the areas of each of the 6 faces of a cube) is given by $SA(s) = 6s^2$, where $SA(s)$ is the surface area of the cube and s is the length of one side of the cube. Find the surface area of a cube that has a side of 10 centimeters.

Solution $SA(s) = 6s^2$

$SA(10) = 6(10)^2$ • Replace s by 10.

$= 6(100)$ • Simplify.

$= 600$

The surface area is 600 square centimeters

YOU TRY IT 8

If m points are placed in the plane, no three of which are on the same line, then the number of different line segments that can be drawn between the points, $N(m)$, is given by $N(m) = \dfrac{m(m-1)}{2}$. Find the number of different line segments that can be drawn between 12 different points in the plane.

Solution See page S7.

5 points
10 line segments

EXAMPLE 9

A spherical snowball is melting in such a way that the volume of the snow ball can be approximated by $V(t) = 20\pi(2 - \frac{t}{90})^3$, where $V(t)$ is the volume, in cubic inches, of the snowball t minutes after it begins to melt.

a. Find the volume of the snowball when $t = 30$. Round to the nearest hundredth.
b. Explain why the domain of this function is the interval [0, 180].

Solution

a. $V(t) = 20\pi\left(2 - \dfrac{t}{90}\right)^3$

$\qquad = 20\pi\left(2 - \dfrac{30}{90}\right)^3$ • Replace t by 30.

$\qquad = 20\pi\left(2 - \dfrac{1}{3}\right)^3 = 20\pi\left(\dfrac{5}{3}\right)^3$ • Simplify.

$\qquad \approx 290.89$

The volume is 290.89 cubic inches.

b. The snowball begins melting when $t = 0$, so the least value of t is 0. If t is greater than 180, then $\left(2 - \frac{t}{90}\right)^3$ is less than zero. This would mean the volume of the snowball was negative, which is not possible.

YOU TRY IT 9

An environmental study determined that the amount of carbon monoxide in the air surrounding a city depends on the population of the city and can be approximated by $C(p) = 0.15\sqrt{p^2 + 4p + 10}$, where p is the population in thousands and $C(p)$ is the concentration of carbon monoxide in parts per million (ppm).

a. Find the concentration of carbon monoxide in a city whose population is 100,000. Round to the nearest tenth.
b. What is the concentration of carbon monoxide when $p = 0$? Round to the nearest tenth. What is the significance of this number in the context of the problem?

Solution   See page S7.

See Appendix A:
Radical Expressions

2.2 EXERCISES

Topics for Discussion

1. Describe the concepts of relation and function. How are they the same? How are they different?

2. Are all functions relations? Are all relations functions?

3. What is the domain of a function? What is the range of a function?

4. What is the value of a function?

5. What does it mean to evaluate a function?

6. Is it possible for a function to have the same output value for two different input values? Explain.

7. Is it possible for a function to have two different output values for the same input value? Explain.

▪ Introduction to Relations and Functions

For Exercises 8 to 15, give the domain and range of the relation. Is the relation a function?

8. $\{(-2, 0), (2, 1), (4, 2), (6, 3), (8, 4)\}$

9. $\{(-3, -5), (-2, -7), (-1, -9), (0, -11), (1, -13)\}$

10. $\{(1, 2), (2, 3), (3, 4), (3, 2), (2, 1)\}$

11. $\{(-4, 6), (-2, 8), (0, 10), (-4, 8), (2, 12)\}$

12. $\{(-1, 3), (0, 7), (1, 9), (4, 7), (7, 3)\}$

13. $\{(2, -6), (3, -3), (4, -6), (5, 6), (6, -6)\}$

14. $\{(-2, 5), (-1, 5), (0, 5), (1, 5), (2, 5)\}$

15. $\{(-4, 0), (-2, 0), (0, 0), (3, 0), (5, 0)\}$

▪ Functional Notation

For Exercises 16 to 25, evaluate the function at the given value.

16. $f(x) = 2x + 7; x = -2$

17. $y(x) = 1 - 3x; x = -4$

18. $f(t) = t^2 - t - 3; t = 3$

19. $P(n) = n^2 - 4n - 7; n = -3$

20. $v(s) = s^3 + 3s^2 - 4s - 2; s = -2$

21. $f(x) = 3x^3 - 4x^2 + 7; x = 2$

22. $T(p) = \dfrac{p^2}{p - 2}; p = 0$

23. $s(t) = \dfrac{4t}{t^2 + 2}; t = 2$

24. $r(x) = 2^x - x^2; x = 3$

25. $ABS(x) = |2x - 7|; x = -3$

▪ Graphs of Functions

For Exercises 26 to 35, complete the input/output table, and graph the function without using a graphing calculator. Check your answer by using a graphing calculator.

26. $f(x) = 2x - 4$

x	-2	-1	0	1	2
y					

27. $f(x) = 2 - 2x$

x	-2	-1	0	1	2
y					

28. $f(x) = -\dfrac{1}{2}x + 3$

x	-4	-2	0	2	4
y					

29. $f(x) = -\dfrac{2x}{3} + 4$

x	-6	-3	0	3	6
y					

30. $f(x) = -x^2 + 2$

x	-3	-2	-1	0	1	2	3
y							

31. $f(x) = x^2 - 2$

x	-3	-2	-1	0	1	2	3
y							

32. $f(x) = x^2 + 6x + 2$

x	-6	-5	-4	-3	-2	-1	0
y							

33. $f(x) = -x^2 + 2x - 1$

x	-2	-1	0	1	2	3	4
y							

34. $f(x) = 3$

x	-4	-3	-2	-1	0	1	2
y							

35. $f(x) = -2$

x	-2	-1	0	1	2	3	4
y							

36. Describe the graph of the function $G(x) = -4$.

37. Describe the graph of the function $H(x) = 1$.

For Exercises 38 to 43, use a graphing calculator to graph each function in the integer viewing window. Then use the TRACE feature to find the x-coordinate for the given y-coordinate. Check your work by evaluating the function at the x-coordinate.

38. $f(x) = -3x + 6; y = 12$

39. $f(x) = 2x - 7; y = 13$

40. $g(x) = -\dfrac{5}{4}x + 10; y = 15$

41. $g(x) = \dfrac{2}{3}x + 8; y = -10$

42. $F(x) = 5 - \dfrac{7}{5}x; y = 26$

43. $y(x) = 9 - \dfrac{15}{8}x; y = -6$

For Exercises 44 to 49, graph the function in the standard viewing window. Use the TRACE feature to evaluate the function. Verify the results algebraically.

44. $f(x) = x^2 - 3x - 1; f(-2)$

45. $f(x) = x^2 + 2x - 5; f(3)$

46. $g(x) = x^3 - 4x - 1; g(2)$

47. $g(x) = x^3 + 4x^2 - 2;$ $g(-3)$

48. $F(x) = x^3 - 3x^2 + x - 1;$ $F\left(\dfrac{3}{2}\right)$

49. $F(x) = x^3 + 4x^2 - x - 3;$ $F\left(-\dfrac{5}{2}\right)$

■ Domain and Range

50. Given $f(x) = x^2 + 3x$ with domain $\{-4, -3, -2, -1, 0, 1, 2, 3, 4\}$, find the range of f.

51. Given $g(x) = 10 - x^2$ with domain $\{-4, -3, -2, -1, 0, 1, 2, 3, 4\}$, find the range of g.

52. Given $s(t) = t^3 - t^2 + 3t - 5$ with domain $\{-4, -2, 0, 2, 4\}$, find the range of s.

53. Given $P(n) = \dfrac{n(n + 1)}{2}$ with domain $\{1, 2, 3, 4, 5, 6, 7\}$, find the range of P.

54. Given $R(x) = \dfrac{1}{x + 2}$ with domain $\{-1, 0, 1, 2, 3, 4, 5\}$, find the range of R.

55. Given $v(s) = \frac{s}{s^2 + 1}$ with domain $\{-3, -2, -1, 0, 1, 2, 3\}$, find the range of v. Express the values of the range as fractions in simplest form.

For Exercises 56 to 70, determine which, if any, of the given numbers are *not* in the domain of the function.

56. $h(x) = x^2$; $x = -3, 0, 4$

57. $f(t) = 2t - 4$; $t = -1, 0, 2$

58. $R(s) = \frac{5}{s - 3}$; $s = -3, 0, 3$

59. $f(x) = \frac{x}{x + 5}$; $x = -5, 0, 2$

60. $g(v) = \frac{v + 1}{v^2 - 4}$; $v = -2, -1, 2$

61. $F(x) = \frac{x - 1}{x^2 - 2x - 3}$; $x = -1, 1, 3$

62. $h(x) = x^3$; $x = -2, 0, 3$

63. $f(t) = 3t + 1$; $t = -6, 0, 5$

64. $f(x) = \frac{x}{x - 5}$; $x = -3, 0, 5$

65. $g(v) = \frac{v + 1}{v + 4}$; $v = -4, -1, 0$

66. $F(x) = \frac{x + 1}{x}$; $x = -1, 0, 1$

67. $F(x) = \frac{2x - 4}{x + 2}$; $x = -2, 0, 2$

68. $R(s) = \frac{s^2 + s}{5}$; $s = -1, 0, 1$

69. $z(t) = \frac{t}{t^2 + 1}$; $t = -1, 0, 2$

70. $ABS(x) = |2x - 4|$; $x = -2, 0, 2$

For Exercises 71 to 76, graph the function in the decimal viewing window. Trace along the curve to find a number that is *not* in the domain of the function.

71. $f(x) = \frac{2}{x - 1}$

72. $f(x) = \frac{1}{x + 2}$

73. $g(x) = \frac{x}{x + 3}$

74. $g(x) = \frac{x}{x - 2}$

75. $F(x) = \frac{x}{2x - 3}$

76. $F(x) = \frac{x}{2x + 5}$

For Exercises 77 to 82, graph the function in the decimal viewing window. Trace along the curve to find two numbers that are *not* in the domain of the function.

77. $f(x) = \frac{1}{x^2 - 1}$

78. $f(x) = \frac{1}{x^2 - x - 2}$

79. $g(x) = \frac{x}{x^2 - 2x - 3}$

80. $g(x) = \frac{x}{x^2 - 9}$

81. $F(x) = \frac{1}{2x^2 - x - 1}$

82. $F(x) = \frac{2}{2x^2 - x - 3}$

■ Applications

83. *Geometry* The perimeter P of a square is a function of the length of one of its sides s and is given by $P(s) = 4s$.

    a. Find the perimeter of a square whose side is 4 meters.
    b. Find the perimeter of a square whose side is 5 feet.

84. *Geometry* The area of a circle is a function of its radius and is given by $A(r) = \pi r^2$.

    a. Find the area of a circle whose radius is 3 inches. Round to the nearest tenth.
    b. Find the area of a circle whose radius is 12 centimeters. Round to the nearest tenth.

85. *Sports* The height h, in feet, of a baseball that is released 4 feet above the ground with an initial upward velocity of 80 feet per second is a function of the time t, in seconds, and is given by $h(t) = -16t^2 + 80t + 4$.

    a. Find the height of the baseball above the ground 2 seconds after it is released.
    b. Find the height of the baseball above the ground 4 seconds after it is released.

86. *Forestry* The distance d, in miles, that a forest fire ranger can see from an observation tower is a function of the height h, in feet, of the tower above the ground and is given by $d(h) = 1.5\sqrt{h}$.

    a. Find the distance a ranger can see whose eye level is 20 feet above the ground. Round to the nearest tenth.
    b. Find the distance a ranger can see whose eye level is 35 feet above the ground. Round to the nearest tenth.

87. *Physics* The speed s, in feet per second, of sound in air depends on the temperature t of the air, in degrees Celsius, and is given by

$$s(t) = \frac{1087\sqrt{t + 273}}{16.52}.$$

    a. What is the speed of sound in air when the temperature is 25°C? Round to the nearest whole number.
    b. Does the speed of sound in air increase or decrease as temperature increases?

88. *Business* The number of personal digital assistants (PDAs) that a company can sell per month depends on the price of the PDA and is given by $D(p) = \frac{480{,}000}{100 + 5p}$, where p is price of the PDA, in dollars, and $D(p)$ is the number of PDAs that can be sold per month at that price.

    a. How many PDAs can be sold per month when the price is $300?
    b. Will the number of PDAs that can be sold per month increase or decrease as the price increases?

89. *Sports*   In a softball league in which each team plays every other team three times, the number N of games that must be scheduled depends on the number of teams in the league and is given by $N(n) = \frac{3}{2}n^2 - \frac{3}{2}n$.

    a. How many games must be scheduled for a league that has 5 teams?

    b. How many games must be scheduled for a league that has 6 teams?

90. *Solutions*   The percent concentration, P, of salt in a salt–water solution depends on the number of grams x of salt that is added to the solution and is given by $P(x) = \frac{100x + 100}{x + 10}$, where x is the number of grams of salt that is added.

    a. What is the percent concentration of salt after an additional 5 grams of salt is added to the solution?

    b. What is the percent concentration of salt when $x = 0$ and what is the significance of this result in the context of this problem?

91. *Physics*   The time T, in seconds, it takes a pendulum to make one swing depends on the length of the pendulum and is given by $T(L) = 2\pi\sqrt{\frac{L}{32}}$, where L is the length of the pendulum in feet.

    a. Find the time it takes the pendulum to make one swing if the length of the pendulum is 3 feet. Round to the nearest hundredth.

    b. Find the time it takes the pendulum to make one swing if the length of the pendulum is 9 inches. Round to the nearest hundredth.

Applying Concepts

92. Create a set of five ordered pairs that is a function. Create a set of five ordered pairs that is a relation but not a function.

93. **a.** Define a function that has domain = {1, 4, 6} and range = {2, 7, 9}.

    b. Define a function that has domain = {1, 2, 3} and range = {4}.

94. **a.** Suppose $f(2) = 7$ and $f(4) = 7$. Is it possible for f to be a function?

    b. Suppose $g(7) = 2$ and $g(7) = 4$. Is it possible for g to be a function?

95. Create a function whose domain does not contain 5.

96. Modular functions have many different applications. One such application is in creating codes for secure communications so that, for instance, credit card information can be transmitted over the Internet. We define $a \equiv b$ mod n if a has remainder b when divided by n. (It is traditional to use $\equiv$ rather than $=$ for the mod function.) For instance,

$5 \equiv 2 \bmod 3$ because the remainder when 5 is divided by 3 is 2. On the other hand, $7 \not\equiv 2 \bmod 3$ because the remainder when 7 is divided by 3 is not 2.

a. Is $8 \equiv 3 \bmod 5$?
b. Is $7 \equiv 1 \bmod 3$?
c. Find three positive integers x for which $x \equiv 2 \bmod 5$.
d. Find the least positive integer x for which $2x \equiv 1 \bmod 11$.
e. Find the least positive integer x for which $x + 4 \equiv 0 \bmod 11$.

97.   All books published in the United States have an ISBN (International Standard Book Number). Write a report that explains how mod 11 is used for ISBNs. (See Exercise 96.)

EXPLORATION

1. *Functions of More Than One Variable*   The value of some functions may depend on several variables. For instance, the perimeter of a rectangle depends on the length L and the width W. We can write this as

$$P(L, W) = 2L + 2W.$$

To evaluate this function, we need to be given the value of L and W. Here is an example: To find the perimeter of a rectangle whose length is 5 feet and whose width is 3 feet, evaluate $P(L, W)$ when $L = 5$ and $W = 3$.

$$P(L, W) = 2L + 2W$$
$$P(5, 3) = 2(5) + 2(3) \qquad \bullet \text{ Replace } L \text{ by 5 and } W \text{ by 3.}$$
$$= 10 + 6 = 16$$

The perimeter is 16 feet.

a. Evaluate $f(a, b) = 2a + 3b$ when $a = 3$ and $b = 4$.
b. Evaluate $R(s, t) = 2st - t^2$ when $s = -1$ and $t = 2$.
c. Although we normally do not think of addition as a function, it is a function of two variables. If we define the function *Add* as $Add(a, b) = a + b$, find $Add(3, 7)$.
d. Write the area of a triangle as a function of two variables.

e. Give an example of a function whose value depends on more than one variable.

SECTION **2.3** **Properties of Functions**

- Vertical-Line Test
- Intercepts
- Intersections of the Graphs of Two Functions

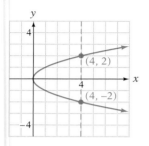

Vertical-Line Test

Consider the graph shown at the left. Note that two ordered pairs that belong to the graph are (4, 2) and (4, −2) and that these points lie on a vertical line. These two ordered pairs have the same first coordinates but different second coordinates, and therefore, the graph is not the graph of a function. With this observation in mind, we can give a quick method to determine whether a graph is the graph of a function.

> **Vertical-Line Test for the Graph of a Function**
> A graph defines a function if any vertical line intersects the graph at no more than one point.

This graphical interpretation of a function is often described by saying that each value in the domain of the function is paired with *exactly one* value in the range of the function.

TAKE NOTE

For the second graph on the right, note that there are values of *x* for which there is only one value of *y*. For instance, when *x* = −5, *y* = 4. In a function, however, *every* value of *x* in the domain of the function must have exactly one value of *y*. If there is even one value of *x* that has two or more values of *y*, the condition for a function is not met.

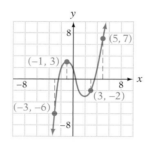

For each x there is exactly one value of y. This is the graph of a function.

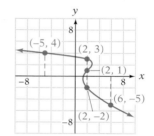

Some values of x can be paired with more than one value of y. For instance, 2 can be paired with −2, 1, and 3. This is not the graph of a function.

EXAMPLE 1

Use the vertical-line test to determine whether the graph is the graph of a function.

a.
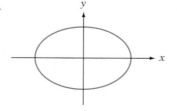

b.
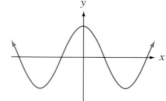

Solution

a. As shown at the right, there are vertical lines that intersect the graph at more than one point. Therefore, the graph is not the graph of a function.

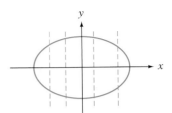

b. For the graph at the right, every vertical line intersects the graph at most once. Therefore, the graph is the graph of a function.

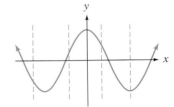

YOU TRY IT 1

Use the vertical-line test to determine whether the graph is the graph of a function.

a.

b.

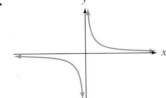 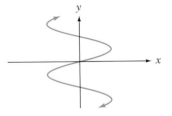

Solution See page S7.

■ Intercepts

When choosing a window in which to graph a function, we usually choose the window so that the important characteristics of the graph are displayed. One important characteristic of a graph is its *intercepts*. A **y-intercept** is a point at which a graph crosses the y-axis. An **x-intercept** is a point at which a graph crosses the x-axis.

Consider the graph of $f(x) = x^2 + x - 2$ shown at the right. Note that **the x-coordinate of the y-intercept is zero.** To find the y-intercept, evaluate the function at $x = 0$.

$$f(x) = x^2 + x - 2$$
$$f(0) = 0^2 + 0 - 2 \qquad \bullet \text{ To find the y-intercept,}$$
$$= -2 \qquad\qquad\qquad \text{evaluate the function at } 0.$$

The y-intercept is $(0, -2)$.

Look again at the graph of $f(x) = x^2 + x - 2$ and note that the x-coordinates of the x-intercepts are -2 and 1. Note also that **the y-coordinate of an x-intercept is zero.** We can verify this by evaluating the function at -2 and 1.

$$f(x) = x^2 + x - 2$$
$$f(-2) = (-2)^2 + (-2) - 2 \qquad \bullet \text{ Evaluate } f \text{ at } -2.$$
$$= 4 - 2 - 2$$
$$= 0 \qquad\qquad\qquad\quad \bullet \text{ The value of the function is 0.}$$

$$f(x) = x^2 + x - 2$$
$$f(1) = (1)^2 + (1) - 2 \qquad \bullet \text{ Evaluate } f \text{ at } 1.$$
$$= 1 + 1 - 2$$
$$= 0 \qquad\qquad\qquad\quad \bullet \text{ The value of the function is 0.}$$

The numbers -2 and 1 are called **zeros of the function** because the value of the function at these numbers is 0. From a graphical perspective, the x-coordinates of the x-intercepts of the graph of a function are zeros of the function. This idea is used by many graphing calculators to determine the x-intercepts of a graph.

See Appendix A:
Zero

To illustrate the procedure for using a graphing calculator to determine the x-intercepts of the graph of a function, we will use $f(x) = x^2 + x - 2$, the function discussed above. To begin, use the Y= editor to enter the expression for the function, and then graph the function in any viewing window that shows the x-intercepts. The standard viewing window is a good place to start. Once the graph is displayed, the ZERO feature of the calculator is used to find the x-intercepts. Some typical screens are shown below.

CALCULATOR NOTE

The ZERO option on the graphing calculator calculates the value of x when y is zero. In other words, it finds the x-coordinates of the x-intercepts.

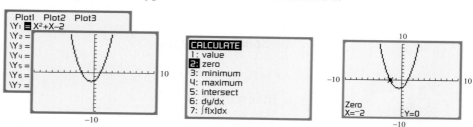

An x-intercept of the graph of $f(x) = x^2 + x - 2$ is $(-2, 0)$.

To find the second x-intercept, we repeat the process. The graph is shown at the right. A second x-intercept of the graph of $f(x) = x^2 + x - 2$ is $(1, 0)$.

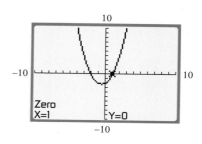

EXAMPLE 2

Find **a.** the y-intercept and **b.** the x-intercepts for the graph of $f(x) = x^2 + 2x - 2$. Round to the nearest hundredth.

Solution

a. To find the y-intercept, evaluate the function at zero.

$$f(x) = x^2 + 2x - 2$$
$$f(0) = 0^2 + 2(0) - 2 = -2$$

The y-intercept is $(0, -2)$.

b. To find the x-intercepts, we need to determine where the graph crosses the x-axis. The x-coordinate of an x-intercept is a zero of the function. Graph $f(x) = x^2 + 2x - 2$, and use the ZERO option of a graphing calculator to find the x-coordinates of the x-intercepts of the function.

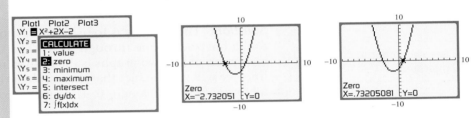

To the nearest hundredth, the x-coordinates of the x-intercepts are -2.73 and 0.73.

To the nearest hundredth, the x-intercepts are $(-2.73, 0)$ and $(0.73, 0)$.

YOU TRY IT 2

Find **a.** the y-intercept and **b.** the x-intercepts for the graph of $g(x) = 2x^2 - 5x + 2$.

Solution See page S7.

■ Intersections of the Graphs of Two Functions

In the last section, we discussed how we could determine an output for a given input. We can also solve the opposite problem of finding an input for a given output. Although there are algebraic methods for doing this, we will use a graphical approach here.

The graph of $f(x) = 2x + 1$ is shown at the right. To determine the value of x (the input) in the domain of f that will result in a given output of 7 in the range of f, draw a horizontal line from 7 on the y-axis to the graph of f. Now draw a vertical line to the x-axis. The x-coordinate (3, in this case) of the point where the vertical line touches the x-axis is the desired value. This can be verified by evaluating the function at this number.

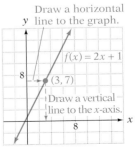

Draw a horizontal line to the graph.

Draw a vertical line to the x-axis.

TAKE NOTE

The problem of finding the x-intercept is more difficult than finding the y-intercept because we must find the value of x for which $f(x)$ is zero rather than just evaluating the function at zero. In this chapter, we are using a graphical technique to solve this problem. In the next chapter, we will begin a discussion of algebraic techniques to solve the problem.

$$f(x) = 2x + 1$$
$$f(3) = 2(3) + 1 \qquad \bullet \text{ Replace } x \text{ by } 3.$$
$$= 6 + 1$$
$$= 7 \qquad \bullet \text{ The output is 7, the given number.}$$

The coordinates of the point at which the horizontal line through (0, 7) intersects the graph is (3, 7). This observation is the basis of a graphing calculator solution to this problem.

Example 3 illustrates how a graphing calculator can be used to find a number in the domain of a function that corresponds to a given output of that function.

EXAMPLE 3

Find the number in the domain of $f(x) = -\frac{2}{3}x + 2$ for which the output is 4.

 See Appendix A: Intersect

Solution   The strategy is to use a calculator to graph both $f(x) = -\frac{2}{3}x + 2$ and a horizontal line through (0, 4). The x-coordinate of the point of intersection of the two graphs is the desired number. To draw the horizontal line, we will use the fact that the graph of the constant function $g(x) = 4$ is a horizontal line through (0, 4). Some typical screens are shown below.

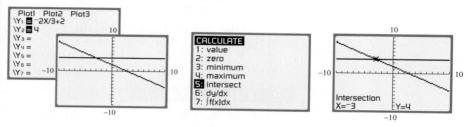

The point of intersection is (−3, 4).

The number −3 in the domain of f produces an output of 4 in the range of f.

We can verify this algebraically as follows:

$$f(x) = -\frac{2}{3}x + 2$$

$$f(-3) = -\frac{2}{3}(-3) + 2 \qquad \bullet \text{ Replace } x \text{ by } -3.$$

$$= 2 + 2$$

$$= 4 \qquad \bullet \text{ The output is 4, the given number.}$$

YOU TRY IT 3

Find the number in the domain of $G(x) = 1 - 2x$ for which the output is −6.

Solution   See page S7.

In Example 3 and You Try It 3, the graphs of the functions were straight lines. We can solve similar problems for graphs that are not straight lines.

⇒   Find the number in the domain of $f(x) = \sqrt{2x + 1}$ for which the output is 3. We proceed in a manner similar to Example 3. Draw the graph of $f(x) = \sqrt{2x + 1}$ and the graph of $g(x) = 3$, and then use a graphing calculator to find the point of intersection.

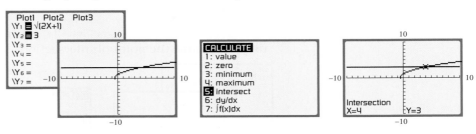

The point of intersection is (4, 3).

The number 4 in the domain of f produces an output of 3 in the range of f.   ⇐

Suppose we want to determine an input that will result in an output of -3 for $f(x) = x^2$. The graph of $f(x) = x^2$ is shown at the right. Note that no matter in which direction a horizontal line through -3 on the y-axis is drawn, it will not intersect the graph of f. This means that there is no input for f that will produce an output of -3. Another way of saying this is that -3 is not in the range of f.

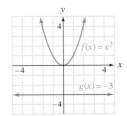

A problem that is related to finding the input for a given output is that of finding the input values for which the values of two functions are equal. The graphs of $f(x) = -2x + 1$ and $g(x) = x - 5$ are shown at the right. The two graphs intersect at the point $(2, -3)$. The values of the functions are equal at the x-coordinate of the point of intersection.

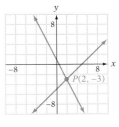

$$f(x) = -2x + 1 \qquad\qquad g(x) = x - 5$$
$$f(2) = -2(2) + 1 \quad \bullet \text{ Replace } x \text{ by 2.} \quad g(2) = 2 - 5 \quad \bullet \text{ Replace } x \text{ by 2.}$$
$$ = -3 \qquad\qquad\qquad\qquad\quad = -3$$

From these evaluations of f and g, $f(2) = -3$ and $g(2) = -3$, which means $f(2) = g(2)$. That is, the value of the functions are equal when $x = 2$.

❓ QUESTION   For the graph at the right, is there a value of x for which the values of the functions f and g are equal?

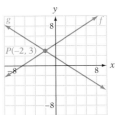

❓ ANSWER   Yes. When $x = -2$, $f(-2) = g(-2)$.

A graphing calculator can be used to find the point of intersection of the graphs of two functions.

EXAMPLE 4

Find the element in the domain of $f(x) = 2x + 4$ and $g(x) = -3x - 1$ for which the values of the functions are equal. Verify the results algebraically.

Solution

Graph $f(x) = 2x + 4$ and $g(x) = -3x - 1$ in the same viewing window, and then determine the point of intersection.

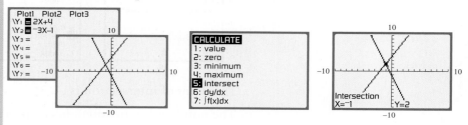

The point of intersection is $(-1, 2)$.

The values of the functions are equal when $x = -1$.

To verify the results algebraically, evaluate the functions at the x-coordinate of the point of intersection.

$$f(x) = 2x + 4 \qquad\qquad g(x) = -3x - 1$$
$$f(-1) = 2(-1) + 4 \quad \bullet \text{ Replace } x \quad g(-1) = -3(-1) - 1 \quad \bullet \text{ Replace}$$
$$= 2 \qquad\qquad \text{ by } -1. \qquad\qquad = 2 \qquad\qquad x \text{ by } -1.$$

The values of the functions are equal when $x = -1$.

YOU TRY IT 4

Find the element in the domain of $f(x) = 2x - 3$ and $g(x) = \frac{x}{2} + 3$ for which the values of the functions are equal. Verify the results algebraically.

Solution See page S8.

There are many applications whose solutions use the techniques of Example 3 and Example 4.

EXAMPLE 5

The distance a forest ranger can see from a lookout tower is given by $d(h) = 1.5\sqrt{h}$, where h is the height, in feet, of the ranger's binoculars above the ground and $d(h)$ is the distance, in miles, the ranger can see at a height of h feet. At what height above the ground must the ranger's eyes be to see 20 miles? Use a domain of $[0, 300]$ and a range of $[0, 30]$. Round to the nearest whole number.

Solution To solve this problem, we need to determine the value of h for which $d = 20$. This is similar to Example 3. Graph $d(h) = 1.5\sqrt{h}$ and $g(h) = 20$, and determine the point of intersection.

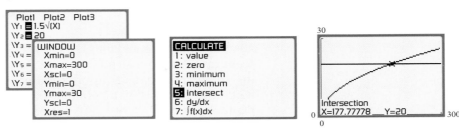

The ranger's eyes must be 178 feet above the ground to see 20 miles.

We can check this result by evaluating $d(h) = 1.5\sqrt{h}$ when $h = 178$.

$$d(h) = 1.5\sqrt{h}$$
$$d(178) = 1.5\sqrt{178}$$
$$\approx 20.012$$

The ranger can see approximately 20 miles at a height of 178 feet above the ground.

YOU TRY IT 5

The distance a marathon runner is from the finish line is given by $s(t) = 26 - 8t$, where t is the time in hours since the beginning of the race and $s(t)$ is the distance, in miles, from the finish line at time t. After how many hours will the runner be 10 miles from the finish line? Use a domain of [0, 5] and a range of [0, 30].

Solution See page S8.

EXAMPLE 6

The value of an investment in t years is given by $V(t) = 400 + 50t$, and the value of a second investment in t years is given by $W(t) = 500 + 30t$. In how many years will the two investments have the same value? Use a domain of [0, 7] and a range of [0, 800].

Solution To solve this problem, we need to determine the value of t for which $W(t) = V(t)$. This is similar to Example 4. Graph $V(t) = 400 + 50t$ and $W(t) = 500 + 30t$, and determine the point of intersection.

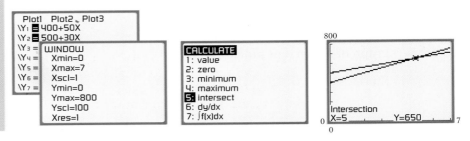

The point of intersection is $(5, 650)$.

The investments will be equal in 5 years. At that time, each investment will be worth $650.

YOU TRY IT 6

A small plane is leaving an airport just as another plane is beginning a descent into the same airport. The height above the ground of the plane leaving the airport can be approximated by $h(t) = 115t$, where $h(t)$ is the height, in feet, of the airplane after t minutes. The height of the second plane is given by $f(t) = 2000 - 135t$, where $f(0)$ is the moment the second plane starts its descent. After how many minutes will the two planes be at the same height? Use a domain of $[0, 10]$ and a range of $[0, 2000]$.

Solution   See page S8.

2.3 EXERCISES

Topics For Discussion

1. What is the vertical-line test?

2. Draw a graph that is the graph of a function. Draw a graph that is not the graph of a function.

3. **a.** What is the value of the x-coordinate of any point on the y-axis?
   b. What is the value of the y-coordinate of any point on the x-axis?

4. Can the graph of a function have more than one y-intercept? Explain.

5. **a.** How are the independent and dependent variables of a function related to the domain and range of the function?
   b. How are the input and output values of a function related to the domain and range of the function?

6. Draw a graph of a constant function.

■ **Vertical-Line Test**

In Exercises 7 to 12, use the vertical-line test to determine whether the graph is the graph of a function.

7.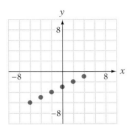

8.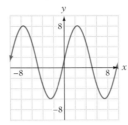

9.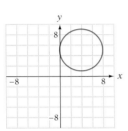

10.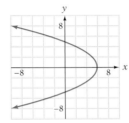

11.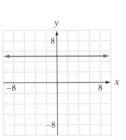

12.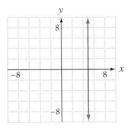

■ **Intercepts**

For Exercises 13 to 24, find the x- and y-intercepts for the graph of the function.

13. $f(x) = 3x + 6$

14. $y(x) = 2x - 5$

15. $h(x) = x^2 - x - 6$

16. $g(x) = x^2 + 3x - 4$

17. $G(x) = 2x^2 + 5x - 3$

18. $H(x) = 2x^2 - 7x + 6$

19. $s(x) = -x^2 + 4x + 5$

20. $F(x) = -x^2 + 4x$

21. $g(x) = x^3 - 4x^2 - 7x + 10$

22. $f(x) = x^3 + 4x^2 - 7x - 10$

23. $P(x) = x^3 - x^2 - 12x$

24. $h(x) = -x^3 - 3x^2 + 4x$

■ Intersections of the Graphs of Two Functions

For Exercises 25 to 36, find the number in the domain of the function for which the output is the given number. If necessary, round to the nearest hundredth.

25. $f(x) = 3x - 4$; 5

26. $g(x) = 2x + 3$; -1

27. $h(x) = -\dfrac{3}{2}x - 4$; -7

28. $s(t) = -\dfrac{3}{4}t + 2$; -1

29. $f(x) = \dfrac{5}{2}x - 2$; 2

30. $v(x) = \dfrac{5}{4}x - 2$; 1

31. $h(t) = 2.1t - 3$; 3.3

32. $g(x) = 3 - 2.4x$; 5.4

33. $f(x) = \dfrac{6}{7}x - 4$; -4

34. $z(x) = 1 - \dfrac{5}{4}x$; 1

35. $f(x) = \dfrac{7}{3}x + 2$; 6

36. $g(x) = -\dfrac{6}{5}x + 3$; -2

For Exercises 37 to 42, find the number in the domain of the function for which the output is the given number. Use a domain of $[-10, 10]$ and a range of $[-10, 10]$.

37. $f(x) = \dfrac{8}{x + 1}$; 2

38. $g(x) = \dfrac{6}{x - 2}$; 3

39. $h(x) = \sqrt{x + 1}$; 3

40. $s(t) = \sqrt{8 - t}$; 2

41. $f(x) = x^3 + 0.5x + 2$; -7

42. $v(s) = s^3 + s - 1$; -3

For Exercises 43 to 54, find the input value for which the two functions have the same value. Verify the results algebraically.

43. $f(x) = 3x - 3$, $g(x) = -2x + 7$

44. $f(x) = -x + 8$, $g(x) = 2x - 1$

45. $f(x) = 2x + 8$, $g(x) = -3x - 2$

46. $f(x) = \dfrac{2}{3}x - 6$, $g(x) = -2x + 2$

47. $f(x) = \dfrac{3}{2}x + 2$, $g(x) = -3x - 7$

48. $f(x) = \dfrac{2x}{5} + 5$, $g(x) = \dfrac{-3x}{2} + 5$

49. $f(x) = 2x - 2$, $g(x) = -2x + 8$

50. $f(x) = \dfrac{3}{4}x$, $g(x) = -2x - 5.5$

51. $f(x) = -2x - 3.25$, $g(x) = 3x + 8.5$

52. $f(x) = -\dfrac{1}{4}x + 4$, $g(x) = \dfrac{7}{4}x + 10$

53. $f(x) = 1.6x - 6$, $g(x) = -2.4x + 2.4$

54. $f(x) = 2.5x + 6$, $g(x) = -1.5x - 3.6$

For Exercises 55 to 58, complete the ordered pairs that belong to the function.

55. Let $h(x) = 4x - 1$.
  a. $(-2, ?)$
  b. $(?, 3)$

56. Let $g(x) = 5 - x$.
  a. $(-4, ?)$
  b. $(?, 6)$

57. Let $F(x) = -\dfrac{x}{3} + 2$.
  a. $(-6, ?)$
  b. $(?, -1)$

58. Let $H(x) = \dfrac{4}{3}x + 7$.
  a. $(-3, ?)$
  b. $(?, -5)$

For Exercises 59 to 69, solve by using a graphing calculator.

59. *Metallurgy*   The amount of gold in an 18-carat gold necklace is given by $Q(w) = 0.75w$, where $Q(w)$ is the number of grams of pure gold in a necklace that weighs w grams. If a necklace contains 33 grams of pure gold, what is the weight of the necklace? Use a domain of $[0, 50]$ and a range of $[0, 40]$.

60. *Investments*   The value of an investment is given by $V(t) = 500 + 3.5t$, where $V(t)$ is the value of the investment, in dollars, after t months. In how many months will the investment be worth \$591? Use a domain of $[0, 30]$ and a range of $[0, 650]$.

This necklace is from Mycenae, a Greek city that flourished around 1500 B.C.

61. *Physics*   The height of a rock that was dropped from a cliff overlooking a ravine is given by $s(t) = 175 - 16t^2$, where $s(t)$ is the height, in feet, of the rock above the ocean t seconds after it is dropped.

  a.   Find the value of t for which $s(t) = 0$. Round to the nearest tenth.
  b.   Write a sentence that explains the meaning of the answer to part a in the context of this problem.

62. *Automotive Technology*   When the driver of a car is presented with a dangerous situation that requires braking, the distance the car will travel before stopping depends on the driver's reaction time and the distance the car travels after the brakes are applied. The distance can be approximated by $d(s) = 0.05s^2 + 1.1s$, where $d(s)$ is the distance, in feet, the car travels before stopping when the car was traveling s miles per hour when the brakes were applied. Find the speed of a car that travels 253 feet after the brakes are applied. Round to the nearest whole number. Use a domain of $[0, 100]$ and a range of $[0, 500]$.

63. *Population Growth*   The population of a city is increasing, and city planners have determined that the population can be modeled by $P(t) = 50 - \dfrac{30}{t + 1}$, where $P(t)$ is the population of the city, in thousands, t years from now. In how many years will the population be 45,000? Use a domain of $[0, 10]$ and a range of $[0, 50]$.

64. *Physics*   The time T, in seconds, it takes a pendulum to make one swing depends on the length of the pendulum and is given by $T(L) = 2\pi\sqrt{\frac{L}{32}}$, where L is the length of the pendulum in feet. How long is a pendulum that takes 1 second to make one swing? Use a domain of $[0, 3]$ and a range of $[0, 3]$. Round to the nearest tenth.

65. *Economics*   For a particular computer game, the number of copies of the game that a company can sell per month depends on the price of the game and is given by $D(p) = \frac{250,000}{80 + 4p}$, where p is the price of the game in dollars and $D(p)$ is the number of games that can be sold per month at that price. At what price can 1500 games be sold per month? Round to the nearest whole number.

66. *Investments*   The value of an investment in t years is given by the function $V(t) = 600 + 48t$, and the value of a second investment in t years is given by $W(t) = 744 + 30t$. In how many years will the two investments have the same value? Use a domain of $[0, 10]$ and a range of $[0, 1200]$.

67. *Sports*   Ramona starts walking along a hiking trail through a nature preserve, and 1 hour later Emily starts along the same trail trying to catch Ramona. The distance Ramona has traveled from the beginning of the trail is given by $g(t) = 3t + 3$, and the distance that Emily has traveled from the beginning of the trail is given by $f(t) = 4.5t$. In each case, t is the number of hours Emily has been walking. The distance each of them has walked is measured in miles. In how many hours will Emily catch up to Ramona? Use a domain of $[0, 4]$ and a range of $[0, 20]$.

68. *Economics*   Suppose that the number of professional digital cameras that will be purchased by consumers each month is given by $n(p) = 8800 - 100p$, where $n(p)$ is the number of cameras that consumers will purchase at a selling price of p dollars. A company that manufactures digital cameras, however, is willing to manufacture the cameras only if the selling price is high enough to earn a profit. Suppose that the number of cameras a company is willing to produce each month is given by $c(p) = 10p$, where $c(p)$ is the number of cameras the manufacturer will produce at a selling price of p dollars. At what price will the number of cameras produced by the manufacturer equal the number of cameras purchased by consumers? Economists call this the *equilibrium price* of the commodity. Use a domain of $[0, 100]$ and a range of $[0, 10\,000]$.

69. *Population Growth*   The population of a certain city t years after the year 2000 can be approximated by $P(t) = 53,000 + 1000t$, and the population of a second city can be approximated by $R(t) = 42,000 + 2000t$. In what year will the populations of the two cities be equal? Use a domain of $[0, 15]$ and a range of $[0, 75\,000]$.

Applying Concepts

In Exercises 25 to 36, you were asked to find the number in the domain of the function for which the output was the given number. Frequently in mathematics, we express directions such as these by using a combination of words and symbols. For instance, in Exercise 25, we could have written "Find the value of a in the domain of $f(x) = 3x - 4$ for which $f(a) = 5$." Recall that $f(a)$ is the output of a function for a given input a. Thus $f(a) = 5$ says the output is 5 for an input of a. We will use this terminology in Exercises 70 to 75.

70. Find the value of a in the domain of $f(x) = 2x + 5$ for which $f(a) = -3$.

71. Find the value of a in the domain of $g(x) = -2x - 1$ for which $g(a) = -5$.

72. Find the value of a in the domain of $h(x) = \dfrac{3}{2}x - 2$ for which $h(a) = 4$.

73. Find the value of a in the domain of $F(x) = -\dfrac{5}{4}x - 1$ for which $F(a) = 9$.

74. For $f(x) = x^3 - 4x - 1$, how many different values, a, in the domain of f satisfy the condition that $f(a) = 1$? (You do not have to find the values; just determine number of possible values for a.)

75. For $f(x) = 0.01(x^4 - 49x^2 + 36x + 252)$, how many different values, a, in the domain of f satisfy the condition that $f(a) = 1$? (You do not have to find the values; just determine number of possible values for a.)

In Exercises 76 to 79, find two numbers in the domain of the functions for which the values of the functions are equal. *Hint:* Apply the method of finding the point of intersection of two graphs twice, once to each point of intersection.

76. $f(x) = x^2 + 4x - 1, g(x) = 3x + 5$

77. $f(x) = x^2 - x - 1, g(x) = -3x + 2$

78. $f(x) = 2x - 7, g(x) = x^2 - 4x - 2$

79. $f(x) = x + 4, g(x) = x^2 + 3x - 4$

EXPLORATION

1. *Calculator Viewing Windows*   A graphing calculator screen consists of **pixels,**[2] which are small rectangles of light that can be turned on or off. When a calculator draws the graph of an equation, it is turning on the pixels that represent the ordered-pair solutions of the equation. The jagged appearance of the graph is a consequence of the solutions being approximations; the pixel nearest the ordered pair is turned on.

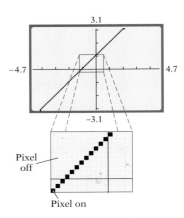

[2] Digital cameras are rated in pixels; some cameras have over 3 million pixels. A typical graphing calculator has just over 5800 pixels. Because of this, the graphs on these screens are not so sharp as an image in a digital camera.

Recall that Δ can be read "the change in." For a Texas Instruments TI-83 or TI-83 Plus, there are 94 horizontal pixels. Accordingly, the change in x, Δx, each time the left arrow key is pressed in TRACE mode is calculated by the formula

$$\Delta x = \frac{\text{Xmax} - \text{Xmin}}{94} \qquad \bullet \text{ Formula 1}$$

For the decimal viewing window, Xmin $= -4.7$ and Xmax $= 4.7$. Therefore,

$$\Delta x = \frac{\text{Xmax} - \text{Xmin}}{94}$$

$$= \frac{4.7 - (-4.7)}{94} = \frac{9.4}{94}$$

$$= 0.1$$

Thus each time the left or right arrow key is pressed, the value of x changes by 0.1.

The formula for Δx can be rewritten so that you can create a viewing window with your choice for Δx and for Xmin. This formula is

$$\textbf{Xmax = Xmin + 94}(\Delta x) \qquad \bullet \text{ Formula 2}$$

For instance, if we want to begin the graph with Xmin $= -20$ and have $\Delta x = 0.5$, then

$$\text{Xmax} = \text{Xmin} + 94(\Delta x)$$

$$= -20 + 94(0.5) = -20 + 47$$

$$= 27$$

Choosing Xmin $= -20$ and Xmax $= 27$ will result in a viewing window in which x will change by 0.5 each time the left or right arrow key is pressed when the calculator is in TRACE mode.

a. Using Formula 1, determine the change in x each time the left or right arrow key is pressed when the calculator uses the standard viewing window. Draw the graph of $y = 2x + 1$ in the standard viewing window and verify your answer.

b. Using Formula 1, verify that $\Delta x = 1$ for the integer viewing window.

c. Using Formula 2, create a viewing window for which Xmin $= -10$ and $\Delta x = 0.25$.

CHAPTER **2** *SUMMARY*

Key Terms

abscissa [p. 97]
axes [p. 97]
constant function [p. 125]
coordinates [p. 97]
coordinate axes [p. 97]
dependent variable [p. 99]
domain [p. 126]
equation in two variables [p. 98]
evaluating a function [p. 121]
first coordinate [p. 98]
function [p. 119]
functional notation [p. 121]
graph of an equation [p. 103]
graph of a function [p. 123]
graph of an ordered pair [p. 97]
graph a point [p. 97]
independent variable [p. 99]
input/output table [p. 99]
intercepts [p. 139]
linear equation in two variables [p. 103]
ordered pair [p. 97]
ordinate [p. 97]

origin [p. 97]
pixel [p. 151]
plot a point [p. 97]
quadrants [p. 97]
range [p. 126]
rectangular coordinate system [p. 97]
relation [p. 118]
second coordinate [p. 98]
solution of an equation in two variables [p. 98]
standard viewing window [p. 104]
value of a function [p. 121]
viewing window [p. 104]
x-axis [p. 97]
x-coordinate [p. 97]
x-intercept [p. 139]
xy-plane [p. 97]
y-axis [p. 97]
y-coordinate [p. 97]
y-intercept [p. 139]
zero of a function [p. 140]

Essential Concepts

Vertical-Line Test for the Graph of a Function [p. 138]
A graph defines a function if any vertical line intersects the graph at no more than one point.

Graphing Calculator Techniques
Creating an input/output table [Appendix A: Table]
Adjusting the viewing window [Appendix A: Window]
Using the TRACE feature [Appendix A: Trace]
Evaluating a function [Appendix A: Evaluating Functions]
Finding the x-intercepts of a graph [Appendix A: Zero]
Finding the point of intersection of the graphs of two functions [Appendix A: Intersect]
Graphing a function [Appendix A: Graph]

CHAPTER **2** *REVIEW EXERCISES*

1. Without using a calculator, create an input/output table for $y = \frac{1}{2}x - 3$ for $x = -6, -4, -2, 0, 2$ and 4. Check your results using a graphing calculator. Graph the resulting ordered pairs.

2. Without using a calculator, create an input/output table for the equation $y = x^2 + x - 3$ for $x = -3, -2, -1, 0, 1, 2$ and 3. Check your results using a graphing calculator. Graph the resulting ordered pairs.

3. Complete the input/output table for $y = -\frac{1}{3}x + 2$ and graph the equation without using a calculator. Then use a calculator to verify the table and graph.

x	-9	-6	-3	0	3
y					

For Exercises 4 and 5, graph the equation in the integer viewing window. Then trace along the graph to find the requested values.

4. Let $y = -\frac{4}{5}x - 3$.

   a. Find y when $x = 5$.
   b. Find x when $y = 1$.

5. Let $y = \frac{5}{3}x - 1$.

   a. Find y when $x = 3$.
   b. Find x when $y = -6$.

6. Find the domain and range of the relation $\{(-1, -1), (0, 1), (1, 3), (2, 5), (3, 3), (4, 1)\}$. Is the relation a function?

7. Find the range of $h(t) = -2t^2 + 5$ given the domain $\{-4, -3, -2, -1, 0, 1, 2, 3, 4\}$.

For Exercises 8 and 9, determine which numbers, if any, must be excluded from the domain of the function.

8. $F(x) = \dfrac{2x - 4}{x + 2}$, $x = -2, 0, 2$

9. $G(x) = \dfrac{x}{x^2 - 9}$, $x = -3, 0, 3$

For Exercises 10 to 12, complete the input/output table, and graph the function without using a calculator. Check your answer by using a graphing calculator.

10. $f(x) = -2x + 3$

x	-3	-2	-1	0	1
y					

11. $f(x) = -x^2 + 4x - 1$

x	-1	0	1	2	3	4	5
y							

12. $f(x) = -4$

x	-2	-1	0	1	2
y					

For Exercises 13 and 14, graph the function in the integer viewing window. Then use the TRACE feature to find the x-coordinate for the given y-coordinate. Check your work by evaluating the function at the x-coordinate.

13. $f(x) = -\dfrac{5}{4}x + 5; y = -15$

14. $g(x) = 3 - \dfrac{9}{5}x; y = 21$

For Exercises 15 and 16, graph the function in the standard viewing window. Then use the TRACE feature to evaluate the function. Verify the results algebraically.

15. $f(x) = -x^3 - 4x^2 + 2; f(-3)$

16. $F(x) = x^3 - x^2 + 2x - 2; F(-1.5)$

For Exercises 17 and 18, graph the function in the decimal viewing window. Trace along the curve to find a number that is not in the domain of the function.

17. $G(x) = \dfrac{-2}{x + 1}$

18. $F(x) = \dfrac{x}{2x - 4}$

19. Use the vertical-line test to determine whether the graph at the right is the graph of a function.

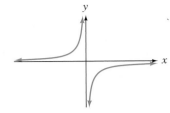

For Exercises 20 and 21, find the x- and y-intercepts of the graph of the function.

20. $F(x) = \dfrac{1}{2}x - 3$

21. $H(x) = x^2 + 2x - 8$

22. Find the number in the domain of $f(x) = \frac{1}{2}x - 3$ for which the output is $-\frac{5}{4}$.

23. Find the number in the domain of $f(x) = -2x + 4$ and $g(x) = \frac{3}{2}x + 11$ for which the values of the functions are equal. Verify the results algebraically.

24. The height of a plane leaving an airport can be given by $h(t) = 75t + 300$, where $h(t)$ is the height, in feet, of the plane above sea level t minutes after it takes off.

   a. In how many minutes will the plane be 750 feet above sea level? Use a domain of $[0, 10]$ and a range of $[0, 1000]$.

   b. What is the height of the airport above sea level?

25. The value, in dollars, of two investments can be given by $V(x) = 400 + 24x$ and $W(x) = 350 + 34x$, where x is the number of years after 2000. In what year will the values of the two investments be equal? Use a domain of $[0, 20]$ and a range of $[0, 1000]$.

CHAPTER **2** TEST

1. Without using a calculator, create an input/output table for the equation $y = -x^2 + 4x + 5$ for $x = -2, -1, 0, 1, 2, 3, 4, 5,$ and 6. Graph the resulting ordered pairs.

2. Complete the input/output table for $f(x) = \frac{2}{3}x - 2$ and then graph the equation.

x	-6	-3	0	3	6	9
y						

3. Graph $y = -\frac{5}{2}x + 4$ in the integer viewing window. Then find the value of x for which $y = -6$.

4. Find the domain and range of the relation $\{(-4, -2), (-2, -1), (0, 0), (2, -1), (4, -2)\}$. Is the relation a function?

5. Given $P(x) = x^2 - 3x - 1$ with domain $\{-2, -1, 0, 1, 2, 3\}$, find the range of P.

6. For $f(x) = \frac{2x + 4}{x - 2}$, which of the following numbers, if any, are *not* in the domain of f?
   a. -2 **b.** 0 **c.** 2

For Exercises 7 and 8, complete the input/output table and graph the function.

7. $f(x) = -\frac{3}{2}x + 4$

x	-2	0	2	4	6
y					

8. $f(x) = -x^2 - 2x + 3$

x	-4	-3	-2	-1	0	1	2
y							

For Exercises 9 and 10, graph the function in the integer viewing window. Then use the TRACE feature to find the x-coordinate for the given y-coordinate. Check your work by evaluating the function at the x-coordinate.

9. $f(x) = -\frac{4}{3}x + 3$ when $y = 11$.

10. $g(x) = \frac{x}{2} - 5$ when $y = -11$.

11. Graph $f(x) = \frac{-2x}{x^2 - 9}$ in the decimal viewing window. Trace along the curve to find two numbers that are *not* in the domain of the function.

12. Draw a graph that is not the graph of a function.

For Exercises 13 and 14, find the x- and y-intercepts of the graph of the function.

13. $G(x) = 3 + \frac{3}{4}x$

14. $p(x) = x^2 - 2x - 3$

15. Find the number in the domain of $f(x) = 2 + \frac{5}{4}x$ for which the output is -3.

16. Find the number in the domain of $f(x) = -\frac{5}{2}x + 4$ and $g(x) = \frac{3}{4}x - 9$ for which the values of the functions are equal. Verify the results algebraically.

17. The percent concentration, P, of acid in a solution depends on the number of grams x of acid that is added to the solution and is given by $P(x) = \frac{100x + 100}{x + 5}$, where x is the number of grams of acid that is added.
   a. What is the percent concentration of acid after an additional 3 grams of acid is added to the solution?
   b. What is the original percent concentration?

18. The height of a roller coaster car above the ground as it is pulled to the highest point on the track is given by $H(t) = 2t + 40$, where $H(t)$ is the height of the car, in feet, after t seconds. In how many seconds will the car be 110 feet above the ground? Use a domain of $[0, 60]$ and a range of $[0, 200]$.

19. The height of a rock that was dropped from a cliff overlooking the ocean is given by $s(t) = 150 - 16t^2$, where $s(t)$ is the height, in feet, of the rock above the ocean t seconds after it is dropped. Find the value of t for which $s(t) = 0$. Round to the nearest tenth.

20. Because of changing economic conditions in two cities, Bradford and Candlewood, the populations of the cities are changing. The population of Bradford is given by $B(t) = 750t + 25{,}000$, and the population of Candlewood is given by $C(t) = 31{,}250 - 500t$, where t is the number of years after 2002. In which year will the two cities have the same population? Use a domain of $[0, 8]$ and a range of $[0, 32\,000]$.

◀ CUMULATIVE REVIEW EXERCISES

1. Write $[-2, 3]$ in set-builder notation.

2. True or false: If $x \in A \cap B$, then $x \in A$.

3. Evaluate: $2 \cdot 3^2 - 4^3 \div (2 - 6)$

4. Evaluate $-a^3b - 4ab^2$ when $a = -2$ and $b = 4$.

5. Evaluate $3a + 2b - c^2$ when $a = \frac{5}{6}$, $b = -\frac{2}{3}$, and $c = -\frac{3}{2}$.

6. Simplify: $3 - 5(2a - 7)$

7. $3(a + b) = (a + b)3$ is an example of what Property of Real Numbers?

8. Complete the following input/output table for $y = \frac{3}{2}x - 3$ and then graph the ordered pairs.

x	-4	-2	0	2	4	6
y						

9. Federal government emission standards limit the grams of nitrous oxides (NO_x) that can be emitted from the exhaust of a car. The number of grams, g, of NO_x emitted into the atmosphere from the exhaust of a certain car is given by $g = 0.4m$, where m is the number of miles the car is driven.

    a. Complete the input/output table below.

Input, distance driven m (in miles)	0	100	150	200	250	300	350
Output, NO_x g (in grams)							

    b. Write a sentence that explains the meaning of the ordered pair $(150, 60)$.

10. Graph $y = 2 - \dfrac{x}{2}$.

11. Graph $f(x) = -\dfrac{2}{3}x$.

12. Complete the input/output table for $f(x) = x^2 - 6x + 1$ and then graph the function.

x	-1	0	1	2	3	4	5
y							

13. Complete the input/output table for $f(x) = -x^2 - 2x + 1$ and then graph the function.

x	-4	-3	-2	-1	0	1	2
y							

14. Graph $y = \frac{4}{3}x - 2$ in the integer viewing window. Then trace along the curve to find x when $y = -14$.

15. Find the number in the domain of $f(x) = -\frac{3}{2}x + 3$ for which the output is -3.

16. For $g(x) = \frac{x + 3}{x - 2}$, which of the following numbers, if any, are *not* in the domain of g?

    a. -3 **b.** 2 **c.** -4

17. Find the x- and y-intercepts for the graph of $f(x) = x^2 + 2x - 3$.

18. Find the input value for which the values of $f(x) = 3x - 4$ and $g(x) = -x + 4$ are equal.

19. A biologist introduces a toxin into a culture of bacteria that causes the number of bacteria in the culture to decrease according to the population model $P(t) = \frac{20}{t + 2}$, where $P(t)$ is the number of bacteria, in thousands, t minutes after the toxin is introduced. In how many minutes will the population be 2000? Use a domain of $[0, 10]$ and a range of $[0, 20]$.

20. According to a certain demographic study, the population of the city of Goldcreek can be approximated by $G(n) = 0.75n + 8$, and the population of the city of Walnut Grove can be approximated by $W(n) = -0.5n + 13$, where the populations are in thousands and n is the number of years after the year 2000. In what year will the populations of the two cities be equal?

CHAPTER

3

First-Degree Equations and Inequalities

3.1 Solving First-Degree Equations

3.2 Applications of First-Degree Equations

3.3 Applications to Geometry

3.4 Inequalities in One Variable

3.5 Absolute Value Equalities and Inequalities

```
TEST  LOGIC
1: =
2: ≠
3: >
4: ≥
5: <
6: ≤
```

Press **2nd** TEST to access the inequality symbols in the TEST menu.

Making decisions is a part of life, and having a good under-standing of the alternatives makes deciding between options much easier. For example, choosing which of two cell phone plans will be more economical may be easier if you know how many minutes you will use the phone each month. With that information, you can determine the "better deal" by writing and solving an inequality, such as the one required to solve ***Exercise 54 on page 214.***

Need help? For online student resources, visit this web site:
Math.college.hmco.com

161

PREP TEST

For Exercises 1 to 4, add, subtract, multiply, or divide.

1. $8 - 12$

2. $-9 + 3$

3. $\dfrac{-18}{-6}$

4. $-\dfrac{3}{4}\left(-\dfrac{4}{3}\right)$

5. Simplify: $3x - 5 + 7x$

6. Simplify: $8x - 9 - 8x$

7. Simplify: $6x - 3(6 - x)$

8. Evaluate: $|-8|$

9. Twenty ounces of a snack mixture contains nuts and pretzels. Let n represents the number of ounces of nuts in the mixture. Express the number of ounces of pretzels in the mixture in terms of n.

GO FIGURE

A pair of perpendicular lines are drawn through the interior of a rectangle, dividing it into four smaller rectangles. The areas of the smaller rectangles are x, 2, 3, and 6. Find the possible values of x.

SECTION **3.1**

- Introduction to Solving Equations
- Solve Equations Using the Addition and Multiplication Properties
- Equations Containing Parentheses

Solving First-Degree Equations

■ Introduction to Solving Equations

When the National Weather Service identifies a hurricane building up over the ocean, it tries to predict when the hurricane will reach land. Meteorologists do this by determining the direction and speed of the hurricane.

Suppose the National Weather Service locates at 9:00 A.M. a hurricane that is 150 miles from land and moving at a constant speed of 25 mph toward land. Then the distance d, in miles, that the hurricane is from land can be given by $d = 150 - 25t$, where t is the time in hours since 9:00 A.M. If the Weather Service wants to give a warning to residents along the coast when the hurricane is 100 miles from land, then they must find the input value for t that results in an output of 100 ($d = 100$).

$$d = 150 - 25t$$
$$100 = 150 - 25t \quad \bullet \text{ We want an input value of } t \text{ for which } d = 100.$$

CALCULATOR NOTE

The independent variable is t, which is input as X, and the dependent variable is d, which is Y_1. We are using a domain of $[0, 6]$ and a range of $[0, 150]$.

   See Appendix A: Intersect

This value of t can be found using a graphing calculator and its INTERSECT feature. Here are some typical screens.

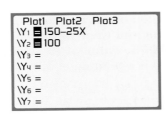

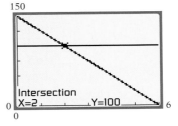

An input value of 2 results in an output value of 100. We can check this algebraically.

$$d = 150 - 25t$$
$$d = 150 - 25(2) \qquad \bullet \text{ Replace } t \text{ with 2.}$$
$$d = 150 - 50$$
$$d = 100 \qquad\qquad \bullet \text{ The input value 2 results in an output value of 100.}$$

The Weather Service should give a warning 2 hours after 9:00 A.M., or at 11:00 A.M.

Now suppose the Weather Service wants to issue another warning when the hurricane is 50 miles from land. The procedure above is repeated with $d = 50$. In this case, we want to find the input value of t that results in d equal to 50.

$$d = 150 - 25t$$
$$50 = 150 - 25t$$

Although saying we need to find the value of t that results in d equal to 50 is fine, this wording is usually rephrased as "Solve the equation $50 = 150 - 25t$ for t." Up to this point, we have accomplished this graphically. We will now begin an algebraic study of solving equations.

An **equation** expresses the equality of two mathematical expressions. The expressions can be either numerical or variable expressions. For the equation $50 = 150 - 25t$, the numerical expression 50 equals the variable expression $150 - 25t$. The expression to the left of the equals sign is the **left side of the equation,** and the expression to the right of the equals sign is the **right side of the equation.**

The equation $x + 3 = 8$ at the right is a **conditional equation.** The equation is true if the variable is replaced by 5. The equation is false if the variable is replaced by 4.

$$x + 3 = 8$$
$$5 + 3 = 8 \qquad \text{A true equation}$$
$$4 + 3 = 8 \qquad \text{A false equation}$$

The replacement values of the variable that will make an equation true are called the **roots,** or **solutions,** of the equation. The solution of the equation $x + 3 = 8$ is 5.

An **identity** is an equation for which any replacement for the variable will result in a true equation. For instance, the equation $2x = x + x$ is an identity.

Some equations have no solutions. For instance, the equation $n = n + 1$ has no solution. There is no number n that is equal to one more than itself.

Given a value for a variable, it is always possible to determine whether that value is a solution of an equation. **Replace the given value of the variable in the equation and then simplify. If the left and right sides of the equation are equal, the value of the variable is a solution of the equation.** As shown below, 4 is a solution of $50 = 150 - 25t$.

$$50 = 150 - 25t$$

50	$150 - 25(4)$	• Replace t by 4.
50	$150 - 100$	• Simplify.
$50 = 50$		• The left and right sides are equal.

Because the left and right sides of the equation are equal when $t = 4$, 4 is a solution of the equation. Four hours after 9:00 A.M. is 1:00 P.M., the time at which the hurricane will be 50 miles from land.

The equation $50 = 150 - 25t$ is a **first-degree equation in one variable.** It is called a first-degree equation because the exponent on the variable is 1. Several other examples of first-degree equations are given at the right.

$$2x - 7 = 15$$
$$3 - 4y = 8y + 1$$
$$6z = 2$$
$$3a - 2(4a + 1) = 7a$$

? QUESTION   Which of the following are first-degree equations?

    a. $5 = 3n + 7$ **b.** $6z^2 + 1 = 7$ **c.** $x = 4$ **d.** $x^3 = 8$

Solving an equation means finding a solution of the equation. The simplest equation to solve is an equation of the form *variable = constant* because the constant is the solution. If $x = 3$, then 3 is the solution of the equation because $3 = 3$ is a true equation. When solving an equation, the goal is to rewrite the given equation in the form

$$variable = constant$$

The Addition Property of Equations can be used to rewrite an equation in this form.

> **The Addition Property of Equations**
>
> If a, b, and c are algebraic expressions, then the equation $a = b$ has the same solutions as the equation $a + c = b + c$.

The Addition Property of Equations states that the same quantity can be added to each side of an equation without changing the solution of the equa-

---

? ANSWER   The equations in parts a and c are first-degree equations; the variable has an exponent of 1. The equations in parts b and d are not first-degree equations. In part b, the exponent on the variable is 2; in part d, the exponent on the variable is 3.

tion. **This property is used to remove a *term* from one side of the equation by adding the opposite of that term to each side of the equation.**

Note the effect of adding, to each side of the equation $x + 6 = 9$, the *opposite of the constant term* 6. After each side of the equation is simplified, the equation is in the form *variable = constant*. The solution is the constant.

$$x + 6 = 9$$
$$x + 6 + (-6) = 9 + (-6)$$
$$x + 0 = 3$$
$$x = 3$$
$$variable = constant$$

Because subtraction is defined in terms of addition, the Addition Property of Equations makes it possible to subtract the same number from each side of an equation without changing the solution of the equation.

➡ Solve: $y + \dfrac{3}{4} = \dfrac{2}{3}$

The goal is to write the equation in the form *variable = constant*.

Add the opposite of the constant term $\frac{3}{4}$ to each side of the equation. This is equivalent to subtracting $\frac{3}{4}$ from each side of the equation. After simplifying, the equation is in the form *variable = constant*.

$$y + \dfrac{3}{4} = \dfrac{2}{3}$$
$$y + \dfrac{3}{4} - \dfrac{3}{4} = \dfrac{2}{3} - \dfrac{3}{4}$$
$$y + 0 = \dfrac{8}{12} - \dfrac{9}{12}$$
$$y = -\dfrac{1}{12}$$

The solution is $-\dfrac{1}{12}$. ⬅

The goal of solving an equation can also be to write the equation as *constant = variable*. This is shown in Example 1.

TAKE NOTE

You should always check your solutions to an equation.

$$y + \dfrac{3}{4} = \dfrac{2}{3}$$

$$-\dfrac{1}{12} + \dfrac{3}{4} \ \Big|\ \dfrac{2}{3}$$

$$-\dfrac{1}{12} + \dfrac{9}{12} \ \Big|\ \dfrac{2}{3}$$

$$\dfrac{8}{12} \ \Big|\ \dfrac{2}{3}$$

$$\dfrac{2}{3} = \dfrac{2}{3}$$

A true equation

EXAMPLE 1

Solve: $7 = x + 9$

Solution

$$7 = x + 9$$
$$7 - 9 = x + 9 - 9 \qquad \bullet \text{ Subtract 9 from each side of the equation.}$$
$$-2 = x \qquad\qquad \bullet \text{ The equation is in the form } constant = variable.$$

The solution is -2.

TAKE NOTE

You should always check your work. Here is the check for Example 1.

$$7 = x + 9$$
$$\dfrac{7 \ \Big|\ -2 + 9}{7 = 7 \ \checkmark}$$

YOU TRY IT 1

Solve: $9 + n = 4$

Solution See page S9.

The Multiplication Property of Equations is also used to rewrite an equation in the form *variable = constant*.

The Multiplication Property of Equations

If a, b, and c are algebraic expressions, and $c \neq 0$, then the equation $a = b$ has the same solutions as the equation $ac = bc$.

The Multiplication Property of Equations states that we can multiply each side of an equation by the same nonzero number without changing the solutions of the equation. **This property is used to rewrite an equation so that the *coefficient* on the variable is 1. This is accomplished by multiplying each side of the equation by the reciprocal of the coefficient.**

➡ Solve: $\dfrac{2}{3}t = -\dfrac{1}{6}$

Note the effect of multiplying each side of the equation by $\dfrac{3}{2}$, the reciprocal of $\dfrac{2}{3}$.

$$\dfrac{2}{3}t = -\dfrac{1}{6}$$

$$\dfrac{3}{2}\left(\dfrac{2}{3}t\right) = \dfrac{3}{2}\left(-\dfrac{1}{6}\right)$$

$$1 \cdot t = -\dfrac{3}{12}$$

After simplifying, the equation is in the form *variable = constant*.

$$t = -\dfrac{1}{4}$$

Remember to check your solution.

The solution is $-\dfrac{1}{4}$. ⬅

Because division is defined in terms of multiplication, the Multiplication Property of Equations enables us to divide each side of an equation by the same nonzero number without changing the solution of the equation.

➡ Solve: $6x = -12$

Multiply each side of the equation by the reciprocal of 6. This is equivalent to dividing each side of the equation by 6.

$$6x = -12$$

$$\dfrac{6x}{6} = \dfrac{-12}{6}$$

After simplifying, the equation is in the form *variable = constant*.

$$x = -2$$

Remember to check your solution.

The solution is -2. ⬅

EXAMPLE 2

Solve: $18 = -12z$

TAKE NOTE

Here is a check for
Example 2.

$$18 = -12z$$

$$18 \;\Big|\; -12\left(-\frac{3}{2}\right)$$

$$18 = 18 \;\; \surd$$

Solution $18 = -12z$

$$\frac{18}{-12} = \frac{-12z}{-12}$$ • Divide each side of the equation by -12.

$$-\frac{3}{2} = z$$ • Write the answer in simplest form.

The solution is $-\dfrac{3}{2}$.

YOU TRY IT 2

Solve: $-4x = -20$

Solution   See page S9.

■ Solve Equations Using the Addition and Multiplication Properties

In the next example, we will apply both the Addition and the Multiplication Properties of Equations.

TAKE NOTE

The goal is to isolate the variable so that the equation can be written in the form *variable = constant*.

EXAMPLE 3

Solve: $8 = 6r + 4$

Solution $8 = 6r + 4$

$$8 - 4 = 6r + 4 - 4$$ • Subtract 4 from each side of the equation.

$$4 = 6r$$ • Simplify.

$$\frac{4}{6} = \frac{6r}{6}$$ • Divide each side of the equation by 6.

$$\frac{2}{3} = r$$ • Write the answer in simplest form.

The solution is $\dfrac{2}{3}$.

 CALCULATOR NOTE

The decimal approximation given at the right can be converted to a fraction.

 See Appendix A:
Math

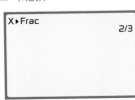

Graphical check:

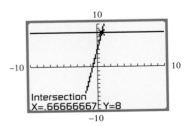

YOU TRY IT 3

Solve: $5 - 4z = 15$

Solution   See page S9.

Now consider an equation such as $2x + 5 = 4x - 1$. The solution of this equation is the value of x that results in the left side and the right side of the equation being equal. That is, we are trying to find the input value x so that the outputs of the functions $f(x) = 2x + 5$ and $g(x) = 4x - 1$ are equal.

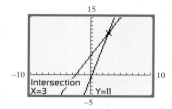

Plot1 Plot2 Plot3
\Y₁ ▪ 2X+5
\Y₂ ▪ 4X−1
\Y₃ =
\Y₄ =
\Y₅ =
\Y₆ =
\Y₇ =

X	Y₁	Y₂
0	5	−1
1	7	3
2	9	7
3	11	11
4	13	15
5	15	19
6	17	23
X=3		

From the table and graph above, note that when $x = 3$, $Y_1 = Y_2$. The solution of $2x + 5 = 4x - 1$ is 3.

The equation $2x + 5 = 4x - 1$ can be solved by using the Addition and Multiplication Properties of Equations.

$$2x + 5 = 4x - 1$$
$$2x - 4x + 5 = 4x - 4x - 1 \qquad \text{• Subtract } 4x \text{ from each side of the equation.}$$
$$-2x + 5 = -1 \qquad \text{• Simplify.}$$
$$-2x + 5 - 5 = -1 - 5 \qquad \text{• Subtract 5 from each side of the equation.}$$
$$-2x = -6 \qquad \text{• Simplify.}$$
$$\frac{-2x}{-2} = \frac{-6}{-2} \qquad \text{• Divide each side of the equation by } -2.$$
$$x = 3 \qquad \text{• Simplify.}$$

The solution is 3. This algebraic solution confirms that the solution that we obtained from the table and graph is correct.

EXAMPLE 4

Solve: $2x + 5 = 5x - 1 - 7x$

Solution $2x + 5 = 5x - 1 - 7x$

$$2x + 5 = -2x - 1 \qquad \text{• Combine like terms.}$$
$$2x + 2x + 5 = -2x + 2x - 1 \qquad \text{• Add } 2x \text{ to each side of the equation.}$$
$$4x + 5 = -1 \qquad \text{• Simplify.}$$
$$4x + 5 - 5 = -1 - 5 \qquad \text{• Subtract 5 from each side of the equation.}$$
$$4x = -6 \qquad \text{• Simplify.}$$
$$\frac{4x}{4} = \frac{-6}{4} \qquad \text{• Divide each side of the equation by 4.}$$
$$x = -\frac{3}{2} \qquad \text{• Simplify.}$$

The solution is $-\dfrac{3}{2}$.

CALCULATOR NOTE

We entered $-2x - 1$ for Y_2

after simplifying $5x - 1 - 7x$.

Graphical check:

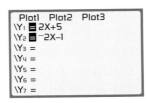

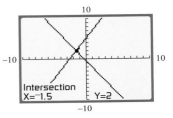

The solution is given as the decimal equivalent of $-\dfrac{3}{2}$.

YOU TRY IT 4

Solve: $6y - 3 + y = 2y + 7$

Solution   See page S9.

■ **Equations Containing Parentheses**

For an equation containing parentheses, the Distributive Property is used to remove the parentheses.

➡ Solve: $3 - x = 3 - 5(2x - 6)$

$$3 - x = 3 - 5(2x - 6)$$

$$3 - x = 3 - 10x + 30 \qquad \bullet \text{ Use the Distributive Property.}$$

$$3 - x = 33 - 10x \qquad \bullet \text{ Add like terms on the right side of the equation.}$$

$$3 - x + 10x = 33 - 10x + 10x \qquad \bullet \text{ Add } 10x \text{ to each side of the equation.}$$

$$3 + 9x = 33 \qquad \bullet \text{ Simplify.}$$

$$3 - 3 + 9x = 33 - 3 \qquad \bullet \text{ Subtract 3 from each side of the equation.}$$

$$9x = 30 \qquad \bullet \text{ Simplify.}$$

$$\frac{9x}{9} = \frac{30}{9} \qquad \bullet \text{ Divide each side of the equation by 9.}$$

$$x = \frac{10}{3} \qquad \bullet \text{ Write the answer in simplest form.}$$

The solution is $\dfrac{10}{3}$. $\bullet$ Remember to check the solution.   ⬅

This example illustrates the steps used to solve a first-degree equation.

Steps in Solving First-Degree Equations
1. Use the Distributive Property to remove parentheses.
2. Combine like terms on each side of the equation.
3. Rewrite the equation with only one variable term.
4. Rewrite the equation with only one constant term.
5. Rewrite the equation so that the coefficient of the variable is 1.

EXAMPLE 5

Solve: $3 - 2(3x - 1) = 1 - 2x$

Solution

$$3 - 2(3x - 1) = 1 - 2x$$

$$3 - 6x + 2 = 1 - 2x \qquad \bullet \text{ Use the Distributive Property.}$$

$$5 - 6x = 1 - 2x \qquad \bullet \text{ Simplify.}$$

$$5 - 6x + 2x = 1 - 2x + 2x \qquad \bullet \text{ Add } 2x \text{ to each side of the equation.}$$

$$5 - 4x = 1 \qquad \bullet \text{ Simplify.}$$

$$5 - 5 - 4x = 1 - 5 \qquad \bullet \text{ Subtract 5 from each side of the equation.}$$

$$-4x = -4 \qquad \bullet \text{ Simplify.}$$

$$\frac{-4x}{-4} = \frac{-4}{-4} \qquad \bullet \text{ Divide each side of the equation by } -4.$$

$$x = 1$$

The solution is 1.

Graphical check:

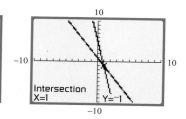

The solution checks.

TAKE NOTE

In Example 4, we simplified the expression on the right side of the equation before entering it. For Example 5, we did not simplify first. You may use either method.

YOU TRY IT 5

Solve: $2(3x + 1) = 4x + 8$

Solution See page S9.

3.1 EXERCISES

Topics For Discussion

1. How does an equation differ from an expression?

2. What is the solution of an equation?

3. Explain the difference between solving an equation and simplifying an expression.

4. The solution of the equation $2x + 3 = 3$ is 0 and the equation $x = x + 1$ has no solution. Is there a difference between zero as a solution and no solution?

5. What is the Addition Property of Equations? When is it used?

6. What is the Multiplication Property of Equations? When is it used?

■ Introduction to Solving Equations

Solve.

7. $x - 2 = 7$

8. $a + 3 = -7$

9. $3x = 12$

10. $18 = 2a$

11. $\dfrac{2}{3}y = 5$

12. $-\dfrac{5}{8}x = \dfrac{4}{5}$

13. $-\dfrac{3}{5} = \dfrac{3b}{10}$

14. $\dfrac{2}{3}y = 5$

15. $0.25x = 1.2$

16. $-0.03z = 0.6$

17. $12 = 3x + 5x$

18. $4t - 7t = 0$

■ Solve Equations Using the Addition and Multiplication Properties

Solve.

19. $3x + 8 = 17$

20. $2 + 5a = 12$

21. $5 = 3x - 10$

22. $4 = 3 - 5x$

23. $\frac{2}{3}x + 5 = 3$

24. $-\frac{1}{2}x + 4 = 1$

25. $2x + 2 = 3x + 5$

26. $2 - 3t = 3t - 4$

27. $3b - 2b = 4 - 2b$

28. $\frac{1}{3} - 2b = 3$

29. $d + \frac{1}{5}d = 2$

30. $\frac{5}{8}z - 3 = 12$

■ Equations Containing Parentheses

Solve.

31. $4(x - 5) = 8$

32. $3(x - 2) = 21$

33. $5 - 2(2x + 3) = 11$

34. $2 + 3(x - 5) = 20$

35. $5(2 - b) = -3(b - 3)$

36. $3 = 2 - 5(3y - 2)$

37. $4 - 3x = 7x - 2(3 - x)$

38. $-3x - 2(4 + 5x) = 14 - 3(2x - 3)$

39. $3y = 2[5 - 3(2 - y)]$

40. $2[3 - 2(z + 4)] = 3(4 - z)$

41. $3[x - (2 - x) - 2x] = 3(4 - x)$

42. $2 + 3[1 - 2(x + 3)] = -7(x + 1)$

Applying Concepts

43. If $3x - 5 = 9x + 4$, evaluate $6x - 3$.

44. If $8 - 2(4x - 1) = 3x - 12$, evaluate $x^4 - x^2$.

45. Solve: $2[3(x + 4) - 2(x + 1)] = 5x + 3(1 - x)$

Solve.

46. $8 \div \dfrac{1}{x} = 3$

47. $\dfrac{1}{\dfrac{1}{x}} = 9$

48. $\dfrac{6}{\dfrac{7}{a}} = -18$

49. $\dfrac{10}{\dfrac{3}{x}} - 5 = 4x$

50. *Sports* The speed v, in feet per second, of a foul tip that goes directly upward is given by $v = 100 - 32t$, where t is the number of seconds after the ball is hit. How many seconds after the ball is released will its speed be 8 feet per second?

51. *Monthly Income* A sales executive for a software company can choose between two different equations that will determine the executive's monthly income, $I = 0.05x + 2500$ or $I = 0.02x + 4000$, where I is the monthly income for selling x dollars worth of software.
   a. For each option, determine the dollar amount the sales executive must sell in order to earn $4500 in one month.
   b. For each option, determine the dollar amount the sales executive must sell in order to earn $5500 in one month.
   c. Determine the dollar amount the sales executive must sell so that the monthly incomes from the two plans are equal.

EXPLORATION

1. *Business Application* Two people decide to open a business reconditioning toner cartridges for copy machines. They rent a building for $7000 per year and estimate that building maintenance, taxes, and insurance will cost $6500 per year. Each person wants to make $12 per hour in the first year and will work 10 hours per day for 260 days of the year. Assume that it costs $28 to restore a cartridge and that they can sell each restored cartridge for $45.
   a. How many cartridges must they restore and sell annually to break even, not including the hourly wage they wish to earn?

   b. How many cartridges must they restore and sell annually just to earn the hourly wage they desire?

   c. Suppose the entrepreneurs are successful in their business and are restoring and selling 25 cartridges each day of the 260 days they are open. What would be their hourly wage for the year?

SECTION **3.2**   **Applications of First-Degree Equations**

■ Value Mixture Problems
■ Uniform Motion Problems

■ Value Mixture Problems

A **value mixture problem** involves combining two ingredients that have different prices into a single blend. For instance, a coffee manufacturer may blend two types of coffee into a single blend.

The solution of a value mixture problem is based on the equation $V = AC$, where V is the value of an ingredient, A is the amount of the ingredient, and C is the cost per unit of the ingredient.

For example, to find the value of 10 pounds of coffee costing $6.60 per pound, use the equation $V = AC$.

$$V = AC$$
$$V = (10)(6.60) \qquad \bullet \ A = 10, C = 6.60$$
$$V = 66$$

The value of the 10 pounds of coffee is $66.

? QUESTION   What is the value of 15 ounces of a silver alloy that costs $8 an ounce?

Now consider the situation of trying to determine how many pounds of peanuts that cost $2.25 per pound should be mixed with 40 pounds of cashews that cost $6.00 per pound to produce a mixture that has a value of $3.50 per pound. We will let x represent the number of pounds of peanuts that are being added to the 40 pounds of cashews. Then, using the equation $V = AC$, we have

Value of 40 Pounds of Cashews	**Value of x Pounds of Peanuts**
$V_1 = 40(6) = 240$	$V_2 = x(2.25) = 2.25x$

From the diagram at the left, note that

Peanuts + Cashews = Mixture

x	40	$x + 40$
2.25	6.00	3.50

$2.25x + 40(6.00) = (x + 40)3.50$

Total *amount* of the mixture = amount of peanuts + amount of cashews
$$= x + 40$$

Total *value* of the mixture = value of the peanuts + value of the cashews
$$= 2.25x + 40(6.00)$$
$$= 2.25x + 240$$

? ANSWER $V = AC = 15(8) = 120$. The value is $120.

To find the value of x, again use the equation $V = AC$, this time for the mixture. The unit cost of the mixture is $3.50 per pound.

$$V = AC$$
$$2.25x + 240 = (x + 40)3.50$$
$$2.25x + 240 = 3.50x + 140$$
$$-1.25x = -100$$
$$x = 80$$

- V is the total value of the mixture, $2.25x + 240$. A is the total amount of the mixture in pounds, $x + 40$. C is the unit cost of the mixture, $3.50.

To produce a mixture that has a value of $3.50 per pound, 80 pounds of peanuts should be added to the 40 pounds of cashews.

The unit cost, or cost per pound, of the cashew–peanut mixture changes as peanuts are added. Solving the equation $V = AC$ for C yields the unit cost of the blend as

$$C = \frac{V}{A} = \frac{2.25x + 240}{x + 40}$$

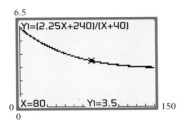

A graph of this equation is shown at the left, where X is the number of pounds of peanuts that have been added and Y_1 is the unit cost (C) of the mixture. By using the TRACE feature, we have positioned the cursor at X = 80. Note that when X = 80 (pounds), Y_1 is 3.5 ($3.50). This confirms the algebraic solution we found above.

Note that the graph at the left is decreasing. This makes sense in the context of the problem: The peanuts have less value per pound than the cashews, so as peanuts are added, the cost per pound of the mixture decreases.

? QUESTION   Suppose peanuts are combined with cashews to make a mixture weighing 20 pounds. If x pounds of peanuts are used, what expression represents the number of pounds of cashews used in the mixture?

EXAMPLE 1

A butcher wishes to combine hamburger that costs $3.00 per pound with hamburger that costs $1.80 per pound. How many pounds of each should be used to make 75 pounds of a mixture costing $2.20 per pound?

State the goal.   The goal is to determine how many pounds of hamburger that costs $3.00 per pound and how many pounds of hamburger that costs $1.80 per pound should be combined to form 75 pounds of hamburger costing $2.20 per pound.

Devise a strategy.   Let x = the number of pounds of $3.00 hamburger that are needed.

? ANSWER   Number of pounds of cashews =
number of pounds in the mixture − number of pounds of peanuts = $20 - x$

Then $75 - x$ = the number of pounds of \$1.80 hamburger that are needed.

Find the value of each of the hamburger meats.

Value of the \$3.00 hamburger: $V = AC = x(3.00) = 3x$

Value of the \$1.80 hamburger: $V = AC = (75 - x)1.80 = 135 - 1.80x$

Value of the mixture (the \$2.20 hamburger):

    = value of the \$3.00 hamburger + value of the \$1.80 hamburger

    $= 3x + 135 - 1.80x$

    $= 1.2x + 135$

To find the value of x, use the equation $V = AC$ for the mixture (the \$2.20 hamburger). The amount A of the mixture is 75 pounds. The unit cost C of the mixture is \$2.20 per pound. Solve the equation for x.

Solve the problem.

$$V = AC$$

$$1.2x + 135 = 75(2.20)$$

- V is the value of the mixture, A is the amount of the mixture, and C is the unit cost of the mixture.

$$1.2x + 135 = 165$$
$$1.2x = 30$$
$$x = 25$$

- This is the number of pounds of the \$3.00 hamburger needed.

$$75 - x = 75 - 25 = 50$$

- Find the number of pounds of the \$1.80 hamburger needed by substituting the value of x into the expression for the amount of \$1.80 hamburger needed.

The butcher needs to combine 25 pounds of the hamburger that costs \$3.00 per pound with 50 pounds of the hamburger that costs \$1.80 per pound.

Check your work. One way to check the solution is to make sure that the value of the \$3.00 hamburger plus the value of the \$1.80 hamburger is equal to the value of the mixture.

Value of the \$3.00 hamburger: $V = AC = 25(3.00) = 75$

Value of the \$1.80 hamburger: $V = AC = 50(1.80) = 90$

Value of the two ingredients = $75 + 90 = 165$

The value of the mixture is $V = AC = 75(2.20) = 165$ (\$165). The solution checks.

A second way to check the solution is to graph the variable expression for the value of the mixture: $V = 1.2x + 135$. Note in the graph at the left that the point (25, 165) is on the line.

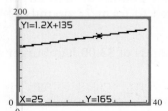

? QUESTION   The graph of the equation $V = 1.2x + 135$ is increasing. Why does this make sense in the context of the problem?

YOU TRY IT 1

How many ounces of gold that costs $320 per ounce must a jeweler mix with 100 ounces of an alloy that costs $100 per ounce to produce a new alloy that costs $160 per ounce?

Solution   See page S9.

■ Uniform Motion Problems

A train that travels constantly in a straight line at 50 miles per hour is in *uniform motion*. **Uniform motion** means that the speed and direction of the object do not change.

The solution of a uniform motion problem is based on the equation $d = rt$. In this equation, d is the distance traveled by the object, r is the speed of the object, and t is the time the object spent traveling.

For instance, suppose a homing pigeon, on its return home, flies at a speed of 50 miles per hour. The distance flown by the pigeon in 2 hours is calculated using the uniform motion equation.

▼ *Point of Interest*

Homing pigeons were first domesticated by the Egyptians around 5000 years ago.

$$d = rt$$
$$d = 50(2) \qquad • \; r = 50, t = 2$$
$$d = 100$$

The pigeon flew 100 miles in 2 hours.

Substituting 50 for r in the equation $d = rt$ produces the equation $d = 50t$. This equation gives the distance d traveled by the pigeon in a certain amount of time t. The table and the graph below show the relationship between the time flying and the distance flown. The variable X represents t, the time in hours, and the variable Y_1 represents d, the distance in miles. The ordered pair $(4, 200)$ means that in 4 hours, the pigeon traveled 200 miles.

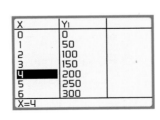
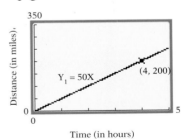

The graph above is called a **time–distance graph** and shows the relationship between the time traveled and the distance traveled. Time is on the horizontal axis, and distance is on the vertical axis.

? ANSWER   The $3 hamburger has more value per pound than the $1.80 hamburger, so as more $3 hamburger is added, the cost per pound of the mixture increases.

Suppose two brothers are going to race. Tom, who can run 7 meters per second, wants to give his younger brother Harry, who runs 5 meters per second, a 4-second head start in a 100-meter race. Let t represent the time Tom runs.

The distance Tom runs: $d = rt$

$$d = 7t$$ • Tom's rate is 7 meters per second.

Harry had a 4-second head start, which means that he has been running 4 seconds longer than Tom. Therefore, the time that Harry has been running is $(t + 4)$ seconds.

The distance Harry runs: $d = rt$

$$d = 5(t + 4)$$ • Harry's rate is 5 meters per second.
Harry runs 4 seconds longer than Tom.

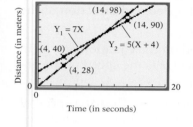

The time–distance graphs of the equations of the two brothers are shown at the left.

The graph shows that after Tom has been running for 4 seconds, he has traveled 28 meters and Harry has traveled 40 meters. The difference between the distances is $40 - 28 = 12$. This means that Harry is 12 meters ahead of Tom. You can also see this by looking at the table of values at the right.

X	Y1	Y2
2	14	30
4	28	40
6	42	50
8	56	60
10	70	70
12	84	80
14	98	90
X=10		

The graph and the table show that Harry is ahead of Tom until Tom has been running for 10 seconds. At that time, Tom catches up to Harry and they have traveled the same distance, 70 meters. After 10 seconds, Tom is ahead of Harry. At the end of 14 seconds, Tom has traveled 98 meters and Harry has traveled 90 meters, so Tom is 8 meters ahead of Harry.

Another method of finding how long it takes Tom to catch up to his brother is to solve an equation. Again, let t be the time Tom is running. Use the fact that when Tom overtakes Harry, both have traveled the same distance.

Distance traveled by Tom	equals	distance traveled by Harry.
$7t$	$=$	$5(t + 4)$

$$7t = 5(t + 4)$$
$$7t = 5t + 20$$
$$2t = 20$$
$$t = 10$$

Tom catches up to Harry in 10 seconds. This confirms the graphical approach discussed above.

? QUESTION Suppose Car A is traveling 5 miles per hour faster than Car B. If the rate of Car B is represented by r, how can the rate of Car A be represented in terms of r?

? ANSWER $r + 5$

EXAMPLE 2

As part of flight training, a student pilot was required to fly from Brown Field to Monterey and then return. The average speed on the way to Monterey was 100 miles per hour, and the average speed returning was 150 miles per hour. Find the distance between the two airports if the total flying time was 6 hours.

State the goal.   The goal is to find the distance between the airports.

Devise a strategy.   If we can determine the time it took the pilot to fly to Monterey, then we can use the equation $d = rt$ to find the distance to that airport.

For instance, suppose it took 2 hours to fly to Monterey. Then the distance to the airport would be

Rate of the plane ⟶ ⟵ Time to the airport

$$d = 100(2) = 200$$

⟵ Distance to the airport

This suggests that we let t represent the time it takes the pilot to fly to Monterey.

The total time of the trip was 6 hours. Therefore, the time to return to Brown Field is the total time for the trip (6 hours) minus the time it took to fly to Monterey (t).

Time to return to Brown Field = 6 hours − the time flying to Monterey
$$= 6 - t$$

Use the equation $d = rt$ to write an equation for the distance traveled from Brown Field to Monterey and an equation for the distance traveled from Monterey to Brown Field.

Distance from Brown Field to Monterey: $d = rt$
$$d = 100t$$
Distance from Monterey to Brown Field: $d = rt$
$$d = 150(6 - t)$$

To assist in writing an equation, draw a diagram showing the distances traveled to and from Monterey.

$d = 100t$

Brown Field   Monterey

$d = 150(6 - t)$

Note that the distance the plane travels to Monterey is the same as the distance the plane travels returning from Monterey. Translating this sentence into an equation, we have $100t = 150(6 - t)$.

Solve the problem.

$100t = 150(6 - t)$ • The distance to Monterey equals the distance back
$100t = 900 - 150t$ to Brown.

$250t = 900$

$t = 3.6$ • The time flying from Brown to Monterey was 3.6 hours.

$d = 100t$ • To find the distance between the airports, substitute 3.6
$d = 100(3.6)$ for t in the equation for the distance from Brown to
$d = 360$ Monterey.

The distance between the airports is 360 miles.

Check your work. It is important to note that the solution of the equation was 3.6 hours but that finding the answer to the question (What is the
distance between the airports?) required substituting 3.6 into the equation
$d = rt$.

As a check of your work, substitute 3.6 as the distance from Monterey to
Brown.

$$d = 150(6 - t) = 150(6 - 3.6) = 150(2.4) = 360$$

This shows that the distance back is equal to the distance out, as it
should be.

YOU TRY IT 2

Two cyclists, the second traveling 5 miles per hour faster than the first,
start at the same time from the same point and travel in opposite directions. In 4 hours, they are 140 miles apart. Find the rate of each cyclist.

Solution   See page S10.

3.2 EXERCISES

Topics for Discussion

1. Use the equation $V = AC$ to explain how to represent the value of x
    quarts of juice that costs $.85 per quart.

2. If a confectioner combines chocolate costing $5.50 per pound with
    caramel costing $4.00 per pound and then sells the candy at $6.00 per
    pound, would the confectioner make a profit or lose money?

3. Suppose a merchant mixes apple juice costing $1.25 per quart with cranberry juice costing $2.00 per quart. Will the merchant always make a profit if the price of the mixture is $3.00 per quart? Will the merchant always make a profit if the price of the mixture is $1.50 per quart? Will the merchant ever make a profit if the price of the mixture is $1.00 per quart?

4. Suppose you combined peanuts and raisins into a mixture that weighed a total of 5 pounds. Use one variable to express the number of pounds of peanuts and the number of pounds of raisins in the mixture.

5. Suppose a jogger starts on a 4-mile course. Two hours later a second jogger starts on the same course. If both joggers arrive at the finish line at the same time, which jogger is running faster?

6. A Boeing 757 airplane leaves San Diego, California, flying to Miami, Florida. One hour later, a Boeing 767 leaves San Diego taking the same route to Miami. Let t represents the time the Boeing 757 has been in the air. Use an expression involving t to represent the time the Boeing 767 has been in the air.

7. If two objects started from the same point and are moving in opposite directions, how can the total distance between the two objects be expressed?

8. Two friends are standing 50 feet apart and begin walking toward each other on a straight sidewalk. When they meet, what is the total distance covered by the two friends?

9. Suppose two planes are heading toward each other. One plane is traveling at 450 miles per hour, and the other plane is traveling at 350 miles per hour. What is the rate at which the distance between the planes is changing?

■ Value Mixture Problems

10. *Food Mixtures*   A restaurant chef mixes 20 pounds of snow peas costing $1.99 per pound with 14 pounds of petite onions costing $1.19 per pound to make a vegetable medley for the evening meal. Find the cost per pound of the mixture.

11. *Food Mixtures*   Find the cost per ounce of a salad dressing made from 64 ounces of olive oil that costs $.13 per ounce and 20 ounces of vinegar that costs $.09 per ounce. Round to the nearest cent.

12. *Food Mixtures*   Forty pounds of cashews costing $5.60 per pound were mixed with 100 pounds of peanuts costing $1.89 per pound. Find the cost of the resulting mixture.

13. *Food Mixtures*   A coffee merchant combined coffee costing $6 per pound with coffee costing $3.50 per pound. How many pounds of each were used to make 25 pounds of a blend costing $5.25 per pound?

14. *Entertainment*   Adult tickets for a play cost $5.00 and children's tickets cost $2.00. For one performance, 460 tickets were sold. Receipts for the performance were $1880. Find the number of adult tickets sold.

15. *Entertainment*   Tickets for a school play sold for $2.50 for each adult and $1.00 for each child. The total receipts for 113 tickets sold were $221. Find the number of adult tickets sold.

16. *Food Mixtures*   A breakfast cook mixes 5 liters of pure maple syrup that costs $9.50 per liter with imitation maple syrup that costs $4.00 per liter. How much imitation maple syrup is needed to make a mixture that costs $5.00 per liter?

17. *Food Mixtures*   To make a flour mixture, a miller combined soybeans that cost $8.50 per bushel with wheat that cost $4.50 per bushel. How many bushels of each were used to make a mixture of 1000 bushels costing $5.50 per bushel?

18. *Metallurgy*   A goldsmith combined pure gold that cost $400 per ounce with an alloy of gold that cost $150 per ounce. How many ounces of each were used to make 50 ounces of gold alloy costing $250 per ounce?

19. *Metallurgy*   A silversmith combined pure silver that cost $5.20 per ounce with 50 ounces of a silver alloy that cost $2.80 per ounce. How many ounces of the pure silver were used to make an alloy of silver costing $4.40 per ounce?

20. *Food Mixtures*   A tea mixture was made from 30 pounds of tea that cost $6.00 per pound and 70 pounds of tea that cost $3.20 per pound. Find the cost per pound of the tea mixture.

21. *Cosmetology*   Find the cost per ounce of a face cream mixture made from 100 ounces of face cream that cost $3.46 per ounce and 60 ounces of face cream that cost $12.50 per ounce.

22. *Food Mixtures*   A fruit stand owner combined cranberry juice that costs $4.20 per gallon with 50 gallons of apple juice that costs $2.10 per gallon. How much cranberry juice was used to make cranapple juice that costs $3.00 per gallon?

23. *Food Mixtures*   Walnuts that cost $4.05 per kilogram were mixed with cashews that cost $7.25 per kilogram. How many kilograms of each were used to make a 50-kilogram mixture costing $6.25 per kilogram? Round to the nearest tenth.

■ Uniform Motion Problems

24. *Travel*   Write the equation for the distance a car traveling at a constant rate of 45 miles per hour travels in t hours. Use a graphing calculator to graph this equation with X as t and Y₁ as d. Use a domain of [0, 7] and a range of [0, 350].

25. *Transportation*   Write the equation for the distance a cyclist traveling at a constant rate of 12 miles per hour travels in t hours. Use a graphing calculator to graph this equation with X as t and Y₁ as d. Use a domain of [0, 5] and a range of [0, 60].

26. *Sports*   Jacob starts on a 16-mile hike on a path through a nature preserve. One hour later, Davadene starts on the same path, walking in the same direction as Jacob. The graphs of the two hikers are shown at the right, where t is the time that Davadene has been walking.
   a.   After Davadene has been walking for 2 hours, has Jacob or Davadene traveled farther?
   b.   Does Davadene ever pass Jacob on this hike? How can you tell?

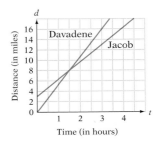

27. *Sports*   Imogene begins a 50-mile bicycle course. Two hours later, Alice starts on the same course, riding in the same direction as Imogene. The graphs of the two cyclists are shown at the right, where t is the time that Alice has been riding.
   a.   After Alice has been riding for 4 hours, has Imogene or Alice traveled farther?
   b.   Does Alice ever pass Imogene on this ride? How can you tell?

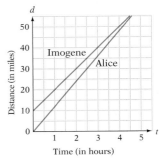

28. *Travel*   Two planes are 1380 miles apart and traveling toward each other. One plane is traveling 80 miles per hour faster than the other plane. The planes meet in 1.5 hours. Find the speed of each plane.

29. *Travel*   Two cars are 295 miles apart and traveling toward each other. One car travels 10 miles per hour faster than the other car. The cars meet in 2.5 hours. Find the speed of each car.

30. *Transportation*   A ferry leaves a harbor and travels to a resort island at an average speed of 18 miles per hour. On the return trip, the ferry travels at an average speed of only 12 miles per hour because of fog. The total time for the trip is 6 hours. How far is the island from the harbor?

31. *Transportation*   A commuter plane that provides transportation from an international airport to the surrounding cities averaged 210 miles per hour flying to a city and 140 miles per hour returning to the international airport. The total flying time was 4 hours. Find the distance between the two airports.

32. *Travel*   Two planes start from the same point and fly in opposite directions. The first plane is flying 50 miles per hour slower than the second plane. In 2.5 hours, the planes are 1400 miles apart. Find the rate of each plane.

33. *Sports*   Two hikers start from the same point and hike in opposite directions around a lake whose shoreline is 13 miles long. One hiker walks 0.5 mile per hour faster than the other hiker. How fast did each hiker walk if they meet in 2 hours?

34. *Transportation*   A student rode a bicycle to the repair shop and then walked home. The student averaged 14 miles per hour riding to the shop and 3.5 miles per hour walking home. The round trip took 1 hour. How far is it between the student's home and the bicycle shop?

35. *Travel*   A passenger train leaves a depot 1.5 hours after a freight train leaves the same depot. The passenger train is traveling 18 miles per hour faster than the freight train. Find the rate of each train if the passenger train overtakes the freight train 2.5 hours after leaving the depot.

36. *Travel*   A plane leaves an airport at 3 P.M. At 4 P.M. another plane leaves the same airport traveling in the same direction at a speed 150 miles per hour faster than that of the first plane. Four hours after the first plane takes off, the second plane is 250 miles ahead of the first plane. How far did the second plane travel?

37. *Sports*   A jogger and a cyclist set out at 9 A.M. from the same point headed in the same direction. The average speed of the cyclist is four times the average speed of the jogger. In 2 hours, the cyclist is 33 miles ahead of the jogger. How far did the cyclist ride?

Applying Concepts

38. *Metallurgy*   Find the cost per ounce of a mixture of 30 ounces of an alloy that costs $4.50 per ounce, 40 ounces of an alloy that costs $3.50 per ounce, and 30 ounces of an alloy that costs $3.00 per ounce.

39. *Food Mixtures*   A grocer combined walnuts that cost $2.60 per pound and cashews that cost $3.50 per pound with 20 pounds of peanuts that cost $2.00 per pound. Find the amount of walnuts and the amount of cashews used to make the 50-pound mixture costing $2.72 per pound.

40. *Food Mixtures*   A grocer creates a blend of two chocolate candies, chocolate mints and chocolate covered almonds. The grocer uses 30 pounds of chocolate mints costing $4.50 per pound and 20 pounds of chocolate covered almonds costing $6.00 per pound. At what price per pound should the grocer mark the blend to realize a $100 profit on the sale of the entire blend?

41.   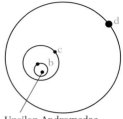 *Space Travel*   In 1999, astronomers confirmed the existence of planets orbiting a star other than the Sun. One of the planets, called Companion b, is approximately three-fourths the size of Jupiter. Companion c is approximately twice the size of Jupiter, and Companion d is four times the size of Jupiter. Each planet orbits the star Upsilon Andromedae, which is approximately 44 light years, or approximately 260 trillion (260,000,000,000,000) miles, from Earth. How many years (to the nearest hundred) after leaving Earth would it take a spacecraft traveling 18 million miles per hour to reach this star? (Note that 18 million miles per hour is about 1000 times faster than current spacecraft can travel.)

Upsilon Andromedae

The orbit of Companion c is approximately the same as the orbit of Earth around the Sun.

42. *Ancient Word Problem*   The following problem appears in a math text written around A.D. 1200. Two birds start flying from the tops of two towers 50 feet apart at the same time and at the same rate. One tower is 30 feet high, and the other tower is 40 feet high. The birds reach a grass seed on the ground at exactly the same time. How far is the grass seed from the 40-foot tower? *Note:* The solution requires use of the Pythagorean Theorem.

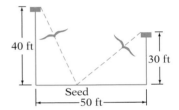

43. *Sports*   At 10 A.M., two campers left their campsite by canoe and paddled downstream at an average speed of 12 miles per hour. They then turned around and paddled back upstream at an average rate of 4 miles per hour. The total trip took 1 hour. At what time did the campers turn around downstream?

EXPLORATION

1. *Challenging Uniform Motion Problems*
   a.   If a parade 2 miles long is proceeding at 3 miles per hour, how long will it take a runner, jogging at 6 miles per hour, to travel from the end of the parade to the start of the parade?

   b.   Two cars are headed directly toward each other at rates of 40 miles per hour and 60 miles per hour. How many miles apart are they 2 minutes before impact?

   c.   A car travels a 1-mile track at an average speed of 30 miles per hour. At what average speed must the car travel the next mile so that the average speed for the 2 miles is 60 miles per hour?

    d. Two horses, one mile apart, are running in a straight line toward each other. Each horse is running at a speed of 15 miles per hour. A bird, flying at 20 miles per hour, flies in a straight line back and forth from the nose of one horse to the nose of the other horse. How many miles will the bird fly before the horses reach one another?

2. *Equations with No Solution*   Some equations have no solution. For instance, $x = x + 1$ has no solution. If we subtract x from each side of the equation, the result is $0 = 1$, which is not a true statement. One possible interpretation of this equation is "A number equals one more than itself." Because there is no number that is one more than itself, the equation has no solution. Now consider the equation $ax + b = cx + d$. Determine what conditions on a, b, c, and d will result in an equation with no solution.

3. *Modular Equations*   An equation of the form $ax + b \equiv c \bmod n$, where a, b, c, and n are integers with $n > 1$, is one form of a *modular equation*. For instance $2x \equiv 3 \bmod 5$ is a modular equation ($a = 2$, $b = 0$, $c = 3$, and $n = 5$). These equations have many important applications. One use is to create codes so that sensitive or personal information can be transmitted electronically without someone other than the intended recipient being able to decode the message.

A solution of a modular equation is a number for which the expressions $ax + b$ and c have the same remainder when divided by n. For instance, 4 is a solution of $2x \equiv 3 \bmod 5$ because $\frac{2(4)}{5} = 1$ remainder 3 and $\frac{3}{5} = 0$ remainder 3. There are other solutions of $2x \equiv 3 \bmod 5$. For instance, 14 is a solution because $\frac{2(14)}{5} = 5$ remainder 3.

For Exercises a through d, find, by trial and error, only those solutions of the equation that are less than n.

    a. $3x \equiv 2 \bmod 4$

    b. $4x \equiv 1 \bmod 3$

    c. $3x + 6 \equiv 1 \bmod 11$

    d. $4x - 1 \equiv 3 \bmod 5$ (*Hint:* Try a decimal ending in five tenths.)

    e. The modular equation $x^2 \equiv a \bmod p$, where p is a prime number, is especially important in applications. Find the two solutions of $x^2 \equiv 9 \bmod 11$.

Applications to Geometry

■ Angles

A **ray** is part of a line that starts at a point, called the **endpoint** of the ray, but has no end. A ray is named by giving its endpoint and some other point on the ray. The ray below is named $\overrightarrow{PQ}$ or $\overrightarrow{PR}$.

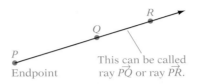

This can be called
ray $\overrightarrow{PQ}$ or ray $\overrightarrow{PR}$.

An **angle** is formed by two rays with a common endpoint. The endpoint is the **vertex** of the angle, and the rays are the **sides of the angle.** If A is a point on one ray of an angle, C is a point on the other ray, and B is the vertex, then the angle is called $\angle B$, $\angle ABC$, or $\angle CBA$, where $\angle$ is the symbol for angle. Note that the angle is named by the vertex, or when the angle is named by giving three points, the vertex is the second point listed.

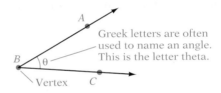

Greek letters are often
used to name an angle.
This is the letter theta.

An angle can also be named by a letter inside the angle. The angle above can be named $\angle \theta$.

One unit of measure for an angle is **degrees** (°). One degree is equal in magnitude to $\frac{1}{360}$ of a complete revolution.

$\frac{1}{360}$ of a revolution of a circle

The measure of $\angle ABC$ is written $m\angle ABC$; the measure of $\angle B$ is written $m\angle B$.

A **right angle** has a measure of 90°. A right-angle symbol, ⌐, is frequently placed inside an angle to indicate a right angle.

Right angle

An angle whose measure is between 0° and 90° is called an **acute angle.** An angle whose measure is between 90° and 180° is called an **obtuse angle.**

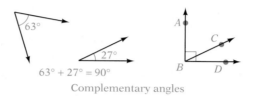

Acute angle   Obtuse angle

Straight angle

A **straight angle** has measure 180°.

Two angles are **complements** of one another if the sum of the measures of the angles is 90°. The angles are called **complementary angles.** A 63° angle and a 27° angle are complementary angles. Angles *ABC* and *CBD* below are complementary angles.

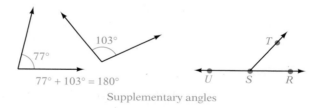

63° + 27° = 90°

Complementary angles

Two angles are **supplements** of one another if the sum of the measures of the angles is 180°. These angles are called **supplementary angles.** A 77° angle and a 103° angle are supplementary angles. Angles *RST* and *TSU* below are supplementary angles.

77° + 103° = 180°

Supplementary angles

EXAMPLE 1

One angle is 3° more than twice its supplement. Find the measure of each angle.

State the goal.   The goal is to find two supplementary angles such that one angle is 3° more than twice the other.

Devise a strategy.   Let x represent the measure of one angle.

The angles are supplements of one another. If the measure of one angle is x, then the measure of the supplementary angle is $180° - x$. Thus we have

Measure of one angle: x

Measure of the supplement: $180 - x$

Note that $x + (180 - x) = 180$, which shows that the angles x and $180 - x$ are supplementary angles.

Solve the problem. ┌─────────┐ ┌──────────────────────────────┐
one angle = 3° more than twice its supplement
└─────────┘ └──────────────────────────────┘

$$x = 2(180 - x) + 3$$
$$x = 360 - 2x + 3$$
$$x = 363 - 2x$$
$$3x = 363$$
$$x = 121$$

One angle is 121°.

To find the measure of the supplement, evaluate $180 - x$ when $x = 121$.

$$180 - x$$
$$180 - 121 = 59$$

The measure of the supplementary angle is 59°.

The measures of the two angles are 121° and 59°.

Check your work.   Note that 121° + 59° = 180°, so the two angles are supplements.

Also observe that 121 = 2(59) + 3, so 121° is 3° more than twice 59°. This confirms that our solution is correct.

YOU TRY IT 1

One angle is 3° less than its complement. Find the two angles.

Solution   See page S10.

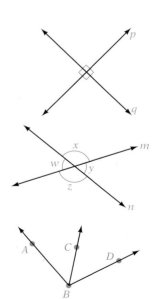

■ Intersecting Lines

▼ *Point of Interest*

Many cities in the New World, unlike those in Europe, were designed using rectangular street grids. Washington, DC, was planned that way except that diagonal avenues were added to provide for quick troop movement in the event the city required defense. As an added precaution, monuments and statues were constructed at major intersections so that attackers would not have a straight shot down a boulevard.

Four angles are formed by the intersection of two lines. If each of the four angles is a right angle, then the two lines are **perpendicular.** Line p is perpendicular to line q. This is written $p \perp q$, where $\perp$ is read "is perpendicular to."

If the two lines are not perpendicular, then two of the angles are acute angles and two of the angles are obtuse angles. The two acute angles are always opposite each other, and the two obtuse angles are always opposite each other. $\angle w$ and $\angle y$ are acute angles; $\angle x$ and $\angle z$ are obtuse angles.

Two angles that have the same vertex and share a common side are called **adjacent angles.** For the figure shown at the right, $\angle ABC$ and $\angle CBD$ are adjacent angles.

Adjacent angles of intersecting lines are supplementary angles. This is summarized by the following equations:

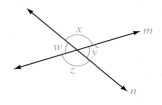

$$m\angle x + m\angle y = 180°$$
$$m\angle y + m\angle z = 180°$$
$$m\angle z + m\angle w = 180°$$
$$m\angle w + m\angle x = 180°$$

The nonadjacent angles formed when two lines intersect are called **vertical angles.** For the intersecting lines m and n above, $\angle x$ and $\angle z$ are vertical angles; $\angle w$ and $\angle y$ are also vertical angles. Vertical angles have the same measure. Thus,

$$m\angle x = m\angle z$$
$$m\angle w = m\angle y$$

EXAMPLE 2

In the figure at the right, what is the value of x?

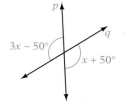

State the goal.   The goal is to find the value of x.

Devise a strategy.   The labeled angles are vertical angles of intersecting lines. Therefore, the angles are equal.

Solve the problem.
$$3x - 50 = x + 50$$
$$2x - 50 = 50$$
$$2x = 100$$
$$x = 50$$

The value of x is 50.

Check your work.   Replace x by 50 in the equation $3x - 50 = x + 50$ to ensure that the solution checks.

YOU TRY IT 2

The measures of two adjacent angles for a pair of intersecting lines are $2x + 20°$ and $3x + 50°$. Find the measure of the larger angle.

Solution   See page S10.

Parallel lines never meet; the distance between them is always the same. The symbol for parallel lines is ‖.

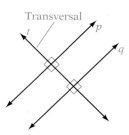

A line that intersects two other lines at two distinct points is called a **transversal.** If the lines cut by a transversal are parallel lines and the transversal is perpendicular to the parallel lines, then all eight angles formed are right angles. For the diagram at the right, $p \parallel q$.

If the lines cut by a transversal are parallel lines and the transversal is not perpendicular to the parallel lines, then all four acute angles have the same measure and all four obtuse angles have the same measure. For the figure at the right:

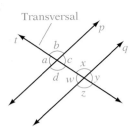

$$m\angle a = m\angle c = m\angle w = m\angle y$$
$$m\angle b = m\angle d = m\angle x = m\angle z$$

Alternate interior angles are two nonadjacent angles that are on opposite sides of the transversal and between the parallel lines. In the figure above, $\angle c$ and $\angle w$ are alternate interior angles; $\angle d$ and $\angle x$ are alternate interior angles. Alternate interior angles have the same measure.

Alternate interior angles have the same measure.

$$m\angle c = m\angle w$$
$$m\angle d = m\angle x$$

Alternate exterior angles are two nonadjacent angles that are on opposite sides of the transversal and outside the parallel lines. In the figure above, $\angle a$ and $\angle y$ are alternate exterior angles; $\angle b$ and $\angle z$ are alternate exterior angles. Alternate exterior angles have the same measure.

Alternate exterior angles have the same measure.

$$m\angle a = m\angle y$$
$$m\angle b = m\angle z$$

For two parallel lines cut by a transversal that is not perpendicular to the parallel lines, **corresponding angles** are two angles that are on the same side of the transversal and are both acute angles or are both obtuse angles. For the figure above, the following pairs of angles are corresponding angles: $\angle a$ and $\angle w$, $\angle d$ and $\angle z$, $\angle b$ and $\angle x$, $\angle c$ and $\angle y$. Corresponding angles have the same measure. (Note that if the transversal is perpendicular to the parallel lines, all corresponding angles are right angles.)

Corresponding angles have the same measure.

$$m\angle a = m\angle w$$
$$m\angle d = m\angle z$$
$$m\angle b = m\angle x$$
$$m\angle c = m\angle y$$

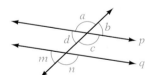

? QUESTION   In the figure at the left, $p \parallel q$. Which of the angles a, b, c, and d have the same measure as $\angle m$? Which angles have the same measure as $\angle n$?

EXAMPLE 3

Given that $p \parallel q$ in the figure at the right and that $m\angle 1 = x + 20°$ and $m\angle 2 = 3x$, find the value of x.

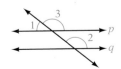

State the goal.   The goal is to find the value of x.

? ANSWER   The angles that have the same measure as angle $\angle m$ are $\angle b$ and $\angle d$. The angles that have the same measure as angle $\angle n$ are $\angle a$ and $\angle c$.

Devise a strategy. Because corresponding angles are equal, we can label $\angle 3$ in the original diagram as $3x$.

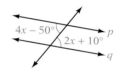

The sum of the measures of adjacent angles of intersecting lines is 180°. Therefore,

$$m\angle 3 + m\angle 1 = 180°$$

Solve the problem.

$$3x + (x + 20) = 180$$
$$4x + 20 = 180$$
$$4x = 160$$
$$x = 40$$

The value of x is 40.

Check your work. By replacing x by 40 in the equation $3x + (x + 20) = 180$, you can verify that the solution is correct.

YOU TRY IT 3

Given that $p \parallel q$, find the value of x in the diagram at the right.

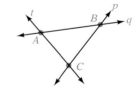

Solution See page S11.

■ Angles of a Triangle

If the lines cut by a transversal are not parallel lines, the three lines will intersect at three points. In the figure at the right, the transversal t intersects lines p and q. The three lines intersect at points A, B, and C. These three points define the three line segments $\overline{AB}$, $\overline{BC}$, and $\overline{AC}$. The plane figure formed by these line segments is a **triangle.**

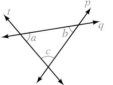

Each of the three points of intersection is the vertex of an angle of the triangle. The angles within the region enclosed by the triangle are called **interior angles.** In the figure at the right, $\angle a$, $\angle b$, and $\angle c$ are interior angles. The sum of the measures of interior angles is 180°.

$$m\angle a + m\angle b + m\angle c = 180°$$

The Sum of the Measures of the Interior Angles of a Triangle

The sum of the measures of the interior angles of a triangle is 180°.

As an example of this, suppose the measures of two angles of a triangle are 25° and 47°. Let x be the measure of the third angle. Then

$x + 25 + 47 = 180$ • The sum of the measures of the angles is 180°.

$x + 72 = 180$ • Add like terms.

$x = 108$ • Solve for x.

The measure of the third angle is 108°.

An angle adjacent to an interior angle of a triangle is an **exterior angle** of the triangle. In the figure at the right, $\angle x$ and $\angle y$ are exterior angles for $\angle a$. The sum of the measures of an interior angle and the adjacent exterior angle of a triangle is 180°.

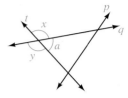

$m\angle a + m\angle x = 180°$

$m\angle a + m\angle y = 180°$

EXAMPLE 4

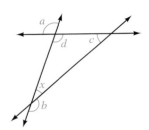

Given that $m\angle a = 110°$ and $m\angle c = 40°$ in the figure at the right, find the measure of $\angle b$.

State the goal. The goal is find the measure of $\angle b$.

Devise a strategy. Note that $\angle b$ is an exterior angle for $\angle x$. Therefore, they are supplementary angles, and $m\angle b = 180° - m\angle x$. This means that we can find the measure of $\angle b$ by first finding the measure of $\angle x$.

$\angle d$ and $\angle a$ are vertical angles and therefore have the same measure.

That is, $m\angle d = m\angle a = 110°$.

We know the measure of $\angle d$ and the measure of $\angle c$. The measure of $\angle x$ can be found by using the fact that the sum of the interior angles of a triangle is 180°.

Solve the problem. $m\angle d + m\angle c + m\angle x = 180°$

$110° + 40° + m\angle x = 180°$

$150° + m\angle x = 180°$

$m\angle x = 30°$

$m\angle b = 180° - m\angle x = 180° - 30° = 150°$

The measure of $\angle b$ is 150°.

Check your work. Check over your work to be sure it is accurate.

YOU TRY IT 4

Given that $m\angle a = 112°$ in the figure at the right, find the $m\angle b$.

Solution See page S11.

■ Angles and Circles

The angles formed by rays that intersect circles have some special properties. In the diagram at the right, $\angle BOC$ is a **central angle** because the vertex is at the center of the circle, O. The sides of the angle are radii of the circle. $\angle BAC$ is an **inscribed angle** because its vertex is on the circumference of the circle and its sides are **chords,** or line segments whose endpoints lie on the circle.

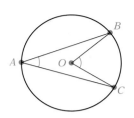

An **arc** is an unbroken part of a circle. In the diagram below, points A and B divide the circle into *minor arc $\widehat{AB}$* and *major arc $\widehat{ACB}$*. Three points are always used to name a major arc. The **measure of an arc** is the measure of the central angle that intersects it. The measure of arc $\widehat{AB}$ below, denoted as $m\widehat{AB}$, is 125°. Because a circle contains 360°, $m\widehat{ACB} = 360° - 125° = 235°$.

> **TAKE NOTE**
>
> If a chord is a diameter of a circle, then the central angle is a straight angle. Thus $m\widehat{ACB} = m\widehat{ADB} = 180°$.

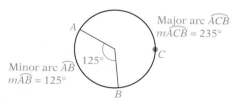

Major arc $\widehat{ACB}$
$m\widehat{ACB} = 235°$

Minor arc $\widehat{AB}$
$m\widehat{AB} = 125°$

? QUESTION   For the figure at the right, what is the measure of $\widehat{ABC}$?

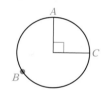

A **tangent** to a circle is a line that is in the same plane as the circle and is perpendicular to a radius of the circle at the point of intersection. See the diagram at the left.

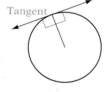

Tangent

The theorems below give some relationships between arcs and inscribed angles.

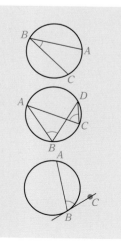

Inscribed-Angle Theorems

If $\angle ABC$ is an inscribed angle of a circle, then
$$m\angle ABC = \tfrac{1}{2}(m\widehat{AC}).$$

Inscribed angles that intersect the same arc are equal. $m\angle ABD = m\angle ACD$

> **TAKE NOTE**
>
> In the second figure at the right, $\angle ABD$ and $\angle ACD$ are inscribed angles that intersect arc AD.

The measure of an angle formed by a tangent and a chord is equal to one-half the measure of the intercepted arc. $m\angle ABC = \tfrac{1}{2}(m\widehat{AB})$

? ANSWER $m\widehat{ABC} = 360° - 90° = 270°$

EXAMPLE 5

Find $m\angle ABD$ given that $\overline{BD}$ is tangent to the circle at B and that $m\angle ACB = 138°$.

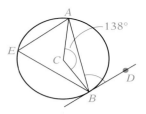

State the goal.   The goal is to find $m\angle ABD$.

Devise a strategy. $\angle ABD$ is formed by the tangent $\overline{BD}$ and a chord of the circle. By the theorem above, $m\angle ABD = \frac{1}{2}(m\overset{\frown}{AB})$. Thus we can find $m\angle ABD$ by finding $m\overset{\frown}{AB}$.

Solve the problem.
$m\overset{\frown}{AB}$ = the measure of the central angle $ACB = 138°$
$m\angle ABD = \frac{1}{2}(m\overset{\frown}{AB}) = \frac{1}{2}(m\angle ACB) = \frac{1}{2}(138°) = 69°$

The measure of $\angle ABD = 69°$.

Check your work.   We can check the reasonableness of the answer by noting that chord $\overline{AB}$ is not a diameter of the circle. Therefore, $m\angle ABD$ must be less than 90°.

YOU TRY IT 5

Use the diagram for Example 5, and find $m\angle AEB$.

Solution   See page S11.

EXAMPLE 6

If $\overline{AC}$ is a diameter of the circle at the right, show that $\angle ABC$ is right angle.

State the goal.   The goal is to show that $\angle ABC$ is a right angle; that is, that $m\angle ABC = 90°$.

Devise a strategy.   Because $\overline{AC}$ is a diameter, $m\overset{\frown}{ADC} = 180°$. From the Inscribed-Angle Theorems, the measure of the inscribed angle ABC is $\frac{1}{2}(m\overset{\frown}{ADC})$. Use this information to write and solve an equation.

Solve the problem. $m\angle ABC = \frac{1}{2}(m\overset{\frown}{ADC})$

$$= \frac{1}{2}(180°) = 90°$$

Because the measure of $\angle ABC$ is 90°, $\angle ABC$ is a right angle.

Check your work.   Be sure to check your work.

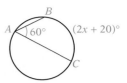

YOU TRY IT 6

Find the value of x in the figure at the right.

Solution   See page S11.

3.3 EXERCISES

Topics for Discussion

1. Describe each of the following: a right angle, an acute angle, an obtuse angle, a straight angle.

2. What are complementary angles? What are supplementary angles?

3. What are vertical angles?

4. Draw a diagram with a transversal intersecting two parallel lines. Identify the corresponding angles, alternate interior angles, and alternate exterior angles.

5. If a transversal cuts two lines p and q, and the alternate interior angles are not equal, what can be said about the lines p and q?

6. What is a chord of a circle? Are all diameters chords of a circle? Are all chords diameters of a circle?

7. What is a central angle of a circle? How is the measure of a central angle related to the measure of the arc intercepted by the angle?

8. What is an inscribed angle of a circle? How is the measure of an inscribed angle related to the measure of the arc intercepted by the angle?

▪ Angles

Solve.

9. Find the complement of a 43° angle.

10. Find the complement of a 53° angle.

11. Find the supplement of a 98° angle.

12. Find the supplement of a 33° angle.

13. Find two complementary angles such that one angle is 6 degrees more than twice the other.

14. Find two complementary angles such that one angle is 15 degrees less than one-half the other.

15. Find two supplementary angles such that one angle is 12 degrees less than three times the other.

16. Find two supplementary angles such that one angle is 10 degrees less than two-thirds the other.

Given that $\angle ABC$ is a right angle, find the value of x.

17.
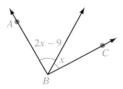

18.

19.
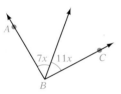

20.
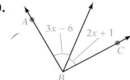

Find the value of x.

21.

22.

23.
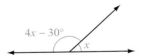

24.
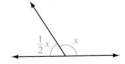

Find the measure of $\angle b$.

25.
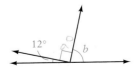

26.
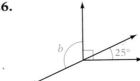

■ **Intersecting Lines**

Find the value of x.

27.

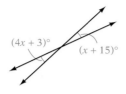

$(4x + 3)°$ $(x + 15)°$

28.

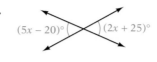

$(5x - 20)°$ $(2x + 25)°$

Given that $p \parallel q$, find $m\angle a$ and $m\angle b$.

29.

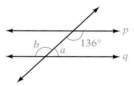

b $136°$ a p q

30.

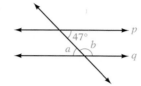

$47°$ b a p q

31.

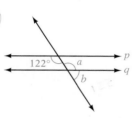

$122°$ a b p q

32.

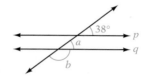

$38°$ a b p q

Given that $p \parallel q$, find the value of x.

33.

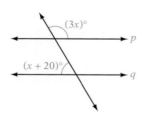

$(3x)°$ $(x + 20)°$ p q

34.

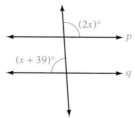

$(2x)°$ $(x + 39)°$ p q

35.

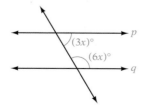

$(3x)°$ $(6x)°$ p q

36.

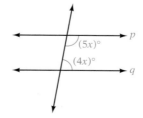

$(5x)°$ $(4x)°$ p q

■ Angles of a Triangle

37. Given that $m\angle a = 45°$ and $m\angle b = 100°$, find $m\angle x$ and $m\angle y$.

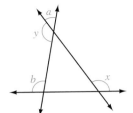

38. Given that $m\angle a = 80°$ and $m\angle b = 25°$, find $m\angle x$ and $m\angle y$.

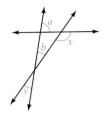

39. Given $m\angle a = 25°$, find $m\angle x$ and $m\angle y$.

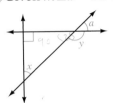

40. Given $m\angle a = 50°$, find $m\angle x$ and $m\angle y$.

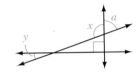

41. The measure of one of the acute angles of a right triangle is two degrees more than three times the measure of the other acute angle. Find the measure of each angle.

42. The measure of the largest angle of a triangle is five times the measure of the smallest angle in the triangle. The measure of the third angle is three times the measure of the smallest angle. Find the measure of the largest angle.

■ Angles and Circles

Find the value of x.

43.

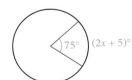

44.

45.

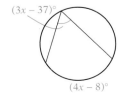

46.

47.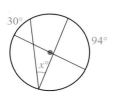
$(5x + 10)°$ $(9x - 30)°$

48.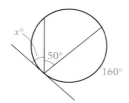
$x°$
$50°$
$160°$

49.
$30°$
$94°$
$x°$

50.
C
$(6x - 3)°$
B
A
$(5x + 18)°$

51.
$(2x + 4)°$
$48°$

52.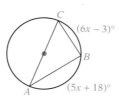
$120°$
$50°$
$30°$
$x°$

Applying Concepts

53. 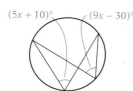 Cut out a paper triangle and then tear off two of the angles, as shown in the figure at the right. Position the pieces you tore off so that $\angle a$ is adjacent to $\angle b$ and $\angle c$ is adjacent to $\angle b$. Describe what you observe. What does this demonstrate?

54. The measure of the supplement of the complement of $\angle a$ is $120°$. What is the measure of $\angle a$?

55. The measure of the complement of the supplement of $\angle a$ is $50°$. What is the measure of $\angle a$?

56. Determine whether the statement is always true, sometimes true, or never true.
   a. Two lines that are parallel to a third line are parallel to each other.
   b. A triangle contains two acute angles.
   c. Vertical angles are complementary angles.
   d. Adjacent angles are supplementary angles.

EXPLORATION

1. *Properties of Triangles* For the figure at the right, explain why $m\angle a + m\angle b = m\angle x$. Write a rule that describes the relationship between an exterior angle of a triangle and the opposite interior angles.

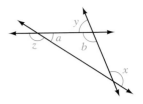

2. *Properties of Triangles* For the figure at the right, find $m\angle x + m\angle y + m\angle z$.

SECTION 3.4

- The Addition and Multiplication Properties of Inequalities
- Compound Inequalities

Inequalities in One Variable

■ The Addition and Multiplication Properties of Inequalities

Recall that an equation contains an equals sign. An **inequality** contains the symbol $>$, $<$, $\geq$, or $\leq$. An inequality expresses the relative order of two mathematical expressions.

Here are some examples of inequalities in one variable:

$$\left.\begin{array}{l} 4x \geq 12 \\ 2x + 7 \leq 9 \\ x^2 + 1 > 3x \end{array}\right\} \quad \text{Inequalities in one variable}$$

A **solution of an inequality in one variable** is a number that, when substituted for the variable, results in a true inequality. For the inequality $x < 6$ shown below, 5, 0, and -4 are solutions of the inequality because replacing the variable by these numbers results in a true inequality.

$x < 6$		$x < 6$		$x < 6$	
$5 < 6$	True	$0 < 6$	True	$-4 < 6$	True

The number 7 is not a solution of the inequality $x < 6$ because $7 < 6$ is a false inequality.

Besides the numbers 5, 0, and -4, there are an infinite number of other solutions of the inequality $x < 6$. Any number less than 6 is a solution; for instance, -5.2, $\frac{5}{2}$, π, and 1 are also solutions of the inequality. The set of all the solutions of an inequality is called the **solution set of the inequality.** The solution set of the inequality $x < 6$ is written in set-builder notation as $\{x \mid x < 6\}$ and in interval notation as $(-\infty, 6)$.

Now consider the inequality $x - 1 < 4$. We can use a graphing calculator to visualize the solution set of this inequality by asking, "When is the graph of $y = x - 1$ less than 4?" To answer this question, graph $Y_1 = X - 1$ and $Y_2 = 4$. Use the INTERSECT feature to determine that the two lines intersect at $(5, 4)$. Observe that the graph of $Y_1 = X - 1$ is less than 4 (the graph is below 4) when $x < 5$.

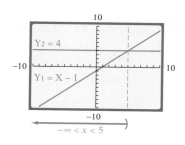

The graph of the solution set of $x - 1 < 4$ is usually displayed on a number line as shown at the right.

The solution set of the inequality $x - 1 < 4$ is $\{x | x < 5\}$ or $(-\infty, 5)$.

This solution set can be checked by using the TEST feature of a graphing calculator. Some typical screens follow.

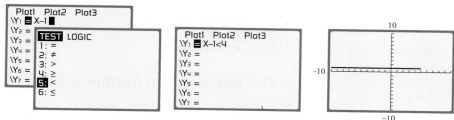

In solving an inequality, the goal is to rewrite the given inequality in the form

$$variable < constant \quad \text{or} \quad variable > constant$$

The Addition Property of Inequalities is used to rewrite an inequality in this form.

See Appendix A: Test

CALCULATOR NOTE
Note that the graphing calculator draws a horizontal line above the x-axis. The numbers below the line drawn are the elements of the solution set.

The Addition Property of Inequalities

If $a > b$ and c is a real number, then the inequalities $a > b$ and $a + c > b + c$ have the same solution set.

If $a < b$ and c is a real number, then the inequalities $a < b$ and $a + c < b + c$ have the same solution set.

The Addition Property of Inequalities states that the same number can be added to each side of an inequality without changing the solution set of the inequality. This property is also true for the symbols $\le$ and $\ge$.

The Addition Property of Inequalities is used to remove a term from one side of an inequality by adding the additive inverse of that term to each side of the inequality. Because subtraction is defined in terms of addition, the same number can be subtracted from each side of an inequality without changing the solution set of the inequality.

EXAMPLE 1

Solve and graph the solution set of $x + 5 > 3$. Write the solution set in set-builder notation and interval notation.

ALGEBRAIC SOLUTION

$$x + 5 > 3$$
$$x + 5 - 5 > 3 - 5 \quad \text{• Subtract 5 from each side of the inequality.}$$
$$x > -2$$

The solution set is $\{x | x > -2\}$ or $(-2, \infty)$.

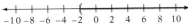

GRAPHICAL CHECK

Put the calculator in dot mode.

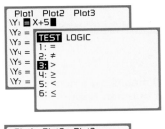

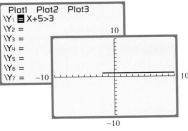

YOU TRY IT 1

Solve and graph the solution set of $x - 4 \le 1$. Write the solution set in set-builder notation and interval notation.

Solution See page S12.

As shown in the example that follows, the Addition Property of Inequalities applies to variable terms as well as to constants.

➡ Solve $3x - 4 \le 2x - 1$. Write the solution set in interval notation.

$$3x - 4 \le 2x - 1$$
$$3x - 2x - 4 \le 2x - 2x - 1 \quad \text{• Subtract } 2x \text{ from each side of the inequality.}$$
$$x - 4 \le -1 \quad \text{• Simplify.}$$
$$x - 4 + 4 \le -1 + 4 \quad \text{• Add 4 to each side of the inequality.}$$
$$x \le 3 \quad \text{• Simplify.}$$

The solution set is $(-\infty, 3]$.

When we multiply or divide an inequality by a number, the inequality symbol may be reversed, depending on whether the number is positive or negative. Look at the following two examples.

$$3 < 5$$
$$2(3) < 2(5)$$
$$6 < 10$$
• Multiply by positive 2. The inequality symbol remains the same. $6 < 10$ is a true statement.

$$3 < 5$$
$$-2(3) > -2(5)$$
$$-6 > -10$$
• Multiply by negative 2. The inequality symbol is reversed in order to make the inequality a true statement.

This is summarized in the Multiplication Property of Inequalities.

The Multiplication Property of Inequalities
Rule 1
If $a > b$ and $c > 0$, then the inequalities $a > b$ and $ac > bc$ have the same solution set.
If $a < b$ and $c > 0$, then the inequalities $a < b$ and $ac < bc$ have the same solution set.
Rule 2
If $a > b$ and $c < 0$, then the inequalities $a > b$ and $ac < bc$ have the same solution set.
If $a < b$ and $c < 0$, then the inequalities $a < b$ and $ac > bc$ have the same solution set.

Rule 1 states that when each side of an inequality is multiplied by a positive number, the inequality symbol remains the same. Rule 2 states that when each side of an inequality is multiplied by a negative number, the inequality symbol must be reversed.

Here are a few more examples of this property.

Rule 1

$-4 < -2$ $\qquad$ $5 > -3$
$2(-4) < 2(-2)$ $\qquad$ $3(5) > 3(-3)$
$-8 < -4$ $\qquad$ $15 > -9$

Rule 2

$1 < 7$ $\qquad$ $-2 > -6$
$-2(1) > -2(7)$ $\qquad$ $-3(-2) < -3(-6)$
$-2 > -14$ $\qquad$ $6 < 18$

Use the Multiplication Property of Inequalities to remove a coefficient other than 1 from one side of an inequality so that the inequality can be written in the form *variable < constant* or *variable > constant*. The Multiplication Property of Inequalities is also true for the symbols $\le$ and $\ge$.

Because division is defined in terms of multiplication, when each side of an inequality is divided by a positive number, the inequality symbol remains the same. When each side of an inequality is divided by a negative number, the inequality symbol must be reversed.

➡ Solve $-3x < 9$. Write the solution set in interval notation.

$-3x < 9$

$\dfrac{-3x}{-3} > \dfrac{9}{-3}$ • Divide each side of the inequality by the coefficient -3 and reverse the inequality symbol.

$x > -3$ • Simplify.

$(-3, \infty)$ • Write the answer in interval notation.

The solution set is $(-3, \infty)$.

EXAMPLE 2

Solve and graph the solution set of $7x < -21$. Write the solution set in set-builder notation and interval notation.

ALGEBRAIC SOLUTION

$7x < -21$

$\dfrac{7x}{7} < \dfrac{-21}{7}$
• Divide each side of the inequality by 7. Because 7 is a positive number, the inequality symbol is not reversed.

$x < -3$
• Simplify.

The solution set is $\{x \mid x < -3\}$ or $(-\infty, -3)$.

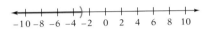

GRAPHICAL CHECK

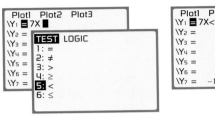

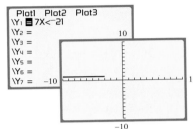

YOU TRY IT 2

Solve and graph the solution set of $-3x \geq 6$. Write the solution set in set-builder notation and interval notation.

Solution   See page S12.

EXAMPLE 3

Solve $x + 3 > 4x + 6$. Write the solution set in set-builder notation.

ALGEBRAIC SOLUTION

$x + 3 > 4x + 6$

$x - 4x + 3 > 4x - 4x + 6$
• Subtract $4x$ from each side of the inequality.

$-3x + 3 > 6$
• Simplify.

$-3x + 3 - 3 > 6 - 3$
• Subtract 3 from each side of the inequality.

$-3x > 3$
• Simplify.

$\dfrac{-3x}{-3} < \dfrac{3}{-3}$
• Divide each side of the inequality by -3 and reverse the inequality symbol.

$x < -1$
• Simplify.

The solution set is $\{x \mid x < -1\}$.
• Write the solution set.

GRAPHICAL CHECK

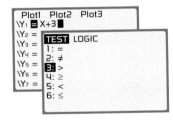

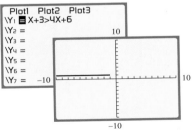

YOU TRY IT 3

Solve $3x - 1 \leq 5x - 7$. Write the solution set in set-builder notation.

Solution   See page S12.

When an inequality contains parentheses, often the first step in solving the inequality is to use the Distributive Property to remove the parentheses.

EXAMPLE 4

Solve $5(x - 2) \geq 9x - 3(2x - 4)$. Write the solution set in interval notation.

ALGEBRAIC SOLUTION   **GRAPHICAL CHECK**

$5(x - 2) \geq 9x - 3(2x - 4)$

$5x - 10 \geq 9x - 6x + 12$ • Use the Distributive Property to remove parentheses.

$5x - 10 \geq 3x + 12$ • Combine like terms on the right side of the equation.

$2x - 10 \geq 12$ • Subtract $3x$ from each side of the equation.

$2x \geq 22$ • Add 10 to each side of the equation.

$x \geq 11$

• Divide each side of the equation by 2.

The solution set is $[11, \infty)$.   • Write the solution set.

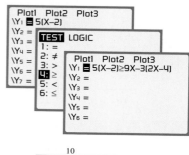

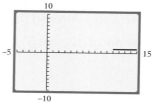

The graph is not visible in the standard viewing window. We had to choose a different window in order to display the graph of x ≥ 11.

YOU TRY IT 4

Solve $3 - 2(3x + 1) < 7 - 2x$. Write the solution set in interval notation.

Solution   See page S12.

Solving application problems requires recognition of the verbal phrases that translate into mathematical symbols. For instance, consider the sentence "To vote in an election for the president of the United States, a person must be *at least* 18 years old." This means the person must be 18 years old or older. If we let A represent a person's age, then this condition is represented mathematically as $A \geq 18$.

Now consider a plaque in a elevator that reads "The *maximum* allowable weight is 1050 pounds." This means that the total weight of all the occupants in the elevator must be 1050 pounds or less. If W represents the total weight of all the occupants, then this condition is expressed mathematically as $W \leq 1050$.

There are additional words and phrases that translate into an inequality symbol. Here is a list of some the phrases used to indicate each of the four inequality symbols.

$<$ is less than

$>$ $\begin{cases} \text{is greater than} \\ \text{is more than} \\ \text{exceeds} \end{cases}$

$\leq$ $\begin{cases} \text{is less than or equal to} \\ \text{maximum} \\ \text{at most} \\ \text{or less} \end{cases}$

$\geq$ $\begin{cases} \text{is greater than or equal to} \\ \text{minimum} \\ \text{at least} \\ \text{or more} \end{cases}$

EXAMPLE 5

In 2002, the computer service America Online offered its customers the option of paying $23.90 per month for unlimited use. Another option was a rate of $4.95 per month with 3 free hours plus $2.50 per hour thereafter (*Source:* AOL web site, March 2002). How many hours per month can you use this second option if it is to cost you less than the first option? Round to the nearest whole number.

State the goal.   The goal is to determine how many hours you can use the second option ($4.95 per month plus $2.50 per hour after the first 3 hours) if it is to cost you less than the first option ($23.90 per month).

Devise a strategy.   Let x represent the number of hours per month you use the service. Then $x - 3$ represents the number of hours you would be paying $2.50 per hour for service under the second option.

$$\text{Cost of first plan: } 23.90$$
$$\text{Cost of second plan: } 4.95 + 2.50(x - 3)$$

Write and solve an inequality that expresses that the second plan is less expensive (less than) the first plan.

Solve the problem. $4.95 + 2.50(x - 3) < 23.90$

$$4.95 + 2.50x - 7.50 < 23.90$$
$$2.50x - 2.55 < 23.90$$
$$2.50x < 26.45$$
$$x < 10.58$$

The greatest whole number less than 10.58 is 10.

In order for the second option to cost you less than the first option, you can use the service for up to 10 hours per month.

Check your work.   One way to check the solution is to review the accuracy of our work. We can also make a partial check by ensuring that the answer makes sense. For instance, suppose you used the service for 11 hours per month. Then

Monthly cost = 4.95 + 2.50(11 − 3) = 4.95 + 2.50(8) = 4.95 + 20 = 24.95

Because 24.95 > 23.90, 11 is not in the solution set.

YOU TRY IT 5

The base of a triangle is 12 inches, and the height is $(x + 2)$ inches. Express as an integer the maximum height of the triangle when the area is less than 50 in².

Solution   See page S12.

■ Compound Inequalities

A **compound inequality** is formed by joining two inequalities with a connective word such as *and* or *or*. The inequalities shown below are compound inequalities.

$$2x − 1 ≥ 4 \text{ and } x + 3 < 4$$
$$1 − 3x < 2 \text{ or } 5x − 7 > 3$$

The solution set of a compound inequality containing the word *and* is the intersection of the solution sets of the two inequalities.

EXAMPLE 6

Solve: $2x + 1 < 9$ and $2 − 3x < −4$

Write the solution set in set-builder notation.

ALGEBRAIC SOLUTION

Solve each inequality.

$$
\begin{array}{ccc}
2x + 1 < 9 & \text{and} & 2 − 3x < −4 \\
2x + 1 − 1 < 9 − 1 & & 2 − 2 − 3x < −4 − 2 \\
2x < 8 & & −3x < −6 \\
\dfrac{2x}{2} < \dfrac{8}{2} & & \dfrac{−3x}{−3} > \dfrac{−6}{−3} \\
x < 4 & & x > 2 \\
\{x | x < 4\} & & \{x | x > 2\}
\end{array}
$$

The solution of the compound inequality is the intersection of the solution sets of the individual inequalities.

$$\{x | x < 4\} \cap \{x | x > 2\} = \{x | 2 < x < 4\}$$

The solution set is $\{x | 2 < x < 4\}$.

GRAPHICAL CHECK

Plot1 Plot2 Plot3
\Y₁ ▤ 2X+1
\Y₂ =
\Y₃ = **TEST** LOGIC
\Y₄ =   1: =
\Y₅ =   2: ≠
\Y₆ =   3: >
\Y₇ =   4: ≥
        5: <
        6: ≤

Plot1 Plot2 Plot3
\Y₁ ▤ 2X+1<9
\Y₂ =
\Y₃ = **TEST** **LOGIC**
\Y₄ =   **1:** and
\Y₅ =   2: or
\Y₆ =   3: xor
\Y₇ =   4: not(

Plot1 Plot2 Plot3
\Y₁ ▤ 2X+1<9 and 2−3X■
\Y₂ =
\Y₃ = **TEST** LOGIC
\Y₄ =   1: =
\Y₅ =   2: ≠
\Y₆ =   3: >
        4: ≥
        5: <
        6: ≤

Plot1 Plot2 Plot3
\Y₁ ▤ 2X+1<9 and 2−3X<⁻4
\Y₂ =
\Y₃ =
\Y₄ =
\Y₅ =
\Y₆ =

YOU TRY IT 6

Solve: $5x - 1 \geq -11$ and $4 - 6x > -14$.

Write the solution set in set-builder notation.

Solution   See page S12.

Some compound inequalities imply the use of the word *and* without actually stating it. This is illustrated in the following problem.

➡ Solve: $-3 \leq 2x + 1 < 7$
Write the solution set in set-builder notation.

This inequality is read "$2x + 1$ is greater than or equal to -3 and less than 7" and is equivalent to the compound inequality $-3 \leq 2x + 1$ and $2x + 1 < 7$.

Solve each inequality. Then find the intersection of the solution sets.

$$
\begin{array}{ll}
-3 \leq 2x + 1 & \text{and} \qquad 2x + 1 < 7 \\
-3 - 1 \leq 2x + 1 - 1 & \qquad 2x + 1 - 1 < 7 - 1 \\
-4 \leq 2x & \qquad 2x < 6 \\
\dfrac{-4}{2} \leq \dfrac{2x}{2} & \qquad \dfrac{2x}{2} < \dfrac{6}{2} \\
-2 \leq x & \qquad x < 3 \\
\{x \mid x \geq -2\} & \qquad \{x \mid x < 3\}
\end{array}
$$

$\{x \mid x \geq -2\} \cap \{x \mid x < 3\} = \{x \mid -2 \leq x < 3\}$ • Find the intersection of the solution sets.

The solution set is $\{x \mid -2 \leq x < 3\}$.

The graph of the solution set is shown at the right.

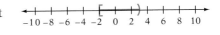

TAKE NOTE

The inequality $-2 \leq x$ is read, from right to left, "x is greater than or equal to -2," which is the inequality $x \geq -2$.

See Appendix A: Test

Graphical Check:

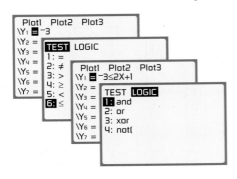

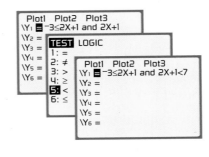

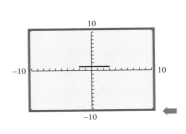

Here is an alternative method for solving the previous inequality.

⮕ Solve: $-3 \le 2x + 1 < 7$

$$-3 \le 2x + 1 < 7$$

$$-3 - 1 \le 2x + 1 - 1 < 7 - 1$$ • Subtract 1 from each part of the inequality.

$$-4 \le 2x < 6$$

$$\frac{-4}{2} \le \frac{2x}{2} < \frac{6}{2}$$ • Divide each part of the inequality by 2.

$$-2 \le x < 3$$

The solution set is $\{x \mid -2 \le x < 3\}$.

The solution set of a compound inequality with the connective word *or* is the union of the solution sets of the two inequalities.

EXAMPLE 7

Solve and graph the solution set $2x + 3 > 7$ or $4x - 1 \le 3$. Write the solution set in interval notation.

ALGEBRAIC SOLUTION

Solve each inequality. Then find the union of the solution sets.

$$\begin{array}{ccc} 2x + 3 > 7 & \text{or} & 4x - 1 \le 3 \\ 2x + 3 - 3 > 7 - 3 & & 4x - 1 + 1 \le 3 + 1 \\ 2x > 4 & & 4x \le 4 \\ \dfrac{2x}{2} > \dfrac{4}{2} & & \dfrac{4x}{4} \le \dfrac{4}{4} \\ x > 2 & & x \le 1 \\ (2, \infty) & & (-\infty, 1] \end{array}$$

The solution set is $(2, \infty) \cup (-\infty, 1]$.   • The solution set is the union of the two intervals.

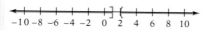

• Graph the solution set.

GRAPHICAL CHECK

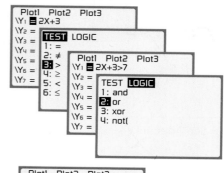

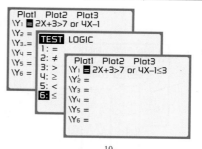

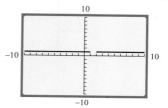

YOU TRY IT 7

Solve and graph the solution set $3 - 4x > 7$ or $4x + 5 > 9$

Write the solution set in interval notation.

Solution See page S13.

Just as with equations, some inequalities may not have real number solutions. In this case the solution set is the empty set.

➡ Solve: $2x - 1 > 5$ and $3x - 2 < 1$

$$2x - 1 > 5 \quad \text{and} \quad 3x - 2 < 1$$
$$2x > 6 \qquad\qquad 3x < 3$$
$$x > 3 \qquad\qquad x < 1$$
$$\{x \mid x > 3\} \qquad\qquad \{x \mid x < 1\}$$
$$\{x \mid x > 3\} \cap \{x \mid x < 1\} = \varnothing$$

Another way of thinking about the solution of this inequality is to ask, "What number is greater than 3 and less than 1?" There is no such number, so the solution set is the empty set.

? QUESTION   Suppose the word *and* in the previous compound inequality is replaced with *or*. Does that change the solution set?

3.4 EXERCISES

Topics for Discussion

1. How are the symbols), (,], and [used to distinguish the graphs of solution sets of inequalities?

2. State the Addition Property of Inequalities and give examples of its use.

3. State the Multiplication Property of Inequalities and give examples of its use.

4. Which set operation is used when a compound inequality is combined with *or*? Which set operation is used when a compound inequality is combined with *and*?

5. Explain why writing $-3 > x > 4$ does not make sense.

? ANSWER   Yes. The solution set is now the union of two sets, $\{x \mid x > 3\} \cup \{x \mid x < 1\}$. Another way of thinking about this is to note that we are looking for a number that is greater than 3 *or* less than 1.

▪ The Addition and Multiplication Properties of Inequalities

Solve and graph the solution set. Write the solution set in set-builder notation.

6. $x + 1 < 3$

7. $x - 5 > -2$

8. $5 + n \geq 4$

9. $-2 + n \geq 0$

10. $8x \leq -24$

11. $-4x < 8$

12. $3n > 0$

13. $-2n \leq -8$

Solve. Write the answer in set-builder notation.

14. $x - 3 < 2$

15. $4x \leq 8$

16. $-2x > 8$

17. $3x - 1 > 2x + 2$

18. $2x - 1 > 7$

19. $5x - 2 \leq 8$

20. $6x + 3 > 4x - 1$

21. $8x + 1 \geq 2x + 13$

22. $4 - 3x < 10$

23. $7 - 2x \geq 1$

24. $-3 - 4x > -11$

25. $4x - 2 < x - 11$

Solve. Write the answer using interval notation.

26. $x + 7 \geq 4x - 8$

27. $3x + 2 \leq 7x + 4$

28. $\dfrac{3}{5}x - 2 < \dfrac{3}{10} - x$

29. $\dfrac{2}{3}x - \dfrac{3}{2} < \dfrac{7}{6} - \dfrac{1}{3}x$

30. $\dfrac{1}{2}x - \dfrac{3}{4} < \dfrac{7}{4}x - 2$

31. $0.5x + 4 > 1.3x - 2.5$

32. $4(2x - 1) > 3x - 2(3x - 5)$

33. $2 - 5(x + 1) \geq 3(x - 1) - 8$

34. $3(4x + 3) \leq 7 - 4(x - 2)$

35. $3 + 2(x + 5) \geq x + 5(x + 1) + 1$

36. $3 - 4(x + 2) \leq 6 + 4(2x + 1)$

37. $12 - 2(3x - 2) \geq 5x - 2(5 - x)$

38. *Mathematics*   Three-fifths of a number is greater than two-thirds. Find the least integer that satisfies the inequality.

39. *Income Tax*   One way a self-employed person can avoid a tax penalty is to pay at least 90% of her or his total annual income tax liability by April 15. What amount of income tax must be paid by April 15 by a person with an annual income tax liability of $3500?

40. *Recycling*   A service organization will receive a bonus of $200 for collecting more than 1850 pounds of aluminum cans during its four collection drives. On the first three drives, the organization collected 505 pounds, 493 pounds, and 412 pounds. How many pounds of cans must the organization collect on the fourth drive to receive the bonus?

41. *Monthly Income*   A sales representative for a stereo store has the option of receiving either a monthly salary of $2000 or a 35% commission on the selling price of each item sold by the representative. What dollar amounts in sales will make the commission more attractive than the monthly salary?

42. *Monthly Income*   The sales agent for a jewelry company is offered a flat monthly salary of $3200 or a salary of $1000 plus an 11% commission on the selling price of each item sold by the agent. If the agent chooses the $3200 salary, what dollar amount does the agent expect to sell per month?

43. *Telecommunications*   A computer bulletin board service charges either a flat fee of $10 per month or $4 per month plus $.10 for each minute the service is used. For how many minutes per month must a person use this service for the cost to exceed $10?

44. *Food Mixtures*   For a product to be labeled orange juice, a state agency requires that at least 80% of the drink be real orange juice. How many ounces of artificial flavors can be added to 32 ounces of real orange juice if the drink is to be labeled orange juice?

45. *Transportation*   A shuttle service taking skiers to a ski area charges $8 per person each way. Four skiers are debating whether to take the shuttle bus or rent a car for $45 plus $.25 per mile. Assuming that the skiers will share the cost of the car and that they want the least expensive method of transportation, how far away is the ski area if they choose to take the shuttle service?

46. *Transportation*   Company A rents cars for $25 per day and $.08 per mile driven. Company B rents cars for $15 per day and $.14 per mile driven. You want to rent a car for one day. Find the maximum number of miles you can drive a Company B car if it is to cost you less than a Company A car.

47. *Telecommunications*   TopPage advertises local paging service for $6.95 per month for up to 400 pages, and $.10 per page thereafter. A competitor advertises service for $3.95 per month for up to 400 pages and $.15 per page thereafter. For what number of pages per month is the TopPage plan less expensive?

48. *Telecommunications*   During a weekday, to call a city 40 miles away from a certain pay phone costs $.70 for the first 3 minutes and $.15 for each additional minute. If you use a calling card, there is a $.35 fee and then the rates are $.196 for the first minute and $.126 for each additional minute. How long must a call last if it is to be cheaper to pay with coins rather than with a calling card?

49. *Temperature*   The temperature range for a week in a mountain town was between 0°C and 30°C. Find the temperature range in Fahrenheit degrees. The equation used to convert Fahrenheit to Celsius is $C = \frac{5(F - 32)}{9}$.

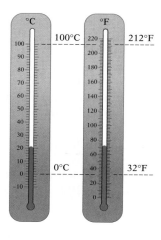

50. *Banking*   Heritage National Bank offers two different checking accounts. The first charges $3 per month and $.50 per check after the first 10 checks. The second account charges $8 per month with unlimited check writing. How many checks can be written per month if the first account is to be less expensive than the second account?

51. *Banking*   Glendale Federal Bank offers a checking account to small businesses. The charge is $8 per month plus $.12 per check after the first 100 checks. A competitor is offering an account for $5 per month plus $.15 per check after the first 100 checks. If a business chooses the first account, how many checks does the business write each month if it is assumed that an account at the Glendale Federal Bank will cost less than the competitor's account?

52. *Education*   In a history class, an average score of 90 or above out of a possible 100 receives an A grade. You have grades of 95, 89, and 81 on three exams. Find the range of scores on the fourth exam that will give you an A for the course.

53. *Education*   An average of 70 to 79 in a mathematics class receives a C grade. A student has grades of 56, 91, 83, and 62 on four tests. If the maximum score on a fifth test is 100, find the range of scores on that test that will give the student a C for the course.

54. ● *Telecommunications*   The America's Choice^{SM} 550 plan offered by Verizon Wireless has a monthly rate of $55, which includes 550 minutes per month for calls. The rate for additional minutes over 550 is $.35 per minute. The America's Choice^{SM} plan has a monthly rate of $75 and includes 900 minutes per month for calls. The rate for additional minutes over 900 is $.35 per minute (*Source:* Verizon Wireless web site, April 2002). Assuming that a person is going to use at least 600 minutes per month but less than 900 minutes per month, how many additional minutes over 600 would the person have to use for the America's Choice^{SM} 550 plan to be less expensive? Round to the nearest whole number.

■ Compound Inequalities

Solve. Write the answer in set-builder notation.

55. $2x < 6$ or $x - 4 > 1$

56. $\dfrac{1}{2}x > -2$ and $5x < 10$

57. $3x < -9$ and $x - 2 < 2$

58. $7x < 14$ and $1 - x < 4$

59. $6x - 2 < -14$ or $5x + 1 > 11$

60. $5 < 4x - 3 < 21$

61. $3x - 5 > 10$ or $3x - 5 < -10$

62. $6x - 2 < 5$ or $7x - 5 < 16$

63. $5x + 12 \geq 2$ or $7x - 1 \leq 13$

64. $3 \leq 7x - 14 \leq 31$

65. $6x + 5 < -1$ or $1 - 2x < 7$

66. $9 - x \geq 7$ and $9 - 2x < 3$

Applying Concepts

Use the roster method to list the positive integers that are solutions of the inequalities.

67. $7 - 2b \leq 15 - 5b$

68. $13 - 8a \geq 2 - 6a$

69. $2(2c - 3) < 5(6 - c)$

70. $-6(2 - d) \geq 4(4d - 9)$

Use the roster method to list the integers that are elements of the intersection of the solution sets of the two inequalities.

71. $5x - 12 \leq x + 8$
$3x - 4 \geq 2 + x$

72. $6x - 5 > 9x - 2$
$5x - 6 < 8x + 9$

73. $4(x - 2) \leq 3x + 5$
$7(x - 3) \geq 5x - 1$

74. $3(x + 2) < 2(x + 4)$
$4(x + 5) > 3(x + 6)$

75. Determine whether the following statements are always true, sometimes true, or never true.
  a. If $a > b$, then $-a < -b$.
  b. If $a < b$ and $a \neq 0$, $b \neq 0$, then $\dfrac{1}{a} < \dfrac{1}{b}$.
  c. When dividing both sides of an inequality by an integer, we must reverse the inequality symbol.
  d. If $a < 1$, then $a^2 < a$.
  e. If $a < b < 0$ and $c < d < 0$, then $ac > bd$.

76. Determine whether the following statements are always true, sometimes true, or never true. If a statement is sometimes true, find conditions that will make it always true.

   a. If $ax < bx$, then $a < b$.

   b. If $a < b$, then $a^2 < b^2$.

   c. If $a < b$, then $ax^2 < bx^2$.

   d. If $a < b$ and $a \neq 0$, $b \neq 0$, then $\frac{1}{a} < \frac{1}{b}$.

   e. If $a > b > 0$, then $\frac{1}{a} < \frac{1}{b}$.

EXPLORATION

1. *Measurements as Approximations*   Recall the rules for rounding a decimal, which are given at the right. Given these rules, some possible values of the number 2.7 that was rounded to the nearest tenth are 2.73, 2.68, 2.65, and 2.749. If V represents the exact value of 2.7 before it was rounded, then the inequality $2.65 \leq V < 2.75$ represents all possible values of 2.7 before it was rounded. This is read "V is greater than or equal to 2.65 and less than 2.75."

Now suppose a rectangle is measured as 3.4 meters by 4.8 meters, each measurement rounded to the nearest tenth of a meter. By using the least and greatest possible values of each measurement, we can find the possible values of the area, A.

$$3.35(4.75) \leq A < 3.45(4.85)$$
$$15.9125 \leq A < 16.7325$$

The area is greater than or equal to 15.9125 square meters and less than 16.7325 square meters.

   a. Suppose the length of a line is measured as 4.2 inches, rounded to the nearest tenth of an inch. Write an inequality that represents the possible lengths of the line.

   b. The length of the side of a square was given as 6.4 centimeters, rounded to the nearest tenth of a centimeter. Write an inequality that represents the possible areas of the square.

   c. The base of a triangle was measured as 5.43 meters and the height as 2.47 meters, each measurement rounded to the nearest hundredth of a meter. Write an inequality that represents the possible areas of the triangle.

   d. A rectangle is measured as 3.0 meters by 4.0 meters, each measurement rounded to the nearest tenth of a meter. Write an inequality that represents the possible areas of the rectangle.

> **TAKE NOTE**
>
> If the digit to the right of the given place value is less than 5, that digit and all the digits to the right are dropped. For example, 2.73 rounded to the nearest tenth is 2.7.
>
> If the digit to the right of the given place value is greater than or equal to 5, increase the number in the given place value by 1 and drop the remaining digits. For example, 2.65 rounded to the nearest tenth is 2.7.

2. *Inequalities and Logic*   Logical operators and inequalities are such an important part of mathematics that these functions are built into graphing calculators. Typical graphing calculator screens follow.

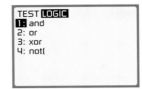

A graphing calculator will display a 1 when a statement is true and a 0 when the statement is false. For instance, the inequality $x > 2$ is true when $x = 3$ but false when $x = -1$. In these cases, the calculator assigns a *value* to the expression. The value of the expression $x > 2$ is 1 when $x = 3$; the value of $x > 2$ is 0 when $x = -1$.

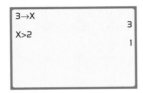

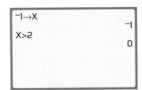

As shown at the right, a graphing calculator can be used to check the answer to a compound inequality. Enter $25 < 50$ and $25 > 10$. The calculator prints a 1 to the screen to mean that the statement is true. If we enter $30 > 50$ or $20 < 10$, a 0 is printed to the screen.

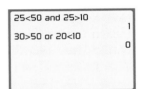

a.   What is the value of $2x - 3 < 7$ when $x = 6$?

b.   What is the value of $2x - 3 < 7$ when $x = 2$?

c.   For what values of x is the value of $2x - 3 < 7$ equal to 1?

d.   What is the value of $4 - 3x \geq 13$ when $x = -4$?

e.   What is the value of $4 - 3x \geq 13$ when $x = 2$?

f.   For what values of x is the value of $4 - 3x \geq 13$ equal to 1?

g.   What is the value of the compound inequality $2x + 1 > 5$ and $3x - 2 < 13$ when $x = 3$?

h.   What is the value of the compound inequality $2x + 1 > 5$ and $3x - 2 < 13$ when $x = 7$?

i.   What is the value of the compound inequality $2x + 1 > 5$ and $3x - 2 < 13$ when $x = 1$?

j.   For what values of x is the value of the compound inequality $2x + 1 > 5$ and $3x - 2 < 13$ equal to 1?

k.   For what values of x is the value of the compound inequality $2x - 5 < 1$ or $4x + 1 > 21$ equal to 1?

Absolute Value Equations and Inequalities

- Absolute Value Equations
- Absolute Value Inequalities

■ Absolute Value Equations

The **absolute value** of a number is its distance from zero on the number line. Distance is always a positive number or zero. Therefore, the absolute value of a number is always a positive number or zero.

The distance from 0 to 6 or from 0 to -6 is 6 units.

$$|6| = 6 \text{ and } |-6| = 6$$

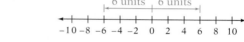

> **TAKE NOTE**
>
> Recall that the symbol for absolute value is $|\ |$.

An equation containing an absolute value symbol is called an **absolute value equation.** Examples of absolute value equations are shown at the right.

$$\left.\begin{array}{l} |x| = 3 \\ |x + 2| = 8 \\ |3x - 4| = 5x - 9 \end{array}\right\} \text{Absolute value equations}$$

The solution of an absolute value equation is based on the following rule.

> **Solutions of Absolute Value Equations**
>
> If $a > 0$ and $|x| = a$, then $x = a$ or $x = -a$. If $a = 0$ and $|x| = a$, then $x = 0$.

> **TAKE NOTE**
>
> We require $a > 0$ because the absolute value of a number other than zero is positive. If $a < 0$, then $|x| = a$ has no solution.

For instance, if $|x| = 6$, then $x = 6$ or $x = -6$.

$$|x| = 6 \qquad\qquad |x| = 6$$
$$|6| = 6 \text{ True} \qquad |-6| = 6 \text{ True}$$

? QUESTION   **a.** What are the solutions of the equation $|x| = 12$?

b. What are the solutions of the equation $|x| = -3$?

? ANSWERS   **a.** 12 and -12 **b.** There are no solutions of the equation because the absolute value of a number is positive or zero.

> Solve: $|x + 3| = 7$
> $$|x + 3| = 7$$

- If $x + 3$ is positive, then $x + 3 = 7$.
  If $x + 3$ is negative, then $x + 3 = -7$.

$$x + 3 = 7 \qquad x + 3 = -7$$
$$x = 4 \qquad x = -10$$

- Remove the absolute value sign and rewrite as two equations. Then solve each equation.

The solutions are -10 and 4.

TAKE NOTE

Be sure to check your solutions.

$|x + 3| = 7$		$|x + 3| = 7$	
$|-10 + 3|$	7	$|4 + 3|$	7
$|-7|$	7	$|7|$	7
7	$= 7$	7	$= 7$

The solutions check.

EXAMPLE 1

Solve.   **a.** $|3x - 5| = 10$ **b.** $6 - |1 - 4x| = 1$

Solution   **a.**
$$|3x - 5| = 10$$
$$3x - 5 = 10 \qquad 3x - 5 = -10$$
$$3x = 15 \qquad 3x = -5$$
$$x = 5 \qquad x = -\frac{5}{3}$$

- Remove the absolute value sign and rewrite as two equations.

The solutions are $-\dfrac{5}{3}$ and 5.

b.
$$6 - |1 - 4x| = 1$$

$$-|1 - 4x| = -5$$

$$|1 - 4x| = 5$$

$$1 - 4x = 5 \qquad 1 - 4x = -5$$

$$-4x = 4 \qquad -4x = -6$$

$$x = -1 \qquad x = \frac{3}{2}$$

The solutions are -1 and $\dfrac{3}{2}$.

- First solve for the absolute value expression.

- Subtract 6 from each side of the equation.

- Multiply each side of the equation by -1.

- Remove the absolute value sign and rewrite as two equations.

YOU TRY IT 1

Solve.   **a.** $|5 - 6x| = 1$ **b.** $|3x - 7| + 4 = 2$

Solution   See page S13.

5 units   5 units

-2 -1 0 1 2 3 4 5 6 7 8

■ Absolute Value Inequalities

Recall that absolute value represents the distance between two points. For example, the solutions of the absolute value equation $|x - 3| = 5$ are the numbers whose distance from 3 is 5 units. Therefore, the solutions are -2 and 8.

The solutions of the absolute value inequality $|x - 3| < 5$ are the numbers whose distance from 3 is less than 5 units. Therefore, the solutions are the numbers greater than -2 and less than 8. The solution set is $\{x \mid -2 < x < 8\}$.

5 units   5 units

-2 -1 0 1 2 3 4 5 6 7 8

Another way to visualize the solution set of $|x - 3| < 5$ is to graph $Y_1 = \text{abs}(X - 3)$ and then draw the line $Y_2 = 5$. Using the INTERSECT feature of the calculator, we find that the graph of $Y_1 = \text{abs}(X - 3)$ intersects the graph of $Y_2 = 5$ at $(-2, 5)$ and $(8, 5)$. Observe that the graph of $Y_1 = \text{abs}(X - 3)$ is less than 5 (the graph is below 5) when $-2 < X < 8$.

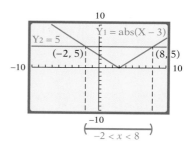

Absolute Value Inequalities of the Form $|ax + b| < c$

To solve an absolute value inequality of the form $|ax + b| < c,\ c > 0$, solve the equivalent compound inequality $-c < ax + b < c$.

For instance, if $|x| < 6$, then $-6 < x < 6$. The absolute value of all the numbers between -6 and 6 is less than 6.

❓ QUESTION **a.** What are the solutions of $|x| < 12$?

b. What are the solutions of $|x| < -3$?

In the previous statement on absolute value inequalities of the form $|ax + b| < c$, it is given that $c > 0$. If c is less than zero, then an absolute value inequality has no solution, as in part b of the Question.

❓ ANSWER **a.** $-12 < x < 12$ **b.** There are no solutions because there are no numbers whose absolute value are less than -3; the absolute value of a number is positive or zero.

EXAMPLE 2

Solve $|3x + 2| < 5$. Write the solution set in set-builder notation.

ALGEBRAIC SOLUTION

$$|3x + 2| < 5$$

$$-5 < 3x + 2 < 5$$
  • Write an equivalent inequality.

$$-5 - 2 < 3x + 2 - 2 < 5 - 2$$
  • Subtract 2 from each part of the inequality.

$$-7 < 3x < 3$$
  • Simplify.

$$\frac{-7}{3} < \frac{3x}{3} < \frac{3}{3}$$
  • Divide each part of the inequality by 3.

$$-\frac{7}{3} < x < 1$$
  • Simplify.

The solution set is $\left\{ x \,\middle|\, -\dfrac{7}{3} < x < 1 \right\}$.

GRAPHICAL CHECK

Graph $Y_1 = \text{abs}(3X + 2)$ and $Y_2 = 5$. Use the INTERSECT feature of the calculator to find the intersections of the two equations: $\left(-\frac{7}{3}, 5\right)$ and $(1, 5)$. Observe that the graph of $Y_1 = \text{abs}(3X + 2)$ is less than 5 (the graph is below 5) when $-\frac{7}{3} < X < 1$.

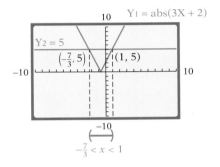

YOU TRY IT 2

Solve $|2x - 5| \leq 7$. Write the solution set in set-builder notation.

Solution   See page S13.

The solutions of the absolute value inequality $|x + 2| > 5$ are the numbers whose distance from -2 is greater than 5 units. Therefore, the solutions are the numbers less than -7 *or* greater than 3. Because the word *or* is used, the solution set is the union of $\{x \,|\, x < -7\}$ and $\{x \,|\, x > 3\}$. The solution set is

$$\{x \,|\, x < -7\} \cup \{x \,|\, x > 3\} = \{x \,|\, x < -7 \text{ or } x > 3\}$$

Another way to visualize the solution set of $|x + 2| > 5$ is to graph $Y_1 = \text{abs}(X + 2)$ and $Y_2 = 5$. Using the INTERSECT feature of the calculator, we find that the graph of $Y_1 = \text{abs}(X + 2)$ intersects the graph of $Y_2 = 5$ at $(-7, 5)$ and $(3, 5)$. Observe that the graph of $Y_1 = \text{abs}(X + 2)$ is greater than 5 (the graph is above 5) when $X < -7$ or when $X > 3$.

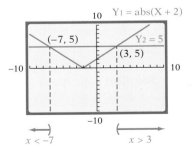

TAKE NOTE

Closely note the difference between solving an absolute value inequality of the form $|ax + b| < c$, discussed previously, and one of the form $|ax + b| > c$, discussed here.

Absolute Value Inequalities of the Form $|ax + b| > c$

To solve an absolute value inequality of the form $|ax + b| > c$, solve the equivalent compound inequality $ax + b > c$ or $ax + b < -c$.

For instance, if $|x| > 6$, then $x < -6$ or $x > 6$.

? QUESTION **a.** What are the solutions of $|x| > 12$?

b. What are the solutions of $|x| > -3$?

EXAMPLE 3

Solve $|1 - 2x| > 7$. Write the solution set in set-builder notation.

ALGEBRAIC SOLUTION

$|1 - 2x| > 7$

$1 - 2x > 7$ or $1 - 2x < -7$ • Write an equivalent inequality.

$1 - 1 - 2x > 7 - 1$ $1 - 1 - 2x < -7 - 1$ • Subtract 1 from each side.

$-2x > 6$ $-2x < -8$

$\dfrac{-2x}{-2} < \dfrac{6}{-2}$ $\dfrac{-2x}{-2} > \dfrac{-8}{-2}$ • Divide each side by -2. Because we are dividing by -2, the inequality symbol must be reversed.

$x < -3$ $x > 4$

$\{x | x < -3\}$ or $\{x | x > 4\}$

The solution set is the union of the solution sets of the two inequalities.

$$\{x | x < -3\} \cup \{x | x > 4\} = \{x | x < -3 \text{ or } x > 4\}$$

The solution set is $\{x | x < -3 \text{ or } x > 4\}$.

GRAPHICAL CHECK

Graph $Y_1 = \text{abs}(1 - 2X)$ and $Y_2 = 7$. Use the INTERSECT feature of the calculator to find the intersections of the two equations: $(-3, 7)$ and $(4, 7)$. Observe that the graph of $Y_1 = \text{abs}(1 - 2X)$ is greater than 7 (the graph is above 7) when $X < -3$ or $X > 4$.

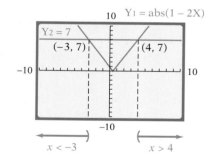

YOU TRY IT 3

Solve $|5x + 4| \geq 16$. Write the solution set in set-builder notation.

Solution   See page S13.

? ANSWERS **a.** $x < -12$ or $x > 12$ **b.** The numbers greater than -3 include 0 and all the positive numbers. The absolute value of any number is positive or zero. Therefore, the solutions are all the real numbers.

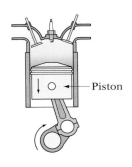
Piston

The **tolerance** of a component, or part, is the acceptable amount by which the component may vary from a given measurement. For example, the diameter of a piston may vary from the given measurement of 9 centimeters by 0.001 centimeter. This is written as 9 centimeters ± 0.001 centimeter, which is read "9 centimeters plus or minus 0.001 centimeter." The maximum diameter, or **upper limit,** of the piston is 9 centimeters + 0.001 centimeter = 9.001 centimeters. The minimum diameter, or **lower limit,** of the piston is 9 centimeters − 0.001 centimeter = 8.999 centimeters.

The lower and upper limits of the diameter can also be found by solving the absolute value inequality $|d - 9| \le 0.001$, where d is the diameter of the piston.

$$|d - 9| \le 0.001$$
$$-0.001 \le d - 9 \le 0.001$$
$$-0.001 + 9 \le d - 9 + 9 \le 0.001 + 9$$
$$8.999 \le d \le 9.001$$

The lower and upper limits are 8.999 centimeters and 9.001 centimeters.

EXAMPLE 4

A doctor has prescribed 2 cc (cubic centimeters) of medication for a patient. The tolerance is 0.03 cc. Find the lower and upper limits of the amount of medication to be given.

State the goal.   The goal is to find the lower and upper limits of the amount of medication to be given.

Devise a strategy.   Let p represent the prescribed amount of medication, T the tolerance, and m the given amount of medication. Solve the absolute value inequality $|m - p| \le T$ for m.

Solve the problem. $|m - p| \le T$
$$|m - 2| \le 0.03$$
$$-0.03 \le m - 2 \le 0.03$$
$$1.97 \le m \le 2.03$$

The lower and upper limits of the amount of medication to be given to the patient are 1.97 cc and 2.03 cc.

Check your work.   Be sure to check your work by doing a thorough check of your calculations. As an estimate, the answers appear reasonable in that the amounts of medication are close to 2 cc.

YOU TRY IT 4

A machinist must make a bushing that has a tolerance of 0.003 inch. The diameter of the bushing is 2.55 inch. Find the lower and upper limits of the diameter of the bushing.

Solution   See page S13.

EXAMPLE 5

A statistician is willing to state that a coin is fair if, when it is tossed 1000 times, the number of tails, t, satisfies the inequality $\left|\dfrac{t - 500}{15.81}\right| < 2.33$. Determine what values of t will cause the statistician to state that the coin is fair.

State the goal.   The goal is to find the number of tails that must be obtained when tossing a coin 1000 times to suggest that the coin is fair.

Devise a strategy.   Solve the inequality $\left|\dfrac{t - 500}{15.81}\right| < 2.33$ for t.

Solve the problem. $\dfrac{t - 500}{15.81} < 2.33$

$-2.33 < \dfrac{t - 500}{15.81} < 2.33$ • Write a compound inequality.

$-36.8373 < t - 500 < 36.8373$ • Multiply each part of the inequality by 15.81.

$463.1627 < t < 536.8373$ • Add 500 to each part of the inequality.

There must be between 464 tails and 536 tails, inclusive, for the statistician to state the coin is fair.

Check your work.   Be sure to check your calculations.

> ### TAKE NOTE
>
> Note how the rounding was done for the answer. Since $t > 463.1527$ and t is a whole number, the lower bound is 464. Similarly, $t < 536.8373$, so the upper bound is 536.

YOU TRY IT 5

According to the registrar of a college, there is a 95% chance that a student applying for admission will have an SAT score, x, that satisfies the inequality $\left|\dfrac{x - 950}{98}\right| < 1.96$. Determine the values of x that the registrar expects from a student applicant.

Solution   See page S13.

3.5 EXERCISES

Topics for Discussion

1. Determine whether the statement is always true, sometimes true, or never true.
    a. If $a > 0$ and $|x| = a$, then $x = a$ or $x = -a$.
    b. The absolute inequality $|x| < a$, $a > 0$, is equivalent to the compound inequality $x > a$ or $x < -a$.
    c. If $|x + 3| = 12$, then $|x + 3| = 12$ and $|x + 3| = -12$.
    d. An absolute value equation has two solutions.
    e. If $|x + b| < c$, then $x + b < -c$ or $x + b > c$.

2.   If the absolute value of a number must be positive or zero, why can the solution of an absolute value equation be a negative number?

3.   Which of the following inequalities have no solution? Which have all real numbers as the solution set?
   a. $|3x + 5| \geq -9$
   b. $|4x - 8| \leq -7$
   c. $|2x + 1| > -6$
   d. $|-x - 10| < -3$
   e. $|7 - 5x| \geq 0$
   f. $|9 - x| \leq -4$

4.   The solution set of which inequality, $|ax + b| > c$ or $|ax + b| < c$, where in both cases $c > 0$, is the union of two solution sets and which is the intersection of two solution sets?

5.   How does the solution set of $|ax + b| < c$, $c > 0$, differ from the solution set of $|ax + b| \leq c$.

▪ Absolute Value Equations

Solve.

6. $|x| = 7$

7. $|a| = 2$

8. $|-t| = 3$

9. $|-a| = 9$

10. $|-t| = -3$

11. $|-y| = -2$

12. $|x + 2| = 3$

13. $|x + 5| = 2$

14. $|y - 5| = 3$

15. $|y - 8| = 4$

16. $|a - 2| = 0$

17. $|a + 7| = 0$

18. $|x - 2| = -4$

19. $|x + 8| = -2$

20. $|2x - 5| = 4$

21. $|4 - 3x| = 4$

22. $|2 - 5x| = 2$

23. $|2x - 3| = 0$

24. $|5x + 5| = 0$

25. $|3x - 2| = -4$

26. $|2x + 5| = -2$

27. $|x - 2| - 2 = 3$

28. $|x - 9| - 3 = 2$

29. $|3a + 2| - 4 = 4$

30. $|8 - y| - 3 = 1$

31. $|2x - 3| + 3 = 3$

32. $|4x - 7| - 5 = -5$

33. $|2x - 3| + 4 = -4$

34. $|3x - 2| + 1 = -1$

35. $|6x - 5| - 2 = 4$

36. $|4b + 3| - 2 = 7$

37. $|3t + 2| + 3 = 4$

38. $|5x - 2| + 5 = 7$

39. $3 - |x - 4| = 5$

40. $2 - |x - 5| = 4$

41. $|2x - 8| + 12 = 2$

42. $|3x - 4| + 8 = 3$

43. $2 + |3x - 4| = 5$

44. $5 + |2x + 1| = 8$

45. $5 - |2x + 1| = 5$

46. $3 - |5x + 3| = 3$

47. $8 - |1 - 3x| = -1$

■ Absolute Value Inequalities

Solve.

48. $|x| > 3$

49. $|x| < 5$

50. $|x + 1| > 2$

51. $|x - 2| > 1$

52. $|x - 5| \leq 1$

53. $|x - 4| \leq 3$

54. $|2 - x| \geq 3$

55. $|3 - x| \geq 2$

56. $|2x + 1| < 5$

57. $|3x - 2| < 4$

58. $|5x + 2| > 12$

59. $|7x - 1| > 13$

60. $|4x - 3| \leq -2$

61. $|5x + 1| \leq -4$

62. $|2x + 7| > -5$

63. $|3x - 1| > -4$

64. $|4 - 3x| > 5$

65. $|7 - 2x| > 9$

66. $|5 - 4x| \leq 13$

67. $|3 - 7x| < 17$

68. $|6 - 3x| \leq 0$

69. $|10 - 5x| \geq 0$

70. $|2 - 9x| > 20$

71. $|5x - 1| < 16$

72. *Mechanics*   The diameter of a bushing is 1.75 inches. The bushing has a tolerance of 0.008 inch. Find the lower and upper limits of the diameter of the bushing.

1.75 in.

73. *Mechanics* A machinist must make a bushing that has a tolerance of 0.004 inch. The diameter of the bushing is 3.48 inches. Find the lower and upper limits of the diameter of the bushing.

74. *Medicine* A doctor has prescribed 2.5 cc of medication for a patient. The tolerance is 0.2 cc. Find the lower and upper limits of the amount of medication to be given.

75. *Electricity* A power strip is utilized on a computer to prevent the loss of programming by electrical surges. The power strip is designed to allow 110 volts plus or minus 16.5 volts. Find the lower and upper limits of voltage to the computer.

76. *Electricity* An electric motor is designed to run on 220 volts plus or minus 25 volts. Find the lower and upper limits of voltage on which the motor will run.

77. *Mechanics* A piston rod for an automobile is $10\frac{3}{8}$ inches long with a tolerance of $\frac{1}{32}$ inch. Find the lower and upper limits of the length of the piston rod.

78. *Mechanics* The diameter of a piston for an automobile is $3\frac{5}{16}$ inches with a tolerance of $\frac{1}{64}$ inch. Find the lower and upper limits of the diameter of the piston.

79. *Electronics* Find the lower and upper limits of a 29,000-ohm resistor with a 2% tolerance.

80. *Electronics* Find the lower and upper limits of a 15,000-ohm resistor with a 10% tolerance.

81. *Electronics* Find the lower and upper limits of a 25,000-ohm resistor with a 5% tolerance.

82. *Electronics* Find the lower and upper limits of a 56-ohm resistor with a 5% tolerance.

83. *Fair Play* In order to be reasonably sure that a coin is fair, the number of heads, h, in 500 tosses of the coin should satisfy the inequality $\frac{|h - 250|}{11.18} < 1.96$. Determine the values of h that would allow one to be reasonably sure that the coin is fair.

84. *Fair Play*   The spinner for a game is shown at the right. If the spinner is fair (that is, the pointer is equally likely to land in each one of the sectors), then in 1000 spins, the number of times the spinner lands in sector 3 should satisfy the inequality $\frac{|x - 250|}{13.69} < 2.33$. What values of x will indicate that the spinner is fair?

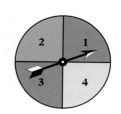

85. *Agriculture*   Pumpkins harvested from a certain farm had a mean diameter of 12.4 inches with a standard deviation of 2.6 inches. On the basis of these data, there is a 5% probability that a randomly selected pumpkin would have a diameter that satisfied the inequality $\frac{|x - 12.4|}{2.6} > 1.96$. Find the diameters of pumpkins that satisfy this condition. Round to the nearest tenth of an inch.

Applying Concepts

Solve.

86. $|2x + 1| = |x - 4|$ **87.** $|1 - 3x| = |x + 2|$ **88.** $|x| + |x - 1| = 3$

89. $|2x - 4| + |x| = 5$ **90.** $|3 - |x|| = 1$ **91.** $|x + 4| = 4x$

Solve. Write the answer in set-builder notation.

92. $|2x - 1| > |x + 2|$ **93.** $|3x - 2| < |x - 3|$ **94.** $x + |x| = 0$

95. Solve each inequality for x. In each inequality, $a > 0$, $b > 0$.
   a. $|x + a| \le b$
   b. $|x - a| > b$
   c. $|x + a| > a$
   d. $|x - a| \le a$

96. *Probability*   In a survey of the heights of 1000 women college students, the mean height was 64 inches, and the standard deviation of the heights was 2.5 inches. Statisticians, using this information, have determined that there is approximately a 1% probability that a woman chosen from this group will have a height that satisfies the inequality $\frac{|x - 64|}{2.5} > 2.58$. What are the women's heights for which the probability is approximately 1%?

97. Express the fact that both -7 and 3 are 5 units from -2 using absolute value.

98. Use absolute value to represent the inequality $-3 \le x \le 5$.

99. Explain how the solution set of $|x - 4| \leq c$ changes for $c > 0$, $c = 0$, and $c < 0$.

EXPLORATION

1. *Graphing in Restricted Domains*   This Exploration builds on Question 2 of the Exploration in Section 3.4, in which we discussed the *value* of an expression as being 1 or 0, depending on whether the expression is true or false for a particular value of a variable.

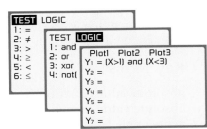

a. Consider the inequality $|x - 2| < 1$, which is equivalent to the compound inequality $x > 1$ and $x < 3$. When a graphing calculator evaluates an expression containing *and*, the calculator *multiplies* the values of the two expressions. Using the Y= editor, enter this expression into your calculator. Now create a table using a starting value of 0, and an increment of 0.25. Explain why the value of the expression is 0 for some values of x and is 1 for other values of x.

b. Consider the inequality $|x - 2| > 1$, which is equivalent to the compound inequality $x < 1$ or $x > 3$. When a graphing calculator evaluates an expression containing *or*, the calculator *adds* the values of the two expressions. Using the Y= editor, enter this expression into your calculator. Now create a table using a starting value of 0, an ending value of 4, and an increment of 0.25. Explain why the value of the expression is 0 for some values of x and 1 for other values of x.

c. Using the standard viewing window and the graph mode as dot rather than connected, enter and then graph $Y_1 = ((X > -2)$ and $(X < 5))(2X - 1)$. Explain why the graph displays as it does.

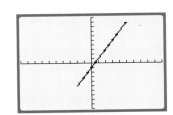

d. Using the standard viewing window and dot mode, graph $y = x^2$ for $0 < x < 3$.

e. Using the standard viewing window and dot mode, graph $y = 2x + 2$ when $x < -2$ or when $x > 3$.

f. Using the standard viewing window and dot mode, graph $y = |x + 1|$ for $-5 < x < 3$.

g. Using Xmin $= -5$, Xmax $= 5$, Ymin $= -1$, Ymax $= 25$ and dot mode, graph $y = x^2$ when $x < -2$ or when $x > 3$.

CHAPTER **3** SUMMARY

Key Terms

absolute value equation [p. 218]
absolute value inequality [p. 220]
acute angle [p. 188]
adjacent angles [p. 189]
angle [p. 187]
arc [p. 194]
central angle [p. 194]
chord [p. 194]
complementary angles [p. 188]
complements [p. 188]
compound inequality [p. 208]
conditional equation [p. 163]
corresponding angles [p. 191]
degrees [p. 187]
endpoint [p. 187]
equation [p. 163]
exterior angle of a triangle [p. 193]
first-degree equation in one variable [p. 164]
identity [p. 163]
inequality [p. 201]
inscribed angle [p. 194]
interior angles of a triangle [p. 192]
left side of an equation [p. 163]
lower limit [p. 223]
major arc [p. 194]
measure of an arc [p. 194]

minor arc [p. 194]
obtuse angle [p. 188]
parallel lines [p. 190]
perpendicular lines [p. 189]
ray [p. 187]
right angle [p. 187]
right side of an equation [p. 163]
root of an equation [p. 163]
sides of an angle [p. 187]
solution of an equation [p. 163]
solution of an inequality in one variable [p. 201]
solution set of an inequality [p. 201]
solving an equation [p. 164]
straight angle [p. 188]
supplementary angles [p. 188]
supplements [p. 188]
tangent [p. 194]
time-distance graph [p. 177]
tolerance [p. 223]
transversal [p. 190]
triangle [p. 192]
uniform motion [p. 177]
upper limit [p. 223]
value mixture problem [p. 174]
vertex [p. 187]
vertical angles [p. 190]

Essential Concepts

The Addition Property of Equations
If a, b, and c are algebraic expressions, then the equation $a = b$ has the same solutions as the equation $a + c = b + c$. [p. 164]

The Multiplication Property of Equations
If a, b, and c are algebraic expressions, and $c \neq 0$, then the equation $a = b$ has the same solutions as the equation $ac = bc$. [p. 166]

Steps in Solving First-Degree Equations
1. Use the Distributive Property to remove parentheses.
2. Combine like terms on each side of the equation.
3. Rewrite the equation with only one variable term.
4. Rewrite the equation with only one constant term.
5. Rewrite the equation so that the coefficient of the variable is 1. [p. 170]

A **value mixture problem** involves combining two ingredients that have different prices into a single blend. The solution of a value mixture problem is based on the equation $V = AC$, where V is the value of an ingredient, A is the amount of the ingredient, and C is the cost per unit of the ingredient. [p. 174]

Uniform motion means that the speed and direction of the object do not change. The solution of a uniform motion problem is based on the equation $d = rt$. In this equation, d is the distance traveled, r is the speed of the object, and t is the time spent traveling. [p. 177]

A **time–distance graph** shows the relationship between the time of travel and the distance traveled. Time is on the horizontal axis, and distance is on the vertical axis. [p. 177]

When a transversal intersects parallel lines, and the transversal is not perpendicular to the parallel lines, the following pairs of angles with equal measure are formed.
- **Alternate interior angles** are two nonadjacent angles that are on opposite sides of the transversal and between the parallel lines. [p. 191]
- **Alternate exterior angles** are two nonadjacent angles that are on opposite sides of the transversal and outside the parallel lines. [p. 191]
- **Corresponding angles** are two angles that are on the same side of the transversal and are both acute angles or are both obtuse angles. [p. 191]

The Sum of the Measures of the Interior Angles of a Triangle
The sum of the measures of the interior angles of a triangle is 180°. [p. 192]

Inscribed-Angle Theorems

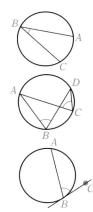

If $\angle ABC$ is an inscribed angle of a circle, then $m\angle ABC = \dfrac{1}{2}(m\widehat{AC})$.

Inscribed angles that intersect the same arc are equal. $m\angle ABD = m\angle ACD$

The measure of an angle formed by a tangent and a chord is equal to one-half the measure of the intercepted arc. $m\angle ABC = \dfrac{1}{2}(m\widehat{AB})$. [p. 195]

The Addition Property of Inequalities
If $a > b$ and c is a real number, then the inequalities $a > b$ and $a + c > b + c$ have the same solution set.
If $a < b$ and c is a real number, then the inequalities $a < b$ and $a + c < b + c$ have the same solution set. [p. 202]

The Multiplication Property of Inequalities
Rule 1
If $a > b$ and $c > 0$, then the inequalities $a > b$ and $ac > bc$ have the same solution set.
If $a < b$ and $c > 0$, then the inequalities $a < b$ and $ac < bc$ have the same solution set.
Rule 2
If $a > b$ and $c < 0$, then the inequalities $a > b$ and $ac < bc$ have the same solution set.
If $a < b$ and $c < 0$, then the inequalities $a < b$ and $ac > bc$ have the same solution set. [p. 203]

Solutions of Absolute Value Equations
If $a > 0$ and $|x| = a$, then $x = a$ or $x = -a$. If $a = 0$ and $|x| = a$, then $x = 0$.
[p. 218]

Absolute Value Inequalities of the Form $|ax + b| < c$
To solve an absolute value inequality of the form $|ax + b| < c$, $c > 0$, solve the equivalent compound inequality $-c < ax + b < c$. [p. 220]

Absolute Value Inequalities of the Form $|ax + b| > c$
To solve an absolute value inequality of the form $|ax + b| > c$, solve the equivalent compound inequality $ax + b < -c$ or $ax + b > c$. [p. 222]

CHAPTER **3** REVIEW EXERCISES

1. Solve: $m - \dfrac{3}{5} = -\dfrac{1}{4}$

2. Solve: $\dfrac{3}{2}y = 4$

3. Solve: $9 - 4b = 5b + 8$

4. Solve: $2[x + 3(4 - x) - 5x] = 6(x + 4)$

5. Solve $5x - 3 < x + 9$. Write the answer in set-builder notation.

6. Solve $-1 \le 3x + 5 \le 8$. Write the answer in interval notation.

7. Solve $5x - 2 > 8$ or $3x + 2 < -4$. Write the answer in interval notation.

8. Solve: $|6x + 4| - 3 = 7$

9. Solve $|5 - 4x| > 3$. Write the answer in set-builder notation.

10. Solve $\left| \dfrac{3x - 1}{5} \right| < 4$. Write the answer in set-builder notation.

11. Find the value of x.

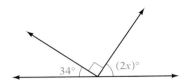

12. Given that $m\angle a = 103°$ and $m\angle b = 143°$, find $m\angle x$ and $m\angle y$.

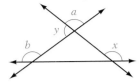

13. Given that $l_1 \| l_2$, find the measures of angles a and b.

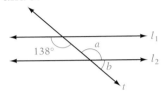

14. Find the value of x.

15. Find the supplement of a 32° angle.

16. A statistics professor gives a pretest on the first day of a semester. On the basis of past experience, the professor knows that 95% of the students will have scores that satisfy the inequality $\left|\dfrac{x - 70}{10}\right| < 1.96$. Find the range of scores that 95% of the students taking the pretest will have.

17. At 1:00 P.M., two planes were 800 miles apart and flying toward each other at different altitudes. The rate of one plane was 320 miles per hour, and the rate of the second plane was 280 miles per hour. At what time will they pass each other?

18. The diameter of a bushing is 2.75 inches. The bushing has a tolerance of 0.003 inch. Find the lower and upper limits of the diameter of the bushing.

19. An average score of 80 to 90 in a psychology class receives a B grade. A student has grades of 92, 66, 72, and 88 on four exams. Find the range of scores on the fifth exam that will give the student a B in the course. Assume 100 is the highest possible score.

20. How much apple juice that costs $3.20 per gallon must a grocer mix with 40 gallons of cranberry juice that costs $5.50 per gallon to make cranapple juice that costs $4.20 per gallon?

CHAPTER **3** TEST

1. Solve: $\dfrac{2}{3} = b + \dfrac{3}{4}$

2. Solve: $\dfrac{2}{3}d = \dfrac{4}{9}$

3. Solve: $4x + 1 = 7x - 7$

4. Solve: $5x - 4(x + 2) = 7 - 2(3 - 2x)$

5. Solve $2 - 2(7 - 2x) \le 4(5 - 3x)$. Write the answer in set-builder notation.

6. Solve $2 - 5(x + 1) \ge 3(x - 1) - 8$. Write the answer in set-builder notation.

7. Solve $-5 < 4x - 1 < 7$. Write the answer in interval notation.

8. Solve $3x - 2 > -4$ or $7x - 5 < 3x + 3$. Write the answer in interval notation.

9. Solve $9x - 2 > 7$ and $3x - 5 < 10$. Write the answer in set-builder notation.

10. Solve: $|2x - 3| = 8$

11. Solve $|2x - 5| \le 3$. Write the answer in set-builder notation.

12. Solve $|4x - 7| \ge 5$. Write the answer in set-builder notation.

13. Solve: $|5x - 4| < -2$

14. Find the value of x.

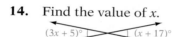

15. Given that $l_1 \| l_2$, find the measures of angles a and b.

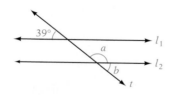

16. Find the value of x.

17. The measure of one of the acute angles of a right triangle is twice the measure of the other acute angle. Find the measure of each angle.

18. Two planes are 1680 miles apart and traveling toward each other. One plane is traveling 80 mph faster than the other plane. The planes meet in 1.75 hours. Find the speed of each plane.

19. A tea mixture was made from 40 pounds of tea costing $6.40 per pound and 65 pounds of tea costing $3.80 per pound. Find the cost per pound of the tea mixture.

20. A doctor prescribed 5 milligrams of medication for a patient. The tolerance is 0.2 milligram. Find the lower and upper limits of the amount of medication to be given.

CUMULATIVE REVIEW EXERCISES

1. 1K31K4 represents a six-digit number that is a multiple of 12 but not a multiple of 9. Find the value of K.

2. Give the order of the following statements so that the first two statements listed make it possible to use deductive reasoning to arrive at the third statement listed.
(A) An eagle has feathers.
(B) All birds have feathers.
(C) An eagle is a bird.

3. Use the roster method to list the odd natural numbers less than 9.

4. Let $E = \{0, 3, 6, 9, 12\}$ and $F = \{-6, -4, -2, 0, 2, 4, 6\}$. Find $E \cup F$ and $E \cap F$.

5. Evaluate the variable expression $2(b + c) - 2a^2$ for $a = -1$, $b = 3$, and $c = -2$.

6. Find the temperature after a rise of 12°C from −8°C.

7. Evaluate $y - z$ for $y = -3.597$ and $z = -4.826$.

8. The formula for the area of a trapezoid is $A = \frac{1}{2} h(a + b)$, where A is the area, h is the height, and a and b are the lengths of the bases. Find the area of the trapezoid shown at the right.

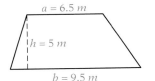

9. Simplify: $5(3y - 8) - 4(1 - 2y)$

10. Translate "a number minus the sum of the number and twenty" into a variable expression. Then simplify the expression.

11. If a car averages 28 miles per gallon, then the distance d, in miles, that a car can travel on g gallons of gasoline is given by $d = 28g$.
a. Complete the following input/output table.

Input, quantity of gasoline g (in gallons)	0	2	4	6	8	10	12
Output, distance traveled d (in miles)							

b. Write a sentence that explains the meaning of the ordered pair (10, 280).

12. Evaluate $f(t) = t^2 + t - 4$ at $t = -2$.

13. Given $s(t) = 2t^3 - t^2 - 3t + 4$ with domain $\{-4, -2, 0, 2, 4\}$, find the range of s.

14. Find the x- and y-intercepts for the graph of $F(x) = x^2 + x - 6$.

15. Find the input value for which the two functions $f(x) = 4x - 2$ and $g(x) = -3x + 5$ have the same value.

16. Solve: $3(2x - 3) + 1 = 2(1 - 2x)$

17. Solve $3x - 2 \geq 6x + 7$. Write the solution set in interval notation.

18. Solve: $3 - |2x - 3| = -8$

19. Solve: $|3x - 5| \leq 4$

20. Two planes are 1400 miles apart and traveling toward each other. One plane is traveling 120 mph faster than the other plane. The planes meet in 2.5 hours. Find the speed of the faster plane.

4

Linear Functions

```
Plot1  Plot2  Plot3
On Off
Type: ▰▰  ⬚    ⬚⬚⬚
      ⬚⬚·· ·⬚⬚·  ⬚
Xlist: L₁
Ylist: L₂
Mark: ▫  +  ·
```

Press **2nd** STAT PLOT **ENTER** to access the **STAT PLOTS** options.

In order to monitor species that are or are becoming endangered, scientists need to determine the present population of that species. Scientists have tracked the increase in the population of the grey wolf in regions of Idaho since its re-introduction in the mid-1990s. This has led to the modeling of the size of the population with a linear function, as shown in **Exercise 9 on page 289.** *From the equation, we can determine how fast the population is growing and make estimates about its future growth.*

Need help? For online student resources, visit this web site:
Math.college.hmco.com

237

PREP TEST

1. Simplify: $-4(x - 3)$

2. Simplify: $y - (-5)$

3. Simplify: $\dfrac{1}{4}(3x - 16)$

4. Simplify: $\dfrac{3 - (-5)}{2 - 6}$

5. Evaluate $8r + 240$ for $r = 0$.

6. Evaluate $\dfrac{a - b}{c - d}$ when $a = 3$, $b = -2$, $c = -3$, and $d = 2$.

7. Given $3x - 4y = 12$, find the value of x when $y = 0$.

8. Solve: $3x + 6 = 0$

9. Solve: $y + 8 = 0$

10. Which of the following are solutions of the inequality $-4 < x + 3$?
    a. 0   **b.** -3 **c.** 5   **d.** -7 **e.** -10

GO FIGURE

Two fractions are inserted between $\frac{1}{4}$ and $\frac{1}{2}$ so that the difference between any two successive fractions is the same. Find the sum of the four fractions.

SECTION 4.1

Slopes and Graphs of Linear Functions

■ Slope of a Line
■ Equations of the Form $Ax + By = C$

■ Slope of a Line

The graph at the left shows the pressure on a diver as the diver descends into the ocean. The graph of this equation can be represented by $P(d) = 64d + 2100$, where $P(d)$ is the pressure in pounds per square foot on a diver d feet below the surface of the ocean. By evaluating the function for various values of d, we can determine the pressure on the diver at that depth.

For instance, when $d = 2$, we have

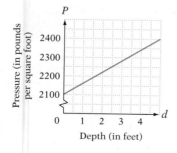

$$P(d) = 64d + 2100$$
$$P(2) = 64(2) + 2100$$
$$= 128 + 2100$$
$$= 2228$$

The pressure on a diver 2 feet below the ocean surface is 2228 pounds per square foot.

The function $P(d) = 64d + 2100$ is an example of a *linear function*.

> **Linear Function**
>
> A **linear function** is one that can be written in the form $f(x) = mx + b$, where m is the coefficient of x and b is a constant.

Here are some examples of linear functions.

$$f(x) = 2x + 5 \qquad \bullet \ m = 2, b = 5$$

$$g(t) = \frac{2}{3}t - 1 \qquad \bullet \ m = \frac{2}{3}, b = -1$$

$$v(s) = -2s \qquad \bullet \ m = -2, b = 0$$

$$h(x) = 3 \qquad \bullet \ m = 0, b = 3$$

$$f(x) = 2 - 4x \qquad \bullet \ m = -4, b = 2$$

Note that for a linear function, the exponent on the variable is 1. Also note that, as shown above, different variables can be used to designate a linear function.

? QUESTION   Which of the following are linear functions?

    a. $f(x) = 2x^2 + 5$ **b.** $g(x) = 1 - 3x$ **c.** $H(x) = \dfrac{1}{x}$

Evaluating at 0 the linear function that modeled the pressure on a diver, we have

$$P(d) = 64d + 2100$$

$$P(0) = 64(0) + 2100 = 2100$$

In this case, the P-intercept (the intercept on the vertical axis) is $(0, 2100)$. In the context of this application, this means that the pressure on a diver 0 feet below the ocean surface is 2100 pounds per square inch. Another way of saying "zero feet below the ocean surface" is to say "at sea level." Thus the pressure on a diver, or anyone else for that matter, is 2100 pounds per square foot at sea level.

Consider again the linear function $P(d) = 64d + 2100$ that models the pressure on a diver as the diver descends below the ocean surface. From the graph at the

---

? ANSWER   **a.** Because the exponent on the variable is 2, not 1, the function is not a linear function.   **b.** $1 - 3x = -3x + 1$. $g(x) = -3x + 1$ is a function of the form $f(x) = mx + b$. It is a linear function.   **c.** The variable is in the denominator. It is not a linear function.

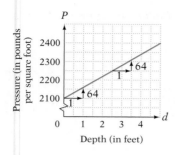

Pressure (in pounds per square foot)

Depth (in feet)

left, note that as the depth of the diver increases by 1 foot, the pressure on the diver increases by 64 pounds per square foot. This can be verified algebraically.

$$P(0) = 64(0) + 2100 = 2100$$ • Pressure at sea level
$$P(1) = 64(1) + 2100 = 2164$$ • Pressure after descending 1 foot
$$2164 - 2100 = 64$$ • Change in pressure

If we choose two other depths that differ by 1 foot, such as 2.5 and 3.5 (as in the graph at the left), the change in pressure is the same.

$$P(2.5) = 64(2.5) + 2100 = 2260$$ • Pressure at 2.5 feet below surface
$$P(3.5) = 64(3.5) + 2100 = 2324$$ • Pressure at 3.5 feet below surface
$$2324 - 2260 = 64$$ • Change in pressure

The **slope** of a line is the change in the vertical direction caused by a 1-unit change in the horizontal direction. **In a linear function of the form $f(x) = mx + b$, m is the symbol used for slope.**

For the function $P(d) = 64d + 2100$, the slope is 64. In the context of this problem, the slope means that the pressure on a diver increases by 64 pounds per square foot for each additional foot the diver descends.

$$f(x) = mx + b$$
$$\updownarrow$$
$$P(d) = 64d + 2100$$

EXAMPLE 1

After a parachute is deployed, a function that models the height of the parachutist above the ground is $f(t) = -10t + 2800$, where $f(t)$ is the height, in feet, of the parachutist t seconds after the chute is deployed. What does the slope of this function mean in the context of this problem?

Solution The function is of the form $f(x) = mx + b$, where m is the slope.

For the function $f(t) = -10t + 2800$, the slope m is -10.

The slope means that the height of the parachutist decreases 10 feet per second.

Note: The *negative* slope in $f(t) = -10t + 2800$ indicates a *decrease* in height; the *positive* slope in the function $P(d) = 64d + 2100$ indicates an *increase* in pressure.

YOU TRY IT 1

A function that models a certain small plane as it descends is given by $g(t) = -20t + 8000$, where $g(t)$ is the height, in feet, of the plane t seconds after it begins its descent. What does the slope of this function mean in the context of this problem?

Solution See page S14.

In general, for the linear function $f(x) = mx + b$, we define the slope as follows:

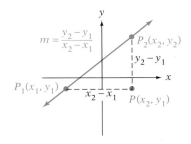

Slope of a Line

Let $P_1(x_1, y_1)$ and $P_2(x_2, y_2)$ be two points on a line. Then the **slope** m of the line through the two points is the ratio of the change in the y-coordinates to the change in the x-coordinates.

$$m = \frac{\text{change in } y}{\text{change in } x} = \frac{y_2 - y_1}{x_2 - x_1}, x_1 \neq x_2$$

TAKE NOTE

$\begin{array}{cc} P_1(x_1, y_1) & P_2(x_2, y_2) \\ \downarrow \ \downarrow & \downarrow \ \downarrow \\ P_1(-4, -3) & P_2(-1, 1) \end{array}$

In the formula for slope, let
$x_1 = -4$,
$y_1 = -3$,
$x_2 = -1$, and
$y_2 = 1$

TAKE NOTE

It does not matter which point is named P_1 and which P_2; the slope will be the same. For the example at the right, let $P_1 = (1, -3)$ and $P_2 = (-2, 3)$. Then

$m = \dfrac{y_2 - y_1}{x_2 - x_1}$

$= \dfrac{3 - (-3)}{-2 - 1}$

$= \dfrac{6}{-3} = -2$

This is the same slope calculated using $P_1 = (-2, 3)$ and $P_2 = (1, -3)$.

? QUESTION Why is the restriction $x_1 \neq x_2$ required in the definition of slope?

→ Find the slope of the line between the points $P_1(-4, -3)$ and $P_2(-1, 1)$.

Let $(x_1, y_1) = (-4, -3)$ and $(x_2, y_2) = (-1, 1)$.

$$m = \frac{y_2 - y_1}{x_2 - x_1} = \frac{1 - (-3)}{-1 - (-4)} = \frac{4}{3}$$

The slope is $\dfrac{4}{3}$.

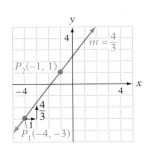

A *positive* slope indicates that the line slopes *upward* to the right.

For this line, the value of y *increases* by $\dfrac{4}{3}$ when x increases by 1. ◄

→ Find the slope of the line between the points $P_1(-2, 3)$ and $P_2(1, -3)$.

Let $(x_1, y_1) = (-2, 3)$ and $(x_2, y_2) = (1, -3)$.

$$m = \frac{y_2 - y_1}{x_2 - x_1} = \frac{-3 - 3}{1 - (-2)} = \frac{-6}{3} = -2$$

The slope is -2.

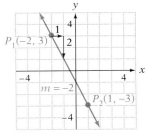

A *negative* slope indicates that the line slopes *downward* to the right.

For this line, the value of y *decreases* by 2 when x increases by 1. ◄

? ANSWER If $x_1 = x_2$, then the difference $x_2 - x_1 = 0$. This would make the denominator 0, and division by 0 is undefined.

➡ Find the slope of the line between the points $P_1(-1, -3)$ and $P_2(4, -3)$.

Let $(x_1, y_1) = (-1, -3)$ and $(x_2, y_2) = (4, -3)$.

$$m = \frac{y_2 - y_1}{x_2 - x_1} = \frac{-3 - (-3)}{4 - (-1)} = \frac{0}{5} = 0$$

The slope is 0.

A *zero* slope indicates that the line is *horizontal*.

For this particular line, the value of y stays the same when x increases by 1.

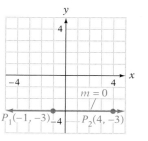

➡ Find the slope of the line between the points $P_1(4, 3)$ and $P_2(4, -1)$.

Let $(x_1, y_1) = (4, 3)$ and $(x_2, y_2) = (4, -1)$.

$$m = \frac{y_2 - y_1}{x_2 - x_1} = \frac{-1 - 3}{4 - 4} = \frac{-4}{0} \quad \text{undefined}$$

If the denominator of the slope formula is zero, the line has *no slope*. We say that the slope of the line is *undefined*.

The slope is undefined.

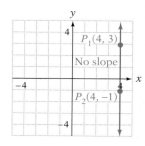

EXAMPLE 2

Find the slope of the line between the two points.

a. $P_1(-6, 1)$ and $P_2(-4, 2)$ **b.** $P_1(-3, 3)$ and $P_2(4, 3)$

Solution   **a.** $(x_1, y_1) = (-6, 1)$, $(x_2, y_2) = (-4, 2)$

$$m = \frac{y_2 - y_1}{x_2 - x_1} = \frac{2 - 1}{-4 - (-6)} = \frac{1}{2}$$

The slope is $\frac{1}{2}$.

b. $(x_1, y_1) = (-3, 3)$, $(x_2, y_2) = (4, 3)$

$$m = \frac{y_2 - y_1}{x_2 - x_1} = \frac{3 - 3}{4 - (-3)} = \frac{0}{7} = 0$$

The slope is 0.

> **YOU TRY IT 2**
>
> Find the slope of the line between the two points.
>
> **a.** $P_1(-6, 5)$ and $P_2(4, -5)$ **b.** $P_1(-5, 0)$ and $P_2(-5, 7)$
>
> **Solution**   See page S14.

TAKE NOTE

Whether we write $f(t) = 6t$ or $d = 6t$, the equation represents a linear function. $f(t)$ and d are different symbols for the same quantity.

Suppose a jogger is running at a constant speed of 6 miles per hour. Then the linear function $d = 6t$ relates the time t spent running to the distance d traveled. Some of the entries in an input/output table are shown below.

Time t (in hours)	0	0.5	1	1.5	2	2.5
Distance d (in miles)	0	3	6	9	12	15

Because the equation $d = 6t$ represents a linear function, the slope of the graph is 6. This can be confirmed by choosing any two points on the graph at the right and finding the slope of the line between the two points. The points (0.5, 3) and (2, 12) are used here.

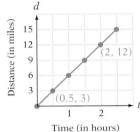

$$m = \frac{\text{change in } d}{\text{change in } t} = \frac{12 \text{ miles} - 3 \text{ miles}}{2 \text{ hours} - 0.5 \text{ hours}}$$

$$= \frac{9 \text{ miles}}{1.5 \text{ hours}} = 6 \text{ miles per hour}$$

This example demonstrates that the slope of the graph of an object in uniform motion is the speed of the object. In a more general way, we can say that anytime we discuss the speed of an object, we are discussing the slope of the graph that describes the relationship between the time the object travels and the distance it travels.

The value of the slope of a line gives the change in y for a *1-unit* change in x. For instance, a slope of -3 means that y changes by -3 as x changes by 1. We can write the slope as $\frac{-3}{1}$. A slope of $\frac{4}{3}$ means that y changes by $\frac{4}{3}$ as x changes by 1. Because it is difficult to graph a change of $\frac{4}{3}$, for fractional slopes it is easier to think of slope as integer changes in x and y.

For a slope of $\frac{4}{3}$, we have

$$m = \frac{\text{change in } y}{\text{change in } x} = \frac{4}{3}$$

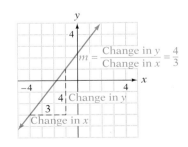

EXAMPLE 3

Graph the line that passes through $P(-2, 4)$ and has slope $-\dfrac{3}{4}$.

Solution Rewrite the slope $-\dfrac{3}{4}$ as $\dfrac{-3}{4}$.

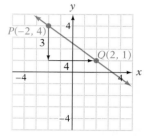

Draw a dot at $(-2, 4)$.

Starting at $(-2, 4)$, move 3 units down (the change in y) and then 4 units to the right (the change in x). Draw a dot at $(2, 1)$.

Draw a line through the two points.

YOU TRY IT 3

Graph the line that passes through $P(2, 4)$ and has slope -1.

Solution See page S14.

Recall that we can find the y-intercept of a linear equation by letting $x = 0$.

To find the y-intercept of $y = 3x + 4$, let $x = 0$.

$$y = 3x + 4$$
$$y = 3(0) + 4$$
$$y = 0 + 4$$
$$y = 4$$

The y-intercept is $(0, 4)$.

The constant term of $y = 3x + 4$ is the y-coordinate of the y-intercept.

In general, **for any equation of the form $y = mx + b$, the y-intercept is $(0, b)$.**

Because the slope and the y-intercept can be determined directly from the equation $f(x) = mx + b$, this equation is called the slope–intercept form of a straight line.

TAKE NOTE

For a function of the form $f(x) = mx + b$, m is the slope and b is the y-intercept.

Slope–Intercept Form of a Straight Line

The equation $y = mx + b$ is called the **slope–intercept form of a straight line.** The slope of the line is m, the coefficient of x. The y-intercept is $(0, b)$.

When an equation is in slope–intercept form, it is possible to draw a graph of the function quickly.

EXAMPLE 4

Graph $f(x) = -\frac{2}{3}x + 4$ by using the slope and y-intercept.

Solution   From the equation, the slope is $-\frac{2}{3}$ and the y-intercept is $(0, 4)$.

Rewrite the slope $-\frac{2}{3}$ as $\frac{-2}{3}$.

Place a dot at the y-intercept.

Starting at the y-intercept, move down 2 units (the change in y) and to the right 3 units (the change in x).

Place a dot at that location.

Draw a line through the two points.

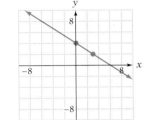

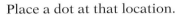

YOU TRY IT 4

Graph $y = \frac{3}{4}x - 1$ by using the slope and the y-intercept.

Solution   See page S14.

■ Equations of the Form *Ax + By = C*

Sometimes the equation of a line is written in the form $Ax + By = C$. This is called the **standard form of the equation of a line.** For instance, the equation $3x + 4y = 12$ is in standard form. For the equation $3x + 4y = 12$, $A = 3$, $B = 4$, and $C = 12$.

Here are two more examples of linear equations in standard form:

$$-2x + 5y = -10 \qquad (A = -2, B = 5, C = -10)$$
$$6x - y = 6 \qquad (A = 6, B = -1, C = 6)$$

Note that a linear equation written in standard form cannot be entered on a graphing calculator. The equation must be solved for y before it can be entered into the Y= editor of the calculator.

If an equation is in standard form, write the equation in slope–intercept form by solving the equation for y.

$$3x + 4y = 12 \qquad \bullet \text{ Standard form.}$$
$$3x - 3x + 4y = -3x + 12 \qquad \bullet \text{ Subtract } 3x \text{ from each side.}$$
$$4y = -3x + 12 \qquad \bullet \text{ Simplify.}$$
$$\frac{4y}{4} = \frac{-3x + 12}{4} \qquad \bullet \text{ Divide each side by 4.}$$
$$y = -\frac{3}{4}x + 3 \qquad \bullet \text{ Divide each term of } -3x + 12 \text{ by 4.}$$
$$\phantom{y = -\frac{3}{4}x + 3} \qquad \text{ The equation is now in slope–intercept form.}$$

TAKE NOTE

Note that $\dfrac{8 + 12}{4}$ can be simplified by first adding the terms in the numerator or by first dividing each term in the numerator by the denominator.

$$\frac{8 + 12}{4} = \frac{20}{4} = 5$$

$$\frac{8 + 12}{4} = \frac{8}{4} + \frac{12}{4}$$
$$= 2 + 3 = 5$$

It is this second method that is used to write the equation at the right in slope–intercept form.

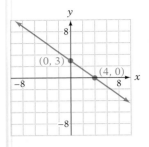

Once the equation is written in slope–intercept form, we can use the technique illustrated in Example 4 to graph the equation. The graph is shown at the left.

Another way to create the graph of a line when the equation is in standard form is to find the x- and y-intercepts (the points where the graph crosses the x- and y-axes). This is shown below for the equation $3x + 4y = 12$.

To find the x-intercept, let $y = 0$ and then solve for x.	To find the y-intercept, let $x = 0$ and then solve for y.
$3x + 4y = 12$	$3x + 4y = 12$
$3x + 4(0) = 12$	$3(0) + 4y = 12$
$3x = 12$	$4y = 12$
$x = 4$	$y = 3$
The x-intercept is $(4, 0)$.	The y-intercept is $(0, 3)$.

Plot the two intercepts. Then draw a line through the two points, as shown in the figure at the left above.

EXAMPLE 5

Write the equation $4x - 3y = 6$ in slope–intercept form. Then identify the slope and y-intercept.

Solution

$$4x - 3y = 6$$

• The goal is to solve the equation for y.

$$4x - 4x - 3y = -4x + 6$$

• Subtract $4x$ from each side of the equation.

$$-3y = -4x + 6$$

• Simplify the left side of the equation.

$$\frac{-3y}{-3} = \frac{-4x + 6}{-3}$$

• Divide each side of the equation by -3.

$$y = \frac{4}{3}x - 2$$

• Simplify. On the right side, divide each term in the numerator by the denominator.

The slope is $\dfrac{4}{3}$. The y-intercept is $(0, -2)$.

YOU TRY IT 5

Write the equation $3x + 2y = -6$ in slope–intercept form. Then identify the slope and y-intercept.

Solution See page S14.

EXAMPLE 6

Graph $2x - 5y = 10$ by finding the x- and y-intercepts.

Solution   To find the x-intercept,   To find the y-intercept,
let $y = 0$ and solve for x.   let $x = 0$ and solve for y.

$$2x - 5y = 10$$ $$2x - 5y = 10$$
$$2x - 5(0) = 10$$ $$2(0) - 5y = 10$$
$$2x = 10$$ $$-5y = 10$$
$$x = 5$$ $$y = -2$$

The x-intercept is $(5, 0)$.   The y-intercept is $(0, -2)$.

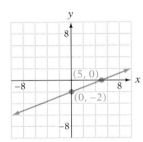

Graph $3x + y = 6$ by finding the x- and y-intercepts.

Solution   See page S14.

A linear equation in which one of the variables is missing has a graph that is either a horizontal or a vertical line. The equation $y = -2$ can be written in standard form as

$$0x + y = -2 \quad \bullet \ A = 0, B = 1, \text{ and } C = -2$$

Because $0x = 0$ for all values of x, the value of y is -2 for all values of x.

Some of the possible ordered-pair solutions of $y = -2$ are given in the following table. The graph is shown at the left.

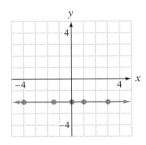

x	-4	-1.5	0	1	3
y	-2	-2	-2	-2	-2

The equation $y = -2$ represents a function. In functional notation we write $f(x) = -2$. Some of the ordered pairs of this function are $(-4, -2)$, $(-1.5, -2)$, $(0, -2)$, $(1, -2)$, and $(3, -2)$. This function is an example of a *constant function*. No matter what value of x is selected, $f(x) = -2$.

Definition of a Constant Function

A function given by $f(x) = b$, where b is a constant, is a **constant function**. The graph of a constant function is a horizontal line passing through $(0, b)$.

For each value in the domain of a constant function, the value of the function (the range) is the same (that is, it is constant). For instance, if $f(x) = 4$, then $f(-2) = 4$, $f(3) = 4$, $f(\pi) = 4$, $f(\sqrt{2}) = 4$, and so on. The value of $f(x)$ is 4 for all values of x.

> **? QUESTION**   What is the value of $P(t) = 5$ when $t = 2$?

For the equation $y = -2$, the coefficient of x is zero. For the equation $x = 3$, the coefficient of y is zero. The equation $x = 3$ can be written in standard form as

$$x + 0y = 3 \qquad \bullet \; A = 1, B = 0, \text{ and } C = 3$$

Because $0y = 0$ for all values of y, the value of x is 3 for all values of y.

Some of the possible ordered-pair solutions of $x = 3$ are given in the following table. The graph is shown at the left.

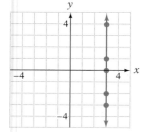

x	3	3	3	3	3
y	-3	-2	0	1	4

Because $(3 -3)$, $(3, -2)$, $(3, 0)$, $(3, 1)$, and $(3, 4)$ are ordered pairs of this graph, the graph is not the graph of a function: there are ordered pairs with the same first coordinate and different second coordinates.

The graph of $x = a$ is not the graph of a function. It is a vertical line passing through the point $(a, 0)$.

EXAMPLE 7

Graph: $y + 1 = 0$

Solution   Solve the equation for y by subtracting 1 from each side of the equation.

$$y + 1 = 0$$
$$y = -1$$

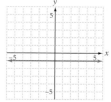

This is a constant function. The graph of a constant function is a horizontal line passing through $(0, b)$.

The graph of $y = -1$ is a horizontal line through $(0, -1)$.

TAKE NOTE

Recall that a horizontal line has 0 slope.

YOU TRY IT 7

Graph: $y - 5 = 0$

Solution   See page S14.

? ANSWER $P(t) = 5$ is a constant function. Therefore, $P(2) = 5$.

EXAMPLE 8

Graph: $x = -7$.

Solution   This is an equation of the form $x = a$.

The graph of $x = a$ is a vertical line passing through the point $(a, 0)$.

The graph of $x = -7$ is a vertical line passing through the point $(-7, 0)$.

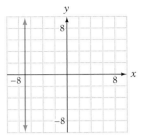

TAKE NOTE

Recall that the slope of a vertical line is undefined.

YOU TRY IT 8

Graph: $x = 1$

Solution   See page S14.

4.1 EXERCISES

Topics for Discussion

1. Give an example of a linear equation in two variables that **a.** is in slope–intercept form and **b.** is in standard form.

2. What is the formula for slope? Explain what each variable in the formula represents.

3. Explain the difference between zero slope and no slope.

4. Is the graph of $Ax + By = C$ always a straight line?

5. Is the graph of a line always the graph of a function? If not, give an example of the graph of a line that is not the graph of a function.

6. What is a constant function? Give an example of a constant function.

7. Describe the graph of $x = a$ and the graph of $y = b$.

8. For each of the following slopes of a straight line, discuss how the value of y changes when x changes by 1: $m = 2$, $m = \frac{2}{3}$, $m = -\frac{3}{4}$, $m = -3$.

Slope of a Line

Is the function a linear function? Explain.

9. $f(x) = -\dfrac{3x}{4} + 1$

10. $f(c) = \dfrac{2}{5c} - 6$

11. $f(a) = a^2 + 7$

12. $F(x) = -10$

Find the slope of the line containing the points P_1 and P_2.

13. $P_1(1, 3), P_2(3, 1)$

14. $P_1(2, 3), P_2(5, 1)$

15. $P_1(-1, 4), P_2(2, 5)$

16. $P_1(3, -2), P_2(1, 4)$

17. $P_1(-1, 3), P_2(-4, 5)$

18. $P_1(-1, -2), P_2(-3, 2)$

19. $P_1(0, 3), P_2(4, 0)$

20. $P_1(-2, 0), P_2(0, 3)$

21. $P_1(2, 4), P_2(2, -2)$

22. $P_1(4, 1), P_2(4, -3)$

23. $P_1(2, 5), P_2(-3, -2)$

24. $P_1(4, 1), P_2(-1, -2)$

25. $P_1(2, 3), P_2(-1, 3)$

26. $P_1(3, 4), P_2(0, 4)$

27. $P_1(0, 4), P_2(-2, 5)$

28. $P_1(-2, 3), P_2(-2, 5)$

29. $P_1(-3, -1), P_2(-3, 4)$

30. $P_1(-2, -5), P_2(-4, -1)$

31. Graph the line that passes through the point $(-1, -3)$ and has slope $\dfrac{4}{3}$.

32. Graph the line that passes through the point $(-2, -3)$ and has slope $\dfrac{5}{4}$.

33. Graph the line that passes through the point $(-3, 0)$ and has slope -3.

34. Graph the line that passes through the point $(2, 0)$ and has slope -1.

Graph by using the slope and the *y*-intercept.

35. $y = \dfrac{1}{2}x + 2$ **36.** $y = \dfrac{2}{3}x - 3$ **37.** $y = -\dfrac{3}{2}x$

38. $y = \dfrac{3}{4}x$ **39.** $y = \dfrac{1}{3}x - 1$ **40.** $y = -\dfrac{3}{2}x + 6$

41. *Telecommunications* The graph below shows the total cost of a cellular phone call. Find the slope of the line. Write a sentence that states the meaning of the slope.

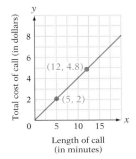

42. *Aviation* The graph below shows how the altitude of an airplane above the runway changes after takeoff. Find the slope of the line. Write a sentence that states the meaning of the slope.

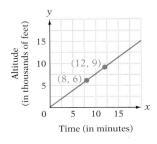

43. *Computers* The graph below shows the relationship between the time, in seconds, it takes to download a file and the size of the file, in megabytes. Find the slope of the line. Write a sentence that states the meaning of the slope.

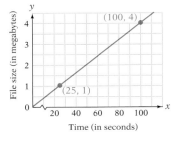

44. *Computers* The graph below shows the relationship between the size of a document and the time required to print the document using a laser printer. Find the slope of the line. Write a sentence that states the meaning of the slope.

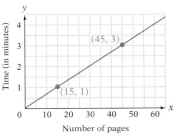

45. *Temperature* The graph below shows the relationship between the temperature inside an oven and the time since the oven was turned off. Write a sentence that states the meaning of the slope.

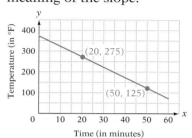

46. *Home Maintenance* The graph below shows the number of gallons of water remaining in a pool t minutes after a valve is opened to drain the pool. Find the slope of the line. Write a sentence that states the meaning of the slope.

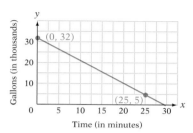

47. *Uniform Motion* The graph below shows the relationship between the distance traveled by a motorist and the time of travel. Find the slope of the line between the two points shown on the graph. Write a sentence that states the meaning of the slope.

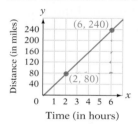

48. *Depreciation* The graph below shows the relationship between the value of a building and the depreciation allowed for income tax purposes. Find the slope of the line between the two points shown on the graph. Write a sentence that states the meaning of the slope.

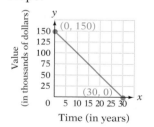

49. *Income Taxes* The graph below shows the relationship between the amount of tax and the amount of taxable income between $22,101 and $54,500. Find the slope of the line between the two points shown on the graph. Write a sentence that states the meaning of the slope.

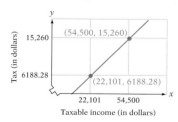

50. *Mortgages* The graph below shows the relationship between the payment on a mortgage and the amount of the mortgage. Find the slope of the line between the two points shown on the graph. Write a sentence that states the meaning of the slope.

51. 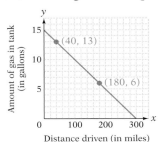 *Fuel Consumption*   The graph below shows how the amount of gas in the tank of a car decreases as the car is driven. Find the slope of the line. Write a sentence that states the meaning of the slope.

52. 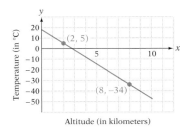 *Earth Science*   The troposphere extends from the surface of Earth to an elevation of approximately 11 kilometers. The graph below shows the decrease in temperature of the troposphere as altitude increases. Find the slope of the line. Write a sentence that states the meaning of the slope.

53. *Biology*   There is a relationship between the number of times a cricket chirps per minute and the air temperature. A linear model of this relationship is given by $f(x) = 7x - 30$, where x is the temperature in degrees Celsius and $f(x)$ is the number of chirps per minute.
  a.   Find and discuss the meaning of the x-intercept.
  b.   What does the slope of this function mean in the context of this problem?

54. *Aviation*   An approximate linear model that gives the remaining distance a plane must travel from Los Angeles to Paris is given by $s(t) = 6000 - 500t$, where $s(t)$ is the remaining distance t hours after the flight begins.
  a.   Find and discuss the meaning of the intercepts on the vertical and horizontal axes.
  b.   What does the slope of this function mean in the context of this problem?

55. *Refrigeration*   The temperature of an object taken from a freezer gradually increases and can be modeled by $T(x) = 20x - 100$, where $T(x)$ is the Fahrenheit temperature of the object x hours after being removed from the freezer.
  a.   Find and discuss the meaning of the intercepts on the vertical and horizontal axes.
  b.   What does the slope of this function mean in the context of this problem?

56. *Investments* A retired botanist begins withdrawing money from a retirement account according to the linear model $A(t) = 100{,}000 - 2500t$, where $A(t)$ is the amount remaining in the account t months after withdrawals begin.

   a. Find and discuss the meaning of the intercepts on the vertical and horizontal axes.

   b. What does the slope of this function mean in the context of this problem?

57. *Temperature* The function $T(x) = -6.5x + 20$ approximates the temperature $T(x)$, in degrees Celsius, x kilometers above sea level. What is the slope of this function? Write a sentence that explains the meaning of the slope in the context of this problem.

58. *Sound* The distance sound travels through air when the temperature is 75°F can be approximated by $d(t) = 1125t$, where d is the distance, in feet, that sound travels in t seconds. What is the slope of this function? What is the meaning of the slope in the context of this problem?

59. *Biology* The distance that a homing pigeon can fly can be approximated by $d(t) = 50t$, where $d(t)$ is the distance, in miles, flown by the pigeon in t hours. What is the slope of this function? What is the meaning of the slope in the context of this problem?

60. *Construction* The American National Standards Institute (ANSI) states that the slope for a wheelchair ramp must not exceed $\frac{1}{12}$.

   a. Does a ramp that is 6 inches high and 5 feet long meet the requirements of ANSI?

   b. Does a ramp that is 12 inches high and 170 inches long meet the requirements of ANSI?

61. 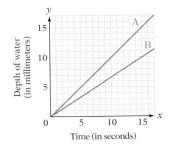 *Construction*   A certain ramp for a wheelchair must be 14 inches high. What is the minimum length of this ramp so that it will meet the ANSI requirements stated in Exercise 60.

62. If (2, 3) are the coordinates of a point on a line that has slope 2, what is the *y*-coordinate of the point on the line whose *x*-coordinate is 4?

63. If (−1, 2) are the coordinates of a point on a line that has slope −3, what is the *y*-coordinate of the point on the line whose *x*-coordinate is 1?

64. If (1, 4) are the coordinates of a point on a line that has slope $\frac{2}{3}$, what is the *y*-coordinate of the point on the line whose *x*-coordinate is −2?

65. If (−2, −1) are the coordinates of a point on a line that has slope $\frac{3}{2}$, what is the *y*-coordinate of the point on the line whose *x*-coordinate is −6?

66. *Sports*   Lois and Tanya start from the same place on a jogging course. Lois is jogging at 9 kilometers per hour, and Tanya is jogging at 6 kilometers per hour. The graphs below show the total distance traveled by each jogger and the total distance between Lois and Tanya. Which lines represent which distances?

67. *Gardening*   A gardener is filling two cans from a faucet that releases water at a constant rate. Can 1 has a diameter of 20 millimeters, and Can 2 has a diameter of 30 millimeters. The depth of the water in each can is shown in the graph below. On the graph, which line represents the depth of the water for which can?

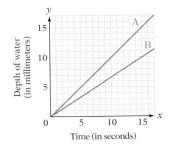

■ Equations of the Form $Ax + By = C$

Write the equation in slope–intercept form.

68. $3x + y = 10$　　**69.** $2x + y = 5$　　**70.** $4x - y = 3$　　**71.** $5x - y = 7$

72. $2x + 7y = 14$　　**73.** $3x + 2y = 6$　　**74.** $2x + 3y = 9$　　**75.** $2x - 5y = 10$

76. $5x - 2y = 4$　　**77.** $x + 3y = 6$　　**78.** $x - 4y = 12$　　**79.** $6x - 5y = 10$

Find the x- and y-intercepts and graph.

80. $x - 2y = -4$　　**81.** $3x + y = 3$　　**82.** $2x - 3y = 6$

83. $4x - y = 8$　　**84.** $2x - y = 4$　　**85.** $2x + y = 6$

86. $3x + 5y = 15$　　**87.** $4x - 3y = 12$　　**88.** $5x + 4y = 20$

89. $2x - 3y = 18$

90. $3x - 5y = 15$

91. $4x - 3y = 24$

Graph.

92. $x = 2$

93. $y = -3$

94. $y - 4 = 0$

95. Given that f is a linear function for which $f(1) = -6$ and $f(-1) = -6$, determine $f(4)$.

96. Given that f is a linear function for which $f(-3) = 2$ and $f(8) = 2$, determine $f(-5)$.

Applying Concepts

97.   Explain how you can use the slope of a line to determine whether three given points lie on the same line. Then use your procedure to determine whether all of the following points lie on the same line.
   a. $(2, 5), (-1, -1), (3, 7)$
   b. $(-1, 5), (0, 3), (-3, 4)$

98. a.   What effect does increasing the coefficient of x have on the graph of $y = mx + b$?
   b.   What effect does decreasing the coefficient of x have on the graph of $y = mx + b$?
   c.   What effect does increasing the constant term have on the graph of $y = mx + b$?
   d.   What effect does decreasing the constant term have on the graph of $y = mx + b$?

99. Do the graphs of all straight lines have a y-intercept? If not, give an example of one that does not.

100. If two lines have the same slope and the same y-intercept, must the graphs of the lines be the same? If not, give an example.

101. A line with slope 3 passes through the point whose coordinates are $(8, 12)$. If the ordered pair $(C, -3)$ belongs to the line, find C.

102. A secant is a line that passes through two points on a curve. To find the slope of the secant, the formula for slope is written in functional notation as $m = \dfrac{f(x_2) - f(x_1)}{x_2 - x_1}$, $x_1 \neq x_2$. For the graph at the right, $f(x) = x^2 - 2x - 1$, $x_1 = -1$, and $x_2 = 2$. Therefore,

$$m = \frac{f(2) - f(-1)}{2 - (-1)}$$

$$= \frac{[2^2 - 2(2) - 1] - [(-1)^2 - 2(-1) - 1]}{2 - (-1)}$$

$$= \frac{-1 - 2}{2 + 1} = \frac{-3}{3} = -1$$

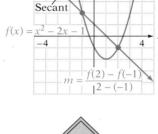

For each of the following, find the slope of the secant line for the given x-coordinates.

a. $f(x) = 2x - 1$, $x_1 = -2$, $x_2 = 3$ **b.** $f(x) = x^2$, $x_1 = -1$, $x_2 = 4$

c. $f(x) = x^2 - x$, $x_1 = 0$, $x_2 = 4$ **d.** $f(x) = \sqrt{x - 2}$, $x_1 = 3$, $x_2 = 6$

103. A warning sign for drivers on a mountain road might read, "Caution: 6% down-grade next 2 miles." Explain this statement in the context of slope.

EXPLORATION

1. *Designing a Staircase* When you climb a staircase, the flat part of a stair that you step on is called the **tread** of the stair. The **riser** is the vertical part of the stair. The slope of a staircase is the quotient of the length of the riser and the length of the tread. Because the design of a staircase may affect safety, most cities have building codes that give rules for the design of a staircase.

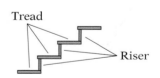

a. The traditional design of a staircase called for a 9-inch tread and a 8.25-inch riser. What is the slope of this staircase?

b. A newer design for a staircase uses an 11-inch tread and a 7-inch riser. What is the slope of this staircase?

c. An architect is designing a house with a staircase that is 8 feet high and 12 feet long. Is the architect using the traditional design given in part a or the newer design given in part b? Explain your answer.

d. Staircases that have a slope between 0.5 and 0.7 are usually considered safer than those with a slope greater than 0.7. Design a safe staircase that goes from the first floor of a house to the basement, which is 9 feet below the first floor.

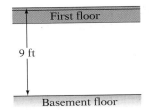

e. Measure the tread and riser for three staircases you encounter. Do these staircases match the traditional design in part a or the newer design in part b?

f. If there is an escalator in a building in your area, measure the tread and rise on a fully extended step of the escalator. Does it match the traditional design in part a or the newer design in part b?

2. *Intercept Form of a Straight Line*   We have discussed two equations whose graph is a straight line: $y = mx + b$ and $Ax + By = C$. There are other equations that represent straight lines. One such equation is $\frac{x}{a} + \frac{y}{b} = 1$, $a \neq 0, b \neq 0$. This is called the **intercept form of a straight line.**

a. Find the x- and y-intercepts of $\frac{x}{3} + \frac{y}{4} = 1$. Draw the graph of the equation.

b. Find the x- and y-intercepts of $\frac{x}{2} - \frac{y}{5} = 1$. Draw the graph of the equation.

c. Show that the x-intercept of $\frac{x}{a} + \frac{y}{b} = 1$ is $(a, 0)$ and that the y-intercept is $(0, b)$.

d. Explain why this form of a linear equation is called the intercept form.

e. Write the equation $3x + 5y = 15$ in intercept form.

f. Write the equation $y = 2x - 4$ in intercept form.

g. Write the equation $3x - 4y = 8$ in intercept form.

SECTION **4.2**

Finding Equations of Straight Lines

- Find Equations of Lines Using $y = mx + b$
- Find Equations of Lines Using the Point–Slope Formula
- Parallel and Perpendicular Lines

▪ Find Equations of Lines Using $y = mx + b$

Suppose that a car uses 0.05 gallon of gas per mile driven and that the fuel tank, which holds 18 gallons of gas, is full. Using this information, we can determine a linear model for the amount of fuel remaining in the gas tank.

Recall that a linear function is one that can be written in the form $f(x) = mx + b$, where m is the slope of the line and b is the y-intercept. The slope is the rate at which the car is using fuel. Because the car is consuming the fuel, the amount of fuel in the tank is decreasing. Therefore, the slope is negative and we have $m = -0.05$.

The amount of fuel in the tank depends on the number of miles, x, the car is driven. Before the car starts (that is, when $x = 0$), there are 18 gallons of gas in the tank. The y-intercept is (0, 18).

Using this information, we can create the linear function by replacing m and b in the equation $f(x) = mx + b$ by their values.

$$f(x) = mx + b$$
$$f(x) = -0.05x + 18 \qquad \text{• Replace } m \text{ by } -0.05; \text{ replace } b \text{ by } 18.$$

The linear function that models the amount of fuel remaining in the tank is given by $f(x) = -0.05x + 18$, where $f(x)$ is the amount of fuel remaining after driving x miles. The graph of the function is shown at the right.

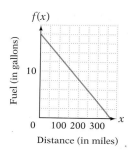

The x-intercept of this graph is the point at which $f(x) = 0$. For this application, $f(x) = 0$ means that there are 0 gallons of fuel remaining in the tank. Thus, replacing $f(x)$ by 0 in $f(x) = -0.5x + 18$ and solving for x will give the number of miles that can be driven before running out of gas.

$$f(x) = -0.05x + 18$$
$$0 = -0.05x + 18 \qquad \text{• Replace } f(x) \text{ by } 0.$$
$$-18 = -0.05x \qquad \text{• Subtract 18 from each side.}$$
$$360 = x \qquad \text{• Divide each side by } -0.05.$$

The car can travel 360 miles before running out of gas.

The domain of this function is the number of miles driven. Because the fuel tank is empty when the car has traveled 360 miles, the domain of this function is [0, 360]. The range of the function is the number of gallons of fuel in the tank. Therefore, the range is [0, 18].

TAKE NOTE

When we are creating a linear model, the slope will be the quantity that is expressed by using the word *per*. The car discussed at the right uses 0.05 gallon per mile. The slope is negative because the amount of fuel in the tank is decreasing.

TAKE NOTE

Recall that [0, 360] is interval notation and represents the set $\{x \mid 0 \le x \le 360\}$. The interval [0, 18] represents the set $\{x \mid 0 \le x \le 18\}$.

? QUESTION Why does it not make sense for the domain of $f(x) = -0.05x + 18$, discussed above, to exceed 360?

EXAMPLE 1

Suppose a 20-gallon gas tank contains 2 gallons when a motorist decides to fill up the tank. The gas pump fills the tank at a rate of 0.08 gallon per second. Find a linear function that models the amount of fuel in the tank x seconds after fueling begins.

Solution Because there are 2 gallons of gas in the tank when fueling begins (at $x = 0$), the y-intercept is $(0, 2)$.

The slope is the rate at which fuel is being added to the tank. Because the amount of fuel in the tank is increasing, the slope is positive and we have $m = 0.08$.

To find the linear function, replace m and b in $f(x) = mx + b$ by their values.

$$f(x) = mx + b$$
$$f(x) = 0.08x + 2 \qquad \bullet \text{ Replace } m \text{ by } 0.08; \text{ replace } b \text{ by } 2.$$

The linear function is $f(x) = 0.08x + 2$, where $f(x)$ is the number of gallons of fuel in the tank x seconds after fueling begins.

YOU TRY IT 1

The boiling point of water at sea level is 100°C. The boiling point decreases 3.5°C for each 1-kilometer increase in altitude. Find a linear function that gives the boiling point of water as a function of altitude.

Solution See page S14.

■ Find Equations of Lines Using the Point–Slope Formula

For each of the previous examples, the known point on the graph of the linear function was the y-intercept. This information enabled us to determine b for the linear function $f(x) = mx + b$. In some instances, a point other than the y-intercept is given. In this case, the *point–slope formula* is used to find the equation of the line.

Point–Slope Formula of a Straight Line

Let $P_1(x_1, y_1)$ be a point on a line, and let m be the slope of the line. Then the equation of the line can be found using the point–slope formula

$$y - y_1 = m(x - x_1)$$

? ANSWER If $x > 360$, then $f(x) < 0$. This would mean that the tank contained negative gallons of gas. For instance, $f(400) = -2$.

➡ Find the equation of the line that contains the point $(4, -1)$ and has slope $-\frac{3}{4}$.

TAKE NOTE

$(x_1, y_1) = (4, -1)$. Substitute 4 for x_1 and -1 for y_1.

$$y - y_1 = m(x - x_1)$$
• The slope and a point other than the y-intercept are given. Use the point–slope formula.

$$y - (-1) = -\frac{3}{4}(x - 4)$$
• $(x_1, y_1) = (4, -1)$ and $m = -\frac{3}{4}$.

$$y + 1 = -\frac{3}{4}x + 3$$
• Simplify the left side. Use the Distributive Property on the right side.

$$y = -\frac{3}{4}x + 2$$
• Subtract 1 from each side of the equation. The equation is now in the form $y = mx + b$.
⬅

EXAMPLE 2

Find the equation of the line that passes through $P(1, -3)$ and that has slope -2.

TAKE NOTE

Recall that $f(x)$ and y are different symbols for the same quantity, the value of the function at x.

Solution

$$y - y_1 = m(x - x_1)$$
• Use the point–slope formula.

$$y - (-3) = -2(x - 1)$$
• $m = -2$, $(x_1, y_1) = (1, -3)$

$$y + 3 = -2x + 2$$

$$y = -2x - 1$$

In this example, we wrote the equation of the line as $y = -2x - 1$. We could have written the equation in functional notation as $f(x) = -2x - 1$.

YOU TRY IT 2

Find the equation of the line that passes through $P(-2, 2)$ and has slope $-\frac{1}{2}$.

Solution   See page S15.

EXAMPLE 3

Find the equation of the line that passes through $P(5, -1)$ and has 0 slope.

Solution

$$y - y_1 = m(x - x_1)$$
• Use the point–slope formula.

$$y - (-1) = 0(x - 5)$$
• $m = 0$, $(x_1, y_1) = (5, -1)$

$$y + 1 = 0$$

$$y = -1$$

Recall that a line that has 0 slope is a horizontal line with equation $y = b$.

YOU TRY IT 3

Find the equation of the line that passes through $P(4, 3)$ and whose slope is undefined.

Solution   See page S15.

EXAMPLE 4

Judging on the basis of data from the Kelley Blue Book, the value of a certain car decreases approximately $250 per month. If the value of the car 2 years after it was purchased was $14,000, find a linear function that models the value of the car after x months of ownership. Use this function to find the value of the car after 3 years of ownership.

State the goal.   Find a linear model that gives the value of the car after x months of ownership. Then use the model to find the value of the car after 3 years.

Devise a strategy.   Because the function will predict the value of the car, let y represent the value of the car after x months.

Then $y = 14{,}000$ when $x = 24$ (2 years is 24 months).

The value of the car is decreasing $250 per month. Therefore, the slope is -250.

Use the point–slope formula to find the linear model.

To find the value of the car after 3 years (36 months), evaluate the function when $x = 36$.

Solve the problem.
$$y - y_1 = m(x - x_1)$$
$$y - 14{,}000 = -250(x - 24)$$
$$y - 14{,}000 = -250x + 6000$$
$$y = -250x + 20{,}000$$

A linear function that models the value of the car is $f(x) = -250x + 20{,}000$.

$$f(x) = -250x + 20{,}000$$
$$f(36) = -250(36) + 20{,}000 \qquad \bullet \text{ Evaluate the function at } x = 36.$$
$$= -9000 + 20{,}000$$
$$= 11{,}000$$

The value of the car is $11,000 after 36 months of ownership.

Check your work.   An answer of $11,000 seems reasonable. This value is less than $14,000, the value of the car after 2 years.

The graph of the function is shown at the right. Pressing ⬚TRACE⬚ 24 shows that the or-

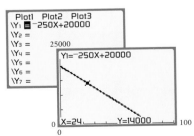

dered pair (24, 14,000) is on the graph. Pressing TRACE 36 shows that the ordered pair (36, 11,000) is also on the graph.

YOU TRY IT 4

In 1950, there were 13 million adults 65 years old or older in the United States. Data from the U.S. Census Bureau show that the population of these adults has been increasing at a constant rate of approximately 0.5 million per year. This rate of increase is expected to continue through the year 2010. Find a linear function that approximates the population of adults 65 years old or older in terms of the year. Use your equation to approximate the population of these adults in 2005.

Solution   See page S15.

There are instances in which it may be necessary **to find the equation of a line between two points.** The process involves two steps:

- Find the slope of the line between the two points.
- Use the point–slope formula to find the equation of the line.

Here is an example.

EXAMPLE 5

Find the equation of the line that contains the points (6, −4) and (3, 2).

Solution   Find the slope of the line between the two points.

$$m = \frac{y_2 - y_1}{x_2 - x_1} = \frac{2 - (-4)}{3 - 6} = \frac{6}{-3} = -2$$

Use the point–slope formula to find the equation of the line. Use either the point (6, −4) or the point (3, 2). The point (6, −4) is used here.

$$y - y_1 = m(x - x_1)$$
$$y - (-4) = -2(x - 6) \qquad \bullet \; m = -2, x_1 = 6, y_1 = -4$$
$$y + 4 = -2x + 12$$
$$y = -2x + 8$$

YOU TRY IT 5

Find the equation of the line containing the points (−2, 3) and (4, 1).

Solution   See page S15.

EXAMPLE 6

Gabriel Daniel Fahrenheit invented the mercury thermometer in 1717. In terms of readings on this thermometer, water freezes at 32°F and boils at 212°F. In 1742 Anders Celsius invented the Celsius temperature scale. On this scale, water freezes at 0°C and boils at 100°C.

Determine a linear function that can be used to predict the Celsius temperature when the Fahrenheit temperature is known. Use the function to find the temperature in degrees Celsius when it is 70°F. Round to the nearest whole number.

State the goal.   Find a linear model that gives the temperature in degrees Celsius when the temperature in degrees Fahrenheit is given. Then use the model to find the temperature in degrees Celsius when the temperature is 70°F.

Devise a strategy.   Because the function will predict the temperature in degrees Celsius, let y represent the temperature in degrees Celsius. Then x represents the temperature in degrees Fahrenheit.

From the given data, two ordered pairs of the function are (32, 0) and (212, 100).

Use the two ordered pairs to find the slope of the line.

Use the point–slope formula to find the linear model.

To find the temperature in degrees Celsius when it is 70°F, evaluate the linear function at $x = 70$.

Solve the problem.   Let $(x_1, y_1) = (32, 0)$ and $(x_2, y_2) = (212, 100)$.

$$m = \frac{y_2 - y_1}{x_2 - x_1} = \frac{100 - 0}{212 - 32} = \frac{100}{180} = \frac{5}{9}$$ • The slope is $\frac{5}{9}$.

$$y - y_1 = m(x - x_1)$$ • Use the point–slope formula.

$$y - 0 = \frac{5}{9}(x - 32)$$ • $m = \frac{5}{9}, x_1 = 32, y_1 = 0.$

$$y = \frac{5}{9}x - \frac{160}{9}$$

The linear function is $f(x) = \frac{5}{9}x - \frac{160}{9}$.

$$f(x) = \frac{5}{9}x - \frac{160}{9}$$

$$f(70) = \frac{5}{9}(70) - \frac{160}{9}$$ • Evaluate the function at $x = 70$.

$$\approx 21$$

When the temperature is 70°F, it is approximately 21°C.

Check your work.   The graph of the function is shown at the right. Use the TRACE feature to show that the ordered pairs (32, 0) and (212, 100) are on the graph. Use the same feature to show that when $x = 70$, $y \approx 21$.

See Appendix A: Trace

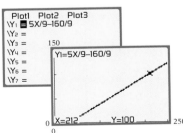

YOU TRY IT 6

There are approximately 126 calories in a 2-ounce serving of lean hamburger and approximately 189 calories in a 3-ounce serving. Write a linear equation for the number of calories in lean hamburger in terms of the size of the serving. Use your equation to estimate the number of calories in a 5-ounce serving of lean hamburger.

Solution   See page S15.

■ Parallel and Perpendicular Lines

The graph of $g(x) = 2x - 3$ and the graph of $f(x) = 2x + 4$ are shown at the right. Note from the equations that the lines have the same slope and different y-intercepts. Lines that have the same slope and different y-intercepts are **parallel lines**; the graphs of the lines never meet.

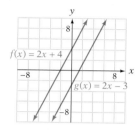

Parallel Lines

Two nonvertical lines with slopes m_1 and m_2 are **parallel lines** if and only if $m_1 = m_2$. Vertical lines are also parallel lines.

➡ Is the line that contains the points $P_1(-2, 1)$ and $P_2(-5, -1)$ parallel to the line that contains the points $Q_1(1, 0)$ and $Q_2(4, 2)$?

To determine whether the lines are parallel, find the slope of each line.

Slope of the line containing P_1 and P_2:

$$m_1 = \frac{y_2 - y_1}{x_2 - x_1} = \frac{-1 - 1}{-5 - (-2)} = \frac{-2}{-3} = \frac{2}{3}$$

Slope of the line containing Q_1 and Q_2: $m_2 = \dfrac{y_2 - y_1}{x_2 - x_1} = \dfrac{2 - 0}{4 - 1} = \dfrac{2}{3}$

$m_1 = m_2$: the slopes are equal. Therefore, the lines are parallel.   ⬅

? **QUESTION**   Is the graph of $y = -\frac{1}{2}x + 2$ parallel to the graph of $y = -x + 2$?

? **ANSWER**   No. The slope of one line is $-\frac{1}{2}$ and the slope of the other line is -1. The slopes are not equal, so the graphs are not parallel.

EXAMPLE 7

Find the equation of the line that is parallel to the graph of $y = \frac{1}{2}x - 4$ and contains the point (2, 3).

Solution   The slope of the given line is $\frac{1}{2}$.

Because parallel lines have the same slope, the slope of the unknown line is also $\frac{1}{2}$. We know the slope of the line and a point on the line. We can use the point–slope formula to find the equation of the line.

$$y - y_1 = m(x - x_1)$$

$$y - 3 = \frac{1}{2}(x - 2) \qquad \bullet \ m = \frac{1}{2}, x_1 = 2, y_1 = 3$$

$$y - 3 = \frac{1}{2}x - 1$$

$$y = \frac{1}{2}x + 2 \qquad \bullet \ \text{Check: The slope of this line is } \frac{1}{2}, \text{ and (2, 3) is a}$$
$$\text{solution of this equation.}$$

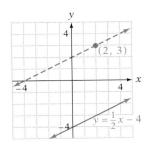

YOU TRY IT 7

Find the equation of the line that is parallel to the graph of $y = -3x + 1$ and contains the point $(-5, -4)$.

Solution   See page S16.

EXAMPLE 8

Find the equation of the line that is parallel to the graph of $2x - 3y = 12$ and passes through the point $(6, -1)$.

Solution   Because the lines are parallel, the slope of the unknown line is the same as the slope of the given line. To determine the slope of the given line, write $2x - 3y = 12$ in slope–intercept form by solving the equation for y.

$$2x - 3y = 12$$

$$-3y = -2x + 12 \qquad \bullet \ \text{Subtract } 2x \text{ from each side of the equation.}$$

$$\frac{-3y}{-3} = \frac{-2x + 12}{-3} \qquad \bullet \ \text{Divide each side of the equation by } -3.$$

$$y = \frac{2}{3}x - 4 \qquad \bullet \ \text{The equation is in slope–intercept form.}$$

The slope of the given line is $\frac{2}{3}$.

Because parallel lines have the same slope, the slope of the unknown line is also $\frac{2}{3}$.

The slope of the line and a point on the line are known. Use the point–slope formula to find the equation of the line.

$$y - y_1 = m(x - x_1)$$

$$y - (-1) = \frac{2}{3}(x - 6) \qquad \bullet \ m = \frac{2}{3}, x_1 = 6, y_1 = -1$$

$$y + 1 = \frac{2}{3}x - 4$$

$$y = \frac{2}{3}x - 5 \qquad \bullet \ \text{Check: The slope of this line is } \frac{2}{3}, \text{ and } (6, -1) \text{ is a solution of this equation.}$$

YOU TRY IT 8

Find the equation of the line that is parallel to the graph of $3x + 5y = 15$ and passes through the point $P(-2, 3)$.

Solution See page S16.

For Example 8, we left the answer in slope–intercept form. However, we could have rewritten the equation in standard form.

$$y = \frac{2}{3}x - 5$$

$$3y = 3\left(\frac{2}{3}x - 5\right) \qquad \bullet \ \text{Multiply each side by 3.}$$

$$3y = 2x - 15$$

$$-2x + 3y = -15 \qquad \bullet \ \text{Subtract } 2x \text{ from each side. The equation is in standard form. } A = -2, B = 3, \text{ and } C = -15.$$

Two lines that intersect at right angles are **perpendicular** lines. A theorem allows us to determine whether the graphs of two lines are perpendicular.

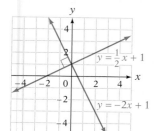

Slopes of Perpendicular Lines

If m_1 and m_2 are the slopes of two lines, neither of which is vertical, then the lines are perpendicular if and only if $m_1 \cdot m_2 = -1$.

A vertical line is perpendicular to a horizontal line.

Solving $m_1 \cdot m_2 = -1$ for m_1 gives $m_1 = -\frac{1}{m_2}$. This last equation states that the slopes of perpendicular lines are **negative reciprocals** of each other. The negative reciprocal of $-\frac{3}{4}$ is $\frac{4}{3}$. The negative reciprocal of 5 is $-\frac{1}{5}$.

? QUESTION   **a.** What is the negative reciprocal of $\frac{7}{2}$?*
                 b. What is the negative reciprocal of -6?

➡ Is the line that contains the points $P_1(4, 2)$ and $P_2(-2, 5)$ perpendicular to the line that contains the points $Q_1(-4, 3)$ and $Q_2(-3, 5)$?

To determine whether the lines are perpendicular, find the slope of each line.

Slope of the line containing P_1 and P_2:

$$m_1 = \frac{y_2 - y_1}{x_2 - x_1} = \frac{5 - 2}{-2 - 4} = \frac{3}{-6} = -\frac{1}{2}$$

Slope of the line containing Q_1 and Q_2:

$$m_2 = \frac{y_2 - y_1}{x_2 - x_1} = \frac{5 - 3}{-3 - (-4)} = \frac{2}{1} = 2$$

m_1 is the negative reciprocal of m_2.

The lines are perpendicular.   ⬅

? QUESTION   Is the graph of $f(x) = -\frac{2}{3}x + 3$ perpendicular to the graph of $g(x) = \frac{2}{3}x - 3$? †

Graphs on a graphing calculator may give the impression that two lines are not perpendicular when in fact they are. This is due to the size of the pixels (picture elements). For instance, the graph of $y = -\frac{1}{2}x + 4$ and the graph of $y = 2x - 3$ are shown at the right in the standard viewing window. Although the graphs are perpendicular, they do not appear to be from the graph. This apparent distortion can be fixed, however, by using the square viewing window.

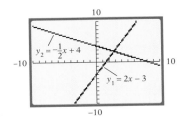

See Appendix A:
Window

_____

? ANSWERS   *a. $-\frac{2}{7}$ b. $\frac{1}{6}$ †No. The slope of f is $-\frac{2}{3}$ and the slope of g is $\frac{2}{3}$. The slopes are not negative reciprocals.

The graphs of $y = -\frac{1}{2}x + 4$ and $y = 2x - 3$ are shown at the right in the *square* viewing window. Note that the graphs now appear to be perpendicular. The main point of this discussion is that the appearance of a graph will change as the size of the viewing window changes.

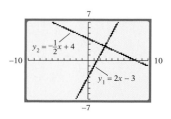

EXAMPLE 9

Find the equation of the line that is perpendicular to $y = \frac{2}{5}x + 1$ and passes through the point (5, 3).

Solution Because the lines are perpendicular, the value of the slope of the unknown line is the negative reciprocal of the slope of the given line.

The slope of the given line is $\frac{2}{5}$. Therefore, the slope of the unknown perpendicular line is $-\frac{5}{2}$.

The slope of the line and a point on the line are known. Use the point–slope formula to find the equation of the line.

$$y - y_1 = m(x - x_1)$$

$$y - 3 = -\frac{5}{2}(x - 5) \qquad \bullet \ m = -\frac{5}{2}, (x_1, y_1) = (5, 3).$$

$$y - 3 = -\frac{5}{2}x + \frac{25}{2}$$

$$y = -\frac{5}{2}x + \frac{31}{2} \qquad \bullet \ \text{Check: The slope of the line is } -\frac{5}{2}, \text{ and } (5, 3) \text{ is a solution of this equation.}$$

YOU TRY IT 9

Find the equation of the line that is perpendicular to the graph of $y = -\frac{4}{3}x - 1$ and passes through the point $(-4, 3)$.

Solution See page S16.

EXAMPLE 10

Find the equation of the line that is perpendicular to $2x - y = -3$ and passes through the point $(4, -5)$.

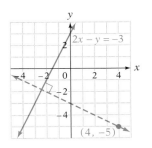

Solution Because the lines are perpendicular, the slope of the unknown line is the negative reciprocal of the slope of the given line. To determine the slope of the given line, write $2x - y = -3$ in slope–intercept form by solving the equation for y.

$$2x - y = -3$$
$$-y = -2x - 3$$
$$y = 2x + 3$$

The slope of the given line is 2.

The slope of a perpendicular line is $-\dfrac{1}{2}$.

The slope of the line and a point on the line are known. Use the point–slope formula to find the equation of the line.

$$y - y_1 = m(x - x_1)$$
$$y - (-5) = -\frac{1}{2}(x - 4) \qquad \bullet\ m = -\frac{1}{2}, x_1 = 4, y_1 = -5$$
$$y + 5 = -\frac{1}{2}x + 2$$
$$y = -\frac{1}{2}x - 3 \qquad \bullet\ \text{Check: The slope of this line is } -\tfrac{1}{2}, \text{ and } (4, -5)$$
$$\text{is a solution of this equation.}$$

YOU TRY IT 10

Find the equation of the line that is perpendicular to the graph of $5x - 3y = 15$ and passes through the point $P(-5, -2)$.

Solution See page S16.

There are many applications of the concept of perpendicular. We will consider one here.

Suppose a ball is being twirled on the end of a string. If the string breaks, the initial path of the ball is on a line that is perpendicular to the radius of the circle.

EXAMPLE 11

Suppose that a ball is being twirled on the end of a string and that the center of rotation is the origin of a coordinate system. See the figure at the right. If the string breaks when the ball is at the point whose coordinates are $P(6, 3)$, find the initial path of the ball.

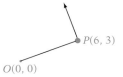

State the goal.   The goal is to find the equation of the line that is perpendicular to the line containing the points (0, 0) and (6, 3) and goes through point (6, 3).

Devise a strategy.   The initial path of the ball is perpendicular to the line through OP. Therefore, the slope of the initial path of the ball is the negative reciprocal of the slope of the line between O and P.

We need to find the slope of the line through OP.

The slope of the line we are looking for is the negative reciprocal of that slope.

We will then have the slope of the line and a point on the line. We can use the point–slope formula to find the equation of the line.

Solve the problem.

Slope of the line between OP: $m = \dfrac{y_2 - y_1}{x_2 - x_1} = \dfrac{3 - 0}{6 - 0} = \dfrac{1}{2}$

The slope of the line that is the initial path of the ball is the negative reciprocal of $\frac{1}{2}$. Therefore, the slope of a perpendicular line is -2.

$$y - y_1 = m(x - x_1)$$ • Use the point–slope formula.
$$y - 3 = -2(x - 6)$$ • $m = -2, x_1 = 6, y_1 = 3$
$$y - 3 = -2x + 12$$
$$y = -2x + 15$$

The initial path of the ball is along the line whose equation is $y = -2x + 15$.

Check your work.   The graphs of $f(x) = -2x + 15$ and $f(x) = \frac{1}{2}x$ are shown at the right in the square viewing window of a graphing calculator. The lines appear to be perpendicular. Use the TRACE feature to show that the ordered pair (6, 3) is on the graph.

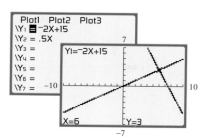

YOU TRY IT 11

Suppose that a ball is being twirled on the end of a string and that the center of rotation is the origin of a coordinate system. See the figure at the right. If the string breaks when the ball is at the point whose coordinates are (2, 8), find the initial path of the ball.

Solution   See page S16.

4.2 EXERCISES

Topics For Discussion

1. Explain why the equation $y = mx + b$ is called the slope–intercept form of a straight line.

2. What is the point–slope formula and how is it used?

3. Suppose a biologist determined that there was a linear model that related the height of a tree, y, to its age, x. In the equation $y = mx + b$, would you expect m to be positive or negative? Why?

4. Suppose a baked potato is taken from a hot oven and placed on a plate to cool. If y represents the temperature of the potato and x represents the time the potato has been out of the oven, would you expect m to be positive or negative in the equation $y = mx + b$? Why?

5. **a.** Explain how to determine whether two lines are parallel.
   b. Explain how to determine whether two lines are perpendicular.

6. Are the lines $x = 0$ and $y = 0$ perpendicular? What is another name for these lines?

■ Writing Equations of Lines in the Form $y = mx + b$

7. Find the equation of the line that has slope -2 and y-intercept $(0, -1)$.

8. Find the equation of the line that has slope $\frac{5}{3}$ and y-intercept $(0, -6)$.

9. Find the equation of the line that has slope $-\frac{1}{4}$ and passes through the point $(0, 2)$.

10. Find the equation of the line that has slope 5 and passes through the point $(0, -3)$.

11. Find the equation of the line that has slope $\frac{1}{6}$ and passes through the point $(0, 0)$.

12.   Find the equation of the line that has slope -1 and passes through the point $(0, -8)$.

13.   Find the equation of the line that has slope 2 and passes through the point $(0, 5)$.

14.   Find the equation of the line that has slope $\frac{1}{2}$ and passes through the point $(2, 3)$.

15.   Find the equation of the line that has slope $-\frac{5}{4}$ and passes through the point $(4, 0)$.

16.   Find the equation of the line that has slope -3 and passes through the point $(-1, 7)$.

17.   Find the equation of the line that has slope 3 and passes through the point $(2, -3)$.

18.   Find the equation of the line that has slope $-\frac{2}{3}$ and passes through the point $(3, 5)$.

19.   Find the equation of the line that contains the point $(-2, -3)$ and has zero slope.

20.   Find the equation of the line that contains the point $(5, 8)$ and has zero slope.

21.   Find the equation of the line that contains the point $(3, -4)$ and whose slope is undefined.

22.   Find the equation of the line that contains the point $(-5, -1)$ and whose slope is undefined.

23.   Find the equation of the line that contains the points $(0, 2)$ and $(3, 5)$.

24.   Find the equation of the line that contains the points $(0, -3)$ and $(-4, 5)$.

25.   Find the equation of the line containing the points $(0, 0)$ and $(4, 3)$.

26.   Find the equation of the line containing the points $(2, -5)$ and $(0, 0)$.

27.   Find the equation of the line that passes through the points $(-2, -3)$ and $(-1, -2)$.

28. Find the equation of the line that passes through the points $(3, -1)$ and $(-2, 4)$.

29. Find the equation of the line that contains the points $(2, 0)$ and $(4, -3)$.

30. Find the equation of the line that contains the points $(4, 1)$ and $(-4, -3)$.

31. Find the equation of the line that passes through the points $(-1, 3)$ and $(2, 4)$.

32. Find the equation of the line that passes through the points $(2, 3)$ and $(5, 5)$.

33. Find the equation of the line that contains the points $(3, -4)$ and $(-2, -4)$.

34. Find the equation of the line that contains the points $(-3, 3)$ and $(-2, 3)$.

35. Find the equation of the line that passes through the points $(-2, 5)$ and $(-2, -5)$.

36. Find the equation of the line that passes through the points $(3, 2)$ and $(3, -4)$.

37. *Aviation*   The pilot of a Boeing 757 jet takes off from Boston's Logan Airport, which is at sea level, and climbs to a cruising altitude of 32,000 feet at a constant rate of 1200 feet per minute. Write a linear equation for the height of the plane in terms of the time after take-off. Use your equation to find the height of the plane 11 minutes after take-off.

38. *Telecommunications*   A cellular phone company offers several different options for using a cellular telephone. One option, for people who plan on using the phone only in emergencies, costs the user $4.95 per month plus $.59 per minute for each minute the phone is used. Write a linear equation for the monthly cost of the phone in terms of the number of minutes the phone is used. Use your equation to find the cost of using the cellular phone for 13 minutes in 1 month.

39. *Aviation*   An Airbus 320 plane takes off from Denver International Airport in Denver, Colorado, which is 5200 feet above sea level, and climbs to 30,000 feet at a constant rate of 1000 feet per minute. Write a linear equation for the height of the plane in terms of the time after take-off. Use your equation to find the height of the plane 8 minutes after take-off.

40. *Construction* A general building contractor estimates that the cost to build a new home is $30,000 plus $85 for each square foot of floor space in the house. Determine a linear function that will give the cost of building a house that contains a given number of square feet. Use this model to determine the cost to build a house that contains 1800 square feet.

41. *Boiling Points* At sea level, the boiling point of water is 100°C. At an altitude of 2 kilometers, the boiling point of water is 93°C. Write a linear equation for the boiling point of water in terms of the altitude above sea level. Use your equation to predict the boiling point of water on top of Mount Everest, which is approximately 8.85 kilometers above sea level. Round to the nearest degree.

42. *Uniform Motion* A plane travels 830 miles in 2 hours. Determine a linear model that will predict the number of miles the plane can travel in a given amount of time. Use this model to predict the distance the plane will travel in $4\frac{1}{2}$ hours.

43. *Computers* According to the U.S. Department of Commerce, there were 24 million homes with computers in 1991. The average rate of growth in computers in homes was expected to increase by 2.4 million homes per year through 2005. Write a linear equation for the number of computers in homes in terms of the year. Let $x = 90$ represent 1990. Use your equation to find the number of computers expected to be in homes in 2004.

44. *Fuel Consumption* The gas tank of a certain car contains 16 gallons when the driver of the car begins a trip. Each mile driven by the driver decreases the amount of gas in the tank by 0.032 gallon per mile. Write a linear equation for the number of gallons of gas in the tank in terms of the number of miles driven. Use your equation to find the number of gallons in the tank after the car has been driven 150 miles.

45. *Sound* Whales, dolphins, and porpoises communicate using high-pitched sounds that travel through the water. The speed at which the sound travels depends on many factors, one of which is the depth of the water. At approximately 1000 meters below sea level, the speed of sound is 1480 meters per second. Below 1000 meters, the speed of sound increases at a constant rate of 0.017 meters per second for each additional meter below 1000 meters. Write a linear equation for the speed of sound in terms of the number of meters below sea level. Use your equation to approximate the speed of sound 2500 meters below sea level. Round to the nearest meter per second.

46. *Compensation* An account executive receives a base salary plus a commission. On $20,000 in monthly sales, the account executive receives $1800. On $50,000 in monthly sales, the account executive receives $3000. Determine a linear function that will yield the compensation of the sales executive for a given amount of monthly sales. Use this model to determine the account executive's compensation for $85,000 in monthly sales.

47. *Business* A manufacturer of pickup trucks has determined that 50,000 trucks per month can be sold at a price of $9000. At a price of $8750, the number of trucks sold per month would increase to 55,000. Determine a linear function that will predict the number of trucks that would be sold at a given price. Use this model to predict the number of trucks that would be sold at a price of $8500.

48. *Business* A manufacturer of graphing calculators has determined that 10,000 calculators per week will be sold at a price of $95. At a price of $90, it is estimated that 12,000 calculators would be sold. Determine a linear function that will predict the number of calculators that would be sold at a given price. Use this model to predict the number of calculators per week that would be sold at a price of $75.

49. *Business* The operator of a hotel estimates that 500 rooms per night will be rented if the room rate per night is $75. If the room rate per night is $85, then 494 rooms will be rented. Determine a linear function that will predict the number of rooms that will be rented for a given price per room. Use this model to predict the number of rooms that will be rented if the room rate is $100 per night.

50. *Boiling Points* When sugar is added to water, the solution has a higher boiling point than pure water. The table at the right gives the boiling point (in degrees Celsius) of a certain quantity of water as various amounts of sugar are added to the water.
  a. Find a linear model for the boiling point of the solution in terms of the number of grams of sugar added.
  b. Write a sentence explaining the meaning of the slope of the line in the context of this problem.
  c. Using this model, determine the boiling point when 50 grams of sugar has been added to this quantity of pure water.

Sugar (in grams)	Boiling Point (in °C)
20	100.104
30	100.156
40	100.208
60	100.312
80	100.416

51. *Freezing Points* When sugar is added to water, the solution has a lower freezing point than pure water. The table at the right gives the freezing point (in degrees Celsius) of a certain quantity of water as various amounts of sugar are added to the water.
  a. Find a linear model for the freezing point of the solution in terms of the number of grams of sugar added.
  b. Write a sentence explaining the meaning of the slope of the line in the context of this problem.
  c. Using this model, determine the freezing point when 50 grams of sugar has been added to this quantity of pure water.

Sugar (in grams)	Freezing Point (in °C)
20	−0.372
30	−0.558
40	−0.744
60	−1.116
80	−1.488

52.  *Aviation*   In 1927, Charles Lindbergh made history by making the first transatlantic flight from New York to Paris. It took Lindbergh approximately 33.5 hours to make the trip. In 1997, the Concorde could make the trip in approximately 3.3 hours. Write a linear equation for the time, in hours, it takes to cross the Atlantic in terms of the year the trip is made. Use your equation to predict how long a flight between the two cities would have taken in 1967. Round your answer to the nearest tenth. On the basis of your answer, do you think a linear model accurately predicts how the flying time between New York and Paris has changed? Explain your answer.

▪ Parallel and Perpendicular Lines

53. Is the line $x = -2$ perpendicular to the line $y = 3$?

54. Is the line $y = \frac{1}{4}$ perpendicular to the line $y = -4$?

55. Is the line $x = -3$ parallel to the line $y = -3$?

56. Is the line $x = 4$ parallel to the line $x = -4$?

57. Is the line $y = -\frac{3}{2}x + 4$ parallel to the line $y = -\frac{3}{2}x - 1$?

58. Is the line $y = 5x - 6$ parallel to the line $y = -5x - 6$?

59. Is the line that contains the points $(3, 2)$ and $(1, 6)$ parallel to the line that contains the points $(-1, 3)$ and $(-1, -1)$?

60. Is the line that contains the points $(4, -3)$ and $(2, 5)$ parallel to the line that contains the points $(-2, -3)$ and $(-4, 1)$?

61. Find the equation of the line that is parallel to $y = -3x - 1$ and passes through $P(1, 4)$.

62. Find the equation of the line that is parallel to $y = \frac{2}{3}x + 2$ and passes through $P(-3, 1)$.

63. Find the equation of the line that contains the point $(-2, -4)$ and is parallel to the line $2x - 3y = 2$.

64. Find the equation of the line that contains the point $(3, 2)$ and is parallel to the line $3x + y = -3$.

65. Is the line $y = -\frac{5}{2}x + 4$ perpendicular to the line $y = -\frac{2}{5}x - 1$?

66. Is the line $y = 4x - 8$ perpendicular to the line $y = -\frac{1}{4}x + 2$?

67. Is the line that contains the points $(-3, 2)$ and $(4, -1)$ perpendicular to the line that contains the points $(1, 3)$ and $(-2, -4)$?

68. Is the line that contains the points $(4, -1)$ and $(-4, 5)$ perpendicular to the line that contains the points $(6, -2)$ and $(-3, 6)$?

69. Find the equation of the line that contains the point $(4, 1)$ and is perpendicular to the line $y = -3x + 4$.

70. Find the equation of the line that contains the point $(2, -5)$ and is perpendicular to the line $y = \frac{5}{2}x - 4$.

71. Find the equation of the line that contains the point $(-1, -3)$ and is perpendicular to the line $3x - 5y = 2$.

72. Find the equation of the line that contains the point $(-1, 3)$ and is perpendicular to the line $2x + 4y = -1$.

73. *Physical Forces*   Suppose that a ball is being twirled on the end of a string and that the center of rotation is the origin of a coordinate system. If the string breaks when the ball is at the point whose coordinates are $(1, 9)$, find the initial path of the ball.

74. *Geometry*   A theorem from geometry states that a line passing through the center of a circle and through a point P on the circle is perpendicular to the tangent line at P. (See the figure at the right.) If the coordinates of P are $(5, 4)$ and the coordinates of C are $(3, 2)$, what is the equation of the tangent line?

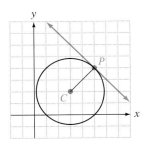

Applying Concepts

Is there a linear equation that contains all the given ordered pairs? If there is, find the equation.

75. $(5, 1), (4, 2), (0, 6)$ **76.** $(-2, -4), (0, -3), (4, -1)$

77. $(-1, -5), (2, 4), (0, 2)$ **78.** $(3, -1), (12, -4), (-6, 2)$

The given ordered pairs are solutions to the same linear equation. Find n.

79. $(0, 1), (4, 9), (3, n)$ **80.** $(2, 2), (-1, 5), (3, n)$

81. $(2, -2), (-2, -4), (4, n)$

82. $(1, -2), (-2, 4), (4, n)$

83.   Suppose A_1, A_2, B_1, and B_2 are all not equal to zero. If the graphs of $A_1 x + B_1 y = C_1$ and $A_2 x + B_2 y = C_2$ are parallel, express $\frac{A_1}{B_1}$ in terms of A_2 and B_2.

84.   Suppose A_1, A_2, B_1, and B_2 are all not equal to zero. If the graphs of $A_1 x + B_1 y = C_1$ and $A_2 x + B_2 y = C_2$ are perpendicular, express $\frac{A_1}{B_1}$ in term of A_2 and B_2.

85.   A line contains the points $(4, -1)$ and $(2, 1)$. Find the coordinates of three other points that are on this line.

86.   Given that f is a linear function for which $f(1) = 3$ and $f(-1) = 5$, determine $f(4)$.

87.   The graphs of $y = -\frac{1}{2} x + 2$ and $y = \frac{2}{3} x - 5$ intersect at the point whose coordinates are $(6, -1)$. Find the equation of a line whose graph intersects the graphs of the given lines to form a right triangle. (*Hint:* There is more than one answer to this question.)

88.   A linear function includes the ordered pairs $(2, 4)$ and $(4, 10)$. Find the value of the function at $x = -1$.

89.   *Uniform Motion*   Assume the maximum speed your car will go varies linearly with the steepness of the hill it is climbing or descending. If the hill is 5° up, your car can go 77 kilometers per hour. If the hill is 2° down $(-2°)$, your car can go 154 kilometers per hour. When your top speed is 99 kilometers per hour, how steep is the hill? State your answer in degrees, and note whether it is up or down.

EXPLORATION

1.   *Linear Parametric Equations*   Consider the situation of a person who can row at a rate of 3 miles per hour in calm water and is trying to cross a river for which there is a current, running perpendicular to the direction of rowing, of 4 miles per hour. See the figure at the right. Because of the current, the boat is being pushed downstream at the same time it is moving across the river. Because the boat is traveling 3 miles per hour in the x direction, its position after t hours is given by $x = 3t$. The current is pushing the boat in the negative y direction at 4 miles per hour. Therefore, its position after t hours is given by $y = -4t$, where we use -4 to indicate that the boat is moving down. The equations $x = 3t$ and $y = -4t$ are called **parametric equations,** and t is called the **parameter.**

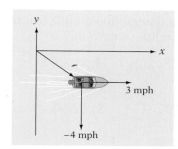

a. Assume the boat starts at the point (0, 0). What is the location of the boat after 15 minutes (0.25 hour)?

b. If the river is 1 mile wide, how far down river will the boat be when it reaches the other shore? (*Suggestion*: Find the time it takes the boat to cross the river by solving $x = 3t$ for t when $x = 1$. Now replace t by this value in $y = -4t$ and simplify.)

c. For the parametric equations $x = 3t$ and $y = -4t$, write y in terms of x by solving $x = 3t$ for t and then substituting this expression into $y = -4t$.

d. In the diagram at the right, a plane flying at 5000 feet above sea level begins a gradual ascent. Determine parametric equations for the path of the plane.

e. What is the altitude of the plane 5 minutes after it begins its ascent?

f. What is the altitude of the plane after it has traveled 12,000 feet in the positive x direction? Round to the nearest whole number.

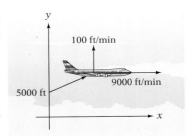

Linear Regression

■ Fit a Line to Data
■ Linear Regression

■ Fit a Line to Data

There are many instances when a linear function can be used to approximate collected data. For instance, the table below shows the recommended maximum exercise heart rates for individuals of various ages who exercise regularly.

Age, x	20	25	30	32	43	55	28	42	50	55	62
Heart rate, y	160	150	148	145	140	130	155	140	132	125	125

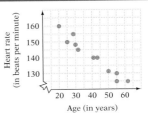

The graph at the right, called a **scatter diagram,** shows a graph of the ordered pairs given in the table. These ordered pairs suggest that the maximum exercise heart rate for an individual decreases as the person's age increases.

Although these points do not lie on a straight line, it is possible to find a line that *approximately fits* the data. One way to do this is to select two data points. You want the line through the two points you select to be one that is close to all the data points. We chose (25, 150) to be P_1 and (55, 130) to be P_2. The slope of the line between these two points is

$$m = \frac{y_2 - y_1}{x_2 - x_1} = \frac{130 - 150}{55 - 25} = \frac{-20}{30} = -\frac{2}{3}$$

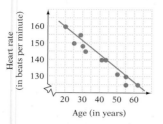

The graph of $y = -\dfrac{2}{3} x + \dfrac{500}{3}$

Now use the point–slope formula to find the equation of the line through the two points.

$$y - y_1 = m(x - x_1)$$

$$y - 150 = -\frac{2}{3}(x - 25)$$ • $m = -\dfrac{2}{3}, x_1 = 25, y_1 = 150$

$$y - 150 = -\frac{2}{3}x + \frac{50}{3}$$ • Use the Distributive Property on the right side.

$$y = -\frac{2}{3}x + \frac{500}{3}$$ • Add 150 to each side of the equation.

The graph of $y = -\dfrac{2}{3} x + \dfrac{500}{3}$ is shown at the left. It *approximates* the data.

You may get a better approximation to the data if, rather than selecting two of the data points, you visually determine a line that closely fits the data and then use a straight-edge to draw that line. The goal is to draw on the graph the **line of best fit**—that is, the line that most closely approximates all the points. Here is an example.

EXAMPLE 1

The table below shows the actual and projected sales of DVDs, in billions of dollars, from 1998 through 2003 (*Source:* Adams Media Research). Sketch a line of best fit through a scatter diagram of the data. Then find a linear equation for the line you drew. Use decimals rather than fractions for the slope and y-intercept in the equation.

Year, x	1998	1999	2000	2001	2002	2003
DVD sales, y (in billions of dollars)	0.4	1.5	3.1	4.9	6.6	8.2

Solution The data points are plotted in the scatter diagram at the right. Although the points do not lie on a straight line, they are close to linear.

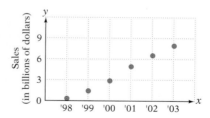

The goal is to draw on the graph the line of best fit. Use a straightedge to draw the line.

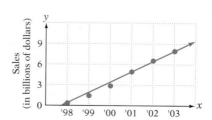

Approximate the location of any two points on the line. We chose $(2001, 5)$ to be P_1 and $(2003, 8)$ to be P_2.

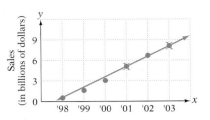

Use the two points selected to find the slope of the line.

$$m = \frac{y_2 - y_1}{x_2 - x_1} = \frac{8 - 5}{2003 - 2001} = \frac{3}{2} = 1.5$$

Now use the point–slope formula to find the equation of the line through the two points.

$$y - y_1 = m(x - x_1)$$
$$y - 5 = 1.5(x - 2001)$$
$$y - 5 = 1.5x - 3001.5$$
$$y = 1.5x - 2996.5$$

The equation for our line is $y = 1.5x - 2996.5$.

YOU TRY IT 1

The table below shows the actual and projected average price of a DVD, in dollars, from 1998 through 2003 (*Source:* Adams Media Research). Sketch a line of best fit through a scatter diagram of the data. (A scatter diagram is provided below the table.) Then find a linear equation for the line. Use decimals rather than fractions for the slope and y-intercept in the equation.

Year, x	1998	1999	2000	2001	2002	2003
Average price of a DVD, y (in dollars)	23.90	23.15	22.30	21.19	19.91	18.52

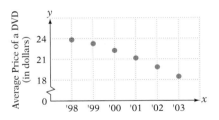

Solution   See page S17.

■ Linear Regression

Consider again the heart rate data presented at the beginning of this section. The equation of the line we found by choosing two data points produces an approximate linear model to the data. If we had chosen different points, the result would have been a slightly different equation.

Among all the equations that could have been chosen, statisticians have determined that the line of best fit is the **regression line.** The equation of the regression line for the data presented there is $y = -0.827x + 174$. The graph of the regression line is shown at the right.

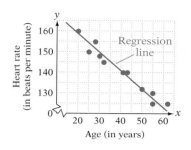

Using the equation of the regression line, an exercise physiologist can determine the recommended maximum exercise heart rate for an individual.

For instance, suppose an individual is 28 years old. Then the physiologist would replace x by 28 and determine the value of y.

$$y = -0.827x + 174$$
$$y = -0.827(28) + 174 \quad \bullet \text{ Replace } x \text{ by } 28.$$
$$y = 150.844$$

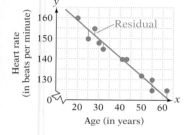

The recommended maximum exercise heart rate for a 28-year-old person is approximately 151 beats per minute.

In Example 1 above, we calculated a linear equation that modeled the data on sales of DVDs. We did this by first sketching a line through the data points and approximating the location of two points on this line. A graphing calculator, however, mathematically determines the line of best fit, or the regression line. The equation of the regression line for the DVD sales data is $y = 1.603x - 3202.399$.

The regression equation predicts that in 2005, sales of DVDs will be \$11.616 billion.

$$y = 1.603x - 3202.399$$
$$y = 1.603(2005) - 3202.399$$
$$= 11.616$$

The example that follows illustrates the calculation of a regression line using a graphing calculator.

The table below shows the data recorded by a chemistry student who was trying to determine a relationship between the temperature (in degrees Celsius) and volume (in liters) at a constant pressure for 1 gram of oxygen. Chemists call this relationship Charles's Law.

See Appendix A: Regression

Temperature, T (in °C)	−100	−75	−50	−25	0	25	50
Volume, V (in liters)	0.43	0.5	0.57	0.62	0.7	0.75	0.81

A graphing calculator can be used to calculate the regression line. Some typical screens follow.

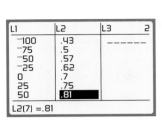

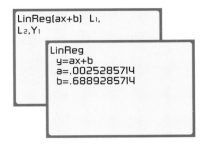

Note that the graphing calculator uses the variable a instead of m; the equation is of the form $y = ax + b$.

For this set of data, the regression equation is $V = 0.0025286T + 0.68892857$.

To determine the volume of 1 gram of oxygen when the temperature is $-30°C$, replace T in the regression equation by -30 and evaluate the expression. This can be done with your calculator. The volume will be displayed as approximately 0.61 liter.

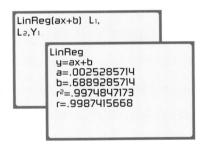

You may have noticed the results of some other calculations on the screen when the regression equation was calculated. The variable r is the **correlation coefficient** and r^2 is the **coefficient of determination.** Statisticians use these numbers to determine how well the regression equation approximates the data. If $r = 1$, the data exactly fit a line of positive slope. If $r = -1$, the data exactly fit a line of negative slope. In general, the closer r^2 is to 1, the closer the data fit a linear model. For these data points, the r^2 value is 0.997, which is very close to 1; the regression line is quite a good fit to the data.

CALCULATOR NOTE

If your calculator does not display the values of r and r^2, see Appendix A:
Correlation Coefficient

EXAMPLE 2

Sodium thiosulfate is used by photographers to develop some types of film. The amount of this chemical that will dissolve in water depends on the temperature of the water. The table that follows gives the number of grams of sodium thiosulfate that will dissolve in 100 milliliters of water for various temperatures.

Temperature, x (in °C)	20	35	50	60	75	90	100
Grams, y	50	80	120	145	175	205	230

a. Find the linear regression line for the data. Round decimals to the nearest thousandth.

b. How many grams of sodium thiosulfate does the model predict will dissolve in 100 milliliters of water when the temperature is 70°C? Round to the nearest tenth.

c. What does the slope of the regression line mean in the context of the problem?

d. What does the *y*-intercept mean in the context of the problem?

Solution **a.** Use a calculator to determine the regression line for the data.

The regression equation is $y = 2.252x + 5.248$.

b. Evaluate the regression equation when $x = 70$.

$y = 2.252x + 5.248$

$= 2.252(70) + 5.248$

$= 162.888$

Approximately 162.9 grams of sodium thiosulfate will dissolve when the temperature is 70°C.

c. The slope of 2.252 means that for every 1°C increase in temperature, an additional 2.252 grams of sodium thiosulfate will dissolve in the water.

d. The *y*-intercept of 5.248 means that at 0°C, 5.248 grams of sodium thiosulfate will dissolve in the water.

A scatter diagram of the data is shown at the left, along with the graph of the regression line. Note that the regression line is a very good fit for the data and that the r^2 value of 0.997959, shown in the graphing calculator screen at the left above, is very close to 1.

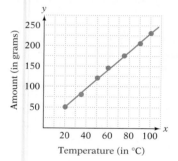

```
LinReg
 y=ax+b
 a=2.25177305
 b=5.24822695
 r²=.9979591614
 r=.9989790596
```

YOU TRY IT 2

The heights and weights of women swimmers on a college swim team are given in the table that follows.

Height, x (in inches)	68	64	65	67	62	67	65
Weight, y (in pounds)	132	108	108	125	102	130	105

a. Find the linear regression line for these data.

b. Use your regression equation to estimate the weight of a woman on a college swim team who is 63 inches tall. Round to the nearest whole number.

c. What does the slope of the regression line mean in the context of the problem?

d. What does the *y*-intercept mean in the context of the problem?

Solution See page S17.

One important use of a scatter diagram is to determine the relationship between two variables before performing regression on the data. In this section, we are investigating two-variable data in which the relationship is linear. Therefore, the data values should lie close to a straight line.

The table from Example 2 is repeated below, and a scatter diagram for the data is shown at the left. Note that the points lie close to a straight line.

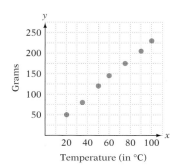

Temperature, x (in °C)	20	35	50	60	75	90	100
Grams, y	50	80	120	145	175	205	230

A graphing calculator can display data in a scatter diagram. Some typical screens follows.

See Appendix A:
Stat Plot

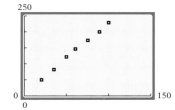

Note that in the scatter diagram, all the points lie close to a straight line. Therefore, linear regression is appropriate for the data.

The following data are from a biology experiment in which the growth of bacteria was recorded. A scatter diagram of the data is shown at the left. Note that the points do not lie close to a straight line. Linear regression would not be appropriate for the data.

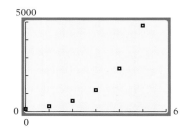

Time, x (in hours)	0	1	2	3	4	5
Population, y	150	300	600	1200	2400	4800

In the last section, we found the equation of a line between two points by first finding the slope of the line between the two points and then using the point–slope formula. Linear regression can also be used to find the equation of a line given two points on the line. Example 3 illustrates the procedure.

EXAMPLE 3

Use linear regression to find the equation of the line containing the points $(6, -4)$ and $(3, 2)$.

Solution   The points $(6, -4)$ and $(3, 2)$ are represented in the input/output table.

x	6	3
y	-4	2

```
LinReg
 y=ax+b
 a=-2
 b=8
 r²=1
 r=-1
```

Enter the *x* values in one list of a calculator and the *y* values in another. Then use the calculator to determine the regression line for the data.

The equation is $y = -2x + 8$.

YOU TRY IT 3

Use linear regression to find the equation of the line containing the points $(-2, 3)$ and $(4, 1)$.

Solution See page S17.

? QUESTION For the regression equation in Example 3, why is the value of *r* equal to -1?

4.3 EXERCISES

Topics for Discussion

1. What does it mean to "fit a line to data"?

2. What is a regression line?

3. What might be the purpose of determining the regression equation for a set of data?

4. Determine whether the statement is always true, sometimes true, or never true.
   a. For linear regression to be performed on two-variable data, the points corresponding to the data values must lie on a straight line.
   b. If the correlation coefficient is equal to 1, the data exactly fit the regression line. If the correlation coefficient is equal to -1, the data do not fit the regression line.
   c. A scatter diagram is a graph of ordered pairs.

5. Suppose an infant's weight is measured once a month for 2 years. If a regression equation were calculated for the weight of the infant in terms of the age of the infant, in months, would *r* be positive, zero, or negative? Why?

? ANSWER The given points lie exactly on the line $y = -2x + 8$, and the slope of the line is negative.

6. Suppose a person purchases a used car. If data were collected giving the value of the car in terms of its age, would r be positive, zero, or negative? Why?

7. Suppose that in a college history class, data are collected giving the height of a student and the student's score on an exam. If a regression equation were calculated on the data, would r be positive, zero, or negative? Why?

Fit a Line to Data

8. *Demography*   The table and scatter diagram show the projected number of U.S. high school graduates, in millions (*Source:* National Center for Education Statistics).

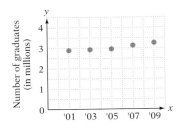

Year, x	'01	'03	'05	'07	'09
Number of graduates, y (in millions)	2.90	2.98	2.99	3.13	3.25

  a. Find the equation of a line that approximately fits the data by selecting two data points and finding the equation of the line through those two points.

  b. What does the slope of your line mean in the context of the problem?

  c. What does the y-intercept mean in the context of the problem?

9. *Zoology*   The table and scatter diagram show the increase in the grey wolf population in regions of Idaho after that species's re-introduction in the mid-1990s (*Source:* U.S. Fish and Wildlife Service).

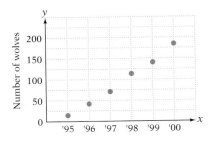

Year, x	'95	'96	'97	'98	'99	'00
Number of wolves, y	14	42	71	114	141	185

  a. Find the equation of a line that approximately fits the data by selecting two data points and finding the equation of the line through those two points.

  b. What does the slope of your line mean in the context of the problem?

10. 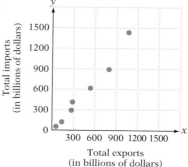 *Commerce* The table shows the total U.S. exports and imports, in billions of dollars, for selected years (*Source:* U.S. Department of Commerce, Bureau of Economic Analysis). The scatter diagram represents the total exports along the horizontal axis and the total imports along the vertical axis.

Year	Total Exports	Total Imports
1970	56.6	54.4
1975	132.6	120.2
1980	271.8	291.2
1985	288.8	410.9
1990	537.2	618.4
1995	795.1	891.0
2000	1068.4	1438.1

a. Sketch a line of best fit through the scatter diagram of the data. Then find a linear equation for the line. Use decimals for the slope and *y*-intercept in the equation.

b. What does the slope of your line mean in the context of the problem?

11. 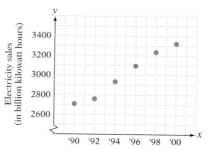 *Energy Consumption* The table and scatter diagram show electricity sales, in billions of kilowatt hours, in the United States for selected years (*Source:* U.S. Department of Energy).

Year	Electricity Sales (in billion kilowatt hours)
1990	2713
1992	2763
1994	2935
1996	3098
1998	3240
2000	3325

a. Sketch a line of best fit through the scatter diagram of the data. Then find a linear equation for the line. Use decimals for the coefficient and constant in the equation.

b. What does the slope of your line mean in the context of the problem?

Linear Regression

12. *Health* A research hospital did a study on the relationship between stress and diastolic blood pressure. The results from 8 patients in the study are given in the table that follows.

Stress, x	55	62	58	78	92	88	75	80
Blood pressure, y	70	85	72	85	96	90	82	85

a. Find the regression line for the data.

b. Use the regression line to determine the blood pressure of a person whose stress test score was 85. Round to the nearest whole number.

c. Explain why the slope of the regression line indicates that blood pressure increases when stress increases.

13. *Energy Consumption*   An automotive engineer studied the relationship between the speed of a car and the number of miles per gallon consumed at that speed. The results of the study are shown in the table that follows.

Speed, x (in miles per hour)	40	25	30	50	60	80	55	35	45
Consumption, y (in miles per gallon)	26	27	28	24	22	21	23	27	25

a. Find the regression line for the data.

b. Use the regression line to determine the expected number of miles per gallon for a car traveling 65 miles per hour. Round to the nearest whole number.

c. Explain why the slope of the regression line indicates that the number of miles per gallon decreases as speed increases.

14. *Earth Science*   A meteorologist studied the high temperature at various latitudes for January of a certain year. The results of the study are shown in the table that follows.

Latitude, x (in °N)	22	30	36	42	56	51	48
Temperature, y (in °F)	80	65	47	54	21	44	52

a. Find the regression line for this data.

b. Use the regression line to determine the expected temperature at a latitude of 45°N. Round to the nearest whole number.

c. What does the slope of the regression line mean in the context of the problem?

d. What does the y-intercept mean in the context of the problem?

15. *Zoology*   A zoologist studied the running speed of animals in terms of the animal's body length. The results of the study are shown in the table that follows.

Body length, x (in centimeters)	1	9	15	16	24	25	60
Running speed, y (in meters per second)	1	2.5	7.5	5	7.4	7.6	20

a. Find the regression line for the data.

b. Use the regression line to determine the expected running speed of a deer mouse whose body length is 10 centimeters. Round to the nearest tenth.

c. What does the slope of the regression line mean in the context of the problem?

d. What does the y-intercept mean in the context of the problem?

16. *Paleontology*   The data below shows the length, in centimeters, of the humerus and the total wingspan, in centimeters, of several pterosaurs, which are extinct flying reptiles of the order Pterosauria (*Source:* Southwest Educational Development Laboratory).

Pterosaur Data (in centimeters)

Humerus	Wingspan	Humerus	Wingspan
24	600	20	500
32	750	27	570
22	430	15	300
17	370	15	310
13	270	9	240
4.4	68	4.4	55
3.2	53	2.9	50
1.5	24		

a. Find the linear regression equation for the data.

b. On the basis of the linear regression model, what is the projected wingspan of the pterosaur *Quetzalcoatlus northropi*, which is thought to have been the largest of the prehistoric birds, if its humerus is 54 centimeters? Round to the nearest whole number.

17. *Demography*   According to the U.S. Census Bureau, there were 69.9 million children under age 18 in the United States in 1998. In 1999 there were 70.2 million children under age 18 in the United States. It is projected that the number will increase to 77.2 million in 2020.

a. Let the year be the independent variable where x = 98 represents the year 1998, x = 99 represents the year 1999, and x = 120 represents the year 2020. Let the number of children, in millions, be the dependent variable. Find the regression line for the data.

b. What is the correlation coefficient? What does this mean about the fit of the data to the regression line?

c. Use the regression line to determine the expected number of children under age 18 in the United States in 2010. Round to the nearest hundred thousand.

d. ✎ What does the slope of the regression line mean in the context of the problem?

e. ✎ What does the y-intercept mean in the context of the problem?

18. *Air Density* The density of air changes as temperature changes. These changes in density affect the resistance a cyclist experiences while riding. The table at the right gives the density of air, in kilograms per cubic meter, for various temperatures in degrees Celsius.

a. Find the linear regression equation of density in terms of temperature.

b. Use the regression equation to predict the density when the temperature is 27°C.

c. ✎ Write a sentence explaining the meaning of the slope of the repression line.

Temperature (in degrees Celsius)	Density of air (in kilograms per cubic meter)
0	1.292
15	1.225
20	1.204
25	1.184
30	1.165
35	1.146
40	1.127

19. *Electoral College* Listed at the right are the number of electoral college votes allotted to each of the 50 states and the District of Columbia (*Source:* Office of the Federal Register). Also listed is the population of each state (*Source:* U.S. Census Bureau).

a. Using population as the independent variable and number of electoral college votes as the dependent variable, find the regression line for the data.

b. ✎ What does the slope of the regression line mean in the context of the problem?

c. ✎ What does the y-intercept mean in the context of the problem?

d. ✎ Why is the r value not exactly equal to 1?

States	Population (in millions)	Electoral College Votes	States	Population (in millions)	Electoral College Votes
Alabama	4.4	9	Montana	0.9	3
Alaska	0.6	3	Nebraska	1.7	5
Arizona	5.1	10	Nevada	2.0	5
Arkansas	2.7	6	New Hampshire	1.2	4
California	33.9	55	New Jersey	8.4	15
Colorado	4.3	9	New Mexico	1.8	5
Connecticut	3.4	7	New York	19.0	31
Delaware	0.8	3	North Carolina	8.0	15
D.C.	0.6	3	North Dakota	0.6	3
Florida	16.0	27	Ohio	11.4	20
Georgia	8.2	15	Oklahoma	3.5	7
Hawaii	1.2	4	Oregon	3.4	7
Idaho	1.3	4	Pennsylvania	12.3	21
Illinois	12.4	21	Rhode Island	1.0	4
Indiana	6.1	11	South Carolina	4.0	8
Iowa	3.0	7	South Dakota	0.8	3
Kansas	2.7	6	Tennessee	5.7	11
Kentucky	4.0	8	Texas	20.9	34
Louisiana	4.5	9	Utah	2.2	5
Maine	1.3	4	Vermont	0.6	3
Maryland	5.3	10	Virginia	7.1	13
Massachusetts	6.3	12	Washington	5.9	11
Michigan	9.9	17	West Virginia	1.8	5
Minnesota	4.9	10	Wisconsin	5.4	10
Mississippi	2.8	6	Wyoming	0.5	3
Missouri	5.6	11			

20. Each screen shows a scatter diagram and the corresponding linear regression line. Match each screen with the corresponding correlation coefficient.

a.

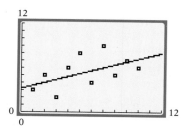

b.

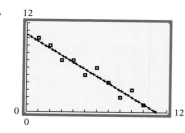

i. $r = -0.515$

ii. $r = -0.970$

iii. $r = 0.515$

iv. $r = 0.970$

c.

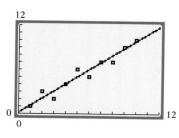

d.

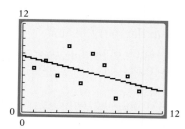

21. Each screen shows a scatter diagram and the corresponding linear regression line. Match each screen with the corresponding correlation coefficient.

a.

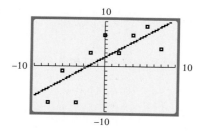

b.

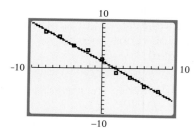

i. $r = -0.787$

ii. $r = 0.787$

iii. $r = -0.995$

iv. $r = 0.995$

c.

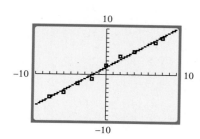

d.

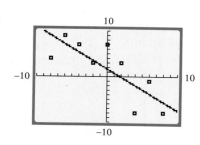

22. Use linear regression to find the equation of the line containing the points $(1, 3)$ and $(5, -3)$.

23. Use linear regression to find the equation of the line containing the points $(2, 4)$ and $(4, -1)$.

24. *Demography*   Refer to the data on the number of high school graduates in Exercise 8.
   a.   Find the regression line for these data. Use $x = 1$ for 2001, $x = 3$ for 2003, and so on.
   b.   If the figure for 2009 were changed from 3.25 to 4.25, what would be the effect on the value of r^2? Why?

25. *Zoology*   Refer to the data on the grey wolf population in Exercise 9.
   a.   Find the regression line for these data. Use $x = 95$ for 1995, $x = 96$ for 1996, and so on.
   b.   If the figure for 1998 were changed from 114 to 50, what would be the effect on the value of r^2? Why?

Applying Concepts

26. Use linear regression to find the equation of the line containing the points $(5, 1)$ and $(5, -2)$. Explain the result.

27. What is wrong with the statement "The r value is 1.35"?

28. *Economics*   The following quote was printed on the web site **www.eia.doe.gov**. Provide an explanation of its meaning. "A strong correlation between economic growth and electricity use accounts for the variation in coal demand projections across the economic growth cases, with domestic coal consumption in 2020 projected to range from 1,245 to 1,426 million tons in the low and high economic growth cases, respectively."

Average SAT Scores

Verbal	Math
543	516
543	516
540	517
537	512
532	513
530	509
523	506
521	505
512	498
509	497
507	496
507	494
505	493
502	492
502	492
504	493
503	494
504	497
509	500
509	500
507	501
505	501
504	502
500	501
499	500
500	501
500	503
499	504
504	506
505	508
505	511
505	512
505	511
505	514

29. *Standardized Tests*   The table at the right shows the average verbal SAT score and the average math SAT score for each year from 1967 through 2000 (*Source:* **www.collegeboard.org**).

   a. Let the average verbal SAT score be the independent variable and the average math SAT score be the dependent variable. Find the regression line for these data and the corresponding correlation coefficient.

   b. Let the average math SAT score be the independent variable and the average verbal SAT score be the dependent variable. Find the regression line for these data and the corresponding correlation coefficient. (*Note:* You do not need to reenter the data. You are able to instruct the calculator to treat the data in the second list as the independent variable and the data in the first list as the dependent variable. For assistance, see Appendix A: Regression.)

   c. Do you consider the average verbal SAT score to be a good predictor of the average math SAT score? Do you consider the average math SAT score to be a good predictor of the average verbal SAT score?

EXPLORATION

1. *Elasticity Experiment*

For this experiment, you will need:

a styrofoam cup with two holes cut, on opposite sides of the cup, just below the top rim
a piece of string several inches long
a wide elastic band
a large paper clip
about 100 pennies
heavy-duty tape
a measuring tape or ruler with units in centimeters

Thread the string through the two holes in the cup. Tie off the string on both sides of the cup. Attach the elastic band to the string. Attach the other end of the elastic band to the paper clip. Open the paper clip so that the cup can hang off the side of a desk or table. Tape the paper clip to the table.

Use the tape measure to record the distance, in centimeters, from the top of the rubber band to the bottom of the cup. This is the initial distance. Record this trial in the table that follows. Put a number of pennies in the cup (anywhere from 10 to 25). Measure the distance to the bottom of the cup. Record this trial in the table. Continue adding pennies and recording the results in the table.

Number of pennies					
Distance to bottom of cup					

a. Make a scatter plot of the data. Describe any patterns you see.

b. Use your graphing calculator to generate a regression line.

c. What is the correlation coefficient of your line? What does this tell you?

d. What does the slope of your line mean in the context of the experiment?

e. What does the *y*-intercept of your line mean in the context of the experiment?

f. What is a reasonable domain of your equation? What is a reasonable range of your equation?

g. Use your model to predict what the distance from the top of the rubber band to the bottom of the cup would be if you placed 125 pennies in the cup.

h. If the elastic band were less elastic (tighter), what would you expect to happen to the slope of the line?

i. If the elastic band were more elastic (stretchier), what would you expect to happen to the slope of the line?

j. If the objects you were putting in the cup were lighter, how would that affect the slope of the line?

k. If the objects you were putting in the cup were heavier, how would that affect the slope of the line?

l. If instead of measuring from the top of the elastic to the bottom of the cup, you measured from the top of the paper clip to the bottom of the cup, how would that affect the equation of the line?

m. If instead of measuring from the top of the elastic to the bottom of the cup, you measured from the floor to the bottom of the cup, how would that affect the equation of the line?

■ Solution Sets of Inequalities in Two Variables

Linear Inequalities in Two Variables

■ Solution Sets of Inequalities in Two Variables

The graph of the linear equation $y = x + 1$ sep-
arates the plane into three sets: the set of points
on the line, the set of points above the line, and
the set of points below the line.

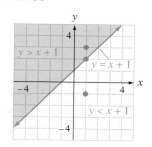

The point whose coordinates are $(1, 2)$ is a solution of $y = x + 1$ and is a point on the line.

The point whose coordinates are $(1, 3)$ is a solution of $y > x + 1$ and is a point above the line.

The point whose coordinates are $(1, -1)$ is a solution of $y < x + 1$ and is a
point below the line.

The set of points on the line are the solutions of the equation $y = x + 1$. The
set of points above the line are the solutions of the inequality $y > x + 1$. These
points form a **half-plane.** The set of points below the line are solutions of the
inequality $y < x + 1$. These points also form a half-plane.

? QUESTION Which ordered pairs are solutions of the inequality
$y < 2x - 3$?

a. $(-1, 4)$ **b.** $(0, 5)$ **c.** $(3, 1)$ **d.** $(-2, -7)$ **e.** $(2, -3)$

An inequality of the form $y > mx + b$ or $Ax + By > C$ is a **linear inequality in
two variables.** (The inequality symbol could be replaced by $<$, $\leq$, or $\geq$.) The
solution set of a linear inequality in two variables is a half-plane.

The following illustrates the procedure for graphing the solution set of a linear inequality in two variables.

➡ Graph the solution set of $2x - 5y > 10$.

Solve the inequality for y.

$$2x - 5y > 10$$
$$-5y > -2x + 10$$
$$\frac{-5y}{-5} < \frac{-2x + 10}{-5}$$
$$y < \frac{2}{5}x - 2$$

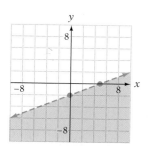

? ANSWER **a.** No. $4 < -5$ is not true. **b.** No. $5 < -3$ is not true. **c.** Yes. $1 < 3$ is true.
d. No. $-7 < -7$ is not true. **e.** Yes. $-3 < 1$ is true.

Change the inequality $y < \frac{2}{5}x - 2$ to the equality $y = \frac{2}{5}x - 2$, and graph the line.

After solving the equation for y, look at the inequality symbol. **If the inequality symbol is $\leq$ or $\geq$, the line belongs to the solution set and is shown by a solid line. If the inequality symbol is $<$ or $>$, the line is not part of the solution set and is shown by a dashed line.**

If the inequality contains $>$ or $\geq$, shade the upper half-plane. If the inequality contains $<$ or $\leq$, shade the lower half-plane. Every point in the shaded half-plane is in the solution set of the inequality.

As a check, use the ordered pair $(0, 0)$ to determine whether the correct region of the plane has been shaded. **If $(0, 0)$ is a solution of the inequality, then $(0, 0)$ should be in the shaded region. If $(0, 0)$ is not a solution of the inequality, then $(0, 0)$ should not be in the shaded region.**

To check whether $(0, 0)$ is a solution of the inequality, substitute 0 for x and 0 for y in the original inequality. For the example above,

$$\frac{2x - 5y > 10}{2(0) - 5(0) \mid 10}$$
$$0 > 10 \qquad \text{False. } (0, 0) \text{ is not a solution of the inequality.}$$
$$\qquad\qquad (0, 0) \text{ should not be in the shaded region.}$$

If the line passes through the point $(0, 0)$, another point, such as $(0, 1)$, must be used as a check.   ⬅

From the graph of $y < \frac{2}{5}x - 2$, note that for a given value of x, more than one value of y can be paired with the value of x. For instance, $(5, -1)$ and $(5, -2)$ are ordered pairs that are solutions of the inequality.

$y < \dfrac{2}{5}x - 2$			$y < \dfrac{2}{5}x - 2$	
-1	$\dfrac{2}{5}(5) - 2$		-2	$\dfrac{2}{5}(5) - 2$
-1	$2 - 2$		-2	$2 - 2$
$-1 < 0$		True	$-2 < 0$	True

Because there are ordered pairs with the same first component and different second components, the inequality does not represent a function. The inequality is a relation but not a function.

A graphing calculator can be used to graph the solution set of an inequality in two variables. Some typical screens for graphing the solution set of $y \leq 2x - 3$ on a graphing calculator follow.

See Appendix A:
Graphing Linear
Inequalities

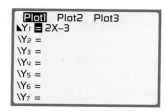

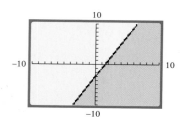

An inequality with the symbol $\geq$ or $\leq$ should be graphed as a solid line, and an inequality with the symbol $>$ or $<$ should be graphed as a dashed line. However, a graphing calculator does not distinguish between a solid line and a dashed line.

EXAMPLE 1

Graph the solution set of $x + 2y \geq 6$. Is $(6, -4)$ in the solution set?

Solution   Solve the inequality for y.

$$x + 2y \geq 6$$
$$2y \geq -x + 6$$
$$\frac{2y}{2} \geq \frac{-x + 6}{2}$$
$$y \geq -\frac{1}{2}x + 3$$

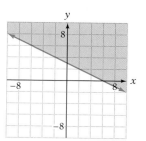

Graph $y = -\frac{1}{2}x + 3$ as a solid line.

Shade the upper half-plane.

From the graph, we can see that the point $(6, -4)$ is not in the solution set of the inequality.

GRAPHICAL CHECK:	**ALGEBRAIC CHECK:**

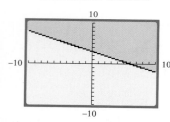

$$y \geq -\frac{1}{2}x + 3$$

-4	$-\frac{1}{2}(6) + 3$
-4	$-3 + 3$
$-4 \geq 0$	False.

The point $(6, -4)$ is not in the solution set.

YOU TRY IT 1

Graph the solution set of $2x - 3y < 12$. Is $(3, -1)$ in the solution set?

Solution   See page S17.

Just as we can draw graphs of equations such as $x = 3$ and $y = -4$, we can draw graphs of similar inequalities.

EXAMPLE 2

Graph the solution set.

a. $x > -4$ **b.** $y \leq 2$

Solution   **a.** Graph $x = -4$ as a dashed line.

$0 > -4$ is a true inequality.
The point $(0, 0)$ satisfies the inequality.
The point $(0, 0)$ should be in the shaded region.
Shade the half-plane to the right of the line.

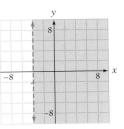

b. Graph $y = 2$ as a solid line.

$0 \leq 2$ is a true inequality.
The point $(0, 0)$ satisfies the inequality.
The point $(0, 0)$ should be in the shaded region.
Shade the half-plane below the line.

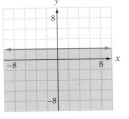

YOU TRY IT 2

Graph the solution set.

a. $x \geq 1$ **b.** $y < -5$

Solution   See page S17.

4.4 EXERCISES

Topics for Discussion

1. Is it possible to write a linear inequality in two variables that has no solution?

2. What is a half-plane?

3. Does a linear inequality in two variables define a function? Why or why not?

4. How does the graph of a linear inequality in two variables differ when $<$ is used from when $\leq$ is used?

■ Solution Sets of Inequalities in Two Variables

Graph the solution set. State whether the given ordered pair is in the solution set.

5. $y \leq \dfrac{3}{2}x - 3$; $(4, -3)$

6. $y \geq \dfrac{4}{3}x - 4$; $(-6, 0)$

7. $y < -\dfrac{1}{3}x + 2$; $(-3, 6)$

8. $y < \dfrac{3}{5}x - 3$; $(-5, -2)$

9. $y < \dfrac{4}{5}x - 2$; $(5, -1)$

10. $y < -\dfrac{4}{3}x + 3$; $(3, -3)$

11. $x + 3y < 6$; $(1, 2)$

12. $2x - 5y \leq 10$; $(5, 0)$

13. $2x + 3y \geq 6$; $(6, -1)$

14. $3x + 2y < 4$; $(-4, -1)$

15. $-x + 2y > -8$; $(5, -3)$

16. $-3x + 2y > 2$; $(-2, -3)$

17. $y < 4$; $(0, 2)$

18. $y > 3$; $(-3, 4)$

19. $6x + 5y < 15$; $(-6, 0)$

20. $3x - 5y < 10;$ $(0, -2)$ **21.** $-5x + 3y \geq -12;$ $(2, -2)$ **22.** $3x + 4y \geq 12;$ $(0, 3)$

23. $x \geq -2;$ $(1, 1)$ **24.** $x < 3;$ $(5, -1)$ **25.** $y \leq -2;$ $(-4, 3)$

Applying Concepts

Graph the solution set.

26. $y - 5 < 4(x - 2)$

27. $y + 3 < 6(x + 1)$

28. $3x - 2(y + 1) \leq y - (5 - x)$

29. $2x - 3(y + 1) \geq y - (4 - x)$

Write the inequality given its graph.

30.

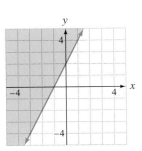

31.

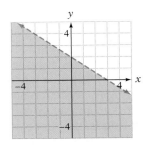

32. Are there any points whose coordinates satisfy both $y \leq x + 3$ and $y \geq -\frac{1}{2}x + 1$? If so, give the coordinates of three such points. If not, explain why not.

33. Are there any points whose coordinates satisfy both $y \leq x - 1$ and $y \geq x + 2$? If not, explain why not.

EXPLORATION

1. *Constraints*   Linear inequalities are used as constraints (conditions that must be satisfied) for some application problems. For these problems, the focus of attention is only the first quadrant, so a solution outside the first quadrant is not considered. For each of the following, shade the region of the first quadrant that satisfies the constraints.

   a. Suppose a manufacturer makes two types of computer monitors, 15-inch and 17-inch. Because of the production requirements for these monitors, the maximum number of monitors that can be produced in one day is 100. Shade the region of the first quadrant whose ordered pairs satisfy the constraint. (*Hint:* Let $x =$ the number of 15-inch monitors and $y =$ the number of 17-inch monitors. Write an inequality. Solve the inequality for y. Graph the inequality.)

   b. A manufacturer makes two types of bicycle gears, standard and deluxe. It takes 4 hours of labor to produce a standard gear and 6 hours of labor to produce a deluxe gear. If there are a maximum of 480 hours of labor available, shade the region of the first quadrant whose ordered pairs satisfy the constraint. (*Hint:* Let $x =$ the number of standard gears produced and $y =$ the number of deluxe gears produced. Write an inequality for the number of hours of labor. Solve the inequality for y. Graph the inequality.)

   c. Suppose a single tablet of the diet supplement SuperC contains 150 milligrams of calcium and that one tablet of the diet supplement CalcPlus contains 200 milligrams of calcium. A health care professional recommends that a patient take at least 2000 milligrams of calcium per day. Shade the region of the first quadrant whose ordered pairs satisfy these constraints. (*Hint:* Let $x =$ the number of SuperC tablets and $y =$ the number of CalcPlus tablets.)

   d. A farmer is planning to raise wheat and barley. Each acre of wheat yields a profit of $50, and each acre of barley yields a profit of $70. The farmer wants to make a profit of at least $3500. Shade the region of the first quadrant whose ordered pairs satisfy the constraint. (*Hint:* Let $x =$ the number of acres of wheat and $y =$ the number of acres of barley.)

CHAPTER **4** *SUMMARY*

Key Terms

coefficient of determination [p. 285]
constant function [p. 247]
correlation coefficient [p. 285]
half-plane [p. 300]
linear function [p. 239]
linear inequality in two variables
 [p. 298]
linear regression [p. 284]
line of best fit [p. 282]

negative reciprocals [p. 269]
parallel lines [p. 266]
perpendicular lines [p. 268]
regression line [p. 284]
scatter diagram [p. 281]
slope [p. 240]
solution set of a linear inequality in
 two variables [p. 298]

Essential Concepts

Slope of a Line
Let $P_1(x_1, y_1)$ and $P_2(x_2, y_2)$ be two points on a line. Then the slope m of the line through the two points is the ratio of the change in the y-coordinates to the change in the x-coordinates. [p. 241]

$$m = \frac{\text{change in } y}{\text{change in } x} = \frac{y_2 - y_1}{x_2 - x_1}, x_1 \neq x_2$$

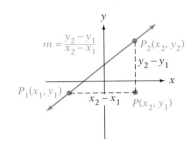

Slope–Intercept Form of a Straight Line
The equation $y = mx + b$ is called the slope–intercept form of a straight line. The slope of the line is m, the coefficient of x. The y-intercept is $(0, b)$. [p. 244]

Standard Form of the Equation of a Line
The equation of a line written in the form $Ax + By = C$ is called the standard form of the equation of a line. [p. 245]

Constant Function
A function given by $f(x) = b$, where b is a constant, is a constant function. The graph of a constant function is a horizontal line passing through $(0, b)$. [p. 247]

Point–Slope Formula of a Straight Line
Let $P_1(x_1, y_1)$ be a point on a line, and let m be the slope of the line. Then the equation of the line can be found by using the point–slope formula $y - y_1 = m(x - x_1)$. [p. 261]

To Find the Equation of a Line Between Two Points
Find the slope of the line between the two points. Then use the point–slope formula to find the equation of the line. [p. 264]

Parallel Lines
Two nonvertical lines with slopes m_1 and m_2 are parallel lines if and only if $m_1 = m_2$. Vertical lines are also parallel lines. [p. 266]

Perpendicular Lines
If m_1 and m_2 are the slopes of two lines, neither of which is vertical, then the lines are perpendicular if and only if $m_1 \cdot m_2 = -1$. A vertical line is perpendicular to a horizontal line. [p. 268]

CHAPTER **4** *REVIEW EXERCISES*

1. Find the slope of the line that contains the points $(-1, 3)$ and $(-2, 4)$.

2. Find the slope of the line that passes through the points $(-6, 5)$ and $(-6, 4)$.

3. Graph the line that has slope $\frac{1}{2}$ and passes through the point $(-2, 4)$.

4. Graph $y = -\frac{2}{3}x + 4$ by using the slope and y-intercept.

5. Graph $x + 2y = -4$.

6. Graph $y = 3$.

7. Find the equation of the line that has slope $-\frac{4}{3}$ and passes through the point $(0, -5)$.

8. Find the equation of the line that has slope 4 and passes through the point $(1, 2)$.

9. Find the equation of the line that passes through the points $(2, 6)$ and $(-4, 9)$.

10. Find the equation of the line that passes through the points $(3, -4)$ and $(-2, -4)$.

11. Is the line that contains the points $(4, 3)$ and $(6, 2)$ parallel to the line that contains the points $(3, 2)$ and $(1, 4)$?

12. Find the equation of the line that is parallel to the line $3x + y = 4$ and contains the point $(3, -2)$.

13. Is the line that contains the points $(3, 5)$ and $(-3, 3)$ perpendicular to the line that contains the points $(2, -5)$ and $(-4, 4)$?

14. Find the equation of the line that is perpendicular to $y = -\frac{2}{3}x + 6$ and contains the point $(2, 5)$.

15. Graph the solution set of $y \leq -\frac{3}{2}x + 6$.

16. A contractor estimates that it costs $60,000 plus $90 per square foot to build a house. Write a linear equation for the cost to build a house. Use your equation to find the cost to build a 2500-square-foot house.

17. The graph at the right shows the relationship between the age of a person and the recommended maximum exercise heart rate for a person who exercises regularly. Find the slope of the line between the two points shown on the graph. Write a sentence that states the meaning of the slope in the context of this problem.

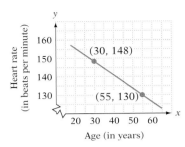

18. Water is being added to a pond that already contains 1000 gallons of water. The table at the right shows the number of gallons of water in the pond after selected times, in minutes.
    a. Find a linear model for the number of gallons of water in the tank after t minutes.
    b. Write a sentence that explains the meaning of the slope of the line in the context of this problem.
    c. Assuming that water continues to flow into the pond at the same rate, how many gallons of water will be in the tank after 6 hours?

Time (in minutes)	Water (in gallons)
30	1750
60	2500
80	3000
120	4000

19. A linear model for a monthly cellular phone bill is given by $F(x) = 0.25x + 19.95$, where $F(x)$ is the monthly cellular phone bill and x is the number of minutes the phone was used during the month.
    a. Write a sentence that explains the meaning of the slope of this function in the context of this problem.
    b. Write a sentence that explains the meaning of the y-intercept in the context of this problem.

20. The "apparent temperature" takes into consideration not only the temperature but the relative humidity as well. The following table gives the apparent temperature when the actual temperature is 85°F for various humidities.
    a. Find a linear regression equation that gives apparent temperature in terms of the relative humidity.
    b. Use the regression equation to find the apparent temperature when the relative humidity is 75. Round to the nearest tenth.

Relative humidity, x (in percents)	30	40	50	60	70	80	90
Apparent temperature, y (in °F)	84	86	88	90	93	97	102

CHAPTER **4** *TEST*

1. Find the slope of the line that contains the points $(-2, 6)$ and $(-1, 4)$.

2. Find the slope of the line that passes through the points $(-4, 3)$ and $(-8, 3)$.

3. Graph the line that has slope $-\frac{3}{2}$ and passes through the point $(-2, 3)$.

4. Graph $y = \frac{2}{3}x - 4$ by using the slope and y-intercept.

5. Graph $2x + y = 2$.

6. Graph $y = -2$.

7. Write the equation $3x - 4y = 8$ in slope–intercept form.

8. Graph the solution set of $6x - y > 6$.

9. Find the equation of the line that has slope $-\frac{5}{3}$ and passes through the point $(0, -4)$.

10. Find the equation of the line that has slope $\frac{1}{2}$ and passes through the point $(3, -2)$.

11. Find the equation of the line containing the points $(0, 1)$ and $(-1, 0)$.

12. Find the equation of the line that passes through the points $(4, -2)$ and $(-4, 8)$.

13. Is the line that contains the points $(3, 3)$ and $(-3, 7)$ parallel to the line that contains the points $(6, -5)$ and $(-6, 3)$?

14. Find the equation of the line that is parallel to the line $4x - y = 2$ and contains the point $(-3, 1)$.

15. Is the line that contains the points $(4, 1)$ and $(-2, 4)$ perpendicular to the line that contains the points $(-1, -6)$ and $(3, 2)$?

16. Find the equation of the line that is perpendicular to $y = 3x + 2$ and contains the point $(3, 4)$.

17. The table at the right shows the monthly profit for Sportlete.com for January, March, and May. Assume that profits continue in the same manner.
  a. Find a linear model for the data.
  b. Write a sentence that explains the meaning of the slope of this line in the context of this problem.
  c. Use the model to predict the profit in December.

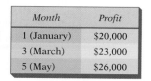

Month	Profit
1 (January)	$20,000
3 (March)	$23,000
5 (May)	$26,000

18. The increases in fuel prices for the first 6 months of a recent year are shown in the graph at the right. Find the slope of the line between the two points shown on the graph. Write a sentence that states the meaning of the slope in the context of this problem.

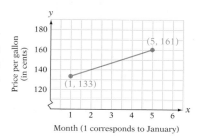

19. A molten piece of metal is allowed to cool in a controlled environment. The temperature, in degrees Fahrenheit, of the metal after it is removed from a smelter for various times *t*, in minutes, is shown at the right.

Time (in minutes)	Temperature (in degrees Fahrenheit)
15	2500
20	2400
30	2200

    a. Find a linear model for the temperature of the metal after *t* minutes.
    b. Write a sentence that explains the meaning of the slope of this line in the context of this problem.
    c. Assuming that temperature continues to decrease at the same rate, what will be the temperature in 2 hours?

20. The data in the following table show the curb weight, in pounds, and horsepower of the 10 best cars of 2001 as ranked by *Car and Driver* magazine (*Source: Car and Driver* web site, **www.10bestcars. com.**)
    a. Find a linear regression equation that gives horsepower in terms of weight.
    b. Use the regression equation to find the horsepower when the curb weight is 2700 pounds. Round to the nearest whole number.

Curb Weight and Horsepower of 10 Selected Cars

Car Model	Weight	Horsepower	Car Model	Weight	Horsepower
Audi A6	3750	300	Ford Focus	2550	130
Audi TT	2900	225	Honda Accord	3000	200
BMW 3 Series	3250	225	Honda S2000	2800	240
BMW 5 Series	3450	282	Mazda MX-5	2400	155
Chrysler PT Cruiser	3150	150	Porsche Boxster	2800	250

◀ CUMULATIVE REVIEW EXERCISES

1. In how many different ways can a panel of four on–off switches be set if no two adjacent switches can be off?

2. Given the operation $a @ b = a + ab$, evaluate $(x @ y) @ z$ for $x = 2$, $y = 3$, $z = 4$.

3. Let $E = \{0, 5, 10, 15\}$ and $F = \{-10, -5, 0, 5, 10\}$. Find $E \cup F$ and $E \cap F$.

4. Evaluate the variable expression $2(a - d)^2 + (bc)^2$ for $a = -2$, $b = -1$, $c = 3$, and $d = -4$.

5. The formula for the volume of a regular pyramid is $V = \frac{1}{3}s^2h$, where V is the volume, s is the length of a side of the square base, and h is the height. Find the volume of the regular pyramid shown at the right.

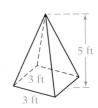
5 ft
3 ft
3 ft

6. Simplify: $-3[4x - (2x - 1)]$

7. Translate "the product of twenty and one-fifth of a number" into a variable expression. Then simplify the expression.

8. Without using a calculator, create an input/output table for $y = x^2 - 2$ for $x = -2, -1, 0, 1,$ and 2. Check your results using a graphing calculator. Graph the resulting ordered pairs.

9. Give the domain and range of the relation. Is the relation a function? $\{(-1, 0), (0, 1), (1, 2), (1, 0), (0, -1)\}$

10. Evaluate $p(s) = -2s^2 + 5s - 4$ when $s = -1$.

11. Find the x- and y-intercepts for the graph of the function $h(x) = x^2 - 2x - 3$.

12. Use a graphing calculator to find the input value for which the two functions $f(x) = 3x - 4$ and $g(x) = 6x + 5$ have the same value. Verify the results algebraically.

13. Solve: $3t - 8t = 0$

14. Solve: $8 - z = 6z - 3(4 - z)$

15. A merchant combines coffee that costs $6 per pound with coffee that costs $4 per pound. How many pounds of each should be used to make 60 pounds of a blend that costs $4.50 per pound?

16. Given that $l_1 \parallel l_2$, find the measures of angles a and b.

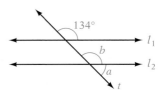

17. Solve $2 - 4(x + 1) \geq 11 + 3(2x - 6)$. Write the solution set in interval notation.

18. Solve: $2 + |3x + 1| = 7$

19. Graph $4x - 6y = 12$.

20. Find the equation of the line that contains the point (2, 5) and is perpendicular to the line $y = -\frac{2}{3}x + 6$.

5

Systems of Linear Equations and Inequalities

```
CALCULATE
1: value
2: zero
3: minimum
4: maximum
5: intersect
6: dy/dx
7: ∫f(x)dx
```

Press **2nd** CALC to access the
intersect option.

*Pharmacists not only dispense pre-packaged pills and medications, they are also trained healthcare professionals who can offer advice about minor ailments and medicine usage. They can suggest over-the-counter treatments for symptoms of common ailments such as colds or allergies. Pharmacists are also called upon to mix different ingredients in proportions that satisfy certain criteria, thereby creating specific treatments and remedies for their customers. This is illustrated in **Exercise 37 on page 322**, in which a system of equations is used to determine the amount of each ingredient in the mixture.*

Need help? For online student resources, visit this web site: Math.college.hmco.com

PREP TEST

1. Simplify: $10\left(\frac{3}{5}x + \frac{1}{2}y\right)$

2. Evaluate $3x + 2y - z$ for $x = -1$, $y = 4$, and $z = -2$.

3. Given $3x - 2z = 4$, find the value of x when $z = -2$.

4. Solve: $3x + 4(-2x - 5) = -5$

5. Solve: $0.45x + 0.06(-x + 4000) = 630$

6. Graph: $y = \frac{1}{2}x - 4$

7. Graph: $3x - 2y = 6$

8. Graph: $y > -\frac{3}{5}x + 1$

GO FIGURE

I have two more sisters than brothers. Each of my sisters has two more sisters than brothers. How many more sisters than brothers does my youngest brother have?

SECTION 5.1

- Solve Systems of Equations by Graphing
- Solve Systems of Equations by the Substitution Method

Solving Systems of Linear Equations by Graphing and by the Substitution Method

■ Solve Systems of Equations by Graphing

Suppose Maria and Michael drove from California to Connecticut and that the total driving time was 48 hours. We now pose the question, "How long did Maria drive?" From the given information, it is impossible to tell. Maria may have driven 30 hours and Michael 18 hours; she may have driven 1 hour and Michael 47 hours; or many other possibilities. If we let x be the number of hours Michael drove and y the number of hours Maria drove, then the equation $x + y = 48$ expresses the fact that the total driving time was 48 hours. The graph of this equation is shown at the right.

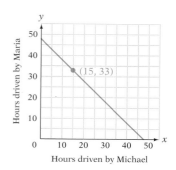

Any ordered pair on the graph represents possible driving times for Maria and Michael. For instance, the ordered pair $(15, 33)$ means that Michael drove 15 hours and Maria drove 33 hours.

Now suppose that we obtain the additional information that Maria drove twice as many hours as Michael. This can be expressed as the equation $y = 2x$. The graph of this equation is shown at the right, along with $x + y = 48$. The point of intersection $(16, 32)$ satisfies both conditions of the problem: The total number of hours driven were 48 [16 + 32 = 48] and Maria drove twice as many hours as Michael [32 = 2(16)].

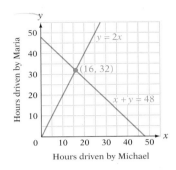

$$x + y = 48$$
$$y = 2x$$

A **system of equations** is two or more equations considered together. The system of equations for Maria and Michael is shown at the right. Because each equation of the system is a linear equation, this is a **system of linear equations in two variables.**

A **solution of a system of equations in two variables** is an ordered pair that is a solution of each equation of the system. For instance, as the following shows, $(16, 32)$ is a solution of the system of equations for the driving times of Michael and Maria.

$$\frac{x + y = 48}{16 + 32 \mid 48}$$
$$48 = 48$$

$$\frac{y = 2x}{32 \mid 2(16)}$$
$$32 = 32$$

- Replace x by 16 and y by 32. Because the ordered pair is a solution of each equation, it is a solution of the system of equations.

The solution of the system of equations is the ordered pair whose values of x and y simultaneously satisfy the conditions imposed by the equations.

A solution of a system of linear equations can be found by graphing the lines of the system on the same coordinate axes. **The coordinates of the point of intersection of the lines is the solution of the system of equations.**

EXAMPLE 1

Solve by graphing: $\begin{array}{l} 5x - 2y = 9 \\ 3x + 2y = -1 \end{array}$

Solve each equation for y.

$$5x - 2y = 9 \qquad\qquad 3x + 2y = -1$$
$$-2y = -5x + 9 \qquad\qquad 2y = -3x - 1$$
$$y = \frac{5}{2}x - \frac{9}{2} \qquad\qquad y = -\frac{3}{2}x - \frac{1}{2}$$

Enter the two equations into Y_1 and Y_2 and then graph them. If necessary, adjust the viewing window so that the point of intersection shows on the screen.

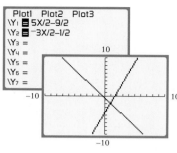

Use the INTERSECT feature of the calculator to find the point of intersection.

The solution is $(1, -2)$.

Algebraic Check:

Replace x by 1 and y by -2 in each equation of the system of equations.

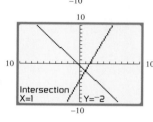

$$\begin{array}{c|c} 5x - 2y = 9 & \\ \hline 5(1) - 2(-2) & 9 \\ 5 + 4 & \\ 9 = 9 \quad \surd \end{array} \qquad \begin{array}{c|c} 3x + 2y = -1 & \\ \hline 3(1) + 2(-2) & -1 \\ 3 - 4 & \\ -1 = -1 \quad \surd \end{array}$$

The solution checks.

YOU TRY IT 1

Solve by graphing:
$$y = -\frac{2}{3}x + 1$$
$$2x + y = -3$$

Solution See page S18.

When the graphs of a system of equations intersect at only one point, the system of equations is called an **independent system of equations.** The system of equations in Example 1 is an independent system of equations.

? QUESTION Is the system of equations for Michael and Maria an independent system of the equations?

Recall that two lines with the same slope are parallel lines. If the y-intercepts are not equal, parallel lines do not intersect. Therefore, a system of equations that contains equations whose slopes are equal but whose y-intercepts are different has no solution. This is called an **inconsistent system of equations.**

➡ Show that the system of equations is inconsistent:
$$2x - 3y = 6$$
$$4x - 6y = -18$$

? ANSWER The graphs intersect at one point. Yes, the system of equations is independent.

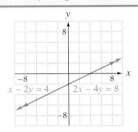

TAKE NOTE

Keep in mind the differences among independent, dependent, and inconsistent systems of equations. You should be able to express your understanding of these terms by using graphs.

ALGEBRAIC SOLUTION

Solve each equation for y.

$$2x - 3y = 6 \qquad\qquad 4x - 6y = -18$$
$$-3y = -2x + 6 \qquad -6y = -4x - 18$$
$$y = \frac{2}{3}x - 2 \qquad\qquad y = \frac{2}{3}x + 3$$

The lines have the same slope and different y-intercepts. Therefore, the lines are parallel and do not intersect. The system of equations is inconsistent and has no solution.

GRAPHICAL CHECK

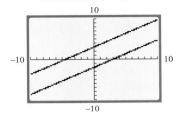

The lines are parallel. The system of equations has no solution.

Now consider the system of equations $\begin{array}{l} x - 2y = 4 \\ 2x - 4y = 8 \end{array}$. Solving each equation for y, we have

$$x - 2y = 4 \qquad\qquad 2x - 4y = 8$$
$$-2y = -x + 4 \qquad -4y = -2x + 8$$
$$y = \frac{1}{2}x - 2 \qquad\qquad y = \frac{1}{2}x - 2$$

In this case, both the slopes and the y-intercepts are equal. Therefore, the equations represent the same line. This is a **dependent system of equations.**

When the equations of this system of equations are graphed, one line will graph on top of the other line. The solutions of this system of equations are the ordered pairs that satisfy each equation. Because both equations represent the same line, the solutions are the ordered pairs (x, y), where $y = \frac{1}{2}x - 2$. This is sometimes written $(x, \frac{1}{2}x - 2)$, where y has been replaced by the expression it is equal to.

■ Solve Systems of Equations by the Substitution Method

A graphical solution of a system of equations is based on approximating the coordinates of a point of intersection. An algebraic method called the **substitution method** can be used to find a solution of a system of equations. To use the substitution method, we must write one of the equations of the system in terms of x or in terms of y.

EXAMPLE 2

Solve by the substitution method: $\begin{array}{ll} (1) & 3x + y = 5 \\ (2) & 4x + 5y = 3 \end{array}$

Solution Solve Equation (1) for y. The result is labeled Equation (3).

$$3x + y = 5$$
$$(3) \qquad y = -3x + 5$$

Substitute $-3x + 5$ for y in Equation (2) and solve for x.

$$4x + 5y = 3$$ • This is Equation (2).
$$4x + 5(-3x + 5) = 3$$ • From Equation (3), replace y by $-3x + 5$.
$$4x - 15x + 25 = 3$$ • Solve for x.
$$-11x + 25 = 3$$
$$-11x = -22$$
$$x = 2$$

Replace x in Equation (3) by 2 and solve for y.

$$y = -3x + 5$$ • This is Equation (3).
$$= -3(2) + 5$$ • Replace x by 2.
$$= -1$$

The solution is $(2, -1)$.

Graphical Check:

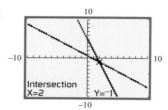

See Appendix A:
Intersect

YOU TRY IT 2

Solve by the substitution method:
(1) $\quad y = 2x + 3$
(2) $\quad 2x + 3y = 17$

Solution See page S18.

Here is an illustration of what happens when the substitution method is applied to an inconsistent system of equations.

➡ Solve: (1) $2x + 3y = 6$
(2) $\quad x = -\dfrac{3}{2}y + 4$

ALGEBRAIC SOLUTION

Replace x in Equation (1) by $-\dfrac{3}{2}y + 4$ from Equation (2) and solve for y.

$$2x + 3y = 6$$ • This is Equation (1).
$$2\left(-\dfrac{3}{2}y + 4\right) + 3y = 6$$ • Replace x by $-\dfrac{3}{2}y + 4$.
$$-3y + 8 + 3y = 6$$
$$8 = 6$$ • This is not a true equation.

The system of equations is inconsistent and has no solution.

GRAPHICAL CHECK

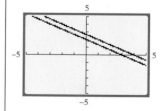

The lines are parallel. The system of equations has no solution.

TAKE NOTE

When a system of equations in two variables is inconsistent, the substitution method will always result in an equation that is not true. For the system of equations at the right, the false equation $8 = 6$ was reached.

Here is an example of a dependent system of equations.

EXAMPLE 3

Solve by the substitution method: (1) $3x + 4y = 12$
                                       (2) $y = -\dfrac{3}{4}x + 3$

Solution

Replace y in Equation (1) by $-\frac{3}{4}x + 3$ from Equation (2) and solve for x.

$$3x + 4y = 12$$

$$3x + 4\left(-\frac{3}{4}x + 3\right) = 12$$

$$3x - 3x + 12 = 12$$

$$12 = 12 \quad \bullet \text{ This is a true equation.}$$

This means that if x is any real number and $y = -\frac{3}{4}x + 3$, then the ordered pair (x, y) is a solution of the system of equations. The solutions are the ordered pairs $\left(x, -\frac{3}{4}x + 3\right)$, where we have replaced y by $-\frac{3}{4}x + 3$.

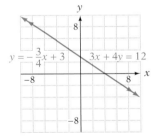

Before leaving this problem, it is important to understand that **there are infinitely many solutions of this system of equations.** Because the graph of one equation lies on top of the graph of the other equation, the two lines intersect at an infinite number of points. The graph is shown at the left. To find some ordered-pair solutions, replace x in $\left(x, -\frac{3}{4}x + 3\right)$ by any real number and then simplify. This is shown at the right for selected values of x. Some of the ordered-pair solutions are $(-8, 9)$, $(4, 0)$, $(0, 3)$, and $\left(\frac{4}{3}, 2\right)$.

$$\left(x, -\frac{3}{4}x + 3\right)$$

$(-8, 9) \quad \bullet \ x = -8$

$(4, 0) \quad \bullet \ x = 4$

$(0, 3) \quad \bullet \ x = 0$

$\left(\dfrac{4}{3}, 2\right) \quad \bullet \ x = \dfrac{4}{3}$

YOU TRY IT 3

Solve by the substitution method: (1) $3x + y = 2$
                                      (2) $9x + 3y = 6$

Solution   See page S18.

Application problems that contain two unknown quantities can be solved by using a system of equations.

EXAMPLE 4

A community theater sold 550 tickets for a benefit concert. Two types of tickets were sold. Orchestra tickets were $50 each, and loge tickets were $30 each. If income from the sales of tickets was $22,500, how many of each type were sold?

State the goal.   The goal is to determine the number of orchestra and loge tickets that were sold.

Devise a strategy.   Let x represent the number of orchestra tickets sold, and let y represent the number of loge tickets sold. A total of 550 tickets were sold. Therefore,

$$x + y = 550$$

The price of each orchestra ticket was $50. Therefore, $50x$ represents the income from the sale of orchestra seats. Similarly, the income from the sale of loge tickets was $30y$. Because the total income was $22,500, we have

$$50x + 30y = 22,500$$

Solve the system of equations formed from the two equations.

Solve the problem.
$$(1) \qquad x + y = 550$$
$$(2) \quad 50x + 30y = 22,500$$

Solve Equation (1) for y.

$$x + y = 550$$
$$(3) \qquad y = -x + 550$$

Substitute $-x + 550$ for y in Equation (2) and solve for x.

$$50x + 30y = 22,500 \qquad \bullet \text{ This is Equation (2).}$$
$$50x + 30(-x + 550) = 22,500 \qquad \bullet \text{ Replace } y \text{ by } -x + 550.$$
$$50x - 30x + 16,500 = 22,500$$
$$20x + 16,500 = 22,500$$
$$20x = 6000$$
$$x = 300$$

Substitute the value of x into Equation (3) and solve for y.

$$y = -x + 550$$
$$y = -300 + 550 = 250$$

There were 300 orchestra tickets and 250 loge tickets sold.

Check your work.   The sum of the orchestra tickets sold and the loge tickets sold is 550, which is the number sold by the theater. Also, the income from orchestra tickets is $300(50) = 15,000$, and the income from loge tickets is $250(30) = 7500$. The total income from the sale of the tickets is $15,000 + 7500 = 22,500$, which is the income received by the theater. The solution checks.

CALCULATOR NOTE

For a graphical check, choose a viewing window that contains the point of intersection.

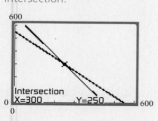

YOU TRY IT 4

In an isosceles triangle, the sum of the measures of the two equal angles is equal to the measure of the third angle. Find the measure of each angle. (Recall that in an isosceles triangle, two angles have the same measure, and that the sum of the measures of the interior angles of a triangle is 180°.)

Solution   See page S18.

Some problems that involve investing money can be solved using a system of equations. The annual simple interest that an investment earns is given by the equation $I = Pr$, where P is the principal, or the amount invested, r is the simple interest rate, and I is the simple interest earned.

For instance, if you invest $750 at an annual simple interest rate of 6%, then the interest earned after 1 year is calculated as follows:

$$I = Pr$$
$$I = 750(0.06) \qquad \bullet \text{ Replace } P \text{ by } 750 \text{ and } r \text{ by } 0.06.$$
$$I = 45$$

The amount of interest earned is $45.

EXAMPLE 5

Suppose an investor deposits a total of $5000 into two simple interest accounts. On one account, the money market fund, the annual simple interest rate is 3.5%. On the second account, a bond fund, the annual simple interest rate is 7.5%. If the investor wishes to earn $245 in interest from the two investments, how much money should be placed in each account?

Solution

State the goal.   The goal is to find the amounts of money that should be invested at 3.5% and at 7.5% so that the total interest earned is $245.

Devise a strategy.   Let x represent the amount invested at 3.5%, and let y represent the amount invested at 7.5%. The total amount invested is $5000. Therefore,

$$x + y = 5000$$

Using the equation $I = Pr$, we can determine the interest earned from each account.

Interest earned at 3.5%: $0.035x$

Interest earned at 7.5%: $0.075y$

The total interest earned is $245. Therefore,

$$0.035x + 0.075y = 245$$

Solve the system of equations formed by the two equations.

Solve the problem.   (1) $x + y = 5000$
                               (2) $0.035x + 0.075y = 245$

Solve Equation (1) for y.

$$x + y = 5000$$
(3) $$y = -x + 5000$$

Substitute into Equation (2) and solve for x.

$$0.035x + 0.075y = 245$$ • This is Equation (2).
$$0.035x + 0.075(-x + 5000) = 245$$ • Replace y by $-x + 5000$.
$$0.035 - 0.075x + 375 = 245$$
$$-0.04x + 375 = 245$$
$$-0.04x = -130$$
$$x = 3250$$

Substitute the value of x into Equation (3) and solve for y.

$$y = -x + 5000$$
$$y = -3250 + 5000 = 1750$$

The amount that should be invested at 3.5% is $3250. The amount that should be invested at 7.5% is $1750.

Check your work.   Note that $3250 + 1750 = 5000$. This confirms that the total amount invested is $5000. Also note that $0.035(3250) = 113.75$, that $0.075(1750) = 131.25$, and that $113.75 + 131.25$ is 245, the amount of interest to be earned. The solution checks.

YOU TRY IT 5

An investment club invests $13,600 in two simple interest accounts. On one account, the annual simple interest rate is 4.2%. On the other, the annual simple interest rate is 6%. How much should be invested in each account so that both accounts earn the same annual interest?

Solution   See page S18.

5.1 EXERCISES

Topics for Discussion

1. How is the solution of a system of linear equations in two variables represented?

2. For a system of two linear equations in two variables, explain, in graphical terms, each of the following: dependent system of equations, independent system of equations, and inconsistent system of equations.

3. Explain how to determine, when solving a system of equations by the substitution method, whether the system of equations is dependent or inconsistent.

4. Can a system of two linear equations in two variables have exactly two solutions? Explain your answer.

▪ Solve Systems of Equations by Graphing

Solve by graphing.

5. $y = 2x - 1$
   $y = -x + 5$

6. $y = x + 3$
   $y = -x + 5$

7. $x + y = 1$
   $3x - y = -5$

8. $x - y = -2$
   $x + 2y = 10$

9. $-3x + 2y = 11$
   $2x + 5y = 18$

10. $4x - 3y = 3$
    $2x + 5y = -31$

11. $2x - 5y = 10$
    $y = \dfrac{2}{5}x - 2$

12. $3x - 2y = 6$
    $4y - 6x = -12$

13. $x - 2y = 8$
    $y = \dfrac{1}{2}x - 2$

14. $2x + 3y = 6$
    $4x + 6y = 5$

15. $4x + 3y = -1$
    $2x - 2y = -11$

16. $3x + 2y = 15$
    $x - 4y = -16$

▪ Solve Systems of Equations by the Substitution Method

Solve by the substitution method.

17. $3x - 2y = 4$
    $x = 2$

18. $2x + 3y = 4$
    $y = -2$

19. $4x - 3y = 5$
    $y = 2x - 3$

20. $x = 2y + 4$
    $4x + 3y = -17$

21. $5x + 4y = -1$
    $y = 2 - 2x$

22. $7x - 3y = 3$
    $x = 2y + 2$

23. $2x + 2y = 7$
    $y = 4x + 1$

24. $3x + y = 5$
    $2x + 3y = 8$

25. $x + 3y = 5$
    $2x + 3y = 4$

26. $3x + 4y = 14$
    $2x + y = 1$

27. $3x + 5y = 0$
    $x - 4y = 0$

28. $5x - 3y = -2$
    $-x + 2y = -8$

29. $y = 3x + 2$
    $y = 2x + 3$

30. $6x - 2y = 4$
    $y = 3x - 2$

31. $y = -2x + 1$
    $6x + 3y = 3$

32. *Carpentry*   A carpenter purchased 50 feet of redwood and 90 feet of pine for a total cost of $31.20. A second purchase, at the same prices, included 200 feet of redwood and 100 feet of pine for a total cost of $78. Find the cost per foot of redwood and of pine.

33. *Energy Consumption* During one month, a homeowner used 400 units of electricity and 120 units of gas for a total cost of $147.20. The next month, 350 units of electricity and 200 units of gas were used for a total cost of $144. Find the cost per unit of gas.

34. *Coin Problem* The total value of the quarters and dimes in a coin bank is $6.90. If the quarters were dimes and the dimes were quarters, the total value of the coins would be $7.80. Find the number of quarters in the bank.

35. *Geometry* In a right triangle, the measure of one acute angle is twice the measure of the second acute angle. Find the measure of the two acute angles. (Recall that a right triangle has a right angle whose measure is 90° and that the sum of the measures of the angles of a triangle is 180°.)

36. *Manufacturing* A company manufactures both liquid crystal display (LCD) and cathode ray tube (CRT) color monitors. The cost of materials for a CRT monitor is $50, whereas the cost of materials for a LCD monitor is $150. The cost of labor to manufacture a CRT monitor is $80, whereas the cost of labor to manufacture a LCD monitor is $130. During a week when the company has budgeted $9600 for materials and $8760 for labor, how many LCD monitors does the company plan to manufacture?

37. *Pharmacology* A pharmacist has two vitamin-supplement powders. The first powder is 25% vitamin B1 and 15% vitamin B2. The second is 15% vitamin B1 and 20% vitamin B2. How many milligrams of each of the two powders should the pharmacist use to make a mixture that contains 117.5 milligrams of vitamin B1 and 120 milligrams of vitamin B2?

38. *Investments* An investment of $12,000 is deposited into two simple interest accounts. On one account the annual simple interest rate is 5.5%. On the other, the annual simple interest rate is 6.5%. How much should be invested in each account so that both accounts earn the same interest?

39. *Investments* A total of $10,000 is deposited in two accounts. On one account the simple interest rate is 9.5%. On the other the annual simple interest rate is 7.5%. How much is invested in each account if the total annual interest earned is $870?

Applying Concepts

For what values of k will the system of equations be inconsistent?

40. $2x - 2y = 5$
    $kx - 2y = 3$

41. $6x - 3y = 4$
    $3x - ky = 1$

42. $6y + 6 = x$
    $kx - 3y = 6$

43. $2y + 2 = x$
    $kx - 8y = 2$

Solve. (*Hint:* These equations are not linear equations. First rewrite the equations as linear equations by substituting x for $\frac{1}{a}$ and y for $\frac{1}{b}$. For example, rewrite $\frac{2}{a} + \frac{3}{b} = 4$ as $2x + 3y = 4$.)

44. $\dfrac{2}{a} + \dfrac{3}{b} = 4$
$\dfrac{4}{a} + \dfrac{1}{b} = 3$

45. $\dfrac{2}{a} + \dfrac{1}{b} = 1$
$\dfrac{8}{a} - \dfrac{2}{b} = 0$

46. $\dfrac{1}{a} + \dfrac{3}{b} = 2$
$\dfrac{4}{a} - \dfrac{1}{b} = 3$

47. $\dfrac{3}{a} + \dfrac{4}{b} = -1$
$\dfrac{1}{a} + \dfrac{6}{b} = 2$

48. Write three different systems of equations:
   a. A system that has $(-3, 5)$ as its only solution
   b. A system for which there is no solution
   c. A dependent system of equations

49. If x and y are real numbers and $|x + y - 17| + |x - y - 5| = 0$, find the numerical value of y.

50. Find the equation of the line that passes through the solution of the system of equations $\begin{array}{l} 2x - 3y = 13 \\ x + 4y = -10 \end{array}$ and has slope 2.

EXPLORATION

1. *Ill-Conditioned Systems of Equations*   Solving systems of equations algebraically as we did in this chapter is not practical for systems of equations that contain a large number of variables. In those cases, a computer solution is the only hope. Computer solutions are not without some problems, however.

Consider the following system of equations.

$$0.24567x + 0.49133y = 0.73700$$
$$0.84312x + 1.68623y = 2.52935$$

It is easy to verify that the solution of this system of equations is $(1, 1)$. However, change the constant 0.73700 to 0.73701 (add 0.00001) and the constant 2.52935 to 2.52936 (add 0.00001), and the solution is now $(3, 0)$. Thus a very small change in the constant terms produced a dramatic change in the solution. A system of equations of this sort is said to be an *ill-conditioned* system.

These types of systems are important because computers generally cannot store numbers beyond a certain number of significant digits. Your calculator, for example, probably allows you to enter no more than 10 significant digits. If an exact number cannot be entered, then an approximation to that number is necessary. When a computer is solving an equation or system of equations, the hope is that approximations of the coefficients it uses will give reasonable approximations to the solutions. For ill-conditioned systems of equations, this is not always true.

In the system of equations, small changes in the constant terms caused a large change in the solution. It is possible that small changes in the coefficients of the variables will also cause large changes in the solution.

In the two systems of equations that follow, examine the effects on the solutions of approximating the fractional coefficients. Try approximating each fraction to the nearest hundredth, to the nearest thousandth, to the nearest ten-thousandth, and then to the limits of your calculator. The exact solution of the first system of equations is $(27, -192, 210)$. The exact solution of the second system of equations is $(-64, 900, -2520, 1820)$.

System 1

$$x + \frac{1}{2}y + \frac{1}{3}z = 1$$

$$\frac{1}{2}x + \frac{1}{3}y + \frac{1}{4}z = 2$$

$$\frac{1}{3}x + \frac{1}{4}y + \frac{1}{5}z = 3$$

System 2

$$x + \frac{1}{2}y + \frac{1}{3}z + \frac{1}{4}w = 1$$

$$\frac{1}{2}x + \frac{1}{3}y + \frac{1}{4}z + \frac{1}{5}w = 2$$

$$\frac{1}{3}x + \frac{1}{4}y + \frac{1}{5}z + \frac{1}{6}w = 3$$

$$\frac{1}{4}x + \frac{1}{5}y + \frac{1}{6}z + \frac{1}{7}w = 4$$

Note how the solutions change as the approximations change and thus how important it is to know whether a system of equations is ill-conditioned. For systems that are not ill-conditioned, approximations of the coefficients yield reasonable approximations of the solution. For ill-conditioned systems of equations, that is not always true.

Solving Systems of Linear Equations by the Addition Method

■ Solve Systems of Two Linear Equations in Two Variables by the Addition Method

The addition method is an alternative method for solving a system of equations. This method is based on the Addition Property of Equations and is the basis for solving systems of equations with more than two variables.

Note, for the system of equations at the right, the effect of adding Equation (2) to Equation (1). Because $-3y$ and $3y$ are additive inverses, adding the equations results in an equation with only one variable.

$$(1) \quad 5x - 3y = 14$$
$$(2) \quad \underline{2x + 3y = -7}$$
$$7x + 0y = 7$$
$$7x = 7$$
$$x = 1$$

The second component is found by substituting the value of x into Equation (1) or Equation (2) and then solving for y. Equation (1) is used here.

$$(1) \quad 5x - 3y = 14$$
$$5(1) - 3y = 14$$
$$5 - 3y = 14$$
$$-3y = 9$$
$$y = -3$$

The solution is $(1, -3)$.

Sometimes adding the two equations does not eliminate one of the variables. In this case, **use the Multiplication Property of Equations to rewrite one or both of the equations so that when the equations are added, one of the variables is eliminated.** To do this, first choose which variable to eliminate. The coefficients of that variable must be additive inverses. Multiply each equation by a constant that will produce coefficients that are additive inverses. This is illustrated in Example 1.

EXAMPLE 1

Solve by the addition method:
$$(1) \quad 3x + 4y = 2$$
$$(2) \quad 2x + 5y = -1$$

Solution   We can choose to eliminate either x or y. We will eliminate x.

$$2 \diagdown (3x + 4y) = 2(2)$$
$$-3 \diagup (2x + 5y) = -3(-1)$$

- Multiply Equation (1) by 2 and multiply Equation (2) by -3.
- The negative sign is chosen so that the resulting coefficients are additive inverses.

$$6x + 8y = 4$$
$$\underline{-6x - 15y = 3}$$
$$-7y = 7$$
$$y = -1$$

- 2 times Equation (1).
- -3 times Equation (2).
- Add the equations.
- Solve for y.

Substitute the value of *y* into one of the equations and solve for *x*. Equation (1) is used here.

$$3x + 4y = 2$$ • This is Equation (1).
$$3x + 4(-1) = 2$$ • Replace *y* by -1.
$$3x - 4 = 2$$ • Solve for *x*.
$$3x = 6$$
$$x = 2$$

The solution is $(2, -1)$.

A graphical check (shown at the right) was created by solving each equation of the system for *y*, producing its graph, and then finding the point of intersection. For the equations of this system, we have $y = -\frac{3}{4}x + \frac{1}{2}$ and $y = -\frac{2}{5}x - \frac{1}{5}$.

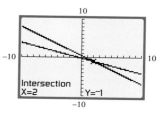

Intersection
X=2   Y=-1

YOU TRY IT 1

Solve by the addition method: (1) $2x - 5y = 4$
(2) $3x - 7y = 15$

Solution   See page S19.

Example 2 shows the addition method applied to an inconsistent system of equations.

EXAMPLE 2

Solve by the addition method: (1) $4x - 2y = 5$
(2) $6x - 3y = -3$

Solution   We will choose to eliminate *x*. Multiply Equation (1) by 3 and Equation (2) by -2.

$$3(4x - 2y) = 3(5)$$ • 3 times Equation (1).
$$-2(6x - 3y) = -2(-3)$$ • -2 times Equation (2).

$$12x - 6y = 15$$
$$\underline{-12x + 6y = 6}$$
$$0 = 21$$ • Add the equations. This is not a true equation.

The system of equations is inconsistent. The system does not have a solution.

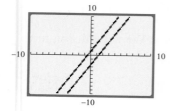

A graphical check is shown at the left. From the graphs, it appears that the lines are parallel and therefore do not intersect. The only way to be sure, however, is to solve each equation in the system of equations for y and verify that the slopes are the same but the y-intercepts are different.

YOU TRY IT 2

Solve by the addition method: (1) $x + 2y = 6$
(2) $3x + 6y = 6$

Solution See page S19.

In Example 3, the addition method is used to solve a dependent system of equations.

EXAMPLE 3

Solve by the addition method: (1) $6x + 2y = 12$
(2) $3x + y = 6$

Solution We will choose to eliminate x. Multiply Equation (2) by -2.

$$6x + 2y = 12 \qquad \bullet \text{ This is Equation (1).}$$
$$-2(3x + y) = -2(6) \qquad \bullet \; -2 \text{ times Equation (2).}$$

$$6x + 2y = 12$$
$$-6x - 2y = -12$$

$$ 0 = 0 \qquad \bullet \text{ Add the equations. This is a true equation.}$$

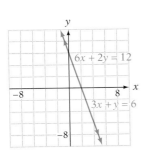

The system of equations is dependent. To find the ordered-pair solutions, solve one of the equations for y. Equation (2) is used here.

$$3x + y = 6$$
$$y = -3x + 6$$

The solutions are the ordered pairs $(x, -3x + 6)$.

A graphical check is shown at the left. Note that the graph of one line is on top of that of the other line.

YOU TRY IT 3

Solve by the addition method: (1) $2x + 5y = 10$
(2) $8x + 20y = 40$

Solution See page S19.

■ Solve Systems of Three Linear Equations in Three Variables by the Addition Method

An equation of the form $Ax + By + Cz = D$, where A, B, and C are coefficients and D is a constant, is a **linear equation in three variables.** Examples of these equations are shown at the right.

$$3x - 2y + z = 4$$
$$2x + y - 4z = 1$$

Graphing an equation in three variables requires a third coordinate axis perpendicular to the *xy*-plane. The third axis is commonly called the *z*-axis. The result is a three-dimensional coordinate system called the ***xyz*-coordinate system.** To help visualize a three-dimensional coordinate system, think of a corner of a room: The floor is the *xy*-plane, one wall is the *yz*-plane, and the other wall is the *xz*-plane. A three-dimensional coordinate system is shown at the right.

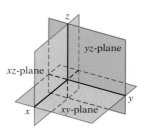

The graph of a point in an *xyz*-coordinate system is an **ordered triple** (x, y, z). Graphing an ordered triple requires three moves, the first along the *x*-axis, the second parallel to the *y*-axis, and the third parallel to the *z*-axis. The graphs of the points $(-4, 2, 3)$ and $(3, 4 - 2)$ are shown at the right.

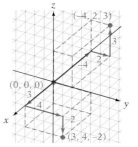

The graph of a linear equation in three variables is a plane. That is, if all the solutions of a linear equation in three variables were plotted in an *xyz*-coordinate system, the graph would look like a large piece of paper with infinite extent. The graph of $x + y + z = 3$ is shown at the right.

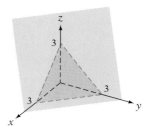

There are different ways in which three planes can be oriented in an *xyz*-coordinate system. The systems of equations represented by the planes below are inconsistent. There is no one point that lies on all three planes.

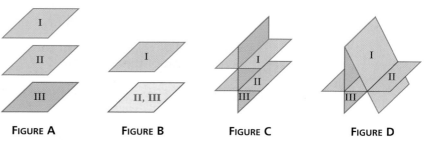

| FIGURE A | FIGURE B | FIGURE C | FIGURE D |

Graphs of Inconsistent Systems of Equations

For a system of three equations in three variables to have a solution, the graphs of the planes must intersect at a single point, they must intersect along a common line, or all equations must have a graph that is the same plane. Let's look at each of these situations.

The three planes shown in Figure E intersect at a point *P*. A system of equations represented by planes that intersect at a point is **independent.** The planes shown in Figures F and G intersect along a common line. The system of equations represented by the planes in Figure H has a graph that is the same plane. The systems of equations represented by Figures F, G, and H are **dependent.**

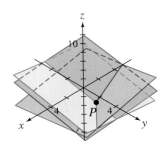

FIGURE E *An Independent System of Equations*

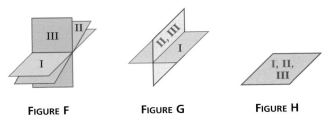

| FIGURE F | FIGURE G | FIGURE H |

Dependent Systems of Equations

CALCULATOR NOTE

Most graphing calculators cannot solve a system of three equations in three unknowns graphically and use an algebraic process instead. The method we show below forms a basis for the algebraic methods of a calculator.

Just as a solution of an equation in two variables is an ordered pair (x, y), a **solution of an equation in three variables** is an ordered triple (x, y, z). For example, $(2, -1, 3)$ is a solution of the equation $2x - 3y + 5z = 22$. The ordered triple $(1, 3, 2)$ is not a solution.

A **system of linear equations in three variables** is shown at the right. A **solution of a system of equations in three variables** is an ordered triple that is a solution of each equation of the system.

$$2x - y + z = 7$$
$$x + 2y + z = 12$$
$$x - 2y - z = -8$$

A system of linear equations in three variables can be solved by using the addition method. First, eliminate one variable from any two of the given equations. Then eliminate the same variable from any other two equations. The result will be a system of two equations in two variables. Solve this system by the addition method.

➡ Solve:
$$(1) \quad 2x - 3y + 2z = -7$$
$$(2) \quad x + 4y - z = 10$$
$$(3) \quad 3x + 2y + z = 4$$

Eliminate z from Equations (1) and (2) by multiplying Equation (2) by 2 and then adding to Equation (1).

$$2x - 3y + 2z = -7 \qquad \bullet \text{ This is Equation (1).}$$
$$\underline{2x + 8y - 2z = 20} \qquad \bullet \text{ 2 times Equation (2).}$$
$$(4) \qquad\qquad 4x + 5y = 13 \qquad \bullet \text{ Add the equations.}$$

Eliminate z from Equations (2) and (3) by adding the two equations.

$$x + 4y - z = 10 \qquad \bullet \text{ This is Equation (2).}$$
$$\underline{3x + 2y + z = 4} \qquad \bullet \text{ This is Equation (3).}$$
$$(5) \qquad\qquad 4x + 6y = 14 \qquad \bullet \text{ Add the equations.}$$

Using Equations (4) and (5), solve the system of two equations in two variables.

$$(4) \qquad 4x + 5y = 13$$

$$(5) \qquad 4x + 6y = 14$$

Eliminate x by multiplying Equation (5) by -1 and then add to Equation (4).

$$4x + 5y = 13$$ • This is Equation (4).
$$\underline{-4x - 6y = -14}$$ • -1 times Equation (5).
$$-y = -1$$ • Add the equations.
$$y = 1$$

Substitute this value of y into Equation (4) or Equation (5) and solve for x. Equation (4) is used here.

$$4x + 5y = 13$$ • This is Equation (4).
$$4x + 5(1) = 13$$ • $y = 1$.
$$4x + 5 = 13$$ • Solve for x.
$$4x = 8$$
$$x = 2$$

Substitute the value of x and the value of y into one of the equations in the original system of equations and solve for z. Equation (1) is used here.

$$2x - 3y + 2z = -7$$ • This is Equation (1).
$$2(2) - 3(1) + 2z = -7$$ • $x = 2, y = 1$.
$$1 + 2z = -7$$ • Solve for z.
$$2z = -8$$
$$z = -4$$

The solution is $(2, 1, -4)$.

Just as a system of two equations in two variables may not have a solution, it is possible for a system of three equations in three variables not to have a solution. Here is an example:

$$\text{Solve: } \begin{array}{ll} (1) & 2x - 3y - z = -1 \\ (2) & x + 4y + 3z = 2 \\ (3) & 4x - 6y - 2z = 5 \end{array}$$

Eliminate x from Equations (1) and (3).

$$-4x + 6y + 2z = 2$$ • -2 times Equation (1).
$$\underline{4x - 6y - 2z = 5}$$ • This is Equation (3).
$$0 = 7$$ • Add the equations.

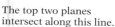

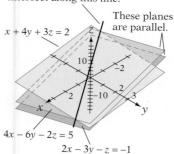

The top two planes intersect along this line.

These planes are parallel.

$x + 4y + 3z = 2$

$4x - 6y - 2z = 5$

$2x - 3y - z = -1$

The equation $0 = 7$ is not a true equation. The system of equations is inconsistent and therefore has no solution. A graph of the system of equations is shown at the left. Note that two of the planes are parallel and therefore never intersect.

EXAMPLE 4

$$\text{Solve by the addition method: } \begin{array}{ll} (1) & 2x - y + z = 8 \\ (2) & x + 2y + z = -3 \\ (3) & x - 2y - z = 7 \end{array}$$

Solution   You can choose any variable to eliminate first. We will choose x. We first eliminate x from Equation (1) and Equation (2) by multiplying Equation (2) by -2 and then adding to Equation (1).

$$2x - y + z = 8$$

- This is Equation (1).

$$-2(x + 2y + z) = -2(-3)$$

- -2 times Equation (2).

$$
\begin{array}{r}
2x - y + z = 8 \\
-2x - 4y - 2z = 6 \\
\hline
-5y - z = 14 \quad (4)
\end{array}
$$

- Add the equations. This is Equation (4).

Eliminate x from Equation (2) and Equation (3) by multiplying Equation (3) by -1 and then adding it to Equation (2).

$$x + 2y + z = -3$$

- This is Equation (2).

$$-1(x - 2y - z) = -1(7)$$

- -1 times Equation (3).

$$
\begin{array}{r}
x + 2y + z = -3 \\
-x + 2y + z = -7 \\
\hline
4y + 2z = -10 \quad (5)
\end{array}
$$

- Add the equations. This is Equation (5).

Now form a system of two equations in two variables using Equation (4) and Equation (5). We will solve this system of equations by multiplying Equation (4) by 2 and then adding to Equation (5).

$$-5y - z = 14$$

- This is Equation (4).

$$4y + 2z = -10$$

- This is Equation (5).

$$2(-5y - z) = 2(14)$$

- 2 times Equation (4).

$$4y + 2z = -10$$

$$
\begin{array}{r}
-10y - 2z = 28 \\
4y + 2z = -10 \\
\hline
-6y = 18
\end{array}
$$

- Add the equations. Then solve for y.

$$y = -3$$

Substitute -3 for y in Equation (4) or (5) and solve for z. We will use Equation (4).

$$-5y - z = 14$$

- This is Equation (4).

$$-5(-3) - z = 14$$

- Replace y by -3.

$$15 - z = 14$$

$$-z = -1$$

$$z = 1$$

Now replace y by -3 and z by 1 in one of the original equations of the system. Equation (1) is used here.

$$2x - y + z = 8$$ • This is Equation (1).
$$2x - (-3) + 1 = 8$$ • Replace y by -3 and replace z by 1.
$$2x + 4 = 8$$
$$2x = 4$$
$$x = 2$$

The solution of the system of equations is $(2, -3, 1)$.

YOU TRY IT 4

Solve by the addition method:
(1) $3x - y - 2z = 11$
(2) $x - 2y + 3z = 12$
(3) $x + y - 2z = 5$

Solution   See page S19.

▪ Rate-of-Wind and Rate-of-Current Problems

If a motorboat is on a river that is flowing at a rate of 4 mph, then the boat will float down the river at a speed of 4 mph even though the motor is not on. Now suppose the motor is turned on and the power adjusted so that the boat would travel 10 mph without the aid of the current. Then if the boat is moving with the current, its effective speed is the speed of the boat using power plus of the speed of the current: 10 mph + 4 mph = 14 mph. However, if the boat is moving in the direction opposite to the current, the current slows the boat down, and the effective speed of the boat is the speed of the boat using power minus the speed of the current: 10 mph − 4 mph = 6 mph.

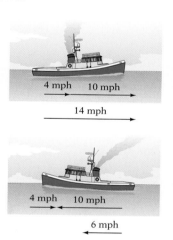

 QUESTION   The speed of a plane is 500 mph. There is a headwind of 50 mph. What is the speed of the plane relative to an observer on the ground?

EXAMPLE 5

A motorboat traveling with the current can travel 24 miles in 2 hours. Against the current, it takes 3 hours to travel the same distance. Find the rate of the boat in calm water and the rate of the current.

State the goal.   The goal is to find the rate of the boat in calm water and the rate of the current.

 ANSWER   500 mph − 50 mph = 450 mph

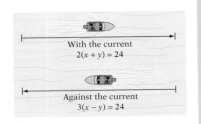

With the current
$2(x + y) = 24$

Against the current
$3(x - y) = 24$

Devise a strategy.   Let x represent the rate of the boat in calm water, and let y represent the rate of the current. Traveling with the current, the speed of the boat in calm water is increased by the rate of the current. Traveling against the current, the speed of the boat in calm water is decreased by the rate of the current. This can be expressed as follows:

Rate of boat with the current: $x + y$

Rate of boat against the current: $x - y$

Now use the equation $rt = d$ to express the distance traveled by the boat with the current and the distance traveled against the current in terms of the rate of the boat and the time traveled

Distance traveled with the current: $2(x + y) = 24$

Distance traveled against the current: $3(x - y) = 24$

These two equations form a system of equations.

Solve the problem. $2(x + y) = 24 \Rightarrow x + y = 12$ • Divide each side by 2.

$3(x - y) = 24 \Rightarrow \underline{x - y = 8}$ • Divide each side by 3.

$2x = 20$ • Add the equations.

$x = 10$ • Solve for x.

Substitute the value of x into one of the equations and solve for y. We will use $x + y = 12$.

$x + y = 12$
$10 + y = 12$
$y = 2$

The rate of the boat in calm water is 10 mph; the rate of the current is 2 mph.

Check your work.   With the current the boat can travel 10 mph + 2 mph = 12 mph, or 24 miles in 2 hours. Against the current the boat can travel 10 mph − 2 mph = 8 mph, or 24 miles in 3 hours. The answer is reasonable.

YOU TRY IT 5

Flying with the wind, a plane flew 1000 miles in 5 hours. Flying against the wind, the plane could fly only 500 miles in 5 hours. Find the rate of the plane in calm air and the rate of the wind.

Solution   See page S20.

■ Percent Mixture Problems

The quantity of a substance in a solution can be given as a percent of the total solution. For instance, in an 8% salt–water solution, 8% of the total solution is salt. The remaining 92% of the solution is water.

The equation $Q = Ar$ relates the quantity, Q, of a substance in a solution to the amount, A, of solution and the percent concentration, r, of the solution. For example, suppose 40 ounces of a salt–water solution is 8% salt. Then the quantity of salt in the solution is

$$Q = Ar$$
$$= 40(0.08) \qquad \bullet \text{ The total amount, } A, \text{ of solution is 40 ounces.}$$
$$= 3.2 \qquad\qquad \text{The percent concentration, } r, \text{ is } 8\% = 0.08.$$

There are 3.2 ounces of salt in the solution. Because the total amount of solution is 40 ounces, there are $40 - 3.2 = 36.8$ ounces of water in the solution.

Now suppose two different solutions are mixed together. For instance, suppose a 200-gram solution that is 15% sugar is mixed with 300 grams of a solution that is 25% sugar. Then the total amount of solution is the sum of the amounts in each solution.

$$200 + 300 = 500 \qquad \bullet \text{ Grams of solution after mixing}$$

The quantity of sugar in the new solution is the sum of the quantities in the two original solutions. To find the quantity in the new solution, we use the equation $Q = Ar$.

$$200(0.15) + 300(0.25) = 30 + 75 = 105 \qquad \bullet \text{ Grams of sugar after mixing}$$

Using the number of grams of solution after mixing the two solutions, the number of grams of sugar in the mixture, and the equation $Q = Ar$, we can find the percent concentration of sugar in the new solution.

$$Q = Ar$$
$$105 = 500r$$
$$\frac{105}{500} = \frac{500r}{500}$$
$$0.21 = r$$

The new solution is 21% sugar.

Problems involving mixtures expressed as percent are solved using the ideas discussed above.

EXAMPLE 6

A chemist mixes an 11% acid solution with a 4% acid solution. How many milliliters of each solution should the chemist use to make a 700-milliliter solution that is 6% acid?

State the goal. The goal is to find how many milliliters of each of the solutions must be mixed together to produce a 700-milliliter, 6% acid solution.

Devise a strategy. Let x represent the number of milliliters of the 11% acid solution, and let y represent the number of milliliters of the 4% solution. After mixing, the new solution is 700 milliliters. Therefore,

$$x + y = 700 \qquad \bullet \text{ This is Equation (1).}$$

The amount of acid in each solution can be found by using $Q = Ar$.

Quantity of acid in a solution: $Ar = rA$

Quantity of acid in the 11% solution: $0.11x$

Quantity of acid in the 4% solution: $0.04y$

Quantity of acid in the 6% solution (the mixture): $0.06(700)$

Write an equation using the fact that the sum of the quantity of acid in the 11% solution and the quantity of acid in the 4% solution equals the quantity of acid in the 6% solution.

$$0.11x + 0.04y = 0.06(700)$$
$$0.11x + 0.04y = 42 \qquad \bullet \text{ This is Equation (2).}$$

Equations (1) and (2) form a system of equations.

Solve the problem.
$$(1) \qquad x + y = 700$$
$$(2) \quad 0.11x + 0.04y = 42$$

Eliminate x by multiplying Equation (1) by -0.11 and then adding it to Equation (2).

$$
\begin{array}{ll}
-0.11x - 0.11y = -77 & \bullet \ -0.11 \text{ times Equation (1).} \\
\underline{0.11x + 0.04y = 42} & \bullet \text{ This is Equation (2).} \\
\qquad\quad -0.07y = -35 & \bullet \text{ Add the equations.} \\
\qquad\qquad\quad\; y = 500 & \bullet \text{ Solve for } y.
\end{array}
$$

Substitute the value of y into Equation (1) and solve for x.

$$x + y = 700$$
$$x + 500 = 700$$
$$x = 200$$

Because x represents the number of milliliters of the 11% solution, the chemist must use 200 milliliters of the 11% solution. Because y represents the number of milliliters of the 4% solution, the chemist must use 500 milliliters of the 4% solution.

Check your work.   One way to check the solution is to calculate the percent concentration of the solution after mixing to be sure it is 6%.

Quantity of Acid in the 11% Solution	**Quantity of Acid in the 4% Solution**
$Q_1 = 0.11(200) = 22$	$Q_2 = 0.04(500) = 20$

The quantity of acid in the mixture is $22 + 20 = 42$ milliliters. The amount of mixture is 700 milliliters. To find the percent concentration of acid, solve $Q = Ar$ for r given that $Q = 42$ and $A = 700$.

$$Q = Ar$$
$$42 = 700r$$
$$\frac{42}{700} = r$$
$$0.06 = r$$

The percent concentration is 6%. The solution checks.

> ### *YOU TRY IT 6*
>
> A hospital staff mixed a 55% disinfectant solution with a 15% disinfectant solution. How many liters of each were used to make 50 liters of a 25% disinfectant solution?
>
> **Solution**   See page S20.

5.2 EXERCISES

Topics for Discussion

1. When you solve a system of two linear equations in two variables by the addition method, how can you tell whether the system of equations is inconsistent?

2. When you solve a system of two linear equations in two variables by the addition method, how can you tell whether the system of equations is dependent?

3. What is a three-dimensional coordinate system?

4. Describe the graph of a linear equation in three variables.

5. Describe how the planes of an independent system of three linear equations in three variables intersect.

6. Give an example of how the graphs of three planes would intersect for an inconsistent system of equations.

7. If a 10% apple juice solution is mixed with a 20% apple juice solution, is the resulting mixture less than 10% apple juice, between 10% and 20% apple juice, or greater than 20% apple juice?

8. If a 50% gold alloy is mixed with pure gold, is the resulting alloy more than 50% gold or less than 50% gold?

9. Suppose you have a powerboat with the throttle set to move the boat at 8 miles per hour in calm water, and the rate of the current in the river the boat is on is 4 miles per hour. What is the speed of the boat when it is traveling with the current?

10. If a cargo ship can travel 25 miles per hour in calm water, what speed can the cargo ship travel when moving against a 5-mile-per-hour river current?

■ Solve Systems of Equations by the Addition Method

Solve by the addition method.

11. $x - y = 5$
$x + y = 7$

12. $3x + y = 4$
$x + y = 2$

13. $3x + y = 7$
$x + 2y = 4$

14. $3x - y = 4$
$6x - 2y = 8$

15. $2x + 5y = 9$
$4x - 7y = -16$

16. $4x - 6y = 5$
$2x - 3y = 7$

17. $3x - 5y = 7$
$x - 2y = 3$

18. $3x + 2y = 16$
$2x - 3y = -11$

19. $4x + 4y = 5$
$2x - 8y = -5$

20. $5x + 4y = 0$
$3x + 7y = 0$

21. $3x - 6y = 6$
$9x - 3y = 8$

22. $5x + 2y = 2x + 1$
$2x - 3y = 3x + 2$

23. $\dfrac{2}{3}x - \dfrac{1}{2}y = 3$
$\dfrac{1}{3}x - \dfrac{1}{4}y = \dfrac{3}{2}$

24. $\dfrac{2}{5}x - \dfrac{1}{3}y = 1$
$\dfrac{3}{5}x + \dfrac{2}{3}y = 5$

25. $\dfrac{3}{4}x + \dfrac{2}{5}y = -\dfrac{3}{20}$
$\dfrac{3}{2}x - \dfrac{1}{4}y = \dfrac{3}{4}$

26. $4x - 5y = 3y + 4$
$2x + 3y = 2x + 1$

27. $2x + 5y = 5x + 1$
$3x - 2y = 3y + 3$

28. $x - 3y = 2x - 5y$
$4x - y = x + y$

29. $x + 2y - z = 1$
$2x - y + z = 6$
$x + 3y - z = 2$

30. $x + 3y + z = 6$
$3x + y - z = -2$
$2x + 2y - z = 1$

31. $2x - y + 2z = 7$
$x + y + z = 2$
$3x - y + z = 6$

32. $x - 2y + z = 6$
$x + 3y + z = 16$
$3x - y - z = 12$

33. $3x - 2y + 3z = -4$
$2x + y - 3z = 2$
$3x + 4y + 5z = 8$

34. $3x + y = 5$
$3y - z = 2$
$x + z = 5$

35. $2x + 4y - 2z = 3$
$x + 3y + 4z = 1$
$x + 2y - z = 4$

36. $x - 3y + 2z = 1$
$x - 2y + 3z = 5$
$2x - 6y + 4z = 3$

37. $3x + 2y - 3z = 8$
$2x + 3y + 2z = 10$
$4x + 3y + 5z = 28$

38. $2x + 2y + 3z = 13$
$-3x + 4y - z = 5$
$5x - 3y + z = 2$

39. $2x - 3y + 7z = 0$
$4x - 5y + 2z = -11$
$x - 2y + 3z = -1$

40. $3x - y + 2z = 2$
$4x + 2y - 7z = 0$
$2x + 3y - 5z = 7$

41. $2x + y - z = 5$
$x + 3y + z = 14$
$3x - y + 2z = 1$

42. $3x - 3y + 4z = 6$
$4x - 5y + 2z = 10$
$x - 2y + 3z = 4$

43. $5x + 3y - z = 5$
$3x - 2y + 4z = 13$
$4x + 3y + 5z = 22$

44. *Rate-of-Wind Problem*   Flying with the wind, a small plane flew 320 miles in 2 hours. Against the wind, the plane could fly only 280 miles in the same amount of time. Find the rate of the plane in calm air and the rate of the wind.

45. *Rate-of-Wind Problem*   A turbo-prop plane flying with the wind flew 600 miles between two cities in 2 hours. The return trip against the wind took 3 hours. Find the rate of the plane in calm air and the rate of the wind.

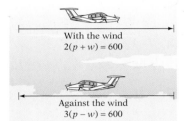

With the wind
$2(p + w) = 600$

Against the wind
$3(p - w) = 600$

46. *Rate-of-Current Problem*   A cabin cruiser traveling with the current went 48 miles in 3 hours. Against the current, it took 4 hours to travel the same distance. Find the rate of the cabin cruiser in calm water and the rate of the current.

47. *Rate-of-Current Problem*   A motorboat traveling with the current went 88 kilometers in 4 hours. Against the current, the boat could go only 64 kilometers in the same amount of time. Find the rate of the boat in calm water and the rate of the current.

48. *Rate-of-Wind Problem*   A plane flying with a tailwind flew 360 miles in 3 hours. Against the wind, the plane required 4 hours to fly the same distance. Find the rate of the plane in calm air and the rate of the wind.

49. *Rate-of-Current Problem*   A motorboat traveling with the current went 54 miles in 3 hours. Against the current, it took 3.6 hours to travel the same distance. Find the rate of the boat in calm water and the rate of the current.

50. *Percent Mixture Problem*   A goldsmith mixed 10 grams of a 50% gold alloy with 40 grams of a 15% gold alloy. What is the percent concentration of the resulting alloy?

51. *Percent Mixture Problem*   A silversmith mixed 25 grams of a 70% silver alloy with 50 grams of a 15% silver alloy. What is the percent concentration of the resulting alloy?

52. *Percent Mixture Problem*   A butcher has some hamburger that is 20% fat and some hamburger that is 12% fat. How many pounds of each should be mixed to make 80 pounds of hamburger that is 17% fat?

53. *Percent Mixture Problem*   A chemist mixed a 3% hydrogen peroxide solution with a 12% hydrogen peroxide solution. The resulting 50-milliliter solution was 8.4% hydrogen peroxide. How many milliliters of each solution was used?

54. *Percent Mixture Problem*   A metallurgist mixed a 24% copper alloy with a 36% copper alloy to produce 300 pounds of an alloy that is 31% copper. Find the number of pounds of each alloy that was used.

55. *Percent Mixture Problem*   A goldsmith mixed a 25% gold alloy with pure gold to produce a 120-gram alloy that was 75% gold. Find the amount of each substance used by the goldsmith.

56. *Percent Mixture Problem*   A pharmacist wants to make a 200-milliliter salt solution that is 2% salt by mixing a 5% salt solution with pure water. How many milliliters of the two solutions are required?

57. *Manufacturing*   On Monday, a computer manufacturing company sent out three shipments. The first order, which contained a bill for $114,000, was for 4 Model II, 6 Model VI and 10 Model IX computers. The second shipment, which contained a bill for $72,000, was for 8 Model II, 3 Model VI and 5 Model IX computers. The third shipment, which contained a bill for $81,000, was for 2 Model II, 9 Model VI, and 5 Model IX computers. What does the manufacturer charge for a Model VI computer?

58. *Not-for-Profit Organizations*   A relief organization supplies blankets, cots, and lanterns to victims of fires, floods, and other natural disasters. One week the organization purchased 15 blankets, 5 cots, and 10 lanterns for a total cost of $1250. The next week, at the same prices, the organization purchased 20 blankets, 10 cots, and 15 lanterns for a total cost of $2000. The next week, at the same prices, the organization purchased 10 blankets, 15 cots, and 5 lanterns for a total cost of $1625. Find the cost of one blanket, the cost of one cot, and the cost of one lantern.

59. *Investments*   An investor has a total of $18,000 deposited in three different accounts, which earn annual interest of 9%, 7%, and 5%. The amount deposited in the 9% account is twice the amount in the 5% account. If the three accounts earn total annual interest of $1340, how much money is deposited in each account?

60. *Investments*   An investor has a total of $15,000 deposited in three different accounts, which earn annual interest of 9%, 6%, and 4%. The amount deposited in the 6% account is $2000 more than the amount in the 4% account. If the three accounts earn total annual interest of $980, how much money is deposited in each account?

61. *Investments*   A financial planner invested $33,000 of a client's money, part at 9%, part at 12%, and the remainder at 8%. The total annual income from these three investments was $3290. The amount invested at 12% was $5000 less than the combined amounts invested at 9% and 8%. Find the amount invested at each rate.

62. *Chemistry*   The following table shows the active chemical content of three different soil additives.

Additive	Ammonium Nitrate	Phosphorus	Iron
1	30%	10%	10%
2	40%	15%	10%
3	50%	5%	5%

A soil chemist wants to prepare two chemical samples. The first sample requires 380 grams of ammonium nitrate, 95 grams of phosphorus, and 85 grams of iron. The second sample requires 380 grams of ammonium nitrate, 110 grams of phosphorus, and 90 grams of iron. How many grams of each additive are required for sample 1, and how many grams of each additive are required for sample 2?

63. *Nutrition* The following table shows the carbohydrate, fat, and protein content of three food types.

Food Type	Carbohydrate	Fat	Protein
I	60%	10%	20%
II	10%	4%	60%
III	70%	0%	10%

A nutritionist must prepare two diets from these three food groups. The first diet must contain 220 grams of carbohydrate, 18 grams of fat, and 160 grams of protein. The second diet must contain 210 grams of carbohydrate, 28 grams of fat, and 170 grams of protein. How many grams of each food type are required for the first diet, and how many grams of each food type are required for the second diet?

Applying Concepts

64. The point of intersection of the graphs of the equations $Ax + 2y = 2$ and $2x + By = 10$ is $(2, -2)$. Find A and B.

65. The point of intersection of the graphs of the equations $Ax - 4y = 9$ and $4x + By = -1$ is $(-1, -3)$. Find A and B.

66. Given that the graphs of the equations $2x - y = 6$, $3x - 4y = 4$, and $Ax - 2y = 0$ all intersect at the same point, find A.

67. Given that the graphs of the equations $3x - 2y = -2$, $2x - y = 0$, and $Ax + y = 8$ all intersect at the same point, find A.

68. Find an equation such that the system of equations formed by your equation and $2x - 5y = 9$ will have $(2, -1)$ as a solution.

69. Let L be the line in which planes $2x + y - z = 13$ and $x - 2y + z = -4$ intersect. If the point $(x, 3, z)$ lies on L, find the value of $(x - z)$.

For Exercises 70 and 71, use the system of equations
$$\begin{aligned} x - 3y - 2z &= A^2 \\ 2x - 5y + Az &= 9 \\ 2x - 8y + z &= 18 \end{aligned}$$

70. Find all values of A for which the system has no solution.

71. Find all values of A for which the system has a unique solution.

72. *Rate-of-Wind Problem*   A plane is flying the 3500 miles from New York City to London. The speed of the plane in calm air is 375 mph, and there is a 50-mph tailwind. The *point of no return* is the point at which the flight time required to return to New York City is the same as the flight time to travel on to London. For this flight, how far from New York is the point of no return? Round to the nearest whole number.

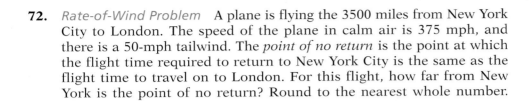

EXPLORATION

1.   *Multiplying an Equation in a System of Equations by a Constant*   When the addition method is used to solve a system of linear equations in two variables, sometimes it is necessary to multiply one or both equations by a constant and then add the equations. Multiplying and then adding equations does not change the solution of the system of equations. In this Exploration, you will investigate this fact.

a. Graph the equations of the system $\begin{array}{ll}(1) & 2x - 5y = -4 \\ (2) & 4x + 3y = 18\end{array}$ and find the solution of the system of equations.

b. Multiply Equation (1) by 3 and add it to Equation (2). Call this Equation (3). Graph Equation (3) on the same coordinate grid as in part a. Does the system of equations made up of Equation (1) and Equation (3) have the same solution as the original system of equations? Explain.

c. Explain how the answer to part b illustrates that replacing an equation in a system of equations by the sum of that equation and a multiple of another equation does not change the solution of the system of equations.

d. Return to the original system of equations. Multiply Equation (1) by -2 and add it to Equation (2). Call this Equation (4). Graph Equation (4) on the same coordinate grid as in part a. Does the system of equations made up of Equation (1) and Equation (4) have the same solution as the original system of equations? Explain.

e. Explain why multiplying Equation (1) by -2 as in part d is better than multiplying it by 3 as in part b.

SECTION **5.3** **Solving Systems of Linear Equations Using Matrices**

- Elementary Row Operations
- Solve Systems of Equations Using the Gaussian Elimination Method

■ Elementary Row Operations

A **matrix** is a rectangular array of numbers. Each number of a matrix is called an **element** of the matrix. The matrix at the right, with three rows and four columns, is called a 3×4 (read "3 by 4") matrix.

$$A = \begin{bmatrix} 2 & -3 & -6 & 0 \\ 7 & 4 & -2 & 5 \\ 1 & 6 & 0 & 3 \end{bmatrix}$$

A matrix of m rows and n columns is said to be of **order $m \times n$.** The order of matrix A on the previous page is 3×4. The notation a_{ij} refers to the element of the matrix in the ith row and jth column. For matrix A, $a_{23} = -2$ and $a_{31} = 1$.

❓ QUESTION For matrix A, what is a_{12}?

The elements $a_{11}, a_{22}, a_{33}, \ldots, a_{nn}$ form the **main diagonal** of a matrix. The elements 2, 4, and 0 form the main diagonal of matrix A given on the previous page.

▼ Point of Interest

Working with systems of equations is only one of the many ways in which we use matrices. Besides this application, matrices are used in such diverse fields as economics, biology, chemistry, and physics.

One application of matrices is solving a system of equations. For each system of equations, there is an associated matrix called an **augmented matrix.** This matrix consists of the coefficients of the variables and the constant terms.

System of Equations

$$2x - y + 3z = 5$$
$$x + 4y = -2$$
$$4x + 3y - z = 3$$

Augmented Matrix

$$\begin{bmatrix} 2 & -1 & 3 & | & 5 \\ 1 & 4 & 0 & | & -2 \\ 4 & 3 & -1 & | & 3 \end{bmatrix}$$

• Typically, a vertical line is drawn between the coefficients of the variables and the constant terms.

Note that when a term is missing from one of the equations (there is no z term in the second equation), the coefficient of that term is 0, and 0 is entered in the matrix.

A system of equations can be written from an augmented matrix.

Augmented Matrix

$$\begin{bmatrix} 2 & 0 & -1 & | & 4 \\ 3 & -1 & 1 & | & 5 \\ 1 & 2 & -4 & | & -3 \end{bmatrix}$$

System of Equations

$$2x - z = 4$$
$$3x - y + z = 5$$
$$x + 2y - 4z = -3$$

EXAMPLE 1

Write the augmented matrix for $\begin{array}{l} 2x - 3y = 4 \\ x + 5y = 0 \end{array}$.

Solution The augmented matrix is $\begin{bmatrix} 2 & -3 & | & 4 \\ 1 & 5 & | & 0 \end{bmatrix}$.

YOU TRY IT 1

Write the system of equations that corresponds to the augmented matrix
$$\begin{bmatrix} 2 & -3 & 1 & | & 4 \\ 1 & 0 & -2 & | & 3 \\ 0 & 1 & 2 & | & -3 \end{bmatrix}.$$

Solution See page S21.

❓ ANSWER $a_{12} = -3$

See Appendix A:
Matrix

A matrix can be entered into a graphing calculator using **EDIT** under the matrix key. There are 10 matrices with names A through J. By pressing the down arrow key, you can see the additional names.

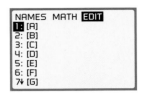

A typical graphing calculator screen displaying the 2×3 matrix $\begin{bmatrix} 2 & -3 & 4 \\ 1 & 5 & 3 \end{bmatrix}$ is shown at the right.

A system of equations can be solved by writing the system as an augmented matrix and then performing operations on the matrix similar to those performed on the equations of the system. These operations are called **elementary row operations.**

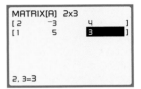

Elementary Row Operations

1. Interchange two rows.
2. Multiply all the elements in a row by the same nonzero number.
3. Replace a row by the sum of that row and a multiple of any other row.

Each of these elementary row operations has as its basis the operations that can be performed on a system of equations. These operations do not change the solution of the system of equations. Here are some examples of each row operation.

1. Interchange two rows.

Original System

This notation means to interchange rows 1 and 2.

New System

$2x - 3y = 1$
$4x + 5y = 13$
$\begin{bmatrix} 2 & -3 & | & 1 \\ 4 & 5 & | & 13 \end{bmatrix}$ $R_1 \longleftrightarrow R_2$ $\begin{bmatrix} 4 & 5 & | & 13 \\ 2 & -3 & | & 1 \end{bmatrix}$ $4x + 5y = 13$
$2x - 3y = 1$

The solution is (2, 1).   The solution is (2, 1).

2. Multiply all the elements in a row by the same nonzero number.

Original System

This notation means to multiply row 2 by 3.

New System

$2x - 3y = 1$
$4x + 5y = 13$
$\begin{bmatrix} 2 & -3 & | & 1 \\ 4 & 5 & | & 13 \end{bmatrix}$ $3R_2 \longrightarrow$ $\begin{bmatrix} 2 & -3 & | & 1 \\ 12 & 15 & | & 39 \end{bmatrix}$ $2x - 3y = 1$
$12x + 15y = 39$

The solution is (2, 1).   The solution is (2, 1).

3. Replace a row by the sum of that row and a multiple of any other row.

Original System

This notation means to replace row 2 by the sum of that row and -2 times row 1.

New System

$2x - 3y = 1$
$4x + 5y = 13$
$\begin{bmatrix} 2 & -3 & | & 1 \\ 4 & 5 & | & 13 \end{bmatrix}$ $-2R_1 + R_2 \longrightarrow$ $\begin{bmatrix} 2 & -3 & | & 1 \\ 0 & 11 & | & 11 \end{bmatrix}$ $2x - 3y = 1$
$11y = 11$

The solution is (2, 1).   The solution is (2, 1).

Note that we replace the row that follows the plus sign. See the Take Note at the left.

EXAMPLE 2

Let $A = \begin{bmatrix} 1 & 3 & -4 & 6 \\ 3 & 2 & 0 & -1 \\ -2 & -5 & 3 & 4 \end{bmatrix}$. Perform the following elementary row operations on A.

a. $R_1 \longleftrightarrow R_3$ **b.** $-2R_3$ **c.** $2R_3 + R_1$

Solution

a. $R_1 \longleftrightarrow R_3$ means to interchange row 1 and row 3.

$$\begin{bmatrix} 1 & 3 & -4 & 6 \\ 3 & 2 & 0 & -1 \\ -2 & -5 & 3 & 4 \end{bmatrix} \quad R_1 \longleftrightarrow R_3 \quad \begin{bmatrix} -2 & -5 & 3 & 4 \\ 3 & 2 & 0 & -1 \\ 1 & 3 & -4 & 6 \end{bmatrix}$$

b. $-2R_3$ means to multiply row 3 by -2.

$$\begin{bmatrix} 1 & 3 & -4 & 6 \\ 3 & 2 & 0 & -1 \\ -2 & -5 & 3 & 4 \end{bmatrix} \quad -2R_3 \longrightarrow \quad \begin{bmatrix} 1 & 3 & -4 & 6 \\ 3 & 2 & 0 & -1 \\ 4 & 10 & -6 & -8 \end{bmatrix}$$

c. $2R_3 + R_1$ means to multiply row 3 by 2 and then add the result to row 1. Only Row 1 will be changed.

$$\begin{bmatrix} 1 & 3 & -4 & 6 \\ 3 & 2 & 0 & -1 \\ -2 & -5 & 3 & 4 \end{bmatrix} \quad 2R_3 + R_1 \longrightarrow \quad \begin{bmatrix} -3 & -7 & 2 & 14 \\ 3 & 2 & 0 & -1 \\ -2 & -5 & 3 & 4 \end{bmatrix}$$

YOU TRY IT 2

Let $B = \begin{bmatrix} 1 & 8 & -2 & 3 \\ 2 & -3 & 4 & 1 \\ 3 & 5 & -7 & 3 \end{bmatrix}$. Perform the following elementary row operations on B.

a. $R_2 \longleftrightarrow R_3$ **b.** $3R_2$ **c.** $-3R_1 + R_3$

Solution   See page S21.

See Appendix A:
Matrix

The elementary row operations can be performed using a graphing calculator. A typical screen from a graphing calculator is shown below.

Interchange rows

Multiply a row
by a constant

Multiply a row
by a constant
and then add to
another row

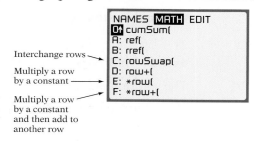

The operation row+(shown by ▢: is to add two rows. This is really the same as F: where the constant is 1.

Here are the calculator versions of the elementary row operations as they apply to Example 2.

```
rowSwap([A],1,3)

[ [⁻2  ⁻5   3   4]
  [3    2   0  ⁻1]
  [1    3  ⁻4   6] ]
```
$R_1 \leftrightarrow R_3$

```
*row(⁻2,[A],3)
   [ [1    3  ⁻4   6]
     [3    2   0  ⁻1]
     [4   10  ⁻6  ⁻8] ]
```
$2R_3$

```
*row+(2,[A],3,1)

[ [⁻3  ⁻7   2  14]
  [3    2   0  ⁻1]
  [⁻2  ⁻5   3   4] ]
```
$2R_3 + 2R_1$

Elementary row operations are used to solve a system of equations. **The goal is to use the elementary row operations to rewrite the augmented matrix with 1's down the main diagonal and 0's to the left of the 1's in all rows except the first.** This is called a **row echelon form** of the matrix. Examples of echelon form are shown below.

$$\begin{bmatrix} 1 & 3 & -2 \\ 0 & 1 & 3 \end{bmatrix} \qquad \begin{bmatrix} 1 & -2 & 3 & 1 \\ 0 & 1 & 2.5 & -4 \\ 0 & 0 & 1 & 2 \end{bmatrix} \qquad \begin{bmatrix} 1 & 4 & \frac{1}{2} & -3 \\ 0 & 1 & 3 & 0 \\ 0 & 0 & 1 & -\frac{2}{3} \end{bmatrix} \qquad \begin{bmatrix} 1 & -2 & 3 & 4 \\ 0 & 1 & 5 & -6 \\ 0 & 0 & 0 & 5 \end{bmatrix}$$

We will follow a very definite procedure to rewrite an augmented matrix in row echelon form. For a 2×3 augmented matrix, use elementary row operations to

1. Change a_{11} to a 1.
2. Change a_{21} to a 0.
3. Change a_{22} to a 1.

$$\begin{bmatrix} a_{11} & a_{12} & a_{13} \\ a_{21} & a_{22} & a_{23} \end{bmatrix}$$

➡ Write the matrix $\begin{bmatrix} 3 & -6 & 12 \\ 2 & 1 & -3 \end{bmatrix}$ in row echelon form.

ALGEBRAIC SOLUTION

1. Change a_{11} to 1. One way to do this is to multiply row 1 by the reciprocal of a_{11}.

$$\begin{bmatrix} 3 & -6 & 12 \\ 2 & 1 & -3 \end{bmatrix} \xrightarrow{\frac{1}{3}R_1} \begin{bmatrix} 1 & -2 & 4 \\ 2 & 1 & -3 \end{bmatrix}$$

2. Change a_{21} to 0 by multiplying row 1 by the opposite of a_{21} and then adding to row 2.

$$\begin{bmatrix} 1 & -2 & 4 \\ 2 & 1 & -3 \end{bmatrix} \xrightarrow{-2R_1 + R_2} \begin{bmatrix} 1 & -2 & 4 \\ 0 & 5 & -11 \end{bmatrix}$$

3. Change a_{22} to 1 by multiplying by the reciprocal of a_{22}.

$$\begin{bmatrix} 1 & -2 & 4 \\ 0 & 5 & -11 \end{bmatrix} \xrightarrow{\frac{1}{5}R_2} \begin{bmatrix} 1 & -2 & 4 \\ 0 & 1 & -2.2 \end{bmatrix}$$

GRAPHICAL CHECK

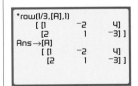

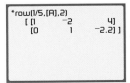

TAKE NOTE

Sometimes it is not possible, as shown in the fourth matrix at the right, to have all 1's on the main diagonal. In this case, we try as best we can to write the matrix with 1's on the main diagonal and rows with 0's following these. For instance, the following matrix is not in row echelon form.

$$\begin{bmatrix} 1 & -2 & 3 & 4 \\ 0 & 0 & 0 & 5 \\ 0 & 1 & 5 & -6 \end{bmatrix}$$

CALCULATOR NOTE

To rewrite a matrix in row echelon form, we make a series of changes to the matrix. After each step, we must replace [A] by the new matrix. The operation Ans->[A] replaces the matrix in [A] with the new matrix. If you need to keep the original matrix, you can make a copy of it and store it in another matrix, say [B].

A row echelon form of the matrix is $\begin{bmatrix} 1 & -2 & 4 \\ 0 & 1 & -2.2 \end{bmatrix}$.

The row echelon form of a matrix is not unique and depends on the elementary row operations that are used. For instance, suppose we again start with $\begin{bmatrix} 3 & -6 & 12 \\ 2 & 1 & -3 \end{bmatrix}$ and follow the elementary row operations below.

$$\begin{bmatrix} 3 & -6 & 12 \\ 2 & 1 & -3 \end{bmatrix} \xrightarrow{-1R_2 + R_1} \begin{bmatrix} 1 & -7 & 15 \\ 2 & 1 & -3 \end{bmatrix} \xrightarrow{-2R_1 + R_2}$$

$$\begin{bmatrix} 1 & -7 & 15 \\ 0 & 15 & -33 \end{bmatrix} \xrightarrow{\frac{1}{15}R_2} \begin{bmatrix} 1 & -7 & 15 \\ 0 & 1 & -2.2 \end{bmatrix}$$

In this case, we get $\begin{bmatrix} 1 & -7 & 15 \\ 0 & 1 & -2.2 \end{bmatrix}$ as the row echelon form rather than $\begin{bmatrix} 1 & -2 & 4 \\ 0 & 1 & -2.2 \end{bmatrix}$, which we got in the first case. Row echelon form is not unique.

The order in which the elements in a 3×4 matrix are changed is as follows:

1. Change a_{11} to a 1.
2. Change a_{21} and a_{31} to 0's.
3. Change a_{22} to a 1.
4. Change a_{32} to a 0.
5. Change a_{33} to a 1.

$$\begin{bmatrix} a_{11} & a_{12} & a_{13} & a_{14} \\ a_{21} & a_{22} & a_{23} & a_{24} \\ a_{31} & a_{32} & a_{33} & a_{34} \end{bmatrix}$$

EXAMPLE 3

Write $\begin{bmatrix} 2 & 1 & 3 & -1 \\ 1 & 3 & 5 & -1 \\ -3 & -1 & 1 & 2 \end{bmatrix}$ in row echelon form.

Solution

ALGEBRAIC SOLUTION

1.   Change a_{11} to 1 by interchanging row 1 and row 2. *Note:*

We could have chosen to multiply row 1 by $\frac{1}{2}$. The sequence of steps to get to row echelon form is not unique.

$$\begin{bmatrix} 2 & 1 & 3 & -1 \\ 1 & 3 & 5 & -1 \\ -3 & -1 & 1 & 2 \end{bmatrix} \xrightarrow{R_1 \longleftrightarrow R_2} \begin{bmatrix} 1 & 3 & 5 & -1 \\ 2 & 1 & 3 & -1 \\ -3 & -1 & 1 & 2 \end{bmatrix}$$

GRAPHICAL CHECK

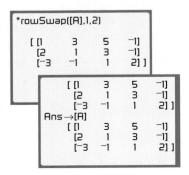

2. Change a_{21} to 0 by multiplying row 1 by the opposite of a_{21} and then adding to row 2.

$$\begin{bmatrix} 1 & 3 & 5 & -1 \\ 2 & 1 & 3 & -1 \\ -3 & -1 & 1 & 2 \end{bmatrix} \xrightarrow{-2R_1 + R_2} \begin{bmatrix} 1 & 3 & 5 & -1 \\ 0 & -5 & -7 & 1 \\ -3 & -1 & 1 & 2 \end{bmatrix}$$

Change a_{31} to 0 by multiplying row 1 by the opposite of a_{31} and then adding to row 3.

$$\begin{bmatrix} 1 & 3 & 5 & -1 \\ 0 & -5 & -7 & 1 \\ -3 & -1 & 1 & 2 \end{bmatrix} \xrightarrow{3R_1 + R_3} \begin{bmatrix} 1 & 3 & 5 & -1 \\ 0 & -5 & -7 & 1 \\ 0 & 8 & 16 & -1 \end{bmatrix}$$

3. Change a_{22} to 1 by multiplying row 2 by the reciprocal of a_{22}.

$$\begin{bmatrix} 1 & 3 & 5 & -1 \\ 0 & -5 & -7 & 1 \\ 0 & 8 & 16 & -1 \end{bmatrix} \xrightarrow{-\frac{1}{5}R_2} \begin{bmatrix} 1 & 3 & 5 & -1 \\ 0 & 1 & \frac{7}{5} & -\frac{1}{5} \\ 0 & 8 & 16 & -1 \end{bmatrix}$$

4. Change a_{32} to 0 by multiplying row 2 by the opposite of a_{32} and then adding to row 3.

$$\begin{bmatrix} 1 & 3 & 5 & -1 \\ 0 & 1 & \frac{7}{5} & -\frac{1}{5} \\ 0 & 8 & 16 & -1 \end{bmatrix} \xrightarrow{-8R_2 + R_3} \begin{bmatrix} 1 & 3 & 5 & -1 \\ 0 & 1 & \frac{7}{5} & -\frac{1}{5} \\ 0 & 0 & \frac{24}{5} & \frac{3}{5} \end{bmatrix}$$

5. Change a_{33} to 1 by multiplying row 3 by the reciprocal of a_{33}.

$$\begin{bmatrix} 1 & 3 & 5 & -1 \\ 0 & 1 & \frac{7}{5} & -\frac{1}{5} \\ 0 & 0 & \frac{24}{5} & \frac{3}{5} \end{bmatrix} \xrightarrow{\frac{5}{24}R_3} \begin{bmatrix} 1 & 3 & 5 & -1 \\ 0 & 1 & \frac{7}{5} & -\frac{1}{5} \\ 0 & 0 & 1 & \frac{1}{8} \end{bmatrix}$$

A row echelon form of the matrix is $\begin{bmatrix} 1 & 3 & 5 & -1 \\ 0 & 1 & \frac{7}{5} & -\frac{1}{5} \\ 0 & 0 & 1 & \frac{1}{8} \end{bmatrix}$.

YOU TRY IT 3

Write $\begin{bmatrix} 1 & -3 & 2 & 1 \\ -4 & 14 & 0 & -2 \\ 2 & -5 & -3 & 16 \end{bmatrix}$ in row echelon form.

Solution   See page S21.

```
*row+(⁻2,[A],1,2)
   [ [1    3    5   ⁻1]
     [0   ⁻5   ⁻7    1]
     [⁻3  ⁻1    1    2] ]
```

```
*row+(3,[A],1,3)
   [ [1    3    5   ⁻1]
     [0   ⁻5   ⁻7    1]
     [0    8   16   ⁻1] ]
```

```
*row(⁻1/5,[A],2)
   [ [1    3    5   ⁻1]
     [0    1   1.4  ⁻.2]
     [0    8   16   ⁻1] ]
```

```
*row+(⁻8,[A],2,3)
   [ [1    3    5   ⁻1]
     [0    1   1.4  ⁻.2]
     [0    0   4.8  .6] ]
```

```
*row(5/24,[A],3)
   [ [1    3    5   ⁻1]
     [0    1   1.4  ⁻.2]
     [0    0    1   .125] ]
```

CALCULATOR NOTE

For the graphical check above, we have shown the result of interchanging rows. Remember that you must store the result in [A] after each step.

The ref(function on a graphing calculator performs all of the elementary row operations on a matrix and directly produces a row echelon form of a matrix. The abbreviation **ref** stands for **r**ow **e**chelon **f**orm. A typical screen is shown at the right for the matrix in Example 3, where we have also used the ▶Frac command to write the matrix with fractions rather than decimals. Again observe that this form is different from the form we created in Example 3. The echelon form that you produce by means of a calculator may not be the same one that you produce without a calculator.

ref([A])
[[1   .3333333333   ...
  [0   1   ...
  [0   0   ...

[[1   .3333333333   ...
  [0   1   ...
  [0   0   ...
Ans▶Frac
[[1   1/3   −1/3   −2...
  [0   1   2   −1...
  [0   0   1   1/...

Solve Systems of Equations Using the Gaussian Elimination Method

If an augmented matrix is in row echelon form, the corresponding system of equations can be solved by substitution. For instance, consider the following matrix in row echelon form and the corresponding system of equations.

$$\begin{bmatrix} 1 & -3 & 4 & | & 7 \\ 0 & 1 & 3 & | & -6 \\ 0 & 0 & 1 & | & -1 \end{bmatrix} \qquad \begin{aligned} x - 3y + 4z &= 7 \\ y + 3z &= -6 \\ z &= -1 \end{aligned}$$

From the last equation of the system above, we have $z = -1$. Substitute this value into the second equation and solve for y. Thus $y = -3$.

$$\begin{aligned} y + 3z &= -6 \\ y + 3(-1) &= -6 \\ y - 3 &= -6 \\ y &= -3 \end{aligned}$$

Substitute $y = -3$ and $z = -1$ in the first equation of the system and solve for x. Thus $x = 2$.

The solution of the system of equations is $(2, -3, -1)$.

$$\begin{aligned} x - 3y + 4z &= 7 \\ x - 3(-3) + 4(-1) &= 7 \\ x + 9 - 4 &= 7 \\ x + 5 &= 7 \\ x &= 2 \end{aligned}$$

The process of solving a system of equations by using elementary row operations is called the **Gaussian elimination method.**

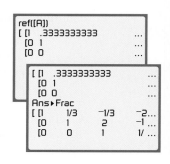

EXAMPLE 4

Solve using the Gaussian elimination method: $\begin{aligned} 2x - 5y &= 19 \\ 3x + 4y &= -6 \end{aligned}$

Solution Write the augmented matrix and then use elementary row operations to rewrite the matrix in row echelon form.

$$\begin{bmatrix} 2 & -5 & | & 19 \\ 3 & 4 & | & -6 \end{bmatrix} \xrightarrow[\frac{1}{2}R_1]{\text{Change } a_{11} \text{ to } 1.} \begin{bmatrix} 1 & -\frac{5}{2} & | & \frac{19}{2} \\ 3 & 4 & | & -6 \end{bmatrix}$$

• Note that we multiplied R_1 by the reciprocal of a_{11}.

$$\begin{bmatrix} 1 & -\dfrac{5}{2} & \bigg| & \dfrac{19}{2} \\ 3 & 4 & \bigg| & -6 \end{bmatrix}$$ $\xrightarrow[\substack{-3R_1 + R_2}]{\text{Change } a_{21} \text{ to } 0.}}$ $$\begin{bmatrix} 1 & -\dfrac{5}{2} & \bigg| & \dfrac{19}{2} \\ 0 & \dfrac{23}{2} & \bigg| & -\dfrac{69}{2} \end{bmatrix}$$ • Note that we multiplied R_1 by the opposite of a_{21}.

$$\begin{bmatrix} 1 & -\dfrac{5}{2} & \bigg| & \dfrac{19}{2} \\ 0 & \dfrac{23}{2} & \bigg| & -\dfrac{69}{2} \end{bmatrix}$$ $\xrightarrow[\substack{\frac{2}{23}R_2}]{\text{Change } a_{22} \text{ to } 1.}}$ $$\begin{bmatrix} 1 & -\dfrac{5}{2} & \bigg| & \dfrac{19}{2} \\ 0 & 1 & \bigg| & -3 \end{bmatrix}$$ • This is row echelon form.

(1) $x - \dfrac{5}{2}y = \dfrac{19}{2}$

(2) $y = -3$

• Write the system of equations corresponding to the matrix that is in row echelon form.

$$x - \dfrac{5}{2}(-3) = \dfrac{19}{2}$$

$$x + \dfrac{15}{2} = \dfrac{19}{2}$$

$$x = 2$$

• Substitute -3 for y in Equation (1) and solve for x.

The solution is $(2, -3)$.

If a graphing calculator is used to find a row echelon form for $\begin{bmatrix} 2 & -5 & \big| & 19 \\ 3 & 4 & \big| & -6 \end{bmatrix}$, the result is as shown below. This gives a different corresponding system of equations. However, the final answer is the same.

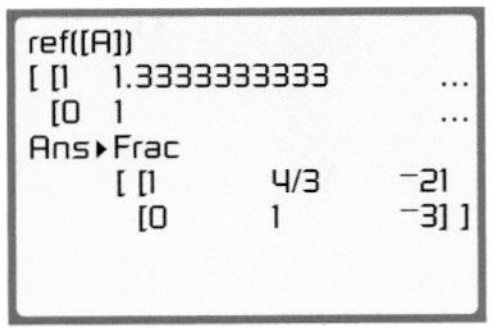

```
ref([A])
[[1  1.3333333333
 [0  1              ...
Ans▸Frac
      [[1    4/3    -2]
       [0    1     -3] ]
```

(1) $x + \dfrac{4}{3}y = -2$

(2) $y = -3$

$\xrightarrow[\text{and solve for } x.]{\substack{\text{Replace } y \text{ in} \\ \text{Equation (1)}}}$

$x + \dfrac{4}{3}y = -2$

$x + \dfrac{4}{3}(-3) = -2$

$x - 4 = -2$

$x = 2$

The solution is $(2, -3)$.

YOU TRY IT 4

Solve by using the Gaussian elimination method: $\begin{aligned} 4x - 5y &= 17 \\ 3x + 2y &= 7 \end{aligned}$

Solution   See page S21.

The Gaussian elimination method can be used with dependent and inconsistent systems of equations. Here is an example of a dependent system of equations.

➡ Solve by the Gaussian elimination method: $\begin{aligned} x - 3y &= 6 \\ -2x + 6y &= -12 \end{aligned}$

$$\begin{bmatrix} 1 & -3 & | & 6 \\ -2 & 6 & | & -12 \end{bmatrix} \xrightarrow[\;2R_1 + R_2\;]{\substack{a_{11} \text{ is } 1. \text{ Change} \\ a_{21} \text{ to } 0.}} \begin{bmatrix} 1 & -3 & | & 6 \\ 0 & 0 & | & 0 \end{bmatrix}$$

- This is row echelon form.

- Write the system of equations corresponding to the matrix that is in row echelon form.

$$x - 3y = 6$$
$$0 = 0$$

Because the equation $0 = 0$ is true, the solutions of the system of equations are the solutions of $x - 3y = 6$. Solving for y, we have $y = \frac{1}{3}x - 2$.

The ordered-pair solutions are $\left(x, \frac{1}{3}x - 2\right)$. The graph of the system of equations is shown at the left. Note that the graphs are identical. The system of equations is dependent. ⬅

Here is an example of an inconsistent system of equations.

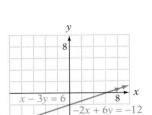

➡ Solve by the Gaussian elimination method: $\begin{aligned} 4x + 2y &= 6 \\ 2x + y &= -4 \end{aligned}$

$$\begin{bmatrix} 4 & 2 & | & 6 \\ 2 & 1 & | & -4 \end{bmatrix} \xrightarrow[\;\frac{1}{4}R_1\;]{\text{Change } a_{11} \text{ to } 1.} \begin{bmatrix} 1 & \frac{1}{2} & | & \frac{3}{2} \\ 2 & 1 & | & -4 \end{bmatrix}$$

$$\begin{bmatrix} 1 & \frac{1}{2} & | & \frac{3}{2} \\ 2 & 1 & | & -4 \end{bmatrix} \xrightarrow[\;-2R_1 + R_2\;]{\text{Change } a_{21} \text{ to } 0.} \begin{bmatrix} 1 & \frac{1}{2} & | & \frac{3}{2} \\ 0 & 0 & | & -7 \end{bmatrix}$$

- This is row echelon form.

$$x + \frac{1}{2}y = \frac{3}{2}$$
$$0 = -7$$

- Write the system of equations corresponding to the matrix that is in row echelon form.

Because the equation $0 = -7$ is not true, the system of equations has no solution. The graphs of the lines are parallel and do not intersect. The system of equations is inconsistent. The graph is shown at the left. ⬅

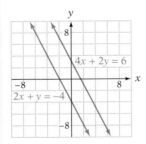

The Gaussian elimination method can be extended to systems of equations with more than two variables.

EXAMPLE 5

Solve by using the Gaussian elimination method:

$$x + 2y - z = 9$$
$$2x - y + 2z = -1$$
$$-2x + 3y - 2z = 7$$

Solution

$$\begin{bmatrix} 1 & 2 & -1 & | & 9 \\ 2 & -1 & 2 & | & -1 \\ -2 & 3 & -2 & | & 7 \end{bmatrix} \xrightarrow[\;-2R_1 + R_2\;]{\substack{a_{11} \text{ is } 1. \text{ Change} \\ a_{21} \text{ to } 0.}} \begin{bmatrix} 1 & 2 & -1 & | & 9 \\ 0 & -5 & 4 & | & -19 \\ -2 & 3 & -2 & | & 7 \end{bmatrix}$$

$$\begin{bmatrix} 1 & 2 & -1 & | & 9 \\ 0 & -5 & 4 & | & -19 \\ -2 & 3 & -2 & | & 7 \end{bmatrix} \xrightarrow[\text{2}R_1 + R_3]{\text{Change } a_{31} \text{ to } 0.} \begin{bmatrix} 1 & 2 & -1 & | & 9 \\ 0 & -5 & 4 & | & -19 \\ 0 & 7 & -4 & | & 25 \end{bmatrix}$$

$$\begin{bmatrix} 1 & 2 & -1 & | & 9 \\ 0 & -5 & 4 & | & -19 \\ 0 & 7 & -4 & | & 25 \end{bmatrix} \xrightarrow[-\frac{1}{5}R_2]{\text{Change } a_{22} \text{ to } 1.} \begin{bmatrix} 1 & 2 & -1 & | & 9 \\ 0 & 1 & -\frac{4}{5} & | & \frac{19}{5} \\ 0 & 7 & -4 & | & 25 \end{bmatrix}$$

$$\begin{bmatrix} 1 & 2 & -1 & | & 9 \\ 0 & 1 & -\frac{4}{5} & | & \frac{19}{5} \\ 0 & 7 & -4 & | & 25 \end{bmatrix} \xrightarrow[-7R_2 + R_3]{\text{Change } a_{32} \text{ to } 0.} \begin{bmatrix} 1 & 2 & -1 & | & 9 \\ 0 & 1 & -\frac{4}{5} & | & \frac{19}{5} \\ 0 & 0 & \frac{8}{5} & | & -\frac{8}{5} \end{bmatrix}$$

$$\begin{bmatrix} 1 & 2 & -1 & | & 9 \\ 0 & 1 & -\frac{4}{5} & | & \frac{19}{5} \\ 0 & 0 & \frac{8}{5} & | & -\frac{8}{5} \end{bmatrix} \xrightarrow[\frac{5}{8}R_3]{\text{Change } a_{33} \text{ to } 1.} \begin{bmatrix} 1 & 2 & -1 & | & 9 \\ 0 & 1 & -\frac{4}{5} & | & \frac{19}{5} \\ 0 & 0 & 1 & | & -1 \end{bmatrix}$$

- This is row echelon form.

(1) $\quad x + 2y - z = 9$

(2) $\qquad y - \dfrac{4}{5}z = \dfrac{19}{5}$

(3) $\qquad\qquad z = -1$

- Write the system of equations corresponding to the matrix that is in row echelon form.

$$y - \frac{4}{5}(-1) = \frac{19}{5}$$

$$y + \frac{4}{5} = \frac{19}{5}$$

$$y = 3$$

- Substitute -1 for z in Equation (2) and solve for y.

$$x + 2y - z = 9$$

$$x + 2(3) - (-1) = 9$$

$$x + 7 = 9$$

$$x = 2$$

- Substitute -1 for z and 3 for y in Equation (1) and solve for x.

The solution is $(2, 3, -1)$.

If a graphing calculator is used to find a row echelon form for $\begin{bmatrix} 1 & 2 & -1 & | & 9 \\ 2 & -1 & 2 & | & -1 \\ -2 & 3 & -2 & | & 7 \end{bmatrix}$, the result is as shown on the next page. This gives a different corresponding system of equations. However, the final answer is the same.

```
ref([A])
[[1    -.5    1    -.5...
 [0     1   -.8   3.8...
 [0     0    1    -1 ...
```

(1) $x - 0.5y + z = -0.5$
(2) $y - 0.8z = 3.8$
(3) $z = -1$

$$y - 0.8(-1) = 3.8$$
$$y + 0.8 = 3.8$$
$$y = 3$$

• Replace z by -1 in Equation (2) and solve for y.

$$x - 0.5(3) + (-1) = -0.5$$
$$x - 2.5 = -0.5$$
$$x = 2$$

• Replace z by -1 and y by 3 in Equation (1) and solve for x.

The solution is $(2, 3, -1)$. This again illustrates that different row echelon forms of the same augmented matrix will yield the same solution of the system of equations.

YOU TRY IT 5

Solve by using the Gaussian elimination method:

$$2x + 3y + 3z = -2$$
$$x + 2y - 3z = 9$$
$$3x - 2y - 4z = 1$$

Solution   See page S22.

Just as we can write the equation of a line in slope–intercept form as $y = mx + b$ or in standard form as $Ax + By = C$, we can write the equation of a plane in different ways. We can solve the equation in standard form of a plane, $Ax + By + Cz = D$, for z.

$$Ax + By + Cz = D$$
$$Cz = -Ax - By + D$$
$$z = -\frac{A}{C}x - \frac{B}{C}y + \frac{D}{C}$$

The last equation is usually written as $z = ax + by + c$, where $a = -\frac{A}{C}$, $b = -\frac{B}{C}$, and $c = \frac{D}{C}$. We will use the form $z = ax + by + c$ to find the equation of a plane.

EXAMPLE 6

Find the equation of the plane that passes through the points $P_1(1, 3, 6)$, $P_2(3, 2, 10)$, and $P_3(4, -1, 7)$.

State the goal.   The goal is to find the equation of the plane that contains the given points.

Devise a strategy.   To find the equation of the plane, we must determine the constants a, b, and c for the equation $z = ax + by + c$. Because the given ordered triples belong to a plane, they must satisfy that equation. Substitute the coordinates of each point into $z = ax + by + c$ and solve the resulting system of equations.

$$z = ax + by + c$$
$$6 = a(1) + b(3) + c \qquad \bullet \; P_1: x = 1, y = 3, z = 6$$
$$10 = a(3) + b(2) + c \qquad \bullet \; P_2: x = 3, y = 2, z = 10$$
$$7 = a(4) + b(-1) + c \qquad \bullet \; P_3: x = 4, y = -1, z = 7$$

Simplify and write the system of equations as an augmented matrix.

$$
\begin{array}{l}
6 = a + 3b + c \\
10 = 3a + 2b + c \\
7 = 4a - b + c
\end{array}
\quad
\xrightarrow{\text{Augmented matrix}}
\quad
\left[
\begin{array}{ccc|c}
1 & 3 & 1 & 6 \\
3 & 2 & 1 & 10 \\
4 & -1 & 1 & 7
\end{array}
\right]
$$

Solve the system of equations by using the Gaussian elimination method.

Solve the problem.   A graphing calculator is used below to write the augmented matrix in row echelon form. We have used the ▶Frac command to write the augmented matrix with fractions.

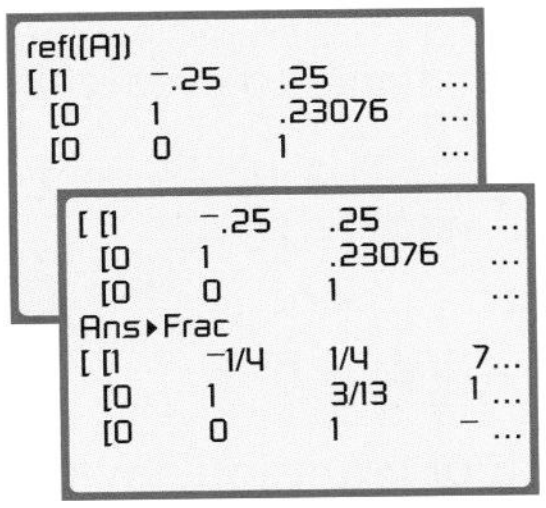

```
ref([A])
[[1      -.25    .25     ...
 [0       1    .23076    ...
 [0       0       1      ...

   [[1     -.25    .25      ...
    [0      1    .23076     ...
    [0      0       1       ...
   Ans▶Frac
   [[1     -1/4   1/4    7...
    [0      1    3/13   1...
    [0      0      1     -...
```

$$(1) \qquad a - \frac{1}{4}b + \frac{1}{4}c = \frac{7}{4}$$

$$(2) \qquad b + \frac{3}{13}c = \frac{17}{13}$$

$$(3) \qquad c = -3$$

Solve the resulting system of equations by substitution.

$$
\begin{aligned}
b + \frac{3}{13}(-3) &= \frac{17}{13} \\
b - \frac{9}{13} &= \frac{17}{13} \\
b &= 2
\end{aligned}
$$
• Replace c by -3 in Equation (2) and solve for b.

$$
\begin{aligned}
a - \frac{1}{4}(2) + \frac{1}{4}(-3) &= \frac{7}{4} \\
a - \frac{2}{4} - \frac{3}{4} &= \frac{7}{4} \\
a &= 3
\end{aligned}
$$
• Replace c by -3 and b by 2 in Equation (1) and solve for a.

We have $a = 3$, $b = 2$, and $c = -3$. The equation of the plane is $z = 3x + 2y - 3$.

Check your work.   Verify that each given ordered triple is a solution of the equation by substituting into the equation of the plane. For instance, the check using P_1 is shown at the left. $P_1(1, 3, 6)$ checks. Now verify that the other points check.

$$
\begin{array}{l}
z = 3x + 2y - 3 \\
\hline
6 \mid 3(1) + 2(3) - 3 \\
6 = 6
\end{array}
$$

YOU TRY IT 6

Recall that a quadratic function can be written in the form $y = ax^2 + bx + c$. Find the equation of the quadratic function whose graph passes through $P_1(2, 3)$, $P_2(-1, 0)$, and $P_3(0, -3)$.

Solution   See page S22.

EXAMPLE 7

An artist is creating a mobile from which three objects will be suspended from a light rod that is 18 inches long, as shown below at the left. The weight, in ounces, of each object is shown in the diagram. For the mobile to balance, the objects must be positioned so that $w_1 d_1 + w_2 d_2 = w_3 d_3$. The artist wants d_1 to be 1.5 times d_2. Find the distances d_1, d_2, and d_3 so that the mobile will balance.

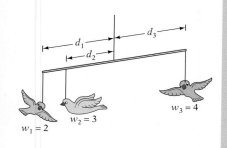

State the goal. The goal is to find the values of d_1, d_2, and d_3 so that the mobile will balance.

Devise a strategy. There are three unknowns in this problem. Using the figure and information from the problem, write a system of three equations in three unknowns. The length of the rod is 18 inches. Therefore, $d_1 + d_3 = 18$. Because the artist wants d_1 to be 1.5 times d_2, we have $d_1 = 1.5 d_2$. Using the equation $w_1 d_1 + w_2 d_2 = w_3 d_3$, we have

$$w_1 d_1 + w_2 d_2 = w_3 d_3$$
$$2d_1 + 3d_2 = 4d_3 \quad \bullet \text{ From the diagram, } w_1 = 2, w_2 = 3, w_3 = 4.$$

Use the three equations to create a system of three equations in three unknowns.

$$
\begin{array}{rcl}
d_1 \qquad\quad + d_3 &=& 18 \\
d_1 - 1.5 d_2 \qquad &=& 0 \\
2d_1 + 3d_2 - 4d_3 &=& 0
\end{array}
\qquad \underrightarrow{\text{Augmented matrix}} \qquad
\left[
\begin{array}{rrr|r}
1 & 0 & 1 & 18 \\
1 & -1.5 & 0 & 0 \\
2 & 3 & -4 & 0
\end{array}
\right]
$$

Solve the system of equations by using the Gaussian elimination method.

Solve the problem. A graphing calculator is used below to write the augmented matrix in row echelon form. We have used the ▶Frac command to write the augmented matrix with fractions.

```
ref([A])
[ [1    1.5    -2      ...
  [0    1    -.66666   ...
  [0    0     1        ...
```
```
[ [1    1.5    -2      ...
  [0    1    -.66666   ...
  [0    0     1        ...
Ans▶Frac
[ [1    3/2    -2      0]
  [0    1    -2/3      0]
  [0    0     1        9] ]
```

(1) $\quad d_1 + \dfrac{3}{2} d_2 - 2d_3 = 0$

(2) $\qquad\qquad d_2 - \dfrac{2}{3} d_3 = 0$

(3) $\qquad\qquad\qquad\qquad d_3 = 9$

Solve the resulting system of equations by substitution.

$d_2 - \dfrac{2}{3}(9) = 0$ • Replace d_3 by 9 in Equation (2) and solve for d_2. $d_1 + \dfrac{3}{2}(6) - 2(9) = 0$ • Replace d_3 by 9 and d_2 by 6 in Equation (1) and solve for d_1.

$\qquad d_2 - 6 = 0$ $d_1 + 9 - 18 = 0$

$\qquad\quad d_2 = 6$ $d_1 = 9$

The values are $d_1 = 9$ inches, $d_2 = 6$ inches, and $d_3 = 9$ inches.

Check your work. You can check your solution by substituting the known values for w_1, w_2, and w_3 and the computed values for d_1, d_2, and d_3 into $w_1 d_1 + w_2 d_2 = w_3 d_3$ and verifying that the solution checks.

YOU TRY IT 7

A science museum charges $10 for an admission ticket, but members receive a discount of $3, and students are admitted for half the regular admission price. Last Saturday, 750 tickets were sold for a total of $5400. If 20 more student tickets than full-price tickets were sold, how many of each type of ticket were sold?

Solution   See page S23.

5.3 EXERCISES

Topics for Discussion

1. What is a matrix?
2. What is an augmented matrix?

3. What are the three elementary row operations on a matrix?

4. What is the next step toward writing the matrix $\begin{bmatrix} 1 & 3 & -5 \\ 4 & 3 & 2 \end{bmatrix}$ in row echelon form?

■ Elementary Row Operations

5. Which of the following matrices are not in row echelon form?

a. $\begin{bmatrix} 1 & -2 & 0 \\ 0 & 0 & 3 \end{bmatrix}$ b. $\begin{bmatrix} 0 & 1 & 2 \\ 1 & 2 & 3 \end{bmatrix}$ c. $\begin{bmatrix} 1 & -1 & 3 & 0 \\ 0 & 1 & 4 & 0 \\ 0 & 0 & 1 & 0 \end{bmatrix}$ d. $\begin{bmatrix} 1 & -1 & -2 & 3 \\ 0 & 1 & 1 & 3 \\ 0 & 0 & 0 & 0 \end{bmatrix}$

Without using a calculator, write each matrix in row echelon form.

6. $\begin{bmatrix} 1 & -5 & 1 \\ 2 & -9 & 4 \end{bmatrix}$

7. $\begin{bmatrix} 1 & 4 & -1 \\ -3 & -13 & 7 \end{bmatrix}$

8. $\begin{bmatrix} 2 & -4 & 1 \\ 3 & -7 & -1 \end{bmatrix}$

9. $\begin{bmatrix} 4 & 2 & -2 \\ 7 & 4 & -1 \end{bmatrix}$

10. $\begin{bmatrix} 5 & -2 & 3 \\ -7 & 3 & 1 \end{bmatrix}$

11. $\begin{bmatrix} 2 & 5 & -4 \\ 3 & 1 & 2 \end{bmatrix}$

12. $\begin{bmatrix} 1 & 4 & 1 & -2 \\ 3 & 11 & -1 & 2 \\ 2 & 3 & 1 & 4 \end{bmatrix}$

13. $\begin{bmatrix} 1 & 2 & 2 & -1 \\ -4 & -10 & -1 & 3 \\ 3 & 4 & 2 & -2 \end{bmatrix}$

14. $\begin{bmatrix} 3 & 6 & -3 & 4 \\ -2 & -6 & -1 & 3 \\ 2 & 1 & 2 & 5 \end{bmatrix}$

15. $\begin{bmatrix} -2 & 6 & -1 & 3 \\ 1 & -2 & 2 & 1 \\ 3 & -6 & 7 & 6 \end{bmatrix}$

16. $\begin{bmatrix} 2 & 6 & 10 & 3 \\ 3 & 8 & 15 & 0 \\ 1 & 2 & 3 & -1 \end{bmatrix}$

17. $\begin{bmatrix} 4 & -6 & 9 & 4 \\ 2 & 2 & 1 & -5 \\ 3 & 3 & -5 & 1 \end{bmatrix}$

■ Solve Systems of Equations Using the Gaussian Elimination Method

18. What is the solution of the system of equations that has $\begin{bmatrix} 1 & -1 & 3 & -2 \\ 0 & 1 & -1 & 1 \\ 0 & 0 & 1 & 3 \end{bmatrix}$ as the row echelon form of the augmented matrix for the system of equations?

19. What is the solution of the system of equations that has $\begin{bmatrix} 1 & -3 & 2 & 4 \\ 0 & 1 & -2 & 3 \\ 0 & 0 & 1 & -1 \end{bmatrix}$ as the row echelon form of the augmented matrix for the system of equations?

Solve by using the Gaussian elimination method. Do not use a calculator.

20. $3x + y = 6$
$2x - y = -1$

21. $2x + y = 3$
$x - 4y = 6$

22. $x - 3y = 8$
$3x - y = 0$

23. $2x + 3y = 16$
$x - 4y = -14$

24. $y = 4x - 10$
$2y = 5x - 11$

25. $2y = 4 - 3x$
$y = 1 - 2x$

26. $2x - y = -4$
$y = 2x - 8$

27. $3x - 2y = -8$
$y = \frac{3}{2}x - 2$

28. $4x - 3y = -14$
$3x + 4y = 2$

29. $5x + 2y = 3$
$3x + 4y = 13$

30. $5x + 4y + 3z = -9$
$x - 2y + 2z = -6$
$x - y - z = 3$

31. $x - y - z = 0$
$3x - y + 5z = -10$
$x + y - 4z = 12$

32. $5x - 5y + 2z = 8$
$2x + 3y - z = 0$
$x + 2y - z = 0$

33. $2x + y - 5z = 3$
$3x + 2y + z = 15$
$5x - y - z = 5$

34. $2x + 3y + z = 5$
$3x + 3y + 3z = 10$
$4x + 6y + 2z = 5$

35. $x - 2y + 3z = 2$
$2x + y + 2z = 5$
$2x - 4y + 6z = -4$

36. $3x + 2y + 3z = 2$
$6x - 2y + z = 1$
$3x + 4y + 2z = 3$

37. $2x + 3y - 3z = -1$
$2x + 3y + 3z = 3$
$4x - 4y + 3z = 4$

38. $5x - 5y - 5z = 2$
$5x + 5y - 5z = 6$
$10x + 10y + 5z = 3$

39. $3x - 2y + 2z = 5$
$6x + 3y - 4z = -1$
$3x - y + 2z = 4$

40. $2x - y = 3$
$3x + 2z = 7$
$2y - 3z = -8$

41. $3y - 2z = -9$
$2x + 3z = 13$
$3x - y = 7$

42. $3x + y - 2z = 7$
$2x - y = 2$
$3x + 4z = -5$

43. $2y - 5z = 12$
$3x + y - 4z = 9$
$2x - 5z = 10$

44. Find an equation of a plane that contains the points $(2, 1, 1)$, $(-1, 2, 12)$, and $(3, 2, 0)$.

45. Find an equation of a plane that contains the points $(1, -1, 5)$, $(2, -2, 9)$, and $(-3, -1, -1)$.

46. Find an equation of the form $y = ax^2 + bx + c$ whose graph passes through the points $(2, 3)$, $(-2, 7)$, and $(1, -2)$.

47. Find an equation of the form $y = ax^2 + bx + c$ whose graph passes through the points $(3, -4)$, $(2, -2)$, and $(1, -2)$.

48. *Art*   A sculptor is creating a mobile from which three objects will be suspended from a light rod that is 15 inches long. The weight, in ounces, of each object is shown in the diagram at the right. For the mobile to balance, the objects must be positioned so that $w_1d_1 = w_2d_2 + w_3d_3$. The artist wants d_3 to be three times d_2. Find the distances d_1, d_2, and d_3 so that the mobile will balance.

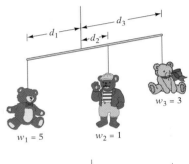

49. *Art*   A mobile is made by suspending three objects from a light rod that is 20 inches long. The weight, in ounces, of each object is shown in the diagram at the right. For the mobile to balance, the objects must be positioned so that $w_1d_1 + w_2d_2 = w_3d_3$. The artist wants d_3 to be twice d_2. Find the distances d_1, d_2, and d_3 so that the mobile will balance.

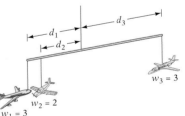

Applying Concepts

50. *Biology*   Biologists use capture–recapture models to estimate how many animals live in a certain area. Say a sample of a certain number of fish is caught and tagged. When subsequent samples of fish are caught, a biologist can use a capture history matrix to record (with a 1) which, if any, of the fish in the original sample are caught again. The rows of the capture history matrix at the right represent particular fish (each has its own identification number), and the columns represent the number of the sample in which the fish was caught.

	Samples			
	1	2	3	4
Fish A	1	0	0	1
Fish B	0	1	1	1
Fish C	0	0	1	1

a.   What is the meaning of the 1 in row A, column 4?

b.   Which fish was recaptured the most times?

51. *Biology* Biologists can use a predator–prey matrix to study the relationships among animals in an ecosystem. Each row and each column represents an animal in that system. A 1 is used as an element in the matrix to indicate that the animal represented by that row preys on the animal in that column. A 0 is used to indicate that the animal in that row does not prey on the animal in that column. A simple predator–prey matrix is shown at the right. The abbreviations are H = hawk, R = rabbit, S = snake, C = coyote.

$$\begin{array}{c} \\ H \\ R \\ S \\ C \end{array} \begin{array}{cccc} H & R & S & C \\ \begin{bmatrix} 0 & 1 & 1 & 0 \\ 0 & 0 & 0 & 0 \\ 1 & 1 & 0 & 0 \\ 0 & 1 & 1 & 0 \end{bmatrix} \end{array}$$

   a. What is the meaning of the 0 in row 2, column 1?

   b. What is the meaning of the 1 in row 3, column 2?

   c. What is the meaning of there being all zeros in column C?

   d. What is the meaning of all zeros in row R?

52. The point of intersection of the graphs of $Ax + 3y = 6$ and $2x + By = -4$ is $(3, -2)$. Find A and B.

53. The point of intersection of the graphs of $Ax + 3y + 2z = 8$, $2x + By - 3z = -12$, and $3x - 2y + Cz = 1$ is $(3, -2, 4)$. Find A, B, and C.

The following are not systems of linear equations. However, they can be solved by using a modification of the addition method. Solve each system of equations.

54.
$$\frac{1}{x} - \frac{2}{y} = 3$$
$$\frac{2}{x} + \frac{3}{y} = -1$$

55.
$$\frac{1}{x} + \frac{2}{y} = 3$$
$$\frac{1}{x} - \frac{3}{y} = -2$$

56. Suppose a system of equations contains three linear equations in two variables. Describe geometrically what must be true if the system of equations is to have a unique solution.

57. Describe the graph of each of the following equations in an *xyz*-coordinate system.
   a. $x = 3$ **b.** $y = 4$ **c.** $z = 2$ **d.** $y = x$

58. Solve the system and express the answer in the form (a, b, c, d).
$$a + b + c = 0$$
$$b + c + d = 1$$
$$a + c + d = 2$$
$$a + b + d = 3$$

EXPLORATION

1. *Reduced Row Echelon Form*   Another form in which an augmented matrix can be written is called *reduced row echelon form*. In this form, the matrix has 1's along the main diagonal and 0's above and below the main diagonal. The matrices at the right are in reduced row echelon form.

$$\begin{bmatrix} 1 & 0 & -2 \\ 0 & 1 & 3 \end{bmatrix}$$

$$x = -2$$
$$y = 3$$

The solution is $(-2, 3)$.

The advantage of having an augmented matrix in reduced row echelon form is that the corresponding system of equations is very easy to solve. The corresponding system of equations for each of the matrices at the right is shown below the matrix, along with the solution of the system of equations. The disadvantage, at least algebraically, is that it takes more steps to get the matrix in this form. However, a graphing calculator can be used to write a matrix in reduced row echelon form. Enter the augmented matrix into the calculator and then select the rref(function instead of ref(. Some sample screens are shown below.

$$\begin{bmatrix} 1 & 0 & 0 & 3 \\ 0 & 1 & 0 & -2 \\ 0 & 0 & 1 & 4 \end{bmatrix}$$

$$x = 3$$
$$y = -2$$
$$z = 4$$

The solution is $(3, -2, 4)$.

Enter the matrix. | *Select* **MATH** *under the* **MATRIX** *key.* | *Scroll through the options to find* rref(.

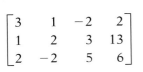 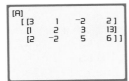 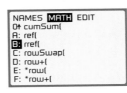 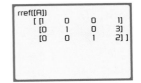

$$\begin{bmatrix} 3 & 1 & -2 & 2 \\ 1 & 2 & 3 & 13 \\ 2 & -2 & 5 & 6 \end{bmatrix}$$

$$\begin{bmatrix} 1 & 0 & 0 & 1 \\ 0 & 1 & 0 & 3 \\ 0 & 0 & 1 & 2 \end{bmatrix}$$

Find the reduced row echelon form for each matrix.

a. $\begin{bmatrix} 3 & 4 & 25 \\ 2 & 1 & 10 \end{bmatrix}$

b. $\begin{bmatrix} 3 & 2 & 16 \\ 2 & -3 & -11 \end{bmatrix}$

c. $\begin{bmatrix} 2 & 1 & -1 & 5 \\ 1 & 3 & 1 & 14 \\ 3 & -1 & 2 & 1 \end{bmatrix}$

d. $\begin{bmatrix} 2 & -3 & 7 & 0 \\ 1 & 4 & -4 & -2 \\ 3 & 2 & 5 & 1 \end{bmatrix}$

Solve the system of equations by finding the reduced row echelon form of the augmented matrix corresponding to the system of equations.

e. $2x - 5y = 13$
    $5x + 3y = 17$

f. $4x + 4y = 5$
    $2x - 8y = -5$

g. $5x + 3y - z = 5$
    $3x - 2y + 4z = 13$
    $4x + 3y + 5z = 22$

h. $3x - y - 2z = 11$
    $2x + y - 2z = 11$
    $x + 3y - z = 8$

SECTION **5.4**

Systems of Linear Inequalities

■ Graph the Solution Set of a System of Linear Inequalities

■ Graph the Solution Set of a System of Linear Inequalities

Two or more inequalities considered together are called a **system of inequalities.** The **solution set of a system of inequalities** is the intersection of the solution sets of the individual inequalities. To graph the solution set of a system of inequalities, first graph the solution set of each inequality. The solution set of the system of inequalities is the region of the plane represented by the intersection of the shaded areas.

➡ Graph the solution set: $\begin{array}{l} 2x - y \le 3 \\ 3x + 2y > 8 \end{array}$

Solve each inequality for y.

$$2x - y \le 3 \qquad\qquad 3x + 2y > 8$$
$$-y \le -2x + 3 \qquad\qquad 2y > -3x + 8$$
$$y \ge 2x - 3 \qquad\qquad y > -\frac{3}{2}x + 4$$

Graph $y = 2x - 3$ as a solid line. Because the inequality is $\ge$, shade above the line.

Graph $y = -\frac{3}{2}x + 4$ as a dashed line. Because the inequality is $>$, shade above the line.

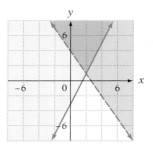

The solution set is the region of the plane represented by the intersection of the solution sets of the individual inequalities.

A graphing calculator can be used to draw the solution set of a system of inequalities. Begin as we have above by solving each equation for y.

$$y \ge 2x - 3$$
$$y > -\frac{3}{2}x + 4$$

See Appendix A: Inequalities

Use the Y= editor window to enter the expressions, and then choose shading above or below the graph. The solution set is the intersection of the solution sets of the individual inequalities. Some typical graphing calculator screens are shown at the right.

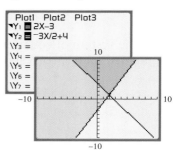

❓ QUESTION Is the point (3, 2) in the solution set of the system $\begin{array}{l} 3x + 4y \ge 12 \\ 3x - 4y \ge 4 \end{array}$?

❓ ANSWER $3(3) + 4(2) = 17 \ge 12$; $3(3) - 4(2) = 1 \not\ge 4$. No, since (3, 2) is not a solution of each inequality in the system, it is not in the solution set of the system of inequalities.

▼ *Point of Interest*

Large systems of inequalities containing over 200 inequalities have been used to solve application problems in such diverse areas as providing health care, analyzing the economies of developing countries, and protecting nuclear silos.

➡ Graph the solution set: $-x + 2y \geq 4$
$$x - 2y \geq 6$$

Solve each inequality for y.

$-x + 2y \geq 4$ $x - 2y \geq 6$

     $2y \geq x + 4$ $-2y \geq -x + 6$

       $y \geq \dfrac{1}{2}x + 2$ $y \leq \dfrac{1}{2}x - 3$

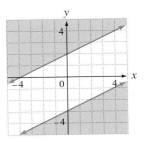

Graph $y = \frac{1}{2}x + 2$ as a solid line. Because the inequality is $\geq$, shade above the line.

Graph $y = \frac{1}{2}x - 3$ as a solid line. Because the inequality is $\leq$, shade below the line.

Because the solution sets of the two inequalities do not intersect, the solution set of the system of inequalities is the empty set. ⬅

EXAMPLE 1

Graph the solution set: $y \geq x - 1$
$$y < -2x$$

Solution   Shade the area above the solid line $y = x - 1$.

Shade the area below the dashed line $y = -2x$.

The solution of the system of inequalities is the intersection of the solution sets of the individual inequalities. A graphing calculator check is shown at the left.

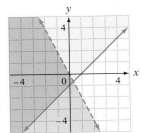

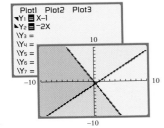

YOU TRY IT 1

Graph the solution set: $y \geq 2x - 3$
$$y > -3x$$

Solution   See page S23.

5.4 EXERCISES

Topics for Discussion

1. Explain how to find the solution set of a system of linear inequalities.

2. After graphing the inequalities in a system of inequalities, how do you determine the solution set of the system?

3. What must be true if an ordered pair is a solution of a system of linear inequalities?

4. If the solution set of a system of linear inequalities in two variables is the empty set, what can be said about the slopes of the lines of the corresponding linear equations?

■ Graph the Solution Set of a System of Linear Inequalities

Which ordered pair is a solution of the system of inequalities?

5. $2x - y < 4$
   $x - 3y \geq 6$
   a. $(5, 1)$ **b.** $(-3, -5)$

6. $3x - 2y \geq 6$
   $x + y < 5$
   a. $(-2, 3)$ **b.** $(3, -2)$

Graph the solution set.

7. $y \leq x - 3$
   $y \leq -x + 5$

8. $y > 2x - 4$
   $y < -x + 5$

9. $y > 3x - 3$
   $y \geq -2x + 2$

10. $x + 2y \leq 6$
    $x - y \leq 3$

11. $2x + y \geq -2$
    $6x + 3y \leq 6$

12. $x + y \geq 5$
    $3x + 3y \leq 6$

13. $3x - 2y < 6$
    $y \leq 3$

14. $x \leq 2$
    $3x + 2y > 4$

15. $y > 2x - 6$
    $x + y < 0$

16. $x < 3$
$y < -2$

17. $x + 1 \geq 0$
$y - 3 \leq 0$

18. $5x - 2y \geq 10$
$3x + 2y \geq 6$

19. $2x + y \geq 4$
$3x - 2y < 6$

20. $3x - 4y < 12$
$x + 2y < 6$

21. $x - 2y \leq 6$
$2x + 3y \leq 6$

22. $x - 3y > 6$
$2x + y > 5$

23. $x - 2y \leq 4$
$3x + 2y \leq 8$
$x > -1$

24. $3x - 2y < 0$
$5x + 3y > 9$
$y < 4$

25. $2x + 3y \leq 15$
$3x - y \leq 6$
$y \geq 0$

26. $x + y \leq 6$
$x - y \leq 2$
$x \geq 0$

27. $x - y \leq 5$
$2x - y \geq 6$
$y \geq 0$

28. $x - 3y \leq 6$
$5x - 2y \geq 4$
$y \geq 0$

29. $2x - y \leq 4$
$3x + y < 1$
$y \leq 0$

30. $x - 4 \leq y$
$2x + 3y > 6$
$x \geq 0$

Applying Concepts

Write a system of inequalities to represent the shaded region.

31.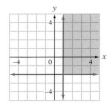

32.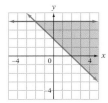

33.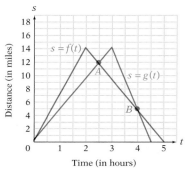

34.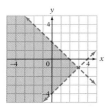

EXPLORATION

Analyzing Graphs of Two Functions

1. *Sports*   Cara and Daren begin from the same point on a bicycle trail and return to that point some time later. The blue graph at the right shows Cara's distance, in miles, from the starting point t hours after starting the trip. The graph in red shows the same information for Daren.

   a.   In which intervals on the t-axis is $f(t) \le g(t)$?
   b.   In which intervals on the t-axis is $f(t) \ge g(t)$?
   c.   Based on your answer to part a, when is Daren closer to the starting point than Cara?
   d.   Based on your answer to part b, when is Cara closer to the starting point than Daren?
   e.   In the context of this problem, what is the significance of the points labeled A and B?
   f.   How do points A and B differ in terms of Daren's and Cara's movement toward or away from the starting point?
   g.   Who returns to the starting point first?

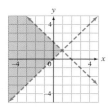

2. *Business*   When a company's income or revenue, R, exceeds its expenses or costs, C, the company has a profit. The graph at the right shows the revenue of a company and its costs to produce and sell n cell phones.

   a.   In which intervals on the n-axis is $f(n) \le g(n)$?
   b.   In which intervals on the n-axis is $f(n) \ge g(n)$?
   c.   Based on your answer to part a, how many cell phones should the company produce to be profitable?
   d.   At which points is the company "breaking even"? That is, at which points does revenue equal cost?
   e.   Is the *profit* greatest when $n = 250$, $n = 750$, or $n = 1000$?

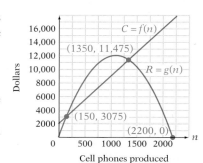

CHAPTER **5** *SUMMARY*

Key Terms

augmented matrix [p. 342]

dependent system of equations [p. 315]

element of a matrix [p. 341]

gaussian elimination method [p. 348]

inconsistent system of equations [p. 314]

independent system of equations [p. 314]

linear equation in three variables [p. 327]

main diagonal [p. 342]

matrix [p. 341]

ordered triples [p. 328]

order $m \times n$ or dimension of a matrix [p. 342]

row echelon form [p. 345]

solution of a system of equations in three variables [p. 313]

solution of a system of equations in two variables [p. 328]

solution of an equation in three variables [p. 329]

solution set of a system of inequalities [p. 360]

substitution method [p. 315]

system of equations [p. 313]

system of inequalities [p. 360]

system of linear equations in three variables [p. 313]

system of linear equations in two variables [p. 329]

three-dimensional coordinate system [p. 328]

xyz-coordinate system [p. 328]

Essential Concepts

Solve a system of equations by graphing:
Graph each equation and graphically determine the point of intersection. [p. 313]

Solve a system of equations by the substitution method:
Write one of the equations of the system in terms of x or y. Then substitute the variable expression for x or y into another equation of the system. [p. 315]

Solve a system of equations by the addition method:
Use the Multiplication Property of Equations to rewrite two equations in the system of equations so that the coefficients of one variable are additive inverses. Then add the two equations. [p. 325]

Elementary row operations on a matrix
1. Interchange two rows.
2. Multiply all the elements in a row by the same nonzero constant.
3. Replace a row by the sum of that row and a multiple of any other row. [p. 343]

Solve a system of equations by the Gaussian elimination method:
Write the system of equations as an augmented matrix. Then use the elementary row operations to write the augmented matrix in row echelon form. Use the substitution method to solve the system of equations corresponding to row echelon form. [p. 348]

CHAPTER **5** REVIEW EXERCISES

1. Solve by substitution: $2x - 6y = 15$
$$x = 4y + 8$$

2. Solve by the addition method: $3x + 2y = 2$
$$x + y = 3$$

3. Solve by graphing: $x + y = 3$
$$3x - 2y = -6$$

4. Solve by substitution: $2x - y = 4$
$$y = 2x - 4$$

5. Solve by the addition method: $5x - 15y = 30$
$$x - 3y = 6$$

6. Solve by the addition method: $3x - 4y - 2z = 17$
$$4x - 3y + 5z = 5$$
$$5x - 5y + 3z = 14$$

7. Solve by graphing: $2x - 3y = -6$
$$2x - y = 2$$

8. Write the augmented matrix for the system of equations shown at the right.
$$2x - 3y - z = 1$$
$$3x + \quad -4z = -2$$
$$4y - 5z = 0$$

9. Write the system of equations corresponding to the augmented matrix shown at the right.
$$\begin{bmatrix} 1 & 3 & 0 & | & -2 \\ 2 & -1 & 1 & | & 0 \\ 3 & 2 & -5 & | & 4 \end{bmatrix}$$

10. Write in row echelon form:
$$\begin{bmatrix} 3 & 6 & -3 & 9 \\ -3 & -5 & 1 & 4 \\ 2 & 3 & 5 & 2 \end{bmatrix}$$

11. Solve using the Gaussian elimination method:
$$2x + 5y = -1$$
$$3x - 4y = 10$$

12. Solve using the Gaussian elimination method:
$$3x + 2y = 5$$
$$4x + 5y = 2$$

13. Solve using the Gaussian elimination method:
$$x + 3y + z = 6$$
$$2x + y - z = 12$$
$$x + 2y - z = 13$$

14. Solve using the Gaussian elimination method:
$$x + y + z = 0$$
$$x + 2y + 3z = 5$$
$$2x + y + 2z = 3$$

15. Graph the solution set: $x + 3y \leq 6$
$$2x - y \geq 4$$

16. Graph the solution set: $2x + 4y \geq 8$
$$x + y \leq 3$$

17. A cabin cruiser traveling with the current went 60 miles in 3 hours. Against the current, it took 5 hours to travel the same distance. Find the rate of the cabin cruiser in calm water and the rate of the current.

18. A plane flying with the wind flew 600 miles in 3 hours. Flying against the wind, the plane required 4 hours to travel the same distance. Find the rate of the plane in calm air and the rate of the wind.

19. At a movie theater, admission tickets are $5 for children and $8 for adults. The receipts for one Friday evening were $2500. The next day there were three times as many children as the preceding evening and half the number of adults as the night before; the receipts were $2500. Find the number of children who attended the Friday evening show.

20. A chef wants to prepare a low-fat, low-sodium meal using lean meat, roasted potatoes, and green beans. A 1-ounce serving of meat contains 50 calories, 20 grams of protein, and 16 milligrams of sodium. A 1-ounce serving of potatoes contains 9 calories, 1 gram of protein, and 3 milligrams of sodium. A 1-ounce serving of green beans contains 12 calories, 2 grams of protein, and 17 milligrams of sodium. If the chef wants to prepare the meal that contains 243 calories, 73 grams of protein, and 131 milligrams of sodium, how many ounces of each ingredient should be prepared?

CHAPTER **5** TEST

1. Solve by substitution: $3x + 2y = 4$
$$x = 2y - 1$$

2. Solve by the addition method: $4x - 6y = 5$
$$6x - 9y = 4$$

3. Solve by graphing: $3x - y = 7$
$$2x + y = 3$$

4. Solve by substitution: $5x + 2y = -23$
$$2x + y = -10$$

5. Solve by the addition method: $4x - 12y = 12$
$$x - 3y = 3$$

6. Solve by the addition method: $3x + 2y + 2z = 2$
$$x - 2y - z = 1$$
$$2x - 3y - 3z = -3$$

7. Solve by graphing: $x - 2y = -5$
$$3x + 4y = -15$$

8. Write the augmented matrix for the system of equations shown at the right.
$$3x - y + 2z = 4$$
$$x + 4y = -1$$
$$5y - z = 3$$

9. Write the system of equations corresponding to the augmented matrix shown at the right.
$$\begin{bmatrix} 2 & -1 & 3 & | & 4 \\ 1 & 5 & -2 & | & 6 \\ -3 & 0 & -4 & | & 1 \end{bmatrix}$$

10. Write in row echelon form:
$$\begin{bmatrix} 2 & 3 & -2 \\ 4 & 1 & 1 \end{bmatrix}$$

11. Solve using the Gaussian elimination method:
$3x + 4y = -2$
$2x + 5y = 1$

12. Solve using the Gaussian elimination method:
$x - y = 3$
$2x + y = -4$

13. Solve using the Gaussian elimination method:
$x - y - z = 5$
$2x + z = 2$
$3y - 2z = 1$

14. Solve using the addition method:
$x - y + z = 2$
$2x - y - z = 1$
$x + 2y - 3z = -4$

15. Graph the solution set: $3x - 2y \geq 4$
$x + y < 3$

16. Graph the solution set: $x + y > 2$
$2x - y < -1$

17. A plane flying with the wind went 350 miles in 2 hours. The return trip, flying against the wind, took 2.8 hours. Find the rate of the plane in calm air and the rate of the wind.

18. A clothing manufacturer purchased 60 yards of cotton and 90 yards of wool for a total cost of $1800. Another purchase, at the same prices, included 80 yards of cotton and 20 yards of wool for a total cost of $1000. Find the cost per yard of the cotton and of the wool.

19. A motorboat traveling with the current went 80 miles in 4 hours. Against the current, it took 5 hours to travel the same distance. Find the rate of the motorboat in calm water and the rate of the current.

20. On a balance scale, a red block balances a green block and a blue block, 5 green blocks balance a red block and a blue block, and a yellow block balances a red block and a green block. If a blue block weighs 4 pounds, how much does a yellow block weigh?

◄ **CUMULATIVE REVIEW EXERCISES**

1. Let P represent the product of all the positive prime numbers less than 100. What is the units digit of the product P?

2. In a class election, one candidate received more than 94%, but less than 100%, of the votes cast. What is the least possible number of votes cast in the election?

3. Evaluate $1 + 3$, $1 + 3 + 5$, $1 + 3 + 5 + 7$, and $1 + 3 + 5 + 7 + 9$. Then use inductive reasoning to explain the pattern and use your reasoning to determine $1 + 3 + 5 + 7 + 9 + 11$.

4. Determine whether the following argument is an example of inductive or deductive reasoning. "All movies directed by Steven Spielberg are blockbusters. The movie *Saving Private Ryan* was directed by Steven Spielberg. Therefore, *Saving Private Ryan* was a blockbuster."

5. Find the range of $g(x) = x^2 - 4x$ given the domain $\{-3, -2, -1, 0, 1, 2, 3\}$.

6. Use a graphing calculator to graph $H(x) = 2x^2 - 4x + 1$ using the viewing window Xmin $= -4.7$, Xmax $= 4.7$, Xscl $= 1$, Ymin $= -5$, Ymax $= 5$, Yscl $= 1$. Then use the TRACE feature to find the two x-coordinates for the y-coordinate 1.

7. Find the x- and y-intercepts for the graph of the function $G(x) = x^3 + 5x^2 + 2x - 8$.

8. An architect charges a fee of $750 plus $3.50 per square foot to design a house. The equation that represents the architect's fee is $F = 3.50s + 750$, where F is the fee, in dollars, and s is the number of square feet in the house. Create an input/output table for this equation for increments of 100 square feet, beginning with $s = 1500$ and ending with $s = 2100$.

9. Solve: $3n = 4(n - 3) - (2n + 1)$

10. Solve and write the answer in interval notation: $3(2t - 1) \geq 5t - 3(t + 9)$

11. Solve and write the answer in set-builder notation: $7 < 4x - 5 < 19$

12. Solve: $|6 - 3x| - 5 = -2$

13. Find the equation of the line that passes through the points $(3, -2)$ and $(-1, 2)$.

14. Solve by the substitution method:
$4x - y = 11$
$3x - 5y = 21$

15. Solve by the addition method:
$3x - 5y = -1$
$4x + 3y = -11$

16. Solve by graphing: $4x - y = 8$
$2x + y = 4$

17. Write in row echelon form: $x - y + z = 1$
$2x + 3y - z = 3$
$-x + 2y - 4z = 4$

18. Solve using the Gaussian elimination method: $x - 2y + z = 5$
$3x - 2y - z = 3$
$4x + 5y - 4z = -9$

19.   The percent of the world's population living in rural areas is shown in the table (*Source:* Food and Agricultural Organization of the United Nations).

Year, x	1950	1960	1970	1980	1990	2000	2010*
Percent, y	70	66	63	61	57	52	48

*Projection

a.   Find the linear regression line for the data.

b.   Use the regression line to determine the percent of the world's population expected to be living in rural areas in 2020. Round to the nearest percent.

c.   Explain why the slope of the regression line indicates that the percent of the population living in rural areas is decreasing.

20.   Traveling with the current, a cruise ship sailed between two islands, a distance of 90 miles, in 3 hours. The return trip against the current required 4 hours and 30 minutes. Find the rate of the cruise ship in calm water and the rate of the current.

CHAPTER

6 Polynomials

6.1 Operations on Monomials and Scientific Notation

6.2 Addition and Subtraction of Polynomials

6.3 Multiplication and Division of Polynomials

```
6.01ᴇ⁻3
                    .00601
5.25ᴇ5
                    525000
```

Press 2nd EE and then the exponent on 10 to enter a number in scientific notation.

This is a photo of Mars as viewed from the Hubble telescope. Images such as this, transmitted to Earth, travel a distance of over 100 million miles. Distances this great, as well as very small measurements, are generally expressed in scientific notation, as illustrated in **Exercises 123 to 132 on pages 391 and 392**.

Need help? For online student resources, visit this web site: Math.college.hmco.com

PREP TEST

1. Simplify: $-4(3y)$

2. Simplify: $(-2)^3$

3. Simplify: $-4a - 8b + 7a$

4. Simplify: $3x - 2[y - 4(x + 1) + 5]$

5. Simplify: $-(x - y)$

GO FIGURE

You are planning a large dinner party. If you seat 5 people at each table, you end up with only 2 people at the last table. If you seat 3 people at each table, you have 9 people left over with no place to sit. There are fewer than 10 tables. How many guests are coming to the dinner party?

SECTION 6.1

- Addition and Subtraction of Monomials
- Multiplication of Monomials
- Division of Monomials
- Scientific Notation

Operations on Monomials and Scientific Notation

■ Addition and Subtraction of Monomials

The floorplan of a mobile home is shown below. All dimensions given are in feet. Not shown in the diagram is the fact that the height of each room is 8 feet.

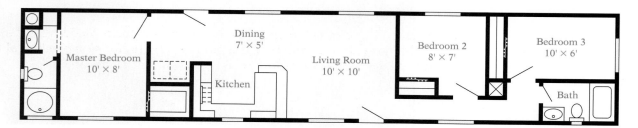

→ What is the combined length of the dining room and the living room?

The length of the dining room is 7 ft.

The length of the living room is 10 ft.

$$7 \text{ ft} + 10 \text{ ft} = 17 \text{ ft}$$

The combined length of the dining room and the living room is 17 ft. ←

→ What is the combined area of the two smaller bedrooms?

The area of bedroom 3 is 10 ft × 6 ft = 60 ft².

The area of bedroom 2 is 8 ft × 7 ft = 56 ft².

$$60 \text{ ft}^2 + 56 \text{ ft}^2 = 116 \text{ ft}^2$$

The combined area of the two smaller bedrooms is 116 ft². ←

⇒ What is the difference between the areas of the two smaller bedrooms?

$$60 \text{ ft}^2 - 56 \text{ ft}^2 = 4 \text{ ft}^2$$

The difference between the areas of the two smaller bedrooms is 4 ft². ⇐

As shown above, we can find the sum of two areas or the sum of two lengths. However, we cannot find the sum of an area and a length. For example, the area of the dining room is 7 ft × 5 ft = 35 ft². The length of the living room is 10 ft.

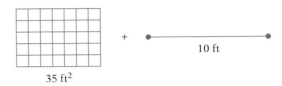

35 ft²   +   10 ft

The sum 35 ft² + 10 ft cannot be simplified.

Just as we cannot add square feet and feet, **we cannot add algebraic terms that do not have the same variable part. The same is true for subtraction.**

$$60x^2 + 56x^2 = 116x^2$$
$$60x^2 - 56x^2 = 4x^2$$

- Both $60x^2$ and $56x^2$ have the same variable part: x^2. Add or subtract the coefficients; the variable part stays the same.

$$35x^2 + 10x$$

- $35x^2$ and $10x$ do not have the same variable part. The terms cannot be combined.

When adding and subtracting like terms, we are actually adding and subtracting monomials. A **monomial** is a number, a variable, or a product of a number and variables. For instance.

7	b	$\dfrac{2}{3}a$	$12xy^2$
A number	A variable	A product of a number and a variable	A product of a number and variables

The expression $3\sqrt{x}$ is not a monomial because $\sqrt{x}$ cannot be written as a product of variables.

The expression $\dfrac{2x}{y^2}$ is not a monomial because it is a quotient of variables.

TAKE NOTE

Addition of monomials involves using the distributive property:
$14x^3y^2z + 8x^3y^2z + 7x^3y^2z$
$= (14 + 8 + 7)x^3y^2z$
$= 29x^3y^2z$

EXAMPLE 1

Simplify: $14x^3y^2z + 8x^3y^2z + 7x^3y^2z$

Solution　$14x^3y^2z + 8x^3y^2z + 7x^3y^2z$

$= 29x^3y^2z$

• The terms have the same variable part. Add the coefficients. The variable part stays the same.

YOU TRY IT 1

Simplify: $16a^4b^3 + 10a^4b^3 + 5a^4b^3$

Solution　See page S23.

EXAMPLE 2

Simplify: $29c^4d^5 - 6c^4d^5$

Solution　$29c^4d^5 - 6c^4d^5$

$= 23c^4d^5$

• The terms have the same variable part. Subtract the coefficients. The variable part stays the same.

YOU TRY IT 2

Simplify: $37m^3n^2p - 14m^3n^2p$

Solution　See page S23.

■ Multiplication of Monomials

➡ What is the volume of air that must be heated in the master bedroom of the mobile home pictured at the beginning of this section? Note that the height of each room is 8 ft.

The volume of air in the master bedroom = 10 ft × 8 ft × 8 ft

= (10 ft × 8 ft) × 8 ft

= 80 ft² × 8 ft

= 640 ft³

There is 640 ft³ of air to heat in the master bedroom.　⬅

This illustrates that we can multiply square feet by feet. The result is cubic feet, or volume.

Let's look at multiplication with monomials.

Recall that the exponential expression 3^4 means to multiply 3, the base, 4 times.

Therefore, $3^4 = 3 \cdot 3 \cdot 3 \cdot 3 = 81$. For the variable exponential expression x^6, x is the base and 6 is the exponent. **The exponent indicates the number of times the base occurs as a factor.** Therefore,

$$\overbrace{x^6 = x \cdot x \cdot x \cdot x \cdot x \cdot x}^{\text{Multiply } x \text{ 6 times}}$$

▼ **Point of Interest**

A billion, which is 10^9, is too large a number for most of us to comprehend. If a computer were to start counting from 1 to 1 billion, writing to the screen one number every second of every day, it would take over 31 years for the computer to complete the task.

And if a billion is a large number, consider a googol. A googol is 1 with 100 zeros after it, or 10^{100}. Edward Kasner is the mathematician credited with thinking up this number, and his nine-year-old nephew is said to have thought up the name. The two then coined the word googolplex, which is 10^{googol}.

The product of exponential expressions with the *same* base can be simplified by writing each expression in factored form and writing the result with an exponent.

$$x^3 \cdot x^2 = \overbrace{(x \cdot x \cdot x)}^{3 \text{ factors}} \cdot \overbrace{(x \cdot x)}^{2 \text{ factors}}$$

$$\underbrace{\qquad\qquad\qquad}_{5 \text{ factors}}$$

$$= x \cdot x \cdot x \cdot x \cdot x$$
$$= x^5$$

Note that adding the exponents results in the same product.

$$x^3 \cdot x^2 = x^{3+2} = x^5$$

This suggests the following rule for multiplying exponential expressions.

> **Rule for Multiplying Exponential Expressions**
> If m and n are positive integers, then $x^m \cdot x^n = x^{m+n}$.

EXAMPLE 3

Simplify: $a^4 \cdot a^5$

Solution $a^4 \cdot a^5 = a^{4+5} = a^9$ • The bases are the same. Add the exponents.

YOU TRY IT 3

Simplify: $t^3 \cdot t^8$

Solution   See page S23.

EXAMPLE 4

Simplify: $c^3 \cdot c^4 \cdot c$

Solution $c^3 \cdot c^4 \cdot c = c^{3+4+1}$ • The bases are the same. Add the exponents. Note that $c = c^1$.

$$= c^8$$

YOU TRY IT 4

Simplify: $n^6 \cdot n \cdot n^2$

Solution   See page S23.

❓ QUESTION   Why can the exponential expression x^5y^3 not be simplified?

❓ ANSWER   The bases are not the same. The Rule for Multiplying Exponential Expressions applies only to expressions with the *same* base.

EXAMPLE 5

Simplify: $(a^3b^2)(a^4)$

Solution $(a^3b^2)(a^4) = a^{3+4}b^2$ • Multiply variables with the same
   $= a^7b^2$ base by adding the exponents.

YOU TRY IT 5

Simplify: $c^9(c^5d^8)$

Solution   See page S23.

EXAMPLE 6

Simplify: $(4x^3)(2x^6)$

Solution $(4x^3)(2x^6) = (4 \cdot 2)(x^3 \cdot x^6)$ • Use the Commutative and Associative Properties of Multiplication to
group the coefficients and variables
with the same base.

   $= 8x^{3+6}$ • Multiply the coefficients. Multiply
   $= 8x^9$ variables with the same base by
adding the exponents.

YOU TRY IT 6

Simplify: $(5y^4)(3y^2)$

Solution   See page S23.

EXAMPLE 7

Simplify: $(-2v^3z^5)(7v^2z^6)$

Solution $(-2v^3z^5)(7v^2z^6)$
   $= [-2(7)](v^{3+2})(z^{5+6})$ • Multiply the coefficients of the
monomials. Multiply variables
with the same base by adding
the exponents.
   $= -14v^5z^{11}$

YOU TRY IT 7

Simplify: $(12p^4q^3)(-3p^5q^2)$

Solution   See page S23.

> **TAKE NOTE**
>
> Note on page 378 that
> 10 ft × 8 ft × 8 ft
> = (10 · 8 · 8) (ft · ft · ft)
> = 640 (ft^{1+1+1})
> = 640 ft^3

The expression $(x^4)^3$ is an example of a *power of a monomial*; the monomial x^4 is raised to a power of 3.

The power of a monomial can be simplified by writing the power in factored form and then using the Rule for Multiplying Exponential Expressions.

$(x^4)^3 = x^4 \cdot x^4 \cdot x^4$
$= x^{4+4+4} = x^{12}$

Note that multiplying the exponent inside the parentheses by the exponent outside the parentheses results in the same product.

$(x^4)^3 = x^{4 \cdot 3} = x^{12}$

This suggests the following rule for simplifying powers of monomials.

> **Rule for Simplifying the Power of an Exponential Expression**
> If m and n are positive integers, then $(x^m)^n = x^{m \cdot n}$.

? QUESTION   Which expression is the multiplication of two exponential expressions and which is the power of an exponential expression?*

a. $q^4 \cdot q^{10}$ **b.** $(q^4)^{10}$

EXAMPLE 8

Simplify: $(z^2)^5$

Solution $(z^2)^5 = z^{2 \cdot 5} = z^{10}$ • z^2 is raised to the power of 5. Simplify the power of an exponential expression by multiplying the exponents.

YOU TRY IT 8

Simplify: $(t^3)^6$

Solution   See page S24.

TAKE NOTE

$(a^2b^3)^2$ is a *product* of exponential expressions raised to a power, whereas $(a^2 + b^3)^2$ is a *sum* of exponential expressions raised to a power. These two expressions are not simplified in the same manner.

The expression $(a^2b^3)^2$ is the *power of the product* of two exponential expressions, a^2 and b^3. The power of the product of exponential expressions can be simplified by writing the product in factored form and then using the Rule for Multiplying Exponential Expressions.

Write the exponential expression in factored form. Use the Rule for Multiplying Exponential Expressions.

$$(a^2b^3)^2 = (a^2b^3)(a^2b^3)$$
$$= a^{2+2}b^{3+3}$$
$$= a^4b^6$$

Note that multiplying each exponent inside the parentheses by the exponent outside the parentheses results in the same product.

$$(a^2b^3)^2 = a^{2 \cdot 2}b^{3 \cdot 2}$$
$$= a^4b^6$$

> **Rule for Simplifying Powers of Products**
> If m, n, and p are positive integers, then $(x^my^n)^p = x^{m \cdot p}y^{n \cdot p}$.

? QUESTION   In the expression $(a^8b^6)^5$, what is the product and what is the power?†

? ANSWERS   *a. This is the multiplication of two exponential expressions. q^4 is multiplied times q^{10}.   **b.** This is the power of an exponential expression. q^4 is raised to the 10th power.
† The product is a^8b^6; a^8 is multiplied times b^6. The power is 5; a^8b^6 is raised to the 5th power.

EXAMPLE 9

Simplify: $(x^4y)^6$

Solution $(x^4y)^6 = x^{4\cdot6}y^{1\cdot6}$ • Multiply each exponent inside the parentheses by the exponent outside the parentheses. Remember that $y = y^1$.

$= x^{24}y^6$

YOU TRY IT 9

Simplify: $(bc^7)^8$

Solution See page S24.

EXAMPLE 10

Simplify: $(5z^3)^2$

Solution $(5z^3)^2 = 5^{1\cdot2}z^{3\cdot2}$ • Multiply each exponent inside the parentheses by the exponent outside the parentheses. Note that $5 = 5^1$.

$= 5^2z^6$

$= 25z^6$ • Evaluate 5^2.

YOU TRY IT 10

Simplify: $(4y^6)^3$

Solution See page S24.

EXAMPLE 11

Simplify: $(3m^5p^2)^4$

Solution $(3m^5p^2)^4 = 3^{1\cdot4}m^{5\cdot4}p^{2\cdot4}$ • Multiply each exponent inside the parentheses by the exponent outside the parentheses.

$= 3^4m^{20}p^8$

$= 81m^{20}p^8$ • Evaluate 3^4.

YOU TRY IT 11

Simplify: $(2v^6w^9)^5$

Solution See page S24.

EXAMPLE 12

Simplify: $(-a^5b^8)^6$

Solution $(-a^5b^8)^6 = (-1)^{1\cdot6}a^{5\cdot6}b^{8\cdot6}$ • Multiply each exponent inside the parentheses by the exponent outside the parentheses. Note that $-a^5b^8 = -1a^5b^8 = (-1)^1a^5b^8$.

$= (-1)^6a^{30}b^{48}$

$= a^{30}b^{48}$ • Evaluate $(-1)^6$. $(-1)^6 = 1$.

YOU TRY IT 12

Simplify: $(-2x^3y^7)^3$

Solution See page S24.

In some products, it is necessary to use the Rule for Simplifying Powers of Products and the Rule for Multiplying Exponential Expressions.

➡ Simplify: $(3x^4)^2 (4x^3)$

$$(3x^4)^2(4x^3) = (3^{1 \cdot 2}x^{4 \cdot 2})(4x^3)$$ • Use the Rule for Simplifying Powers of Products to simplify $(3x^4)^2$.

$$= (3^2x^8)(4x^3)$$

$$= (9x^8)(4x^3)$$

$$= (9 \cdot 4)(x^8 \cdot x^3)$$ • Use the Rule for Multiplying Exponential Expressions.

$$= 36x^{8+3}$$

$$= 36x^{11}$$

⬅

EXAMPLE 13

Simplify: $(2a^2b)(2a^3b^2)^3$

Solution $(2a^2b)(2a^3b^2)^3$

$$= (2a^2b)(2^{1 \cdot 3}a^{3 \cdot 3}b^{2 \cdot 3})$$ • Use the Rule for Simplifying Powers of Products.

$$= (2a^2b)(2^3a^9b^6)$$

$$= (2a^2b)(8a^9b^6)$$

$$= (2 \cdot 8)(a^{2+9})(b^{1+6})$$ • Use the Rule for Multiplying Exponential Expressions.

$$= 16a^{11}b^7$$

YOU TRY IT 13

Simplify: $(-xy^4)(-2x^3y^2)^2$

Solution   See page S24.

■ Division of Monomials

The quotient of two exponential expressions with the *same* base can be simplified by writing each expression in factored form, dividing by the common factors, and then writing the result with an exponent.

$$\frac{x^6}{x^2} = \frac{\overset{1}{\cancel{x}} \cdot \overset{1}{\cancel{x}} \cdot x \cdot x \cdot x \cdot x}{\underset{1}{\cancel{x}} \cdot \underset{1}{\cancel{x}}} = x^4$$

Note that subtracting the exponents results in the same quotient.

$$\frac{x^6}{x^2} = x^{6-2} = x^4$$

This example suggests that to divide monomials with like bases, we subtract the exponents.

Rule for Dividing Exponential Expressions

If m and n are positive integers and $x \neq 0$, then $\dfrac{x^m}{x^n} = x^{m-n}$.

EXAMPLE 14

Simplify: $\dfrac{c^8}{c^5}$

Solution $\dfrac{c^8}{c^5} = c^{8-5}$ • The bases are the same. Subtract the exponents.

$\qquad\qquad = c^3$

YOU TRY IT 14

Simplify: $\dfrac{t^{10}}{t^4}$

Solution See page S24.

? QUESTION   Why can the expression $\dfrac{x^8}{y^2}$ not be simplified?

EXAMPLE 15

Simplify: $\dfrac{x^5 y^7}{x^4 y^2}$

Solution $\dfrac{x^5 y^7}{x^4 y^2} = x^{5-4} \cdot y^{7-2}$ • Use the Rule for Dividing Exponential Expressions by subtracting the exponents of like bases. Note that $x^{5-4} = x^1$, but the exponent 1 is not written.

$\qquad\qquad = xy^5$

YOU TRY IT 15

Simplify: $\dfrac{a^7 b^6}{ab^3}$

Solution See page S24.

The expression at the right has been simplified in two ways: by dividing by common factors, and by using the Rule for Dividing Exponential Expressions.

$$\frac{x^3}{x^3} = \frac{\overset{1}{\cancel{x}} \cdot \overset{1}{\cancel{x}} \cdot \overset{1}{\cancel{x}}}{\underset{1}{\cancel{x}} \cdot \underset{1}{\cancel{x}} \cdot \underset{1}{\cancel{x}}} = 1$$

Because $\frac{x^3}{x^3} = 1$ and $\frac{x^3}{x^3} = x^0$, 1 must equal x^0. Therefore, the following definition of zero as an exponent is used.

$$\frac{x^3}{x^3} = x^{3-3} = x^0$$

Zero as an Exponent

If $x \neq 0$, then $x^0 = 1$. The expression 0^0 is undefined.

? ANSWER   The bases are not the same. The Rule for Dividing Exponential Expressions applies only to expressions with the *same* base.

EXAMPLE 16

Simplify: $(-15y^4)^0$, $y \neq 0$

Solution $(-15y^4)^0 = 1$ • Any nonzero expression to the zero power is 1.

YOU TRY IT 16

Simplify: $(-8x^2y^7)^0$

Solution   See page S24.

EXAMPLE 17

Simplify: $-(6r^3t^2)^0$, $r \neq 0$, $t \neq 0$

Solution $-(6r^3t^2)^0 = -1$ • $(6r^3t^2)^0 = 1$. The negative sign in front of the parentheses can be read "the opposite of." The opposite of 1 is -1.

YOU TRY IT 17

Simplify: $-(9c^7d^4)^0$, $c \neq 0$, $d \neq 0$

Solution   See page S24.

The expression at the right has been simplified in two ways: by dividing by common factors, and by using the Rule for Dividing Exponential Expressions.

$$\frac{x^3}{x^5} = \frac{\overset{1}{\cancel{x}} \cdot \overset{1}{\cancel{x}} \cdot \overset{1}{\cancel{x}}}{\underset{1}{\cancel{x}} \cdot \underset{1}{\cancel{x}} \cdot \underset{1}{\cancel{x}} \cdot x \cdot x} = \frac{1}{x^2}$$

Because $\frac{x^3}{x^5} = \frac{1}{x^2}$ and $\frac{x^3}{x^5} = x^{-2}$, $\frac{1}{x^2}$ must equal x^{-2}. Therefore, the following definition of a negative exponent is used.

$$\frac{x^3}{x^5} = x^{3-5} = x^{-2}$$

Definition of Negative Exponents

If n is a positive integer and $x \neq 0$, then $x^{-n} = \frac{1}{x^n}$ and $\frac{1}{x^{-n}} = x^n$.

An exponential expression is in simplest form when there are no negative exponents in the expression.

➡ Simplify: y^{-7}

$y^{-7} = \dfrac{1}{y^7}$ • Use the Definition of Negative Exponents to rewrite the expression with a positive exponent.

➡ Simplify: $\dfrac{1}{c^{-4}}$

$\dfrac{1}{c^{-4}} = c^4$ • Use the Definition of Negative Exponents to rewrite the expression with a positive exponent.

QUESTION: How are **a.** b^{-8} and **b.** $\frac{1}{w^{-5}}$ rewritten with positive exponents?

EXAMPLE 18

Simplify: $\dfrac{3n^{-5}}{4}$

Solution $\dfrac{3n^{-5}}{4} = \dfrac{3}{4}n^{-5} = \dfrac{3}{4} \cdot \dfrac{1}{n^5}$

$= \dfrac{3}{4n^5}$

• Use the Definition of Negative Exponents to rewrite the expression with a positive exponent.

YOU TRY IT 18

Simplify: $\dfrac{2}{c^{-4}}$

Solution See page S24.

> **TAKE NOTE**
>
> Note from the example at the right that 2^{-3} is a *positive* number. A negative exponent does not indicate a negative number.

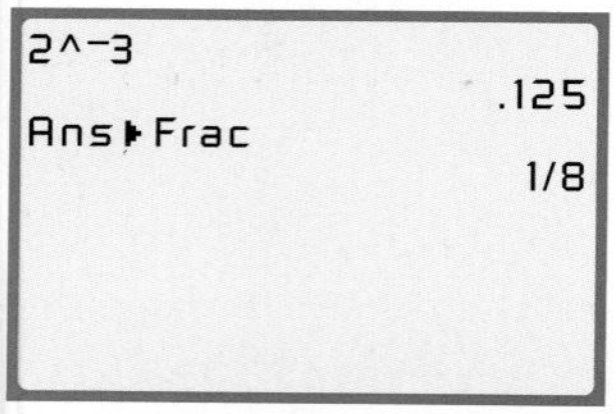
2^-3
.125
Ans▸Frac
1/8

A numerical expression with a negative exponent can be evaluated by first rewriting the expression with a positive exponent.

➡ Evaluate: 2^{-3}

$2^{-3} = \dfrac{1}{2^3}$ • Use the Definition of Negative Exponents to rewrite the expression with a positive exponent.

$= \dfrac{1}{8}$ • Evaluate 2^3,

This answer can be checked using a calculator, as shown at the left. Note that $0.125 = \frac{1}{8}$.

Sometimes applying the Rule for Dividing Exponential Expressions results in a quotient that contains a negative exponent. If this happens, use the Definition of Negative Exponents to rewrite the expression with a positive exponent.

➡ Simplify: $\dfrac{6x^2}{8x^9}$

$\dfrac{6x^2}{8x^9} = \dfrac{3x^2}{4x^9} = \dfrac{3x^{2-9}}{4}$ • Divide the coefficients by their common factors. Then use the Rule for Dividing Exponential Expressions.

$= \dfrac{3x^{-7}}{4} = \dfrac{3}{4} \cdot \dfrac{x^{-7}}{1} = \dfrac{3}{4} \cdot \dfrac{1}{x^7}$ • Rewrite the expression with only positive exponents.

$= \dfrac{3}{4x^7}$

ANSWERS **a.** $b^{-8} = \frac{1}{b^8}$ **b.** $\frac{1}{w^{-5}} = w^5$

EXAMPLE 19

Simplify: $\dfrac{-35a^6b^{-2}}{25a^{-3}b^5}$

Solution $\dfrac{-35a^6b^{-2}}{25a^{-3}b^5} = -\dfrac{7a^6b^{-2}}{5a^{-3}b^5} = -\dfrac{7a^{6-(-3)}b^{-2-5}}{5} = -\dfrac{7a^9b^{-7}}{5} = -\dfrac{7a^9}{5b^7}$

YOU TRY IT 19

Simplify: $\dfrac{12x^{-8}y}{-16xy^{-3}}$

Solution   See page S24.

The expression $\left(\dfrac{x^3}{y^4}\right)^2$ is the *power of the quotient* of two exponential expressions, x^3 and y^4. This expression can be simplified by squaring $\dfrac{x^3}{y^3}$—that is, by multiplying each exponent in the quotient by the exponent outside the parentheses.

$$\left(\dfrac{x^3}{y^4}\right) = \left(\dfrac{x^3}{y^4}\right)\left(\dfrac{x^3}{y^4}\right) = \dfrac{x^3 \cdot x^3}{y^4 \cdot y^4} = \dfrac{x^{3+3}}{y^{4+4}} = \dfrac{x^6}{x^8} \qquad \left(\dfrac{x^3}{y^4}\right)^2 = \dfrac{x^{3\cdot2}}{y^{4\cdot2}} = \dfrac{x^6}{y^8}$$

TAKE NOTE

The Rule for Simplifying Powers of Products states that we can multiply each exponent in the product by the exponent outside the parentheses.

$$(x^m y^n)^p = x^{m \cdot p} y^{n \cdot p}$$

The Rule for Simplifying Powers of Quotients states that we can multiply each exponent in the quotient by the exponent outside the parentheses.

$$\left(\dfrac{x^m}{y^n}\right)^p = \dfrac{x^{m \cdot p}}{y^{n \cdot p}}$$

Rule for Simplifying Powers of Quotients

If m, n, and p are integers and $y \neq 0$, then $\left(\dfrac{x^m}{y^n}\right)^p = \dfrac{x^{m \cdot p}}{y^{n \cdot p}}$.

? **QUESTION**   In the expression $\left(\dfrac{c^4}{d^6}\right)^5$, what is the quotient and what is the power?

EXAMPLE 20

Simplify: $\left(\dfrac{a^4}{b^3}\right)^{-2}$

Solution $\left(\dfrac{a^4}{b^3}\right)^{-2} = \dfrac{a^{4(-2)}}{b^{3(-2)}} = \dfrac{a^{-8}}{b^{-6}}$

- Multiply each exponent inside the parentheses by the exponent outside the parentheses.
- Rewrite the expression with positive exponents.

$$= \dfrac{b^6}{a^8}$$

YOU TRY IT 20

Simplify: $\left(\dfrac{m^{-6}}{n^{-8}}\right)^3$

Solution   See page S24.

? ANSWER   The quotient is $\dfrac{c^4}{d^6}$; c^4 is divided by d^6. The power is 5; $\dfrac{c^4}{d^6}$ is raised to the 5th power.

The rules for simplifying exponential expressions and powers of exponential expressions apply to all integers. These rules are restated here.

Rules of Exponents

If m, n, and p are integers, then

$$x^m \cdot x^n = x^{m+n} \qquad (x^m)^n = x^{m \cdot n} \qquad (x^m y^n)^p = x^{m \cdot p} y^{n \cdot p}$$

$$\frac{x^m}{x^n} = x^{m-n}, x \neq 0 \qquad \left(\frac{x^m}{y^n}\right)^p = \frac{x^{m \cdot p}}{y^{n \cdot p}}, y \neq 0 \qquad x^{-n} = \frac{1}{x^n}, \frac{1}{x^{-n}} = x^n, x \neq 0$$

$$x^0 = 1, x \neq 0$$

Simplifying the expressions in Example 21 requires a combination of the rules of exponents.

EXAMPLE 21

Simplify. **a.** $(-2x)(3x^{-2})^{-3}$ **b.** $\left(\dfrac{3a^2 b^{-1}}{27a^{-3} b^{-4}}\right)^{-2}$

Solution

a. $(-2x)(3x^{-2})^{-3}$

$= (-2x)(3^{-3}x^6)$

$= \dfrac{-2x \cdot x^6}{3^3}$

$= -\dfrac{2x^7}{27}$

- Use the Rule for Simplifying Powers of Products.
- Write the expression with positive exponents.
- Use the Rule for Multiplying Exponential Expressions. Simplify 3^3.

b. $\left(\dfrac{3a^2 b^{-1}}{27a^{-3} b^{-4}}\right)^{-2}$

$= \left(\dfrac{a^2 b^{-1}}{9a^{-3} b^{-4}}\right)^{-2}$

$= \dfrac{a^{2(-2)}b^{(-1)(-2)}}{9^{1(-2)}a^{(-3)(-2)}b^{(-4)(-2)}}$

$= \dfrac{a^{-4}b^2}{9^{-2}a^6 b^8}$

$= 9^2 a^{-4-6} b^{2-8}$

$= 81a^{-10} b^{-6} = \dfrac{81}{a^{10}b^6}$

- Simplify $\frac{3}{27}$.
- Use the Rule for Simplifying Powers of Quotients.
- Simplify and rewrite the expression with positive exponents.

YOU TRY IT 21

Simplify: **a.** $(-2ab)(2a^3 b^{-2})^{-3}$ **b.** $\left(\dfrac{2x^2 y^{-4}}{4x^{-2} y^{-5}}\right)^{-3}$

Solution   See page S24.

■ Scientific Notation

Very large and very small numbers are encountered in the fields of science and engineering. For example, the charge of an electron is

0.0000000000000000000160 coulomb.

These numbers can be written more easily in scientific notation. **In scientific notation, a number is expressed as a product of two factors, one a number between 1 and 10 and the other a power of 10.**

To change a number written in decimal notation to one written in scientific notation, write it in the form $a \times 10^n$, where $1 \le a < 10$ and n is an integer.

For numbers greater than 10, move the decimal point to the right of the first digit. The exponent n is positive and equal to the number of places the decimal point has been moved.

$$240{,}000 = 2.4 \times 10^5$$

$$93{,}000{,}000 = 9.3 \times 10^7$$

For numbers less than 1, move the decimal point to the right of the first nonzero digit. The exponent n is negative. The absolute value of the exponent is equal to the number of places the decimal point has been moved.

$$0.00030 = 3.0 \times 10^{-4}$$

$$0.0000832 = 8.32 \times 10^{-5}$$

Look at the last example above: $0.0000832 = 8.32 \times 10^{-5}$. Using the Definition of Negative Exponents,

$$10^{-5} = \frac{1}{10^5} = \frac{1}{100{,}000} = 0.00001$$

Because $10^{-5} = 0.00001$, we can write

$$8.32 \times 10^{-5} = 8.32 \times 0.00001 = 0.0000832$$

which is the number we started with. We have not changed the value of the number; we have just written it in another form.

EXAMPLE 22

Write the number in scientific notation.

a. 824,300,000,000   **b.** 0.000000961

Solution

a. $824{,}300{,}000{,}000 = 8.243 \times 10^{11}$

Graphical check:

- Move the decimal point 11 places to the left. The exponent on 10 is 11.
- Note how a graphing calculator writes a number in scientific notation. It displays the number between 1 and 10, followed by E, and then the exponent on 10.

b. $0.000000961 = 9.61 \times 10^{-7}$

- Move the decimal point 7 places to the right. The exponent on 10 is -7.

Graphical check: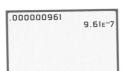

- 9.61E-7 represents 9.61×10^{-7}. The answer checks.

YOU TRY IT 22

Write the number in scientific notation.

a. 57,000,000,000   **b.** 0.000000017

Solution   See page S24.

Changing a number written in scientific notation to decimal notation also requires moving the decimal point.

When the exponent on 10 is positive, move the decimal point to the right the same number of places as the exponent.

$$3.45 \times 10^9 = 3,450,000,000$$

$$2.3 \times 10^8 = 230,000,000$$

When the exponent on 10 is negative, move the decimal point to the left the same number of places as the absolute value of the exponent.

$$8.1 \times 10^{-3} = 0.0081$$

$$6.34 \times 10^{-6} = 0.00000634$$

EXAMPLE 23

Write the number in decimal notation.

a. 7.329×10^6 **b.** 6.8×10^{-10}

Solution

a. $7.329 \times 10^6 = 7,329,000$

- The exponent on 10 is positive. Move the decimal point 6 places to the right.

Graphical check:

- Enter into a graphing calculator the number 7.329×10^6, in scientific notation. The calculator will return the number in decimal notation.

See Appendix A: Scientific Notation

b. $6.8 \times 10^{-10} = 0.00000000068$

- The exponent on 10 is negative. Move the decimal point 10 places to the left.

Graphical check:

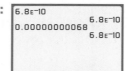

- If you enter 6.8E-10, the calculator returns 6.8E-10. Instead, enter the answer .00000000068 and check that the calculator displays the given expression, 6.8×10^{-10}.

YOU TRY IT 23

Write the number in decimal notation.

a. 5×10^{12} **b.** 4.0162×10^{-9}

Solution   See page S24.

? QUESTION   Is the expression written in scientific notation?

   a. 2.84×10^{-4} **b.** 36.5×10^{7} **c.** 0.91×10^{-12}

The rules for multiplying and dividing with numbers in scientific notation are the same as those for operating on algebraic expressions. The power of 10 corresponds to the variable part and the number between 1 and 10 corresponds to the coefficient of the variable.

	Algebraic Expressions	Scientific Notation
Multiplication	$(4x^{-3})(2x^{5}) = 8x^{2}$	$(4 \times 10^{-3})(2 \times 10^{5}) = 8 \times 10^{2}$
Division	$\dfrac{6x^{5}}{3x^{-2}} = 2x^{5-(-2)} = 2x^{7}$	$\dfrac{6 \times 10^{5}}{3 \times 10^{-2}} = 2 \times 10^{5-(-2)} = 2 \times 10^{7}$

EXAMPLE 24

Multiply or divide. **a.** $(3.0 \times 10^{5})(1.1 \times 10^{-8})$ **b.** $\dfrac{7.2 \times 10^{13}}{2.4 \times 10^{-3}}$

Solution

a. $(3.0 \times 10^{5})(1.1 \times 10^{-8}) = 3.3 \times 10^{-3}$

- Multiply 3.0 times 1.1. Add the exponents on 10.

Graphical check:

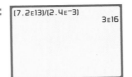

- The calculator returns the answer in decimal notation, .0033. The number .0033 in scientific notation is 3.3×10^{-3}. The answer checks.

b. $\dfrac{7.2 \times 10^{13}}{2.4 \times 10^{-3}} = 3 \times 10^{16}$

- Divide 7.2 by 2.4. Subtract the exponents on 10.

Graphical check: (7.2E13)/(2.4E⁻3)   3E16

- 3E16 represents 3×10^{16}. The answer checks.

YOU TRY IT 24

Multiply or divide.

a. $(2.4 \times 10^{-9})(1.6 \times 10^{3})$ **b.** $\dfrac{5.4 \times 10^{-2}}{1.8 \times 10^{-4}}$

Solution   See page S24.

? ANSWERS   **a.** 2.84×10^{-4} is written in scientific notation.   **b.** 36.5×10^{7} is not written in scientific notation. 36.5 is not a number between 1 and 10.   **c.** 0.91×10^{-12} is not written in scientific notation. 0.91 is not a number between 1 and 10.

6.1 EXERCISES

Topics for Discussion

1. Explain why each of the following is or is not a monomial.

   a. $32a^3b$

   b. $\dfrac{5n^3}{7}$

   c. $\dfrac{6c^4}{25d}$

2. Explain each of the following. Provide an example of each.

   a. The Rule for Multiplying Exponential Expressions

   b. The Rule for Simplifying the Power of an Exponential Expression

   c. The Rule for Simplifying Powers of Products

   d. The Rule for Dividing Exponential Expressions

   e. The Rule for Simplifying Powers of Quotients

3. Explain the error in each of the following. Then correct the error.

   a. $6x^{-3} = \dfrac{1}{6x^3}$

   b. $xy^{-2} = \dfrac{1}{xy^2}$

   c. $\dfrac{1}{8a^{-4}} = 8a^4$

   d. $\dfrac{1}{b^{-5}c} = b^5c$

4. In your own words, explain how you know that a number is written in scientific notation.

Operations on Monomials

Simplify.

5. $a^4 \cdot a^5$

6. $y^5 \cdot y^8$

7. $z^3 \cdot z \cdot z^4$

8. $b \cdot b^2 \cdot b^6$

9. $(x^3)^5$

10. $(b^2)^4$

11. $(x^2y^3)^6$

12. $(m^4n^2)^3$

13. $12s^4t^3 + 5s^4t^3$

14. $8b^6c^5 + 9b^6c^5$

15. 27^0

16. $-(17)^0$

17. $\dfrac{a^8}{a^2}$

18. $\dfrac{c^{12}}{c^5}$

19. $(-m^3n)(m^6n^2)$

20. $(-r^4t^3)(r^2t^9)$

21. $(2x)(3x^2)(4x^4)$

22. $(5a^2)(4a)(3a^5)$

23. $(-2a^2)^3$

24. $(-3b^3)^2$

25. $11p^4q^5 - 7p^4q^5$

26. $16c^2d^3 - 9c^2d^3$

27. $(6r^2)(-4r)$

28. $(7v^3)(-2v)$

29. $(2a^3bc^2)^3$

30. $(4xy^3z^2)^2$

31. $\dfrac{m^4n^7}{m^3n^5}$

32. $\dfrac{a^5b^6}{a^3b^2}$

33. $(3x)^0$

34. $(2a)^0$

35. $\dfrac{-16a^7}{24a^6}$

36. $\dfrac{18b^5}{-45b^4}$

37. $(9mn^4p)(-3mp^2)$

38. $(-3v^2wz)(-4vz^4)$

39. $(-xy^5)(3x^2)(5y^3)$

40. $(-6m^3n)(-mn^2)(m)$

41. $\dfrac{x^4}{x^9}$

42. $\dfrac{b}{b^5}$

43. $(-2n^2)(-3n^4)^3$

44. $(-3m^3n)(-2m^2n^3)^3$

45. $\dfrac{14x^4y^6z^2}{16x^3y^9z}$

46. $\dfrac{25x^4y^7z^2}{20x^5y^9z^{11}}$

47. $(-2x^3y^2)^3(-xy^2)^4$

48. $(-m^4n^2)^5(-2m^3n^3)^3$

Simplify. Remember that an exponential expression is in simplest form when it contains only positive exponents.

49. w^{-8}

50. m^{-9}

51. $\dfrac{1}{a^{-5}}$

52. $\dfrac{1}{c^{-6}}$

53. 4^{-3}

54. 5^{-2}

55. $\dfrac{1}{3^{-5}}$

56. $\dfrac{1}{2^{-4}}$

57. $4x^{-7}$

58. $-6y^{-1}$

59. $\dfrac{2x^{-2}}{y^4}$

60. $\dfrac{a^3}{4b^{-2}}$

61. $x^{-4}x^4$

62. $x^{-3}x^{-5}$

63. $\dfrac{x^{-3}}{x^2}$

64. $\dfrac{x^4}{x^{-5}}$

65. $(3x^{-2})^2$

66. $(5x^2)^{-3}$

67. $\dfrac{1}{3x^{-2}}$

68. $\dfrac{2}{5c^{-6}}$

69. $(x^2 y^{-4})^3$

70. $(x^3 y^5)^{-4}$

71. $(3x^{-1} y^{-2})^2$

72. $(5xy^{-3})^{-2}$

73. $(2x^{-1})(x^{-3})$

74. $(-2x^{-5})(x^7)$

75. $\dfrac{3x^{-2}y^2}{6xy^2}$

76. $\dfrac{2x^{-2}y}{8xy}$

77. $\dfrac{2x^{-1}y^{-4}}{4xy^2}$

78. $\dfrac{3a^{-2} b}{ab}$

79. $(x^{-2} y)^2 (xy)^{-2}$

80. $(x^{-1} y^2)^{-3} (x^2 y^{-4})^{-3}$

81. $\left(\dfrac{x^2y^{-1}}{xy}\right)^{-4}$

82. $\left(\dfrac{x^{-2}y^{-4}}{x^{-2}y}\right)^{-2}$

83. $\left(\dfrac{4a^{-2}b}{8a^3b^{-4}}\right)^2$

84. $\left(\dfrac{6ab^{-2}}{3a^{-2}b}\right)^{-2}$

85. *Geometry* Find the length of line segment *AC*.

86. *Geometry* Find the length of line segment *DF*.

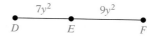

87. *Geometry* The length of line segment *LN* is $27a^2b$. Find the length of line segment *MN*.

88. *Geometry* The length of line segment *QS* is $18c^3$. Find the length of line segment *QR*.

89. *Geometry* Find the area of the square. The dimension given is in meters.

90. *Geometry* Find the area of the rectangle. The dimensions given are in feet.

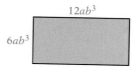

91. *Geometry* Find the perimeter of the rectangle. The dimensions given are in miles.

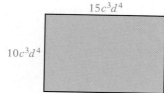

92. *Geometry* Find the perimeter of the square. The dimension given is in centimeters.

93. *Geometry* Find the area of the rectangle. The dimensions given are in kilometers.

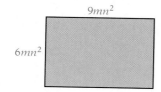

94. *Geometry* Find the area of the parallelogram. The dimensions given are in inches.

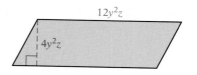

95. *Geometry* The area of the rectangle is $24a^3b^5$ square yards. Find the length of the rectangle.

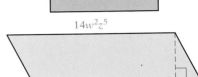

$4ab^2$

96. *Geometry* The area of the parallelogram is $56w^4z^6$ square meters. Find the height of the parallelogram.

$14w^2z^5$

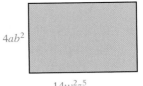

97. The product of a monomial and $4b$ is $12a^2b$. Find the monomial.

98. The product of a monomial and $8y^2$ is $32x^2y^3$. Find the monomial.

■ Scientific Notation

Write the number in scientific notation.

99. 2,370,000 **100.** 75,000 **101.** 0.00045 **102.** 0.000076

103. 309,000 **104.** 819,000,000 **105.** 0.000000601 **106.** 0.00000000096

107. 57,000,000,000 **108.** 934,800,000,000 **109.** 0.000000017 **110.** 0.0000009217

Write the number in decimal notation.

111. 7.1×10^5 **112.** 2.3×10^7 **113.** 4.3×10^{-5} **114.** 9.21×10^{-7}

115. 6.71×10^8 **116.** 5.75×10^9 **117.** 7.13×10^{-6} **118.** 3.54×10^{-8}

119. 5×10^{12} **120.** 1.0987×10^{11} **121.** 8.01×10^{-3} **122.** 4.0162×10^{-9}

Solve.

123. *Physics* Light travels approximately 16,000,000,000 miles in one day. Write this number in scientific notation.

124. *Geology* The mass of the planet Earth is approximately 5,980,000,000,000,000,000,000,000 kilograms. Write this number in scientific notation.

125. *The Arts* The graph at the right shows the box office income, in millions, for three movies through the first two weekends after the release of each film (*Source:* AC-Nielsen EDI). Write in scientific notation the dollar amount of income for *Star Wars, Episode I: The Phantom Menace.*

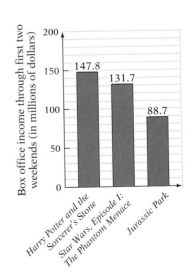

126. *Light* The length of an infrared light wave is approximately 0.0000037 meters. Write this number in scientific notation.

127. *Electricity* The charge on an electron is 0.00000000000000000016 coulomb. Write this number in scientific notation.

128. *Computers* A unit used to measure the speed of a computer is the picosecond. One picosecond is 0.000000000001 second. Write this number in scientific notation.

129. *Chemistry* Avogadro's number is used in chemistry. Its value is approximately 602,300,000,000,000,000,000,000. Write this number in scientific notation.

130. 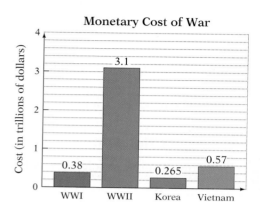 *The Military* The graph at the right shows the monetary cost of four wars (*Source:* Congressional Research Service, using numbers from the *Statistical Abstract of the United States*). Write the monetary cost of World War II in scientific notation.

131. *Astronomy* A parsec is a distance measurement that is used by astronomers. One parsec is 3,086,000,000,000,000,000 centimeters. Write this number in scientific notation.

132. *Astronomy* One light year is the distance traveled by light in one year. One light year is 5,880,000,000,000 miles. Write this number in scientific notation.

Simplify.

133. $(1.9 \times 10^{12})(3.5 \times 10^7)$

134. $(4.2 \times 10^7)(1.8 \times 10^{-5})$

135. $(2.3 \times 10^{-8})(1.4 \times 10^{-6})$

136. $(3 \times 10^{-20})(2.4 \times 10^9)$

137. $\dfrac{6.12 \times 10^{14}}{1.7 \times 10^9}$

138. $\dfrac{6 \times 10^{-8}}{2.5 \times 10^{-2}}$

139. $\dfrac{5.58 \times 10^{-7}}{3.1 \times 10^{11}}$

140. $\dfrac{9.03 \times 10^6}{4.3 \times 10^{-5}}$

Applying Concepts

141. Evaluate.
   a. $8^{-2} + 2^{-5}$ **b.** $9^{-2} + 3^{-3}$

142. Determine whether the statement is always true, sometimes true, or never true.
   a. The phrase *a power of a monomial* means a monomial is the base of an exponential expression.
   b. To multiply $x^m \cdot x^n$, multiply the exponents.
   c. The rules of exponents can be applied to expressions that contain an exponent of zero or contain negative exponents.
   d. The expression 3^{-2} represents the reciprocal of 3^2.

143. Evaluate 2^x and 2^{-x} when $x = -2, -1, 0, 1$, and 2.

144. Write in decimal notation.
  a. 2^{-4}
  b. 25^{-2}

145. If $m = n + 1$ and $a \neq 0$, then $\dfrac{a^m}{a^n} =$ _____.

146. Solve: $(-8.5)^x = 1$

EXPLORATION

1. *Scientific Notation and Order Relations*
  a. Place the correct symbol, $<$ or $>$, between the two numbers.
      (i) 5.23×10^{18} ? 5.23×10^{17}
      (ii) 3.12×10^{13} ? 3.12×10^{12}
      (iii) 3.45×10^{-14} ? 3.45×10^{-15}
      (iv) 4.2×10^8 ? 9.7×10^9
      (v) 2.7×10^{-11} ? 6.8×10^{-10}

  b. Write a rule for ordering two numbers written in scientific notation.

2. *Expressions with Negative Exponents*

  a. If x is a nonzero real number, is x^{-2} always positive, always negative, or positive or negative depending on whether x is positive or negative? Explain your answer.

  b. If x is a nonzero real number, is x^{-3} always positive, always negative, or positive or negative depending on whether x is positive or negative? Explain your answer.

3. *Negative Exponents on Fractional Expressions*
  a. Simplify each of the following expressions.

      (i) $\left(\dfrac{a^2}{b^3}\right)^{-2}$ (ii) $\left(\dfrac{x^4}{y}\right)^{-3}$ (iii) $\left(\dfrac{c^5}{d^2}\right)^{-4}$ (iv) $\left(\dfrac{2^3}{3^4}\right)^{-1}$

  b. Write a rule for rewriting with a positive exponent a fraction raised to a negative exponent.

Addition and Subtraction of Polynomials

■ Introduction to Polynomials

Some forecasters predicted that revenue generated by business on the Internet from 1997 to 2002 could be approximated by the function

$$R(t) = 15.8t^2 - 17.2t + 10.2,$$

where R is the annual revenue in billions of dollars and t is the time in years, with $t = 0$ corresponding to the year 1997. Use this function to approximate the annual revenue in the year 2000.

Because $t = 0$ corresponds to 1997, $t = 3$ corresponds to the year 2000. Evaluate the given function for $t = 3$.

$$R(t) = 15.8t^2 - 17.2t + 10.2$$
$$R(3) = 15.8(3)^2 - 17.2(3) + 10.2$$
$$= 15.8(9) - 17.2(3) + 10.2$$
$$= 142.2 - 51.6 + 10.2$$
$$= 100.8$$

According to this function, in the year 2000, the revenue generated by business conducted on the Internet was approximately $100.8 billion.

In the function $R(t) = 15.8t^2 - 17.2t + 10.2$, the variable expression

$$15.8t^2 - 17.2t + 10.2$$

is a polynomial. A **polynomial** is a variable expression in which the terms are monomials. The polynomial $15.8t^2 - 17.2t + 10.2$ has three terms: $15.8t^2$, $-17.2t$, and 10.2. Note that each of these three terms is a monomial.

A polynomial of *one* term is a **monomial.** $-7x^2$ is a monomial.

A polynomial of *two* terms is a **binomial.** $4y + 3$ is a binomial.

A polynomial of *three* terms is a **trinomial.** $6b^2 + 5b - 8$ is a trinomial.

? QUESTION   Is the expression a polynomial? If it is a polynomial, is it a monomial, a binomial, or a trinomial?

a. $16a^2 - 9b^2$ **b.** $-\dfrac{2}{3}xy$ **c.** $x^2 + 2xy - 8$ **d.** $\dfrac{3}{x} - 5$

The terms of a polynomial in one variable are usually arranged so that the exponents of the variable decrease from left to right. This is called **descending order.** The polynomials at the right are written in descending order.

$2x^3 - 3x^2 + 6x - 1$

$5y^4 - 9y^3 + y^2 - 7y + 8$

$t - 4$

? ANSWERS   **a.** It is a polynomial. It is a binomial because it has two terms ($16a^2$ and $-9b^2$). **b.** It is a polynomial. It is a monomial because it has one term.   **c.** It is a polynomial. It is a trinomial because it has three terms (x^2, $2xy$, and -8).   **d.** $\dfrac{3}{x}$ is not a monomial, so $\dfrac{3}{x} - 5$ is not a polynomial.

? QUESTION   Is the polynomial written in descending order?

> **a.** $3a^2 - 2a^3 + 4a$ **b.** $6d^5 + 4d^3 - 7$

The **degree of a polynomial in one variable** is its greatest exponent.

The degree of $t - 4$ is 1. It is a first-degree or **linear polynomial.**
The degree of $6b^2 + 5b - 8$ is 2. It is a second-degree or **quadratic polynomial.**
The degree of $2x^3 - 3x^2 + 6x - 1$ is 3. It is a third-degree or **cubic polynomial.**
The degree of $5y^4 - 9y^3 + y^2 - 7y + 8$ is 4. It is a fourth-degree polynomial.

▼ *Point of Interest*

The dimples on a golf ball have a dramatic effect on its flight. A golf ball with a well-designed dimple pattern will travel 2 to 3 times farther than a ball with no dimples.

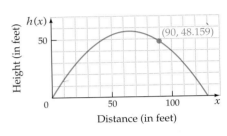

Polynomial functions are used to model many different situations. For instance, ignoring forces other than that of gravity, the height, h, of a golf ball x feet from the point from where it was hit is given by the polynomial function $h(x) = -0.0133x^2 + 1.7321x$. By evaluating this function, we can determine the height of the ball at various distances from the point at which it was struck. The graph above shows that the ball is 48.159 feet high at a distance of 90 feet from the point where it was hit. Evaluating the polynomial when $x = 90$, we have

$$h(x) = -0.0133x^2 + 1.7321x$$
$$h(90) = -0.0133(90)^2 + 1.7321(90) \qquad \bullet \text{ Replace } x \text{ by } 90.$$
$$= 48.159$$

The polynomial function above gave the height of the ball in terms of its *distance* from where it was hit. That is, the height depended on distance. A different polynomial function can be written that will give the height of the ball in terms of the amount of *time* the ball is in flight. Using this function, you can determine the height of the ball at various times during its flight. This is shown in Example 1.

EXAMPLE 1

The height h, in feet, of a golf ball t seconds after it has been struck is given by $h(t) = -16t^2 + 60t$. Determine the height of the ball 3 seconds after it is hit.

Solution $h(t) = -16t^2 + 60t$
$$h(3) = -16(3)^2 + 60(3) \qquad \bullet \text{ Replace } t \text{ by } 3.$$
$$= 36$$

The golf ball is 36 feet high 3 seconds after being hit. See the graph at the left.

? ANSWER   **a.** No. The exponents on a (2 and 3) do not decrease from left to right. $-2a^3 + 3a^2 + 4a$ is the same polynomial written in descending order.   **b.** Yes. The exponents on d (5 and 3) decrease from left to right.

YOU TRY IT 1

If $2000 is deposited into an individual retirement account (IRA), then the value, V, of that investment 3 years later is given by the cubic polynomial function $V(r) = 2000r^3 + 6000r^2 + 6000r + 2000$, where r is the interest rate (as a decimal) earned on the investment. Determine the value after 3 years of $2000 deposited in an IRA that earns an interest rate of 7%.

Solution   See page S24.

■ Addition and Subtraction of Polynomials

Polynomials can be added by combining like terms.

EXAMPLE 2

Add: $(3x^2 - 7x + 4) + (5x^2 + 2x - 8)$

Solution $(3x^2 - 7x + 4) + (5x^2 + 2x - 8)$

$$= (3x^2 + 5x^2) + (-7x + 2x) + (4 - 8)$$

• Use the Properties of Addition to rearrange and group like terms.

$$= 8x^2 - 5x - 4$$

• Combine like terms. Write the polynomial in descending order.

YOU TRY IT 2

Add: $(-4d^2 - 3d + 2) + (3d^2 - 4d)$

Solution   See page S24.

For Example 2, you can use a graphing calculator to check your work. Here are some typical graphing calculator screens that you might use to produce the graphs.

Enter the polynomials to be added.

Enter the sum.
Enter your answer.

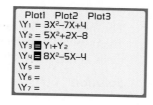

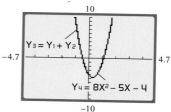

When the graphs above are produced, the graph of Y₃ lies on top of the graph of Y₄. This means that the two graphs are the same. It does not ensure that the addition is correct; however, if the two graphs do not match exactly, the addition is definitely incorrect.

Recall that **the definition of subtraction is addition of the opposite.**

$$a - b = a + (-b)$$

This definition holds true for polynomials. Polynomials can be subtracted by adding the opposite of the second polynomial to the first. The **opposite of a polynomial** is the polynomial with the sign of every term changed.

The opposite of the polynomial $x^2 - 2x + 3$ is $-x^2 + 2x - 3$.
The opposite of the polynomial $-4y^3 + 5y - 8$ is $4y^3 - 5y + 8$.

? QUESTION   What is the opposite of the polynomial $5d^4 - 6d^2 + 9$?

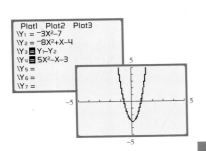

EXAMPLE 3

Subtract: $(-3a^2 - 7) - (-8a^2 + a - 4)$

Solution $(-3a^2 - 7) - (-8a^2 + a - 4)$

$= (-3a^2 - 7) + (8a^2 - a + 4)$ • Rewrite subtraction as addition of the opposite.

$= (-3a^2 + 8a^2) - a + (-7 + 4)$ • Use the Properties of Addition to rearrange and group like terms.

$= 5a^2 - a - 3$ • Combine like terms. Write the polynomial in descending order.

A graphical check is shown at the left.

YOU TRY IT 3

Subtract: $(5x^2 - 3x + 4) - (-6x^3 - 2x + 8)$

Solution   See page S24.

A company's **revenue** is the money the company earns by selling its products. A company's **cost** is the money it spends to manufacture and sell its products. A company's **profit** is the difference between its revenue and cost. This relationship is expressed by the formula $P = R - C$, where P is the profit, R is the revenue, and C is the cost. This formula is used in Example 4 and You Try It 4.

EXAMPLE 4

A company manufactures and sells woodstoves. The total monthly cost, in dollars, to produce n woodstoves is $30n + 2000$. The company's revenue, in dollars, obtained from selling all n woodstoves is $-0.4n^2 + 150n$. Express in terms of n the company's monthly profit.

State the goal.   Our goal is to write a variable expression for the company's profit from manufacturing and selling n woodstoves.

Devise a strategy.   Use the formula $P = R - C$. Substitute the given polynomials for R and C. Then subtract the polynomials.

? ANSWER   The opposite of $5d^4 - 6d^2 + 9$ is $-5d^4 + 6d^2 - 9$.

```
Plot1  Plot2  Plot3
\Y₁ = ⁻.4X²+150X
\Y₂ = 30X+2000
\Y₃ ▊ Y₁-Y₂
\Y₄ ▊ ⁻.4X²+120X-2000
\Y₅ =
\Y₆ =        7500
\Y₇ =
```

−5   400

−500

Solve the problem.

$P = R - C$

$P = (-0.4n^2 + 150n) - (30n + 2000)$ • $R = -0.4n^2 + 150n$, $C = 30n + 2000$

$P = (-0.4n^2 + 150n) + (-30n - 2000)$ • Rewrite subtraction as addition of the opposite.

$P = -0.4n^2 + (150n - 30n) - 2000$ • Combine like terms.

$P = -0.4n^2 + 120n - 2000$

The company's monthly profit, in dollars, is $-0.4n^2 + 120n - 2000$.

Check your work.   A graphical check of the solution is shown at the left.

YOU TRY IT 4

A company's total monthly cost, in dollars, for manufacturing and selling n videotapes per month is $35n + 2000$. The company's monthly revenue, in dollars, from selling all n videotapes is $-0.2n^2 + 175n$. Express in terms of n the company's monthly profit.

Solution   See page S24.

6.2 EXERCISES

Topics for Discussion

1. State whether the polynomial is a monomial, a binomial, or a trinomial. Explain your answer.
   a. $8x^4 - 6x^2$
   b. $4a^2b^2 + 9ab + 10$

   c. $7x^3y^4$

2. Explain each of the following terms. Give an example of each.
   a. Polynomial
   b. Monomial
   c. Binomial
   d. Trinomial

3. State whether the expression is a polynomial. Explain your answer.
   a. $\frac{1}{5}x^3 + \frac{1}{2}x$

   b. $\frac{1}{5x^2} + \frac{1}{2x}$

   c. $x + \sqrt{5}$

4. Determine whether the statement is always true, sometimes true, or never true.
   a. The terms of a polynomial are monomials.
   b. Subtraction is addition of the opposite.

■ Introduction to Polynomials

5. *Geometry*   As sand that is very fine is poured into a pile, the volume, V, of the cone-shaped pile is given by $V(h) = \frac{8}{3}\pi h^3$, where h is the height of the cone. Find the volume of a sand pile that is 2 feet high. Round to the nearest hundredth.

6. *Geometry*   The area, A, of a rectangle with a perimeter of 100 meters is given by $A(w) = 50w - w^2$, where w is the width of the rectangle. What is the area of this rectangle when the width is 10 meters?

10 m

7. *Oceanography*   The wavelength L, in meters, of a deep-water wave can be approximated by the function $L(v) = 0.6411v^2$, where v is the wave speed in meters per second. Find the length of a deep-water wave that has a speed of 30 meters per second.

8. *Polygonal Numbers*   In the diagram at the right, the total number of circles, T, when there are n rows is given by $T = 0.5n^2 + 0.5n$. Verify the formula for the four figures shown. What is the total number of circles when there are 10 rows?

9. *Sports*   The height h, in feet, of a cliff diver t seconds after beginning a dive can be modeled by the function $h(t) = -16t^2 + 5t + 50$. How high is the cliff from which the diver is jumping? (*Hint:* Determine the value of t before the diver starts the dive.)

10. *Oceanography*   The height H, in feet, of the tide at a certain beach in Encinitas, California, can be approximated by

$$H(t) = -0.00013t^5 + 0.00839t^4 - 0.186t^3 + 1.635t^2 - 4.8t + 3.40$$

where t is the number of hours after midnight. Find the height of the tide at 9:00 A.M. Round to the nearest tenth.

11. *Physics*   The amount of force F, in pounds, on one side of a triangular trough is given by $F(x) = -14.2x^3 + 63.9x^2$, where x is the height of the water in feet. What is the force on one side of this trough when the water is 3 feet deep?

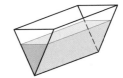

12. *Probability*   The probability, P, that all three security lights in a garage will not fail is given by the function $P(x) = 1 - 3x + 3x^2 - x^3$, where x is the probability that one light will fail. Find the probability that all three lights will not fail if the probability that one light will fail is 0.01. Write the answer to the nearest tenth of a percent.

13. *Energy*   The amount of energy E, in foot-pounds, that is required to pump the water out of a certain conical tank 12 feet tall that contains x feet of water is given by $E(x) = 62.4\pi\left(-\frac{x^4}{64} + \frac{5x^3}{16}\right)$. How much energy is required to pump out the water when the depth of the water is 8 feet? Round to the nearest whole number.

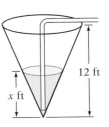

12 ft

x ft

14. *Pollution*   One source of the pollutant carbon monoxide is our exhaling the air we breathe. Suppose the amount of carbon monoxide due to exhaling, in parts per million, is given by

$$P(x) = -0.02x^4 + 0.2x^3 + 1,$$

where x is the population in hundred thousands. Evaluate this polynomial when $x = 2$. Write a sentence that explains the meaning of the value of the polynomial when $x = 2$.

■ Addition and Subtraction of Polynomials

Add or subtract.

15. $(x^2 + 7x) + (-3x^2 - 4x)$

16. $(3y^2 - 2y) + (5y^2 + 6y)$

17. $(x^2 - 6x) - (x^2 - 10x)$

18. $(y^2 + 4y) - (y^2 + 10y)$

19. $(4b^2 - 5b) + (3b^2 + 6b - 4)$

20. $(2c^2 - 4) + (6c^2 - 2c + 4)$

21. $(2y^2 - 4y) - (-y^2 + 2)$

22. $(-3a^2 - 2a) - (4a^2 - 4)$

23. $(2a^2 - 7a + 10) + (a^2 + 4a + 7)$

24. $(-6x^2 + 7x + 3) + (3x^2 + x + 3)$

25. $(x^2 - 2x + 1) - (x^2 + 5x + 8)$

26. $(3x^2 + 2x - 2) - (5x^2 - 5x + 6)$

27. $(-2x^3 + x - 1) - (-x^2 + x - 3)$

28. $(2x^2 + 5x - 3) - (3x^3 + 2x - 5)$

29. $(x^3 - 7x + 4) + (2x^2 + x - 10)$

30. $(3y^3 + y^2 + 1) + (-4y^3 - 6y - 3)$

31. $(5x^3 + 7x - 7) + (10x^2 - 8x + 3)$

32. $(3y^3 + 4y + 9) + (2y^2 + 4y - 21)$

33. $(2y^3 + 6y - 2) - (y^3 + y^2 + 4)$

34. $(-2x^2 - x + 4) - (-x^3 + 3x - 2)$

35. $(4y^3 - y - 1) - (2y^2 - 3y + 3)$

36. $(3x^2 - 2x - 3) - (2x^3 - 2x^2 + 4)$

37. *Geometry*   Find the length of line segment AC.

$$\overset{\displaystyle 3x^2 - 4x + 5 \qquad\quad 8x^2 + 6x - 1}{\underset{A \qquad\qquad\quad B \qquad\qquad\qquad\quad C}{\bullet\!\!\!\rule[0.5ex]{2cm}{0.4pt}\!\!\!\bullet\!\!\!\rule[0.5ex]{2.5cm}{0.4pt}\!\!\!\bullet}}$$

38. *Geometry*   Find the length of line segment DF.

$$\overset{\displaystyle 5y^2 - y \qquad\quad 7y^2 + 4}{\underset{D \qquad\quad E \qquad\qquad F}{\bullet\!\!\!\rule[0.5ex]{1.5cm}{0.4pt}\!\!\!\bullet\!\!\!\rule[0.5ex]{2cm}{0.4pt}\!\!\!\bullet}}$$

39. *Geometry*   The length of line segment LN is $7a^2 + 4a - 3$. Find the length of line segment MN.

$$\overset{\displaystyle 2a^2 + a + 6}{\underset{L \qquad\quad M \qquad\qquad N}{\bullet\!\!\!\rule[0.5ex]{1.5cm}{0.4pt}\!\!\!\bullet\!\!\!\rule[0.5ex]{2cm}{0.4pt}\!\!\!\bullet}}$$

40. *Geometry*   The length of line segment QS is $12c^3 + 4c^2 - 6$. Find the length of line segment QR.

$$\overset{\displaystyle 5c^3 - 3c + 9}{\underset{Q \qquad\qquad R \qquad\qquad S}{\bullet\!\!\!\rule[0.5ex]{2cm}{0.4pt}\!\!\!\bullet\!\!\!\rule[0.5ex]{2cm}{0.4pt}\!\!\!\bullet}}$$

41. *Geometry* Find the perimeter of the rectangle. The dimensions given are in kilometers.

$3d^2 + 5d - 4$

$d^2 + d + 6$

42. *Geometry* Find the perimeter of the rectangle. The dimensions given are in meters.

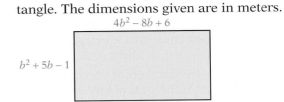

$4b^2 - 8b + 6$

$b^2 + 5b - 1$

43. *Business* The total monthly cost, in dollars, for a company to produce and sell n guitars per month is $240n + 1200$. The company's monthly revenue, in dollars, from selling all n guitars is $-2n^2 + 400n$. Express in terms of n the company's monthly profit. Use the formula $P = R - C$.

44. *Business* A company's total monthly cost, in dollars, for manufacturing and selling n cameras per month is $40n + 1800$. The company's monthly revenue, in dollars, from selling all n cameras is $-n^2 + 250n$. Express in terms of n the company's monthly profit. Use the formula $P = R - C$.

45. What polynomial must be added to $3x^2 - 4x - 2$ so that the sum is $-x^2 + 2x + 1$?

46. What polynomial must be added to $-2x^3 + 4x - 7$ so that the sum is $x^2 - x - 1$?

47. What polynomial must be subtracted from $6x^2 - 4x - 2$ so that the difference is $2x^2 + 2x - 5$?

48. What polynomial must be subtracted from $2x^3 - x^2 + 4x - 2$ so that the difference is $x^3 + 2x - 8$?

Applying Concepts

49. Determine whether the statement is always true, sometimes true, or never true.

   a. Like terms have the same coefficient and the same variable part.

   b. The opposite of the polynomial
   $ax^3 - bx^2 + cx - d$ is $-ax^3 + bx^2 - cx + d$.

   c. A binomial is a polynomial of degree 2.

50. Is it possible to add two polynomials, each of degree 3, and have the sum be a polynomial of degree 2? If so, give an example. If not, explain why not.

51. For what value of k is the given equation an identity?

   a. $(2x^3 + 3x^2 + kx + 5) - (x^3 + 2x^2 + 3x + 7) = x^3 + x^2 + 5x - 2$

   b. $(6x^3 + kx^2 - 2x - 1) - (4x^3 - 3x^2 + 1) = 2x^3 - x^2 - 2x - 2$

EXPLORATION

1. *Sums of Consecutive Integers*   Given that x is an integer, $x + 1$ is the next consecutive integer. Three consecutive integers can be represented as x, $x + 1$, and $x + 2$.

   a.   Represent the sum of two consecutive integers. Simplify.
   b.   Show that the sum of any two consecutive integers is an odd number.
   c.   Represent the sum of three consecutive integers. Simplify.
   d.   Show that the sum of any three consecutive integers is divisible by 3.
   e.   Represent the sum of four consecutive integers. Simplify.
   f.   Show that the sum of any four consecutive integers is an even number.
   g.   Represent the sum of five consecutive integers. Simplify.
   h.   What is true about the sum of any five consecutive integers?
   i.   Is the sum of any six consecutive numbers an even or an odd number?

SECTION   **6.3**

Multiplication and Division of Polynomials

- Multiplication of Polynomials
- Division of Polynomials
- Synthetic Division

▪ Multiplication of Polynomials

To multiply a polynomial by a monomial, use the Distributive Property and the Rule for Multiplying Exponential Expressions.

The monomial $-2x$ is multiplied by the trinomial $x^2 - 4x - 3$ as follows:

$$-2x(x^2 - 4x - 3)$$
$$= -2x(x^2) - (-2x)(4x) - (-2x)(3)$$
$$= -2(x^{1+2}) - (-2 \cdot 4)(x^{1+1}) - (-2 \cdot 3)x$$
$$= -2x^3 + \cdot 8x^2 + 6x$$

- Use the Distributive Property.
- Use the Rule for Multiplying Exponential Expressions.

TAKE NOTE

Distribute $-2x$ over each term inside the parentheses.

$$-2x(x^2 - 4x - 3)$$

EXAMPLE 1

Multiply.   **a.** $(5y + 4)(-2y)$ **b.** $x^3(2x^2 - 3x + 2)$

Solution   **a.** $(5y + 4)(-2y) = 5y(-2y) + 4(-2y)$
$$= -10y^2 - 8y$$

      b. $x^3(2x^2 - 3x + 2) = x^3(2x^2) - x^3(3x) + x^3(2)$
$$= 2x^5 - 3x^4 + 2x^3$$

Check:

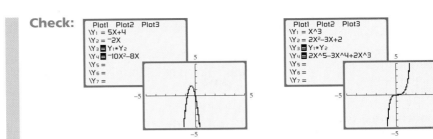

YOU TRY IT 1

Multiply. **a.** $(-2d + 3)(-4d)$ **b.** $-a^3(3a^2 + 2a - 7)$

Solution See page S24.

Multiplication of two polynomials requires the repeated application of the Distributive Property.

Shown below is the binomial $y - 2$ multiplied by the trinomial $y^2 + 3y + 1$.

$(y - 2)(y^2 + 3y + 1)$

$= (y - 2)(y^2) + (y - 2)(3y) + (y - 2)(1)$ • Use the **Distributive Property** to multiply $y - 2$ times each term of the trinomial.

$= y^3 - 2y^2 + 3y^2 - 6y + y - 2$ • Use the Distributive Property.

$= y^3 + y^2 - 5y - 2$ • Combine like terms.

Two polynomials can also be multiplied using a vertical format similar to that used for multiplication of whole numbers. Note that the factors in the multiplication below are the same as those used in the previous example.

$$
\begin{array}{r}
y^2 + 3y + 1 \\
y - 2 \\
\hline
-2y^2 - 6y - 2 \\
y^3 + 3y^2 + \ y \\
\hline
y^3 + \ y^2 - 5y - 2
\end{array}
$$

• Multiply each term in the trinomial by -2.

• Multiply each term in the trinomial by y. Like terms must be written in the same column.

• Add the terms in each column.

EXAMPLE 2

Multiply: $(2b^3 - b + 1)(2b + 3)$

Solution

$$
\begin{array}{r}
2b^3 - b + 1 \\
2b + 3 \\
\hline
6b^3 \qquad - 3b + 3 \\
4b^4 \qquad - 2b^2 + 2b \\
\hline
4b^4 + 6b^3 - 2b^2 - \ b + 3
\end{array}
$$

• This is $3(2b^3 - b + 1)$.

• This is $2b(2b^3 - b + 1)$. Like terms are in the same column.

• Add the terms in each column.

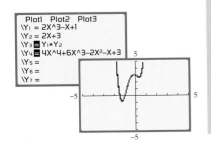

Check: A graphical check is shown at the left.

YOU TRY IT 2

Multiply: $(3c^3 - 2c^2 + c - 3)(2c + 5)$

Solution   See page S24.

The product of two binomials can be found by using a method called **FOIL**, which is based on the Distributive Property. The letters of FOIL stand for **F**irst, **O**uter, **I**nner, and **L**ast.

To multiply $(2x + 3)(x + 5)$:

Multiply the **F**irst terms.	$(2x + 3)(x + 5)$	$2x \cdot x = 2x^2$
Multiply the **O**uter terms.	$(2x + 3)(x + 5)$	$2x \cdot 5 = 10x$
Multiply the **I**nner terms.	$(2x + 3)(x + 5)$	$3 \cdot x = 3x$
Multiply the **L**ast terms.	$(2x + 3)(x + 5)$	$3 \cdot 5 = 15$

Add the products. $(2x + 3)(x + 5)$

$$\begin{array}{cccc} \text{F} & \text{O} & \text{I} & \text{L} \\ = 2x^2 & + 10x & + 3x & + 15 \end{array}$$

Combine like terms. $= 2x^2 + 13x + 15$

EXAMPLE 3

Multiply.   **a.** $(4x - 3)(3x - 2)$ **b.** $(3x - 2y)(x + 4y)$

Solution   **a.** This is the product of two binomials. Use the FOIL method.

$$(4x - 3)(3x - 2)$$
$$= 4x(3x) + (4x)(-2) + (-3)(3x) + (-3)(-2)$$
$$= 12x^2 - 8x - 9x + 6$$
$$= 12x^2 - 17x + 6$$

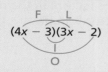

b. This is the product of two binomials. Use the FOIL method.

$$(3x - 2y)(x + 4y)$$
$$= 3x(x) + (3x)(4y) + (-2y)(x) + (-2y)(4y)$$
$$= 3x^2 + 12xy - 2xy - 8y^2$$
$$= 3x^2 + 10xy - 8y^2$$

YOU TRY IT 3

Multiply. **a.** $(4y - 5)(3y - 3)$ **b.** $(3a + 2b)(3a - 5b)$

Solution   See page S24.

The expression $(a + b)^2$ is the **square of a binomial.** We are squaring $(a + b)$, which means that we are multiplying it times itself.

$$(a + b)^2 = (a + b)(a + b)$$

$(a + b)(a + b)$ is the product of two binomials. Use the FOIL method to multiply.

$$(a + b)^2 = (a + b)(a + b) = a^2 + ab + ab + b^2 = a^2 + 2ab + b^2$$

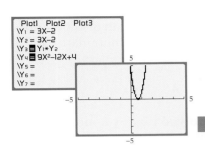

EXAMPLE 4

Multiply: $(3x - 2)^2$

Solution $(3x - 2)^2$ • This is the square of a binomial.

$= (3x - 2)(3x - 2)$ • Multiply $(3x - 2)$ times itself.

$= 9x^2 - 6x - 6x + 4$ • Use the FOIL method.

$= 9x^2 - 12x + 4$ • Combine like terms.

Check: A graphical check is shown at the left.

YOU TRY IT 4

Multiply: $(3x + 2y)^2$

Solution See page S25.

EXAMPLE 5

A rectangular piece of cardboard measures 12 inches by 16 inches. An open box is formed by cutting four squares that measure x inches on a side from the corners of the cardboard and then folding up the sides, as shown in the figure at the left. Determine the volume of the box in terms of x. Use your equation to find the volume of the box when x is 2 inches.

State the goal. The goal is to determine the volume of the box in terms of x and then to find the volume when $x = 2$.

Devise a strategy. To determine the volume of the box in terms of x, use the formula for the volume of a box, $V = LWH$. Substitute variable expressions for L, W, and H. Then multiply.

To determine the volume when $x = 2$, substitute 2 for x in the equation. Then simplify the numerical expression.

Solve the problem.

$V = LWH$

$V = (16 - 2x)(12 - 2x)x$ • $L = 16 - 2x$, $W = 12 - 2x$, $H = x$

$V = (4x^2 - 56x + 192)x$ • Multiply $(16 - 2x)(12 - 2x)$. Write the terms in descending order.

$V = 4x^3 - 56x^2 + 192x$ • Multiply the trinomial by x.

The volume of the box in terms of x is $(4x^3 - 56x^2 + 192x)$ cubic inches.

$V = 4x^3 - 56x^2 + 192x$

$V = 4(2)^3 - 56(2)^2 + 192(2)$ • Replace x by 2.

$V = 192$

When x is 2 inches, the volume of the box is 192 cubic inches.

Check your work. A graphical check of the product $4x^3 - 56x^2 + 192x$ can be performed on a graphing calculator.

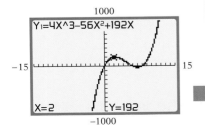

YOU TRY IT 5

The radius of a circle is $(x - 4)$ feet. Find the area of the circle in terms of the variable x. Leave the answer in terms of π.

Solution See page S25.

■ Division of Polynomials

As shown below, $\frac{8 + 4}{2}$ can be simplified by first adding the terms in the numerator and then dividing the result by the denominator. It can also be simplified by first dividing each term in the numerator by the denominator and then adding the results.

$$\frac{8 + 4}{2} = \frac{12}{2} = 6 \qquad \frac{8 + 4}{2} = \frac{8}{2} + \frac{4}{2} = 4 + 2 = 6$$

It is this second method that is used **to divide a polynomial by a monomial: Divide each term in the numerator by the denominator, and then write the sum of the quotients.**

TAKE NOTE

Recall that the fraction bar can be read "divided by."

To divide $\frac{6x^2 + 4x}{2x}$, divide each term of the polynomial $6x^2 + 4x$ by the monomial $2x$. Then simplify each quotient.

$$\frac{6x^2 + 4x}{2x} = \frac{6x^2}{2x} + \frac{4x}{2x}$$
$$= 3x + 2$$

EXAMPLE 6

Divide: $\dfrac{6x^3 - 3x^2 + 9x}{3x}$

Solution $\dfrac{6x^3 - 3x^2 + 9x}{3x}$

$$= \frac{6x^3}{3x} - \frac{3x^2}{3x} + \frac{9x}{3x} \qquad \text{• Divide each term in the numerator}$$
$$\text{by the denominator.}$$
$$= 2x^2 - x + 3 \qquad\qquad \text{• Simplify each quotient.}$$

Check: A graphical check is shown at the left.

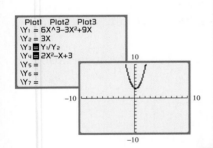

YOU TRY IT 6

Divide: $\dfrac{4x^3y + 8x^2y^2 - 4xy^3}{2xy}$

Solution   See page S25.

The method illustrated above is appropriate only when the divisor is a monomial. To divide two polynomials in which the divisor is not a monomial, we use a method similar to that used for division of whole numbers.

To divide $(x^2 - 5x + 8) \div (x - 3)$:

Step 1

$$\begin{array}{r} x \\ x - 3\overline{)x^2 - 5x + 8} \\ \underline{x^2 - 3x} \\ -2x + 8 \end{array}$$

Think: $x\overline{)x^2} = \dfrac{x^2}{x} = x$

Multiply: $x(x - 3) = x^2 - 3x$
Subtract: $(x^2 - 5x) - (x^2 - 3x) = -2x$
Bring down the $+8$.

Step 2

$$x - 3\overline{)x^2 - 5x + 8}$$ quotient $x - 2$

$$\underline{x^2 - 3x}$$
$$-2x + 8$$

Think: $x\overline{)-2x} = \dfrac{-2x}{x} = -2$

$$\underline{-2x + 6}$$
$$2$$

Multiply: $-2(x - 3) = -2x + 6$
Subtract: $(-2x + 8) - (-2x + 6) = 2$
The remainder is 2.

The same equation we use to check division of whole numbers is used to check polynomial division.

(Quotient × Divisor) + Remainder = Dividend

Check: $(x - 2)(x - 3) + 2 = x^2 - 3x - 2x + 6 + 2 = x^2 - 5x + 8$

$(x^2 - 5x + 8) \div (x - 3) = x - 2 + \dfrac{2}{x - 3}$

TAKE NOTE

Note that the remainder is used to write a fraction with the remainder over the divisor. This is similar to arithmetic, in which the answer to $15 \div 4$ is written $3\frac{3}{4}$.

EXAMPLE 7

Divide: $(6x + 2x^3 + 26) \div (x + 2)$

Solution   Arrange the terms of the dividend in descending order. There is no x^2 term in $2x^3 + 6x + 26$. Insert $0x^2$ for the missing term so that like terms will be in columns.

$$x + 2\overline{)2x^3 + 0x^2 + 6x + 26}$$ quotient $2x^2 - 4x + 14$

$$\underline{2x^3 + 4x^2}$$
$$-4x^2 + 6x$$
$$\underline{-4x^2 - 8x}$$
$$14x + 26$$
$$\underline{14x + 28}$$
$$-2$$

Check: $(x + 2)(2x^2 - 4x + 14) - 2 = 2x^3 + 6x + 28 - 2 = 2x^3 + 6x + 26$

$(6x + 2x^3 + 26) \div (x + 2) = 2x^2 - 4x + 14 - \dfrac{2}{x + 2}$

TAKE NOTE

Inserting the term $0x^2$ is similar to using zero as a placeholder in division.

$45\overline{)702}$ • The 0 represents zero tens.

YOU TRY IT 7

Divide: $(x^3 - 7 - 2x) \div (x - 2)$

Solution   See page S25.

EXAMPLE 8

Given that $x + 1$ is a factor of $x^3 + x^2 + 4x + 4$, find another factor of $x^3 + x^2 + 4x + 4$.

Solution   Recall that a factor of a number divides that number evenly. A factor of a polynomial divides that polynomial evenly. The quotient is another factor of the polynomial.

$$\begin{array}{r} x^2 + 4 \\ x + 1\overline{)x^3 + x^2 + 4x + 4} \\ \underline{x^3 + x^2} \\ 0 + 4x + 4 \\ \underline{4x + 4} \\ 0 \end{array}$$

Check: $(x + 1)(x^2 + 4) = x^3 + 4x + x^2 + 4 = x^3 + x^2 + 4x + 4$

Another factor of $x^3 + x^2 + 4x + 4$ is $x^2 + 4$.

YOU TRY IT 8

Given that $x + 5$ is a factor of $x^4 + 5x^3 + 2x + 10$, find another factor of $x^4 + 5x^3 + 2x + 10$.

Solution See page S25.

EXAMPLE 9

$x - 3$

The area of a rectangle is $(2x^2 - 3x - 9)$ square meters. The width of the rectangle is $(x - 3)$ meters. Find the length of the rectangle in terms of the variable x. Use the formula $L = \frac{A}{W}$, where L is the length, A is the area, and W is the width of a rectangle.

State the goal. The goal is to write a variable expression for the length of a rectangle that has an area of $(2x^2 - 3x - 9)$ square meters and a width of $(x - 3)$ meters.

Devise a strategy. Using the formula $L = \frac{A}{W}$, substitute the given polynomials for A and W. Then divide the polynomials.

Solve the problem.

$$L = \frac{A}{W} = \frac{2x^2 - 3x - 9}{x - 3} \qquad\qquad \begin{array}{r} 2x + 3 \\ x - 3\overline{)2x^2 - 3x - 9} \\ \underline{2x^2 - 6x} \\ 3x - 9 \\ \underline{3x - 9} \\ 0 \end{array}$$

The length of the rectangle is $(2x + 3)$ meters.

Check your work. $(x - 3)(2x + 3) = 2x^2 + 3x - 6x - 9 = 2x^2 - 3x - 9$

YOU TRY IT 9

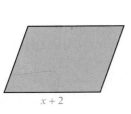

$x + 2$

The area of a parallelogram is $(3x^2 + 2x - 8)$ square feet. The length of the base is $(x + 2)$ feet. Find the height of the parallelogram in terms of the variable x. Use the formula $h = \frac{A}{b}$, where h is the height, A is the area, and b is the length of the base of a parallelogram.

Solution See page S25.

■ Synthetic Division

Synthetic division is a shorter method of dividing a polynomial by a binomial of the form $x - a$. This method of dividing uses only the coefficients of the variable terms.

Both long division and synthetic division are used below to divide the polynomial $3x^2 - 4x + 6$ by $x - 2$.

LONG DIVISION

Compare the coefficients in this problem worked by long division with the coefficients in the same problem worked by synthetic division.

$$
\begin{array}{r}
3x + 2 \\
x - 2\overline{)3x^2 - 4x + 6} \\
\underline{3x^2 - 6x} \\
2x + 6 \\
\underline{2x - 4} \\
10
\end{array}
$$

$$(3x^2 - 4x + 6) \div (x - 2) = 3x + 2 + \frac{10}{x - 2}$$

TAKE NOTE

You can check the answer to a synthetic division problem in the same way that you check an answer to a long division problem.

SYNTHETIC DIVISION

$x - a = x - 2; a = 2$

	Value of a	Coefficients of the dividend		
	2	3	-4	6

Bring down the 3.

		3		

Multiply $2 \cdot 3$ and add the product (6) to -4.

	2	3	-4	6
			6	
		3	2	

Multiply $2 \cdot 2$ and add the product (4) to 6.

	2	3	-4	6
			6	4
		3	2	10

Coefficients of the quotient   Remainder

The degree of the first term of the quotient is one degree less than the degree of the first term of the dividend.

$$(3x^2 - 4x + 6) \div (x - 2) = 3x + 2 + \frac{10}{x - 2}$$

Check: $(3x + 2)(x - 2) + 10$

$$= 3x^2 - 6x + 2x - 4 + 10$$
$$= 3x^2 - 4x + 6$$

? QUESTION Suppose you are going to divide $2x^3 + 13x^2 + 15x - 5$ by $x + 5$ using synthetic division.

   a. What are the coefficients of the dividend?
   b. What is the value of a?
   c. What is the degree of the first term of the quotient?

? ANSWERS **a.** The coefficients of the dividend are 2, 13, 15, and -5.
b. $x - a = x + 5 = x - (-5); a = -5$ **c.** The degree of the first term of the dividend is 3; therefore, the degree of the first term of the quotient is 2.

➡ Divide: $(2x^3 + 3x^2 - 4x + 8) \div (x + 3)$

$x - a = x + 3 = x - (-3); a = -3$

Write down the value of a and the coefficients of the dividend. Bring down the 2. Multiply $-3 \cdot 2$ and add the product (-6) to 3. Continue until all the coefficients have been used.

$$
\begin{array}{r|rrrr}
-3 & 2 & 3 & -4 & 8 \\
   &   & -6 & 9 & -15 \\
\hline
   & 2 & -3 & 5 & -7
\end{array}
$$

Coefficients of the quotient   Remainder

Write the quotient. The degree of the quotient is one less than the degree of the dividend.

$(2x^3 + 3x^2 - 4x + 8) \div (x + 3)$

$= 2x^2 - 3x + 5 - \dfrac{7}{x + 3}$

⬅

EXAMPLE 10

Divide. **a.** $(5x^2 - 3x + 7) \div (x - 1)$ **b.** $(3x^4 - 8x^2 + 2x + 1) \div (x + 2)$

Solution   **a.**
$$
\begin{array}{r|rrr}
1 & 5 & -3 & 7 \\
  &   & 5 & 2 \\
\hline
  & 5 & 2 & 9
\end{array}
$$
• $x - a = x - 1; a = 1$

$(5x^2 - 3x + 7) \div (x - 1) = 5x + 2 + \dfrac{9}{x - 1}$

b.
$$
\begin{array}{r|rrrrr}
-2 & 3 & 0 & -8 & 2 & 1 \\
   &   & -6 & 12 & -8 & 12 \\
\hline
   & 3 & -6 & 4 & -6 & 13
\end{array}
$$
• Insert a zero for the missing cubic term. $x - a = x + 2$; $a = -2$

$(3x^4 - 8x^2 + 2x + 1) \div (x + 2) = 3x^3 - 6x^2 + 4x - 6 + \dfrac{13}{x + 2}$

YOU TRY IT 10

Divide. **a.** $(6x^2 + 8x - 5) \div (x + 2)$ **b.** $(2x^4 - 3x^3 - 8x^2 - 2) \div (x - 3)$

Solution   See page S25.

6.3 EXERCISES

Topics for Discussion

1. When is the FOIL method used?

2. Why is $(a + b)^2$ not equal to $a^2 + b^2$?

3. Given that $\frac{x^3 + 1}{x + 1} = x^2 - x + 1$. Name two factors of $x^3 + 1$.

4. If a polynomial of degree 3 is multiplied by a polynomial of degree 2, what is the degree of the resulting polynomial?

5. Determine whether the statement is always true, sometimes true, or never true.

   a. The FOIL method is used to multiply two polynomials.
   b. Using the FOIL method, the terms $3x$ and 5 are the "First" terms in $(3x + 5)(2x + 7)$.
   c. To square a binomial means to multiply it times itself.

6. What is synthetic division?

7. When synthetic division is used to divide a polynomial by a binomial of the form $x - a$, how is the degree of the quotient related to the degree of the dividend?

■ Multiplication and Division of Polynomials

Multiply.

8. $-b(5b^2 + 7b - 35)$

9. $x^2(3x^4 - 3x^2 - 2)$

10. $y^3(-4y^3 - 6y + 7)$

11. $2y^2(-3y^2 - 6y + 7)$

12. $(-2b^2 - 3b + 4)(b - 5)$

13. $(-a^2 + 3a - 2)(2a - 1)$

14. $(x^3 - 3x + 2)(x - 4)$

15. $(y^3 + 4y^2 - 8)(2y - 1)$

16. $(y + 2)(y^3 + 2y^2 - 3y + 1)$

17. $(2a - 3)(2a^3 - 3a^2 + 2a - 1)$

18. $(x + 1)(x + 3)$

19. $(y + 2)(y + 5)$

20. $(a - 3)(a + 4)$

21. $(b - 6)(b + 3)$

22. $(y - 7)(y - 3)$

23. $(a - 8)(a - 9)$

24. $(2x + 1)(x + 7)$

25. $(y + 2)(5y + 1)$

26. $(3x - 1)(x + 4)$

27. $(7x - 2)(x + 4)$

28. $(4x - 3)(x - 7)$

29. $(2x - 3)(4x - 7)$

30. $(3y - 8)(y + 2)$

31. $(5y - 9)(y + 5)$

32. $(7a - 16)(3a - 5)$

33. $(5a - 12)(3a - 7)$

34. $(3b + 13)(5b - 6)$

35. $(x + y)(2x + y)$

36. $(2a + b)(a + 3b)$

37. $(3x - 4y)(x - 2y)$

38. $(2a - b)(3a + 2b)$

39. $(5a - 3b)(2a + 4b)$

40. $(d - 6)(d + 6)$

41. $(y - 5)(y + 5)$

42. $(2x + 3)(2x - 3)$

43. $(4x - 7)(4x + 7)$

44. $(x + 1)^2$

45. $(y - 3)^2$

46. $(3a - 5)^2$

47. $(6x - 5)^2$

Divide.

48. $\dfrac{2x + 2}{2}$

49. $\dfrac{5y + 5}{5}$

50. $\dfrac{10a - 25}{5}$

51. $\dfrac{16b - 40}{8}$

52. $\dfrac{3a^2 + 2a}{a}$

53. $\dfrac{6y^2 + 4y}{y}$

54. $\dfrac{4b^3 - 3b}{b}$

55. $\dfrac{12x^2 - 7x}{x}$

56. $\dfrac{3x^2 - 6x}{3x}$

57. $\dfrac{10y^2 - 6y}{2y}$

58. $\dfrac{5x^2 - 10x}{-5x}$

59. $\dfrac{3y^2 - 27y}{-3y}$

60. $\dfrac{x^3 + 3x^2 - 5x}{x}$

61. $\dfrac{a^3 - 5a^2 + 7a}{a}$

62. $\dfrac{x^6 - 3x^4 - x^2}{x^2}$

63. $\dfrac{a^8 - 5a^5 - 3a^3}{a^2}$

64. $\dfrac{5x^2y^2 + 10xy}{5xy}$

65. $\dfrac{8x^2y^2 - 24xy}{8xy}$

66. $(b^2 - 14 + 49) \div (b - 7)$

67. $(x^2 - x - 6) \div (x - 3)$

68. $(2x^2 + 5x + 2) \div (x + 2)$

69. $(2y^2 - 13y + 21) \div (y - 3)$

70. $(x^2 + 1) \div (x - 1)$

71. $(x^2 + 4) \div (x + 2)$

72. $(6x^2 - 7x) \div (3x - 2)$

73. $(6y^2 + 2y) \div (2y + 4)$

74. $(a^2 + 5a + 10) \div (a + 2)$

75. $(b^2 - 8b - 9) \div (b - 3)$

76. $(2y^2 - 9y + 8) \div (2y + 3)$

77. $(3x^2 + 5x - 4) \div (x - 4)$

78. $(8x + 3 + 4x^2) \div (2x - 1)$

79. $(10 + 21y + 10y^2) \div (2y + 3)$

80. $(x^3 + 3x^2 + 5x + 3) \div (x + 1)$

81. $(x^3 - 6x^2 + 7x - 2) \div (x - 1)$

82. $(x^4 - x^2 - 6) \div (x^2 + 2)$

83. $(x^4 + 3x^2 - 10) \div (x^2 - 2)$

84. *Geometry*   Find the area of the square. The dimension given is in meters.

2x + 1

85. *Geometry*   Find the area of the square. The dimension given is in yards.

3a − 2

86. *Geometry*   Find the area of the rectangle. The dimensions given are in miles.

5x
2x − 7

87. *Geometry*   Find the area of the rectangle. The dimensions given are in feet.

2x + 3
x − 6

88. *Geometry*   The radius of a circle is $(x + 4)$ inches. Find the area of the circle in terms of the variable x. Leave the answer in terms of π.

x + 4

89. *Geometry*   The radius of a circle is $(x - 3)$ centimeters. Find the area of the circle in terms of the variable x. Leave the answer in terms of π.

x − 3

90. *Geometry*   The length of a side of a cube is $(4x + 1)$ inches. Find the volume of the cube in terms of the variable x.

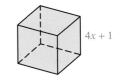
4x + 1

91. *Geometry*   A rectangular box has a length of $(5x + 3)$ centimeters, a width of $(2x - 1)$ centimeters, and a height of $4x$ centimeters. Find the volume of the box in terms of the variable x.

92. *Geometry*   The base of a triangle is $4x$ meters and the height is $(2x + 5)$ meters. Find the area of the triangle in terms of the variable x.

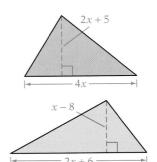
2x + 5
4x

93. *Geometry*   The base of a triangle is $(2x + 6)$ inches and the height is $(x - 8)$ inches. Find the area of the triangle in terms of the variable x.

94. *Geometry*   The width of a rectangle is $(3x + 1)$ inches. The length of the rectangle is twice the width. Find the area of the rectangle in terms of the variable x.

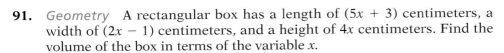
x − 8
2x + 6

95. *Geometry*   The width of a rectangle is $(4x - 3)$ centimeters. The length of the rectangle is twice the width. Find the area of the rectangle in terms of the variable x.

96. *Geometry*   The area of a rectangle is $(3x^2 - 22x - 16)$ square feet. The width of the rectangle is $(x - 8)$ feet. Find the length of the rectangle in terms of the variable x. Use the formula $L = \frac{A}{W}$, where L is the length, A is the area, and W is the width of a rectangle.

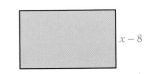
x − 8

97. *Geometry* The area of a rectangle is $(10x^2 + 7x - 12)$ square meters. The length of the rectangle is $(5x - 4)$ meters. Find the width of the rectangle in terms of the variable x. Use the formula $W = \frac{A}{L}$, where W is the width, A is the area, and L is the length of a rectangle.

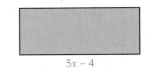

5x − 4

98. *Geometry* The area of a parallelogram is $(2x^3 - 9x^2 - 6x + 5)$ square inches. The height is $(x - 5)$ inches. Find the length of the base of the parallelogram in terms of the variable x. Use the formula $b = \frac{A}{h}$, where b is the length of the base, A is the area, and h is the height of a parallelogram.

$x - 5$

99. *Geometry* The area of a parallelogram is $(2x^3 + 6x^2 - 4x - 12)$ square meters. The length of the base is $(x + 3)$ meters. Find the height of the parallelogram in terms of the variable x. Use the formula $h = \frac{A}{b}$, where h is the height, A is the area, and b is the length of the base of a parallelogram.

$x + 3$

100. *Sports* A softball diamond has dimensions 45 feet by 45 feet. A base path border x feet wide lies on both the first-base side and the third-base side of the diamond. Express the total area of the softball diamond and the base paths in terms of the variable x.

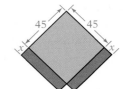

45   45

101. *Sports* An athletic field has dimensions 30 yards by 100 yards. An end zone that is w yards wide borders each end of the field. Express the total area of the field and the end zones in terms of the variable w.

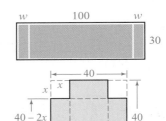

w 100 w

30

102. *Packaging* An open box is made from a square piece of cardboard that measures 40 inches on each side. To construct the box, squares that measure x inches on a side are cut from each corner. Express the volume of the box in terms of x. What is the volume of the box when x is 3 inches?

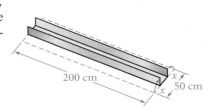

40

x x

$40 - 2x$ 40

$40 - 2x$

103. *Metallurgy* A sheet of tin 50 centimeters wide and 200 centimeters long is made into a trough by bending up two sides, each of length x, until they are perpendicular to the bottom. Express the volume of the trough in terms of x. What is the volume of the trough when x is 10 centimeters?

200 cm

x
x 50 cm

104. What polynomial has quotient $x^2 + 2x - 1$ when divided by $x + 3$?

105. What polynomial has quotient $3x - 4$ when divided by $4x + 5$?

106. Given that $x + 5$ is a factor of $x^3 + 12x^2 + 36x + 5$, find another factor of $x^3 + 12x^2 + 36x + 5$.

107. Given that $x - 2$ is a factor of $x^3 + 2x^2 - 9x + 2$, find another factor of $x^3 + 2x^2 - 9x + 2$.

108. Subtract $4x^2 - x - 5$ from the product of $x^2 + x + 3$ and $x - 4$.

109. Add $x^2 + 2x - 3$ to the product of $2x - 5$ and $3x + 1$.

110. The quotient of a polynomial and $2x + 1$ is $2x - 4 + \dfrac{7}{2x + 1}$. Find the polynomial.

111. The quotient of a polynomial and $x - 3$ is $x^2 - x + 8 + \dfrac{22}{x - 3}$. Find the polynomial.

112. Let $f(x) = \dfrac{x^3 - 10x^2 + 33x - 36}{x^2 - 6x + 9}$, $x \neq 3$. Simplify the expression $\dfrac{x^3 - 10x^2 + 33x - 36}{x^2 - 6x + 9}$ and then graph it using a graphing calculator. What is the relationship between the quotient and the graph?

■ Synthetic Division

Divide by using synthetic division.

113. $(x^3 - 6x^2 + 11x - 6) \div (x - 3)$

114. $(x^3 - 4x^2 + x + 6) \div (x + 1)$

115. $(2x^3 - x^2 + 6x + 9) \div (x + 1)$

116. $(3x^3 + 10x^2 + 6x - 4) \div (x + 2)$

117. $(6x - 3x^2 + x^3 - 9) \div (x + 2)$

118. $(5 - 5x + 4x^2 + x^3) \div (x - 3)$

119. $(x^3 + x - 2) \div (x + 1)$

120. $(x^3 + 2x + 5) \div (x - 2)$

121. $(3x^2 - 4) \div (x - 1)$

122. $(4x^2 - 8) \div (x - 2)$

123. $\dfrac{16x^2 - 13x^3 + 2x^4 - 9x + 20}{x - 5}$

124. $\dfrac{3 - 13x - 5x^2 + 9x^3 - 2x^4}{x - 3}$

125. $\dfrac{3x^4 + 3x^3 - x^2 + 3x + 2}{x + 1}$

126. $\dfrac{4x^4 + 12x^3 - x^2 - x + 2}{x + 3}$

127. $\dfrac{2x^4 - x^2 + 2}{x - 3}$

128. $\dfrac{x^4 - 3x^3 - 30}{x + 2}$

129. *Geometry*   A rectangular box has a volume of $(x^3 + 11x^2 + 38x + 40)$ cubic inches. The height of the box is $(x + 2)$ inches. The length of the box is $(x + 5)$ inches. Find the width of the box in terms of x.

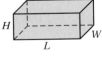

130. *Geometry*   The volume of a right circular cylinder is

$$\pi(x^3 + 7x^2 + 15x + 9)$$

cubic centimeters. The height of the cylinder is $(x + 1)$ centimeters. Find the area of the base of the cylinder in terms of x.

131. Three linear factors of $x^4 + x^3 - 7x^2 - x + 6$ are $x - 1$, $x - 2$, and $x + 3$. Find the other linear factor of $x^4 + x^3 - 7x^2 - x + 6$.

132. Three linear factors of $x^4 + 3x^3 - 8x^2 - 12x + 16$ are $x + 2$, $x - 1$, and $x + 4$. Find the other linear factor of $x^4 + 3x^3 - 8x^2 - 12x + 16$.

Applying Concepts

133. Determine whether the statement is always true, sometimes true, or never true.

    a. To multiply two polynomials, multiply each term of one polynomial by the other polynomial.

    b. The square of a binomial is a trinomial.

134. Is it possible to multiply a polynomial of degree 2 by a polynomial of degree 2 and have the product be a polynomial of degree 3? If so, give an example. If not, explain why not.

135. *Packaging* An open box is made from a square piece of cardboard that measures 20 inches on each side. To construct the box, squares that measure x inches on a side are cut from each corner. Express the volume of the box in terms of x. Can x be 10 inches? Explain your answer.

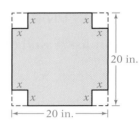

For what value of k will the remainder be zero?

136. $(x^3 - 3x^2 - x + k) \div (x - 3)$ **137.** $(x^3 - 2x^2 + x + k) \div (x - 2)$

138. $(x^2 + kx - 6) \div (x - 3)$ **139.** $(x^3 + kx + k - 1) \div (x - 1)$

140. When $x^2 + x + 2$ is divided by a polynomial, the quotient is $x + 4$, and the remainder is 14. Find the polynomial.

141. Find the value of t given that $x + 1$ is a factor of $3x^3 - 2x^2 + tx - 4$.

142. When a polynomial $P(x)$ is divided by a polynomial $d(x)$, it produces a quotient $q(x)$ and remainder $r(x)$. This can be stated mathematically as

$$P(x) = d(x) \cdot q(x) + r(x)$$

Suppose $P(x) = x^2 + 5x + 8$, and $d(x) = x + 1$. Find possible polynomials for $q(x)$ and $r(x)$.

143. Find the ordered pair of numbers (a, b) for which $x - 3$ is a factor of both $x^2 - (a + b)x + 3b$ and $(a - 1)x^2 + bx + a$.

144. A polynomial $P(x)$ has remainder 3 when divided by $x - 1$ and remainder 5 when divided by $x - 3$. Find the remainder when $P(x)$ is divided by $(x - 1)(x - 3)$.

EXPLORATION

1. *Patterns in Products of Polynomials*

    a. Multiply: $(x + 1)(x - 1)$
    b. Multiply: $(x + 1)(-x^2 + x - 1)$
    c. Multiply: $(x + 1)(x^3 - x^2 + x - 1)$
    d. Multiply: $(x + 1)(-x^4 + x^3 - x^2 + x - 1)$
    e. Use the pattern of the answers to parts a through d to multiply $(x + 1)(x^5 - x^4 + x^3 - x^2 + x - 1)$.
    f. Use the pattern of the answers to parts a through e to multiply $(x + 1)(-x^6 + x^5 - x^4 + x^3 - x^2 + x - 1)$.

2. *Patterns in Quotients of Polynomials*

Part I

    a. Divide each polynomial given below by $x - y$.

$$x^3 - y^3 \qquad x^5 - y^5 \qquad x^7 - y^7 \qquad x^9 - y^9$$

    b. Explain the pattern, and use the pattern to write the quotient of $(x^{11} - y^{11}) \div (x - y)$.

Part II: Determine whether the second polynomial is a factor of the first.

    c. $x^3 + 8; x + 2$ **d.** $x^3 - 8; x + 2$ **e.** $x^3 + 8; x - 2$ **f.** $x^3 - 8; x - 2$
    g. $x^4 + 16; x + 2$ **h.** $x^4 - 16; x + 2$ **i.** $x^4 + 16; x - 2$ **j.** $x^4 - 16; x - 2$

Use your answers to parts c through j to determine whether the statement is true or false.

    k. For $n > 0$, $x - y$ is a factor of $(x^n - y^n)$.
    l. For $n > 0$ and n an even integer, $x + y$ is a factor of $(x^n - y^n)$.
    m. For $n > 0$ and n an odd integer, $x + y$ is a factor of $(x^n - y^n)$.
    n. For $n > 0$ and n an even integer, $x + y$ is a factor of $(x^n + y^n)$.
    o. For $n > 0$ and n an odd integer, $x + y$ is a factor of $(x^n + y^n)$.

3. *Diagramming the Square of a Binomial*

    a. Explain why the diagram at the right represents $(a + b)^2 = a^2 + 2ab + b^2$.
    b. Draw diagrams representing each of the following.

$$(x + 3)^2 = x^2 + 6x + 9$$
$$(y + 5)^2 = y^2 + 10y + 25$$
$$(x + y)^2 = x^2 + 2xy + y^2$$

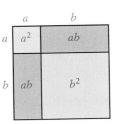

CHAPTER **6** SUMMARY

Key Terms

binomial [p. 394]
cubic polynomial [p. 395]
degree of a polynomial in one
   variable [p. 395]
descending order [p. 394]
linear polynomial [p. 395]
monomial [pp. 373 and 394]

opposite of a polynomial [p. 397]
polynomial [p. 394]
power of a monomial [p. 376]
quadratic polynomial [p. 395]
square of a binomial [p. 404]
synthetic division [p. 409]
trinomial [p. 394]

Essential Concepts

Rule for Multiplying Exponential Expressions [p. 375]
$x^m \cdot x^n = x^{m+n}$

Rule for Simplifying the Power of an Exponential Expression [p. 377]
$(x^m)^n = x^{m \cdot n}$

Rule for Simplifying Powers of Products [p. 377]
$(x^m y^n)^p = x^{m \cdot p} y^{n \cdot p}$

Rule for Dividing Exponential Expressions
For $x \neq 0$, $\dfrac{x^m}{x^n} = x^{m-n}$. [p. 379]

Zero as an Exponent
For $x \neq 0$, $x^0 = 1$. [p. 380]

Definition of Negative Exponents
For $x \neq 0$, $x^{-n} = \dfrac{1}{x^n}$ and $\dfrac{1}{x^{-n}} = x^n$. [p. 381]

Rule for Simplifying Powers of Quotients
For $y \neq 0$, $\left(\dfrac{x^m}{y^n}\right)^p = \dfrac{x^{m \cdot p}}{y^{n \cdot p}}$. [p. 383]

Addition of Polynomials
To add polynomials, add the coefficients of the like terms. [p. 396]

Subtraction of Polynomials
To subtract two polynomials, add the opposite of the second polynomial to the first. [p. 397]

Multiplication of Polynomials
To multiply two polynomials, multiply each term of one polynomial times each term of the other polynomial. [p. 403]

The FOIL Method
To multiply two binomials, add the products of the **F**irst terms, the **O**uter terms, the **I**nner terms, and the **L**ast terms. [p. 404]

Division of Polynomials

To divide a polynomial by a monomial, divide each term of the polynomial by the monomial. If the divisor is not a monomial, use the long-division method similar to that used for division of whole numbers. [pp. 406–407]

Equation Used to Check Division [p. 407]

(Quotient × Divisor) + Remainder = Dividend

Scientific Notation

To express a number in scientific notation, write it in the form $a \times 10^n$, where a is a number between 1 and 10 and n is an integer. If the number is greater than 10, the exponent on 10 will be positive. If the number is less than 1, the exponent on 10 will be negative.

$$367{,}000{,}000 = 3.67 \times 10^8$$
$$0.0000059 = 5.9 \times 10^{-6}$$

To change a number written in scientific notation to decimal notation, move the decimal point to the right if the exponent on 10 is positive and to the left if the exponent on 10 is negative. Move the decimal point the same number of places as the absolute value of the exponent on 10. [p. 385]

$$2.418 \times 10^7 = 24{,}180{,}000$$
$$9.06 \times 10^{-5} = 0.0000906$$

CHAPTER **6** *REVIEW EXERCISES*

1. Subtract: $47a^2b^3c - 23a^2b^3c$

2. Subtract: $(3y^2 - 5y + 8) - (-2y^2 + 5y + 8)$

3. Multiply: $(5xy^2)(-4x^2y^3)$

4. Simplify: $\dfrac{12x^2}{-3x^{-4}}$

5. Simplify: $(2ab^{-3})(3a^{-2}b^4)$

6. Divide: $\dfrac{16x^5 - 8x^3 + 20x}{4x}$

7. Multiply: $-3y^2(-2y^2 + 3y - 6)$

8. Simplify: $(2x - 5)^2$

9. Simplify: $(-3a^2b^{-3})^2$

10. Write 0.0000029 in scientific notation.

11. Multiply: $(4y - 3)(4y + 3)$

12. Multiply: $(2a - 7)(5a^2 - 2a + 3)$

13. Simplify: $\dfrac{-2a^2b^3}{8a^4b^8}$

14. Divide: $(8x^2 + 4x - 3) \div (2x - 3)$

15. Write 3.5×10^{-8} in decimal notation.

16. Multiply: $(5x^2yz^4)(-2xy^3z^{-1})(7x^{-2}y^{-2}z^3)$

17. Divide by using synthetic division: $(x^3 - 6x^2 + 16x - 20) \div (x - 3)$

18. The length of the side of a square is $(2x + 3)$ meters. Find the area of the square in terms of the variable x.

$2x + 3$

19. The mass of the moon is 8.103×10^{19} tons. Write this number in standard form.

20. The height h, in feet, of a golf ball t seconds after it has been struck is given by $h(t) = -16t^2 + 60t$. Determine the height of the ball 2 seconds after it is hit.

CHAPTER **6** *TEST*

1. Add: $(12y^2 + 17y - 4) + (9y^2 - 13y + 3)$

2. Multiply: $(6a^2\, b^5)(-3a^6b)$

3. Multiply: $4x^2(3x^3 + 2x - 7)$

4. Simplify: $\dfrac{-6x^{-2}y^4}{3xy}$

5. Simplify: $(5a^{-1}\, b^{-4})(-2a^2\, b^3)$

6. Divide: $\dfrac{12b^7 + 36b^5 - 3b^3}{3b^3}$

7. Simplify: $(-2a^4\, b^{-5})^3$

8. Write 78,000,000,000 in scientific notation.

9. Evaluate: $\dfrac{6^2}{6^{-2}}$

10. Multiply: $(6y - 5)(6y + 5)$

11. Simplify: $(5.2 \times 10^{-3})(1.4 \times 10^7)$

12. Multiply: $(2a + 3)(3a^2 + 4a - 7)$

13. Subtract: $(6x^3 - 7x^2 + 6x - 7) - (4x^3 - 3x^2 + 7)$

14. Divide: $(x^3 - 5x^2 + 5x + 5) \div (x - 3)$

15. Write 2.971×10^7 in decimal notation.

16. Simplify: $(-3x^{-2}\, y^{-3})^{-2}$

17. What polynomial must be added to $12x^2 + 3x - 4$ so that the sum is $6x^2 - x + 1$?

18. The length of a rectangle is $(5x + 3)$ centimeters. The width is $(2x - 7)$ centimeters. Find the area of the rectangle in terms of the variable x.

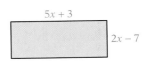
$5x + 3$
$2x - 7$

19. Light from the sun supplies Earth with 2.4×10^{14} horsepower. Write this number in standard form.

20. The wavelength L, in meters, of a deep-water wave can be approximated by the function $L(v) = 0.6411v^2$, where v is the wave speed in meters per second. Find the length of a deep-water wave that has a speed of 30 meters per second.

◀ CUMULATIVE REVIEW EXERCISES

1. If $5 \le a \le 10$ and $20 \le b \le 30$, find the maximum value of $\dfrac{a}{b}$.

2. Evaluate $-2a^2 \div (2b) - c$ when $a = -4$, $b = 2$, and $c = -1$.

3. Identify the property that justifies the statement.
$$(3 + 8) + 7 = 3 + (8 + 7)$$

4. Multiply: $-\dfrac{3}{4}(-24x^2)$

5. Find the domain and range of the relation $\{(-5, -4), (-3, -2), (-1, 0), (1, 2), (3, 4)\}$. Is the relation a function?

6. Find the range of the function given by the equation $f(x) = \dfrac{4}{5}x - 3$ if the domain is $\{-10, -5, 0, 5, 10\}$.

7. Solve: $4 + 3(x - 2) = 13$

8. Solve $-4x - 2 \ge 10$. Write the solution set in interval notation.

9. Graph $3x - 4y = 12$ by using the x- and y-intercepts.

10. Graph $f(x) = -3x - 3$.

11. Graph the solution set of $-3x + 2y < 6$.

12. Find the equation of the line that contains the points $(-5, 2)$ and $(5, 6)$.

13. Solve by the addition method: $2x - 3y = -4$
$\qquad\qquad\qquad\qquad\qquad\qquad 5x + y = 7$

14. Simplify: $(-2x^{-4}y^2)^3$

15. Subtract: $(3y^3 - 5y^2 - 6) - (2y^2 - 8y + 1)$

16. Divide: $(8x^2 + 4x - 3) \div (2x - 3)$

17. Two trains, one traveling at twice the speed of the other, start at the same time from stations that are 240 miles apart and travel toward each other. In 2.5 hours, the trains pass each other. Find the rate of each train.

18. How many ounces of pure gold that costs $360 per ounce must be mixed with 80 ounces of an alloy that costs $120 per ounce to make a mixture that costs $200 per ounce?

19. A 1000-mile trip from one city to another takes 4 hours when a plane is flying with the wind. The return trip against the wind takes 5 hours. Find the rate of the plane in calm air and the rate of the wind.

20. The graph shows the relationship between the distance traveled, in miles, and the time of travel, in hours. Find the slope of the line between the two points on the graph. Write a sentence that states the meaning of the slope.

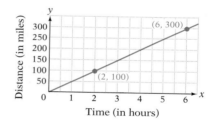

Keystroke Guide for the TI-83 and TI-83 Plus

This appendix contains some keystroke suggestions for many graphing calculator operations that are featured in this text. The keystrokes are for the TI-83 and TI-83 Plus calculators. The descriptions in the margin are the same as those used in the text and are arranged alphabetically. Please see your manual for additional information about your calculator.

Basic Operations

Numerical calculations are performed on the **home screen.** You can always return to the home screen by pressing [2nd] QUIT. Pressing [CLEAR] erases the home screen.

To evaluate the expression $-2(3 + 5) - 8 \div 4$, use the following keystrokes.

[(−)] 2 [(] 3 [+] 5 [)] [−] 8 [÷] 4 [ENTER]

> Note: There is a difference between the key to enter a negative number, [(−)], and the key for subtraction, [−]. You cannot use these keys interchangeably.

The [2nd] key is used to access the commands in gold writing above a key. For instance, to evaluate the $\sqrt{49}$, press [2nd] √ 49 [)] [ENTER].

The [ALPHA] key is used to place a letter on the screen. One reason to do this is to store a value of a variable. The following keystrokes give A the value of 5.

5 [STO▸] [ALPHA] A [ENTER]

This value is now available in calculations. For instance, we can find the value of $3a^2$ by using the following keystrokes: 3 [ALPHA] A [x²]. To display the value of the variable on the screen, press [2nd] RCL [ALPHA] A.

> Note: When you use the [ALPHA] key, only capital letters are available on the TI-83 calculator.

Screen	
⁻2(3+5)−8/4	-18

Screen	
√(49)	7

Screen	
5→A	5

Screen	
3A²	75

Complex Numbers

To perform operations on complex numbers, first press [MODE] and then use the arrow keys to select a+bi. Then press [ENTER] [2nd] QUIT.

Addition of complex numbers To add $(3 + 4i) + (2 - 7i)$, use the keystrokes

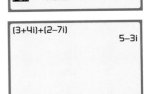

[(] 3 [+] 4 [2nd] i [)] [+]
[(] 2 [−] 7 [2nd] i [)] [ENTER].

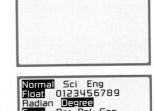

Normal Sci Eng
Float 0123456789
Radian **Degree**
Func Par Pol Seq
Connected Dot
Sequential Simul
Real **a+bi** re^θi
Full Horiz G−T

Screen	
(3+4i)+(2−7i)	5−3i

Division of complex numbers. To divide $\dfrac{26 + 2i}{2 + 4i}$, use the keystrokes (26 + 2 2nd *i*) ÷ (2 + 4 2nd *i*) ENTER .

Note: Operations for subtraction and multiplication are similar.

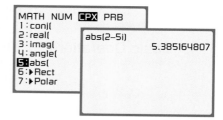

Additional operations on complex numbers can be found by selecting **CPX** under the MATH key.

To find the absolute value of $2 - 5i$, press MATH (scroll to **CPX**) (scroll to **abs**) ENTER (2 — 5 2nd *i*) ENTER .

Correlation Coefficient

The value of the correlation coefficient for a regression equation calculation is not shown unless the **DiagnosticOn** feature is enabled. To enable this feature, press 2nd CATALOG D (scroll to **DiagnosticOn**) ENTER ENTER .

To calculate the correlation coefficient, proceed as if calculating a regression equation.

Evaluating Functions

There are various methods of evaluating a function but all methods require that the expression be entered as one of the ten functions Y_1 to Y_0. To evaluate $f(x) = \dfrac{x^2}{x - 1}$ when $x = -3$, enter the expression into, for instance, Y_1, and then press VARS ▸ 11 ((—) 3) ENTER .

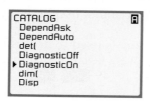

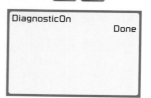

Note: If you try to evaluate a function at a number that is not in the domain of the function, you will get an error message. For instance, 1 is not in the domain of $f(x) = \dfrac{x^2}{x - 1}$. If we try to evaluate the function at 1, the error screen at the right appears.

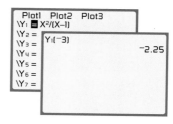

Evaluating Variable Expressions

To evaluate a variable expression, first store the values of each variable. Then enter the variable expression. For instance, to evaluate $s^2 + 2sl$ when $s = 4$ and $l = 5$, use the following keystrokes.

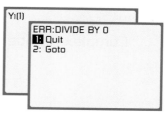

4 STO▸ ALPHA S ENTER 5 STO▸ ALPHA L ENTER ALPHA S x^2 + 2 ALPHA S ALPHA L ENTER

Graph

To graph a function, use the ⬤Y= key to enter the expression for the function, select a suitable viewing window, and then press ⬤GRAPH. For instance, to graph $f(x) = 0.1x^3 - 2x - 1$ in the standard viewing window, use the following keystrokes.

⬤Y= 0.1 ⬤X,T,θ,n ⬤^ 3 ⬤− 2 ⬤X,T,θ,n ⬤− 1 ⬤ZOOM (scroll to 6) ⬤ENTER

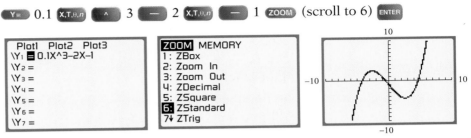

Note: For the keystrokes above, you do not have to scroll to 6. Alternatively, use ⬤ZOOM 6. This will select the standard viewing window and automatically start the graph. Use the ⬤WINDOW key to create a custom window for a graph.

Graphing Inequalities

To illustrate this feature, we will graph $y \le 2x - 1$. Enter $2x - 1$ into Y1. Because $y \le 2x - 1$, we want to shade below the graph. Move the cursor to the left of Y1 and press ⬤ENTER three times. Press ⬤GRAPH.

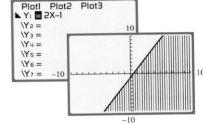

Note: To shade above the graph, move the cursor to the left of Y1 and press ⬤ENTER two times. An inequality with the symbol $\le$ or $\ge$ should be graphed with a solid line, and an inequality with the symbol $<$ or $>$ should be graphed with a dashed line. However, the graph of a linear inequality on a graphing calculator does not distinguish between a solid line and a dashed line.

To graph the solution set of a system of inequalities, solve each inequality for y and graph each inequality. The solution set is the intersection of the two inequalities. The solution set of $\begin{array}{l} 3x + 2y > 10 \\ 4x - 3y \le 5 \end{array}$ is shown at the right.

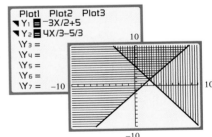

Intersect

The INTERSECT feature is used to solve a system of equations. To illustrate this feature, we will use the system of equations $\begin{array}{l} 2x - 3y = 13 \\ 3x + 4y = -6 \end{array}$.

Note: Some equations can be solved by this method. See the section "Solve an equation" below. Also, this method is used to find a number in the domain of a function for a given number in the range. See the section "Find a domain element."

Solve each of the equations in the system of equations for y. In this case, we have $y = \frac{2}{3}x - \frac{13}{3}$ and $y = -\frac{3}{4}x - \frac{3}{2}$.

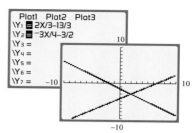

Use the Y-editor to enter $\frac{2}{3}x - \frac{13}{3}$ into Y_1 and $-\frac{3}{4}x - \frac{3}{2}$ into Y_2. Graph the two functions in the standard viewing window. (If the window does not show the point of intersection of the two graphs, adjust the window until you can see the point of intersection.)

Press 2nd CALC (scroll to 5, intersect) ENTER.

Alternatively, you can just press 2nd CALC 5.

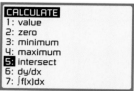

First curve? is shown at the bottom of the screen and identifies one of the two graphs on the screen. Press ENTER.

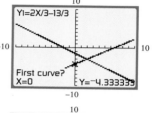

Second curve? is shown at the bottom of the screen and identifies the second of the two graphs on the screen. Press ENTER.

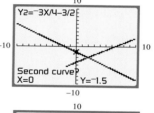

Guess? shown at the bottom of the screen asks you to use the left or right arrow key to move the cursor to the *approximate* location of the point of intersection. (If there are two or more points of intersection, it does not matter which one you choose first.) Press ENTER.

The solution of the system of equations is $(2, -3)$.

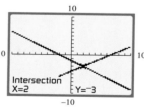

Solve an equation   To illustrate the steps involved, we will solve the equation $2x + 4 = -3x - 1$. The idea is to write the equation as the system of equations $\begin{array}{l} y = 2x + 4 \\ y = -3x - 1 \end{array}$ and then use the steps for solving a system of equations.

Use the Y-editor to enter the left and right sides of the equation into Y_1 and Y_2. Graph the two functions and then follow the steps for Intersect.

The solution is -1, the x-coordinate of the point of intersection.

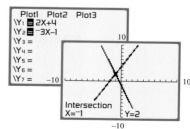

Find a domain element   For this example, we will find a number in the domain of $f(x) = -\frac{2}{3}x + 2$ that corresponds to 4 in the range of the function. This is like solving the system of equations $y = -\frac{2}{3}x + 2$ and $y = 4$.

Use the Y= editor to enter the expression for the function in Y_1 and the desired output, 4, in Y_2. Graph the two functions and then follow the steps for Intersect.

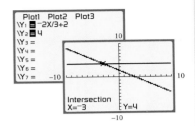

The point of intersection is $(-3, 4)$. The number -3 in the domain of f produces an output of 4 in the range of f.

Math Pressing MATH gives you access to many built-in functions. The following keystrokes will convert 0.125 to a fraction: .125 MATH 1 ENTER .

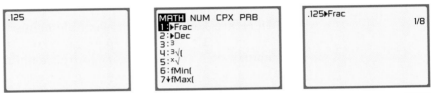

Additional built-in functions under MATH can be found by pressing MATH ▶ . For instance, to evaluate $-|-25|$, press (−) MATH ▶ 1 (−) 25) ENTER .

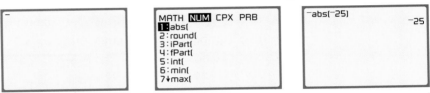

See your owner's manual for assistance with other functions under the MATH key.

Matrix On a TI-83, **matrix operations** are accessed by pressing MATRIX. On a TI-83 Plus, press 2nd MATRX to access the matrix menu.

To enter the elements of a matrix, select the matrix key. Then use the right arrow to select EDIT. Now use the down arrow key to select the name of the matrix. There are 10 matrices with names A through J. By pressing the down arrow key, you can see the additional names. Once you have selected the name of the matrix, press ENTER .

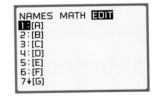

For instance, to enter the matrix $\begin{bmatrix} 2 & -3 & 4 \\ 1 & 5 & 3 \end{bmatrix}$ with 2 rows and 3 columns, access the matrix menu, arrow right to EDIT, and press ENTER . Now enter the dimension and the elements of the matrix, pressing ENTER after each number. You can change an element by using the arrow keys to select that element. After you have entered all the elements, press 2nd QUIT to return to the home screen.

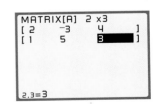

Elementary row operations   Elementary row operations are performed by selecting **MATH** from the matrix menu. Use the down arrow key to scroll to those operations. Your screen should look something like this:

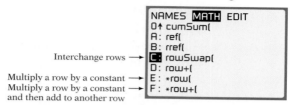

The operation `row+(` shown by **D:** is to add two rows. This is really the same as **F:** where the constant is 1.

Here are keystrokes for each elementary row operation. We will use the matrix $\begin{bmatrix} 1 & 3 & -4 & 6 \\ 3 & 2 & 0 & -1 \\ -2 & -5 & 3 & 4 \end{bmatrix}$ for this demonstration and assume it is stored in matrix [B].

Interchange rows: Access the matrix menu and highlight **MATH**. Scroll down to **C:rowSwap(**. Press `ENTER`. Access the matrix menu. Scroll to [B]; then press `ENTER`. Press `,` 1 `,` 3 `)` `ENTER`. (This interchanges row 1 and row 3. Change these numbers to interchange other rows.)

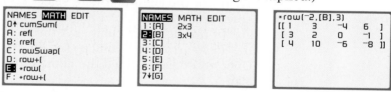

Multiply a row by a constant: Access the matrix menu and highlight **MATH**. Scroll down to **E:*row(**. Press `ENTER` `(-)` 2. (This is the constant that will multiply a row.) Press `,`. Access the matrix menu. Scroll to [B] and then press `ENTER`. Press `,` 3 `)` `ENTER`. (Row 3 is being multiplied.)

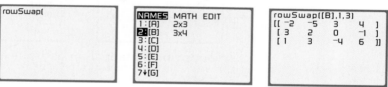

Multiply a row by a constant and then add it to another row: Access the matrix menu and highlight **MATH**. Scroll down to **F:*row+(**. Press `ENTER` 2. (This is the constant that will multiply a row.) Press `,`. Access the matrix menu. Scroll to [B]; then press `ENTER`. Press `,` 1 `,` 3 `)` `ENTER`. (Row 1 is being multiplied by 2 and then added to row 3.)

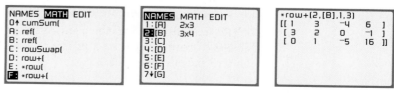

Row echelon form   The ref(function performs all of the elementary row operations on a matrix and directly produces a row echelon form of a matrix. The abbreviation ref stands for **r**ow **e**chelon **f**orm.

To write $\begin{bmatrix} 2 & 1 & 3 & -1 \\ 1 & 3 & 5 & -1 \\ -3 & -1 & 1 & 2 \end{bmatrix}$ in row echelon form, enter the matrix in, for instance, [A].

Press (2nd) QUIT. Then access the matrix menu and highlight MATH, scroll to ref(and press (ENTER), access the matrix menu, select [A], and press (ENTER) ( ) (ENTER). This will produce a matrix in row echelon form. Pressing (MATH) 1 (ENTER) will rewrite the matrix with fractions rather than decimals. (See MATH for assistance with the fraction command.)

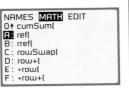
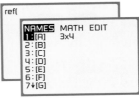

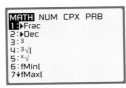
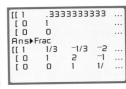

Min and Max

The local minimum and the local maximum values of a function are calculated by accessing the CALC menu. For this demonstration, we will find the minimum value and the maximum value of $f(x) = 0.2x^3 + 0.3x^2 - 3.6x + 2$.

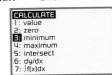

Enter the function into Y₁. Press (2nd) CALC (scroll to 3 for minimum of the function) (ENTER).

Alternatively, you can just press (2nd) CALC 3.

Left Bound? shown at the bottom of the screen asks you to use the left or right arrow key to move the cursor to the *left* of the minimum. Press (ENTER).

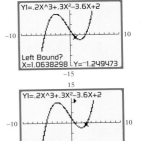

Right Bound? shown at the bottom of the screen asks you to use the left or right arrow key to move the cursor to the *right* of the minimum. Press (ENTER).

Guess? shown at the bottom of the screen asks you to use the left or right arrow key to move the cursor to the *approximate* location of the minimum. Press (ENTER).

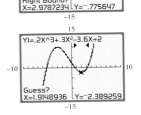

The minimum value of the function is the *y*-coordinate. For this example, the minimum value of the function is −2.4.

The *x*-coordinate for the minimum is 2. However, because of rounding errors in the calculation, it is shown as a number close to 2.

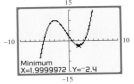

To find the maximum value of the function, follow the same steps as above except select maximum under the CALC menu. The screens for this calculation are shown below.

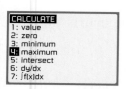 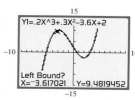 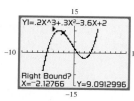 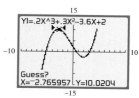 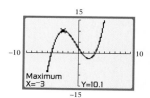

The maximum value of the function is 10.1.

Radical Expressions

To evaluate a square-root expression, press (2nd) $\sqrt{}$.

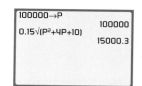

For instance, to evaluate $0.15\sqrt{p^2 + 4p + 10}$ when $p = 100,000$, first store 100,000 in P. Then press 0.15 (2nd) $\sqrt{}$ (ALPHA) P (x^2) (+) 4 (ALPHA) P (+) 10 ()) (ENTER).

To evaluate a radical expression other than a square root, access $\sqrt[x]{}$ by pressing (MATH). For instance, to evaluate $\sqrt[4]{67}$, press 4 (the index of the radical) (MATH) (scroll to 5) (ENTER) 67 (ENTER).

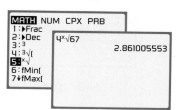

Regression

For the discussion of linear regression, we will use the data in this table.

Temperature, x (in °C)	20	35	50	60	75	90	100
Grams of sugar, y	50	80	120	145	175	205	230

All calculations and graphs involving statistical data begin by entering the data using the Edit option, which is accessed by pressing (STAT).

For the data above, press (STAT) to access the statistics menu. Press 1 to Edit or enter data. To delete data already in a list, press the up arrow until the cursor is highlighting the list name. For instance, to delete data in L_1, highlight L_1. Then press (CLEAR) and (ENTER). Now enter each value of the independent variable in L_1, pressing (ENTER) after each entry. Use the up and down arrow keys to change a value. When all values of the independent variable are entered, press (▶). This will put you in the next column to enter the values of the dependent variable in L_2.

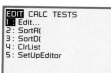 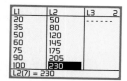

Create a scatter diagram   Press (2nd) STATPLOT (use the down arrow key to select Plot1, Plot2, or Plot3) (ENTER). Use arrow keys to move the cursor to ON and then press (ENTER). The first graph type is for a scatter diagram. Move the cursor over that symbol and press (ENTER). Be sure that Xlist and Ylist are the names of the lists into which you stored data. You can change these by pressing  and then selecting the appropriate list, L₁ through L₆. Prepare to graph the data by adjusting the viewing window by pressing **WINDOW** and entering appropriate values. Now press **GRAPH** .

  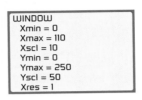 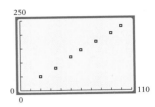

Note: You can tell that **STAT PLOTS** is active by pressing **Y=** . For one screen at the right, observe that **PLOT1** is highlighted, indicating it is active. To turn **STAT PLOTS** off, use the up arrow key to highlight it, and then press **ENTER** . Now use the arrow key to move the cursor to the right of the equals sign for Y₁.

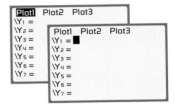

Find a linear regression equation Press **STAT** ▶ (scroll to 4) **ENTER** **2nd** L₁ **,** **2nd** L₂ **,** **VARS** ▶ 1 1 **ENTER** . The values of the slope and *y*-intercept of the linear regression equation will be displayed on the screen. If **DiagnosticOn** is enabled (see Correlation coefficient), then the coefficient of determination r^2 and the correlation coefficient *r* are also shown.

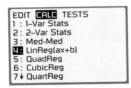  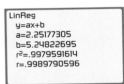

Note: If data are stored in L₁ and L₂, the keystrokes **2nd** L₁ **,** **2nd** L₂ are not necessary. The keystrokes **VARS** ▶ 11 **ENTER** place the regression equation in Y₁. These keystrokes are not necessary but are helpful if you need to graph the regression equation or evaluate the equation at a given value of the independent variable. See below for more details.

Graph a linear regression equation Press **STAT** ▶ (scroll to 4) **ENTER** **2nd** L₁ **,** **2nd** L₂ **,** **VARS** ▶ 11 **ENTER** . This will store the regression equation in Y₁. Now press **GRAPH** . It may be necessary to adjust the viewing window.

Evaluate a regression equation Complete the steps to graph a regression equation, but do not graph the equation. To evaluate the equation when $x = 50$, press **VARS** ▶ 11 **(** 50 **)** **ENTER** .

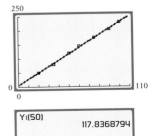

Other regression equations can be calculated. For instance, to find a regression equation of the form $y = ax^b$, called a power regression equation, enter the data and then select PwrReg from the CALC menu under the STAT menu.

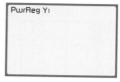

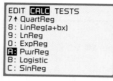

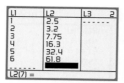

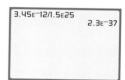

L1	L2	L3	2
1	2.5	-----	
2	3.2		
3	7.75		
4	16.3		
5	32.4		
6	61.8		

L2(7) =

```
EDIT  CALC  TESTS
7↑ QuartReg
8 : LinReg(a+bx)
9 : LnReg
0 : ExpReg
A: PwrReg
B : Logistic
C : SinReg
```

```
PwrReg Y1
```

```
PwrReg
y=a*x^b
a=1.533042316
b=1.817355148
r²=.8907910201
r=.9438172599
```

Note: Because the data were entered into L1 and L2, it was not necessary to include them in PwrReg. We did include the optional Y1. This is good practice because it makes evaluating and graphing a regression equation much easier.

Scientific Notation

To enter a number in scientific notation, use 2nd EE. For instance, to find $\frac{3.45 \times 10^{-12}}{1.5 \times 10^{25}}$, press 3.45 2nd EE (−) 12 ÷ 1.5 2nd EE 25 ENTER. The answer is 2.3×10^{-37}.

```
3.45E-12/1.5E25
                  2.3E-37
```

Sequences and Series

The terms of a sequence and the sum of a series can be calculated by using the 2nd LIST feature.

Store a sequence   A sequence is stored in one of the lists L1 through L6. For instance, to store the sequence 1, 3, 5, 7, 9 in L1, use the following keystrokes.

2nd { 1 , 3 , 5 , 7 ,
9 2nd } STO➡ 2nd L1 ENTER

```
{1,3,5,7,9}→L1
            {1,3,5,7,9}
```

Display the terms of a sequence   The terms of a sequence are displayed by using the function seq(expression, variable, begin, end, increment). For instance, to display the 3rd through 8th terms of the sequence given by $a_n = n^2 + 6$, enter the following keystrokes.

2nd LIST ▶ (scroll to 5)

ENTER X,T,θ,n x² + 6

, X,T,θ,n , 3 , 8

, 1 ENTER STO➡ 2nd L1 ENTER

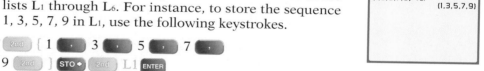

```
NAMES  OPS  MATH
1 : SortA(
2 : SortD(
3 : dim(
4 : Fill(
5: seq(
6 : cumSum(
7↓ΔList(
```
```
seq(X²+6,X,3,8,1)
        {15 22 31 42 55...
```

The keystrokes STO➡ 2nd L1 ENTER store the terms of the sequence in L1. This is not necessary but is sometimes helpful if additional work will be done with that sequence.

Find a sequence of partial sums   To find a sequence of partial sums, use the cumSum(function. For instance, to find the sequence of partial sums for 2, 4, 6, 8, 10, use the following keystrokes.

2nd LIST ▶ (scroll to 6)

ENTER 2nd { 2 , 4 , 6

, 8 , 10 2nd }) ENTER

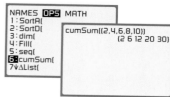

```
NAMES  OPS  MATH
1 : SortA(
2 : SortD(
3 : dim(
4 : Fill(
5 : seq(
6: cumSum(
7↓ΔList(
```
```
cumSum({2,4,6,8,10})
        {2 6 12 20 30}
```

If a sequence is stored as a list in L_1, then the sequence of partial sums can be calculated by pressing [2nd] LIST [▶] (scroll to 6 [or press 6]) [ENTER] [2nd] L1 [ )] [ENTER].

Find the sum of a series   The sum of a series is calculated using sum<list, start, end>. For instance, to find $\sum_{n=3}^{6} (n^2 + 2)$, enter the following keystrokes.

[2nd] LIST [▶] [▶] (scroll to 5)

[ENTER] [2nd] LIST [▶] (scroll to 5 [or press 5])

[ENTER] [X,T,θ,n] [x²] [+] 2 [,] [X,T,θ,n] [,] 3

[,] 6 [,] 1 [ )] [ENTER]

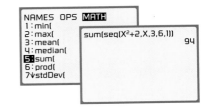

Table   There are three steps in creating an input/output table for a function. First use the [Y=] editor to input the function. The second step is setting up the table, and the third step is displaying the table.

To set up the table, press [2nd] TBLSET. TblStart is the first value of the independent variable in the input/output table. $\triangle$Tbl is the difference between successive values. Setting this to 1 means that, for this table, the input values are $-2, -1, 0, 1, 2. \ldots$ If $\triangle$Tbl $= 0.5$, then the input values are $-2, -1.5, -1, -0.5, 0, 0.5, \ldots$

Indpnt is the independent variable. When this is set to Auto, values of the independent variable are automatically entered into the table. Depend is the dependent variable. When this is set to Auto, values of the dependent variable are automatically entered into the table.

To display the table, press [2nd] TABLE. An input/output table for $f(x) = x^2 - 1$ is shown at the right.

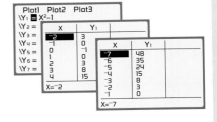

Once the table is on the screen, the up and down arrow keys can be used to display more values in the table. For the table at the right, we used the up arrow key to move to $x = -7$.

An input/output table for any given input can be created by selecting Ask for the independent variable. The table at the right shows an input/output table for $f(x) = \dfrac{4x}{x - 2}$ for selected values of x. Note the word ERROR when 2 was entered. This occurred because f is not defined when $x = 2$.

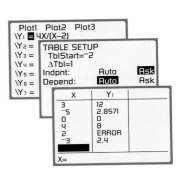

Note: Using the table feature in Ask mode is the same as evaluating a function for given values of the independent variable. For instance, from the table at the right, we have $f(4) = 8$.

Test

The TEST feature has many uses, one of which is to graph the solution set of a linear inequality in one variable. To illustrate this feature, we will graph the solution set of $x - 1 < 4$. Press (Y=) (X,T,θ,n) (−) 1 (2nd) TEST (scroll to 5) (ENTER) 4 (GRAPH).

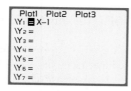 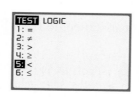 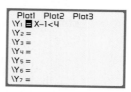 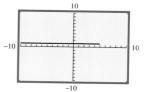

Trace

Once a graph is drawn, pressing (TRACE) will place a cursor on the screen, and the coordinates of the point below the cursor are shown at the bottom of the screen. Use the left and right arrow keys to move the cursor along the graph. For the graph at the right, we have $f(4.8) = 3.4592$, where $f(x) = 0.1x^3 - 2x + 2$ is shown at the top left of the screen.

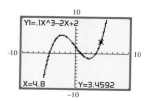

In TRACE mode, you can evaluate a function at any value of the independent variable that is within Xmin and Xmax. To do this, first graph the function. Now press (TRACE) (the value of x) (ENTER). For the graph at the left below, we used $x = -3.5$. If a value of x is chosen outside the window, an error message is displayed.

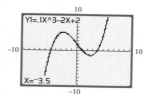 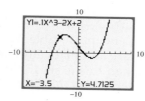 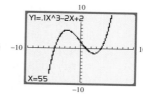 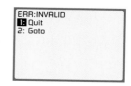

In the example above where we entered -3.5 for x, the value of the function was calculated as 4.7125. This means that $f(-3.5) = 4.7125$. The keystrokes (2nd) QUIT (VARS) (▶) 11 (MATH) 1 (ENTER) will convert the decimal value to a fraction.

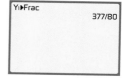

When the TRACE feature is used with two or more graphs, the up and down arrow keys are used to move between the graphs. The graphs below are for the functions $f(x) = 0.1x^3 - 2x + 2$ and $g(x) = 2x - 3$. By using the up and down arrows, we can place the cursor on either graph. The right and left arrows are used to move along the graph.

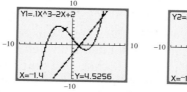 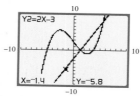

Window

The viewing window for a graph is controlled by pressing (WINDOW). Xmin and Xmax are the minimum value and maximum value, respectively, of the independent variable shown on the graph. Xscl is the distance between tic marks on the x-axis. Ymin and Ymax are the minimum value and maximum value, respectively, of the dependent variable shown on the graph. Yscl is the distance between tic marks on the y-axis. Leave Xres as 1.

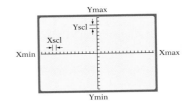

Note: In the standard viewing window, the distance between tic marks on the x-axis is different from the distance between tic marks on the y-axis. This will distort a graph. A more accurate picture of a graph can be created by using a square viewing window. See ZOOM.

 The ⟨Y=⟩ editor is used to enter the expression for a function. There are ten possible functions, labeled Y_1 to Y_0, that can be active at any one time. For instance, to enter $f(x) = x^2 + 3x - 2$ as Y_1, use the following keystrokes.

⟨Y=⟩ ⟨X,T,θ,n⟩ ⟨x²⟩ ⟨+⟩ 3 ⟨X,T,θ,n⟩ ⟨−⟩ 2

Note: If an expression is already entered for Y_1, place the cursor anywhere on that expression and press ⟨CLEAR⟩.

To enter $s = \dfrac{2v - 1}{v^3 - 3}$ into Y_2, place the cursor to the right of the equals sign for Y_2. Then press ⟨(⟩ 2 ⟨X,T,θ,n⟩ ⟨−⟩ 1 ⟨)⟩ ⟨÷⟩ ⟨(⟩ ⟨X,T,θ,n⟩ ⟨^⟩ 3 ⟨−⟩ 3 ⟨)⟩.

Note: When we enter an equation, the independent variable, v in the expression above, is entered using ⟨X,T,θ,n⟩. The dependent variable, s in the expression above, is one of Y_1 to Y_0. Also note the use of parentheses to ensure the correct order of operations.

Observe the black rectangle that covers the equals sign for the two examples we have shown. This rectangle means that the function is "active." If we were to press ⟨GRAPH⟩, then the graph of both functions would appear. You can make a function inactive by using the arrow keys to move the cursor over the equals sign of that function and then pressing ⟨ENTER⟩. This will remove the black rectangle. We have done that for Y_2, as shown at the right. Now if ⟨GRAPH⟩ is pressed, only Y_1 will be graphed.

It is also possible to control the appearance of the graph by moving the cursor on the ⟨Y=⟩ screen to the left of any Y. With the cursor in this position, pressing ⟨ENTER⟩ will change the appearance of the graph. The options are shown at the right.

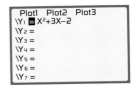

Zero   The ZERO feature of a graphing calculator is used for various calculations: to find the x-intercepts of a function, to solve some equations, and to find the zero of a function.

***x*-intercepts**   To illustrate the procedure for finding *x*-intercepts, we will use $f(x) = x^2 + x - 2$.

First, use the Y-editor to enter the expression for the function and then graph the function in the standard viewing window. (It may be necessary to adjust this window so that the intercepts are visible). Once the graph is displayed, use the keystrokes below to find the *x*-intercepts of the graph of the function.

Press [2nd] CALC (scroll to 2 for **zero** of the function) [ENTER].

Alternatively, you can just press [2nd] CALC 2.

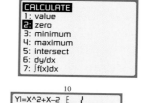

Left Bound? shown at the bottom of the screen asks you to use the left or right arrow key to move the cursor to the *left* of the desired *x*-intercept. Press [ENTER].

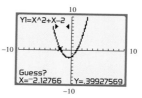

Right Bound? shown at the bottom of the screen asks you to use the left or right arrow key to move the cursor to the *right* of the desired *x*-intercept. Press [ENTER].

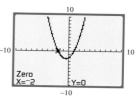

Guess? shown at the bottom of the screen asks you to use the left or right arrow key to move the cursor to the *approximate* location of the desired *x*-intercept. Press [ENTER].

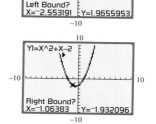

The *x*-coordinate of an *x*-intercept is -2. Therefore, an *x*-intercept is $(-2, 0)$.

To find the other *x*-intercept, follow the same steps as above. The screens for this calculation are shown below.

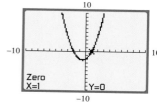

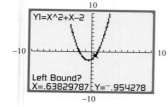 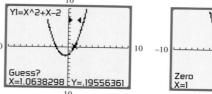 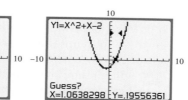

A second *x*-intercept is $(1, 0)$.

Solve an equation   To use the ZERO feature to solve an equation, first rewrite the equation with all terms on one side. For instance, one way to solve $x^3 - x + 1 = -2x + 3$ is first to rewrite the equation as $x^3 + x - 2 = 0$. Enter $x^3 + x - 2$ into Y_1 and then follow the steps for finding *x*-intercepts.

Find the real zeros of a function   To find the real zeros of a function, follow the steps for finding x-intercepts.

Zoom

Pressing ZOOM allows you to select some preset viewing windows. This key also gives you access to **ZBox**, **Zoom In**, and **Zoom Out**. These functions enable you to redraw a selected portion of a graph in a new window. Some windows used frequently in this text are shown below.

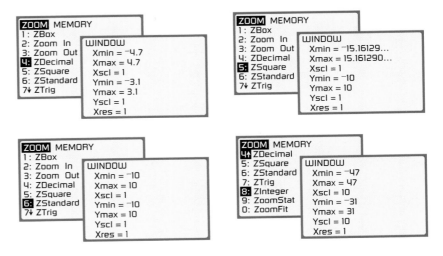

SECTION 1.1

You Try It 1

Goal We want to find three numbers whose product is 4590 and that are elements of the set {13, 14, 15, 16, 17, 18, 19}. None of the three numbers are the same.

Strategy By dividing 4590 by each element of the set, we can determine which elements of the set are factors of 4590 and which are not. (If a number is not a factor of 4590, it cannot be one of the three numbers whose product equals 4590.)

Solution 4590 is not evenly divisible by 13.
4590 is not evenly divisible by 14.
$4590 \div 15 = 306$
4590 is not evenly divisible by 16.
$4590 \div 17 = 270$
$4590 \div 18 = 255$
4590 is not evenly divisible by 19.

Only 15, 17, and 18 are factors of 4590. The ages of the teenagers are 15, 17, and 18. The oldest of the teens is 18 years old.

Check $15(17)(18) = 4590$

The solution checks.

You Try It 2

The pattern of the red beads is
$$1, 2, 3, 4, 5, 6, 7, \ldots$$
The pattern of the blue beads is
$$2, 4, 8, 16, 32, 64, 128, \ldots$$
We can see the group of 4 red beads before the break in the string, and we can see the group of 7 red beads after the break. Therefore, not shown along the break in the string are

5 red beads

6 red beads

We can see 2 of the group of 16 blue beads before the break. We can see 5 of the group of 64 blue beads after the break (and before the 7 red beads). Therefore, not shown along the break in the string are

14 blue beads in the group of 16

32 blue beads in the group of 32

59 blue beads in the group of 64

$$5 + 6 + 14 + 32 + 59 = 116$$

Along the dashed portion of the string, 116 beads are not shown.

You Try It 3

$$\frac{2}{33} = 0.060606\ldots; \frac{10}{33} = 0.303030\ldots; \frac{25}{33} = 0.757575\ldots$$

Note that $2(3) = 6$, $10(3) = 30$, and $25(3) = 75$. The repeating digits of the decimal representation of the fraction equal 3 times the numerator of the fraction.

The decimal representation of a proper fraction with a denominator of 33 is a repeating decimal in which the repeating digits are the product of the numerator and 3.

$$19(3) = 57$$

By this reasoning, $\frac{19}{33} = 0.575757\ldots$.

You Try It 4

Because ¥¥¥ = △△△△ and △△△△ = ΩΩ, ¥¥¥ = ΩΩ.

Because 3 ¥'s = 2 Ω's, 9 ¥'s = 6 Ω's.

That is, ¥¥¥¥¥¥¥¥¥ = ΩΩΩΩΩΩ.

You Try It 5

The conclusion is based on a principle. Therefore, it is an example of deductive reasoning.

You Try It 6

From statement 1, Mike is not the treasurer. In the chart on page S2, write X1 for this condition.

From statement 2, Clarissa is not the secretary or the president. Roger is not the secretary or the president. In the chart, write X2 for these conditions.

From statement 3, Betty is not the president, since we know from statement 2 that the president has lived there the longest. Write X3 for this condition. There are now X's for three of the four people in the president's column; therefore, Mike must be the president. Place a √ in that box. Since Mike is the president, he cannot be either the vice president or the secretary. Write X3 for these conditions. There are now three X's in the secretary's column. Therefore, Betty must be the secretary. Place a √ in that box. Since Betty is the secretary, she cannot be either the vice president or the treasure. Write X3 for these conditions.

From statement 4, together with statement 2, Clarissa is the vice president. Place a √ in that box. Now Clarissa cannot be the treasurer. Write an X4 for that condition. Since there are three X's in the treasurer's column, Roger must be the treasurer. Place a √ in that box.

	President	Vice Pres.	Secretary	Treasurer
Mike	√	X3	X3	X1
Clarissa	X2	√	X2	X4
Roger	X2	X4	X2	√
Betty	X3	X3	√	X3

Therefore, Mike is the president, Clarissa is the vice president, Roger is the treasurer, and Betty is the secretary.

SECTION 1.2

YOU TRY IT 1 {1, 3, 5, 7, 9}

YOU TRY IT 2 $\{x \mid x > 19, x \in \text{real numbers}\}$

YOU TRY IT 3 The set is the real numbers greater than -3. Draw a left parenthesis at -3, and darken the number line to the right of -3.

YOU TRY IT 4 $E \cup F = \{-5, -2, -1, 0, 1, 2, 5\}$

YOU TRY IT 5 The set is the numbers greater than or equal to 1 and less than or equal to -3.

YOU TRY IT 6 **a.** $A \cap B = \{0\}$

b. There are no odd integers that are also even integers.
$$C \cap D = \varnothing$$

YOU TRY IT 7 The set is $\{x \mid -1 \le x \le 2\}$.

YOU TRY IT 8 **a.** The set is the real numbers greater than or equal to -8 and less than -1.
$$[-8, -1)$$

b. The set is the numbers greater than -12.
$$\{x \mid x > -12\}$$

YOU TRY IT 9 $(-\infty, -2) \cup (-1, \infty)$ is the set of real numbers less than -2 and greater than -1.

SECTION 1.3

YOU TRY IT 1 **a.** $|47| = 47$
b. $|-50| = 50$
c. $-|-89| = -89$

YOU TRY IT 2 **a.** $|-18| = 18, |9| = 9$
$|-18| > |9|$
$-18 + 9 = -9$

b. $|-52| = 52, |36| = 36$
$52 - 36 = 16$
$|-52| > |36|$
$-52 + 36 = -16$

YOU TRY IT 3 **a.** $46 - 72 = 46 + (-72)$
$= -26$

b. $-8 - (-26) = -8 + 26$
$= 18$

c. $-15 - 12 - 9 - (-36)$
$= -15 + (-12) + (-9) + 36$
$= -27 + (-9) + 36$
$= -36 + 36$
$= 0$

YOU TRY IT 4 **a.** $-18(-21) = 378$
b. $-5(33) = -165$

YOU TRY IT 5 **a.** $\dfrac{96}{-8} = -12$

b. $-121 \div (-11) = 11$
c. $-24 \div 0$ is undefined.

YOU TRY IT 6 **a.** $4^3 = 4 \cdot 4 \cdot 4 = 16 \cdot 4 = 64$
b. $3^3(5^2) = (3 \cdot 3 \cdot 3)(5 \cdot 5)$
$= 27 \cdot 25 = 675$
c. $(-8)^4 = (-8)(-8)(-8)(-8) = 4096$

YOU TRY IT 7 **a.** $48 \div 2^3 - 2 \cdot 3$
$= 48 \div 8 - 2 \cdot 3$
$= 6 - 2 \cdot 3$
$= 6 - 6$
$= 0$

b. $(-4)(6 - 8)^2 - |-12 \div 4|$
$= (-4)(-2)^2 - |-12 \div 4|$
$= (-4)(-2)^2 - |-3|$
$= (-4)(-2)^2 - 3$
$= (-4)(4) - 3$
$= -16 - 3$
$= -16 + (-3)$
$= -19$

Goal We must determine the score for a student who answered 48 questions correctly, answered 14 questions incorrectly, and left 8 questions unanswered.

Strategy To find the score, multiply the number of questions answered correctly (48) by 2, the number of questions answered incorrectly (14) by -4, and the number of questions left unanswered (8) by -2. Find the sum of these products.

Solution $48(2) + (14)(-4) + 8(-2)$

$$= 96 + (-56) + (-16)$$
$$= 40 + (-16)$$
$$= 24$$

Check You can check that the answer is reasonable. You can also repeat the calculations to verify that the solution is correct or use a calculator to check the answer.

SECTION 1.4

YOU TRY IT 1 $-\dfrac{3}{8} + \left(-\dfrac{1}{3}\right) = -\dfrac{3}{8} \cdot \dfrac{3}{3} + \left(-\dfrac{1}{3} \cdot \dfrac{8}{8}\right)$

$$= -\dfrac{9}{24} + \left(-\dfrac{8}{24}\right)$$

$$= \dfrac{-9 + (-8)}{24} = \dfrac{-17}{24} = -\dfrac{17}{24}$$

YOU TRY IT 2 $-\dfrac{3}{4} - \dfrac{3}{16} = -\dfrac{12}{16} - \dfrac{3}{16} = \dfrac{-12 - 3}{16}$

$$= \dfrac{-15}{16} = -\dfrac{15}{16}$$

YOU TRY IT 3 $-\dfrac{7}{8} - \dfrac{5}{6} + \dfrac{3}{4} = -\dfrac{21}{24} - \dfrac{20}{24} + \dfrac{18}{24}$

$$= \dfrac{-21 - 20 + 18}{24} = -\dfrac{23}{24}$$

YOU TRY IT 4 $-16.127 - 67.91 = -16.127 + (-67.91)$

$$= -84.037$$

YOU TRY IT 5 **a.** $-\dfrac{3}{8}\left(-\dfrac{5}{12}\right) = \dfrac{3}{8} \cdot \dfrac{5}{12} = \dfrac{3 \cdot 5}{8 \cdot 12} = \dfrac{5}{32}$

b. $-\dfrac{5}{8} \div \left(-\dfrac{5}{40}\right) = \dfrac{5}{8} \div \dfrac{5}{40}$

$$= \dfrac{5}{8} \cdot \dfrac{40}{5}$$

$$= \dfrac{5 \cdot 40}{8 \cdot 5}$$

$$= 5$$

YOU TRY IT 6 **a.** $-4.027(0.49) \approx -1.97$

b. $\dfrac{-2.835}{-1.35} = 2.1$

YOU TRY IT 7

Goal We want to find the average monthly net income for Friendly Ice Cream for the first quarter of 2001.

Strategy To find the average monthly net income, divide Friendly Ice Cream's net income for the first quarter of 2001 (-3.203) by 3, the number of months in one quarter of a year.

Solution $-3.203 \div 3 \approx -1.068$

Friendly Ice Cream's average monthly net income for the first quarter of 2001 was $-\$1.068$ million.

Check $-1.068(3) = -3.204 \approx -3.203$

YOU TRY IT 8 $(4.7 - 6.9)^2 + 4.5 \div (-0.05)$

$$= (-2.2)^2 + 4.5 \div (-0.05)$$
$$= 4.84 + 4.5 \div (-0.05)$$
$$= 4.84 + (-90)$$
$$= -85.16$$

SECTION 1.5

YOU TRY IT 1 $1.50g$

$1.50(9.7) = 14.55$

The cost for 9.7 gallons of gas is \$14.55.

YOU TRY IT 2 **a.** The input variable is t, the number of hours since the plane left Los Angeles. The output variable is d, the distance, in miles, the plane is from Boston.

t	d
0	2650
0.5	2387.5
1	2125
1.5	1862.5
2	1600
2.5	1337.5
3	1075
3.5	812.5
4	550

b. The number 1862.5 is the output when the input is 1.5. The number 1862.5 means that the plane is 1862.5 miles from Boston 1.5 hours after it leaves Los Angeles.

You Try It 3   **a.** Because the question asks for the amount of garbage generated per person per day (Y_1) in 1990 (X), look in the table for an input value of 1990. The corresponding output value is 4.5. Thus 4.5 pounds of garbage was generated per person per day in 1990.

      b. Because the question asks for the year (X) when the amount of garbage generated per person per day (Y_1) will be 5.75 pounds, look in the table for an output value of 5.75. You need to scroll down the table. The corresponding input value is 2015. Thus the amount of garbage generated per person per day will be 5.75 pounds in 2015.

You Try It 4 $P = 2L + 2W$

$P = 2(8.5) + 2(3.5)$

$P = 17 + 7$

$P = 24$

The perimeter is 24 meters.

You Try It 5 $3xy^2 - 3x^2y$

$3(-2)(5)^2 - 3(-2)^2(5)$

$= 3(-2)(25) - 3(-2)^2(5)$

$= 3(-2)(25) - 3(4)(5)$

$= -6(25) - 3(4)(5)$

$= -150 - 3(4)(5)$

$= -150 - 12(5)$

$= -150 - 60$

$= -150 + (-60)$

$= -210$

SECTION 1.6

You Try It 1   **a.** $4(3x) = (4 \cdot 3)x$

      b. $12 + (-12) = 0$

You Try It 2   **a.** $-5(-3a) = [-5(-3)]a = 15a$

      b. $\left(-\dfrac{1}{2}c\right)2 = 2\left(-\dfrac{1}{2}c\right) = \left[2\left(-\dfrac{1}{2}\right)\right]c$

$= -1c = -c$

You Try It 3   **a.** $3a - 2b + 5a = 3a + 5a - 2b$

$= (3a + 5a) - 2b$

$= 8a - 2b$

      b. $2z^2 - 5z - 3z^2 + 6z$

$= 2z^2 - 3z^2 + 6z - 5z$

$= (2z^2 - 3z^2) + (6z - 5z)$

$= -1z^2 + 1z$

$= -z^2 + z$

You Try It 4   **a.** $-3(5y - 2) = -3(5y) - (-3)(2)$

$= -15y + 6$

      b. $-(6c + 5) = -1(6c + 5)$

$= -1(6c) + (-1)(5)$

$= -6c - 5$

      c. $(3p - 7)(-3) = 3p(-3) - 7(-3)$

$= -9p + 21$

      d. $-2(4x + 2y - 6z)$

$= -2(4x) + (-2)(2y) - (-2)(6z)$

$= -8x - 4y + 12z$

You Try It 5   **a.** $7(-3x - 4y) - 3(3x + y)$

$= -21x - 28y - 9x - 3y$

$= -30x - 31y$

      b. $2y - 3[5 - 3(3 + 2y)]$

$= 2y - 3[5 - 9 - 6y]$

$= 2y - 3[-4 - 6y]$

$= 2y + 12 + 18y$

$= 20y + 12$

You Try It 6   **a.** Let the unknown number be x.

      seven <u>more than</u> the <u>product</u> of a number and twelve

      the product of a number and 12: $12x$

      $12x + 7$

      b. Let the unknown number be x.

      the <u>total</u> of eighteen and the <u>quotient</u> of a number and nine

      the quotient of a number and nine: $\dfrac{x}{9}$

      $18 + \dfrac{x}{9}$

You Try It 7   Let the unknown number be x.

a number <u>minus</u> the <u>difference</u> between the number and seventeen

the difference between the number and seventeen: $x - 17$

$x - (x - 17)$

$= x - x + 17$

$= 0 + 17$

$= 17$

You Try It 8   one number: x

the other number: $10 - x$

You Try It 9   Let h represent the number of hours of overtime worked.

640 + 32 for each hour of overtime worked

$640 + 32h$

SECTION 2.1

You Try It 1   Plot the points $A(-2, 4)$, $B(4, 0)$, $C(0, 3)$, and $D(-3, -4)$.

You Try It 2   The input/output table for $y = x^2 + 2x$ for $x = -4, -3, -2, -1, 0, 1,$ and 2 is shown to the right in a vertical format.

Input, x	Output, $x^2 + 2x = y$
-4	$(-4)^2 + 2(-4) = 8$
-3	$(-3)^2 + 2(-3) = 3$
-2	$(-2)^2 + 2(-2) = 0$
-1	$(-1)^2 + 2(-1) = -1$
0	$(0)^2 + 2(0) = 0$
1	$(1)^2 + 2(1) = 3$
2	$(2)^2 + 2(2) = 8$

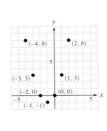

You Try It 3   The input/output table for $y = -\dfrac{x}{2} - 2$ for $x = -6, -4, -2, 0, 2,$ and 4 is shown below in a vertical format.

Input, x	Output, $-\dfrac{x}{2} - 2 = y$
-6	$-\dfrac{(-6)}{2} - 2 = 1$
-4	$-\dfrac{(-4)}{2} - 2 = 0$
-2	$-\dfrac{(-2)}{2} - 2 = -1$
0	$-\dfrac{(0)}{2} - 2 = -2$
2	$-\dfrac{(2)}{(2)} - 2 = -3$
4	$-\dfrac{(4)}{2} - 2 = -4$

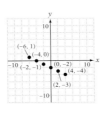

You Try It 4   The temperature T, in degrees Fahrenheit, h hours after 4:00 P.M. one summer day was given by

$$T = \frac{960}{h + 12}.$$

a. The input/output table for $T = \dfrac{960}{h + 12}$ is shown below in a horizontal format.

Input, time h	0	0.5	1	1.5	2	2.5	3
Output, temperature T	80	76.8	73.8	71.1	68.6	66.2	64

b. At 6:00 P.M., the temperature was 68.6° F.

You Try It 5

a. The input/output table for $y = \dfrac{2}{3}x - 3$ is shown below in a horizontal format.

x	-6	-3	0	3	6	9
y	-7	-5	-3	-1	1	3

b.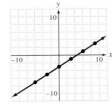

c.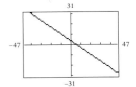

You Try It 6

a. Input $-\dfrac{2}{3}x + 4$ into Y_1 and select the integer viewing window.

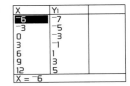

b. Trace along the curve until the x-coordinate is 9.

The value of y is -2 when $x = 9$.

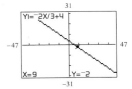

c. Trace along the curve until the y-coordinate is 8.

The value of x is -6 when $y = 8$.

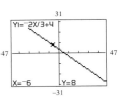

You Try It 7

Enter $\dfrac{1}{2}x + 2$ into Y_1 and then graph the equation in the integer viewing window.

a. Use the TRACE feature of the calculator to find the ordered-pair solution corresponding to $x = -5$.

The ordered-pair solutions is $(-5, -0.5)$.

b. To check the results algebraically, evaluate $\frac{1}{2}x + 2$ when $x = -5$.

$$y = \frac{1}{2}x + 2$$

$$y = \frac{1}{2}(-5) + 2 \quad \bullet \text{ Replace } x \text{ by } -5.$$

$$= -\frac{5}{2} + 2 \quad \bullet \text{ Simplify.}$$

$$= -\frac{1}{2}$$

$$= -0.5$$

The solution checks.

SECTION 2.2

YOU TRY IT 1

The domain of a relation is the set of the first coordinates of the ordered pairs of the relation. The range of a relation is the set of second coordinates of the relation. For the relation {(1, 1), (2, 1), (3, 1), (4, 1), (5, 1), (6, 1), (7, 1)}, the domain is {1, 2, 3, 4, 5, 6, 7}. The range is {1}.

Because no two ordered pairs have the same first coordinate, the relation is a function.

YOU TRY IT 2

a. $f(z) = 2z^3 - 4z$
$f(-1) = 2(-1)^3 - 4(-1)$
$f(-1) = 2(-1) - 4(-1)$
$f(-1) = -2 + 4$
$f(-1) = 2$

b. To find the value of f when $z = -3$ means to evaluate the function when z is -3.
$f(z) = 2z^3 - 4z$
$f(-3) = 2(-3)^3 - 4(-3)$
$f(-3) = 2(-27) - 4(-3)$
$f(-3) = -54 + 12$
$f(-3) = -42$

YOU TRY IT 3

a. Evaluate $h(x) = 2x - 3$ for the given values of x.

x	-2	-1	0	1	2
$h(x)$	-7	-5	-3	-1	1

b. Graph the ordered pairs $(-2, -7)$, $(-1, -5)$, $(0, -3)$, $(1, -1)$, and $(2, 1)$. Then draw a line through the points.

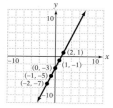

YOU TRY IT 4

The graph of $g(x) = 2$ is a horizontal line through (0, 2).

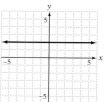

YOU TRY IT 5

To find the range of $f(x) = -x^2 + 2x + 2$ with domain $\{-2, -1, 0, 1, 2, 3\}$, evaluate the function at each element of the domain. The set of outputs is the range of the function for the given domain.

$f(x) = -x^2 + 2x + 2$
$f(-2) = -(-2)^2 + 2(-2) + 2 = -4 - 4 + 2 = -6$
$f(-1) = -(-1)^2 + 2(-1) + 2 = -1 - 2 + 2 = -1$
$f(0) = -(0)^2 + 2(0) + 2 = 0 + 0 + 2 = 2$
$f(1) = -(1)^2 + 2(1) + 2 = -1 + 2 + 2 = 3$
$f(2) = -(2)^2 + 2(2) + 2 = -4 + 4 + 2 = 2$
$f(3) = -(3)^2 + 2(3) + 2 = -9 + 6 + 2 = -1$

The range is $\{-6, -1, 2, 3\}$.

YOU TRY IT 6

Evaluate $P(t) = \frac{t}{t^2 + 1}$ for each of the given values 4, -4, 0, 3.

$$P(t) = \frac{t}{t^2 + 1}$$

$$P(4) = \frac{4}{(4)^2 + 1} = \frac{4}{17} \quad \text{A real number}$$

$$P(-4) = \frac{-4}{(-4)^2 + 1} = -\frac{4}{17} \quad \text{A real number}$$

$$P(0) = \frac{0}{(0)^2 + 1} = 0 \quad \text{A real number}$$

$$P(3) = \frac{3}{(3)^2 + 1} = \frac{3}{10} \quad \text{A real number}$$

Each of the given numbers is in the domain of P. All are included in the domain.

YOU TRY IT 7

Graph $f(x) = \frac{3}{x^2 - x - 6}$ in the decimal viewing window. Then trace along the curve to find the two x-coordinates for which there is no y-coordinate.

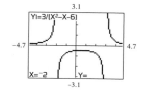 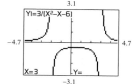

The two numbers that are not in the domain of f are -2 and 3. To verify this algebraically, attempt to evaluate the function for these two numbers.

$$f(x) = \frac{3}{x^2 - x - 6}$$

$$f(-2) = \frac{3}{(-2)^2 - (-2) - 6}$$

$$= \frac{3}{4 + 2 - 6}$$

$$= \frac{3}{0} \quad \text{Not a real number}$$

$$f(x) = \frac{3}{x^2 - x - 6}$$

$$f(3) = \frac{3}{(3)^2 - (3) - 6}$$

$$= \frac{3}{9 - 3 - 6}$$

$$= \frac{3}{0} \quad \text{Not a real number}$$

YOU TRY IT 8

Evaluate the function for $m = 12$.

$$N(m) = \frac{m(m - 1)}{2}$$

$$N(12) = \frac{12(12 - 1)}{2} = \frac{12(11)}{2} = 66$$

66 different line segments can be drawn between 12 different points in the plane.

YOU TRY IT 9

a. Because p is in thousands, a value of 100,000 is given as $p = 100$. Evaluate $C(p) = 0.15\sqrt{p^2 + 4p + 10}$ when $p = 100$.

$$C(p) = 0.15\sqrt{p^2 + 4p + 10}$$

$$C(100) = 0.15\sqrt{100^2 + 4(100) + 10}$$

$$\approx 15.3$$

The carbon monoxide concentration for a city of 100,000 people is 15.3 ppm.

b. Evaluate $C(p)$ when $p = 0$.

$$C(p) = 0.15\sqrt{p^2 + 4p + 10}$$

$$C(0) = 0.15\sqrt{0^2 + 4(0) + 10}$$

$$\approx 0.5$$

If there were no people in an area, the carbon monoxide concentration would be approximately 0.5 ppm.

SECTION 2.3

YOU TRY IT 1

a.

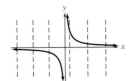

All vertical lines intersect the graph at most once. The graph is the graph of a function.

b.

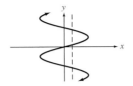

There is at least one vertical line that intersects the graph at more that one point. The graph is not the graph of a function.

YOU TRY IT 2

a. To find the y-intercept, evaluate $g(x) = 2x^2 - 5x + 2$ at $x = 0$.

$$g(x) = 2x^2 - 5x + 2$$

$$g(0) = 2(0)^2 - 5(0) + 2 = 2$$

The y-intercept is $(0, 2)$.

b. To find the x-intercept, graph $g(x) = 2x^2 - 5x + 2$ and then use the ZERO feature of a graphing calculator to find the x-intercepts.

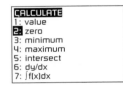

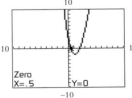
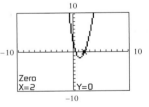

One x-intercept is $(0.5, 0)$.   A second x-intercept is $(2, 0)$.

YOU TRY IT 3

To find the number in the domain of $G(x) = 1 - 2x$ for which the output is -6, use a graphing calculator to graph $G(x) = 1 - 2x$ and $F(x) = -6$ on the same coordinate grid, and then find the point of intersection.

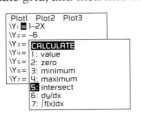
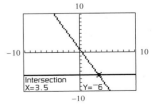

The output of $G(x) = 1 - 2x$ is -6 when $x = 3.5$.

YOU TRY IT 4

To find the element in the domain of $f(x) = 2x - 3$ and $g(x) = \frac{x}{2} + 3$ for which the values of the functions are equal, use a graphing calculator to graph each equation, and then find the point of intersection. The x-coordinate of the point of intersection is the desired value.

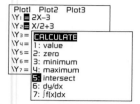 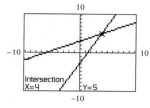

The values of the functions are equal when $x = 4$. To algebraically verify the result, evaluate each function for $x = 4$.

$$f(x) = 2x - 3 \qquad g(x) = \frac{x}{2} + 3$$

$$f(4) = 2(4) - 3 \qquad g(4) = \frac{4}{2} + 3$$

$$= 5 \qquad = 5$$

The value of both functions is 5 when $x = 4$.

YOU TRY IT 5

To solve this problem, we need to determine the value of t for which $s(t) = 10$. This is similar to Example 3. Graph $s(t) = 26 - 8t$ and $g(t) = 10$, and determine the point of intersection. Use a domain of $[0, 5]$ and a range of $[0, 30]$.

 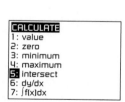

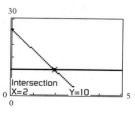

The marathon runner will be 10 miles from the finish line in 2 hours.

We can verify this algebraically as follows:

$$s(t) = 26 - 8t$$
$$s(2) = 26 - 8(2) \qquad \bullet \text{ Replace } t \text{ by 2.}$$
$$= 26 - 16$$
$$= 10$$

The marathon runner will be 10 miles from the finish line in 2 hours.

YOU TRY IT 6

To solve this problem, we need to find the value of t for which $h(t) = f(t)$. This is similar to Example 4. Graph each function on the same coordinate grid, and then determine the point of intersection.

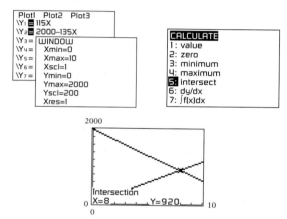

The planes are at the same height after 8 minutes.

SECTION 3.1

YOU TRY IT 1

$$9 + n = 4$$
$$9 - 9 + n = 4 - 9$$
$$n = -5$$

The solution is -5.

YOU TRY IT 2

$$-4x = -20$$
$$\frac{-4x}{-4} = \frac{-20}{-4}$$
$$x = 5$$

The solution is 5.

YOU TRY IT 3

$$5 - 4z = 15$$
$$5 - 5 - 4z = 15 - 5$$
$$-4z = 10$$
$$\frac{-4z}{-4} = \frac{10}{-4}$$
$$z = -\frac{5}{2}$$

The solution is $-\frac{5}{2}$.

YOU TRY IT 4

$$6y - 3 + y = 2y + 7$$
$$7y - 3 = 2y + 7$$
$$7y - 2y - 3 = 2y - 2y + 7$$
$$5y - 3 = 7$$
$$5y - 3 + 3 = 7 + 3$$
$$5y = 10$$
$$\frac{5y}{5} = \frac{10}{5}$$
$$y = 2$$

The solution is 2.

YOU TRY IT 5

$$2(3x + 1) = 4x + 8$$
$$6x + 2 = 4x + 8$$
$$6x - 4x + 2 = 4x - 4x + 8$$
$$2x + 2 = 8$$
$$2x + 2 - 2 = 8 - 2$$

$$2x = 6$$
$$\frac{2x}{2} = \frac{6}{2}$$
$$x = 3$$

The solution is 3.

SECTION 3.2

YOU TRY IT 1

Goal The goal is to find how many ounces of gold costing $320 per ounce should be mixed with 100 ounces of an alloy costing $100 per ounce to produce a new alloy that costs $160 per ounce.

Strategy Let x represent the number of ounces of gold that are needed.

Find the value of each of the metals.

Value of the gold: $V = AC = x(320) = 320x$

Value of the $100-per-ounce alloy:
$V = AC = 100(100) = 10,000$

Value of the $160-per-ounce alloy (the mixture)
= value of the gold + value of the $100-per-ounce alloy
= $320x + 10,000$

Find the amount of the mixture.

Amount of the mixture = amount of gold + amount of the $100-per-ounce alloy
= $x + 100$

To find the value of x, use the equation $V = AC$ for the mixture. The unit cost of the mixture is $160 per ounce. Solve the equation for x.

Solution

$$V = AC$$
$$320x + 10,000 = (x + 100)160$$
$$320x + 10,000 = 160x + 16,000$$
$$160x + 10,000 = 16,000$$
$$160x = 6000$$
$$x = 37.5$$

- V is the value of the mixture, A is the amount of the mixture, C is the unit cost of the mixture.

The jeweler must use 37.5 ounces of gold.

Check One way to check the solution is to substitute the value of x into the original equation and determine whether the left and right sides of the equation are equal.

A second way to check the solution is to calculate the value of the mixture to ensure that its value is $160 per ounce.

Value of 37.5 ounces of gold:
$V = AC = 37.5(320) = 12,000$

Value of 100 ounces of the $100-per-ounce alloy:
$V = AC = 100(100) = 10,000$

Value of the two ingredients =
$12,000 + 10,000 = 22,000$

The mixture contains
100 ounces + 37.5 ounces = 137.5 ounces.

$$\frac{V = AC}{22,000 \;\big|\; 137.5(160)}$$
$22,000 = 22,000$ √ The value of the mixture is $22,000. The solution checks.

You Try It 2

Goal The goal is to determine the speed of each of the two cyclists.

Strategy Let r represents the rate of the first cyclist.

Then the rate of the second cyclist is $r + 5$.

Use the equation $d = rt$ to represent the distance traveled by each cyclist in 4 hours.

First cyclist: $d = rt$
$$d = r(4)$$
$$d = 4r$$

Second cyclist: $d = rt$
$$d = (r + 5)4$$
$$d = 4r + 20$$

The total distance traveled by the two cyclists is 140 miles.

$$\text{Distance traveled by first cyclist} + \text{Distance traveled by second cyclist} = 140 \text{ miles}$$
$$4r \quad + \quad 4r + 20 \quad = 140$$

Solve this equation for r.

Solution $4r + 4r + 20 = 140$
$$8r + 20 = 140$$
$$8r = 120$$
$$r = 15$$

Substitute the value of r into the expression representing the rate of the second cyclist.
$$r + 5 = 15 + 5 = 20$$

The first cyclist is traveling 15 mph. The second cyclist is traveling 20 mph.

Check In 4 hours, the first cyclist travels $4(15) = 60$ miles and the second cyclist travels $4(20) = 80$.

The total distance traveled by the two cyclists in 4 hours is 60 miles + 80 miles = 140 miles.

SECTION 3.3

You Try It 1

Goal The goal is to find the measures of the two complementary angles.

Strategy Let x represent the measure of one angle.

The measure of the complement of x is $90° - x$.

It is given that x is 3° less than the measure of its complement.

"x is 3° less than the measure of its complement" is translated as
$$x = (90 - x) - 3$$
Solve this equation for x.

Solution
$$x = (90 - x) - 3$$
$$x = 90 - x - 3$$
$$x = 87 - x$$
$$x + x = 87 - x + x$$
$$2x = 87$$
$$x = 43.5$$

Substitute the value of x into the expression for the complement of x.
$$90 - x = 90 - 43.5 = 46.5$$
The angles measure 43.5° and 46.5°.

Check
$$43.5° + 46.5° = 90°;$$
the sum of the angles is 90°.
$$46.5° - 43.5° = 3°;$$ one angle is 3° less than the other angle.

You Try It 2

Goal The goal is to find the measure of the larger of two adjacent angles for a pair of intersecting lines.

Strategy Adjacent angles of intersecting lines are supplementary angles (their sum is 180°).
$$(2x + 20) + (3x + 50) = 180$$

Solve this equation for x.
Then substitute the value of x into the expressions $2x + 20$ and $3x + 50$ to determine the larger angle.

Solution $(2x + 20) + (3x + 50) = 180$
$$5x + 70 = 180$$
$$5x = 110$$
$$x = 22$$

$2x + 20 = 2(22) + 20 = 44 + 20 = 64$

$3x + 50 = 3(22) + 50 = 66 + 50 = 116$

The measure of the larger angle is 116°.

Check $64 + 116 = 180$; the sum of the two angles is 180°.

YOU TRY IT 3

Goal   We want to determine the value of x, given two of the angles formed by a transversal and two parallel lines.

Strategy   The angles given are alternate interior angles. Alternate interior angles have the same measure.

$$4x - 50 = 2x + 10$$

Solve this equation for x.

Solution

$$4x - 50 = 2x + 10$$
$$4x - 2x - 50 = 2x - 2x + 10$$
$$2x - 50 = 10$$
$$2x - 50 + 50 = 10 + 50$$
$$2x = 60$$
$$x = 30$$

The value of x is 30°.

Check   We can use the value of x to check that the two angles have the same measure.

$$4x - 50 = 4(30) - 50 = 120 - 50 = 70$$
$$2x + 10 = 2(30) + 10 = 60 + 10 = 70$$

YOU TRY IT 4

Goal   The goal is to find $m\angle b$, the measure of an exterior angle of the triangle pictured.

Strategy   We are given the measure of $\angle a$.

We can use the measure of $\angle a$ to find the measure of the adjacent interior angle of the triangle.

Use the fact that the sum of the measures of an interior angle and the adjacent exterior angle of a triangle is 180°.

We will represent the measure of the adjacent interior angle by $m\angle y$.

Then find the measure of the interior angle adjacent to $\angle b$.

Use the $m\angle y$, the fact that the triangle is a right triangle, and the fact that the sum of the measures of the interior angles of a triangle is 180°.

We will represent the measure of the interior angle adjacent to $\angle b$ by $m\angle z$.

Then find the measure of $\angle b$.

Use the fact that the sum of the measures of an interior angle and the adjacent exterior angle of a triangle is 180°.

Solution $m\angle a + m\angle y = 180°$

$$112° + m\angle y = 180°$$
$$m\angle y = 68°$$
$$m\angle y + m\angle z + 90° = 180°$$
$$68° + m\angle z + 90° = 180°$$
$$158° + m\angle z = 180°$$
$$m\angle z = 22°$$
$$m\angle z + m\angle b = 180°$$
$$22° + m\angle b = 180°$$
$$m\angle b = 158°$$

Check   Check all the steps of the solution.

YOU TRY IT 5

Goal   We want to determine the measure of $\angle AEB$.

Strategy $\angle AEB$ is an inscribed angle because its vertex is on the circumference of the circle and its sides are chords.

According to the Inscribed-Angle Theorems:

If $\angle AEB$ is an inscribed angle of a circle, then $m\angle AEB = \frac{1}{2}m\overarc{AB}$.

The measure of an arc is the measure of the central angle that intersects it.

Therefore, the measure of $\overarc{AB}$ is equal to the measure of central angle ACB, or 138°.

Use the Inscribed-Angle Theorems to find the measure of $\angle AEB$

Solution $m\angle AEB = \dfrac{1}{2}m\overarc{AB}$

$$m\angle AEB = \frac{1}{2}(138°)$$

$$m\angle AEB = 69°$$

The measure of $\angle AEB$ is 69°.

Check   Be sure to check the calculations.

YOU TRY IT 6

Goal   The goal is to find the value of x in the expression $2x + 20$ in the diagram.

Strategy   According to the Inscribed-Angle Theorems:

If $\angle BAC$ is an inscribed angle of a circle, then $m\angle BAC = \frac{1}{2}m\overarc{BC}$.

We are given the measure of $\angle BAC$, so we can use the theorem to write an equation.

$$60° = \frac{1}{2}(2x + 20)°$$

Solve this equation for x.

Solution $60 = \dfrac{1}{2}(2x + 20)$

$60 = x + 10$

$50 = x$

The value of x is 50°.

Check Use the value of x to find the measure of the arc: $2x + 20 = 2(50) + 20 = 100 + 20 = 120$. One-half the measure of the arc is equal to the measure of the inscribed angle: $\dfrac{1}{2}(120) = 60$.

SECTION 3.4

YOU TRY IT 1

$x - 4 \leq 1$

$x - 4 + 4 \leq 1 + 4$

$x \leq 5$

In set-builder notation, the solution set is written $\{x\,|\,x \leq 5\}$.
In interval notation, the solution set is written $(-\infty, 5]$.

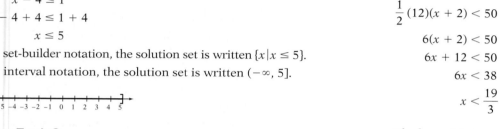

YOU TRY IT 2

$-3x \geq 6$

$\dfrac{-3x}{-3} \leq \dfrac{6}{-3}$

$x \leq -2$

In set-builder notation, the solution set is written $\{x\,|\,x \leq -2\}$.

In interval notation, the solution set is written $(-\infty, -2]$.

YOU TRY IT 3

$3x - 1 \leq 5x - 7$

$3x - 5x - 1 \leq 5x - 5x - 7$

$-2x - 1 \leq -7$

$-2x - 1 + 1 \leq -7 + 1$

$-2x \leq -6$

$\dfrac{-2x}{-2} \geq \dfrac{-6}{-2}$

$x \geq 3$

$\{x\,|\,x \geq 3\}$

YOU TRY IT 4 $3 - 2(3x + 1) < 7 - 2x$

$3 - 6x - 2 < 7 - 2x$

$-6x + 1 < 7 - 2x$

$-4x + 1 < 7$

$-4x < 6$

$x > -\dfrac{3}{2}$

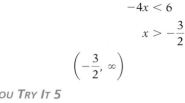

YOU TRY IT 5

Goal The goal is to find the maximum height of the triangle.

Strategy Substitute the given values in the inequality $\dfrac{1}{2}bh < A$ and solve for x.

Solution $\dfrac{1}{2}bh < A$

$\dfrac{1}{2}(12)(x + 2) < 50$

$6(x + 2) < 50$

$6x + 12 < 50$

$6x < 38$

$x < \dfrac{19}{3}$

The largest integer less than $\dfrac{19}{3}$ is 6.

$x + 2 = 6 + 2 = 8$

The maximum height of the triangle is 8 inches.

Check When the height is 8 inches, the area is $\dfrac{1}{2}bh = \dfrac{1}{2}(12)(8) = 48$ square inches.

When the height is 9 inches, the area is $\dfrac{1}{2}bh = \dfrac{1}{2}(12)(9) = 54$ square inches, which is greater than 50 square inches.

The solution checks.

YOU TRY IT 6

$5x - 1 \geq -11$ and $4 - 6x > -14$

$5x - 1 + 1 \geq -11 + 1$ $\quad 4 - 4 - 6x > -14 - 4$

$5x \geq -10$ $\qquad\qquad -6x > -18$

$\dfrac{5x}{5} \geq \dfrac{-10}{5}$ $\qquad\quad \dfrac{-6x}{-6} < \dfrac{-18}{-6}$

$x \geq -2$ $\qquad\qquad\qquad x < 3$

$\{x\,|\,x \geq -2\}$ $\qquad\qquad (x\,|\,x < 3)$

The solution of the compound inequality is the intersection of the solution sets for each inequality.

$\{x\,|\,x \geq -2\} \cap \{x\,|\,x < 3\} = \{x\,|-2 \leq x < 3\}$

YOU TRY IT 7

$$3 - 4x > 7 \qquad \text{or} \qquad 4x + 5 > 9$$
$$3 - 3 - 4x > 7 - 3 \qquad\qquad 4x + 5 - 5 > 9 - 5$$
$$-4x > 4 \qquad\qquad\qquad 4x > 4$$
$$\frac{-4x}{-4} < \frac{4}{-4} \qquad\qquad\qquad \frac{4x}{4} > \frac{4}{4}$$
$$x < -1 \qquad\qquad\qquad x > 1$$
$$(-\infty, -1) \qquad\qquad\qquad (1, \infty)$$

The solution set is the union of the two intervals.

$$(-\infty, -1) \cup (1, \infty)$$

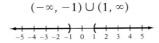

SECTION 3.5

YOU TRY IT 1

a. $|5 - 6x| = 1$

$$5 - 6x = 1 \qquad\qquad 5 - 6x = -1$$
$$-6x = -4 \qquad\qquad -6x = -6$$
$$x = \frac{2}{3} \qquad\qquad x = 1$$

The solutions are $\frac{2}{3}$ and 1.

b. $|3x - 7| + 4 = 2$

$$|3x - 7| = -2$$

The absolute value of a number is positive or zero.
There is no solution.

YOU TRY IT 2

$$|2x - 5| \leq 7$$
$$-7 \leq 2x - 5 \leq 7$$
$$-7 + 5 \leq 2x - 5 + 5 \leq 7 + 5$$
$$-2 \leq 2x \leq 12$$
$$\frac{-2}{2} \leq \frac{2x}{2} \leq \frac{12}{2}$$
$$-1 \leq x \leq 6$$

The solution set is $\{x \mid -1 \leq x \leq 6\}$.

YOU TRY IT 3

$$|5x + 4| \geq 16$$
$$5x + 4 \geq 16 \qquad\qquad 5x + 4 \leq -16$$
$$5x + 4 - 4 \geq 16 - 4 \qquad 5x + 4 - 4 \leq -16 - 4$$
$$5x \geq 12 \qquad\qquad\qquad 5x \leq -20$$
$$\frac{5x}{5} \geq \frac{12}{5} \qquad\qquad\qquad \frac{5x}{5} \leq \frac{-20}{5}$$
$$x \geq \frac{12}{5} \qquad\qquad\qquad x \leq -4$$
$$\left\{x \mid x \geq \frac{12}{5}\right\} \qquad \text{or} \qquad \{x \mid x \leq -4\}$$

The solution set is the union of the solution sets of the two inequalities.

$$\left\{x \mid x \geq \frac{12}{5}\right\} \cup \{x \mid x \leq -4\} = \left\{x \mid x \leq -4 \text{ or } x \geq \frac{12}{5}\right\}$$

YOU TRY IT 4

Goal The goal is to find the lower and upper limits of the diameter of a bushing that has a tolerance of 0.003 inch.

Strategy Let b represent the desired diameter of the bushing, T the tolerance, and d the actual diameter of the bushing. Solve the absolute value inequality $|d - b| \leq T$ for d.

Solution
$$|d - b| \leq T$$
$$|d - 2.55| \leq 0.003$$
$$-0.003 \leq d - 2.55 \leq 0.003$$
$$-0.003 + 2.55 \leq d - 2.55 + 2.55 \leq 0.003 + 2.55$$
$$2.547 \leq d \leq 2.553$$

The lower and upper limits of the diameter of the bushing are 2.547 inches and 2.553 inches.

Check Be sure to check your work by doing a check of your calculations. As an estimate, the answers appear reasonable in that the diameters are close to 2.55 inches.

YOU TRY IT 5

Goal The goal is to determine the SAT scores, x, that satisfy the inequality $\left|\frac{x - 950}{98}\right| < 1.96$.

Strategy Solve the inequality $\left|\frac{x - 950}{98}\right| < 1.96$ for x.

Solution
$$\left|\frac{x - 950}{98}\right| < 1.96$$
$$-1.96 < \frac{x - 950}{98} < 1.96$$
$$98(-1.96) < 98\left(\frac{x - 950}{98}\right) < 98(1.96)$$
$$-192.08 < x - 950 < 192.08$$
$$-192.08 + 950 < x - 950 + 950 < 192.08 + 950$$
$$757.92 < x < 1142.08$$

The values of x that the registrar expects from a student applicant are $\{x \mid 757.92 < x < 1142.08\}$.

Check Be sure to check the calculations.

SECTION 4.1

YOU TRY IT 1 The function is of the form $f(x) = mx + b$, where m is the slope.

For the function $g(t) = -20t + 8000$, the slope m is -20.

The slope means the plane is descending 20 feet per second.

YOU TRY IT 2 **a.** $(x_1, y_1) = (-6, 5)$, $(x_2, y_2) = (4, -5)$

$$m = \frac{y_2 - y_1}{x_2 - x_1} = \frac{-5 - 5}{4 - (-6)} = \frac{-10}{10} = -1$$

The slope is -1.

b. $(x_1, y_1) = (-5, 0)$, $(x_2, y_2) = (-5, 7)$

$$m = \frac{y_2 - y_1}{x_2 - x_1} = \frac{7 - 0}{-5 - (-5)} = \frac{7}{0}$$

The slope is undefined.

YOU TRY IT 3 Rewrite the slope -1 as $\dfrac{-1}{1}$.

Draw a dot at $(2, 4)$.

Starting at $(2, 4)$, move 1 unit down (the change in y) and then 1 unit to the right (the change in x). Draw a dot at $(3, 3)$.

Draw a line through the two points.

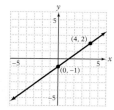

YOU TRY IT 4 $y = \dfrac{3}{4}x - 1$

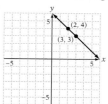

YOU TRY IT 5
$$3x + 2y = -6$$
$$3x - 3x + 2y = -3x - 6$$
$$2y = -3x - 6$$
$$\frac{2y}{2} = \frac{-3x - 6}{2}$$
$$y = -\frac{3}{2}x - 3$$

The slope is $-\dfrac{3}{2}$. The y-intercept is $(0, -3)$.

YOU TRY IT 6 $3x + y = 6$

To find the x-intercept, let $y = 0$ and solve for x.
$$3x + y = 6$$
$$3x + 0 = 6$$
$$3x = 6$$
$$x = 2$$

The x-intercept is $(2, 0)$.

To find the y-intercept, let $x = 0$ and solve for y.
$$3x + y = 6$$
$$3(0) + y = 6$$
$$y = 6$$

The y-intercept is $(0, 6)$.

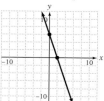

YOU TRY IT 7 $y - 5 = 0$

$$y = 5$$

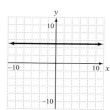

YOU TRY IT 8 $x = 1$

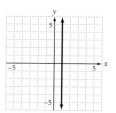

SECTION 4.2

YOU TRY IT 1 Let x represent the number of kilometers above sea level and y represent the boiling point of water.

Since the boiling point of water at sea level is 100°C, $x = 0$ when $y = 100$. The y-intercept is $(0, 100)$.

The slope is the decrease in the boiling point per kilometer increase in altitude.

Since the boiling point decreases 3.5°C per 1-kilometer increase in altitude, the slope is negative; $m = -3.5$.

To find the linear function, replace m and b in $f(x) = mx + b$ by their values.

$$f(x) = mx + b$$
$$f(x) = -3.5x + 100$$

The linear function is $f(x) = -3.5x + 100$, where $f(x)$ is the boiling point of water x kilometers above sea level.

YOU TRY IT 2 $\quad y - y_1 = m(x - x_1)$

$$y - 2 = -\frac{1}{2}[x - (-2)]$$

$$y - 2 = -\frac{1}{2}x - 1$$

$$y = -\frac{1}{2}x + 1$$

YOU TRY IT 3 A line whose slope is undefined is a vertical line that passes through the point $(a, 0)$.

The equation of the line is $x = a$.

The value of x in the given point, $(4, 3)$, is 4.

The equation of the line is $x = 4$.

YOU TRY IT 4

Goal Find a linear model that predicts the population of adults 65 years old or older in terms of the year.

Then use the model to approximate the population of these adults in 2005.

Strategy Because the function will predict the population, let y represent the population in year x.

Then $y = 13$ million when $x = 1950$.

The population is increasing 0.5 million per year. Therefore, the slope is 0.5.

Use the point-slope formula to find the linear model.

To find the population in 2005, evaluate the function when $x = 2005$.

Solution $y - y_1 = m(x - x_1)$
$y - 13 = 0.5(x - 1950)$
$y - 13 = 0.5x - 975$
$\quad\;\; y = 0.5x - 962$

A linear function that models the population is $f(x) = 0.5x - 962$.

$$f(x) = 0.5x - 962$$
$$f(2005) = 0.5(2005) - 962$$
$$= 1002.5 - 962$$
$$= 40.5$$

The predicted population of adults 65 years old or older in 2005 is 40.5 million.

Check The population is increasing 0.5 million per year. $2005 - 1950 = 55$; 2005 is 55 years after 1950.

The expected increase is $(0.5)(55) = 27.5$ million people.

The population in 1950 + the increase in population = 13 million + 27.5 million = 40.5 million.

Our solution checks.

YOU TRY IT 5 $(x_1, y_1) = (-2, 3), (x_2, y_2) = (4, 1)$

$$m = \frac{y_2 - y_1}{x_2 - x_1} = \frac{1 - 3}{4 - (-2)} = \frac{-2}{6} = -\frac{1}{3}$$

$$y - y_1 = m(x - x_1)$$

$$y - 1 = -\frac{1}{3}(x - 4)$$

$$y - 1 = -\frac{1}{3}x + \frac{4}{3}$$

$$y = -\frac{1}{3}x + \frac{7}{3}$$

YOU TRY IT 6

Goal Find a linear model that gives the number of calories in lean hamburger in terms of the number of ounces in the serving.

Then use the model to find the number of calories in a 5-ounce serving of lean hamburger.

Strategy Because the function will predict the number of calories, let y represent the number of calories.

Then x represents the number of ounces in a serving.

From the given data, two ordered pairs of the function are $(2, 126)$ and $(3, 189)$.

Use the two ordered pairs to find the slope of the line.

Use the point-slope formula to find the linear model.

To find the number of calories in a 5-ounce serving of lean hamburger, evaluate the linear function at $x = 5$.

Solution Let $(x_1, y_1) = (2, 126)$ and $(x_2, y_2) = (3, 189)$.

$$m = \frac{y_2 - y_1}{x_2 - x_1} = \frac{189 - 126}{3 - 2} = \frac{63}{1} = 63$$
$$y - y_1 = m(x - x_1)$$
$$y - 126 = 63(x - 2)$$
$$y - 126 = 63x - 126$$
$$y = 63x$$

The linear function is $f(x) = 63x$.

$$f(x) = 63x$$
$$f(5) = 63(5)$$
$$= 315$$

There are 315 calories in a 5-ounce serving of lean hamburger.

Check A 1-ounce serving contains 63 calories, a 2-ounce serving contains $63 + 63 = 126$ calories, a 3-ounce serving contains $126 + 63 = 189$ calories, a 4-ounce serving contains $189 + 63 = 252$ calories, and a 5-ounce serving contains $252 + 63 = 315$ calories. Our solution checks.

YOU TRY IT 7 The slope of the given line is -3.

The slope of any parallel line is also -3.

$$y - y_1 = m(x - x_1)$$
$$y - (-4) = -3[x - (-5)]$$
$$y + 4 = -3(x + 5)$$
$$y + 4 = -3x - 15$$
$$y = -3x - 19$$

YOU TRY IT 8 $3x + 5y = 15$
$$5y = -3x + 15$$
$$\frac{5y}{5} = \frac{-3x + 15}{5}$$
$$y = -\frac{3}{5}x + 3$$

The slope of the given line is $-\frac{3}{5}$.

The slope of any parallel line is also $-\frac{3}{5}$.

$$y - y_1 = m(x - x_1)$$
$$y - 3 = -\frac{3}{5}[x - (-2)]$$
$$y - 3 = -\frac{3}{5}(x + 2)$$
$$y - 3 = -\frac{3}{5}x - \frac{6}{5}$$
$$y = -\frac{3}{5}x + \frac{9}{5}$$

YOU TRY IT 9 The slope of the given line is $-\frac{4}{3}$.

The slope of any perpendicular line is $\frac{3}{4}$.

$$y - y_1 = m(x - x_1)$$
$$y - 3 = \frac{3}{4}[x - (-4)]$$
$$y - 3 = \frac{3}{4}(x + 4)$$
$$y - 3 = \frac{3}{4}x + 3$$

$$y = \frac{3}{4}x + 6$$

YOU TRY IT 10 $5x - 3y = 15$
$$-3y = -5x + 15$$
$$\frac{-3y}{-3} = \frac{-5x + 15}{-3}$$
$$y = \frac{5}{3}x - 5$$

The slope of the given line is $\frac{5}{3}$.

The slope of any perpendicular line is $-\frac{3}{5}$.

$$y - y_1 = m(x - x_1)$$
$$y - (-2) = -\frac{3}{5}[x - (-5)]$$
$$y + 2 = -\frac{3}{5}(x + 5)$$
$$y + 2 = -\frac{3}{5}x - 3$$
$$y = -\frac{3}{5}x - 5$$

YOU TRY IT 11

Goal The goal is to find the equation of the line that is perpendicular to the line containing the points $(0, 0)$ and $(2, 8)$ and goes through $(2, 8)$.

Strategy The initial path of the ball is perpendicular to the line through OP. Therefore, the slope of the initial path of the ball is the negative reciprocal of the slope of the line between O and P.

We need to find the slope of the line through OP.

The slope of the line we are looking for is the negative reciprocal of that slope.

We will then have the slope of the line and a point on the line. We can use the point–slope formula to find the equation of the line.

Solution Slope of the line through OP:

$$m = \frac{y_2 - y_1}{x_2 - x_1} = \frac{8 - 0}{2 - 0} = \frac{8}{2} = 4$$

The slope of the line that is the initial path of the ball is the negative reciprocal of 4.

Therefore, the slope of a perpendicular line is $-\frac{1}{4}$.

$$y - y_1 = m(x - x_1)$$

$$y - 8 = -\frac{1}{4}(x - 2)$$

$$y - 8 = -\frac{1}{4}x + \frac{1}{2}$$

$$y = -\frac{1}{4}x + \frac{17}{2}$$

Check One way to check the solution is to graph $f(x) = -\frac{1}{4}x + \frac{17}{2}$ and $f(x) = -\frac{1}{4}x$ in the square viewing window of a graphing calculator. The lines should appear to be perpendicular. Use the TRACE feature to check that the ordered pair (2, 8) is on the graph.

SECTION 4.3

YOU TRY IT 1

We chose (1999, 23.15) to be P_1 and (2002, 19.91) to be P_2. (Other points are possible.)

$$m = \frac{y_2 - y_1}{x_2 - x_1} = \frac{19.91 - 23.15}{2002 - 1999} = \frac{-3.24}{3} = -1.08$$

$$y - y_1 = m(x - x_1)$$
$$y - 23.15 = -1.08(x - 1999)$$
$$y - 23.15 = -1.08x + 2158.92$$
$$y = -1.08x + 2182.07$$

The equation for our line is $y = -1.08x + 2182.07$. Other equations are possible.

YOU TRY IT 2 **a.** Use a calculator to determine the regression line for the data. The regression equation is $y = 5.6\overline{3}x - 252.86$.

b. $y = 5.6\overline{3}x - 252.86$

$y = 5.6\overline{3}(63) - 252.86$

$y \approx 102$

The weight of a woman on a college swim team who is 63 inches tall would be approximately 102 pounds.

c. The slope indicates the increase in weight for every 1-inch increase in height.

d. A woman 0 in. tall is predicted to weight -253 lb.

YOU TRY IT 3 The points $(-2, 3)$ and $(4, 1)$ are represented in the following input/output table.

x	-2	4
y	3	1

Enter the x values in one list of a calculator and the y values in another. Then use the calculator to determine the regression line for the data.

The equation is $y = -0.\overline{3}x + 2.\overline{3}$.

SECTION 4.4

YOU TRY IT 1 $2x - 3y < 12$

$$-3y < -2x + 12$$

$$\frac{-3y}{-3} > \frac{-2x + 12}{-3}$$

$$y > \frac{2}{3}x - 4$$

Graph $y = \frac{2}{3}x - 4$ as a dashed line.

Shade the upper half-plane.

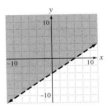

From the graph, we can see that the point $(3, -1)$ is in the solution set of the inequality.

YOU TRY IT 2 **a.** $x \geq 1$

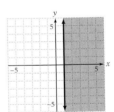

b. $y < -5$

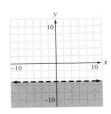

SOLUTIONS to Chapter 5 You Try Its

SECTION 5.1

You Try It 1

$$y = -\frac{2}{3}x + 1$$
$$2x + y = -3$$

$$y = -\frac{2}{3}x + 1$$
$$y = -2x - 3$$

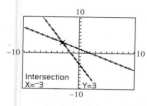

The solution is $(-3, 3)$.

You Try It 2

(1) $\quad y = 2x + 3$
(2) $\quad 2x + 3y = 17$

Substitute $2x + 3$ for y in Equation (2) and solve for x.

$2x + 3y = 17$ • This is Equation (2).
$2x + 3(2x + 3) = 17$
$2x + 6x + 9 = 17$ • Solve for x.
$8x + 9 = 17$
$8x = 8$
$x = 1$

Replace x in Equation (1) by 1 and solve for y.

$y = 2x + 3$ • This is Equation (1).
$= 2(1) + 3$ • Replace x by 1.
$= 5$

The solution is $(1, 5)$.

You Try It 3

(1) $\quad 3x + y = 2$
(2) $\quad 9x + 3y = 6$

Solve Equation (1) for y.

$3x + y = 2$
$y = -3x + 2$

Replace y in Equation (2) by $-3x + 2$ and solve for x.

$9x + 3y = 6$
$9x + 3(-3x + 2) = 6$

$9x - 9x + 6 = 6$
$6 = 6$ • This is a true equation.

This means that if x is any real number and $y = -3x + 2$, then the ordered pair (x, y) is a solution of the system of equations. The solutions are the ordered pairs $(x, -3x + 2)$.

You Try It 4

Goal The goal is to find the measure of each angle of an isosceles triangle.

Strategy An isosceles triangle has two angles of equal measure. Let x be the measure of one of the equal angles, and let y be the measure of the third angle.

The sum of the measures of the angles of a triangle is 180°. Therefore,

$$x + x + y = 180 \text{ or } 2x + y = 180.$$

We are also given that the sum of the measures of the two equal angles is equal to the measure of the third angle. Therefore,

$$x + x = y \text{ or } 2x = y.$$

Solve the system of equations $\begin{array}{l} 2x + y = 180 \\ 2x = y \end{array}$ using the substitution method.

Solution $2x + y = 180$
$2x + 2x = 180$ • $y = 2x$
$4x = 180$
$x = 45$

Substitute this value of x into $y = 2x$ and solve for y.

$$y = 2x$$
$$y = 2(45) = 90$$

The measures of the angles are 45°, 45°, and 90°.

Check Be sure to check your work. In this case, the sum of the measures of the angles is 180°, which indicates that the solution is correct.

You Try It 5

Goal The goal is to find the amount of money that should be invested at 4.2% and the amount at 6% so that both accounts earn the same interest.

Strategy Let x represent the amount invested at 4.2%, and let y represent the amount invested at 6%.

The total amount invested is $13,600.

S18

$$b - \frac{1}{2}(-3) = \frac{1}{2}$$

$$b + \frac{3}{2} = \frac{1}{2}$$

$$b = -1$$

$$a - (-1) + (-3) = 0$$

$$a - 2 = 0$$

$$a = 2$$

The equation is $y = 2x^2 - x - 3$.

Check Verify that each given ordered pair is a solution of the equation by substituting the coordinates into the equation $y = 2x^2 - x - 3$.

YOU TRY IT 7

Goal The goal is to find the number of each type of ticket sold.

Strategy There are three unknowns in this problem. Using the information from the problem, write a system of three equations in three unknowns. Let x be the number of regular admission tickets sold, let y be the number of member discount tickets sold, and let z be the number of student tickets sold.

Because there were 750 tickets sold, we have $x + y + z = 750$.

The receipts for selling these tickets were $5400. Therefore, $10x + 7y + 5z = 5400$.

Because 20 more student tickets than full-price tickets were sold, we have $z = x + 20$, or $-x + z = 20$. Solve the system of equations

$$x + y + z = 750$$
$$10x + 7y + 5z = 5400$$
$$-x + z = 20$$

Write the system as an augmented matrix.

$$\begin{bmatrix} 1 & 1 & 1 & 750 \\ 10 & 7 & 5 & 5400 \\ -1 & 0 & 1 & 20 \end{bmatrix}$$

Solve the system of equations by using the Gaussian elimination method.

Solution

```
[ [1    .7     .5       ...
  [0    1      2.142857 ...
  [0    0      1        ...
Ans▶Frac
 [ [1    7/10   1/2   5...
  [0    1      15/7  8...
  [0    0      1     2...
```

$$x + \frac{7}{10}y + \frac{1}{2}z = 540$$

$$y + \frac{15}{7}z = 800$$

$$z = 210$$

$$y + \frac{15}{7}(210) = 800$$

$$y + 450 = 800$$

$$y = 350$$

$$x + \frac{7}{10}(350) + \frac{1}{2}(210) = 540$$

$$x + 245 + 105 = 540$$

$$x + 350 = 540$$

$$x = 190$$

There were 190 regular admission tickets, 350 member tickets, and 210 student tickets sold.

Check Check the solution by verifying that these numbers satisfy each of the conditions of the problem.

SECTION 5.4

YOU TRY IT 1

Shade above the solid line $y = 2x - 3$. Shade above the dashed line $y = -3x$.

SOLUTIONS to Chapter 6 You Try Its

SECTION 6.1

YOU TRY IT 1 $16a^4b^3 + 10a^4b^3 + 5a^4b^3 = 31a^4b^3$

YOU TRY IT 2 $37m^3n^2p - 14m^3n^2p = 23m^3n^2p$

YOU TRY IT 3 $t^3 \cdot t^8 = t^{3+8} = t^{11}$

YOU TRY IT 4 $n^6 \cdot n \cdot n^2 = n^{6+1+2} = n^9$

YOU TRY IT 5 $c^9(c^5d^8) = c^{9+5}d^8 = c^{14}d^8$

YOU TRY IT 6 $(5y^4)(3y^2) = (5 \cdot 3)(y^4 \cdot y^2) = 15y^{4+2} = 15y^6$

YOU TRY IT 7 $(12p^4q^3)(-3p^5q^2) = [12(-3)]p^{4+5}q^{3+2}$
$$= -36p^9q^5$$

You Try It 8 $(t^3)^6 = t^{3 \cdot 6} = t^{18}$

You Try It 9 $(bc^7)^8 = b^{1 \cdot 8}c^{7 \cdot 8} = b^8 c^{56}$

You Try It 10 $(4y^6)^3 = 4^{1 \cdot 3}y^{6 \cdot 3} = 4^3 y^{18} = 64y^{18}$

You Try It 11 $(2v^6 w^9)^5 = 2^{1 \cdot 5}v^{6 \cdot 5}w^{9 \cdot 5} = 2^5 v^{30}w^{45}$
$$= 32v^{30}w^{45}$$

You Try It 12 $(-2x^3 y^7)^3 = (-2)^{1 \cdot 3}x^{3 \cdot 3}y^{7 \cdot 3} = (-2)^3 x^9 y^{21}$
$$= -8x^9 y^{21}$$

You Try It 13 $(-xy^4)(-2x^3 y^2)^2 = (-xy^4)[(-2)^{1 \cdot 2}x^{3 \cdot 2}y^{2 \cdot 2}]$
$$= (-xy^4)[(-2)^2 x^6 y^4]$$
$$= (-xy^4)(4x^6 y^4)$$
$$= (-1 \cdot 4)(x^{1+6})(y^{4+4})$$
$$= -4x^7 y^8$$

You Try It 14 $\dfrac{t^{10}}{t^4} = t^{10-4} = t^6$

You Try It 15 $\dfrac{a^7 b^6}{ab^3} = a^{7-1}b^{6-3} = a^6 b^3$

You Try It 16 $(-8x^2 y^7)^0 = 1$

You Try It 17 $-(9c^7 d^4)^0 = -1$

You Try It 18 $\dfrac{2}{c^{-4}} = 2 \cdot \dfrac{1}{c^{-4}} = 2 \cdot c^4 = 2c^4$

You Try It 19 $\dfrac{12x^{-8}y}{-16xy^{-3}} = -\dfrac{3x^{-8}y}{4xy^{-3}} = -\dfrac{3}{4}x^{-8-1}y^{1-(-3)}$
$$= -\dfrac{3}{4}x^{-9}y^4 = -\dfrac{3y^4}{4x^9}$$

You Try It 20 $\left(\dfrac{m^{-6}}{n^{-8}}\right)^3 = \dfrac{m^{-6 \cdot 3}}{n^{-8 \cdot 3}} = \dfrac{m^{-18}}{n^{-24}} = \dfrac{n^{24}}{m^{18}}$

You Try It 21 a. $(-2ab)(2a^3 b^{-2})^{-3} = (-2ab)(2^{-3}a^{-9}b^6)$
$$= (-2 \cdot 2^{-3})(a \cdot a^{-9})(b \cdot b^6)$$
$$= \left(-2 \cdot \dfrac{1}{2^3}\right)a^{-8}b^7$$
$$= \left(-2 \cdot \dfrac{1}{8}\right)a^{-8}b^7 = -\dfrac{b^7}{4a^8}$$

b. $\left(\dfrac{2x^2 y^{-4}}{4x^{-2}y^{-5}}\right)^{-3} = \left(\dfrac{x^2 y^{-4}}{2x^{-2}y^{-5}}\right)^{-3} = \dfrac{x^{-6}y^{12}}{2^{-3}x^6 y^{15}}$
$$= 2^3 x^{-6-6}y^{12-15} = 8x^{-12}y^{-3} = \dfrac{8}{x^{12}y^3}$$

You Try It 22 a. $57{,}000{,}000{,}000 = 5.7 \times 10^{10}$
b. $0.000000017 = 1.7 \times 10^{-8}$

You Try It 23 a. $5 \times 10^{12} = 5{,}000{,}000{,}000{,}000$
b. $4.0162 \times 10^{-9} = 0.0000000040162$

You Try It 24 a. $(2.4 \times 10^{-9})(1.6 \times 10^3) = 3.84 \times 10^{-6}$
b. $\dfrac{5.4 \times 10^{-2}}{1.8 \times 10^{-4}} = 3 \times 10^2$

SECTION 6.2

You Try It 1

$$V(r) = 2000r^3 + 6000r^2 + 6000r + 2000$$
$$V(0.07) = 2000(0.07)^3 + 6000(0.07)^2 + 6000(0.07) + 2000$$
$$V(0.07) = 0.686 + 29.4 + 420 + 2000$$
$$V(0.07) = 2450.086$$

After 3 years, the value of $2000 deposited in an IRA that earns 7% interest is $2450.09.

You Try It 2 $(-4d^2 - 3d + 2) + (3d^2 - 4d)$
$$= (-4d^2 + 3d^2) + (-3d - 4d) + 2$$
$$= -d^2 - 7d + 2$$

You Try It 3 $(5x^2 - 3x + 4) - (-6x^3 - 2x + 8)$
$$= (5x^2 - 3x + 4) + (6x^3 + 2x - 8)$$
$$= 6x^3 + 5x^2 + (-3x + 2x) + (4 - 8)$$
$$= 6x^3 + 5x^2 - x - 4$$

You Try It 4

Goal   The goal is to write a variable expression for the company's monthly profit.

Strategy   Use the formula $P = R - C$. Substitute the given polnomials for R and C. Then subtract the polynomials.

Solution $P = R - C$
$$P = (-0.2n^2 + 175n) - (35n + 2000)$$
$$P = (-0.2n^2 + 175n) + (-35n - 2000)$$
$$P = -0.2n^2 + (175n - 35n) - 2000$$
$$P = -0.2n^2 + 140n - 2000$$

The company's monthly profit is $(-0.2n^2 + 140n - 2000)$ dollars.

Check   √

SECTION 6.3

You Try It 1   **a.** $(-2d + 3)(-4d) = -2d(-4d) + 3(-4d)$
$$= 8d^2 - 12d$$

b. $-a^3(3a^2 + 2a - 7)$
$$= -a^3(3a^2) + (-a^3)(2a) - (-a^3)(7)$$
$$= -3a^5 - 2a^4 + 7a^3$$

You Try It 2 $(3c^3 - 2c^2 + c - 3)(2c + 5)$

$$3c^3 - 2c^2 + c - 3$$
$$\underline{\qquad\qquad\qquad 2c + 5}$$
$$\underline{15c^3 - 10c^2 + 5c - 15}$$
$$6c^4 - 4c^3 + 2c^2 - 6c$$
$$\overline{6c^4 + 11c^3 - 8c^2 - c - 15}$$

You Try It 3   **a.** $(4y - 5)(3y - 3)$
$$= 4y(3y) + 4y(-3) + (-5)(3y) + (-5)(-3)$$
$$= 12y^2 - 12y - 15y + 15$$
$$= 12y^2 - 27y + 15$$

b. $(3a + 2b)(3a - 5b)$

$= 3a(3a) + 3a(-5b) + 2b(3a) + 2b(-5b)$

$= 9a^2 - 15ab + 6ab - 10b^2$

$= 9a^2 - 9ab - 10b^2$

YOU TRY IT 4 $(3x + 2y)^2 = (3x + 2y)(3x + 2y)$

$= 9x^2 + 6xy + 6xy + 4y^2$

$= 9x^2 + 12xy + 4y^2$

YOU TRY IT 5

Goal   The goal is to determine the area of the circle in terms of x.

Strategy   To determine the area of the circle in terms of x, use the formula for the area of a circle. $A = \pi r^2$. Substitute the variable expression $(x - 4)$ for r. Then simplify.

Solution $A = \pi r^2$

$A = \pi(x - 4)^2$

$A = \pi(x - 4)(x - 4)$

$A = \pi(x^2 - 4x - 4x + 16)$

$A = \pi(x^2 - 8x + 16)$

$A = \pi x^2 - 8\pi x + 16\pi$

The area of the circle is $(\pi x^2 - 8\pi x + 16\pi)$ ft^2.

Check   Check each step of the solution.

YOU TRY IT 6 $\dfrac{4x^3y + 8x^2y^2 - 4xy^3}{2xy} = \dfrac{4x^3y}{2xy} + \dfrac{8x^2y^2}{2xy} - \dfrac{4xy^3}{2xy}$

$= 2x^2 + 4xy - 2y^2$

YOU TRY IT 7 $(x^3 - 7 - 2x) \div (x - 2)$

$= (x^3 + 0x^2 - 2x - 7) \div (x - 2)$

$$
\begin{array}{r}
x^2 + 2x + 2 \\
x - 2 \overline{)x^3 + 0x^2 - 2x - 7} \\
\underline{x^3 - 2x^2} \\
2x^2 - 2x \\
\underline{2x^2 - 4x} \\
2x - 7 \\
\underline{2x - 4} \\
-3
\end{array}
$$

$(x^3 - 7 - 2x) \div (x - 2) = x^2 + 2x + 2 - \dfrac{3}{x - 2}$

YOU TRY IT 8

$$
\begin{array}{r}
x^3 \qquad\quad + 2 \\
x + 5 \overline{)x^4 + 5x^3 + 2x + 10} \\
\underline{x^4 + 5x^3} \\
0 \qquad 2x + 10 \\
2x + 10 \\
\underline{} \\
0
\end{array}
$$

Another factor of $x^4 + 5x^3 + 2x + 10$ is $x^3 + 2$.

YOU TRY IT 9

Goal   The goal is to write a variable expression for the height of a parallelogram that has an area of $(3x^2 + 2x - 8)$ square feet and a base of length $(x + 2)$ feet.

Strategy   Using the formula $h = \dfrac{A}{b}$, substitute the given polynomials for A and b. Then divide the polynomials.

Solution $h = \dfrac{A}{b}$

$h = \dfrac{3x^2 + 2x - 8}{x + 2}$

$$
\begin{array}{r}
3x - 4 \\
x + 2 \overline{)3x^2 + 2x - 8} \\
\underline{3x^2 + 6x} \\
-4x - 8 \\
\underline{-4x - 8} \\
0
\end{array}
$$

The height is $(3x - 4)$ ft.

Check $(3x - 4)(x + 2) = 3x^2 + 6x - 4x - 8$

$= 3x^2 + 2x - 8$

YOU TRY IT 10

a.

$$
\begin{array}{r|rrr}
-2 & 6 & 8 & -5 \\
& & -12 & 8 \\
\hline
& 6 & -4 & 3
\end{array}
$$

$(6x^2 + 8x - 5) \div (x + 2) = 6x - 4 + \dfrac{3}{x + 2}$

b.

$$
\begin{array}{r|rrrrr}
3 & 2 & -3 & -8 & 0 & -2 \\
& & 6 & 9 & 3 & 9 \\
\hline
& 2 & 3 & 1 & 3 & 7
\end{array}
$$

$(2x^4 - 3x^3 - 8x^2 - 2) \div (x - 3)$

$= 2x^3 + 3x^2 + x + 3 + \dfrac{7}{x - 3}$

PREP TEST

1. 924   **2.** 1244   **3.** 15,873   **4.** 24   **5.** 127.16   **6.** a, c, d   **7.** a and C; b and D; c and A; d and B
8. 24   **9.** 4   **10.** $3 \cdot 7$

1.1 Exercises

1. Understand the problem and state the goal, devise a strategy to solve the problem, solve the problem, and review the solution and check your work.   **3.** Answers may vary.   **5.** Deductive reasoning involves drawing a conclusion that is based on given facts. Examples will vary.   **7.** 2601 tiles   **9.** 1   **11.** M, N   **13.** 6 students   **15.** 8
17. 55 mph   **19.** $\frac{101}{99}$ **21.** 7 children   **23.** $\frac{1}{8}$ and $\frac{1}{10}$ **25.** 28 minutes   **27.** 41   **29.** 216   **31.** 93
33. u   **35.** 111,111,111; 222,222,222; 333,333,333; 444,444,444; 555,555,555. Explanations will vary.
$12,345,679 \cdot 54 = 666,666,666$; $12,345,679 \cdot 63 = 777,777,777$ **37.**   **39.** 12   **41.** 3

43. The difference is always 3087.   **45.** February and March   **47.** deductive reasoning
49. inductive reasoning   **51.** Maria owns the utility stock, Jose the automotive stock, Anita the technology stock, and Tony the oil stock.   **53.** Atlanta held the stamp convention, Chicago the baseball card convention, Philadelphia the coin convention, and Seattle the comic book convention.   **55.** No   **57.** 6   **59.** 3

1.2 Exercises

1. Explanations will vary.   **3.** $\{x \mid x < 5\}$ does not include the element 5, whereas $\{x \mid x \le 5\}$ does include the element 5.
5a. No. Explanations will vary.   **b.** Yes. Explanations will vary.   **7a.** 31, 8600   **b.** 31, 8600
c. 31, −45, −2, 8600   **d.** 31, 8600   **e.** −45, −2   **f.** 31   **9a.** −17   **b.** $-17, 0.3412, \frac{27}{91}, 6.1\overline{2}$
c. $\frac{3}{\pi}, -1.010010001 \ldots$ **d.** all   **11.** $\{-3, -2, -1\}$ **13.** $\{1, 3, 5, 7, 9, 11, 13\}$ **15.** $\{a, b, n\}$ **17.** $\varnothing$
19. $\{x \mid x < -5, x \in \text{integers}\}$ **21.** $\{x \mid x \ge -4\}$ **23.** $\{x \mid -2 < x < 5\}$ **25.** False   **27.** False   **29.** False
31.   **33.**   **35.** $\{2, 3, 5, 8, 9, 10\}$ **37.** $\{x \mid x \in \text{real numbers}\}$
39. $\{4, 6\}$ **41.** $\varnothing$ **43.** $M \cup C = \{1, 2, 3, 4, 5, 6, 7, 8, 9, 10\}$; $M \cap C = \varnothing$ **45.**
47.   **49.**   **51.**
53.   **55.** $\{x \mid -5 \le x \le 7\}$ **57.** $\{x \mid -9 < x \le 5\}$ **59.** $\{x \mid x \ge -2\}$ **61.** $[0, 3]$
63. $[-2, 7)$ **65.** $(-\infty, -5]$ **67.** $(23, \infty)$ **69.**   **71.**
73.   **75.**   **77.**
79. Explanations may vary.   **81.** A set is well defined if it is possible to determine whether any given item is an element of the set. Examples will vary.

1.3 Exercises

1. Sometimes true   **3.** Never true   **5.** Sometimes true
7. Explanations will vary.   **9a.** Add the absolute values of the numbers. Then attach the sign of the addends.
b. Find the absolute value of each number. Then subtract the lesser of these absolute values from the greater one. Attach the sign of the number with the greater absolute value.   **11a.** Multiply the absolute values of the numbers. The product is positive.   **b.** Multiply the absolute values of the numbers. The product is negative.   **13.** −25

15. 34   **17.** 0   **19.** −12   **21.** 16   **23.** −49   **25.** 16   **27.** 32   **29.** −86   **31.** −54
33.

35.

37.

39. 9   **41.** −40   **43.** 9   **45.** 37   **47.** −10   **49.** −14   **51.** 19   **53.** 6   **55.** 0   **57.** 12
59. −138   **61.** 3   **63.** −20   **65.** −10   **67.** −7   **69.** 8   **71.** 48   **73a.** −10, −14, −9, −9, −10, −9, −13, −9, −16   **b.** Woods, Duval, Michelson, Calcavecchia, Izawa, Els, Furyk, Langer, Triplett   **75.** $27,816; $32,101; $27,445; $27,829; $26,115; $25,068;   **77.**

79. −96   **81.** −336   **83.** 0
85. −168   **87.** −84   **89.** 240   **91.** −8   **93.** 6   **95.** 0   **97.** −7   **99.** −84   **101.** −110   **103.** 252
105. −8   **107.** −7   **109.** 24   **111.** −64, 256, −1024   **113.** −216, −1296, −7776   **115.** −$111,968,000
117. −$4,100,000   **119.** 32   **121.** 0   **123.** 2401   **125.** 729   **127.** −64   **129.** 81   **131.** 108
133. −12   **135.** 32   **137.** −864   **139.** −1008   **141.** −8640   **143.** 7   **145.** 9   **147.** 84   **149.** 44
151. 30   **153.** 30   **155.** 357   **157.** −10   **159.** 29   **161.** 13   **163.** −3   **165.** −21   **167.** −1
169. −1°C   **171.** 214 points   **173.** 400 ft; more than the length of a football field   **175.** −16°F   **177.** 21°F
179a. −4 and 6   **b.** −4 and 8   **181a.** negative 7   **b.** the opposite of negative 10   **c.** the opposite of the absolute value of 9   **d.** the opposite of the absolute value of negative 24   **183.** Answers will vary. For example, row 1: −3, 2, 1; row 2: 4, 0 −4; row 3: −1, −2, 3   **185a.** 81   **b.** −17

1.4 Exercises

1. Never true   **3.** Never true   **5.** Always true   **7.** Always true   **9a.** No   **b.** Yes
11. Answers will vary.   **13.** $-\frac{2}{27}$ **15.** $-\frac{25}{18}$ **17.** $\frac{1}{24}$ **19.** $\frac{7}{24}$ **21.** $-\frac{7}{16}$ **23.** $\frac{11}{24}$ **25.** $-\frac{1}{16}$
27. −23.845   **29.** −1.06   **31.** 4.676   **33.** −37.19   **35.** 19.61   **37.** 1   **39.** −10.7893
41. $\frac{11}{12} - \left(-\frac{1}{4}\right)$ **43.** $\frac{1}{21}$ **45.** $\frac{2}{9}$ **47.** $-\frac{7}{30}$ **49.** $-\frac{10}{9}$ **51.** $-\frac{7}{4}$ **53.** $\frac{2}{3}$ **55.** −4.028
57. −13.176   **59.** −37.57   **61.** 0.75   **63.** −5.11   **65.** $-\frac{4}{9}$ **67.** $-\frac{3}{2}$ **69.** $\left(-\frac{8}{9}\right)\left(-\frac{3}{4}\right)$
71. −$103.408 million   **73.** −$43.584 million   **75.** $30.481 million   **77.** 2000; 1975   **79.** $288.6 billion
81. 1999–2000   **83.** −$92.425 billion   **85.** 1.7   **87.** 1.16   **89.** −1   **91.** 1   **93.** $\frac{1}{2}$
95. $-\frac{15}{2}$ **97.** 42°F   **99.** 24°F   **101.** −19.4°F   **103.** $138.499 billion   **105.** 4 times greater
107. −$710.5 million   **109.** $27.2848 billion   **111.** $\frac{19}{24}$

1.5 Exercises

1. A variable is a letter that is used to stand for an unknown quantity or for a quantity that can change or vary.
3. It means to replace the variables in a variable expression with numbers and then simplify the resulting numerical expression.   **5.** Answers will vary.   **7.** Always true   **9.** 6   **11.** 16   **13.** −9   **15.** −15   **17.** 1
19. 5   **21.** 10   **23.** −2   **25.** 20   **27.** 24   **29.** 4.96   **31.** −5.68   **33.** 24   **35.** 220 cm
37. 2800 cm²   **39.** 3 m²   **41.** $48,000   **43.** 136 ft   **45a.** 11   **b.** 1   **47a.** 4   **b.** 3.5   **49a.** 7.125
b. 2.75   **51a.** 19   **b.** 4   **53.** The architect charges a fee of $4740 to design a 1600-square-foot house.
55a. 91°F   **b.** 2450 ft   **57a.** 75.4 min   **b.** 2.5 min   **59a.** 69 ft   **b.** 1.5 s, 2.5 s
61a.

s	2	4	6	8	10	12	14
P	8	16	24	32	40	48	56

b. When the length of a side of a square is 12 in., the perimeter is 48 in.
63a.

s	1	2	3	4	5	6	7
V	1	8	27	64	125	216	343

b. When the length of a side of a cube is 3 m, the volume of the cube is 27 m^3.
65. $\frac{1}{2}$ **67.** 13   **69.** -1 **71.** 4   **73.** 81

1.6 Exercises

1. Always true   **3.** Always true   **5.** Sometimes true   **7.** Always true   **9.** Sometimes true   **11.** Never true
13. The Commutative Property says that two numbers can be added in either order. The Associative Property states that when three numbers are added together, the numbers can be grouped in any order.   **15.** 2   **17.** 17
19. 4   **21.** 4   **23.** 0   **25.** The Multiplication Property of One   **27.** The Addition Property of Zero
29. The Inverse Property of Multiplication   **31.** The Associative Property of Addition
33. The Commutative Property of Multiplication   **35.** $2x^2$, $5x$, $\underline{-8}$ **37.** $-n^4$, $\underline{6}$ **39.** $\underline{7x^2y}$, $6xy^2$ **41.** 1, -9
43. 1, -4, -1 **45.** $21y$ **47.** $-6y$ **49.** The expression is in simplest form.   **51.** $5xy$ **53.** $-14x^2$
55. $-3x - 8y$ **57.** $-2x$ **59.** $22y^2$ **61.** 0   **63.** $-\frac{7}{20}y$ **65.** $12x$ **67.** $-6a$ **69.** x **71.** $2x$ **73.** $3y$
75. $-2a - 14$ **77.** $15x^2 + 6x$ **79.** $-6y^2 + 21$ **81.** $-12a^2 - 20a + 28$ **83.** $a - 7$ **85.** $18y - 51$
87. $4x - 4$ **89.** $\frac{4}{p - 6}$ **91.** $\frac{3}{8}(t + 15)$ **93.** $13 - x$ **95.** $\frac{3}{7}x$ **97.** $5x - 8$ **99.** $7x + 14$ **101.** $(n + n^3) - 6$
103. $11 + \frac{1}{2}x$ **105.** $80 - 13x$ **107.** $7x^2 - 4$ **109.** $x + (x + 10)$; $2x + 10$ **111.** $x - (9 - x)$; $2x - 9$
113. $\frac{1}{5}x - \frac{3}{8}x$; $-\frac{7}{40}x$ **115.** $(x + 9) + 4$; $x + 13$ **117.** $2(3x + 40)$; $6x + 80$ **119.** $16\left(\frac{1}{4}x\right)$; $4x$
121. $9x - 2x$; $7x$ **123.** $(x - 5) + 19$; $x + 14$ **125.** Let p be the cruising speed of a propeller-driven plane; $2p$
127. Let c be the amount of cashews; $4c$ **129.** Let a be the age of the 8¢ stamp; $a + 25$ **131.** Let L be the measure of the largest angle; $\frac{1}{2}L - 3$ **133.** x and $35 - x$ **135.** $640 + 24h$ **137.** $0.3C$ **139.** $-\frac{1}{2}x + \frac{5}{2}y$
141. For example, four less than five times a number.   **143.** For example, the product of five and four less than a number.   **145.** $5n + 10d$ **147.** $2x$

CHAPTER 1 REVIEW EXERCISES

1. 13 first cousins [1.1]   **2.** 22 [1.1]   **3.** 4 [1.1]   **4.** $\{-8, -7, -6, -5, -4, -3\}$ [1.2]
5. $\{x \mid x \leq -10\}$ [1.2]   **6.** $\{2, 3\}$ [1.2]   **7.** $\{x \mid -2 \leq x \leq 3\}$ [1.2]
8. $(-\infty, -44)$ [1.2]   **9.** [1.2]   **10.** [1.2]
11. [1.2]   **12.** $-\frac{1}{7}$ [1.4]   **13.** -0.1 [1.4]   **14.** -441.2 [1.4]
15. $\frac{41}{24}$ [1.4]   **16.** $-\frac{5}{6}$ [1.4]   **17.** 4 [1.3]   **18.** 10 [1.3]
19. $-3°C$ [1.3]   **20.** $395.45°C$ [1.4]   **21.** 37.5 cm [1.5]

22a.

D	2	4	6	8	10	12	14
P	16	17	18	19	20	21	22

b. At a depth of 6 ft, the pressure is 18 lb/in^2. [1.5]
23. 18 [1.5]   **24.** $\frac{2}{7}$ [1.5]   **25.** The Commutative Property of Multiplication [1.6]
26. $24d$ [1.6]   **27.** $3a^2 + 10a$ [1.6]   **28.** $19a - 13$ [1.6]   **29.** $8\left(\frac{2n}{16}\right)$; n [1.6]
30. Let d be the distance from Earth to the sun; $30d$ [1.6]

CHAPTER 1 TEST

1. 211 [1.1]   **2.** {−6, −5, −4, −3, −2, −1, 0} [1.2]   **3.** {x | x ≥ −2} [1.2]   **4.** {−1, 0, 1} [1.2]
5. {x | −4 ≤ x ≤ 6} [1.2]   **6.** [−20, ∞) [1.2]   **7.** ![number line from −5 to 5] [1.2]
8. ![number line from −5 to 5] [1.2]   **9.** 28 [1.3]   **10.** $\frac{1}{10}$ [1.4]   **11.** $\frac{1}{12}$ [1.4]   **12.** 1.229 [1.4]   **13.** $-\frac{3}{10}$ [1.5]
14. 33 [1.5]   **15.** $38,669 [1.5]   **16a.** 49 ft **b.** 1.25 s [1.5]   **17.** $-8y^2 + 9y$ [1.6]   **18.** $5w - 17$ [1.6]
19. $(n - 3) + (n + 2); 2n - 1$ [1.6]   **20.** Let s be the speed of the second car; $s + 15$ [1.6]

ANSWERS to Chapter 2 Exercises

PREP TEST

1. 2 [1.5]   **2.** 11 [1.5]   **3.** 2.5 [1.5]   **4.** 5 [1.5]   **5.** 0 [1.5]   **6.** −7 [1.5]

2.1 Exercises

1. Answers will vary.
3. A solution of an equation in two variables is an ordered pair that makes the equation a true statement.
5. The input variable is t. The output variable is s.
7. ![graph with points A, B, C, D]

9. −2, 0; 0, −3

11. Yes   **13.** No

15.

x	−3	−2	−1	0	1	2	3
y	7	5	3	1	−1	−3	−5

![graph]

17.

x	−8	−4	0	4	8
y	−5	−2	1	4	7

![graph]

19.

x	−3	−2	−1	0	1	2	3
y	10	5	2	1	2	5	10

![graph]

21.

t	−5	−4	−3	−2	−1	0	1
s	2	−3	−6	−7	−6	−3	2

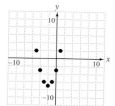

A4

23a.

Input, time t (in seconds)	0	5	10	15	20	25	30
Output, distance d (in feet)	0	55	110	165	220	275	330

b. In 20 s, the jogger runs 220 ft.

25a.

Input, time t (in seconds)	0	0.5	1	1.5	2	2.5	3
Output, distance d (in feet)	0	4	16	36	64	100	144

b. In 1.5 s, the object will fall 36 ft.

27a.

Input, weight of jewelry w (in grams)	0	5	10	15	20	25	30
Output, quantity of gold Q (in grams)	0	3.75	7.5	11.25	15	18.75	22.5

b. In a 15-gram piece of 18-carat gold jewelry, there are 11.25 g of gold.

29a.

Input, time t (in seconds)	0	0.5	1	1.5	2	2.5	3
Output, height h (in feet)	5	36	59	74	81	80	71

b. The ball is 80 ft above the ground 2.5 s after it is released.

31. $y = 2x - 4$

x	-2	-1	0	1	2
y	-8	-6	-4	-2	0

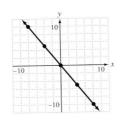

33. $y = \frac{x}{2} + 1$

x	-4	-2	0	2	4
y	-1	0	1	2	3

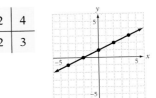

35. $y = \frac{-5x}{4}$

x	-8	-4	0	4	8
y	10	5	0	-5	-10

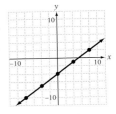

37. $y = \frac{3}{4}x - 4$

x	-8	-4	0	4	8
y	-10	-7	-4	-1	2

39. $y = 2x + 2$

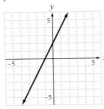

41. $y = \frac{3}{2}x - 3$

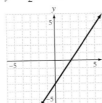

43. $y = -\frac{3}{4}x + 1$

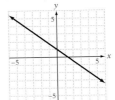

45a. 10 **b.** 5 **47a.** 0 **b.** 22 **49a.** 19 **b.** 8 **51a.** -11 **b.** 28 **53a.** 10 **b.** -6 **55.** $(7.5, 20)$

57. $(-6.3, 20.9)$ **59.** $\left(-\frac{61}{3}, -1\right)$ **61.** $\left(-\frac{57}{10}, -\frac{9}{2}\right)$ **63.** $(12.1, -23.03)$ **65.** 0 **67.** Answers will vary.

For example, $(-3, 2)$ and $(5, 2)$. **69.** $(5, 4)$ and $(-3, -1)$ **71a.** 5 **b.** 3 **73a.** 4 **b.** 7 **75a.** 0 **b.** 2

77. 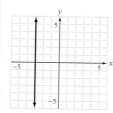 **79.** 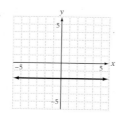 **81.**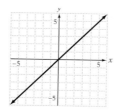

2.2 Exercises

1. A relation is a set of ordered pairs. A function is a relation in which no two ordered pairs have the same first coordinate and different second coordinates. **3.** The domain is the set of first coordinates of the function; the range is the set of second coordinates of the function. **5.** To evaluate a function means to replace the independent variable by a given number and simplify the resulting expression. **7.** No **9.** Domain: $\{-3, -2, -1, 0, 1\}$, Range: $\{-13, -11, -9, -7, -5\}$, Yes **11.** Domain: $\{-4, -2, 0, 2\}$, Range: $\{6, 8, 10, 12\}$, No **13.** Domain: $\{2, 3, 4, 5, 6\}$, Range: $\{-6, -3, 6\}$, Yes **15.** Domain: $\{-4, -2, 0, 3, 5\}$, Range: $\{0\}$, Yes **17.** 13 **19.** 14 **21.** 15 **23.** $\frac{4}{3}$ **25.** 13

27. $f(x) = 2 - 2x$

x	-2	-1	0	1	2
y	6	4	2	0	-2

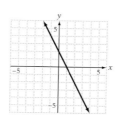

29. $f(x) = -\frac{2x}{3} + 4$

x	-6	-3	0	3	6
y	8	6	4	2	0

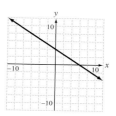

31. $f(x) = x^2 - 2$

x	-3	-2	-1	0	1	2	3
y	7	2	-1	-2	-1	2	7

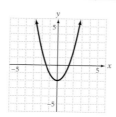

33. $f(x) = -x^2 + 2x - 1$

x	-2	-1	0	1	2	3	4
y	-9	-4	-1	0	-1	-4	-9

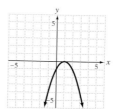

35. $f(x) = -2$

x	-2	-1	0	1	2	3	4
y	-2	-2	-2	-2	-2	-2	-2

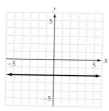

37. The graph is a horizontal line through (0, 1). **39.** 10 **41.** −27 **43.** 8 **45.** 10 **47.** 7 **49.** $\frac{71}{8}$ **51.** $\{-6, 1, 6, 9, 10\}$ **53.** $\{1, 3, 6, 10, 15, 21, 28\}$ **55.** $\left\{-\frac{3}{10}, -\frac{2}{5}, -\frac{1}{2}, 0, \frac{1}{2}, \frac{2}{5}, \frac{3}{10}\right\}$ **57.** None **59.** −5
61. −1, 3 **63.** None **65.** −4 **67.** −2 **69.** None **71.** 1 **73.** −3 **75.** 1.5 **77.** −1, 1
79. −1, 3 **81.** −0.5, 1 **83a.** 16 m **b.** 20 ft **85a.** 100 ft **b.** 68 ft **87a.** 1136 ft/s **b.** increases

89a. 30 games **b.** 45 games   **91a.** 1.92 s **b.** 0.96 s   **93.** Answers will vary. Possibilities are: **a.** {(1, 2), (4, 7), (6, 9)} **b.** {(1, 4), (2, 4), (3, 4)}   **95.** Answers will vary. One possibility is $f(x) = \frac{1}{x-5}$.

2.3 Exercises

1. If every vertical line intersects a graph at most once, then the graph is the graph of a function.   **3a.** 0 **b.** 0
5a. The domain of a function is the set of all values of the independent variable. The range of a function is the set of all values of the dependent variable. **b.** The domain of a function is the set of all input values. The range of a function is the set of all output values.   **7.** Yes   **9.** No   **11.** Yes   **13.** $(-2, 0)$; $(0, 6)$ **15.** $(-2, 0)$, $(3, 0)$; $(0, -6)$
17. $(-3, 0)$, $(0.5, 0)$; $(0, -3)$ **19.** $(-1, 0)$, $(5, 0)$; $(0, 5)$ **21.** $(-2, 0)$, $(1, 0)$, $(5, 0)$; $(0, 10)$ **23.** $(-3, 0)$, $(0, 0)$, $(4, 0)$; $(0, 0)$ **25.** 3   **27.** 2   **29.** 1.6   **31.** 3   **33.** 0   **35.** 1.71   **37.** 3   **39.** 8   **41.** -2 **43.** 2
45. -2 **47.** -2 **49.** 2.5   **51.** -2.35 **53.** 2.1   **55a.** -9 **b.** 1   **57a.** 4 **b.** 9   **59.** 44 g
61a. 3.3 s **b.** The rock hits the bottom of the ravine in 3.3 s.   **63.** 5 years   **65.** $22   **67.** 2 h   **69.** 2011
71. 2   **73.** -8 **75.** 4   **77.** $-3, 1$ **79.** $-4, 2$

CHAPTER 2 REVIEW EXERCISES

1.

x	−6	−4	−2	0	2	4
y	−6	−5	−4	−3	−2	−1

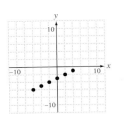

[2.1]

2.

x	−3	−2	−1	0	1	2	3
y	3	−1	−3	−3	−1	3	9

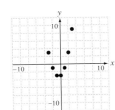

[2.1]

3.

x	−9	−6	−3	0	3
y	5	4	3	2	1

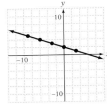

[2.1]

4a. -7 **b.** -5 [2.1]   **5a.** 4 **b.** -3 [2.1]   **6.** Domain: $\{-1, 0, 1, 2, 3, 4\}$, Range: $\{-1, 1, 3, 5\}$; Yes [2.2]
7. $\{-27, -13, -3, 3, 5\}$ [2.2]   **8.** -2 [2.2]   **9.** $-3, 3$ [2.2]
10. $f(x) = -2x + 3$ **11.** $f(x) = -x^2 + 4x - 1$

x	−3	−2	−1	0	1
y	9	7	5	3	1

x	−1	0	1	2	3	4	5
y	−6	−1	2	3	2	−1	−6

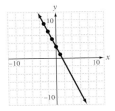

[2.2]

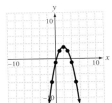

[2.2]

12. $f(x) = -4.$

x	-2	-1	0	1	2
y	-4	-4	-4	-4	-4

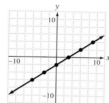

[2.2]

13. 16   [2.2]   **14.** -10   [2.2]   **15.** -7   [2.2]   **16.** -10.625   [2.2]   **17.** -1   [2.2]   **18.** 2   [2.2]
19. Yes; it is a function   [2.3]   **20.** (6, 0); (0, -3)   [2.3]   **21.** (-4, 0), (2, 0); (0, -8)   [2.3]   **22.** 3.5   [2.3]
23. -2   [2.3]   **24a.** 6 min   **b.** 300 ft   [2.3]   **25.** 2005   [2.3]

CHAPTER 2 TEST

1.

x	-2	-1	0	1	2	3	4	5	6
y	-7	0	5	8	9	8	5	0	-7

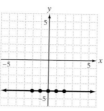

[2.1]

2.

x	-6	-3	0	3	6	9
y	-6	-4	-2	0	2	4

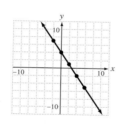

[2.1]

3. 4   [2.1]   **4.** Domain: $\{-4, -2, 0, 2, 4\}$, Range: $\{-2, -1, 0\}$; Yes   [2.2]   **5.** $\{-3, -1, 3, 9\}$ [2.2]   **6.** 2   [2.2]
7. $f(x) = -\frac{3}{2}x + 4$

x	-2	0	2	4	6
y	7	4	1	-2	-5

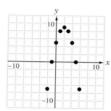

[2.2]

8. $f(x) = -x^2 - 2x + 3$

x	-4	-3	-2	-1	0	1	2
y	-5	0	3	4	3	0	-5

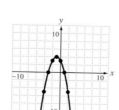

[2.2]

9. -6   [2.2]   **10.** -12   [2.2]   **11.** -3, 3   [2.2]   **12.** Answers will vary.   [2.3]   **13.** (-4, 0); (0, 3)   [2.3]
14. (-1, 0), (3, 0); (0, -3)   [2.3]   **15.** -4   [2.3]   **16.** 4   [2.3]   **17a.** 50%   **b.** 20%   [2.2]
18. 35 s   [2.3]   **19.** 3.1 s   [2.3]   **20.** 2007   [2.3]

1. $\{x \mid -2 \le x \le 3\}$ [1.2]   **2.** True [1.2]   **3.** 34 [1.3]   **4.** 160 [1.5]   **5.** $-\frac{13}{12}$ [1.5]

6. $-10a + 38$ [1.6]   **7.** Commutative Property of Multiplication [1.6]

8.

x	-4	-2	0	2	4	6
y	-9	-6	-3	0	3	6

[2.1]

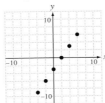

9. a.

Input, distance driven m (in miles)	0	100	150	200	250	300	350
Output, NO_x g (in grams)	0	40	60	80	100	120	140

b. When this car is driven 150 mi, it emits 60 g of NO_x. [2.1]

10. 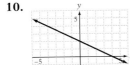 [2.1]   **11.** [2.2]

12.

x	-1	0	1	2	3	4	5
y	8	1	-4	-7	-8	-7	-4

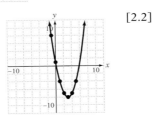 [2.2]

13.

x	-4	-3	-2	-1	0	1	2
y	-7	-2	1	2	1	-2	-7

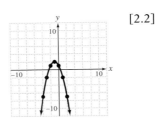 [2.2]

14. -9 [2.1]   **15.** 4 [2.3]   **16.** 2 [2.2]   **17.** $(-3, 0), (1, 0); (0, -3)$ [2.3]   **18.** 2 [2.3]

19. 8 min [2.3]   **20.** 2004 [2.3]

ANSWERS to Chapter 3 Exercises

1. -4 [1.3]   **2.** -6 [1.3]   **3.** 3 [1.3]   **4.** 1 [1.4]   **5.** $10x - 5$ [1.6]   **6.** -9 [1.6]   **7.** $9x - 18$ [1.6]

8. 8 [1.3]   **9.** $20 - n$ [1.6]

3.1 Exercises

1. An equation has an equals sign; an expression does not have an equals sign. **3.** The goal of solving an equation is to find its solutions. The goal of simplifying an expression is to combine like terms and write the expression in simplest form. **5.** The same number can be added to each side of an equation without changing the solution of the equation. This property is used to remove a term from one side of an equation. **7.** 9 **9.** 4 **11.** $\frac{15}{2}$ **13.** -2 **15.** 4.8 **17.** $\frac{3}{2}$ **19.** 3 **21.** 5 **23.** -3 **25.** -3 **27.** $\frac{4}{3}$ **29.** $\frac{5}{3}$ **31.** 7 **33.** -3 **35.** $\frac{1}{2}$ **37.** $\frac{5}{6}$ **39.** $\frac{2}{3}$ **41.** 6 **43.** -12 **45.** The equation has no solution. **47.** 9 **49.** $-\frac{15}{2}$ **51a.** $40,000; $25,000 **b.** $60,000; $75,000 **c.** $50,000

3.2 Exercises

1. $V = x(0.85) = 0.85x$ **3.** Yes. Sometimes; it depends on the ratio of the juices used. No. **5.** The second jogger **7.** The total distance between the two objects = the distance traveled by the first object + the distance traveled by the second object. **9.** 800 mph **11.** $.12 **13.** 17.5 lb of $6 coffee; 7.5 lb of $3.50 coffee **15.** 72 adult tickets **17.** 250 bushels of soybeans; 750 bushels of wheat **19.** 100 oz **21.** $6.85 per ounce **23.** 15.6 kg of walnuts; 34.4 kg of cashews **25.** $d = 12t$

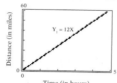

27a. Imogene **b.** No. Her graph does not intersect Imogene's graph. **29.** First car: 54 mph; second car: 64 mph **31.** 336 mi **33.** one hiker: 3 mph; other hiker: 3.5 mph **35.** Freight train: 30 mph; passenger train: 48 mph **37.** 44 mi **39.** Walnuts: 10 lb; cashews: 20 lb **41.** 1600 years **43.** 10:15 A.M.

3.3 Exercises

1. A right angle is an angle whose measure is 90°. An acute angle is an angle whose measure is between 0° and 90°. An obtuse angle is an angle whose measure is between 90° and 180°. A straight angle is an angle whose measure is 180°. **3.** Vertical angles are nonadjacent angles formed by intersecting lines. **5.** They are not parallel. **7.** A central angle is formed by two radii of the circle. The measure of the central angle is equal to the measure of the intercepted arc. **9.** 47° **11.** 82° **13.** 28° and 62° **15.** 48° and 132° **17.** 33° **19.** 5° **21.** 25° **23.** 42° **25.** 78° **27.** 4 **29.** $m\angle a = 44°, m\angle b = 136°$ **31.** $m\angle a = 122°, m\angle b = 58°$ **33.** 40 **35.** 20 **37.** $m\angle x = 125°, m\angle y = 135°$ **39.** $m\angle x = 65°, m\angle y = 155°$ **41.** 22° and 68° **43.** 35 **45.** 33 **47.** 10 **49.** 28 **51.** 64 **53.** The three angles form a straight angle. The sum of the measures of the interior angles of a triangle is 180°. **55.** 140°

3.4 Exercises

1.) and (indicate that the endpoint of an interval is not included in the solution set;] and [indicate that the endpoint point of an interval is included in the solution set. **3.** The Multiplication Property of Inequalities states that when each side of an inequality is multiplied by a positive number, the inequality symbol remains the same; when each side of an inequality is multiplied by a negative number, the inequality symbol must be reversed. **5.** A number cannot be less than -3 *and* greater than 4. **7.** $\{x|x > 3\}$ **9.** $\{n|n \geq 2\}$ **11.** $\{x|x > -2\}$ **13.** $\{n|n \geq 4\}$ **15.** $\{x|x \leq 2\}$ **17.** $\{x|x > 3\}$ **19.** $\{x|x \leq 2\}$ **21.** $\{x|x \geq 2\}$ **23.** $\{x|x \leq 3\}$ **25.** $\{x|x < -3\}$ **27.** $\left[-\frac{1}{2}, \infty\right)$ **29.** $\left(-\infty, \frac{8}{3}\right)$ **31.** $(-\infty, 8.125)$ **33.** $(-\infty, 1]$ **35.** $\left(-\infty, \frac{7}{4}\right]$ **37.** $(-\infty, 2]$ **39.** $3150 or more **41.** More than $5714 **43.** More than 60 min **45.** More than 38 mi **47.** The TopPage plan is less expensive for more than 460 pages per month. **49.** 32°F to 86°F **51.** more than 200 checks **53.** 58 to 100 **55.** $\{x|x < 3 \text{ or } x > 5\}$ **57.** $\{x|x < -3\}$ **59.** $\{x|x < -2 \text{ or } x > 2\}$ **61.** $\left\{x|x > 5 \text{ or } x < -\frac{5}{3}\right\}$ **63.** $\{x|x \in \text{real numbers}\}$

65. $\{x \mid x \in \text{real numbers}\}$ **67.** $\{1, 2\}$ **69.** $\{1, 2, 3\}$ **71.** $\{3, 4, 5\}$ **73.** $\{10, 11, 12, 13\}$
75a. Always true   **b.** Sometimes true   **c.** Sometimes true   **d.** Sometimes true   **e.** Always true

3.5 Exercises

1a. Always true   **b.** Never true   **c.** Never true   **d.** Sometimes true   **e.** Never true   **3.** Parts b, d, and f have no solution. For parts a, c, and e, the solution set is all real numbers.   **5.** The solution set of $|ax + b| \le c$ contains the endpoints. The solution set of $|ax + b| < c$ does not contain the endpoints.   **7.** $-2, 2$ **9.** $-9, 9$
11. The equation has no solution.   **13.** $-7, -3$ **15.** $4, 12$ **17.** -7 **19.** The equation has no solution.
21. $0, \frac{8}{3}$ **23.** $\frac{3}{2}$ **25.** The equation has no solution.   **27.** $-3, 7$ **29.** $-\frac{10}{3}, 2$ **31.** $\frac{3}{2}$ **33.** The equation has
no solution.   **35.** $\frac{11}{6}, -\frac{1}{6}$ **37.** $-\frac{1}{3}, -1$ **39.** The equation has no solution.   **41.** The equation has no solution.
43. $\frac{7}{3}, \frac{1}{3}$ **45.** $-\frac{1}{2}$ **47.** $-\frac{8}{3}, \frac{10}{3}$ **49.** $\{x \mid -5 < x < 5\}$ **51.** $\{x \mid x < 1 \text{ or } x > 3\}$ **53.** $\{x \mid 1 \le x \le 7\}$
55. $\{x \mid x \le 1 \text{ or } x \ge 5\}$ **57.** $\left\{x \mid -\frac{2}{3} < x < 2\right\}$ **59.** $\left\{x \mid x < -\frac{12}{7} \text{ or } x > 2\right\}$ **61.** $\varnothing$ **63.** $\{x \mid x \in \text{real numbers}\}$
65. $\{x \mid x < -1 \text{ or } x > 8\}$ **67.** $\left\{x \mid -2 < x < \frac{20}{7}\right\}$ **69.** $\{x \mid x \in \text{real numbers}\}$ **71.** $\left\{x \mid -3 < x < \frac{17}{5}\right\}$
73. 3.476 in.; 3.484 in.   **75.** 93.5 volts; 126.5 volts   **77.** $10\frac{11}{32}$ in.; $10\frac{13}{32}$ in.   **79.** 28,420 ohms; 29,580 ohms
81. 23,750 ohms; 26,250 ohms   **83.** $228 < h < 272$ **85.** $x < 7.3 \text{ or } x > 17.5$ **87.** $-0.25, 1.5$ **89.** $-\frac{1}{3}, 3$
91. $\frac{4}{3}$ **93.** $\{x \mid -0.5 < x < 1.25\}$ **95a.** $-b - a \le x \le b - a$ **b.** $x < a - b \text{ or } x > a + b$ **c.** $x < -2a \text{ or } x > 0$
d. $0 \le x \le 2a$ **97.** $|x + 2| = 5$ **99.** For $c > 0$, the solution set is $-c \le x - 4 \le c$. For $c = 0$, the solution is 4. For
$c < 0$, the solution set is the empty set.

CHAPTER 3 REVIEW EXERCISES

1. $\frac{7}{20}$ [3.1]   **2.** $\frac{8}{3}$ [3.1]   **3.** $\frac{1}{9}$ [3.1]   **4.** 0 [3.1]   **5.** $\{x \mid x < 3\}$ [3.4]   **6.** $[-2, 1]$ [3.4]
7. $(-\infty, -2) \cup (2, \infty)$ [3.4]   **8.** $1, -\frac{7}{3}$ [3.5]   **9.** $\left\{x \mid x < \frac{1}{2} \text{ or } x > 2\right\}$ [3.5]   **10.** $\left\{x \mid -\frac{19}{3} < x < 7\right\}$ [3.5]
11. 28 [3.3]   **12.** $m\angle x = 140°$; $m\angle y = 77°$ [3.3]   **13.** $m\angle a = 138°$; $m\angle b = 42°$ [3.3]   **14.** 58 [3.3]
15. 148° [3.3]   **16.** $50.4 < x < 89.6$ [3.5]   **17.** 2:20 P.M. [3.2]   **18.** 2.747 in.; 2.753 in. [3.5]
19. $82 \le N \le 100$, where N is the score on the fifth exam [3.4]   **20.** 52 gal [3.2]

CHAPTER 3 TEST

1. $-\frac{1}{12}$ [3.1]   **2.** $\frac{2}{3}$ [3.1]   **3.** $\frac{8}{3}$ [3.1]   **4.** -3 [3.1]   **5.** $\{x \mid x \le 2\}$ [3.4]   **6.** $\{x \mid x \le 1\}$ [3.4]
7. $(-1, 2)$ [3.4]   **8.** $(-\infty, \infty)$ [3.4]   **9.** $\{x \mid 1 < x < 5\}$ [3.4]   **10.** $-\frac{5}{2}, \frac{11}{2}$ [3.5]   **11.** $\{x \mid 1 \le x \le 4\}$ [3.5]
12. $\left\{x \mid x \le \frac{1}{2} \text{ or } x \ge 3\right\}$ [3.5]   **13.** $\varnothing$ [3.5]   **14.** 6 [3.3]   **15.** $m\angle a = 141°, m\angle b = 39°$ [3.3]
16. 82 [3.3]   **17.** 30°, 60°, 90° [3.3]   **18.** 440 mph, 520 mph [3.2]   **19.** \$4.79 per pound [3.2]
20. 4.8 mg; 5.2 mg [3.5]

CUMULATIVE REVIEW EXERCISES

1. 6 [1.1]   **2.** B, C, A [1.1]   **3.** $\{1, 3, 5, 7\}$ [1.2]   **4.** $E \cup F = \{-6, -4, -2, 0, 2, 3, 4, 6, 9, 12\}$;
$E \cap F = \{0, 6\}$ [1.2]   **5.** 0 [1.5]   **6.** 4°C [1.3]   **7.** 1.229 [1.5]   **8.** 40 m² [1.5]   **9.** $23y - 44$ [1.6]
10. $x - (x + 20)$; -20 [1.6]   **11a.** 0, 56, 112, 168, 224, 280, 336   **b.** The car can travel 280 mi on 10 gal of gasoline. [2.1]
12. -2 [2.2]   **13.** $\{-128, -10, 4, 10, 104\}$ [2.2]   **14.** $(-3, 0), (2, 0); (0, -6)$ [2.3]   **15.** 1 [2.3]
16. 1 [3.1]   **17.** $(-\infty, -3]$ [3.4]   **18.** $-4, 7$ [3.5]   **19.** $\left\{x \mid \frac{1}{3} \le x \le 3\right\}$ [3.5]   **20.** 340 mph [3.2]

PREP TEST

1. $-4x + 12$ [1.6]   **2.** $y + 5$ [1.6]   **3.** $\frac{3}{4}x - 4$ [1.6]   **4.** -2 [1.3]   **5.** 240 [1.5]   **6.** -1 [1.5]
7. 4 [3.1]   **8.** -2 [3.1]   **9.** -8 [3.1]   **10.** a, b, c [3.4]

4.1 Exercises

1. Answers will vary. For example, **a.** $y = 3x - 4$, **b.** $2x - 5y = 10$.   **3.** The graph of a line with zero slope is horizontal. The graph of a line with no slope is vertical.   **5.** No. For instance, the graph of $x = 3$ is a line but not the graph of a function.   **7.** The graph of $x = a$ is a vertical line passing through $(a, 0)$. The graph of $y = b$ is a horizontal line passing through $(0, b)$.   **9.** Yes. $-\frac{3x}{4} = -\frac{3}{4}x$. It is a function of the form $f(x) = mx + b$.   **11.** No. The exponent on the variable is 2, not 1.   **13.** -1 **15.** $\frac{1}{3}$ **17.** $-\frac{2}{3}$ **19.** $-\frac{3}{4}$ **21.** Undefined   **23.** $\frac{7}{5}$ **25.** 0   **27.** $-\frac{1}{2}$
29. Undefined   **31.**   **33.** 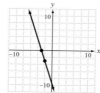   **35.**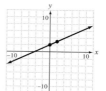

37. 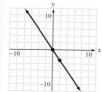   **39.** 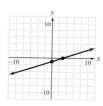   **41.** $m = 0.40$. The cellular call costs $.40 per minute.

43. $m = 0.04$. Each second, 0.04 megabyte is downloaded.   **45.** $m = -5$. The temperature of the oven decreases 5° per minute.   **47.** $m = 40$. The average speed of the motorist is 40 mph.   **49.** $m = 0.28$. The tax rate is 28%.
51. $m = -0.05$. For each mile the car is driven, 0.05 gallon of fuel is used.

53a. The x-intercept is $\left(\frac{30}{7}, 0\right)$. This means that when the temperature is $\frac{30}{7}$°C, the number of chirps per minute is 0. In other words, the cricket no longer chirps.   **b.** The slope of 7 means that the number of chirps per minute increases by 7 chirps for every 1°C increase in the temperature.   **55a.** The intercept on the vertical axis is $(0, -100)$. This means that when the object was taken from the freezer, its temperature was -100°F. The intercept on the horizontal axis is $(5, 0)$. This means that 5 hours after the object was removed from the freezer, its temperature was 0°F.   **b.** The slope of 20 means that the temperature of the object increases 20° per hour.   **57.** $m = -6.5$. The slope of -6.5 means that the temperature is decreasing 6.5°C for each 1-kilometer increase in height above sea level.   **59.** $m = 50$. The slope of 50 means that the pigeon flies 50 mph.   **61.** 168 in.   **63.** -4 **65.** -7 **67.** Line A represents the depth of water for Can 1. Line B represents the depth of water for Can 2.   **69.** $y = -2x + 5$ **71.** $y = 5x - 7$ **73.** $y = -\frac{3}{2}x + 3$
75. $y = \frac{2}{5}x - 2$ **77.** $y = -\frac{1}{3}x + 2$
79. $y = \frac{6}{5}x - 2$ **81.** 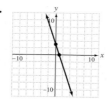   **83.** 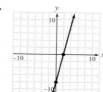   **85.**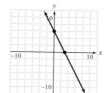

87. 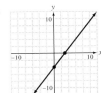   **89.** 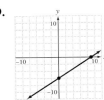   **91.** 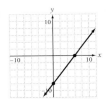   **93.**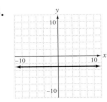

95. -6 **97.** From the three points, A, B, and C, create three pairs of points, A and B, A and C, and B and C. Determine whether the lines containing each pair of points have the same slope.   **a.** The points lie on the same line.   **b.** The points do not lie on the same line.   **99.** No; for example, $x = 2$.   **101.** 3   **103.** Answers will vary.

4.2 Exercises

1. The slope, m, and the y-intercept, $(0, b)$, can be read directly from the equation.   **3.** m would be positive because as the age of the tree increases, the height of the tree increases.   **5a.** Parallel lines have equal slopes.
b. The product of the slopes of perpendicular lines is -1; that is, their slopes are negative reciprocals.

7. $y = -2x - 1$ **9.** $y = -\frac{1}{4}x + 2$ **11.** $y = \frac{1}{6}x$ **13.** $y = 2x + 5$ **15.** $y = -\frac{5}{4}x + 5$ **17.** $y = 3x - 9$

19. $y = -3$ **21.** $x = 3$ **23.** $y = x + 2$ **25.** $y = \frac{3}{4}x$ **27.** $y = x - 1$ **29.** $y = -\frac{3}{2}x + 3$ **31.** $y = \frac{1}{3}x + \frac{10}{3}$

33. $y = -4$ **35.** $x = -2$ **37.** $y = 1200x$; 13,200 ft   **39.** $y = 1000x + 5200$; 13,200 ft

41. $y = -3.5x + 100$; 69°C   **43.** $y = 2.4x - 194.4$; 55.2 million   **45.** $y = 0.017x + 1463$; 1506 m/s

47. $y = -20x + 230{,}000$; 60,000 trucks   **49.** $y = -\frac{3}{5}x + 545$; 485 rooms
51a. $y = -0.0186x$ **b.** For every 1 g of sugar added, the freezing point decreases 0.0186°C.   **c.** -0.93°C   **53.** Yes

55. No   **57.** Yes   **59.** No   **61.** $y = -3x + 7$ **63.** $y = \frac{2}{3}x - \frac{8}{3}$ **65.** No   **67.** Yes   **69.** $y = \frac{1}{3}x - \frac{1}{3}$

71. $y = -\frac{5}{3}x - \frac{14}{3}$ **73.** $y = -\frac{1}{9}x + \frac{82}{9}$ **75.** Yes; $y = -x + 6$ **77.** No   **79.** 7   **81.** -1 **83.** $\frac{A_1}{B_1} = \frac{A_2}{B_2}$

85. Possible answers are $(0, 3)$, $(1, 2)$, and $(3, 0)$.   **87.** Any equation of the form $y = 2x + b$, where $b \neq -13$, or of the form $y = -\frac{3}{2}x + c$, where $c \neq 8$.   **89.** $x = 3$; 3° up

4.3 Exercises

1. Answers will vary.   **3.** Answers will vary. For example, we can use the equation to project possible future outcomes.   **5.** r would be positive because as the number of months increases, the weight increases.
7. r would be close to 0 because there is no correlation between height and history exam scores.
9a. Answers will vary. The equation of the line through the points $(95, 14)$ and $(99, 141)$ is $y = 31.75x - 3002.25$.
b. The slope of 31.75 means that the wolf population increased by approximately 32 wolves per year from 1995 to 2000.   **11a.** Answers will vary. The regression equation is $y = 66.4857x - 129{,}626.\overline{6}$.   **b.** The slope of 66.4857 means that electricity sales increased 66.4857 billion kilowatt hours per year from 1990 to 2000.
13a. $y = -0.1376741486 + 31.23316563$ **b.** 22 miles per gallon   **c.** The slope is negative; as x increases, y decreases.
15a. $y = 0.3213184476x + 0.400318979$ **b.** 3.6 m/s   **c.** With an increase of 1 cm in body length, an animal's running speed increases approximately 0.32 m/s.   **d.** The y-intercept of approximately 0.4 represents the running speed of an animal of length 0 cm.   **17a.** $y = 0.3325054x + 37.2985961$ **b.** $r \approx 0.99999$; The fit of the data to the regression line is very good.   **c.** 73.9 million children   **d.** The slope of approximately 0.333 means that the number of children in the United States is increasing at a rate of about 0.333 million per year.   **e.** The y-intercept of approximately 37.299 means that in 1900 there were 37.299 million children in the United States.   **19a.** $y = 1.551862378x + 1.986390721$
b. The slope of approximately 1.55 means that a state receives 1.55 electoral college votes per 1 million residents.
c. The y-intercept of approximately 1.986 means that a state with a population of 0 people would have 1.986 electoral college votes.   **d.** The r value is not exactly 1 because the data are not completely linear. States cannot have a fractional part of a vote. The number of votes a state receives is rounded to a whole number.   **21a.** ii   **b.** iii   **c.** iv   **d.** i
23. $y = -2.5x + 9$ **25a.** $y = 34.142857x - 3234.4286$ **b.** The r^2 value would decrease because the data values would not as closely fit a straight line.   **27.** The value of r is between -1 and 1; it cannot be greater than 1.
29a. $y = 0.36720042x + 315.62414$; $r \approx 0.6491$ **b.** $y = 1.1474246x - 66.269762$; $r \approx 0.6491$ **c.** No. The r values indicate that there is not a strong relationship between the two variables.

4.4 Exercises

1. No   **3.** No. There are ordered pairs with the same first component and different second components.

5. Yes   **7.** No   **9.** Yes   **11.** No

13. Yes   **15.** No   **17.** Yes   **19.** Yes

21. No   **23.** Yes   **25.** No   **27.**   **29.**

31. $y < -\frac{2}{3}x + 2$

33. No. The solution sets do not intersect, which means that there are no ordered pairs that satisfy both inequalities.

CHAPTER 4 REVIEW EXERCISES

1. -1 [4.1]   **2.** Undefined [4.1]

3. [4.1]   **4.** [4.1]   **5.** [4.1]   **6.** 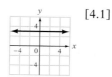 [4.1]

7. $y = -\frac{4}{3}x - 5$ [4.2]   **8.** $y = 4x - 2$ [4.2]   **9.** $y = -\frac{1}{2}x + 7$ [4.2]   **10.** $y = -4$ [4.2]   **11.** No [4.2]

12. $y = -3x + 7$ [4.2]   **13.** No [4.2]   **14.** $y = \frac{3}{2}x + 2$ [4.2]   **15.** [4.4]

16. $y = 90x + 60,000$; $285,000 [4.2]   **17.** The slope is -0.72. The maximum recommended exercise heart rate decreases -0.72 beat per minute for every year older. [4.1]   **18a.** $y = 25x + 1000$ **b.** Water is being added to the pond at a rate of 25 gal/min.   **c.** 10,000 gal   [4.2]   **19a.** It costs $.25 per minute to use the phone.   **b.** The y-intercept is 19.95. When the phone is used for 0 minutes during the month, the phone bill is $19.95. [4.1]
20a. $y = 0.28928571x + 74.07142857$ **b.** $95.8°F$ [4.3]

CHAPTER 4 TEST

1. -2 [4.1]   **2.** 0 [4.1]

3. [4.1]   **4.** [4.1]   **5.** [4.1]   **6.** 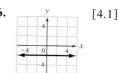 [4.1]

7. $y = \frac{3}{4}x - 2$ [4.1] **8.** [4.4] **9.** $y = -\frac{5}{3}x - 4$ [4.2] **10.** $y = \frac{1}{2}x - \frac{7}{2}$ [4.2]

11. $y = x + 1$ [4.2] **12.** $y = -\frac{5}{4}x + 3$ [4.2] **13.** Yes [4.2] **14.** $y = 4x + 13$ [4.2] **15.** Yes [4.2]

16. $y = -\frac{1}{3}x + 5$ [4.2] **17a.** $y = 1500x + 18,500$ **b.** The slope of 1500 means that the profit is increasing by $1500 per month. **c.** The profit in December will be $36,500. [4.2] **18.** $m = 7$. The prices are increasing 7 cents per month. [4.1] **19a.** $y = -20x + 2800$ **b.** The slope of -20 means the metal is cooling 20°F per minute. **c.** 400°F [4.2] **20a.** $y = 0.098x - 80.079$ **b.** The equation predicts that a car weighs 2700 lb has an engine that delivers approximately 186 hp. [4.3]

CUMULATIVE REVIEW EXERCISES

1. 8 [1.1] **2.** 40 [1.1] **3.** $E \cup F = \{-10, -5, 0, 5, 10, 15\}$; $E \cap F = \{0, 5, 10\}$ [1.2] **4.** 17 [1.5]

5. 15 ft³ [1.5] **6.** $-6x - 3$ [1.6] **7.** $20\left(\frac{1}{5}x\right)$; $4x$ [1.6]

8.

x	-2	-1	0	1	2
y	2	-1	-2	-1	2

 [2.1]

9. Domain: $\{-1, 0, 1\}$, Range: $\{-1, 0, 1, 2\}$, No [2.2] **10.** -11 [2.2] **11.** $(-1, 0)$, $(3, 0)$; $(0, -3)$ [2.3]
12. -3 [2.3] **13.** 0 [3.1] **14.** 2 [3.1] **15.** 15 lb of the $6 coffee; 45 lb of the $4 coffee [3.2]
16. $m\angle a = 46°$, $m\angle b = 134°$ [3.3] **17.** $\left(-\infty, \frac{1}{2}\right]$ [3.4] **18.** $-2, \frac{4}{3}$ [3.5]

19. [4.1] **20.** $y = \frac{3}{2}x + 2$ [4.2]

ANSWERS to Chapter 5 Exercises

PREP TEST

1. $6x + 5y$ [1.6] **2.** 7 [1.5] **3.** 0 [3.1] **4.** -3 [3.1] **5.** 1000 [3.1]
6. 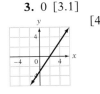 [4.1] **7.** 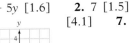 [4.1] **8.** [4.4]

5.1 Exercises

1. Explanations will vary. For example, the solution is represented by an ordered pair (x, y).
3. Explanations will vary. For example, for a dependent system, the resulting equation is true; for an inconsistent system, the resulting equation is false. **5.** $(2, 3)$ **7.** $(-1, 2)$ **9.** $(-1, 4)$ **11.** $\left(x, \frac{2}{5}x - 2\right)$

13. The system of equations has no solution.   **15.** $(-2.5, 3)$ **17.** $(2, 1)$ **19.** $(2, 1)$ **21.** $(3, -4)$

23. $\left(\frac{1}{2}, 3\right)$ **25.** $(-1, 2)$ **27.** $(0, 0)$ **29.** $(1, 5)$ **31.** $(x, -2x + 1)$ **33.** \$.16   **35.** $30°$ and $60°$

37. First powder: 200 mg; second powder: 450 mg   **39.** \$6000 at 9.5%; \$4000 at 7.5%   **41.** $\frac{3}{2}$ **43.** 4

45. $\left(6, \frac{3}{2}\right)$ **47.** $(-1, 2)$ **49.** 6

5.2 Exercises

1. The result of one of the steps will be an equation that is never true.   **3.** A three-dimensional coordinate system is one formed by three mutually perpendicular axes.   **5.** The planes intersect at one point.   **7.** Between 10% and 20% apple juice   **9.** 12 mph   **11.** $(6, 1)$ **13.** $(2, 1)$ **15.** $\left(-\frac{1}{2}, 2\right)$ **17.** $(-1, -2)$ **19.** $\left(\frac{1}{2}, \frac{3}{4}\right)$

21. $\left(\frac{2}{3}, -\frac{2}{3}\right)$ **23.** $\left(x, \frac{4}{3}x - 6\right)$ **25.** $\left(\frac{1}{3}, -1\right)$ **27.** No solution   **29.** $(2, 1, 3)$ **31.** $(1, -1, 2)$

33. $(0, 2, 0)$ **35.** The system of equations has no solution.   **37.** $(6, -2, 2)$ **39.** $(-2, 1, 1)$ **41.** $(1, 4, 1)$

43. $(1, 1, 3)$ **45.** Plane: 250 mph; wind: 50 mph

47. Boat: 19 kilometers per hour; current: 3 kilometers per hour   **49.** Boat: 16.5 mph; current: 1.5 mph

51. $33\frac{1}{3}\%$ **53.** 20 ml of the 3% hydrogen peroxide solution; 30 ml of the 12% hydrogen peroxide solution

55. 40 g of the 25% alloy; 80 g of pure gold   **57.** \$4000   **59.** \$8000 at 9%, \$6000 at 7%, \$4000 at 5%

61. \$14,000 at 12%; \$10,000 at 8%; \$9000 at 9%   **63.** For the first diet, 100 g of food type I, 200 g of food type II, and 200 g of food type III. For the second diet, 200 g of food type I, 200 g of food type II, and 100 g of food type III.

65. $A = 3, B = -1$ **67.** 2   **69.** 6

71. The system of equations has a unique solution when $2A + 13 \neq 0$ or $A \neq -\frac{13}{2}$.

5.3 Exercises

1. A matrix is a rectangular array of numbers.   **3.** 1. Interchange two rows.   2. Multiply a row by a constant.   3. Replace a row by the sum of that row and a nonzero multiple of another row.

5. b   **7.** $\begin{bmatrix} 1 & 4 & -1 \\ 0 & 1 & -4 \end{bmatrix}$ **9.** $\begin{bmatrix} 1 & \frac{1}{2} & -\frac{1}{2} \\ 0 & 1 & 5 \end{bmatrix}$ **11.** $\begin{bmatrix} 1 & \frac{5}{2} & -2 \\ 0 & 1 & -\frac{16}{13} \end{bmatrix}$ **13.** $\begin{bmatrix} 1 & 2 & 2 & -1 \\ 0 & 1 & -\frac{7}{2} & \frac{1}{2} \\ 0 & 0 & 1 & -\frac{2}{11} \end{bmatrix}$

15. $\begin{bmatrix} 1 & -3 & \frac{1}{2} & -\frac{3}{2} \\ 0 & 1 & \frac{3}{2} & \frac{5}{2} \\ 0 & 0 & 1 & 3 \end{bmatrix}$ **17.** $\begin{bmatrix} 1 & -\frac{3}{2} & \frac{9}{4} & 1 \\ 0 & 1 & -\frac{47}{30} & -\frac{4}{15} \\ 0 & 0 & 1 & -\frac{17}{13} \end{bmatrix}$ **19.** $(9, 1, -1)$ **21.** $(2, -1)$ **23.** $(2, 4)$

25. $(-2, 5)$ **27.** The system of equations has no solution.   **29.** $(-1, 4)$ **31.** $(1, 3, -2)$ **33.** $(2, 4, 1)$

35. The system of equations has no solution.   **37.** $\left(\frac{1}{2}, 0, \frac{2}{3}\right)$ **39.** $\left(\frac{2}{3}, -1, \frac{1}{2}\right)$ **41.** $(2, -1, 3)$

43. $(0, 1, -2)$ **45.** $z = \frac{3}{2}x - \frac{5}{2}y + 1$ **47.** $y = -x^2 + 3x - 4$ **49.** $d_1 = 8$ in., $d_2 = 6$ in., $d_3 = 12$ in.

51a. Rabbits do not prey on hawks.   **b.** Snakes prey on rabbits.   **c.** A coyote is not prey for hawks, rabbits, snakes, or coyotes.   **d.** A rabbit does not prey on hawks, rabbits, snakes, or coyotes.   **53.** $A = 2, B = 3, C = -3$ **55.** $(1, 1)$

57a. A plane parallel to the yz-plane passing through $x = 3$.   **b.** A plane parallel to the xy-plane passing through $y = 4$.   **c.** A plane parallel to the xy-plane passing through $x = 2$.   **d.** A plane perpendicular to the xy-plane along the line $y = x$ in the xy-plane.

5.4 Exercises

1. Graph each inequality. Then determine the intersection of the solution sets of the individual inequalities.
3. It must be a solution of every inequality in the system.　　**5.** b

7. 　　**9.** 　　**11.** 　　**13.** 　　**15.** 　　**17.**

19.　　**21.**　　**23.**　　**25.**　　**27.**　　**29.**

31. $y \geq -2$　　**33.** $y > x$
　　　$x \geq 1$　　　　　$y < -x + 2$

CHAPTER 5 REVIEW EXERCISES

1. $\left(6, -\frac{1}{2}\right)$ [5.1]　　**2.** $(-4, 7)$ [5.2]　　**3.** $(0, 3)$ [5.1]　　**4.** $(x, 2x - 4)$ [5.1]　　**5.** $\left(x, \frac{1}{3}x - 2\right)$ [5.2]

6. $(3, -1, -2)$ [5.2]　　**7.** $(3, 4)$ [5.1]　　**8.** $\begin{bmatrix} 2 & -3 & -1 & | & 1 \\ 3 & 0 & -4 & | & -2 \\ 0 & 4 & -5 & | & 0 \end{bmatrix}$ [5.3]　　**9.** $\begin{aligned} x + 3y &= -2 \\ 2x - y + z &= 0 \\ 3x + 2y - 5z &= 4 \end{aligned}$ [5.3]

10. $\begin{bmatrix} 1 & 2 & -1 & 3 \\ 0 & 1 & -2 & 13 \\ 0 & 0 & 1 & \frac{9}{5} \end{bmatrix}$ [5.3]　　**11.** $(2, -1)$ [5.3]　　**12.** $(3, -2)$ [5.3]　　**13.** $(2, 3, -5)$ [5.3]　　**14.** $(-1, -3, 4)$ [5.3]

15. [5.4]　　**16.** [5.4]　　**17.** Cabin cruiser: 16 mph; current: 4 mph [5.2]

18. Plane: 175 mph; wind: 25 mph [5.2]　　**19.** 100 children [5.2]　　**20.** Meat: 3 oz; potatoes: 5 oz; green beans: 4 oz [5.2]

CHAPTER 5 TEST

1. $\left(\frac{3}{4}, \frac{7}{8}\right)$ [5.1]　　**2.** The system of equations has no solution. [5.2]　　**3.** $(2, -1)$ [5.1]　　**4.** $(-3, -4)$ [5.1]

5. $\left(x, \frac{1}{3}x - 1\right)$ [5.2]　　**6.** $(0, -2, 3)$ [5.2]　　**7.** $(-5, 0)$ [5.1]　　**8.** $\begin{bmatrix} 3 & -1 & 2 & | & 4 \\ 1 & 4 & 0 & | & -1 \\ 0 & 5 & -1 & | & 3 \end{bmatrix}$ [5.3]

9. $\begin{aligned} 2x - y + 3z &= 4 \\ x + 5y - 2z &= 6 \\ -3x - 4z &= 1 \end{aligned}$ [5.3]　　**10.** $\begin{bmatrix} 1 & \frac{3}{2} & -1 \\ 0 & 1 & -1 \end{bmatrix}$ [5.3]　　**11.** $(-2, 1)$ [5.3]　　**12.** $\left(-\frac{1}{3}, -\frac{10}{3}\right)$ [5.3]　　**13.** $(2, -1, -2)$ [5.3]

14. $\left(\frac{1}{5}, -\frac{6}{5}, \frac{3}{5}\right)$ [5.2]　　**15.** [5.4]　　**16.** [5.4]　　**17.** Plane: 150 mph; wind: 25 mph [5.2]

18. Cotton: $9; wool: $14 [5.2]　　**19.** Motorboat: 18 mph; current: 2 mph [5.2]　　**20.** 8 lb [5.2]

CUMULATIVE REVIEW EXERCISES

1. 0 [1.1]   **2.** 17 votes [1.1]   **3.** $4 = 2^2$, $9 = 3^2$, $16 = 4^2$, $25 = 5^2$. Answers may vary; for example, each number is the square of the number of odd consecutive integers added. $1 + 3 + 5 + 7 + 9 + 11 = 36 = 6^2$. [1.1]
4. Deductive reasoning [1.1]   **5.** $\{-4, -3, 0, 5, 12, 21\}$ [2.2]   **6.** 0, 2 [2.3]
7. $(-4, 0), (-2, 0), (1, 0), (0, -8)$ [2.3]
8.

s	1500	1600	1700	1800	1900	2000	2100	[2.1]
F	6000	6350	6700	7050	7400	7750	8100	

9. -13 [3.1]   **10.** $[-6, \infty)$ [3.4]   **11.** $\{x \mid 3 < x < 6\}$ [3.4]   **12.** 1, 3 [3.5]
13. $y = -x + 1$ [4.2]   **14.** $(2, -3)$ [5.1]   **15.** $(-2, -1)$ [5.2]   **16.** $(2, 0)$ [5.1]
17. $\begin{bmatrix} 1 & -1 & 1 & | & 1 \\ 0 & 1 & -3 & | & 5 \\ 0 & 0 & 1 & | & -2 \end{bmatrix}$ [5.3]   **18.** $(1, -1, 2)$ [5.3]

19a. $y = -0.357142857x + 766.71429$ **b.** 45%   **c.** The slope is negative; as x increases, y decreases. [4.3]
20. Ship, 25 mph; current, 5 mph [5.2]

ANSWERS to Chapter 6 Exercises

PREP TEST

1. $-12y$ [1.6]   **2.** -8 [1.3]   **3.** $3a - 8b$ [1.6]   **4.** $11x - 2y - 2$ [1.6]   **5.** $-x + y$ [1.6]

6.1 Exercises

1. a. This is a monomial because it is the product of a number, 32, and variables, a and b.
   b. This is a monomial because it is the product of a number, $\frac{5}{7}$, and a variable, n.
   c. This is not a monomial because there is a variable in the denominator.
3. a. The exponent on 6 is positive; it should not be moved to the denominator. $6x^{-3} = \frac{6}{x^3}$
   b. The exponent on x is positive; it should not be moved to the denominator. $xy^{-2} = \frac{x}{y^2}$
   c. The exponent on 8 is positive; it should not be moved to the numerator. $\frac{1}{8a^{-4}} = \frac{a^4}{8}$
   d. The exponent on c is positive; it should not be moved to the numerator. $\frac{1}{b^{-5}c} = \frac{b^5}{c}$
5. a^9 **7.** z^8 **9.** x^{15} **11.** $x^{12}y^{18}$ **13.** $17s^4t^3$ **15.** 1   **17.** a^6 **19.** $-m^9n^3$ **21.** $24x^7$ **23.** $-8a^6$
25. $4p^4q^5$ **27.** $-24r^3$ **29.** $8a^9b^3c^6$ **31.** mn^2 **33.** 1   **35.** $-\frac{2a}{3}$ **37.** $-27m^2n^4p^3$ **39.** $-15x^3y^8$
41. $\frac{1}{x^5}$ **43.** $54n^{14}$ **45.** $\frac{7xz}{8y^3}$ **47.** $-8x^{13}y^{14}$ **49.** $\frac{1}{w^8}$ **51.** a^5 **53.** $\frac{1}{64}$ **55.** 243   **57.** $\frac{4}{x^7}$ **59.** $\frac{2}{x^2y^4}$
61. 1   **63.** $\frac{1}{x^5}$ **65.** $\frac{9}{x^4}$ **67.** $\frac{x^2}{3}$ **69.** $\frac{x^6}{y^{12}}$ **71.** $\frac{9}{x^2y^4}$ **73.** $\frac{2}{x^4}$ **75.** $\frac{1}{2x^3}$ **77.** $\frac{1}{2x^2y^6}$ **79.** $\frac{1}{x^6}$ **81.** $\frac{y^8}{x^4}$
83. $\frac{b^{10}}{4a^{10}}$ **85.** $11xy$ **87.** $15a^2b$ **89.** $64x^4y^2$ m^2 **91.** $50c^3d^4$ mi   **93.** $54m^2n^4$ km^2 **95.** $6a^2b^3$ yd
97. $3a^2$ **99.** 2.37×10^6 **101.** 4.5×10^{-4} **103.** 3.09×10^5 **105.** 6.01×10^{-7} **107.** 5.7×10^{10}
109. 1.7×10^{-8} **111.** 710,000   **113.** 0.000043   **115.** 671,000,000   **117.** 0.00000713
119. 5,000,000,000,000   **121.** 0.00801   **123.** 1.6×10^{10} **125.** $\$1.317 \times 10^8$ **127.** 1.6×10^{-19}

129. 6.023×10^{23} **131.** 3.086×10^{18} **133.** 6.65×10^{19} **135.** 3.22×10^{-14} **137.** 3.6×10^{5}
139. 1.8×10^{-18} **141a.** $\frac{3}{64}$ **b.** $\frac{4}{81}$ **143.** $\frac{1}{4}, \frac{1}{2}, 1, 2, 4; 4, 2, 1, \frac{1}{2}, \frac{1}{4}$ **145.** a

6.2 Exercises

1a. This is a binomial. It contains two terms, $8x^4$ and $-6x^2$ **b.** This is a trinomial. It contains three terms, $4a^2b^2$, $9ab$, and 10.   **c.** This is a monomial. It is one term, $7x^3y^4$. (*Note:* It is a product of a number and variables. There is no addition or subtraction operation in the expression.)   **3a.** Yes. Both $\frac{1}{5}x^3$ and $\frac{1}{2}x$ are monomials. (*Note:* The coefficients of variables can be fractions.)   **b.** No. A polynomial does not have a variable in the denominator of a fraction. **c.** Yes. Both x and $\sqrt{5}$ are monomials. (*Note:* The variable is not under a radical sign.)
5. 67.02 ft^3 **7.** 576.99 m **9.** 50 ft **11.** 191.7 lb **13.** 18,819 foot-pounds   **15.** $-2x^2 + 3x$ **17.** $4x$
19. $7b^2 + b - 4$ **21.** $3y^2 - 4y - 2$ **23.** $3a^2 - 3a + 17$ **25.** $-7x - 7$ **27.** $-2x^3 + x^2 + 2$
29. $x^3 + 2x^2 - 6x - 6$ **31.** $5x^3 + 10x^2 - x - 4$ **33.** $y^3 - y^2 + 6y - 6$ **35.** $4y^3 - 2y^2 + 2y - 4$
37. $11x^2 + 2x + 4$ **39.** $5a^2 + 3a - 9$ **41.** $(8d^2 + 12d + 4) \text{ km}$ **43.** $(-2n^2 + 160n - 1200)$ dollars
45. $-4x^2 + 6x + 3$ **47.** $4x^2 - 6x + 3$ **49a.** Sometimes true **b.** Always true **c.** Sometimes true
51a. $k = 8$ **b.** $k = -4$

6.3 Exercises

1. The FOIL method is used to multiply two binomials.   **3.** $x + 1$ and $x^2 - x + 1$ **5a.** Sometimes true
b. Never true   **c.** Always true   **7.** The degree of the first term of the quotient is one degree less than the degree of the first term of the dividend.   **9.** $3x^6 - 3x^4 - 2x^2$ **11.** $-6y^4 - 12y^3 + 14y^2$ **13.** $-2a^3 + 7a^2 - 7a + 2$
15. $2y^4 + 7y^3 - 4y^2 - 16y + 8$ **17.** $4a^4 - 12a^3 + 13a^2 - 8a + 3$ **19.** $y^2 + 7y + 10$ **21.** $b^2 - 3b - 18$
23. $a^2 - 17a + 72$ **25.** $5y^2 + 11y + 2$ **27.** $7x^2 + 26x - 8$ **29.** $8x^2 - 26x + 21$ **31.** $5y^2 + 16y - 45$
33. $15a^2 - 71a + 84$ **35.** $2x^2 + 3xy + y^2$ **37.** $3x^2 - 10xy + 8y^2$ **39.** $10a^2 + 14ab - 12b^2$ **41.** $y^2 - 25$
43. $16x^2 - 49$ **45.** $y^2 - 6y + 9$ **47.** $36x^2 - 60x + 25$ **49.** $y + 1$ **51.** $2b - 5$ **53.** $6y + 4$ **55.** $12x - 7$
57. $5y - 3$ **59.** $-y + 9$ **61.** $a^2 - 5a + 7$ **63.** $a^6 - 5a^3 - 3a$ **65.** $xy - 3$ **67.** $x + 2$ **69.** $2y - 7$
71. $x - 2 + \frac{8}{x + 2}$ **73.** $3y - 5 + \frac{20}{2y + 4}$ **75.** $b - 5 - \frac{24}{b - 3}$ **77.** $3x + 17 + \frac{64}{x - 4}$ **79.** $5y + 3 + \frac{1}{2y + 3}$
81. $x^2 - 5x + 2$ **83.** $x^2 + 5$ **85.** $(9a^2 - 12a + 4) \text{ yd}^2$ **87.** $(2x^2 - 9x - 18) \text{ ft}^2$
89. $(\pi x^2 - 6\pi x + 9\pi) \text{ cm}^2$ **91.** $(40x^3 + 4x^2 - 12x) \text{ cm}^3$ **93.** $(x^2 - 5x - 24) \text{ in}^2$ **95.** $(32x^2 - 48x + 18) \text{ cm}^2$
97. $(2x + 3) \text{ m}$ **99.** $(2x^2 - 4) \text{ m}$ **101.** $(60w + 3000) \text{ yd}^2$ **103.** $(10{,}000x - 400x^2) \text{ cm}^3$; 60,000 cm³
105. $12x^2 - x - 20$ **107.** $x^2 + 4x - 1$ **109.** $7x^2 - 11x - 8$ **111.** $x^3 - 4x^2 + 11x - 2$ **113.** $x^2 - 3x + 2$
115. $2x^2 - 3x + 9$ **117.** $x^2 - 5x + 16 - \frac{41}{x + 2}$ **119.** $x^2 - x + 2 - \frac{4}{x + 1}$ **121.** $3x + 3 - \frac{1}{x - 1}$
123. $2x^3 - 3x^2 + x - 4$ **125.** $3x^3 - x + 4 - \frac{2}{x + 1}$ **127.** $2x^3 + 6x^2 + 17x + 51 + \frac{155}{x - 3}$ **129.** $(x + 4)$ in.
131. $x + 1$ **133a.** Always true   **b.** Always true   **135.** $(4x^3 - 80x^2 + 400x) \text{ in}^3$; No; Explanations will vary.
137. -2 **139.** 0   **141.** -9 **143.** $(3, -7)$

CHAPTER 6 REVIEW EXERCISES

1. $24a^2b^3c$ [6.1]   **2.** $5y^2 - 10y$ [6.2]   **3.** $-20x^3y^5$ [6.1]   **4.** $-4x^6$ [6.1]   **5.** $\frac{6b}{a}$ [6.1]   **6.** $4x^4 - 2x^2 + 5$ [6.3]
7. $6y^4 - 9y^3 + 18y^2$ [6.3]   **8.** $4x^2 - 20x + 25$ [6.3]   **9.** $\frac{9a^4}{b^6}$ [6.1]   **10.** 2.9×10^{-6} [6.1]   **11.** $16y^2 - 9$ [6.3]
12. $10a^3 - 39a^2 + 20a - 21$ [6.3]   **13.** $-\frac{1}{4a^2b^5}$ [6.1]   **14.** $4x + 8 + \frac{21}{2x - 3}$ [6.3]   **15.** 0.000000035 [6.1]
16. $-70xy^2z^6$ [6.1]   **17.** $x^2 - 3x + 7 + \frac{1}{x - 3}$ [6.3]   **18.** $(4x^2 + 12x + 9) \text{ m}^2$ [6.3]
19. 81,030,000,000,000,000,000 [6.1]   **20.** 56 ft [6.2]

CHAPTER 6 TEST

1. $21y^2 + 4y - 1$ [6.2]   **2.** $-18a^8b^6$ [6.1]   **3.** $12x^5 + 8x^3 - 28x^2$ [6.3]   **4.** $-\frac{2y^3}{x^3}$ [6.1]   **5.** $-\frac{10a}{b}$ [6.1]
6. $4b^4 + 12b^2 - 1$ [6.3]   **7.** $-\frac{8a^{12}}{b^{15}}$ [6.1]   **8.** 7.8×10^{10} [6.1]   **9.** 1296 [6.1]   **10.** $36y^2 - 25$ [6.3]

11. 7.28×10^4 [6.1]   **12.** $6a^3 + 17a^2 - 2a - 21$ [6.3]   **13.** $2x^3 - 4x^2 + 6x - 14$ [6.2]

14. $x^2 - 2x - 1 + \frac{2}{x-3}$ [6.3]   **15.** 29,710,000 [6.1]   **16.** $\frac{x^4 y^6}{9}$ [6.1]   **17.** $-6x^2 - 4x + 5$ [6.2]

18. $(10x^2 - 29x - 21)$ cm² [6.3]   **19.** 240,000,000,000,000 [6.1]   **20.** 576.99 m [6.2]

CUMULATIVE REVIEW EXERCISES

1. $\frac{1}{2}$ [1.1]   **2.** -7 [1.5]   **3.** The Associative Property of Addition [1.6]   **4.** $18x^2$ [1.6]

5. Domain : $\{-5, -3, -1, 1, 3\}$; Range: $\{-4, -2, 0, 2, 4\}$; Yes [2.2]   **6.** $\{-11, -7, -3, 1, 5\}$ [2.2]   **7.** 5 [3.1]

8. $(-\infty, -3]$ [3.4]   **9.**   [4.1]   **10.** 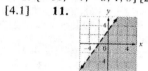   [4.1]   **11.**   [4.4]

12. $y = \frac{2}{5}x + 4$ [4.2]   **13.** $(1, 2)$ [5.2]   **14.** $-\frac{8y^6}{x^{12}}$ [6.1]   **15.** $3y^3 - 7y^2 + 8y - 7$ [6.2]   **16.** $4x + 8 + \frac{21}{2x-3}$ [6.3]

17. 32 mph and 64 mph [3.2]   **18.** 40 oz [3.2]   **19.** Rate of the plane in calm air: 225 mph; rate of the wind: 25 mph [5.2]   **20.** $m = 50$. A slope of 50 means the average speed was 50 mph. [4.1]

I N D E X

INDEX OF APPLICATIONS